Critical Cultural Policy Studies

Critical Cultural Policy Studies
A Reader

Edited by Justin Lewis and Toby Miller

Blackwell
Publishing

350 Main Street, Malden, MA 02148–5018, USA
108 Cowley Road, Oxford OX4 1JF, UK
550 Swanston Street, Carlton, Victoria 3053, Australia
Kurfürstendamm 57, 10707 Berlin, Germany

First published 2003 by Blackwell Publishers Ltd, a Blackwell Publishing company

Library of Congress Cataloging-in-Publication Data

Critical cultural policy studies : a reader / edited by Justin Lewis and Toby Miller.
p. cm.
Includes bibliographical references and index.
ISBN 0-631-22299-5 (alk. paper) – ISBN 0-631-22300-2 (pbk. : alk. paper)
1. Cultural policy. 2. Cultural policy – Study and teaching. 3. Civilization, Modern – 1950–
4. Politics and culture. 5. Popular culture – Political aspects. 6. Popular culture –
Economic aspects. 7. United States – Cultural policy. I. Lewis, Justin, 1958– II. Miller,
Toby.

CB430 .C75 2002   001.3 – dc21   2002066440

A catalogue record for this title is available from the British Library.

Set in 9.5 on 11.5pt Stempel Garamond
by Kolam Information Services Pvt. Ltd, India
Printed and bound in the United Kingdom
by MPG Books Ltd, Bodmin, Cornwall

For further information on
Blackwell Publishing, visit our website:
http://www.blackwellpublishing.com

Contents

Contents

Contributors

Justin Lewis is Professor of Communication and Cultural Industries at the University of Wales, Cardiff.

Toby Miller is Professor of Cultural Studies and Cultural Policy at New York University.

Stuart Cunningham is Professor and Director of the Creative Industries Research and Applications Centre at the Queensland University of Technology.

Jim McGuigan is a Reader and Sociology Programme Director at Loughborough University.

Susan J. Douglas is Catherine Neafie Kellogg Professor of Communication Studies, University of Michigan.

Susan Smulyan is Associate Professor of American Civilization at Brown University.

Nina Huntemann is a Ph.D. student in Communication at the University of Massachusetts at Amherst.

Faye Ginsburg is the David B. Kriser Professor of Anthropology and Director of the Center for Media, Culture & History at New York University.

Sylvia Harvey is Professor of Broadcasting Policy at the School of Cultural Studies, Sheffield Hallam University.

Laurie Ouellette is Assistant Professor of Journalism and Media Studies at Rutgers University.

Isaac Julien is a filmmaker and writer.

Richard Maxwell is Associate Professor of Media Studies at Queens College, City University of New York.

Thomas Streeter is Associate Professor of Sociology at the University of Vermont.

Tony Bennett is Professor of Sociology at the Open University.

Owen Kelly is a community artist.

Pamela Newkirk is Associate Professor of Journalism at New York University.

Jim McKay is Associate Professor of Sociology and Anthropology at the University of Queensland.

Samuel Nunn is Associate Professor, Indiana University School of Public and Environmental Affairs at Indiana University–Purdue University, Indianapolis.

Mark S. Rosentraub is Dean of the Maxine Goodman Levin College of Urban Affairs at Cleveland State University.

Jody Berland is Associate Professor of Humanities at York University in Toronto.

Kembrew McLeod is an Assistant Professor in the Department of Communication at the University of Iowa.

Roy Shuker is Associate Professor of English and Media Studies at Massey University.

Mari Castañeda Paredes is Assistant Professor of Communication, University of Massachussetts, Amherst.

Sandra Braman is Professor of Communication at the University of Alabama.

Arlene Dávila is Assistant Professor of Anthropology at New York University.

Lynn Comella is a Ph.D. student in Communication at the University of Massachussetts, Amherst.

Kenneth T. Jackson is Jacques Barzun Professor of History and the Social Sciences at Columbia University.

Vincent Mosco is Professor of Journalism and Communication at Carleton University.

Acknowledgments

The authors and publishers gratefully acknowledge the following for permission to reproduce copyright material:

Tony Bennett. "The Political Rationality of the Museum," from *The Birth of the Museum: History, Theory and Politics*. London: Routledge, 1995. Reproduced by permission of the publisher and author;

Jody Berland. "Radio Space and Industrial Time: The Case of Music Formats," from *Rock and Popular Music: Politics, Policies, Institutions*, edited by Tony Bennett, Simon Frith, Lawrence Grossberg, John Shepherd, and Graeme Turner. London: Routledge, 1993. Reproduced by permission of the publisher and author;

Sandra Braman. "Trade and Information Policy." *Media, Culture and Society* 12, no. 3 (1990): 361–85. Reproduced by kind permission of Sage Publications Ltd and the author;

Stuart Cunningham. "Cultural Studies from the Viewpoint of Cultural Policy." *Meanjin* 50, nos. 2–3 (1991). Reproduced by kind permission of the author and journal;

Arlene Dávila. "Crafting Culture: Selling and Contesting Authenticity in Puerto Rico's Informal Economy." *Studies in Latin American Popular Culture* 18 (1999): 159–70. Reproduced by kind permission of the author;

Susan Douglas. "The Rise of Military and Corporate Control" from *Inventing American Broadcasting, 1899–1922*. Baltimore: The Johns Hopkins University Press, 1987;

Faye Ginsburg. "Embedded Aesthetics: Creating a Discursive Space for Indigenous Media." Reproduced by permission of the American Anthropological Association from *Cultural Anthropology* 9(3) (1994): 365–82. Not for sale or further reproduction;

Sylvia Harvey. "Doing it My Way – Broadcasting Regulation in Capitalist Cultures: The Case of 'Fairness' and 'Impartiality'." *Media, Culture and Society* 20, no. 4 (1998): 535–56. Reproduced by kind permission of Sage Publications Ltd and the author;

Isaac Julien. "Burning Rubber's Perfume." *Remote Control: Dilemmas of Black Intervention in British Film & TV*. Edited by June Giovanni. London: British Film Institute, 1995, pp. 55–62;

Kenneth Jackson. "All the World's a Mall: Reflections on the Social and Economic Consequences of the American Shopping Center." *American Historical Review* 101, no. 4 (1996): 1111–21. Reproduced by kind permission of the author;

Owen Kelly. "Art," from *Community, Art and the State: Storming the Citadels*. London: Routledge, 1984. Reproduced by permission of the publisher;

Jim McKay. "Hegemonic Masculinity, the State and the Politics of Gender Equity Policy Research." *Culture and Policy* 5 (1993): pp. 233–40. Non-exclusive World English language rights granted by the Australian Key Centre for Cultural and Media Policy;

Richard Maxwell. "The Marketplace Citizen and the Political Economy of Data Trade in the European Union." This article first appeared in *The Journal of International Communication*, issue 6:1 (1999). *JIC* has sole copyright ownership of this article;

Toby Miller. "The Film Industry and the Government: 'Endless Mr Beans and Mr Bonds'?." *British Cinema in the Nineties*. Edited by Robert Murphy. London: British Film Institute, 1999, pp. 37–47;

Vincent Mosco. "Citizenship and the Technopoles." *Communication, Citizenship, and Social Policy: Rethinking the Limits of the Welfare State*. Ed. Andrew Calabrese and Jean-Claude Burgelman. Lanham: Rowman & Littlefield, 1999, pp. 33–45. Reproduced by permission of the publisher;

Pamela Newkirk. "Object Lessons: Fred Wilson Reinstalls Museum Collection to Highlight Sins of Omission." *ARTNews* (January 2000): 156–9. Reproduced by kind permission of the author;

Samuel Nunn and Mark S. Rosentraub. "Sports Wars: Suburbs and Center Cities in a Zero-Sum Game." *Journal of Sport & Social Issues* 21, no. 1, pp. 65–82, copyright © Sage Publications Inc. 1997;

Laurie Ouellette. "TV Viewing as Good Citizenship? Political Rationality, Enlightened Democracy and PBS." *Cultural Studies* 13, no. 1 (1998): 62–90. Reproduced by permission of Taylor and Francis Ltd. http://www.tandf.co.uk/journals;

Roy Shuker. "We are the World: State Music Policy and Cultural Imperialism," chapter 3 of *Understanding Popular Music*. London: Routledge, 1994. Reproduced by permission of the publisher and author;

Susan Smulyan, extract from Chapter 5 of *Selling Radio: The Commercialization of American Broadcasting 1920–1934* by Susan Smulyan. © 1994 by Susan Smulyan. Used by permission of the publisher Smithsonian Institution Press;

Tom Streeter. "'That Deep Romantic Chasm': Libertarianism, Neoliberalism, and the Computer Culture." *Communication, Citizenship, and Social Policy: Rethinking the Limits of the Welfare System*. Ed. Andrew Calabrese and Jean-Claude Burgelman. Lanham: Rowman & Littlefield, 1999, pp. 49–64. Reproduced by permission of the publisher.

The publishers apologize for any errors or omissions in the above list and would be grateful to be notified of any corrections that should be incorporated in the next edition or reprint of this book.

The editors would like to thank Mariana Johnson and Leshu Torchin for their help on various incarnations of this book, and Jayne Fargnoli, Annie Lenth and Anthony Grahame at Blackwell Publishers for their help and guidance.

Introduction

Justin Lewis and Toby Miller

Karl Marx wrote that: "it is impossible to create a moral power by paragraphs of law…*organic* laws supplementing the Constitution" were also needed (Marx, 1978, pp. 27, 35). That "organicism" is sought after and developed through cultural policy, which governments use to address populations with illustrations of patriotism, custom, and art. Sometimes these policies have unintended consequences, as when progressive artists manage to turn arts subvention that was designed to encourage appreciation of the "masters" into an opportunity to support AIDS activism. But broadly speaking, Marx's insight about "moral power" allows us to identify how cultural policy instills fealty in the public.

Cultural policy is, in this sense, a site for the production of cultural citizens, with the cultural industries providing not only a ream of representations about oneself and others, but a series of rationales for particular types of conduct (Miller, 1993). Michel Foucault's historicization of this question encouraged him to develop the idea of governmentality to account for "the way in which the modern state began to worry about individuals" during the Enlightenment (Foucault, 1991b, p. 4). It posed a series of questions: "How to govern oneself, how to be governed, how to govern others, by whom the people will accept being governed, how to become the best possible governor." Daily economic and spiritual government consequently came up for redefinition. When the European state emerged during the sixteenth and seventeenth centuries as a centralizing tendency that sought to normal-ize itself and others, a devolved religious authority left a void via ecclesiastical conflicts and debates about divine right. The doctrine of transcendence fell into crisis, with royalty now representing managerial rather than immanent rule (Foucault, 1991a, pp. 87–90). The government of territory was secondary to the government of things and the social relations between them. Government came to be conceived and actualized, as it is today, in terms of climate, disease, industry, finance, custom, and disaster. It became, literally, a concern with life and death and what could be calculated and managed between them.

Cultural citizenship concerns the maintenance and development of cultural lineage via education, custom, language, religion, and the acknowledgment of difference in and by the mainstream. It is a developing discourse, via the great waves of migration of the past fifty years and an increasingly mobile middle-class workforce generated by a New International Division of Cultural Labor. Today's construction of cultural citizens can be understood in various ways within these coordinates. The establishment and regulation of a cultural economy based on advertising promotes a form of citizenship based on the purchase of commodities – a world in which solutions to social problems are found not in collective action or public advocacy, but through individual acts of consumption. So, for example, we can deal with crime by buying things that make us feel secure (car alarms, padlocks, houses in safer neighborhoods) or we can cope with the thinning ozone layer by lashing on factor 20. Alternatively, as Tony Bennett describes in this volume, the development of a cultural institution like the museum can be seen not only as a form of display, invoking certain histories and suppressing others, but as an appeal to a certain form of well-behaved citizenship that respects authority and the narratives that sustain it. The television commercial and the museum are quite different forms of display. As such, they require different forms of analysis and invoke different forms of power and consent. But they both operate to produce a compliant citizen, who learns self-governance in the interests of the cultural-capitalist polity. As such, these cultural forms are neither arbitrary nor inevitable, but the product of a series of decisions, determinations, and struggles that produce one set of outcomes over another. In short, they are the result of cultural policies.

Cultural policies produce and animate institutions, practices, and agencies. One of their goals is to find, serve, and nurture a sense of belonging, through educational institutions and cultural industries. Such regimens are predicated on the insufficiency of the individual (for whom culture offers possibilities of a more complete self) alongside the generally benevolent sovereign-state. Cultural policies are a means of governance, of formatting public collective subjectivity via what John Stuart Mill termed "the departments of human interests amenable to government control" (Mill, 1974, p. 68). Some of this is done in the name of maintaining culture, to preserve ways of being a person. It can also be managed in terms of economic development generating new modes of expression. The former tend to invoke cultural hierarchies – such as those bound up in glorifying the history of Western civilization. The latter tend to embrace developments in the social technology of culture in ways that talk about the need for a citizenry to have available the latest and the best, whether it is a compact disk or an Internet hook-up.

The creation of cultural citizenship may seem a rather high-flung way to describe the nitty-gritty of policy formations, and such notions are often submerged beneath more pragmatic discourses. But in any of the more panoramic documents of cultural policy, these notions of good citizenship are directly invoked. So, for example, *Mondiacult 1982*, a world conference on cultural policy run by the United Nations Educational, Scientific and Cultural Organisation (UNESCO), announced that:

> culture gives man the ability to reflect upon himself. It is through culture that man expresses himself, becomes aware of himself, recognises his incompleteness, questions his own achievements, seeks untiringly for new meanings and creates works through which he transcends his limitations. (UNESCO, 1982, p. 190)

Similarly, the Canadian Commission for UNESCO – operating in a First World context but with a strong purchase on the tribulations of unequal cultural transfer – called for "proper cultural education" to guarantee appropriate amalgams of social critique and appreciation, making for well-rounded individuals (p. 81).

If cultural policies have, in the past, often implied the management of populations through suggested behavior, any movement towards a progressive or democratic culture – or cultures – depends upon reform. A critical approach to cultural policy is therefore a reformist project that necessitates both an understanding of the ways in which cultural policies have traditionally been deployed, and a disciplined imagining of alternatives. It also relies on making connections with progressive social and cultural movements as well as technical bureaucracies. A critical approach to cultural policy – the scope of this volume – involves both theoretical excavations and practical alternatives. It requires us to understand not only how cultural policies have worked, but how different policies might produce different outcomes.

How we understand cultural policy depends on how we define culture. There is, first of all, an aesthetic notion of culture that focuses on self-consciously "artistic" output, emerging from creative people and judged by aesthetic criteria. This is an artistic definition that generally corresponds to the interests and practices of textual studies, to cultural history and literary criticism. In this world, culture is defined not only by artistic traditions but the scholarly disciplines that define and interpret the select repertoires of great art. It is a straightforwardly elitist notion.

Nowadays, advocates for "the arts" are unlikely to embrace such smuggery overtly, and yet the use of more democratic language in arts advocacy cannot disguise the underlying assumptions that characterize many practices and outcomes of contemporary arts funding. It is, on the whole, a culture chosen and defined by cultural elites, for an audience with the requisite cultural capital.

But running counter to the *politesse* and elevation of these legacies is the spectacularization of culture. This has taken place through the market-driven populism and social-movement relevance of the US art market since the 1960s. The belief, if not the rhetoric, that art appeals to a universal human spirit beyond the reaches of particular interests, is unlikely to survive the soft cynicism of a Warhol soup can, the gendered politics of representation of a Cindy Sherman pose, the muckraking installations of a Hans Haacke, an ACT-UP zap, or a Guerrilla Girls *Blitzkrieg*, not to speak of the sexual politics of Women Against Pornography or the censorious grumblings of the religious Right. Any pretense of an aesthetic detachment floating above the struggles of social life crumbles in the midst of this politicization.

The more orthodox, elevated, notion of culture leads to a particular policy focus – notably the way organizations train, distribute, finance, describe, and reject actors and activities that go under the names of artist or artwork, through the implementation of guidelines, regulations, or directives. Governments, trade unions, colleges, social movements, community groups, and businesses aid, fund, control, promote, teach, and evaluate "creative" persons; in fact, they often decide and implement the very criteria that make possible the use of the word, "creative." This may be done through law courts that permit erotica on the grounds that they are works of art, curricula that require students to read plays on the grounds that they are uplifting, film commissions that sponsor scripts on the grounds that they reflect national concerns, or entrepreneurs who print symphonic program notes justifying an unusual season on the grounds of innovation. In turn, these criteria may themselves derive, respectively, from legal doctrine, citizenship or tourism aims, and the profit plans of impresarios.

A second, less specific meaning than aesthetic discrimination takes culture to be an all-encompassing concept about how we live our lives, the sense of place and person that make us human – what Raymond Williams referred to as a "structure of feeling." This is a more anthropological definition, and the array of policies that guide people through it encompass a much wider field than those envisioned by art agencies – or even by broadcasting authorities.

And if we understand culture in its broader, more anthropological sense, we can also see how a series of policies or guidelines operate to define what takes place and which visions of the social they privilege. References to Aboriginal culture by anthropologists before land-rights tribunals are in part determined by the rules of conduct adopted by the state in the light of colonialist notions of political power. Similarly, references to dot-commer nocturnal culture by journalists are in part determined by the rules of conduct adopted by their editors/proprietors in the light of market segmentation. These "policies" are rarely formulated as such, but once we introduce the notion of policy it assists us in excavating the structures that push cultures in certain directions.

Most of the work in this volume tends towards the spirit of the broader, more anthropological definition of culture, although sometimes with certain operational limits. Those limits are partly enshrined in the structure of this volume: thus, while we reject "high/low" cultural boundaries, we have generally focused on the conventional forms of cultural production (such as film, radio, or pop music). Hence there are no sections, say, on eating and drinking or do-it-yourself fix-uppery, although some sections – notably sport and urban planning – do not involve the same forms of "artistic" or industrial production and consumption that link most of the others. If our categories of culture seem somewhat arbitrary, they were chosen partly because they are areas in which a critical cultural policy literature exists, and where doctrines of cultural uplift and economic development have converged (sometimes in coordinated, sometimes in chaotic and uneven fashion) since the 1980s, especially in Western Europe and certain deindustrializing North American cities.

There is a sense in which most of the domains represented in this volume are understood in relation to specific state or market policies, whether as a "cultural industry" or a form of heritage. This does *not* mean, however, that the policies that shape these domains have always been adopted self-consciously to promote certain outcomes. On the contrary, much of what constitutes cultural policy is somewhat inadvertent. So, for example, the forms of public subsidy that go to college radio stations in the US are not part of a broader strategy to promote diversity in certain genres of the popular music industry, even if that may be one of their outcomes. Similarly, subsidies for road building rather than rapid urban public transportation were not intended to shift cultural locales away from urban centers towards suburban shopping malls; but as Kenneth Jackson argues in this volume, the latter's location was partly determined by the former.

When cultural policies *are* theorized as such, most developed countries tend to adopt one of two rhetorical positions. The first offers the market as a system for identifying and allocating public preferences for culture. This does not mean the state absents itself – rather, it plays the role of a police officer patrolling the precincts of property, deciding who owns what. So, for example, the state will allocate frequencies to corporate broadcasters, thereby providing them with legal protection against anyone else who wishes to use those frequencies. In practice, this means that the state often works to defend certain corporate interests, even while officially eschewing its potential to create cultural possibilities that go beyond corporate requirements. Here, it is argued, there is no policy, only culture. The United States, at least in theory, is perhaps the best example.

The second position identifies certain artifacts as inalienably, transcendentally, laden with value, but vulnerable to the public's inability to remain transcendental in its tastes. Heritage, it is argued, cannot be sustained merely through popular memory and preference. This latter position, dominant in some form in most developed countries outside the Unites States, encourages a *dirigiste* role for the state that may seem to coerce the public into an aesthetic. This position is frequently derided by populist critics for its inevitable cultural magistracy – if the market place fails to support classical ballet, the state must intervene to rescue classical ballet lest it disappear. This is a kind of "endangered species"

approach to culture – but it only seeks to protect those species it likes, while the others are happily consigned to extinction. Radical community artists like Owen Kelly – represented here – see this as a straightforwardly elitist model in which a privileged group designates one set of cultural practices as worthy and another as banal. The entire discipline of cultural studies is, in one sense, a rebellion against this elitism. Cultural studies bypasses hierarchies of value by exploring the significance and meaning of culture, whether it is popular, transitory, or sanctified by traditions of scholarship and patronage.

In this respect, our book takes its lead from cultural studies. The word "critical" in our title specifies forms of analysis that do not simply record or prescribe cultural policy in conventional (e.g. nationalist) frames, but are instead inclined towards a radical-democratic leftism. This being said, not all the work in this volume comes from people who see themselves as cultural studies scholars. Indeed, some, like Robert McChesney, see cultural studies as an intellectual space that fails to speak to their approaches or concerns. But what unifies the pieces in this volume is a rejection of the idea that the only culture worth having a policy about – whether to disseminate or protect – is the culture that many nation-states see as worth subsidizing under the rubric of "art."

One of the more inventive attempts to reinvigorate the tired old hierarchies that guide most arts funding is Ronald Dworkin's rationale for the public support of high culture. Dworkin divides public subvention into "the economic and the lofty." The economic approach suggests that community support for culture is evidenced through the mechanics of price. The lofty approach suggests that community support for culture is necessary because the market emphasizes desire rather than improvement – pleasure over sophistication. Conventional capitalist logic is, of course opposed to the deployment of public funds in the service of an ethically derived set of preferences. Dworkin specifies here the presumption that "it is more worthwhile to look at a Titian on a wall than watch a football game on television." As most people prefer the latter – a preference that can be quantified through a preparedness to pay – it is paternalistic to make them subsidize the former as part of their generic tax burden on the grounds that timeless art can in fact only survive if the vulgate is required to admire it. Art may, however, be reconceived within the economic wing of this Manichean divide as a public good which makes a collective contribution to the aesthetico-intellectual functioning of a community via the mutual impact of popular and high culture.

Dworkin thereby identifies a third way of conceiving support for culture. This involves the establishment of "a rich cultural structure" undergirding the social world of both the contemporary moment and its imagined descendants, a structure which can be identified as valuable not through pleasure or taste but complexity and difference. The availability of a variety of cultural texts thus allows the flexibility to produce pleasure at other times and places. We therefore see a shift in terms, with an emphasis on *choice* rather than *quality*. Dworkin further deflects any charges of paternalism by appealing to the notion of trusteeship – a force conserving the historically contingent in order that currently unfashionable options for pleasure can be made available to future generations. This approach supposedly celebrates difference rather than taste or value (Dworkin, 1985, pp. 221–33). And yet the move from excellence to difference can never be an innocent technical calculation. It presumes a capacity to understand what constitutes important or significant cultural endeavor. In other words, it still presumes to know the difference between what does and does not matter to an era.

This assumption can, of course, lead us back to precisely the elite forms of evaluation that characterize contemporary arts funding. Nevertheless, Dworkin's attempt to avoid the stale old *formulae* of market-driven culture or state intervention on behalf of elite culture raises the important question of how intervention might work differently. Indeed, many of the readings in this volume imply cultural values with the potential to create what we might loosely call a democratic cultural policy.

As we have suggested, while the emphasis is different from one country to the next, attempts to reconcile the "economic and the lofty" animate policy in most developed countries. If this reconciliation conceals certain contradictions between two notions of culture, it is often unified under the general rubric of national identity, an attempt to elaborate the nation to itself. The Australian Labor Party's 1986 policy *Platform*, for instance, maintained that the "basis of Australian society lies to a significant extent in the strength of its own artistic and creative expression. Government has a responsibility to encourage the development of an Australian culture." The subsequent publication of Australia's *Creative Nation* cultural policy document in the 1990s was thus able to combine support for popular cultural industries with old-fashioned arts subsidy in the name of a distinct national culture.

In the US, invoking the importance of culture as a way to "nurture and sustain" the "national character" has failed to create a sustainable political rationale for subsidizing the arts and humanities. Public subvention remains tiny by comparison with most other developed nations. There are various reasons for this, but it has partly floundered *precisely because* of the process it seeks to invoke. The success of big business in defining the "national character" – through everything from advertising to investments in think-tank punditry – has created an image of the United States in which public forms of culture are seen at best as irrelevant and at worst anathematic to the nation's self-image. In other words, the *presence* of a dominant set of marketized images, used to evoke the nation, militates against appeals for public subsidy – whether for public television or the National Endowment for the Arts.

These expressions of Australian and US cultural policy provide a mirror image of one another: the former uses definitions and claims of national cultural identity as a form of defense against the latter's use of culture for an imperialist assertion of dominance. If the first is undeniably less sinister than the second, both evoke ideas of nation that are fraught with political choices about who or what can legitimately represent a national culture. It is partly because these political choices are often implicit that a critical analysis of cultural policy is needed to excavate them.

Angela McRobbie calls cultural policy "the missing agenda" of cultural studies, given that it offers a *program* for change in addition to a distanced critique (1996, p. 335). And yet to step into the domain of policy is to take a set of risks. As cultural critic Stuart Cunningham suggests:

> Many people trained in cultural studies would see their primary role as being critical of the dominant political, economic and social order. When cultural theorists do turn to questions of policy, our command metaphors of resistance and opposition predispose us to view the policy making process as inevitably compromised, incomplete and inadequate, peopled with those inexpert and ungrounded in theory and history or those wielding gross forms of political power for short-term ends. These people are then called to the bar of an abstrusely formulated critical idealism. (1992, p. 9)

Combining theory and practice in ways that can be taken up by policy-making bureaucracies has often been regarded as misplaced in the cultural field, where everyday academic critical practice sidesteps or even disdains such relationships. Cunningham, rightly in our view, attacks this form of critical purity for failing to acknowledge ways in which critique and policy can interact – let alone cultural critics' own, unacknowledged, reliance on the state and industry for their very existence as intellectuals.

The outcomes of applying cultural studies can in fact be progressive. For example, public action on sexism in advertising and the status of women in the workplace have come about because of shifts from utopian critique to implemented policy. The end result may still be subject to vigorous critique, but there is movement in a progressive direction. Cunningham calls for a "political vocation" that draws its energy and direction from "a social democratic view of citizenship and the trainings necessary to activate and motivate it." In a classic metaphor of *Realpolitik*, this means displacing "revolutionary rhetoric" with a "reformist vocation." Its "wellsprings of engagement with policy" can avoid "a politics of the status quo – a sophomoric version of civics," because cultural studies' continued concern with power will always query the Pollyannaisms of liberal pluralism.

Cunningham uses cultural policy studies as a conduit to cultural rights, encompassing such things as access to information held by multinational corporations, the shape of international organizations like the European Community, the balance of power between developed and less-developed countries, and how all these developments have an impact locally (1992, p. 11). Jim McGuigan welcomes this turn in cultural studies, provided it retains radical insights by connecting to political economy's emphasis on public debate and citizenship rights (p. 21).

And yet the history to academic participation in so-called democratic government policy-making is, from a progressive perspective, not especially encouraging. Consider language-spread policy and the part played in it by linguists, or the work of economic advisors (Robert Triffin acting as plenipotentiary for the US to Western Europe and then as a European delegate to the IMF, just a few months apart, in the 1980s), political scientists (Project Camelot in the 1960s), biomedical researchers (relations with pharmaceutical companies), public-relations consultants (a critical concern of the professional associations), anthropologists (cultural-relativist defenses of male violence in court and Atomic Energy Commission-funded experiments on the Yanomami), nuclear physicists (Red-baiting of scientists), and communication studies (God bless the CIA, Wilbur Schramm, and Daniel Lerner). In short, any assumption that an academic presence in policy-making has some inherently progressive tilt is simply naïve.

University consultancies in the US date to nineteenth-century museums, observatories, and agricultural-experimentation outposts, but the shop was really established in the late 1950s. Considerable effort since then has gone into clarifying the significance of tailoring research priorities to contemporary political parties and corporations: "pork-barrel science," as it is known in the US. In an area like media policy, for example, this has often made for a narrow policy framework, its confines determined by the needs of political and financial power-brokers. As Thomas Streeter notes, this "inside-the-beltway" approach excludes, almost by definition, any substantive critique of a corporate-run, government-sanctioned media system. Progressive ideas are thus made irrelevant to the policy process, and entry to this narrow world requires not so much a curtailing of cultural critique as an abandonment of it. Ralph Nader's Center for Universities in the Public Interest was set up because of such concerns, which are even evident to former supporters of government/college/industry relationships (such as

Harvard's Derek Bok) and very traditional sociologists, like Robert Nisbet, who have experienced the obstacles they pose to disinterested research outcomes. Indeed, as Streeter points out, advocacy of a policy focus in cultural studies may be inappropriate in the US, where "policy" connotes a pro-corporate position that turns highly contestable positions into absolutes, with consultant professors simultaneously performing objectivity and applicability. (For example, the policy and program management of America's National Parks has consistently owed much more to bureaucratic *force majeure*, tourism money, and "development" than to ecological science) (*Language Problems and Language Planning*; Ammon, 1992, p. 6; Nisbet, 1970; Beauchamp, 1992; "Special Issue," 1994; Winkelman, 1996; Sholle, 1995, p. 132; Rowe and Brown, 1994, p. 98; Ruscio, 1994, p. 209; Stahler and Tash, 1994; Bowie, 1993, p. 5, 7; deLeon, 1995, p. 886; Dryzek, 1994, p. 117; Streeter, 1996, pp. 16 n. 14, 133, 136; Sellars, 1997, pp. 3–4).

Ironically, because the US has such a strong tradition of academic study financed by governments and foundations, it offers an impressive review of how knowledge is used in sponsored research, and how policy studies intersects with the state and public relations, most notably in think tanks (Hammack, 1995). Paul DiMaggio and Walter Powell (1983), for instance, have done important work on the structure of organizations that suggests a trend towards homologies between sponsoring and consulting bodies – when one institution depends on another for assistance, it tends to mimic its structures and reiterate its concerns.

The history of what might be called a critical cultural policy has a variety of interconnected histories on different continents. In North America, Herbert Gans' path-breaking work on "taste cultures" provided a multiply layered framework for intellectualizing the popular and its relationship to policy in the 1970s (Gans, 1974, pp. 121–59). "Cultural policy studies" was named and undertaken during that decade in part through the formation of the Association of Cultural Economics (which went international in 1994) and the Center for Urban Studies at the University of Akron. This was followed by regular conferences on economics, social theory, and the arts, and major studies of

policy and program evaluation produced at Canada's Institute for New Interpretive Creative Activities, the Cultural Policy Unit of The Johns Hopkins Center for Metropolitan Planning and Research, and Columbia University's Research Center for the Arts and Culture. Publications such as the *Journal of Arts Management, Law, and Society* and the *Journal of Cultural Economics* have long provided a wealth of theoretical speculation and empirical reporting and many of their authors have direct connections to the think-tank Center for Art and Culture in Washington, DC.

In the UK, the move toward cultural policy was inspired by two developments: cultural studies, and the adoption of Pierre Bourdieu's work on class and cultural taste (Bourdieu, 1984; Bourdieu et al., 1991). Both tendencies entered the fray with a critique (one from the humanities, one from the social sciences) of elitist notions of culture, and a determination to engage with popular culture as a site of meaning and social change. But the move was given its political impetus by the election of progressive populist administrations of British local authorities – notably the Greater London Council (GLC) – in the early 1980s. Until that point, institutions like the GLC had equated cultural policy with the high arts: suddenly, insurgent progressives gained power, and looked to academics for assistance in reinventing a more democratic cultural policy. Nicholas Garnham, who had helped introduce Bourdieu's work to the UK, was brought in to help craft a "cultural industries" strategy that would remove class distinctions from cultural policy, and expand the state's view of culture to encompass not only such things as art museums, literature, and opera but television, radio, and pop music. This confluence of political will and cultural critique created one of the most dynamic periods of policy and action in urban cultural policy in British history, with a sparkling array of hits and misses (Lewis, 1990).

All this took place during the Thatcher years, and perhaps inevitably the momentum behind these developments began to wither with the abolition of the GLC and other metropolitan authorities in 1986. The push to expand culture to embrace the popular nonetheless trickled upward, and the British Labour Party institutionalized this shift when it regained power nationally in the late 1990s by broadening ministerial responsibility for the arts to include the electronic media and other popular-cultural industries.

The focal point of a move towards critical cultural policy studies shifted in the late '80s to Australia, where the influence of cultural studies combined with a series of challenges to dominant notions of Australian culture and national identity. The election of successive Labor governments gave this work an entry point into policy-making. The establishment at this time of an Institute for Cultural Policy Studies at Griffith University was the outcome of several interconnected developments. Reformist social-democratic government encouraged more applied university research work, "even" in the humanities. This promised rewards to those scholars who tailored their labors to state priorities. At the same time, several imported scions of British cultural studies were undergoing a conversion from an oppositional discourse influenced by the work of Antonio Gramsci, which celebrated resistance to hegemony, to a liberal model of political activity developed from Foucault's elaboration of governmentality. This confluence made for both opportunities and desires and produced a new engagement with civic life for cultural studies (Miller, 1998).

How far the zigzagging momentum of these various turns towards a critical cultural policy will be developed in the decades to come depends upon movements in the culture and politics of various nation-states, as well as certain whimsies of academic fashion. And yet the impetus for publishing the first reader in critical cultural policy is not simply an attempt to sustain the momentum – it is equally a response to the various ways in which culture is being pushed to the forefront of democratic politics. As the corporate cultural commissars grow larger and more audacious, so their clumsy presence seems to invite irritation and, perhaps, a desire for another way of doing things. So, for example, when most soccer fans in the UK suddenly find games they were accustomed to watching snatched away from their TV screens in order to promote the sale of satellite packages, the failure of cultural policy-makers to do more than wave a feeble hand breeds a grumbling and popular discontent. And if trade agreements sanctioning a move towards global cultural industries once proceeded

quietly (protecting corporate profit and power with an increasingly aggressive regimen of intellectual property law, while shifting production in ways that create a race to the bottom in terms of wages and labor conditions), citizen activism means that they no longer do so. In short, as the cultural industries are caught up in the ruthless push of neo-liberalism, resistance to such moves – regardless of the motivation – creates a rhetorical space for other possibilities, including more progressive cultural policies.

Many of the essays anthologized here address the US and UK contexts. There are several reasons for this. The first is that these nations have, not surprisingly, generated the majority of English-language writing in the area. The second is their prominence in commercial and governmental cultural traditions. The United States has the largest and most powerful set of private culture industries, and while their heritage in commerce is well-known, they have equally important links to the state. It is especially important to emphasize this point at the present moment, when the US model of putative free enterprise is on evangelical export. The United Kingdom has the largest and most powerful set of public cultural industries, via the BBC. It has stood for the model of public provision of culture, where government as well as the market must be overtly involved. Together, these traditions have been exported and also cross-pollinated one another.

This volume is not a manifesto. Nor does it contain a consensus about what these policies should or should not look like. But it does offer a sense of what we have learnt thus far, a space from which we hope the reader will move on. And it is a book of tendency. We acknowledge the importance of both theoretical and empirical work, but veer away from both the elitism of high-culture elevation and the technicism of supposedly objective public-policy scholarship. A critical cultural policy studies must concern itself with progressive politics, and take its touchstone as much from social movements as from policy infrastructures.

References

"Special Issue: Public Relations Ethics." *Public Relations Review* 20, no. 3 (1994).

Ammon, Ulrich. "Editor's Preface." *International Journal of the Sociology of Language*, no. 95 (1992): 5–9.

Australian Labor Party. *Platform, Resolutions and Rules*. Canberra: Australian Labor Party, 1986.

Beauchamp, Tom L. "Ethical Issues in Funding and Monitoring University Research." *Business and Professional Ethics Journal* 11, no. 1 (1992): 5–16.

Bourdieu, Pierre. *Distinction: A Social Critique of the Judgement of Taste*. Trans. Richard Nice. Cambridge, Mass.: Harvard University Press, 1984.

Bourdieu, Pierre, A. Darbel, and D. Schnapper. *The Love of Art: European Art Museums and Their Public*. Stanford: Stanford University Press, 1991.

Bowie, Norman E. "The Clash Between Academic Values and Business Values." *Business and Professional Ethics Journal* 12, no. 4 (1993): 3–19.

Canadian Commission for UNESCO. "A Working Definition of 'Culture'." *Cultures* 4, no. 4 (1977): 78–85.

Cunningham, Stuart. *Framing Culture: Criticism and Policy in Australia*. Sydney: Allen and Unwin, 1992.

deLeon, Peter. "Democratic Values and the Policy Sciences." *American Journal of Political Science* 39, no. 4 (1995): 886–905.

DiMaggio, Paul J. and Walter W. Powell. "The Iron Cage Revisited: Institutional Isomorphism and Collective Rationality in Organizational Fields." *American Sociological Review* 48, no. 2 (1983): 147–60.

Dryzek, John S. *Discursive Democracy: Politics, Policy, and Political Science*. Cambridge: Cambridge University Press, 1994.

Dworkin, Ronald. *A Matter of Principle*. Cambridge, Mass.: Harvard University Press, 1985.

Foucault, Michel. "Governmentality." Trans. Pasquale Pasquino. *The Foucault Effect: Studies in Governmentality*. Ed. Graham Burchell, Colin Gordon, and Peter Miller. London: Harvester Wheatsheaf, 1991a, 87–104.

Foucault, Michel. *Remarks on Marx: Conversations with Duccio Trombadori*. Trans. J. R. Goldstein and J. Cascaito. New York: Semiotext(e), 1991b.

Gans, Herbert J. *Popular Culture and High Culture: An Analysis and Evaluation of Taste*. New York: Basic Books, 1974.

Hammack, David. "Think Tanks and the Invention of Policy Studies." *Nonprofit and Voluntary Service Quarterly* 24, no. 2 (1995): 173–81.

Language Problems & Language Planning.

Leavis, F. R. *Mass Civilization and Minority Culture*. Cambridge: Cambridge University Press, 1930.

Lewis, Justin. *Art, Culture and Enterprise*. London: Routledge, 1990.

Marx, Karl. *The Eighteenth Brumaire of Louis Bonaparte*. Peking: Foreign Language Press, 1978.

McGuigan, Jim. *Culture and the Public Sphere*. London: Routledge, 1996.

McRobbie, Angela. "All the World's a Stage, Screen or Magazine: When Culture is the Logic of Late Capitalism." *Media, Culture and Society* 18, no. 3 (1996): 335–42.

Mill, John Stuart. *On Liberty*. Harmondsworth: Penguin, 1974.

Miller, Toby. *Technologies of Truth: Cultural Citizenship and the Popular Media*. Minneapolis: University of Minnesota Press, 1998.

Miller, Toby. *The Well-Tempered Self: Citizenship, Culture, and the Postmodern Subject*. Baltimore: The Johns Hopkins University Press, 1993.

Nisbet, Robert A. "Project Camelot: An Autopsy." *On Intellectuals: Theoretical Studies. Case Studies*. Ed. Philip Rieff. New York: Anchor, 1970, 307–39.

Rowe, David and Peter Brown. "Promoting Women's Sport: Theory, Policy and Practice." *Leisure Studies* 13, no. 2 (1994): 97–110.

Ruscio, Kenneth P. "Policy Cultures: The Case of Science Policy in the United States." *Science, Technology, and Human Values* 19, no. 2 (1994): 205–22.

Sellars, Richard West. *Preserving Nature in the National Parks: A History*. New Haven: Yale University Press, 1997.

Sholle, David. "Resisting Disciplines: Repositioning Media Studies in the University." *Communication Theory* 5, no. 2 (1995): 130–43.

Stahler, Gerald J. and William R. Tash. "Centers and Institutes in the Research University: Issues, Problems, and Prospects." *Journal of Higher Education* 65, no. 5 (1994): 540–54.

Streeter, Thomas. *Selling the Air: A Critique of the Policy of Commercial Broadcasting in the United States*. Chicago: University of Chicago Press, 1996.

UNESCO. *Final Report of World Conference on Cultural Policies*. Mexico City and Paris: UNESCO, 1982.

Williams, Raymond. *Culture and Society, 1780–1950*. Harmondsworth: Penguin, 1971.

Winkelman, Michael. "Cultural Factors in Criminal Defense Proceedings." *Human Organization* 55, no. 2 (1996): 154–9.

Part I

Cultural Studies and the Cultural Industry

Chapter 1

Cultural Studies from the Viewpoint of Cultural Policy

Stuart Cunningham

As might be expected of any newish field, a growing array of questions has begun to be asked of cultural studies as it moves into a phase of consolidation and some respectability. I think there are three global positions from whence this questioning comes. In placing these on a left-to-right continuum, I am mindful that amongst other things at stake in the current climate is the viability of just such a political set. We might well remember Jean-Luc Godard and Anne-Marie Mieville's caveat in *Numéro Deux*: 'this is not a film of the left or right, but a film of before and behind'.

Feeding from the humanities is a position to the left of an increasingly academicised cultural studies that seeks to question its orthodoxies in the name of a more authentic critical and political practice, or in the name of a more thorough-going deconstruction or postmodernism. This position can invoke the powerful trope of recalling cultural studies to its origins as a brave intervention in established literary and social science orthodoxies.

Meaghan Morris 'Banality in Cultural Studies',[1] for example, attacks the installation of a profoundly banal set of protocols in cultural studies centring on the wilful calling-into-being of progressiveness in texts, resistance in audiences, and a cheerful populism in criticism that too often collapses into little more than a simulacrum of fandom. The critical stances of the traditional humanities disciplines have not

been so clearly dispelled as might have been once imagined, she suggests.

There is a position on the right emerging from the social sciences that identifies the recent sea changes in Eastern Europe and the USSR, the longer-term global shifts toward international-isation and the collapse of movement politics of various kinds as calling into question the continuing relevance of the neo-Marxist 'motor' of cultural studies. From this perspective, the reflex anti-capitalism, anti-consumerism and romanti-cisation of sub-cultural resistance embodied in the classical texts of cultural studies are no longer adequate responses to the big questions con-fronting the articulation of politics and culture in modern Western societies.

With these political re-assessments has come a concomitant revaluation of empirical detail, aligned with a piecemeal approach to the articu-lation of ideology and culture. There is a 'beyond ideology' flavour about much of this work. John Kelly's discussion[2] of Stuart Hall's key text on left renewal in Britain, *The Hard Road to Renewal: Thatcherism and the Crisis of the Left* is a frontal attack on a politics of grand theory that lacks credible empirics. Kelly poses with rhetorical naivete the ultimate empirical question: '*How* does Hall know any of these things [about the roots of the success of Thatcher]?' (emphasis added).

The swelling ranks of apostates from the charmed circle of neo-Marxist orthodoxies, especially in Britain (in the United States cultural studies is still on a growth surge, and substantial questioning of the assumptions of the field from within will not come very soon or very readily), suggests that something more than a faddish search for The Next Thing is afoot.[3]

There is also a 'centrist' policy orientation. This approach seeks to position the perspectives of cultural studies within fields of public policy where academic critical protocols *don't have priority*. Like the 'left-humanities' position, it is aware of the limits of academic discourse. While seeking to respond to the same global concerns as the 'right-social science' position, it is not as concerned to discredit the foundational posture of cultural studies, if that posture is distilled down to the central Enlightenment values of Liberty, Equality and Solidarity.[4] Indeed, it seeks to revivify these core values as the central motor of reformism that can be appealed to in the public sphere of contemporary Western societies. This is the position that I wish to advance as a way forward for cultural studies.

What relations should exist between cultural studies and cultural policy? I employ the term cultural studies (or cultural criticism) as a convenient shorthand for work driven by the major strands of neo-Marxist, structuralist, poststructuralist and postmodernist thought, which treat film, the arts, media and communications, as well as lived, everyday culture. Cultural policy embraces that broad field of public processes involved in formulating, implementing, and contesting governmental intervention in, and support of, cultural activity.

The commonsense reaction to my question, one likely to be offered by the majority of those outside the academy who might be inclined to consider it, would be that the former serves as a kind of 'handmaiden', developing rationales for those at the coalface of public policy. Theory, analysis and commentary should undergird practice; practice implements theory. On closer inspection, however, the relations are far less harmonious than this model suggests. Indeed, in many ways, contemporary practices of theory and policy flatly contradict received wisdom.

Cultural studies, from the viewpoint of cultural policy, might be like the curate's egg – good in part, but even the good parts mightn't be that good! Liz Jacka wrote recently of the 'ever widening gap between cultural critique and cultural policy.'[5] Taking my cue from this, I want to canvass some recent issues in Australian cultural and communications policy where practical opportunities for cultural analysis have been foregone, or worse.

Australian Content on Television

An exhaustive inquiry into Australian Content on Commercial Television, conducted by the Australian Broadcasting Tribunal, concluded its main considerations in December 1989 with the introduction of a new Television Program Standard. The inquiry ran, with a break of three years in the mid-1980s, for about five years.[6]

One of the then members of the Tribunal, Julie James Bailey, commented that there was virtually no input during the several years of the inquiry from academic cultural critics and analysts.[7] However, there was one major contribution, from cultural critic John Docker, and it employed an array of contemporary theory to attack the legitimacy of regulation for Australian content on television.[8]

Such regulation, in Docker's view, actually means the imposition of (British) high cultural values onto popular cultural forms whose appeal is indifferent to national variations and registrations. What viewers actively embrace in television culture, according to Docker, is the carnivalesque overturning of statist official culture and the celebration of working class values and interests. These values and interests are transnational and are inherently subversive of state interventions to preserve national registrations of popular cultural forms.

It is not surprising that Docker's arguments had no effect on the outcomes of the Inquiry. But that should not in itself be cause for good feeling, as Docker's was the only significant contribution to the Inquiry that presented any of the theoretical issues that have concerned theorists, critics and historians for decades. Docker's view of popular television and its audiences may be one idiosyncratic extrapolation of current strands of cultural theory, but it is, in Turner's words, 'directly licensed' by them.[9] To applaud Docker's irrelevance could be tantamount to applauding, from the viewpoint of policy making process, the irrelevance of critical and theoretical input in general.

Advertising and National Culture

This Tribunal inquiry addressed itself to Australian content provisions covering all television programming, *including advertising*. The regulations for television advertising are different from those for other program material. They are directed at prohibiting more than 20 per cent of any advertising being produced overseas, unless Australian crews travel overseas to obtain the footage. They constitute a very high level of protection for local content, and, because they have been in place for thirty years, they have been extremely influential in underwriting the television advertising industry in Australia.

The inquiry into Foreign Content in Advertising has operated virtually as a sidelight to the main act. It is not hard to see why. Advertising is truly the unworthy discourse, as far as both criticism and policy are concerned. If there has been an outstanding consensus amongst critical methods of various persuasions, it is that advertising panders to patriarchal and consumerist mentalities. In the wider scheme of things, this consensus sits comfortably with moves to deregulate a blatantly protected industry. Regulation against foreign advertising content has been the subject of concerted attack from industry – primarily transnational advertisers – as well as high-level economic rationalist sources of advice to government. A recent Industries Assistance Commission (now Industry Commission) report attacked the 'virtual embargo' on foreign-produced ads: 'the sector enjoys an extremely privileged position relative to nearly all other economic activity in Australia'.[10]

The Foreign Content in Advertising segment of the inquiry, therefore, called up the need for a wide-ranging account of the role advertising has played in the formation of national cultural identity, as this has been put forward as the prime rationale for continued regulation.

The argument for making a positive connection between advertising and national culture has to be mounted in two basic areas. From the viewpoint of policy, the weaker argument is the appeal to the effects of deregulation in the area of advertising on the drama production industry. It

is clear that drama production could not have developed its scope and depth without the industrial infrastructure of the Australian advertising industry. Evidence for this link is widely accepted and pieces of it are often cited in film and television histories.[11] For this reason, if for no other, deregulating television advertising would have major cultural consequences. The central argument, however, has to grasp the nettle – the positive contribution advertising itself may make to national culture. To this task, cultural studies, in its present forms, is spectacularly unsuited.

Two main patterns of criticism have remained foundational to the cultural critique of advertising. The first is diachronic, focusing on the history of advertising as a main agent of American cultural imperialism. The MacBride Report for UNESCO established the parameters of this pattern, and Jeremy Tunstall's *The Media are American* and Mattelart and Dorfman's *How to Read Donald Duck* continued it, and the general critical perspective on advertising has never seriously diverted from it. The other pattern is synchronic – informed by the early semiotic guerrilla tactics of Roland Barthes' *Mythologies*, it focuses on the cultural reproduction of dominant ideological values embedded through advertising in bourgeois culture. Its classic statement is Judith Williamson's *Decoding Advertisements*. There have been developments, in particular an increasingly strong emphasis on feminist inflections of semiotic guerrilla warfare. Generally speaking, however, the cultural studies approach to advertising, both in critical writing and in curricula, has not advanced significantly beyond the 1950s and 1960s work of Barthes, MacBride and Mattelart and Dorfman.

Under the umbrella of the Tribunal's content regulation, Australian television advertising has developed a strong grammar of national imaging that parallels film and television fiction, but represents a considerably greater permeation, by volume and by mode and degree of penetration, of the mass market. Advertising occupies an average of some three and a half hours a day on each commercial metropolitan television station compared to recent Australian drama content levels of around two hours a week. By dint of repetition, saturation coverage across the most popular networks, and sophisticated textual strategies that increasingly link programs with their com-merical 'environment', advertising must be seen as having considerable cultural valence.

Such indicators of cultural permeation, though crude and problematic from a critical perspec-tive, are important in policy formulation. The real issue is to what extent can a positive character be imputed to them? This is not a question simply of inverting cultural studies' negativity, putting the Mister Sheen gloss on what the critic has regarded as a tawdry business. It is a matter of evaluating the contribution of television adver-tising in terms other than marking ideological ticks and crosses. It is to describe the impress and influence of advertising in terms that accept that its ideologically regressive elements – its sexism, its chauvinism, its rowdy populism – are bracketed within a more neutral, descriptive cul-tural and audiovisual history.

Such a history would focus on the central role advertising has played in the development of a popular audiovisual 'grammar' of national iden-tity during the 1970s and 1980s. The so-called 'new' nationalism of this period was most visibly expressed in advertising campaigns, despite the large claims made for the contribution of film and television drama. These campaigns were at key moments explicit attempts at social engin-eering – for instance, the Life. Be In It campaign and the Advance Australia campaign of the late 1970s and early 1980s. The published aims of Advance Australia make this clear:

> To heighten community and public awareness and pride in Australian skills, achievements and potential. To highlight the role of individual enterprise in the economy. To encourage im-provements in quality, design, marketing and other characteristics of Australian identity.[12]

This advertising campaign, and others that came in the wake of its high profile (and state-funded cash flow) sought to redress what attitudinal re-search had identified as a widespread lack of 'pride in country' and support for Australian manufacturing.[13] This kind of public service ad-vertising has had its counterparts in purely com-mercial campaigns, which have increasingly over the last fifteen years invented a populist audio-visual grammar of nationalism. Prestige national advertising campaigns now routinely incorpor-ate this established repertoire of Australianist

tropes. The fact that this repertoire is used for evidently contradictory purposes, from promot-ing health to flogging beer and tobacco, and util-ises everything from unacceptably sexist to innovative, even progressive, imaging, simply registers the embeddedness and modularity of advertising's nationalism.

What critical appraisal there is of this enormous portfolio of material, and there is very little that is substantial, is unhelpful in articulating a position sensitive to the policy issues. Stephen Alomes' less-then-trenchant put-down of the course of Australian nationalism 'from jingoism to jingle-ism' in *A Nation at Last?*, Tim Rowse's critique of television populism in the 'humanity' ads, and others engage in critical exercises of the traditional kind.[14]

The kind of 'sophisticated theory of consump-tion' called for by Kathy Myers in Britain[15] and the magisterial descriptivist account of 'advertis-ing as social communication' given by William Leiss, Stephen Kline and Sut Jhally in North America[16] should be applied to the question of Australian national identity in advertising if we are to advance beyond reflex ideological critique and begin to address urgent and practical policy issues embodied in such inquiries as the Tribunal's.

Feminist Cultural Theory and Bureaucratic Reformism

Of course, all need not be sweetness and light for the reconstructed cultural critic in relation to advertising. Turning to questions of sexism, it is notable that Australia lags behind such coun-tries as Canada and some Scandinavian nations in implementing strategies to modify sexist representations in the mass media. Over the last few years, however, there have been signifi-cant initiatives in Australia. The Office of the Status of Women has acted as the co-ordinating secretariat for a body called the National Working Party on the Portrayal of Women in the Media, a body consisting of representatives of the advertising industry, community groups and government departments.

To my knowledge, little or nothing arising from that contemporary feminist scholarship utilising a sophisticated repertoire of theories of representation has been brought to bear on questions of bureaucratic reformism. Indeed, the most willing and effective advocates of institutional change to public representation of women use 'outdated', reflectionist and empiricist research to derive evidence for change, and a liberal humanist feminism to ground their campaigns.

It is not hard to see why advanced feminist theories of representation have weighed so lightly, despite the considerable body of literature that has been developed around exactly the sorts of questions that animate reformist policy initiatives. As Leiss, Kline and Jhally argue, 'representation' critiques of advertising have been subjective, non-quantitative, and have reduced the specificity of advertising to a generalised social critique.

From the viewpoint of policy, they are subjective because they depend to an unacceptable degree on methods that are difficult to replicate without a high degree of interpretative training. In the hands of a Barthes or a Williamson, semiotic method is powerful and convincing, but there has been a lot of obfuscated and redundant 'normal science' in the area. Representation critiques depend on extrapolated pertinence to an equally unacceptable degree – the findings are not underwritten by content analysis based on accepted sampling techniques. And they are guilty of simply using advertising, because it is arguably the most visible and most insistent form of commercialism, as a springboard into a generalised social critique that is unhelpful within the protocols of piecemeal reformism.

For all these reasons, representation accounts have been of little value in policy calculation, even for those predisposed to accept the assumptions from which they stem.

Media Ownership and Cultural Power

Cultural studies has increasingly moved away from the orthodox political economy model which centres great concern on questions of ownership and control of the mass media. The cultural power that is interesting now resides with audiences and, to a lesser extent, producers of media content itself. Set over against these interests are what appear to cultural theorists as rather hackneyed and predictable arguments for greater diversity and less concentration of media ownership. The calls of a David Bowman, a Paul Chadwick, or an Eric Beecher appear hackneyed and predictable because they are voiced within very narrow terms of cultural debate, and partake in what Walter Benjamin memorably called 'left-wing melancholy'. This miserabilism, this prophetic nay-saying, cultural studies is now resolutely setting itself against.

However, political and cultural power exercised through media control remains one of the key blind spots of public policy in Australia. There is considerable evidence that the issue cuts through established party and factional allegiances and will begin to create intolerable anomalies for public policy. The traditional regulatory rationale for distinguishing between the electronic media and the press will begin to break down through convergence, narrowcasting and internationalisation.

I take the view that this issue will certainly not go away in a postmodernist flush of audience sovereignty, and indeed will increase in centrality as media converge and narrow their focus ever more powerfully toward precise demographic and psychographic fine-tuning. Not only that, but the current theoretical fashion for championing the active audience finds an ironic echo in the rhetoric of consumer sovereignty that is offered by the media owners and the deregulators.

Unambiguous economic and political power will increasingly be translatable into unambiguous cultural power. Those who are best positioned to benefit from enhanced technologies of audience targeting, from the convergence of media of carriage, and from pro-competitive public policy parameters, are precisely those who now exercise enormous power through control of the traditional media. Alliances with social democratic advocates of media reform are set to become a crucial defining mark of the relevance of cultural studies in the near future.

Now, Just Wait a Minute!

Of course, the 'handmaiden' model is easy pickings for those inside the academy. Most people trained in the politics of cultural studies would view their primary role as critics of the dominant political, economic and social order. When cultural theorists do turn their hand to questions of policy, our command metaphors of resistance, refusal and oppositionalism predispose us to view the policy making process as inevitably compromised, ad hoc, and always incomplete and inadequate, peopled with those inexpert and ungrounded in theory and history or those wielding gross forms of political power for short term ends. These people and processes are then called to the bar of an abstrusely formulated cultural idealism. This critical idealism would retort that mine is the mealy-mouthed voice of liberal bourgeois compromise.

A more reflective critique of the position I am advancing would raise the issue of the long term, leavening effect of critical idealism. From where does tomorrow's public debate and potential consensus issue? From today's utopian, abstruse, left-of-field thinking, that, at the time of its formulation, might appear counterindicated by the realities of the public world. The clearest example of this is the 'sourcing' of femocrat reformism by feminist movement politics. Similar sourcing relationships hold between the environmental movement and green politics, or between ethnic advocacy and official discourses of multiculturalism. A more pragmatic variant of the same objection is that, if cultural studies doesn't hold to the humanities' traditional critical vocation, who will, particularly in the wake of the breakdown of more broadly-based social movements?

These objections seem reasonable, so I want to respond to them carefully.

First, the model of the lone critic prophesying is one I do not wish to discount at all, indeed such a role is the *sine qua non* of critical practice. However, it is rather disingenuous for the academy to don this mantle, when a great deal of the critical work performed within the academy could not plausibly claim such prophetic status. The most effective public intellectuals on issues of culture in the Australian polity are not vanguard theorists, but those who work within the terms of a given (and, one might readily concede, narrow) set of public interest, liberal democratic and social democratic norms. Vanguard theory, on the evidence we have to date, is less than likely to translate into prophetic criticism.

The second response proceeds from the first. To get to the nub of the problem, what is cultural studies' understanding of its political vocation? What is its vision of a better, more just, equitable, participatory, cultural order? What measures are cultural theorists and analysts taking to have this vision articulated widely, including in the public sphere? What alliances are we forming with cultural activists and policy agents and players, and to what extent are we informing ourselves thoroughly about the historical, existing and emergent policy agenda, and identifying where we might fit?

In an interesting interchange between John Fiske and an unnamed interlocutor, published in Fiske's *Reading the Popular*, the politics of Fiske's influential model of resistive populism are brought to the fore. The resistive strategies imputed to consumers of popular culture are ones which, by definition, are never mobilised into organisations that might seek to influence change in any institutional arrangement or professional practice by which cultural meaning is produced and delivered. While Fiske might assert that 'internal or semiotic resistance…is an essential prerequisite of social change',[17] the resistance he champions actually undermines the strategies of organised reform movements because it sets itself against ideal standards of professional media practice and against empirical audience measurement. Both are essential if reformism is to gain some purchase in public policy processes.

The missing link is a social democratic view of citizenship and the trainings necessary to activate and motivate it. A renewed concept of citizenship should be becoming increasingly central to cultural studies as it moves into the 1990s. Like many developments in one disciplinary area, this development might easily look like the wheel is being re-invented. Political science, government, sociology, journalism, organisation studies, to say nothing of traditional professional trainings such as law: each of these have particular mobilisations of citizenship embodied in their curriculum profiles. Despite this, the emerging evidence for an attention to citizenship in cultural studies signifies an important advance in emphasis and direction. It demonstrates that it is coming to terms with its neo-Marxist heritage as it realises that other political postures can be as radically reformist as neo-Marxism without being automatically marginalised in the public arena through the latter's dependence on a totalistic and confrontational rhetoric. For this reason, the perspectives of

Australian social democratic thinkers like Hugh Stretton in social theory, Donald Horne, Peter Wilenski, and H. C. 'Nugget' Coombs in cultural and communications areas, or Francis Castles in economics, should assume as great an importance for rethinking the vocation of cultural studies than the international fathers (and mothers) of the discipline.

Replacing shop-worn revolutionary rhetoric with the new command metaphor of citizenship commits cultural studies to a reformist strategy within the terms of a social democratic politics, and thus can connect it more organically to the well-springs of engagement with policy. Even though, as Ham and Hill[18] show, the policy process in modern capitalist states has arisen within a liberal pluralist problematic, it need not be limited by liberalism's underdeveloped ideas of power and of the necessity of struggle for access to decision-making processes.

And this concept of citizenship does not by any means imply a politics of the status quo – a sort of primary school version of civics. Donald Horne uses it to advance his Lockean notion of the 'cultural rights' of the citizen in modern social democracies. Graham Murdock and Peter Golding use it to invite thinking about information poverty in our age of increasingly privatised communications. And it is also being employed to pose questions about new forms of citizenship which may embrace larger units than the individual nation state, such as the emergent European community. Similarly, Mattelart, Delcourt and Mattelart propose a linguistic-cultural transnational community – a 'latin audio-visual space' – in their 1984 report to the French Ministry of Culture.[19] Such concerns have been abroad for decades in the ongoing debate in UNESCO concerning the New World Information and Communications Order (NWICO).

Third, it is a fact that the substantial proportion of cultural studies work is performed within academic arrangements that either prioritise vocational trainings or seek to marry a liberal arts education with gestures toward such training. These institutional orientations will become more established, if not necessarily accepted, under current and any likely future government policies. Pragmatically, then, there are powerful reasons to review the current state of cultural studies.

An increasing series of calls to introduce a policy orientation into cultural studies has been evident in recent years.[20] We hear that cultural studies remains fixated on theoretical and textual orientations which provide little purchase in seeking to equip students with knowledge and skills for citizenship and employment in the 1990s. The gap between textually-based studies and policy cannot be bridged merely by further refinements in theories of representation, in new understandings of the audience or the 'progressive text', or in notions of sub-cultural resistance.

Indeed, two of the British cultural studies apostates, Geoff Hurd and Ian Connell, have argued that cultural critique, as a governing educational model, has actively *deskilled* students:

> Cultural organisations, whether state or commercial, have been regarded as targets for criticism and reconstruction in the light of certain cultural theory. While we accept there is a need for cultural appraisal and reconstruction, we would also suggest that the predominant view of cultural organisations within cultural studies has been misleading and that criticism has been placed before understanding. In short, cultural studies has been critical of enterprises whose modes of operation and social significance it does not properly comprehend.[21]

Questions of policy *do* circulate at the margins of the traditional core curricula of cultural studies. In Trevor Barr's words, moving those marginal interests toward the centre of the curriculum ultimately has to do with 'political empowerment'.[22]

And a focus on policy extended to both types of communications curricula – semiotics-based cultural studies on the one hand, and business communication, journalism, public relations, marketing and advertising on the other – offers the opportunity to bridge yawning gaps between opposing traditions. Its integration into liberal arts and media production programs would encourage a firmer grasp of the social and vocational implications of cultural struggle as embodied in governmental and industrial processes. On the other hand, its integration into industry-driven courses would draw students into a broader appreciation of the politics and ethics of their vocations and the reasonable legitimacy of state intervention.

Finally, many of our protocols are disabling because they take scant account of the local conditions in which theory must be developed.

It might seem like a truism to state that cultural studies might appropriately develop different emphases as it is practised in different parts of the world. However, because Australia is a net importer of ideas as much as goods and services, it is all the more crucial for an Australian cultural studies to be self-critical about its agenda, lest it be set, by default, elsewhere. I can't put it better than the report of the Committee to Review Australian Studies in Tertiary Education, when it said that Australianising tertiary education would prevent the intellectual cringe that slides 'between a vacuous cosmopolitanism and an apologetic provincialism.'[23]

To Australianise is not to call for a form of intellectual tariff blockade. On the contrary, it implies a much stronger and more perspicacious engagement with imported traditions than is generally the case. And it in no way implies an *a priori* defence of the status quo, rejecting out of hand possible benefits flowing from greater internationalisation of inquiry. It does suggest that an *Australian* cultural studies engaging with the policy issues that impact on the future of Australian culture would involve, as we have seen, reconceptualising general theories of advertising, considerably upgrading the focus on regulation as a positive underpinning of cultural production, and re-thinking the politics of culture in a non-British, non-North American setting.

Importing British cultural studies has meant privileging subcultural resistance to a repressive and class-defined state and state apparatus. This has much to do with the far-reaching influence of Thatcherism for over a decade as a negative marker of the agenda for the British left, leading to the generally anti-statist tone of much cultural studies, and the search for positive markers of the intrinsic subversiveness of everyday life which is set firmly against a renewed concept of citizenship. The libertarianism implicit in this approach might find a greater echo in the United States (where the state consistently has willingly abetted rather than mollified economic and cultural imperialism) than it ever should in Australia, or for that matter many other countries where state activity has struggled to regulate for the equitable flow of economic and cultural goods and services.

Consider the perennial issue of the nation as an illustration of the importance of localism in intellectual work. The ascendent current of macro-level thought in cultural studies today lays to rest the nation state and invites linking positive opportunities for internationalism with a renewed communalism. This *may* be appropriate for cultural thought in a European context in the present climate, but it is wholly inappropriate in virtually any context outside the First World, including Australia.

There are high stakes involved in the arguments for internationalism and community against the nation. All the major cultural industries in Australia (film, television, the major arts and the many community-based arts programs sponsored by the Australia Council) derive their policy justification from their being national in scope. It is too early, if indeed it will ever be politically strategic, to pit the internationalist-communalist position against the nation in Australia.

Ultimately, despite Australia's byzantine tripartite system of government, making it one of the most 'governed' countries in the world per capita, it is at the national level that debate on cultural futures has to be staged. The optimum realistic future for local, regional, state, subcultural, ethnic, Aboriginal, experimental or innovative futures in cultural production is unavoidably bound into the future of national cultural policies. In terms both of the intellectual resourcing of policy development and in the myriad ways local, state and subcultural sites of activity depend on national provision and support, the national arena will remain the engine room for cultural policy initiatives. For its part, cultural theory must take greater stock of its potential negative influence on progressive public policy outcomes and, if it is to orient itself in a more valuable way toward policy imperatives, must attend to the tasks of consolidating the legitimacy of policy rhetorics which sustain a national cultural infrastructure.

Implications and Conclusions

Is it possible to regard a policy orientation within cultural studies as simply an add-on element, one more offering in the interdisciplinary smorgasbord? I don't think so. I have suggested that the modal political rhetoric under-girding cultural studies would have to be re-examined, the saliency of neo-Marxist in relation to social democratic language reassessed. This alone would indicate a more thorough-going review of the cultural studies enterprise than the smorgasbord model would permit.

There is nothing in what I have said that should be taken to indicate a *less* critical vocation for cultural studies. However, what would count as the critical vocation would change. A cultural studies which grasps and sustains links with policy will inquire across a greatly expanded field, but with methods far less totalistic and abstract, far more modest and specific, than those to which we are accustomed.

To treat policy adequately from a critical perspective, it is necessary to appreciate the coordinated impact of economics, administrative law, cultural history, entertainment financing, government and parliamentary procedures, and so on, on the development of public policy. This means a more subtle and context-sensitive re-education in the roles of the state in mixed capitalist economies, away from monolithic and wooden grand theories inspired more by critical purism than by the requirements for piecemeal, on-going reformism.

Critical policy research thus implies more, rather than less, critical understanding than is found in the traditions of cultural criticism developed exclusively within humanities-based disciplines, and a significantly greater sensitivity to the extra-academic contexts within which such research must circulate for it to exercise its potential leavening function.

In summary, then, a policy orientation in cultural studies would shift the 'command metaphors' of cultural studies away from rhetorics of resistance, progressiveness, and anti-commercialism on the one hand, and populism on the other, toward those of access, equity, empowerment and the divination of opportunities to exercise appropriate cultural leadership. It would not necessarily discount critical strategies and priorities, but may indeed enhance and broaden them. It is not a call simply to add another 'perspective' to the academic sideboard, but would necessitate rethinking the component parts of the field from the ground up. It offers one major means of rapprochement between the critical and the vocational divide that structures the academic field

of cultural and communication studies in Australia, as elsewhere. Finally, it would commit us to a genuine localism, against the abstract theoreticism that usually passes as the currency of international academic rates of exchange.

Notes

1   Meaghan Morris, 'Banality in Cultural Studies', in Patricia Mellencamp (ed.), *Logics of Television* (British Film Institute, London, 1990).

2   John Kelly, 'Iron Lady in a Nanny's Uniform', *Times Higher Education Supplement*, No. 840 (9 December 1988).

3   See, for example, the British journal *Screen*'s new editorial policy (in Vol. 31, No. 1), debate in that and other recent issues, and Richard Collins, *Television: Policy and Culture* (Unwin Hyman, London, 1990).

4   As Manuel Alvarado and John O. Thompson (eds), *The Media Reader* (British Film Institute, London, 1990) do. See also Fred Inglis, *Media Theory: An Introduction* (Blackwell, Oxford, 1990).

5   Elizabeth Jacka, 'Australian Cinema – An Anachronism in the '80s?', in Susan Dermody and Elizabeth Jacka (eds), *The Imaginary Industry: Australian Film in the Late '80s* (Australian Film, Television and Radio School, North Ryde, 1988), p. 118.

6   For discussion, see my 'Figuring the Australian Factor', *Culture & Policy*, Vol. 2, No. 1, 1990.

7   Julie James Bailey, 'Communicating with the Decision Makers: The Role of Research, Scholarship and Teaching in Film and Media Studies', Staff Seminar, Griffith University, 20 October, 1989.

8   John Docker, 'Popular Culture versus the State: an Argument Against Australian Content Regulation for TV', Unpublished ms., Attachment to Federation of Australian Commercial Television Stations (FACTS) submission to ABT Inquiry into Australian Content on Commercial Television, 16 August 1988 (Document D020B, ABT Inquiry File). A shorter version is published as 'Popular Culture versus the State: an Argument Against Australian Content Regulation for TV', *Media Information Australia*, No. 59, 1991. For further discussion, see Stuart Cunningham, Jennifer Craik, Tony Bennett and Ian Hunter, 'Response to Docker', *Media Information Australia*, No. 59, 1991.

9   Graeme Turner, 'It Works for Me: British Cultural Studies, Australian Cultural Studies, Australian Film', Paper delivered to The Future of Cultural Studies Conference, April 1990.

10 Industries Assistance Commission, *International Trade in Services*, Report No. 418 AGPS, 30 June 1989, p. 202.

11 Graham Shirley and Brian Adams, *Australian Cinema: The First Eighty Years* (Angus and Robertson/Currency Press, Sydney, 1983) and Albert Moran, *Images and Industry: Television Drama Production in Australia* (Currency Press, Sydney, 1985).

12 Phillip Lynch, 'Advance Australia', *Bulletin* 2 February 1982, p. 72.

13 See Gary Sturgess, 'The Emerging New Nationalism', *Bulletin* 2 February 1982.

14 Stephen Alomes, *A Nation at Last? The Changing Character of Australian Nationalism 1880–1988* (Angus and Robertson, North Ryde, 1988), p. 338, Tim Rowse and Albert Moran, '"Peculiarly Australian" – The Political Construction of Cultural Identity', in *Australian Society*, 4th edition, eds. Sol Encel and Lois Bryson (Longman Cheshire, Melbourne, 1984) and Noel King and Tim Rowse, '"Typical Aussies": Television and Populism in Australia', *Framework*, Nos. 22/23, Autumn 1983.

15 Kathy Myers, *Understains – the Sense and Seduction of Advertising* (Comedia Publishing Group, London, 1986).

16 William Leiss, Stephen Kline and Sut Jhally, *Advertising as Social Communication: Persons, Products, and Images of Well-Being* (Methuen, Toronto, 1986).

17 John Fiske, *Reading the Popular* (Unwin Hyman, Boston, 1989), p. 179.

18 Christopher Ham and Michael Hill, *The Policy Process in the Modern Capitalist State* (Harvester Press, Brighton, 1984).

19 Donald Horne, 'Think – or Perish! Towards a confident and productive Australia', *Occasional Paper No.8*, Commission for the Future, June 1988, and *The Public Culture* (Pluto Press, Sydney, 1986), Graham Murdock and Peter Golding, 'Information Poverty and Political Inequality: Citizenship in the Age of Privatised Communications', *Journal of Communication* 39, No. 3, Summer 1989, pp. 180–95, Armand Mattelart, Xavier Delcourt and Michele Mattelart, *International Image Markets* (London, Comedia, 1984).

20 For example, Toby Miller, 'Film and Media Citizenship', *Filmnews* February 1990, Miller, 'There are Full Professors in this Place who Read Nothing but Cereal Boxes: Australian Screen in Academic Print', *Media Information Australia*, No. 55, February 1990, Trevor Barr, 'Reflections on Media Education: The Myths and Realities', *Metro Media and Education Magazine*, No. 82, Autumn 1990, Tony Bennett, 'Putting Policy into Cultural Studies', Paper delivered to The Future of Cultural Studies Conference, April 1990.

21 Geoff Hurd, and Ian Connell, 'Cultural Education: A Revised Programme', *Media Information Australia*, No. 53, August 1989, pp. 23–30.

22 Barr, 'Reflections on Media Education', p. 16.

23 *Windows onto Worlds: Studying Australia at Tertiary Level* (The CRASTE Report), Canberra: AGPS, June 1987, p. 18.

Chapter 2

Cultural Policy Studies

Jim McGuigan

Speak truth to power.
Seventeenth-century Quaker epithet

How does cultural studies relate to policy-oriented theorizing and research? As an interdisciplinary field of enquiry, cultural studies has shown considerable interest in *cultural politics*, in the sense of aesthetic practices that challenge the mainstream. Practical engagement with a *politics of culture*, including policy analysis and policy formulation, however, has been restrained by comparison, due perhaps to an excessive critical purity and a suspicion of becoming involved with regulatory processes.[1] The hybrid of "cultural policy studies," proposed by a school of thought inspired by Michel Foucault, is a bid to forge a much stronger relationship between critical analysis and policy orientation in cultural studies. This prospective agenda requires a careful consideration of the actual and potential meanings of cultural policy from the perspectives of social and cultural theory, two leading strands of which are discussed in this chapter. There is, on the one hand, Foucauldian theory with its close connections to "the epistemic shift" associated with poststructuralism and postmodernism; and, there is, on the other hand, Habermasian theory with its persistent commitment to "the unfinished project of modernity," a perspective which has been influential in the critical analysis of communications policy. These rather different yet not necessarily incommensurate theoretical frameworks may be seen to illuminate urgent matters of culture and politics. Such theory also offers a means of clarifying how those most directly involved with formulating, implementing and contesting cultural policies understand what they are doing. Cultural policy studies, then, in both of the contrasting theorizations under discussion, presents new possibilities, not only to theorists and analysts of culture but also to agents of cultural policy.

Here, I am concerned with cultural policy in a sense much broader than is normally meant by the term within the professional discourses of arts management. The words "culture" and "policy" are not restricted to the arts and public administration respectively, although they certainly include those meanings. "Culture," it is often remarked, has two general fields of referent: first, the arts and higher learning; and, second, ways of life. The second of these referential fields, the traditional object of anthropology, has tended increasingly to subsume and transform the first referential field, thereby, in effect, democratizing how we think and talk about culture. However, this expanded notion of culture, in spite of its positive qualities, is not wholly satisfactory since it is too expansive for certain analytical and practical purposes. The anthropological concept of culture encompasses literally everything and, in so doing, obscures important and useful distinctions between that which is principally cultural and that which is not first and foremost about meaning and signification. For example, economic arrangements are cultural: they are human constructs and they are historically and geographically variable in form and operation. They are not, though, primarily to do with the production and circulation of meaning. Economic arrangements are fundamentally about the production and circulation of wealth whatever is being produced, which is not to say they are without meaning.

Raymond Williams (1981: 207) sought to overcome this dual problem of scope and delimitation with "the concept of culture as a *realized signifying system*." From this point of view, "culture" refers specifically to the practices and institutions that make meaning, practices and institutions where symbolic communication is usually, by definition, the main purpose and even an end in itself, like going to the cinema to see a feature film. Film-making and cinemagoing are socio-economic activities but they are, nonetheless, distinguishable from the production and consumption of commodities specifically to sustain life, such as food, or products that function routinely as means rather than ends in themselves, such as transport systems. Food and transport are meaningful but, unlike cinema, that is not their main *raison d'etre*. Of course, one can always bring to mind particular exceptions to a general rule of this kind, for example, wolfing down a hamburger just before going on a rollercoaster ride, which may not be rational but is indeed cultural.

Because culture is so difficult to pin down, so hard to fix in a precise definition or unambiguous mode, the very idea of cultural policy which seems to imply that something so fragile and indeterminate as a "realized signifying system" can be consciously regulated is, to say the very least, problematical. The problem is related to the etymological connection between "policy" and "policing." "Cultural policy" has deeply entrenched connotations of "policing culture," of treating culture as though it were a dangerous lawbreaker or, perhaps, a lost child.

Policing Culture

The Old French word "police" came into English usage during the sixteenth century to refer to government in general and eventually to policy. In 1732, Jonathan Swift could say, "Nothing is held more commendable in all great cities...than what the French call *police*; by which word is meant the government thereof" (*OED*). By the end of the eighteenth century, the word was acquiring its modern and much narrower meaning: "The police of the town is managed by two constables" (Aitkin, 1795, *OED*). Yet still it was possible for Young, following Adam Smith's essay of 1776 on "The Police of Grain," to advocate in 1792, "a good police of corn...a police that shall, by securing a high price to the farmer, encourage his culture enough to secure the people at the same time from famine" (*OED*). Writing to her sister Cassanda in 1813, Jane Austen mentioned an essay she was reading on the "Military Police and Institutions of the British Empire" in a way that blurred the modern distinction between governmental administration in general and the particular duties of a police force. In 1830, however, Lord Wellington was able to congratulate Robert Peel on his successful setting up of the Metropolitan Police in London, at which point the definitive specialization of the term in English had occurred.

While English-speaking Britons forged "policy" out of "police," the French themselves came to use the word "politique" to refer to both politics and policy (the word "Politik" is similarly used in German). Incidentally, in French, the masculine form, "le politique," refers to institutionalized politics whereas the feminine form, "la politique," refers to the science of politics and policy. It is significant that this later French alternative to policy as policing returns to the ancient Greek root of "polis," the city state. The view of policy presented in this chapter emphasizes the relationship of policy to politics as a field of contestation between rival discourses, ideologies and interests rather than confining it to the more technical, though hardly unpolitical, connotation of policy as policing. Cultural policy raises questions of regulation and control but its meaning should not be restricted to an ostensibly apolitical set of practical operations that are merely administered and policed by governmental officials.

Although there are still those who would prefer to keep politics out of culture entirely, to treat culture exclusively as, say, the polishing of personal sensibilities (another semantically available version of cultural policy), culture has always been political and shows no sign of escaping the ruses of power and public controversy. The political heat around culture has generally been greatest in societies where the state has played a manifest role in its regulation, often a manifestly oppressive role, most notably, under conditions of modernity, in communist and fascist states. Where culture is left to the market a cooler politics is usually displayed. It is curious, however, that just at the moment when European communism was disintegrating in the late-1980s, having failed amongst other things to "culturally enlighten" its subjects (White, 1990), "culture wars" broke out spectacularly in the land of free speech and of the free market, the United States of America. These culture wars, albeit generated by sheer ethnic diversity resulting from a complex history of immigration, were focused particularly upon two key issues: public subsidy of the arts and the university humanities curriculum.[2]

The trouble started with Andres Serrano's *Piss Christ*, his photograph of a cheap plastic crucifix immersed in a jar of the artist's own urine. In May 1989, Republican Senator Alphonse D'Amato dramatically tore up a reproduction of the offending work and scattered its pieces on the floor of the United States' Senate. Serrano had been the recipient of a $15,000 prize from the South Eastern Centre for Contemporary Art in Winston-Salem. The money came originally from the National Endowment for the Arts (NEA), the American equivalent of the British Arts Council, founded by a Democratic presidency during the 1960s. Although the NEA had not directly rewarded Serrano for his ambivalent commentary on the status of Jesus Christ in a commercial culture, D'Amato drew the all-too-obvious conservative inference from the relationship, in his eyes, between such blasphemous obscenity and public funding of the arts.

During the following month, an anxious Corcoran Gallery administration in Washington cancelled its presentation of "Robert Mapplethorpe: The Perfect Moment," a retrospective exhibition for the photographer who had died of AIDs in Spring that year. The exhibition, containing the notorious "X Portfolio" from the late-1970s, had already been seen at other publicly subsidized galleries across the country. Mapplethorpe's "X Portfolio" consisted of photographs representing a series of homoerotic images of male genitalia and the remarkable receptivity of human orifices. Amongst these photographs was Mapplethorpe's self-portrait depicting him in devilish guise with a bull whip for a tail hanging from his rectum. In the circumstances it was bold and perhaps deliberately provocative of the Washington Project for the Arts to immediately put on the exhibition that had been dropped by the Corcoran.

Fast on the heels of the journalistic debate over public funding for the arts that followed these events, in July, Jesse Helms, the Republican Senator for North Carolina, proposed an amendment to the procurement bill for voting money to the NEA:

> None of the funds authorized to be appropriated pursuant to this Act may be used to promote, disseminate, or produce –
> (1) obscene or indecent materials, including but not limited to depictions of sadomasochism, homo-eroticism, the exploitation of children, or individuals engaged in sex acts; or
> (2) material which denigrates the objects or beliefs of the adherents of a particular religion or non-religion; or
> (3) material which denigrates, debases, or reviles a person, group or class of citizens on the basis of race, creed, sex, handicap, age, or national origin. (Bolton, 1992: 73–4)

Although much modified when eventually legislated into existence in October 1989 by the inclusion of the standard artistic merit defence, Helms's proposal epitomized, in the judgment of First Amendment liberals and cultural radicals on the Left, the conservative backlash against anything remotely offensive to virtually anyone. Moreover, as Robert Hughes has observed shrewdly, it encapsulated the growing penchant for cultural policing and what he calls a "culture of complaint" that was spreading across the entire political spectrum of American intellectual life: "The most obvious and curious feature of the Helms amendment was that, if it had not issued from a famously right-wing Republican senator, you could have mistaken it – especially in the last two clauses – for any ruling on campus speech limitations recently proposed by the nominally left-wing agitators for political correctness" (Hughes, 1993: 162). The apparent convergence of sections of the Left with the moralizing Right in "the culture of complaint" is not to be taken, however, as an erasure of the actual differences in source and implication between "progressive" and "conservative" positions on "political correctness" and "multiculturalism."

In spite of what appeared to Hughes as a striking consensus on the control of speech and representation, the right-wing political context for the attack on public funding of the arts in the USA must not be underestimated. There were at least three sometimes separate yet more often than not interconnected ideological discourses in play on the Right: cultural elitism, market populism and ethico-political reaction. The cultural elitist strand, which was also most prominent in the attack on "political correctness" in academia, was enunciated particularly by the writers of the *New Criterion* magazine, such as Hilton Kramer and Samuel Lipman, who wished to defend the established canons of American and European art. The public attribution of artistic status to a piss-artist photographer like Andres Serrano was in itself offensive to their highly refined sensibilities. To an extent, however, that merely repeated the historical contest between cultural establishments and various self-styled *avant gardes*.

For populists it was also difficult to see quite how certain kinds of work could be deemed art. Their case rested rather more substantially on the issue of "tax dollars," a key ideological figure in the debate. When accused of censorship, Helms and his allies denied the accusation by arguing the work from which they wanted to withdraw public subsidy should suffer the test of market forces. As Helms himself put it: "Artists who seek to shock and offend can still do so – but at their own expense" (Bolton 1992: 101). Why should the hard-pressed American taxpayer be expected to shield these enemies of the American Dream from the laws of supply and demand? But, again bringing sanity back into the debate, Robert Hughes (1993: 200) has pointed out: "The American taxpayer contributes $0.68 to the support of the arts every year, compared to $27 in Germany and $32 in France." In effect, public subsidy for the arts in the USA functions as modest seedcorn to attract private patronage and corporate sponsorship to concert halls, galleries and theatres. The NEA annual budget was always much less than that of the British Arts Council, which has since the 1940s covered a population one-fifth the size of the USA, although more is spent regionally in the USA.

The debate was not really about money at all, as the more sophisticated critics of the conservative backlash have argued. Richard Bolton (1992) and Carole Vance (1992) placed the attack on public arts subsidy within a much broader right-wing ethico-political agenda fostered by groups such as the American Family Association, an agenda which had hardly been marginalized by the Reagan and Bush administrations through the 1980s and into the '90s. To quote Vance:

In the past ten years, conservative and fundamentalist groups have deployed and perfected techniques of grass-roots and mass mobilization around social issues, usually centred on sexuality, gender and religion. In these campaigns, symbols figure prominently, both as highly condensed statements of moral concern and as powerful spurs to emotion and action. In moral campaigns, fundamentalists select a negative symbol which is highly arousing to their own constituency and which is difficult or problematic for their opponents to defend. The symbol, often taken literally, out of context and always denying the possibility of irony or multiple interpretations, is waved like a red flag before their constituents. The arousing stimulus could be an "un-Christian" passage from an evolution textbook, explicit information from a high school sex-education curriculum or "degrading" pornography said to be available in the local adult bookshop. In the antiabortion campaign, activists favor images of late-term fetuses or better yet, dead babies, displayed in jars. Primed with names and addresses of relevant elected and appointed officials, fundamentalist troops fire off volleys of letters, which cowed politicians take to be the expression of popular sentiment. Right-wing politicians opportunistically ride the ground swell of outrage, while centrists feel anxious and disempowered to stop it – now a familar sight in the political landscape. (1992: 108)

This is a very astute account of how authoritarian embers are fanned into the flames of draconian cultural policing in a liberal democracy, detailing the maneuvers that frequently catch libertarians by surprise and often too late in the process to respond effectively. Ethico-political reaction puts enlightened sections of the community on the defensive in such a way that the only realistic tactic in response is to try and reduce the full force of the backlash. Vance, in addition, identifies two comparatively novel aspects of this ethico-politically motivated reaction with regard to the campaign against the NEA. First, there is the assault on high culture as a valid experimental space and, second, there is the claim that the actual policies proposed do not constitute censorship, which involves "an artfully crafted distinction between absolute censorship and the denial of public funding" (Vance, 1992: 109) that is derived from a coalescence of authoritarianism and populism with free market ideology.

The way in which the issue of "political correctness" in the academy burst into widespread public debate during the early-1990s was another feature of the conservative backlash against cultural leftism. Dinesh D'Souza's 1991 book, *Illiberal Education*, was written with a grant from the American Enterprise Institute and promoted with a grant from the Olin Foundation, both right-wing organizations explicitly committed to reversing the gains of "multiculturalism" in American society (Graff, 1992: 166–7). D'Souza's inaccurate claim that Shakespeare and other members of the pantheon of "dead white male" cultural superstars were being expelled from the American university curriculum reiterated similarly ill-founded claims that had already been made during the 1980s, such as, for example, Christopher Clausen's much quoted and thoroughly unsubstantiated observation that Alice Walker's *The Color Purple* was being taught more widely than all of Shakespeare's plays put together. Inspired by Allan Bloom's 1987 book, *The Closing of the American Mind*, a defence of absolute value enshrined in the great works of Western culture and an attack on its relativistic enemies were thus mounted. This was not only an assault on the study of popular culture, Afrocentrism, Marxist, feminist and gay writing and criticism, but a challenge to an apparently new kind of linguistic policing that put a premium on minding one's 'p's and 'q's and which is based upon a set of assumptions concerning the relationship between ordinary language and various forms of social and cultural oppression.

Although at bottom deadly and even deadeningly earnest, there was a good deal of humour in the debate, initiated it must be said from the Right, which may be illustrated by the American Hyphen Society's tongue-in-cheek definitions of both the "correct" term, "multiculturalism," and the "incorrect" term, "politically correct":

> **multiculturalism.** A broad, pluralistic social movement that, through the celebration of "difference", champions a more tolerant, diverse, inclusive and realistic view of America and (in the memorable words of the New York State Social Studies Review and Development Committee) "the peoples who person it". Indeed, "multiculturalism" encompasses virtually the entire spectrum of views that have come to be known, not always without irony, as "politically correct". Unfortunately, since reactionary critics have co-opted the term in a none-too-subtle attempt to silence the **multiculti**, it is no longer "politically correct" to say "politically correct" ...
> **politically correct.** Culturally sensitive; multiculturally unexceptional; appropriately inclusive. The term "politically correct" co-opted by the white power elite as a tool for attacking multiculturalism is no longer "politically correct". (Beard and Cerf, 1992: 40, 87)

Whereas trivialization of important matters undoubtedly occurred on both sides of the debate, Edward Said (1993: 389) is right (or, is it "correct"?) to have observed that the issue, as it emerged in the wider arena of public discussion, was rather more the product of "a new conservative dogmatism claiming 'political correctness' as its enemy" than resulting directly from the excesses of the cultural Left. It is also necessary, though, to appreciate that there was no smoke without fire. A certain humorless and evangelical radicalism was indeed evident on many campuses. Of much deeper significance than this, however, is the tendency to transform and displace politics in general onto an exclusively academic and cultural terrain, a phenomenon that is probably symptomatic of the comparative powerlessness of oppositional forces in the USA instead of manifesting their decisive incursions into the power structures. Gerald Graff (1992) remarks that, in North American universities, "cultural studies," which was instrumental in heightening the politicization of culture and has done much to theorize the intellectual opposition, has become something of a euphemism for "leftist studies" and, no doubt, it has been marginalized as such. In his sardonic yet even-handed commentary on the American "culture wars," Hughes also makes an acute observation regarding political displacement: "in the universities, what matters is the politics of culture, not the politics of the distribution of wealth and real events in the social sphere, like poverty, drug addiction and the rise of crime" (1993: 76).

Becoming Useful

Cultural studies is vulnerable to both hostile and sympathetic questioning on several counts.[3] From the sympathetic but policy-oriented points of view discussed in this chapter, the most serious deficiency is a gulf between the political pretensions of cultural studies and its practical effects. Connections between cultural critique in the academy and a larger universe of power, the so-called "real world" of politics, are somewhat tenuous. Ironically, however, hostile attacks on cultural studies from outside the field itself only serve to amplify an already exaggerated sense of political importance.

The desire within cultural studies to become useful in a more practical sense than in the past has clearly motivated the Australian development of "cultural policy studies," associated particularly with the Key Centre for Cultural and Media Policy in Brisbane, directed by Tony Bennett until 1998 (he was succeeded by Tom O'Regan). In fact, there are a number of different positions on the relationship between cultural studies and policy-oriented theorizing and research in Australia that may be located, for shorthand purposes, on a Left/Right continuum, which does not, however, stretch all the way over to the Right of the wider political spectrum.[4] Bennett's "rightist" position derives from a dissatisfaction with the politics of neo-Gramscian cultural studies and is inspired by the later work of the French historian of discursive formations, Michel Foucault. The key idea is Foucault's much extended concept of "governmentality":

By this word I mean three things:
1 The ensemble formed by the institutions, procedures, analyses and reflections, the

calculations and tactics that allow the exercise of this very specific albeit complex form of power, which has as its target population, as its principal form of knowledge political economy, and as its essential technical means apparatuses of security.
2 The tendency which, over a long period and throughout the West, has steadily led towards the pre-eminence over all other forms (sovereignty, discipline, etc.) of this type of power which may be termed government, resulting, on the one hand, in the formation of a whole series of specific governmental apparatuses, and, on the other, in the development of a whole complex of savoirs.
3 The process, or rather the result of the process, through which the state of justice of the Middle Ages, transformed into the administrative state during the fifteenth and sixteenth centuries, gradually becomes "governmentalized".   (Foucault,   1991: 102–3)

Embedded in this definition of governmentality are a number of Foucault's major themes: the discursively formed operations of administrative procedure, the complex imbrications of power and knowledge, the always at least implied critique of modern "Reason" and scepticism of historical progress. The impact of such themes on how cultural studies constructs its own history is particularly evident in Ian Hunter's (1988a) "genealogy" of cultural criticism and the disciplinary formation of English as a curriculum subject, *Culture and Government*. Hunter's main adversary, in this revisionist account, is Raymond Williams (1958), whose tracing of the "culture and society" tradition drew the cultural debate towards his own materialist attempt to radicalize Matthew Arnold's idealist "criticism of life." Hunter (1988b) argues that the critical and anthropological notion of culture promoted by Williams's cultural materialism misses the historical point of cultural education. According to him, modern schooling practices in Britain were introduced by state functionaries such as Kay-Shuttleworth in order to operate as "a governmental pedagogy organised by the technology of moral supervision" (Hunter, 1988a: 21) rather than to disseminate the critical ideals of nineteenth-century men of letters. In practice, the idea of culture as criticism of life remained forever a minority pedagogic value aimed, adopting another Foucauldian and indeed Nietzschean theme, at the cultivation of an ethical self (Foucault, 1987 and 1988), that of the sensuous and self-conscious intellectual, and of precious little relevance to majority populations whether for good or evil. Consequently, for Hunter and similarly minded "Right" Foucauldians, the "cultural struggle," as understood and propounded by cultural materialists and neo-Gramscians, is fundamentally ill-conceived and misplaced because it fails to grasp the finely tuned operations of particular technologies and objects of discourse, whether they are applied to the classification and regulation of "populations" or to the cultivated "care of the self."

Tony Bennett (1992a), in his programmatic statement, "Putting Policy into Cultural Studies," stresses the preoccupation of cultural studies with questions of culture and power. This preoccupation, however, places certain practical obligations on cultural studies for which it is badly equipped. The first obligation is to conceptualize "culture" as constituting "a particular field of government," "government" meant not only in the narrow sense of governing the state but much more encompassing than that, including all power/knowledge relations, in effect, the mechanisms of social management. Second, the different "regions" of culture need to be identified and their managerial operations studied. For instance, to give a straightforward example, this involves an appreciation of how the news is regulated differently from, say, painting: both are regulated, but differently. Third, there are specific forms of politics pertaining to each region of culture that must be understood if the cultural policy analyst is serious about engaging with them. For instance, pursuing the same example already used, this would require knowledge of how the flow of news is managed and how legislation on governmental secrecy and freedom of the press work. In the region of fine art, the roles of funding bodies, public and private galleries, and academic standards of taste would be pertinent objects of study. Fourth, research is needed that engages in genuine dialogue with the organizations of cultural governmentality. Dialogue is unlikely to occur if research in cultural policy studies merely displays implacable hostility to such organizations.

Bennett (1992a) does not, however, discuss how a proper balance is to be struck between "useful" knowledge and "critical" knowledge in the field of cultural policy studies. For obvious reasons, knowledge that is produced solely for official use and funded accordingly rarely questions the fundamental aims and objectives of the client organization. Under such conditions, it is very difficult for a policy-oriented research programme to observe the critical aims and responsibilities that have characterized a "disinterested" cultural studies. In any event, cultural studies as normally practiced is in no fit condition to play the policy game, according to Bennett, not because of its critical independence but, instead, because of practical weaknesses to do with the neo-Gramscian theorizing of "culture" and "hegemony" which Bennett, at one time, himself espoused.[5]

To understand what is at stake here, it is necessary to be clear, however schematically, about the complaints against cultural studies that are made by Tony Bennett. The politics and critical practice of cultural studies focus heavily upon textual analysis with the aim, in Bennett's (1992a: 24) words, of "modifying the relationship between persons." Texts, mainly drawn from mass-popular culture, are read from perspectives that seek to reveal how textual processes construct meaning, position reading subjects and how these positionings are adopted, negotiated and resisted. Such practice is routinely concerned with, for instance, issues of gender, sexuality, "race" and identity. Written, visual, aural and audio-visual texts are studied with these matters in mind and with the implicit purpose of producing critical readers and consumers alert to the operations of dominant and subversive discourses. In its most optimistic neo-Gramscian inflection, in particular, the desire of cultural studies was to cultivate oppositional intellectuals capable of contesting prevailing power relations: radical readers who might somehow organically activate radical collectivities. The trouble with this cultural politics, in Bennett's view, is its more or less exclusive concern with significatory processes and the struggle over meaning at the level of the text. For that reason, cultural studies is "liable to the criticism," says Bennett (1992a: 25), of paying "insufficient attention to the institutional conditions that regulate different fields of culture."

Like Hunter, Bennett is also concerned with challenging the legacy of Raymond Williams, whose explication of the meanings of the word "culture" stands at the fountain head of what came to be known as "cultural studies." Bennett criticizes Williams for failing to follow through the full implications of the "culture" and "government" couplet in seventeenth-century English Republican discourse and for providing cultural studies with a very loose, anthropological definition of "culture" in contrast to the aesthetically narrower one. In *Keywords* (1983a [1976]) Williams had, in fact, quoted the Puritan poet John Milton's tract of 1660, *The Ready and Easie Way to Establish a Free Commonwealth* ("the natural heat of Culture and Government"), yet he missed the eventually Foucauldian import of the connection to "governmentality," the very connection which had been uppermost for critics of monarchical absolutism in the period of the English bourgeois revolution. For them, culture was the means and purpose of government, the medium of social regulation. Picking up this lost thread in the culture and society tradition, Bennett (1992a: 26) now finds it preferable to treat culture "as a historically specific set of institutionally embedded relations of government in which forms of thought and conduct of extended populations are targeted for transformation – partly via the extension through the social body of forms, techniques, and regimens of aesthetic and intellectual culture" in relation to discourses of moral regulation.

Bennett cites Foucault's use of the early modern meaning of "police" and its role in the French theorist's concept of "micro-power" to further elaborate upon the culture and governmentality couplet. "Police" once had a wider frame of reference than now, stretching beyond simple nomination of the agents of law and order to signify, roughly, governmental regulation in general. The expansive Foucauldian use of "police" is warranted etymologically and also linked to Foucault's rejection of the conventional zero-sum conception of power, which confines it to a fixed quantum emanating from a central point over which struggle is waged, as in hegemony theory, restricted to the vertical dimension of social control from above, ultimately directed by the state, and resistance by popular forces from below. Foucault's concept of power (Gordon, 1980) is much more diffuse, prolifer-ating horizontally from a multitude of social sites and not, therefore, limited to a finite amount, the sharing out of which is routinely held to be at issue in politics whether conceived in the terms of hegemony theory or otherwise. This Foucauldian idea of politics as extending beyond its official forms has proven especially attractive to cultural studies since it allows power to be conceived of as produced and not only sought from below, bottom-up power, thus giving theoretical force to the ubiquitous notion of "empowerment" that ranges in colloquial usage from feminism through community politics to management training. The associated idea of "capillary power" suggests a sense of power flowing endlessly around the veins and arteries of the body politic, regulating social and cultural relations at innumerable minute points and with specific regional properties. To convey the distinctiveness of this Foucauldian conception of power adequately, it is necessary to quote at some length from the definition that Foucault himself gave in the first volume of *The History of Sexuality*:

[P]ower must be understood in the first instance as the multiplicity of force relations immanent in the sphere in which they operate and which constitute their own organization; as the process which, through ceaseless struggles and confrontations, transforms, strengthens, or reverses them; as the support which these force relations find in one another, thus forming a chain or a system, or on the contrary, the disjunctions and contradictions which isolate them from one another; and lastly, as the strategies in which they take effect, whose general design or institutional crystallization is embodied in the state apparatus, in the formulation of the law, in the various social hegemonies. Power's condition of possibility, or in any case the viewpoint which permits one to understand its exercise, even in its more "peripheral" effects, and which also makes it possible to use its mechanisms as a grid of intelligibility of the social order, must not be sought in the primary existence of a central point, in a unique source of sovereignty from which secondary and descendent forms would emanate; it is the moving substrate of force relations which, by virtue of their inequality, constantly engender states of power, but the latter are always local and unstable. (Foucault, 1981: 92–3)

Another relevant and characteristically Foucauldian idea is that of "cultural technology," which is, again, a concept with a much broader referential field than it would normally have in common-sense usage, going beyond, say, the hardware of communications, in general, or information-processing and transmission systems in particular. It may be taken to reference the "machinery" of institutional and organizational structures and processes that produce particular configurations of knowledge and power. Bennett's main example of a cultural technology, in "Putting Policy into Cultural Studies," is the public museum, a machine for making art and history socially intelligible. The public museum arose as an institution of the modern civilizing process, a means of shaping popular dispositions towards culture through exhibitionary display and thus contributing to the regulation of social conduct.

On the tasks of studying museums as technologies of culture and formulating a practical politics in relation to them, Bennett (1992a) seeks to illustrate the instrumental value of Foucauldian cultural policy studies and he elaborates upon the comparative deficiencies of neo-Gramscian cultural studies. Neo-Gramscianism would tend to conceptualize the public museum as an hegemonic apparatus, yet another instance of vertical and top-down power over which to struggle, a device for inculcating dominant ideologies in a subject population, functioning to misrepresent the past and reproducing culturally-mediated social relations of domination and subordination. Bennett acknowledges the validity up to a point of such an analysis of the public museum's mode of address historically. However, of greater pertinence is that the public museum has been and continues to be, in practice and no doubt in comparison with commercial representations of the past, more an institution for social differentiation and exclusion in the Bourdieuan sense (Bourdieu and Darbel, 1991) than for the reflection of cities and nations, as officially claimed, or for providing the ideological education of majority populations, as neo-Gramscian hegemony theory might suggest. Should, for example, it be the case that the public museum has misrepresented and/or excluded the working class, this is hardly an offence that working-class people are up in arms about. Insofar as the working class persists

as an identifiable collectivity with shared interests, its members are not dashing *en masse* to revolutionize the museum: far from it. The basic weakness of a neo-Gramscian perspective, now for Bennett, is that it is unable to deal adequately with the micro-political level, that is with the specific "regional" properties of the museum and so, therefore, does not really address the social agents who are actually in a position to do something about museum policies. These agents are "museum critics, sectional pressure groups like WHAM, committees of management, teams of designers, curators, sometimes even boards of trustees" (p. 31). If cultural studies has something to say about museums, then, it must be saying it to them.

Bennett quotes Bertolt Brecht's maxim concerning "truth": that it is of no use unless communicated to someone who can do something with it. Like Brecht for his own reasons and Foucault for other reasons, Bennett's conception of truth is exceptionally pragmatic. In effect, "truth," it would seem, is what the social agents engaged in specific institutional practices, such as museum curators, are prepared to believe: in Foucauldian parlance, there are, after all, only "regimes of truth." The consequential logic of such a concept of truth is that a piece of relevant and potentially valid knowledge might just as well be untrue, for practical purposes, when it happens to be disbelieved by those agents who possess the discursive power to put it to use were they, instead, to believe it. Bennett does not explain how this excessively pragmatic conception of truth could be reconciled with a critical conception of truth that does not depend upon ready and willing acceptance by the present agents of power in order to claim validity. Political acceptability in contingent and, therefore, changable circumstances is a questionable criterion of truthful knowledge. One only has to recall Galileo's dilemma concerning politically unpalatable truth, which also interested Brecht, to appreciate the dubious relationship of knowledge to that which is currently politic according to spiritual and temporal authority.

Tom O'Regan (1992: 420) describes the position enunciated by Bennett as "a 'pragmatic' politics as the horizon of the thinkable." Clearly, this relates to the issue raised here concerning pragmatism and truth, which has enormous implications for how critical intellectual work is conducted and what its policy worth is to be or not to be. There are two main grounds of O'Regan's "Left" critique. First, he disputes what appears to be an attempt to revise cultural studies as a whole, to move it lock-stock-and-barrel from "criticism" to "policy." According to O'Regan, such a comprehensive transformation of the field of study is both undesirable and unnecessary. "Cultural studies" is a broad rubric for a wide range of enquiry, not all of which is or need be directly policy-related. Besides, a great deal of cultural studies is of policy relevance, but from the point of view of "the recipient, the victim and the marginal" (p. 409), that is seen from the "bottom-up," not the "top-down." This leads on to O'Regan's second main objection to Bennett's version of "cultural policy studies," its apparently close alignment with the perspectives of administrative and bureaucratic power, which must inevitably set limits on its critical capacities. O'Regan sets out his own alternative and critical agenda for policy-oriented cultural studies that admits a series of different and conflicting purposes:

> – *state purposes* – efficiency, equity, excellence, etc.;
> – *reformist purposes* – which involves working "within" administrative knowledge but with the aim of effecting changes;
> – *antagonistic purposes* – which involve critique and opposition, both general and policy-specific;
> – *diagnostic purposes* – in which policy emerges as a politics of discourse in a descriptive enterprise. (O'Regan, 1992: 418)

Although Bennett (1992b) defends himself strenuously against the accusation that he is polarising critical theory and policy orientation in cultural studies, he still refuses to "pull the punch" on policy. Cultural critique may continue, according to Bennett, but he insists that "all such work is indirectly affected by policy issues and horizons" (p. 395). It would be mistaken to read him as merely saying that in the end cultural analysis is unavoidably political. Bennett (1992b: 406) is quite unambiguous and very precise indeed about his instrumentalist agenda for policing the horizons of cultural studies: "cultural studies might envisage its role as consisting in the training of cultural technicians: that

is, intellectual workers less committed to cultural critique as an instrument for changing consciousness than to modifying the functioning of culture by means of technical adjustments to its governmental deployment."[6]

Remaining Critical

The "Right" Foucauldian wish to relinquish disengaged criticism and turn cultural studies as a whole over to governmental usefulness, an improbable outcome in any event, leads directly onto what is in fact a very familiar terrain, that of administrative research. Such research is, by definition, subject to the pre-existing agendas of policy-making and policy-implementing bodies. In their original distinction, both Paul Lazarsfeld (1941) and Theodor Adorno (1945) contrasted "administrative" research with its opposite, "critical" research, the kind of research that pipes to no paymaster but at the same time runs the risk of political marginalization. The desire to bridge the gulf between critique and practicality in cultural policy studies is not so novel as it imagines itself to be.... Jay Blumler (1978) once postulated a form of communications research that combined the disinterestedness of criticism with the usefulness of administration and dubbed it "meliorative." Tony Bennett's intentions may be similar but one cannot be sure since there are no normative principles other than administrative usefulness made explicit in the "Right" Foucauldian framework for cultural policy studies.

Stuart Cunningham's (1992 and 1993 [1991]) "Centrist" position has the virtue in comparison, of situating itself explicitly and unambiguously within a "real world" ideological and political context, that of Australian social democracy. The Labour Party held office in Australia through the 1980s and until the late 1990s, at a time when the New Right was busy dismantling ameliorative social and cultural policies in Britain and the USA. The very idea of governmental intervention in the field of culture under modern liberal-democratic conditions has been associated historically with social democracy in Western European nation-states and was a distinctive feature of the post-Second World War political settlement in Britain. The growth of public arts subsidy and the keen preservation of public service principles of broadcasting, in effect, represented the cultural branch of the welfare state.

Bennett (1992b) concurs with Cunningham's call for a shift in the "command metaphors" of cultural studies: "a policy orientation in cultural studies would shift its 'command metaphors' away from rhetorics of resistance, oppositionalism and anti-commercialism on the one hand, and populism on the other, towards those of access, equity, empowerment and the divination of opportunities to exercise appropriate cultural leadership" (Cunningham, 1993 [1991]: 137–8). Yet, on endorsing the aims of this passage from Cunningham, Bennett (1992b: 396) turns immediately to a repeat attack on Williams's "misreading" of the "culture and society" tradition instead of addressing himself to the implications of Cunningham's avowedly social-democratic politics of cultural policy. Cunningham (1993 [1991]: 134) could be speaking directly to Bennett's position when he says: "The missing link is a social-democratic view of citizenship and the trainings necessary to activate and motivate it.... Replacing shop-worn revolutionary rhetoric with the new command metaphor of citizenship commits cultural studies to a reformist strategy within the terms of a social-democratic politics, and thus can connect it to the wellsprings of engagement with policy."

To advocate social-democratic citizenship in such a direct manner inevitably raises questions concerning the social rights that were established by the post-Second World War welfare state and, furthermore, suggests a possible category of "cultural citizenship." T. H. Marshall (1992 [1950]) theorized the development of citizenship historically beyond the civil rights necessary to enable a market economy and the political rights of democratic participation onwards into the field of social rights as a matter of distributive justice. To argue, as Peter Townsend (1979) did before the New Right assault on social democracy became hegemonic, that to be without a television set in a modern society is to be poor, indicated how social entitlement was already blurring into cultural entitlement. Marshall (1992 [1950]: 48) himself had said, "Common enjoyment is a common right".

Cunningham argues his social-democratic case in very different circumstances from those of its post-Second World War heyday and, also, in recognition that national policies are increasingly constrained by economic and cultural globalization. Many an old-fashioned social democrat would gag, for instance, on his recommendations for ensuring Australian content in the "unworthy discourse" of advertising (Cunningham, 1992: 71). Cunningham, in effect, refuses to hive off questions of *cultural* policy from those of *communications* policy and he particularly stresses the centrality of television for a policy-oriented cultural studies.

The linking of policy issues around communications and culture has also been of prime concern to the political economy perspective in British media sociology, best exemplified by the writings of Nicholas Garnham (1990), Peter Golding and Graham Murdock (for instance, Golding and Murdock, 1986 and Murdock and Golding, 1989). The political economy approach analyses major institutional transformations and is especially concerned with the relations between capital and technology. It has often been criticized for lacking a discursive form of analysis which is properly sensitive to the complexity of symbolic process and the meaning and use of cultural products in specific contexts, which has been the great strength, in comparison, of cultural studies. There is no necessary incompatibility, however, between political-economic analysis, on the one hand, and textual and contextual interpretation on the other hand (McGuigan, 1997). One of the great strengths of the political economy perspective is to emphasize citizenship rights and the conditions of public debate, in addition to economic analysis, matters which have tended to be neglected in mainstream cultural studies.

For a critical social theory of communications and culture, "the public sphere" and the operations of rational-critical debate, conceptualized and analyzed most famously by the German social philosopher Jürgen Habermas, are of focal concern. Whether one agrees or not with Tony Bennett's version of a Foucauldian framework for cultural policy studies, there is more to be said than it has to say for and about the formation of cultural and governmental relations according to modern principles of democracy. In the spirit of dialectics, then, I shall in the rest of this chapter counterpose the elements of a Habermasian framework to the particular Foucauldian perspective already outlined. In my work on cultural policy, in actual fact,

I make liberal use of the insights of both Foucault and Habermas where appropriate in order to illuminate particular issues of cultural policy.[7]

The cardinal theme of Habermas's work generally concerns how we make sense in public, especially how we negotiate our differences with one another and decide upon common purposes (Holub, 1991). This runs from his *Habilitationshrift*, published in 1962 as *Strukturwandel der Offentlichkeit*, translated into English in 1989 as *The Structural Transformation of the Public Sphere*, and through his two-volume magnum opus of 1981, *Theorie des Kommunikativen Handelns, The Theory of Communicative Action* (English translation, 1984 and 1987). Initially, Habermas was interested in accounting for the emergence of liberal-democratic conversation with the rise of the bourgeoisie in the late-eighteenth and early-nineteenth centuries and how, according to him, such conversation degenerated into manipulative communications with the expansion of modern commercial media and the advent of what he calls "the social-welfare state." Habermas's later work, after his "linguistic turn" of the 1970s, moved towards an abstract and rigorously procedural model of language performance and away from the historically grounded theory of communications and culture represented by his first major book. There is, however, a definite continuity between Habermas's early and later work in spite of the various theoretical revisions he has made to his position over the years.

Public conversation may be considered culturally in two main senses for present purposes. First, it is in itself cultural, enabled by the languages, knowledges, beliefs, and so on, that circulate socially. In a liberal democracy, participation in public conversation, whether it is conducted honestly or dishonestly, with conscious intent or unconscious effect, is a citizenship right, which is the second sense of public conversation germane to the current argument. In principle, as citizens, we are permitted to speak openly about culture and society. Such a right is the rationale for the specialist activities of cultural criticism, and in the general sense that Terry Eagleton (1984) has sought to revive by arguing that literary criticism and theory, in particular, have to a significant extent lost sight of their larger responsibilities for social and political critique even when they seem most radical in the academy.

From a policy-oriented perspective in cultural studies, the angle of vision is shifted partially from attention to the cultural text and its meaningfulness in order to open up questions concerning the *conditions of culture*; and, in this, yet a more general sense, it has a close affinity with the political economy perspective on communications and culture. That is what cultural policy is principally about, the conditions of culture, the material and, also, the discursive determinations in time and space of cultural production and consumption. The study of cultural policy and the practical intent of contributing to the framing of policies does not deny the importance of criticism and textual interpretation but rather puts issues concerning how texts are made and circulated socially into the foreground. Fundamental to the position on cultural policy stated here, then, is the normative view that, in a democratic society, "the public will," however that is understood and constructed, should decisively influence the conditions of culture, their persistence and their potential for change. This is where a Habermasian view parts company most sharply from an exclusively Foucauldian view. The Foucauldian might typically regard such thinking as touchingly idealistic, as rooted in a long-redundant Enlightenment rationality and humanism. Although the Habermasian might be just as suspicious as the Foucauldian of official claims concerning democracy and public accountability, nevertheless, he or she chooses to wager upon the possibility of turning formal claims into substantive truths and acts accordingly.

In Britain, the use of the term "public sphere" became caught up in the academic debate over public service broadcasting. Nicholas Garnham (1983 and 1990) used it in his defence of the ideal of public service broadcasting, not to uncritically endorse the actual history of public service broadcasting, nor simply to protect the BBC as a venerable institution. Without a significant measure of regulation in the interests of the public good in communications, the democratic function of broadcasting, limited though it was in practice, might be lost, he argued. As Richard Collins (1993) has observed, this seemed to equate the public sphere with the public sector and left no space for the market as a stimulus to and provider of broadcast culture. That was not, in fact, the actual position held either by Garnham or by John Keane (1991), whose thinking on these matters is rather similar. Theirs is much more a critique of the problems inherent in an exclusively market-driven media system. Without provision for public accountability and control, and without some attempt to foster alternatives to an overbearing state and untrammelled market forces, the prospects for democratic debate and cultural experiment would be curtailed and, indeed, imperilled. Raymond Williams (1962) put forward a similar argument long ago and, coincidentally, in the same year that Jurgen Habermas's *Strukturwandel der Offentlichkeit* was originally published in Germany. Such arguments, of necessity, draw on liberal-democratic principles of political thought as much as they do, if not more than, upon socialism. This line of argument assumes that liberal principles of democratic freedoms and rights are influential at least residually and open to further development and radicalization. Moreover, the assumption is that, under late-modern conditions, the earlier modern principles of political democracy remain of critical relevance and are increasingly in contradiction with the liberal economics that they originally facilitated and which, in the closing decades of the twentieth century, threatened to eclipse their legitimacy.

The finest study of the historical embodiment of liberal-democratic thought in public communications and culture is Habermas's *The Structural Transformation of the Public Sphere*. Habermas (1989 [1962]) identified the emergence of distinctly new forms of public debate in the advanced European nation-states of Britain, France and Germany during the eighteenth and nineteenth centuries, particularly in the period of the British Industrial Revolution, following the earlier mercantile revolution, and the French Revolution which articulated the modern political ideals of liberty, egalitarianism and solidarity. The ancient Greek city state of Athens had also produced a discourse of democratic citizenship and a meeting place for its articulation, the famous *agora*, but without the ostensible universalism of the bourgeois public sphere. An absolute distinction was made by the ancient Greeks between the men who exercised their citizenship rights by speaking in the city square and women and the slave population who

were denied participation. In comparison, the bourgeois public sphere assumed, in theory, boundless equality. That was a formal claim made for reasons of philosophical consistency and not, in fact, borne out by the actual functioning of public culture and politics in Britain, France and Germany two centuries ago. Only property owners, on strictly capitalistic grounds, were really admitted to the public sphere. Women were excluded, in any case, on patriarchal grounds and confined to what Habermas calls "the intimate sphere" of home and family, which was integrally related, however, to the public sphere insofar as it was the domestic institution, the inviolable personal base, that legitimated the bourgeois gentleman's individual presence in the outside world of politics in addition to the *raison d'etre* of his economic interests in "the private sphere" of business and trade. So, right at the heart of the bourgeois public sphere was a social contradiction, between the formally universal claims of equal citizenship and the substantive exclusions according to class, gender and, indeed, race with few exceptions. Although Habermas is often criticised for idealizing the bourgeois public sphere, he, nonetheless, always stressed its contradictory and partial makeup, which he contrasts, in both his early and later work, with the ideal of a genuinely democratic public sphere where no such exclusions would be permitted.[8]

The eventual decline of the bourgeois public sphere was connected to its founding contradictions as well as resulting from the commercialization and bureaucratization of public communications from the late nineteenth century. However, this should not, according to Habermas, prevent us from appreciating the progressive historical role of the bourgeois public sphere and the principles of rational and critical debate amongst acknowledged equals that it represented. As Terry Eagleton (1984: 17) has commented: "What is at stake in the public sphere, according to its own ideological self-image, is not power but reason. Truth, not authority, is its ground, and rationality, not domination, its daily currency. It is on this radical dissociation of politics and knowledge that its entire discourse is founded; and it is when this dissociation becomes less plausible that the public sphere will begin to crumble." The bourgeois public sphere was the medium through which the middling classes wrested power from absolute rulers and the feudal aristocracy. Its discourse of power and knowledge, which, as Eagleton notes acutely, involved the formal suspension of extraneous force under the proper conditions of debate in order to privilege "Reason," was enunciated informally by the literary culture of the eighteenth century that expressed values of individual freedom and rational critique. The political public sphere was thus *culturally prefigured*. One need only think of the writings of Voltaire and the other *philosophes*, like the *Encyclopaedists*, D'Alembert and Diderot, of pre-revolutionary France to appreciate the political outcomes of such intellectual ferment. In Britain, the London coffee houses were the equivalent of the Parisian *salons* and became the gentlemanly settings for "rational-critical debate". And, Addison and Steele's *Spectator* was the leading journal for circulating the cultural principles of liberal-bourgeois politics.

For the rising bourgeoisie, then, the public sphere which they created came to mediate the relationship of civil society to the state. In fact, it actually produced the conditions for an independent civil society of private persons with demanding public rights. The private spheres of civil society, business (trade and capital accumulation) and the family (the sphere of intimacy and cultural consumption), increasingly achieved representation or protection against arbitrary state power, securing the various liberal freedoms of public expression and personal conscience that a member of a modern liberal democracy might be expected, mistakenly, to take for granted. To quote Habermas's catalogue of liberal-bourgeois rights:

A set of basic rights concerned the sphere of the public engaged in rational-critical debate (freedom of opinion and speech, freedom of press, freedom of assembly and association, etc.) and the political function of private people in this public sphere (rights of petition, equality of vote, etc.) A second set of basic rights concerned the individual's status as a free human being, grounded in the intimate sphere of the patriarchal conjugal family (personal freedom, inviolability of the home, etc.). The third set of basic rights concerned the transactions of the private owners of property in the sphere of civil society (equality before the law, protection of private property, etc.). The basic rights guaranteed: the *spheres* of the public realm and of the private (with the intimate sphere at its core); the *institutions* and *instruments* of the public sphere, on the one hand (press, parties), and the foundation of private autonomy (family and property), on the other; finally, the *functions* of the private people, both their political ones as citizens and their economic ones as owners of commodities (and, as "human beings", those of individual communication, e.g. through inviolability of letters). (Habermas: 1989 [1962]: 83)

Habermas remarks that Karl Marx, writing from the 1840s and '50s, "treated the political public sphere ironically" (p. 123). He saw it as an ideological construct masking the real foundations and interests of bourgeois democracy under the rhetorical cover of "freedom" and "equality"; yet it was not merely to be denounced as a sham. Marx himself operated in both the official public sphere, as a journalist, and also in what Habermas calls "the plebeian public sphere" of radical politics. Habermas is frequently criticized for neglecting the plebeian public sphere, though he did register and name it. More recently he has acknowledged the importance of E. P. Thompson's (1963) historical research for *The Making of the English Working Class*, which was published the year after Habermas's book on the public sphere.[9] Thompson traced a radical intellectual tradition and culture in Britain, inspired by the American and French Revolutions, and functioning through reading groups, corresponding societies and publications that were harried and criminalised by the early-nineteenth century British state. This radical, alternative public sphere, represented by popular newspapers such as *The Poor Man's Guardian*, had a powerful impact upon the bourgeois public sphere, not only in opposition but also as a source of progressive ideas that were, to a considerable extent, incorporated and subsequently realised after much bitter struggle in the nineteenth century, for instance, resulting in suffrage reform and legal recognition of trade union rights. Marx, like the protagonists of the plebeian public sphere in Britain, took the official claims of the bourgeois public sphere very seriously indeed. Such principles and claims had to be viewed as though they were realizable in practice, not only in order to expose the contradictions of liberal democracy but because they would be essential in a socialist democracy (see Williams, 1983b). The irony, of course, eventually rebounded fatally upon Marx and Marxism with the illusory claims of social equality and cultural democracy that were made by the twentieth-century communist states established in his name. According to Habermas, the radical-democratic aspirations of nineteenth-century socialist politics, which sought to hitch onto the bourgeois public sphere and change it into the forum for a democratic culture, failed to realize their anti-capitalist potential in the twentieth century. These aspirations were frustrated in spite or, rather, partly because of the growth of communications media organized for profit and, also, in spite of the real popular gains represented by the foundation of the social-welfare state.

In the second half of *Structural Transformation*, which most commentators regard as the least satisfactory half, Habermas describes a grim view of modern mass-popular culture in the pessimistic terms of his Frankfurt School precursors, Theodor Adorno and Max Horkheimer (1979 [1944]), and constituting what he calls "the re-feudalization of the public sphere." The pleasures of leisure-time consumption and popular entertainment are depicted as essentially alienated and alienating in a society where, to quote Habermas (1989 [1962]: 164), "the conversation itself is administered." The public sphere was hijacked by sophisticated communicational techniques of advertising and public relations; and, rational-critical debate became distorted. Power was not sufficiently devolved with universal suffrage: instead, the partnership between state and capital came to organize the conditions of everyday life and the processes of representation in both the political and cultural senses. Habermas's variant of the mass-culture critique was a good deal more fashionable and widely accepted by critics in the early-1960s than it is in the 1990s. Nevertheless, the claim that the distance between ordinary social and cultural experience, on the one hand, and the processes of public decision-making, on the other hand, has widened rather than narrowed during the twentieth century is not negligible, nor is it without support amongst "postmodernist" commentators. It is similar, for

instance, to Jean Baudrillard's (1988) cool argument that the mass of people just do not care about politics and, in effect, to use Habermasian terminology, do not participate significantly in the public sphere of rational-critical debate. Such debate is for the most part simulated by media personalities and image-conscious politicians who appear on the television day in and day out. The reality is, to be sure, much more complex and contradictory than this vision of an entirely depoliticized mass-popular culture and a public sphere that has degenerated into completely manipulative communications.

John B. Thompson (1993) has usefully clustered the range of criticisms that are made of Habermas's original thesis on the public sphere into four categories. First, it is criticized on historiographical grounds for neglecting the role of popular movements in particular, as we have seen with regard to "the plebeian public sphere." Second, it is criticized for failing to properly address the masculinity of the bourgeois public sphere, not only in the physical exclusion of women but in terms of its ideological constitution as a gentleman's club. Third, it is criticized for misunderstanding the active powers of popular cultural consumption and reception as well as the opportunities that the modern and especially electronic media actually do and potentially afford informed public debate on serious issues. Fourth, the theory of the public sphere is criticized for the vagueness of Habermas's proposals concerning a renewal of rational-critical debate and the conditions for democratization: "the objectively possible minimizing of bureaucratic decisions and a relativizing of structural conflicts of interest according to the standard of a universal interest everyone can acknowledge" (Habermas, 1989 [1962]: 235). Thompson (1993: 186) goes a step further by mentioning his own criticism of the "essentially *dialogical* conception" of the public sphere, which he takes to be founded in a model of exclusively face-to-face interaction. For this reason, Thompson contends, Habermas's theory of the public sphere cannot adequately account for the temporal and spatial displacements of technologically mediated communications. However, like other sympathetic commentators, Thompson believes that the public sphere remains a vital conceptual tool of analysis and, moreover, a normative guide to democratic practice.

An example of the inspiration that is still drawn from Habermas's original idea is James Curran's (1991) model of a radical-democratic public sphere adapted to late-modern conditions and contrasted with liberal, critical Marxist and communist conceptions. Curran's radical-democratic model is based upon the assumption that "a central role for the media should be defined as *assisting the equitable negotiation or arbitration of competing interests through democratic processes*" (1991: 30). Left to its own devices, the market will not bring this about, nor have democratic communications ever been achieved under exclusively state-controlled systems, although public intervention and regulation, in Curran's view, are still necessary requirements. Such arguments are commonly made with regard to democratic entitlement to the culture and information necessary for exercising citizenship rights knowledgably: debate on the communicative properties of the public sphere, institutional and technological change, from the broad perspective of the political economy of communications and culture, usually stresses these considerations. However, Curran goes further by including "entertainment" in his model with the idea of "society communing with itself" (p. 28), inspired by Raymond Williams's hopeful anticipation of the cultural relations and mutual understanding that would be fostered by democratic systems of communication.[10]

In *Culture and the Public Sphere* (McGuigan, 1996), I aim to contribute to the radical-democratic perspective on rational-critical debate concerning communications and culture through discussion of a series of linked and substantive issues of cultural policy. My chosen strategy is to deploy the critical ideal of the public sphere as a normative reference point in its plural and context-specific forms, rather than as a single and abstracted entity, and in relation to a conception of culture and the cultural field which includes art, popular media, everyday forms of pleasure and identity. This approach represents a departure from the usual treatment of the public sphere in communications policy research where the politics of information tends to be privileged over the more affective aspects of culture. Having said this, however, I do not believe nor intend that discussion of "culture" should be conducted in artificial separation from the social and technological development of information and media systems.

The broadly Habermasian perspective outlined here is a corrective to a certain kind of instrumentalism which is implicit in the economic reductionisms and technological determinisms that frame much policy debate in the cultural field and from which a critical political economy of the media is not always immune. While "communications" are treated in this instrumentalist manner, "culture" has been hived off, in the past, and equated simply with "the arts," a marginal yet worthy area of public policy. It has now become common, however, for "culture" to be resituated within the economistic and technicist discourses of public policy and in this way is tied into the governmentality of communications media on industrial and economic grounds. In many respects, this is a major advance for cultural policy and potentially for affective communications, placing them much closer to the centre of politics. What tends to get lost, though, is the specifically cultural, culture as communication and meaning, practices and experiences that are too complex and affective to be treated adequately in the effective terms of economic and bureaucratic models of policy.

The Habermasian perspective focuses upon the operations of discursivity in a fashion that is not entirely dissimilar to Foucauldian discursive formation analysis whilst stressing in contrast, however, the normative conditions for democratic communication. None of these theories and perspectives, Habermasian, Foucauldian, neo-Gramscian, political economy, and so forth, are in themselves sufficient for all analytical and practical purposes. Steven Best and Douglas Kellner (1991) are right to call for a multiperspectival approach in order to address the sheer complexity of a multidimensional social and cultural reality. The analytical framework presented here does not purport to provide such a comprehensive and catholic approach but it does seek to look at cultural policy from a number of points of view. At the heart of consideration, though, is the function of public debate. In consequence, it is necessary to look beyond the purely academic and to engage critical reasoning with the issues that are generated routinely in the practical discourses of culture and society.

Postscript 2000

The present chapter was originally published as the first chapter of my book, *Culture and the Public Sphere*, in 1996. The chapter and, indeed, the book as a whole began life as a critical questioning of Tony Bennett's Foucauldian perspective on cultural policy studies. I wanted to set out a more critical approach than that of Bennett from a broadly Habermasian position. The book was widely reviewed and met with both negative and positive responses.

Tony Bennett, whose position is criticized in this chapter, was asked to review *Culture and the Public Sphere*, as it happened, for *Theory, Culture & Society*. He responded not with a review but with an excellent full-length article addressing some of the issues that I raised in the book. I feel obliged here, then, to reply to Bennett, however briefly, both in gratitude for his serious, insightful and complex engagement with my argument and in order to clarify one or two problems concerning critique and practicality in what, I suppose, has become something of a "debate" between us.

Bennett (2000) puts his finger on a genuinely tortuous problem, the relations between critical intellectuality and practical intellectuality. He rightly accuses me of overstating the schism in the concluding chapter of *Culture and the Public Sphere*. He also argues that I am not a good advocate in my own cause by implying that critical intellectuals – in this case, academics – have nothing to learn from practical intellectuals – specifically, with regard to cultural policy, communication, and cultural managers. All I can say is that I do not believe this be so. As a critical academic, working in a university, I have

a great deal to learn from workers in the communication and cultural industries. University researchers and teachers are not especially privileged, although they may, under the most favorable circumstances that are, in my opinion, not particularly widespread, still be allowed to think for themselves and speak with a critical independence. This is much more mundane than the grand practice of a Chomsky, a Sartre or, for that matter, a Said (1994). I, myself, am lucky in this respect, at present. Undoubtedly, where it is possible to think for oneself and question conventional wisdoms without fear, there is a precious space. That, I readily acknowledge, is not the case everywhere, whether in universities or elsewhere. The critical independence of academia has been under seige in recent years, usually in the name of practicality. I wrote *Culture and the Public Sphere* fifteen years into Thatcherite government in Britain, one effect of which was the deep inculcation of an instrumental reason of a particularly nihilistic kind and new managerialism, which has had profound implications for professional conduct throughout the institutions of British society. It is my admittedly idealistic belief that a critical reflexivity in any occupation should be permitted, but not only in intellectual occupations.

Notes

1   Paul Willis's "common culture" project (1990a, 1990b, and 1991) is a notable exception to cultural studies' general record of neglect concerning practical matters of cultural policy.

2   There is a voluminous literature on the American "culture wars" and "political correctness" in general. See, for instance, Berube (1994) and Dunant (1994).

3   See, for example, my critique of populism in cultural studies (McGuigan, 1992 and 1997).

4   According to Stuart Cunningham's (1993) distribution of political positions, Tony Bennett and his immediate Brisbane associates, such as Ian Hunter, were on the "Right," Tom O'Regan, then of Murdoch University, was on the "Left," whereas Cunningham, of Queensland University of Technology, styled himself a "Centrist." All these writers contributed to the collection of essays that provided a showcase for Australian cultural studies, *Nation, Culture, Text*, edited by Graeme Turner (1993).

5   During the 1980s, in his role as the leading author of the Open University's Popular Culture course, Tony Bennett (1986) advocated a Gramscian turn in cultural studies. The later shift from a Gramscian to a Foucauldian position can be observed in his article on the nineteenth-century "exhibitionary complex" (Bennett, 1988). Bennett's (1995) collection of essays on the history of the museum is entitled *The Birth of the Museum*, a title which echoes and pays homage to Foucault's *Birth of the Clinic*.

6   An instrumentalist version of Foucauldian thought is not peculiar to Bennett and the Australian school of cultural policy studies. It was also recommended as a more "realistic" agenda for education in communications and culture during the Thatcherite 1980s in Britain (Tolson, 1986; Rice and Rice, 1989), the argument being that student empowerment derives from the acquisition of technical and immediately marketable skills rather than the intellectual capacity to critically analyse cultural and social arrangements.

7   See chapters 2 to 9 of McGuigan (1996). The interpretative disputes over Foucault and Habermas, their differences and also their similarities, are well represented in the book edited by Michael Kelly (1994), *Critique and Power – Recasting the Foucault/Habermas Debate*.

8   On its publication in English in 1989, a conference on *The Structural Transformation of the Public Sphere* was held at the University of North Carolina. Habermas himself produced a generous response to the criticisms made of his first major work by contributors to the conference. The conference proceedings, including Habermas's response, are published in the volume *Habermas and the Public Sphere*, edited by Craig Calhoun (1992). One of the critics, Michael Schudson (1992: 160), on challenging the accuracy of Habermas's historical account of the public sphere and indeed its very existence, still concluded by saying,

"the public sphere ... is indispensable as a model of what a good society should achieve."

9   See Habermas's contribution to Calhoun (1992). The deficiencies of a concept of the public sphere modelled upon the "bourgeois" as opposed to the "proletarian" experience is the main theme of Oskar Negt and Alexander Kluge's (1993) *The Public Sphere and Experience*, which had considerable impact on the West German Left when originally published in 1972.

10 In spite of their considerable differences of analytical idiom and national context, there is a certain affinity between Habermas's thinking on the public sphere and Williams's thinking on democratic communications and common culture (see McGuigan, 1993 and 1995).

References

Adorno, T. (1945) "A Social Critique of Radio Music," *Kenyon Review 7*.

Adorno, T. and Horkheimer, M. (1979 [1944]) *Dialectic of Enlightenment*, London: Verso.

Baudrillard, J. (1988) *Selected Writings*, Cambridge: Polity.

Beard, H. and Cerf, C. (1992) *The Official Politically Correct Dictionary & Handbook*, London: Grafton Books.

Bennett, T. (1986) "The Politics of the 'Popular' and Popular Culture," Bennett, T., Mercer, C., and Woollacott, J. eds., *Popular Culture and Social Relations*, Milton Keynes: Open University Press.

Bennett, T. (1988) "The Exhibitionary Complex," *New Formations* 4.

Bennett, T. (1992a) "Putting Policy into Cultural Studies," Grossberg, L., Nelson, C., and Treichler, P., eds., *Cultural Studies*, London and New York: Routledge.

Bennett, T. (1992b) "Useful Culture," *Cultural Studies* 6.3.

Bennett, T. (1995) *The Birth of the Museum*, London and New York: Routledge.

Bennett, T. (2000) "Intellectuals, Cultural Policy – The Technical, the Practical and the Critical," *Theory, Culture and Society* 17.6.

Berube, M. (1994) *Public Access – Literary Theory and American Cultural Politics*, London and New York: Verso.

Best, S. and Kellner, D. (1991) *Postmodern Theory*, London: Macmillan.

Blumler, J. (1978) "Purposes of Mass Communication Research – A Transatlantic Perspective," *Journalism Quarterly*, Summer.

Bolton, R., ed. (1992) *Culture Wars – Documents from the Recent Controversies in the Arts*, New York: New Press.

Bourdieu, P. and Darbel, A., (1991 [1969]) *The Love of Art*, Cambridge: Polity Press.

Calhoun, C., ed. (1992) *Habermas and the Public Sphere*, Cambridge, Mass.: MIT Press.

Collins, R. (1993) "Public Service Versus the Market Ten Years On – Reflections on Critical Theory and the Debate on Broadcasting in the UK," *Screen* 34.3.

Cunningham, S. (1993 [1991]) "Cultural Studies from the Viewpoint of Cultural Policy," Turner, G., ed., *Nation, Culture, Text – Australian Cultural and Media Studies*, London and New York: Routledge. Originally published in *Meanjin* 50.2/3, 1991. Reprinted in Gray, A. and McGuigan, J., eds., (1997, 2nd. edn.) *Studying Culture*, London: Arnold.

Cunningham, S. (1992) *Framing Culture – Criticism and Policy in Australia*, Sydney: Allen and Unwin.

Curran, J. (1991) "Rethinking the Media as a Public Sphere," Dahlgren, P. and Sparks, C., eds., *Communication and Citizenship – Journalism and the Public Sphere in the New Media Age*, London and New York: Routledge.

Dunant, S., ed. (1994) *The War of the Words – The Political Correctness Debate*, London: Virago Press.

Eagleton, T. (1984) *The Function of Criticism – From the Spectator to Post-Structuralism*, London and New York: Verso.

Foucault, M. (1981) *The History of Sexuality, Volume One – An Introduction*, London: Penguin.

Foucault, M. (1987) *The History of Sexuality, Volume Two – The Use of Pleasure*, London: Penguin.

Foucault, M. (1988) *The History of Sexuality, Volume Three – The Care of the Self*, London: Penguin.

Foucault, M. (1991) "Governmentality," Burchill, G., Gordon, C., and Miller, P., eds., *The Foucault Effect – Studies in Governmentality*, Hemel Hempstead: Harvester Wheatsheaf.

Garnham, N. (1983) "Public Service Versus the Market," *Screen* 24.1.

Garnham, N. (1990) *Capitalism and Communication – Global Culture and the Economics of Information*, London, Newbury Park and New Delhi: Sage.

Golding, P. & Murdock, G. (1986) "The New Communications Revolution," Curran, J., Ecclestone, J., Oakley, G., and Richardson, A., eds., *Bending Reality – The State of the Media*, London: Pluto Press.

Gordon, C. ed. (1980) *Michel Foucault – Power/Knowledge*, Brighton: Harvester.

Graff, G. (1992) *Beyond the Culture Wars – How Teaching the Conflicts Can Revitalize American Education*, London and New York: Norton.

Habermas, J. (1984 [1981]) *The Theory of Communicative Action, Volume One – Reason and the Rationalization of Society*, New York: Beacon Press (1991, Cambridge: Polity Press).

Habermas, J. (1987 [1981]) *The Theory of Communicative Action, Volume Two – The Critique of Functionalist Reason*, New York: Beacon Press (1987, Cambridge: Polity Press).

Habermas, J. (1989 [1962]) *The Structural Transformation of the Public Sphere – An Inquiry into a Category of Bourgeois Society*, Cambridge: Polity Press).

Holub, R. (1991) *Jurgen Habermas – Critic in the Public Sphere*, London and New York: Routledge.

Hughes, R. (1993) *Culture of Complaint – The Fraying of America*, New York: Oxford University Press.

Hunter, I. (1988a) *Culture and Government – The Emergence of Literary Education*, London: Macmillan.

Hunter, I. (1988b) "Setting Limits to Culture," *New Formations* 4.

Keane, J. (1991) *The Media and Democracy*, Cambridge: Polity Press.

Kelly, M., ed. (1994) *Critique and Power – Recasting the Foucault/Habermas Debate*, Cambridge, Mass.: MIT Press.

Lazarsfeld, P. (1941) "Administrative and Critical Communications Research," *Studies in Philosophy and Social Science* 9.

Marshall, T. H. (1992 [1950]) *Citizenship and Social Class*, London: Pluto Press.

McGuigan, J. (1992) *Cultural Populism*, London and New York: Routledge.

McGuigan, J. (1993) "Reaching for Control – Raymond Williams on Mass Communication and Popular Culture," Morgan, J. and Preston, P., eds., *Raymond Williams – Politics, Education, Letters*, London: Macmillan, New York: St. Martin's Press.

McGuigan, J. (1995) "'A Slow Reach Again for Control' – Raymond Williams and the Vicissitudes of Cultural Policy", *European Journal of Cultural Policy* 2.1. Reprinted in Wallace, J., Jones, R., and Nield, S., eds., 1997, *Raymond Williams Now – Knowledge, Limits and the Future*, London: Macmillan, New York: St. Martin's Press.

McGuigan, J. (1996) *Culture and the Public Sphere*, London and New York: Routledge.

McGuigan, J. (1997) "Cultural Populism Revisited," Ferguson, M. and Golding, P., eds., *Cultural Studies in Question*, London, Thousand Oaks, and New Delhi: Sage.

Murdock, G. and Golding, P. (1989) "Information Poverty – Citizenship in the Age of Privatized Communications," *Journal of Communication* 39.3.

Negt, O. and Kluge, A. (1993 [1972]) *Public Sphere and Experience – Toward an Analysis of the Bourgeois and Proletarian Public Sphere*, Minneapolis: University of Minnesota Press.

O'Regan, T. (1992) "(Mis)taking Cultural Policy – Notes on the Cultural Policy Debate," *Cultural Studies* 6.3.

Rice, J. and Rice, P. (1989) "Future Imperfect? English and the New Vocationalism," Brooker, P. and Humm, P., eds., *Dialogue and Difference – English Into the Nineties*, London and New York: Routledge.

Said, E. (1993) *Culture and Imperialism*, London: Chatto & Windus.

Said, E. (1994) *Representations of the Intellectual – The 1993 Reith Lectures*, London: Vintage.

Schudson, M. (1992) "Was There Ever a Public Sphere? If So, When? Reflections on the American Case," Calhoun, C., ed., *Habermas and the Public Sphere*, Cambridge, Mass.: MIT Press.

Thompson, E. P. (1963) *The Making of the English Working Class*, London: Victor Gollancz.

Thomspon, J. B. (1993) "The Theory of the Public Sphere," *Theory, Culture & Society* 10.3.

Tolson, A. (1986) "Popular Culture – Notes and Revisions," MacCabe, C., ed., *High Theory/Low Culture – Analysing Popular Film and Television*, Manchester: Manchester University Press.

Townsend, P. (1979) *Poverty in the United Kingdom – A Survey of Household Resources and Standards of Living*, London: Penguin.

Turner, G., ed. (1993) *Nation, Culture, Text – Australian Cultural and Media Studies*, London and New York: Routledge.

Vance, C. (1992) "The War on Culture," Bolton, R., ed., *Culture Wars – Documents from the Recent Controversies in the Arts*, New York: New Press.

White, A. (1990) *De-Stalinization and the House of Culture – Declining State Control Over Leisure in the USSR, Poland and Hungary, 1953–1989*, London and New York: Routledge.

Williams, R. (1958) *Culture and Society, 1780–1950*, London: Chatto & Windus.

Williams, R. (1962) *Communications*, London: Penguin.

Williams, R. (1981) *Culture*, London: Fontana.

Williams, R. (1983a [1976]) *Keywords – A Vocabulary of Culture and Society*, London: Fontana.

Williams, R. (1983b) "Culture," McLellan, D., ed., *Marx – The First 100 Years*, London: Fontana.

Willis, P. (1990a) *Common Culture*, Milton Keynes: Open University Press.

Willis, P. (1990b) *Moving Culture – An Enquiry into the Cultural Activities of Young People*, London: Calouste Gulbenkian Foundation.

Willis P. (1991) "Towards a New Cultural Map," *National Arts and Media Strategy* 18, London: Arts Council of GB.

Part II

Radio

Part II

Introduction to Part II

Justin Lewis

Radio was, in many ways, eclipsed by television several decades ago in the public imaginations of industrialized countries, and the greater prominence of television is reflected in the policy literatures. Outside historical accounts, most of the work in mass communication and media studies either ignores radio entirely or gives it only cursory attention. And yet if radio seems, for many, rather an old and simple technology, it has proved to be an enduring one. Indeed, it is partly because of its simplicity that it endures: it is relatively easy and cheap to produce and to receive, and since it is unencumbered by the need to display images or even the need for moving parts (unlike portable cassette machines, radios have very little that will wear out) it has enormous versatility. We can listen to the radio almost anywhere while doing almost anything.

In policy terms, the presence of radio in media history is profound. The nature of the technology obliges state involvement in ways that print-based media or film do not: firstly, because the airwaves were generally regarded as public property; secondly, because governments have often been involved in the development of radio technology (generally for military purposes); and thirdly, because of the very practical limits of space on the radio spectrum. If nothing else, governments have generally been required to make decisions about who could use frequencies and to police those decisions. Hitherto, government involvement in print-based media or film was restricted, in overt questions of policy, to issues of censorship or taxation. If it was to be permitted to develop, radio forced governments to adopt a series of organizing principles.

It was partly because it was seen as necessary to control the development of radio – and hence conceptualize the airwaves themselves as public rather than private property – that governments became open (in theory, at least) to certain forms of popular or democratic pressure. Indeed, the very notion of the public ownership of the radio airwaves resonated with various forms of socialist politics in the first half of the twentieth century, and allowed the philosophies behind movements for national healthcare or universal public education to influence the development of a mass medium. If governmental deliberations over the future of radio often had as much to do with containment and control as they did with exploring cultural possibilities, the doctrine of public service broadcasting that emerged from those deliberations was a *potentially* radical idea. Thus, for example, while the British Broadcasting Corporation kept radio firmly within the purview of culture and ideas sanctioned if not supported by elites (as the BBC's coverage of the 1926 general strike quickly made clear), it would inevitably be subject to democratic pressures in a way that the press barons were not.

In some ways, the British response to the problem of radio was an easy one: the government dealt with the public airwaves by allowing only government created stations to use them. But in other ways, this approach forced the BBC into the difficult position of justifying itself in

terms of "the public interest," or even to be seen
to embody that very notion. If the BBC began
with a self-assured, straightforwardly "civilizing" discourse, in which culture was dispensed
by upper-middle class non-regional male voices
in ways that were imagined as improving to the
less formally educated masses, the fragility of the
assumption that this represented either the
public or their interests was inevitably exposed.
Since radio was a popular medium, radio broadcasters had no choice to engage with popular
aesthetics, and the friction between rarefied cultural ideals and popular culture quickly raised
questions of voice, style, and representation.

As a number of scholars have documented –
Douglas, and Smulyan in this volume, as well as
Streeter (1996) and McChesney (1994) – the history of radio in the US involved a more complex
formation, one in which the "public interest"
was the dominant legal trope for the development of radio, but within a structure that
allowed government to act as the licensor for –
and guarantor of – the private, corporate development of radio. In essence, this involved the
establishment of an organizing body (the Federal Radio Commission) whose founding principles were replete with the language of public
service broadcasting, but whose appointees were
able to liberally interpret that language in giving
out licenses to privately-owned stations. This
gap between principle and practice can be seen
as the consequence of a series of pragmatic political maneuvers – those constituencies pushing
for public service principles were allowed to
influence the discourses of regulatory principle,
while corporate interests would be the benefi-
ciaries of license allocation.

The US system thereby embraced a contradiction between notions of public and private property, between the free market as the deliverer of
the public interest and the state as the guardian of
those interests. The public resolution of this
contradiction usually involves recourse to the
notion that the private ownership of radio stations adheres to market mechanisms, and hence
the public interest is served through the marketplace. And yet, regardless of the flaws with this
argument on its own terms (flaws perhaps best
illustrated by the French experiment "freeing the
airwaves" in which the bloom of a thousand
flowers quickly withered), it is a fictional resolution. As Streeter explains, the state is central to

the process of station allocation, and, in the US,
"the force of law was used to arbitrarily eliminate a universe of possible alternatives to the cor-
porate-centered, commercial system we have
today: non-legal means of spectrum regulation,
amateur radio operators, and nonprofit broadcasters were all brushed aside or marginalized"
(1996, p. 251). Streeter points out that this is
because the state is bound up in property rights,
and is thus inevitably the guiding arm behind the
"invisible hand" of market logic. But in the case
of radio the impossibility of a "free market" and
the inexorably ideological role of the state in
frequency allocation is especially stark. While
this is well understood when the license to
broadcast is passed exclusively to a public service
broadcaster like the BBC in Britain (see Curran
and Seaton, 1991, and Williams, 1998) the development of radio in a more "open" system like the
US was a victory for corporate interests – and,
often, very specific corporate interests – not because of some simple market mechanism, but
because those interests were favored by regulatory agencies (McChesney, 1994).

In many policy accounts, the importance of
radio is – explicitly or implicitly – often seen in
historical terms. In many countries, the subsequent development of television would take
place largely within the conceptual and legal
frameworks designed for radio broadcasting. If
this historical role is profound, it should not
imply that radio is no longer a significant cultural industry. In many parts of the world, television sets are still luxury items, giving radio a far
more significant reach. Even in countries with
almost universal television ownership (not to
mention an array of other domestic entertainment and information technologies) radio
remains part of many people's daily routines.
In the US, for example, people spend more
time listening to the radio that they do with
any other information or entertainment medium
after television.

Nonetheless, the notion of radio as television
without pictures obscures its many distinctive
features. In particular, the low cost of radio production and its enduring popularity as a medium
has made it much more conducive than television to the expression of ideas outside the sanctioned confines of official spectrum allocations.
Radio has often been regarded as a more democratic and accessible medium than television,

since it allows a greater diversity of broadcasters and is less easily forced into a single state- or corporate-controlled system. While the history of television has tended to be played out in the politer worlds of government commissions and lobby politics, the history of radio has often involved more physical struggles. During both hot and cold wars, radio has regularly been used by the security and military agencies of imperial powers or independent revolutionary groups. And the use of guerilla radio is by no means restricted to civil war zones: the popularity of pirate radio stations in the early 1960s and again in the 1980s in Britain (in the 1980s, surveys suggested that in some areas pirate stations were actually getting more listeners than BBC local radio) forced state-controlled systems to open up and broaden their range.

The low cost of radio production has also made it a more local medium, and the idea of community radio has been embraced and developed in Africa as it has in Europe. It is also local in a global sense, partly because radio programming is not expensive enough to stimulate interest in importing foreign programs (very much an issue with television), and partly because language barriers are, with radio, obviously difficult to surmount. While it could be argued that the radio equivalent of imported TV programming is imported US or British-made music, the economic imperatives involved are quite different (many Third World countries, for example, have no shortage of available locally produced music).

What constitutes "local" – or even community – is, of course, highly contested. So, for example, local radio stations in Britain were challenged in the 1970s for their inattention to a range of local perspectives and concerns. In the same vein, in this section Nina Huntemann describes how corporate mergers in the US radio industry have centralized production while maintaining a pseudo-local identity or feel. If some of the tensions in contesting notions of local or community are inevitable, radio is a medium in which policy guided by a democratic politics of diversity and inclusion requires comparatively little in the way of investment. Radio is, in other words, a medium in which a certain *Realpolitik* (i.e. assuming a parsimonious approach to public funding) is not necessarily at odds with democratic principles. At the same time, its propagandistic potential has made it crucial to projects of neo-colonial domination (such as Radio Marti, or the Voice of America).

References

J. Curran and J. Seaton. *Power Without Responsibility*, London: Routledge, 1991.

R. McChesney. *Telecommunications, Mass Media and Democracy: The Battle for the Control of U.S. Broadcasting, 1928–35*, New York: Oxford University Press, 1994.

T. Streeter. *Selling the Air*, Chicago: University of Chicago Press, 1996.

K. Williams. *Get Me A Murder a Day! A History of Mass Communication in Britain*, London: Arnold, 1998.

Chapter 3

From *Inventing American Broadcasting*

Susan J. Douglas

In the spring of 1922, the radio boom was just beginning. To many people at the time, the entire enterprise seemed filled with uncertainty: Who would be allowed to broadcast? How would interference between competing stations be controlled? Where would the money come from to support broadcasting? Such questions dominated magazine articles, executive board meetings, and the annual Washington Radio Conferences organized by Secretary of Commerce Herbert Hoover from 1922 to 1925. Congestion in the airwaves became intolerable as department stores, newspapers, universities, and churches across the country, as well as AT&T, Westinghouse, and GE, established their own radio stations. In many areas, competition over access to the spectrum required that stations "time-share," taking turns using the same wavelength. When such informal arrangements broke down, cacophony ensued. The cost of broadcasting rose as radio technology became more expensive and as licensing fees to use that technology, and the wages charged by performers, increased dramatically. A range of financing schemes was debated in the press, the industry, and the government, from a licensing fee on sets, to municipal funding, to advertising. At the same time, government officials complained that the Radio Act of 1912 did not provide them with adequate guidelines or power to make broadcasting more orderly. Between 1922 and 1927, broadcasting appeared to be in a state of economic, regulatory, and ethereal chaos.

Despite this chaos and uncertainty, however, critical precedents had been set prior to 1922 that guided how broadcasting would be managed. Most importantly, because radio technology was in the hands of corporations, the ether would have to turn a profit. Members of the radio trust – RCA, GE, Westinghouse, and AT&T – had gained control of radio technology and, like their predecessor Marconi, sought to establish a technological and organizational system impervious to competition. Marconi's model was instructive: create a communications network, seek to monopolize message handling, and sell temporary access to the ether to interested clients. This is precisely what the radio trust did. The trust manufactured millions of dollars worth of apparatus and also set up stations around the country. Through patent suits and the imposition of licensing fees for using trust-controlled technology, the trust was able to reduce competition or make competitors pay for the privilege of broadcasting. The trust had the technical, financial, and organizational resources to shape programming content, to influence public policy, and to determine how broadcasting would maximize profits. AT&T, through its flagship station WEAF, introduced advertising over the airwaves in 1922. AT&T described itself as a communications firm that did not produce its own messages, but that sold access to the airwaves to people who had messages to send. Marconi had established the precedent for this model; now AT&T elaborated and extended it to produce staggering profits.

Regulatory guidelines for resolving disputes in the ether existed, as well. The state would intervene, ostensibly on behalf of "the people," and decide which wavelengths would be allocated to the various competing claimants to the spectrum. In 1912, the state gave the preferred portions of the spectrum to the commercial wireless companies and the military, and relegated individuals unaffiliated with corporations or the government to the least desirable wavelengths. This pattern of regulation was repeated in the 1920s. Herbert Hoover, whose trademark was industry-government cooperation, sought to alleviate etheral congestion in 1923 by dividing radio stations into three classes – high power, medium power, and low power – and assigning the most preferred and least congested wavelengths to the high-power stations, while consigning the low-power stations to the one wavelength (360 meters) that was already overcrowded. It will come as no surprise that the high-power stations were owned by AT&T, GE, and Westinghouse while the low-power stations belonged to universities, churches, and labor unions. These stations were still required to time-share, and many were only allowed to broadcast during the day. This preferential treatment toward the technologically most powerful (and richest) commercial stations, and the regulatory marginalization of smaller, noncommercial stations, persisted through the Radio Act of 1927 and the Communications Act of 1934. As in 1912, the state remained an important ally of corporate interests, legitimating their often preemptive claims to the spectrum, and constraining the transmitting activities of those with less power and money. Certainly the federal government, especially the justice department, was not always friendly to corporate interests, and since 1930 RCA and other members of the radio trust have been subject to antitrust suits and consent decrees. But the government's role in these cases has been to determine when oligopoly went too far, not to challenge its basic legitimacy.

Also in place by 1922 was the dominant conception about what the ether was and who had a legitimate claim on how it was used. As a result of the previous debates among commercial wireless companies, government officials, the amateurs, and the press, the ether was now considered a common property resource in which all Americans had an interest. To protect that interest, however, and to save the resource from being overrun and having its value destroyed, the ether needed custodians. Through the ongoing public discourses about managing "the air," the military had been rejected as appropriate caretaker, and the amateurs cast as agents of etheral anarchy. The badge of legitimacy went to the communications corporations, who burnished its authority by presenting themselves as acting out of benevolent, farsighted paternalism. There were dissenters from this conception of spectrum management, especially among amateurs, educators, and religious groups, and there was some resentment in the 1920s about a potential corporate monopoly of the air. But there was no major break in this ideological frame concerning who was best qualified to serve as warden of the ether.

Technically, economically, legislatively, and ideologically, the elements of America's broadcasting system were, thus, in place by 1922. The constellation of these factors, and how they interacted, had been shaped by the larger historical forces that were redefining American society at the turn of the century. Had the technical developments, the corporate strategies, or the journalistic frameworks been different, or had that period in history not been marked by consolidation and centralization in the public and private sectors, and by the marginalization of diversity in the ideological sphere, the use of radio in America may have been quite different: after all, national networks and radio advertising were not inevitable. There were other alternatives, as demonstrated by the way radio was managed in other countries. That those alternative courses were not taken tells us a great deal about how American society in the early twentieth century rationalized the connections among technology, ideology, and power.

So much had changed in the United States since that fall day in 1899 when Marconi first demonstrated his new invention, the wireless telegraph, before awed Americans. The wireless, which Marconi meant to send Morse code messages between a specific sender and a specific receiver, which he developed for institutional clients, and which he struggled to make secret and private, had become, by 1922, radio, a device marketed to consumers so that they could hear programs broadcast to a vast audience of nonpaying listeners. The technology was under corporate control, and it would be corporations that would decide, for the most part, what was transmitted in the ether and what was not.

The nearly twenty-five-year process that produced this transformation involved the dynamic interplay of individual insights and oversights, organizational ambition and recalcitrance, and technological breakthroughs and errors. Sharply competing ideas about how the invention should be used, and by whom, informed the process from the start. In this interchange among men, machines, and ideas, which affected the social construction of radio broadcasting, the role played by conflict is striking. In this case, although the concept of social construction has been quite valuable, the word *construction* itself is misleading. It suggests a more cooperative process than occurred with radio. Radio broadcasting, despite the references to cultural unity in the press, was the result of battles over technological control and corporate hegemony, and of visions about who should have access to America's newly discovered frontier environment, the electromagnetic spectrum.

The corporations forming the radio trust won these battles in the end. This is not surprising, given that monopolistic capitalism was, by the 1920s, the established way of managing the American economy. But we must remember how they succeeded, because as late as 1920 they were not planning on radio broadcasting. One key to their success was the way they were able to control, and interlink, the three arenas of technology, business strategy, and the press. Here the role that bureaucracy plays in technological change becomes very clear. By the turn of the century, and especially after the panic of 1907, these corporations had what the inventors did not: well-staffed, well-funded, and separate yet related departments to deal specifically with each of these arenas. AT&T, GE, and Westinghouse had industrial research laboratories, and while many engineers in the labs, particularly in the early years, felt the pressure of market considerations, other were more free to work on an emerging technology such as radio. These companies employed carefully selected engineers, who also appreciated market considerations, to serve as the liaisons between the research labs and the company's top brass. Such companies were also establishing their own public relations departments, staffed by men whose specialty was understanding and manipulating the rhetoric surrounding technology and business. Thus, their success was not due solely to the fact that the large electrical firms had more money than the individual inventors; more important was that their financial power was expressed through and reinforced by a carefully articulated bureaucratic structure that addressed, specifically, these three arenas of technology, business strategy, and the press.

That success in all three arenas was critical to controlling this emerging technology was demonstrated by the navy's failure to retain control of radio at the end of World War I. By April 1917, the navy's internal organization had changed to accommodate radio's presence at sea and on shore; the navy was now capable of coordinating technical development and bureaucratic implementation. The war was used to justify the external strategy of navy takeover, suppression of the amateurs, and expansion of military hegemony in the ether. Many of the ideological shifts that occurred during the war, the rhetorical exaggerations that legitimated a range of social changes and excesses, shifted back to prewar frameworks after the armistice, however. The navy's success in the ideological arena between 1915 and 1919 deluded Daniels and his supporters into thinking that this success would be lasting. They did not appreciate that the influence the military enjoys over public discourse during wars can, and usually does, dissipate along with the smoke of the last battle. The press supported private, capitalist control over radio: it had done so prior to 1915 and did so after November 1918. The navy could not overcome the bias against government control of public utilities, which had reached new heights by war's end. Nor did the navy control the technology. Thus, while in 1919 the navy enjoyed titular power over America's radio networks, it was no match for the communications corporations, which had carefully cultivated their turf in all three arenas.

Bureaucratic control over radio had its advantages. Certainly continuous wave technology advanced much more rapidly under the auspices of GE, AT&T, and the U.S. Navy. The patent moratorium during the war, and the subsequent cross-licensing agreements, made possible the coordination of a complete technological system. These organizations simply had the financial, legal, and human resources to achieve these ends, resources unavailable to individuals.

Technological progress and systems building came at a cost, however; the price was individual initiative and freedom in the ether. Control over radio technology put these corporations in an extremely powerful position, not just economically, but culturally, as well. The way the state promoted and protected corporate interests in the airwaves over those of individuals added to corporate power. The radio trust was thus able to co-opt the amateur vision of how radio should be used, and to use the airwaves for commercial ends, to try to promote cultural homogeneity, to mute or screen out diversity and idiosyncracy, and to advance values consonant with consumer capitalism.

The broadcasting boom marks a critical turning point in consumer culture and the corporate role in shaping that culture. Certainly the fact that corporations were sending music and other forms of entertainment into people's homes was revolutionary, as was the eventual sponsorship of these shows by increasingly brazen advertisements. Another major turning point was reached, too; it concerned corporate insight into and sensitivity to the marketplace. While the amateur audience increased every year after 1907, it was catered to only by small companies such as De Forest's or Gernsback's Electro-Importing Company. The amateurs were too inconsequential a subculture in the eyes of GE and AT&T to be considered as anything but a quirky fringe group or a nuisance. Even as late as 1919, when RCA was formed, the oversight persisted. RCA would provide communications to institutional clients, not individual consumers. RCA had the resources to rectify its shortsightedness and to capitalize on the boom, so the myopia was hardly fatal. One cannot help but think that since they were surprised in this way, RCA executives and the many other corporate leaders who witnessed this ambush by the audience cultivated a more calculated, opportunistic outlook toward other American activities seemingly removed from the profit potential. The

concept of who might be considered a potential consumer expanded. This sense of untapped domestic markets, this corporate conviction that there were millions who would willingly reorient their activities, values, and dreams around consumerism, took root and flowered as executives observed, and then managed, the broadcasting boom.

Legitimation of this revolutionary transformation was provided by the mainstream, popular press, which, by the 1920s, had itself invested in the assumptions underlying consumer capitalism. The press was no more objective then than it is now, and its biases caused certain aspects of radio's development to be ignored while other aspects were reviewed and celebrated repeatedly.

What was emphasized and what was ignored? Whether saving lives at sea or bringing lectures to the farmer, radio was consistently cast as the agent of American democracy and altruism. Wireless in 1900 would allow individuals to communicate with whomever they wanted whenever they wanted. Thus, through wireless, Americans could circumvent hated monopolies such as Western Union; the benefits of modern communication would be made available to all. In the 1920s, radio again was portrayed as a democratic agent, leveling class differences, making politicians more accountable to the people, and spreading education "for free." Radio, then, would do nothing less than resurrect the values of the early Republic and, through the power of technology, restore their primacy in an era of monopolistic capitalism.

In the pages of the press, those who stood to benefit financially from radio were able to downplay potential remuneration and to emphasize their humanitarian goals and their commitment to "give the people what they want." Marconi was a modest, selfless hero, and AT&T, in 1915, was a progressive-looking corporation primarily interested in bringing the benefits of modern technology to everyone. Neither Marconi nor Vail was described as a single-minded organization builder determined to establish his firm's corporate hegemony; nor was it suggested that it was profits, not altruism, which fueled such a quest. The theme of altruism, insisting as it did that radio work was guided first and foremost by what "the people" needed and wanted, led to one of the basic myths supporting broadcasting programming since the 1920s. According to the myth, broadcasters are servants of the people, giving the people what they want to hear or see. Because the people can turn their dial, or shut their radio (or television) off entirely, it is the audience, the myth asserts, which ultimately has control over programming content. This illusion of power residing with the audience rather than with the broadcasters was perpetuated in countless articles in the early 1920s and emerged out of the journalistic conventions that cast radio as an agent of altruism, restored democracy, and individual control. References to democracy and to audience participation equated consumption with power. The early 1920s may have been the historical period when the myth of audience power, which rested on the myth of consumer choice, became reified and held up as evidence that Americans possessed unprecedented political and economic freedom. This myth masked the corporate acquisition of control over the content and patterns of mass communication in America, and thus veiled the less romantic and less appealing realities of industrial capitalism.

The emergence and the tenacity of such myths, and the economic and political systems that sustain them, are best understood by linking behind-the-scenes developments in laboratories and offices with the public portrayal of those developments in the popular press. This is why a historical approach that regards technology as socially constructed is so useful, for it requires one to consider how individuals and institutions shaped the design of machines, and to analyze how the uses to which machines are put have been legitimated in the culture at large. The social construction approach demands that we integrate institutional and economic history, individual biography, and the history of technology with a critical perspective on how certain ideas and belief systems became dominant. It requires that the history of technology be construed as cultural history in the broadest possible sense. My aim has been to use this sort of interdisciplinary approach and to show that it is the best way to reconstruct and analyze the connections between technology and ideology, and, thus, between the rise and maintenance of power.

Although a great deal has changed in American broadcasting over the past sixty years, much that was established between 1899 and 1922 remains the same. Major corporations control both broadcasting technology and access to the spectrum, and they shape what kinds of messages we get and the range of ideas to which we are exposed in the public sphere. Corporate-military cooperation in the development of communications technology has reached unprecedented and some would say unsettling proportions. And the myths and heroes through which the mass media justify this state of affairs are strikingly similar to those devised at the beginning of the century. We are still told how much control we have over media content, that what we get is what we demand and want, and that the media are our servants. We are told that because there are at least three networks, plus cable, we have access to a wide diversity of information and perspectives. News stories about emerging technologies, from computers to SDI, are presented as if the stories are completely objective, free of value judgments about who should control technology and why. Just as the press helped shape the early history of radio, so do the mass media today define and delimit the public discourses surrounding how technology is, and should be, embedded in work and leisure, in the existing power structure, and in our very thoughts.

Postscript

In the 1980s, in the history of technology, scholars were trying to debunk three over-simplified but nonetheless persistent misconceptions about the development and diffusion of inventions. The first was the "eureka" myth: the romantic notion that some lone inventor, especially someone like Thomas Edison, sat in his lab thinking and thinking in virtual solitude until the muse descended, whispered into his ear and then he jumped up, yelled "Eureka" and invented the electric light bulb, or the telephone, or the radio. Popular movies, children's books and even museums had helped perpetuate this myth of the lone inventor. The second misconception scholars hoped to put to sleep was technological determinism: the assumption that machines, by themselves, change history, that inventions can be the primary driving force of social change. Again, popular culture and press coverage of technological change helped promote the notion that machines change history, but advertising, with its emphasis on the intertwining of technological change and social progress (newer, improved cars! newer, improved washing machines!) was (and is) central to perpetuating technological determinism. The third misconception was that we could understand technological change best by chronicling the development of discrete inventions, like the incandescent bulb. Wrong, said scholars. We must study and emphasize, instead, the complex technical systems, like power stations, wiring and the distribution of electricity, of which an invention like the light bulb was part, to really understand technological change.

In other words, scholars wanted to get away from the idolatry of heroic, usually male, individuals and away from the mystification of discrete inventions. Inventions emerged out of cooperation, competition, warring visions over what the device should do and how it should look. And they didn't emerge from thin air and then change history on their own terms: people with economic, social, and political interests determined how these devices would be used and who would benefit from them the most.

This emphasis on the many different actors and institutions who shaped how inventions would be designed and used was referred to as the "social construction" of technology, and it powerfully affected my thinking as I wrote about how a device referred to in 1899 as the "wireless telegraph" evolved into something called radio. Radio did not burst on the scene in 1920 out of nowhere, as so many contemporary press accounts suggested. Nor did it have the power, as so many commentators had hoped, to improve a host of ills and inequities in American society.

So now, thirteen years later, would I take back any of what I said? The one thing I have rethought is technological determinism. Yes, inventions like the radio are designed by people who vie with each other over how the device will be used and by whom, and the invention itself gets embedded in economic, political and cultural systems that determine, often powerfully, what kind of an impact the invention will have. But I think now I would emphasize more than I did in 1987 that radio, because of its very particular qualities, had a determining effect on

American culture, politics and the economy, especially in the 1930s. Radio is the only entertainment medium to deny sight to its audience. Because it relies exclusively on our sense of hearing, on listening, radio required that people use their imaginations to picture what was going on, whether it was a baseball game, a comedy, or a report on the Munich crisis. For the first time, millions of Americans listened to exactly the same thing at the same time, and this couldn't help but cultivate a sense of cultural unity and nationalism. Because with radio, it wasn't just that people knew they and others were hearing the same thing at the same time; they knew that others were doing the same kind of imagining, the same kind of cognitive work at the same time. Radio did not eradicate class, ethnic, gender or racial differences; on the contrary, it played on them. But at the same time – and I think this is precisely because radio made you picture things, and because AM broadcasts could, especially at night, travel hundreds of miles – radio was a technology especially well suited to encouraging the sense that listeners were part of this imagined community known as America. So while I don't think I underplayed radio's very distinctive technical qualities, I think now I might be willing to grant the device itself more agency than I did in 1987. This doesn't mean that I think capitalism, or consumer culture, or bourgeois conceits are any less important in shaping radio's development. I still do not believe that technologies change history on their own. But radio is a different technology from television or the movies, and I think now I would be more inclined to foreground the consequences of the device's technical properties. Different technologies do, in fact, encourage different values and behaviors (think about how differently people use e-mail versus the telephone, for example).

As a postscript, I should add that I think the social construction of technology, as an analytical framework, hit a dead end after a while. I think this is because not enough scholars acknowledged the importance of power inequities in these struggles over defining how technologies would be used. This is too bad. Because I still believe that communications technologies are socially constructed by a range of inventors, business people, the press and other media, technical rebels and consumers. But we can never forget that in this construction process, some people and some institutions simply have much, much more power than others. It is when we blend an analysis of power, particularly corporate power, with an understanding of the many people involved in the social construction of communications technologies, that we get the fullest understanding of how the media are used, and abused, in our culture. We also get a richer understanding of the dreams that have – and do – accompany them all, and how and why so many of those dreams are broken.

Chapter 4

The Backlash against Broadcast Advertising

Susan Smulyan

The Protesters and their Agendas

The resistance to commercial radio in the early 1930s brought together a diverse group of people with a wide range of complaints. Educators led the fight but formed different alliances using a variety of tactics, from lobbying Congress to conducting research. Leftist critics joined educators in worrying about the effects of commercialization on American culture, criticizing the lack of choices available to listeners, and bemoaning the fact that radio had not lived up to its potential. Newspapers joined nonprofit educational stations in decrying the increasing dominance of the networks, even if they failed to share concerns about educational programming.

Educational radio stations had the most at stake in the battle against broadcasting commercialism, and they appeared to be losing. There had been 121 educational stations in the mid-1920s; 77 in 1929; and only 53 – occupying just one-sixteenth of the available frequencies – by 1931.[1] In 1925 a group of educational broadcasters attending the Fourth National Radio Conference organized the Association of College and University Broadcasting Stations (ACUBS) because they knew that "the[ir] broadcasting interests...would not be given proper consideration by the...large commercial broadcasting stations."[2] ACUBS members, located at mid-western, state-supported universities, focused at first on survival. Neither the organization nor its members had much money.

The ACUBS financial statement for 1929 reported a small surplus as a result of only $46.97 in expenditures, $69 raised as dues, and a previous balance of $80.[3] Individual member stations and their representatives were experiencing even more difficulty. The secretary of ACUBS wrote, regarding the 1930 annual meeting, that "since I will have to go entirely at my own expense, I am anxious to know about any special provisions for economical rooming and eating while there."[4] As the Depression deepened, stations dropped out because they lacked funds to send personnel to annual meetings or to pay dues.

Despite its limited resources, ACUBS moved on several fronts to challenge the supremacy of the networks. Its members worked to influence radio legislation, maintaining a detailed correspondence with congressional leaders about provisions of the 1927 Radio Act.[5] ACUBS proposed that a reconfigured radio commission, including representatives of education, regulate broadcasting rather than the Secretary of Commerce. ACUBS members voiced disappointment that the 1927 Act did not guarantee "due regard to the requests of educational institutions for opportunities to broadcast educational programs."[6]

After its first annual meeting in 1930, the organization became even more active. With mixed success, it pressured state governments to support educational broadcasting, campaigned for the appointment of sympathetic candidates to the FRC, testified before the FRC, and worked for a reallocation of the radio spectrum that would protect its members.[7] As one supportive observer noted, however, "the Association had little money, and it had given members scarcely more comfort in the difficult days they faced than men without shelter on a winter night might get from huddling together."[8] Its regional focus and membership, plus its limited funding, hampered its effectiveness.

A related group, the National Committee on Education by Radio (NCER), had a national membership, more funding than ACUBS, and a somewhat more focused agenda. NCER sought the reservation of 15 percent of all radio frequencies for educational stations and the "uplift" of American culture through the improvement of radio broadcasting.[9] Founded as a federation of other groups in December 1930, NCER grew out of a conference called by the U.S. Commissioner of Education that had included representatives of various educational organizations, among them ACUBS. NCER received moneys primarily from the Payne Fund, a charitable foundation supporting research into the effects of contemporary institutions on young people.[10] NCER provided a Washington service bureau to help educational stations with federal paperwork and lobbied, provided public information, and sponsored research and experimentation. In addition, it published a weekly bulletin, *Education by Radio*, and financed the preparation and publication of a study, *An Appraisal of Radio Broadcasting in the Land Grant Colleges and State Universities.*[11]

NCER called a national meeting in the spring of 1932 to discuss "The Use of Radio as a Cultural Agency in a Democracy." Representatives from education, government, and nonprofit stations were invited, but the networks and commercial stations were excluded.[12] Cooperation with the networks, NCER activists believed, might "result in further surrenders of power and privilege to the profit-making stations."[13]

Colleges and other nonprofit broadcasters (including labor, municipal, religious, and agricultural stations) had provided alternative programming since the beginning of broadcast radio. In the early 1930s they were joined by other experimenters. The Ohio School of the Air began in January 1929 and broadcast "short periods of instruction which fit into existing

courses" in public schools. By April 1929 100,000 students in twenty-two states listened to these programs broadcast over WEAO (the Ohio State University station) and WLW (the powerful and far-reaching Cincinnati station founded by radio manufacturer Powel Crosley), featuring prominent speakers on current events, health, art appreciation, and science, as well as dramatizations of history, literary masterpieces, and travelogues. The Ohio School continued broadcasting well into the 1930s.[14]

Another unusual proposal for educational programming originated in California with the planning of the Pacific-Western Broadcasting Federation. Begun by "educators, representatives of civic organizations, business men and ministers," the federation sought to build "one genuine UNIVERSITY OF THE AIR." This radio "university" would provide extensive airtime to "learned societies, colleges and universities, civic, social, artistic, and religious bodies," in order to present and popularize the "best in the humanities, social sciences and recreations." It would also provide entertainment – "because the Federation berates banality and bally-hoo in broadcasting, it should not be supposed that there is any lack whatever of realization of the need for relaxation under the terrific pressure of modern life." Programs were to include music, plays, a children's hour, sports, information (especially concerning mental hygiene and public health), discussions of controversial public issues, religious presentations, and charitable appeals. The federation estimated the cost of building its radio station at $1,100,000 and of running it at $530,000 per year. Plans called for obtaining funds from private donors, from cooperating institutions that would subsidize individual programs, and from the sale of time to businesses that sought "indirect publicity."[15] The federation's proposals – apparently never implemented – approached the issues facing radio with unusual creativity, imagining a broadcasting system free from both commercial and governmental control.

While some educators lobbied against radio's growing commercialism and some experimented with noncommercial programming, others favored a form of action more traditional within the academic community: research. The Institute for Education by Radio, part of the Ohio State University Bureau of Educational Research, became the primary research arm of the 1930s protests against commercial radio. Its fifth yearbook noted that the institute "does not shelter present practices; it does not advocate changes," but rather "it specializes in problems where the practical solution seems more immediate." Supported by the Payne Fund, the institute sponsored yearly meetings beginning in 1930 and published the proceedings. ACUBS members were frequent speakers (the ACUBS annual meeting took place in conjunction with the institute's sessions), as were representatives from other nations. In its emphasis on practicality, the institute aligned itself with its cosponsor, the Ohio State Board of Education. Ohio had been a leader in the use of radio in its classrooms, and institute members often heard descriptions of Ohio experiments.[16]

Others approached radio research more theoretically than did the institute. Advertising had turned broadcasting into a search for audiences, and the question of audience lent itself to research and academic debate. In *The Control of Radio*, published in 1934, Jerome Kerwin, a professor of political science at the University of Chicago, criticized radio's uncontrolled monopoly, the organization and personnel of the FRC, the high cost of AT&T's charges for wire lines (which forced the networks to seek too much advertising revenue), and, more generally, the now rampant commercialism.[17] He believed that the search for large audiences and the presentation of educational programming could not be reconciled with broadcasters' search for profits, because "in order to secure the large audiences which the advertisers want and will pay for, it is necessary to stage the least elevating types of program during the best listening hours." Kerwin concluded that "practically every program...suggests a surrender to current standards of taste."[18]

Advocating a chain of government radio stations supported by the federal government, Kerwin, like some other detractors of the networks, cited the British system as a partial model.[19] Many American educators interested in broadcasting sought changes in radio so that the new medium would elevate public taste, as the British Broadcasting Corporation had set out to do. Kerwin presented a somewhat more complex view. On one hand, he found public taste appalling. "If education is to be the aim of radio

broadcasting," Kerwin wrote, "it is absurd to talk at the same time...of giving the public what it wants," because "education must come from above at all times." Yet he also attacked as "callous, indifferent, and irresponsible" the common refrain of broadcasters that "we give the public what it wants." Maintaining that "all the evidence that the people of the country are getting what they want is not in," Kerwin noted that many listeners believed programming complaints were "futile as long as commercialism lies at the base of the broadcasting structure."[20] Kerwin thus articulated the common academic belief that radio listeners needed both "uplift" and protection from excessive commercialism.

Protests against commercialism also came from the American left. Radical thinking avoided, for the most part, the confusion that simultaneously accused broadcasters of underestimating the public and excoriated the public for bad taste in enjoying the programs presented to them. Leftist analysts focused on the corrupting power of commercialism, the public's right to control the airwaves, and a faith in the ability of people, once free of capitalist monopolies, to create a superior culture.

James Rorty, a one-time advertising copywriter and later a founding editor of *The New Masses*, wrote extensively on the evils of commercial broadcasting in Marxist terms, not as a means of production but as part of the superstructure.[21] Daniel Pope has pointed out that, with regard to advertising in general, Rorty contradicted himself by at once reducing advertising to "merely a facet of the conspicuous consumption and conspicuous waste that a business society demanded" and then focusing on the "centrality of advertising in modern America."[22] Rorty treated radio in much the same dualistic way. Radio was a "new instrument of social communication" that contributed "nothing qualitative to the culture" but merely communicated "the pseudo-culture that we had evolved." It was simply "a great mirror in which the social and cultural anomalies of our 'ad-man's civilization' are grotesquely magnified."[23] Yet Rorty also contended that "the control of radio means increasingly the control of public opinion."[24]

Rorty attacked commercial radio both because it influenced public opinion and because it symbolized corporate America's dominance. In the end, he advocated government intervention to bring "order on the air," supporting both the reservation of frequencies for nonprofit stations and comprehensive communications legislation.[25] Rorty worked on his own, but freely expressed opinions about other anticommercial advocates. He applauded the NCER for "militant" actions, but doubted the motives of those newspapers that protested broadcast advertising. Rorty maintained that "the interest of the press in 'reforming' the radio was strictly competitive and pecuniary in quality although, of course, the appeal to public opinion was not made in those terms."[26]

Despite Rorty's scorn, the press played a prominent role in the attacks on commercialized radio. Mainstream newspaper publishers worked on two fronts: against radio news, which seemed to compete directly with them, and against newspaper printing of radio schedules. One notable outbreak of hostilities even came to be called the "press-radio war." In April 1933 the Associated Press, followed by other wire services and under pressure from the American Newspaper Publishers Association (ANPA), refused radio networks the use of news it gathered. NBC and CBS retaliated by founding their own news departments, while independent radio stations continued receiving news from the wire services. The newspaper publishers thus failed to keep news off the radio, but continuing threats by newspapers to drop program listings worried radio advertisers. Network representatives sought a meeting with ANPA. An agreement signed in December 1933 created the Press–Radio Bureau, paid for by NBC and CBS and staffed by the wire services. The bureau daily provided two five-minute news summaries, one to be broadcast after 9:30 a.m. and the other after 9 p.m., so as not to compete with the news presented in morning and evening newspapers. The networks agreed to present the bureau's news unsponsored, and to confine their other news reports to "analysis" or "commentary."[27] This compromise between newspaper publishers and broadcasters led to the development of the radio news commentators and analysts so familiar in the late 1930s and 1940s.[28]

One newspaper, the *Ventura Free Press* of Ventura, California, sponsored a more direct attack on commercial radio. H. O. Davis, publisher of the *Free Press*, bombarded newspaper editors with articles deploring broadcast adver-

tising, the lack of educational programs on radio, and the sinister activities of the radio monopoly. The *Free Press* claimed 746 cooperating newspapers, 523 dailies and 223 weeklies, "in every state in the Union pledging their active support."[29] Its most sustained effort came with the distribution of *Empire of the Air*, fifty articles first sent to newspapers nationwide and then privately published as a book in 1932. In this jeremiad Davis wrote that commercialized stations "so crowd the air channels that the rights of education, labor, and agriculture have suffered," and that "we have seen the ether given over to the advertiser and the home invaded by the salesman." Davis advocated a limit to broadcast advertising, the reservation of channels for education, the supervision of programs by the FRC, and the provision of free programs to local stations to enable them to survive without network affiliation.[30]

The motivation behind the *Ventura Free Press* campaign remained murky. In a letter Davis explained that he had bought the *Ventura Free Press* when he suffered a breakdown "after a career in motion pictures, as reorganizer and editor of *Ladies' Home Journal*, and as regional director for W. R. Hearst." The *Press* proved "sadly run down and neglected," and Davis sought a "broad national issue" in order "to regain local prestige in a hurry."[31] At other times, Davis gave a less personal explanation: he wanted to remove advertising from the air to make room "for channels for education, information, the public service," and "to protect the country's publishers against unfair competition."[32]

Most newspaper publishers believed that radio advertising threatened their profits but, like Davis, they cloaked economic self-interest in seemingly unselfish rhetoric. They emphasized the problems of educational broadcasters and the menace to programming of both radio advertisements and the radio monopoly. Davis urged publishers to attack the radio monopoly in their columns with the *Free Press*'s material.[33] He sent a "Dear Publisher" letter explaining his purpose along with one early release:

> Radio advertising is giving you sharp competition. Radio advertising is a nuisance resented by your radio-owning readers. Radio advertising is the basis on which a dangerous monopoly is being built. The Ventura Free Press, in co-

operation with a thousand other newspapers, is endeavoring to arouse public sentiment for the support of legislation that will defeat the purpose of the radio monopoly and drive direct advertising from the air.[34]

Davis followed up his press releases with lists of "suggestions for the conduct of local campaigns by individual publishers." Realizing that educators and publishers sought the same ends for different reasons, he claimed to be trying to "coordinate" their efforts.[35]

In fact, however, the educators, radicals, and newspaper publishers who objected to commercial radio rarely worked together in the early 1930s. They failed, at this point, to rally around one solution to the problems of commercialization and instead proposed diverse alternatives ranging from model nonprofit stations to revised federal regulations. The government's regulatory mechanisms, however, were easily manipulated by the industry they had been set up to control.

Industry Response to the Protests

The networks and the radio industry, always vigilant concerning complaints that might lead to more government regulation or to a mobilization of public opinion against them, reacted quickly to the backlash against commercialism. Those with a stake in commercialized broadcasting moved to address the criticisms without changing the basis on which radio operated. They spoke out in public to promote commercialized broadcasting; spread their message through sympathetic organizations; and pressured the federal government to ensure, through regulation, that the "American system of broadcasting" would become permanent.

Commercialized broadcasters followed the activities of their opponents in great detail, paying attention to the smallest criticism and calling in favors to find out what the reformers planned. NBC executives received copies of numerous *Ventura Free Press* publications, passed along by newspaper publishers who also owned network-affiliated radio stations.[36] In addition, NBC and RCA directly investigated Davis and the *Ventura Free Press* several times. NBC's manager of press relations met with the *Ventura Free Press* public relations staff in Los Angeles

during September 1931 and reported back to NBC. In October a representative of RCA met with another *Ventura Free Press* employee and sent a confidential report to RCA president David Sarnoff and NBC president Merlin Aylesworth. NBC vice-president Frank Mason also asked the publisher of the *Norfolk Daily News* to seek personal information from friends in Ventura, California, about Davis himself.[37]

These NBC and RCA efforts consisted of information gathering only, with no action planned against the small but annoying *Ventura Free Press*. Neither NBC nor RCA seriously considered changing the practices criticized by Davis or any other protester. The radio industry remained anxious about any opposition that might attract public attention, but only in order to preempt it before it resulted in greater governmental control or a loss in profits.

The networks also undertook public relations activities that seemed to bolster educational programming over the commercial airwaves. Shortly after its own founding, NBC formed a National Advisory Council, composed of people prominent in business, politics, and education, to ensure that "the actions of the company were in the public interest."[38] An education subcommittee of the council reported yearly that the network was cooperating fully with educators and presenting many high-caliber educational programs.[39] The National Advisory Council aimed to help NBC forestall the objections of educators both by identifying prominent citizens who supported the educational policies of the network and by emphasizing its public service activities over its profit-making. CBS joined NBC in touting the educational programs it presented, notably the "American School of the Air." Sometimes in collaboration with the National Association of Broadcasters, NBC undertook other public relations activities to bolster the idea that educational programs belonged on commercial rather than nonprofit stations.[40] The objective was to force nonprofit broadcasters out of business by claiming to do the same job they did.

One organization of educators collaborated in advancing the notion that the networks welcomed educational programming. The National Advisory Council on Radio in Education (NACRE), which shared members with the NBC National Advisory Council and the

National Association of Broadcasters, believed the networks would willingly turn over time for high-quality educational programming.[41] NACRE thus served as a kind of "company union" for the networks. NBC's National Advisory Council reported that NACRE, founded in May 1930, sought to "devise, develop, and sponsor suitable programs" so that the "Council may be recognized as the mouthpiece of American education in respect to educational broadcasting."[42] Funded by John D. Rockefeller, Jr., and the Carnegie Corporation, NACRE prepared programs for both CBS and NBC on economics, psychology, vocational guidance, civics, and labor, and sold nearly 250,000 listeners' guides in 1931 alone.[43]

Speeches at the NACRE assemblies in 1931, 1932, and 1933 revealed both the organization's identification with commercial radio and its low regard for educational stations. Network executives were honored participants at these assemblies, joining government officials, national education association officers, and network-friendly college professors to discuss the development and regulation of radio advertising, broadcasting in the schools, radio legislation, and commercial broadcasting and education.[44] Members of NACRE believed that commercial stations would always have "more unsold time on their hands than they know what to do with," and would give these unsold hours "to educational institutions in the generally vain hope that they will make sensible use of it."[45] In return for the time, and for the access to a varied audience, the educators would have to "disregard many pedagogical practices which have been developed over many decades" in order to produce programs that would "hold an audience."[46] Like the networks, NACRE members complained that the dullness of educational radio stations drove listeners away and decreased the audience for all broadcasting. NACRE saw no conflict between the commercial basis of radio and its use for education, refusing to consider that selling a product and educating a student might be incompatible goals. Rather, it believed that the need of the networks to reach large numbers of consumers complemented the interest of the schools in reaching large audiences for educational purposes.[47]

Reform-minded critics, especially those involved in educational radio stations, did not share NACRE's trust in the commercial networks or its belief that advertising and education were mutually beneficial. James Rorty attacked NACRE for accepting free radio time and asserted that the networks used radio only "in their own private commercial interest and that of the commercial advertisers," a purpose inimical to "genuine education."[48] Jerome Kerwin held that what the networks gave they could also take away, noting that the ease "with which educational programs are brushed aside for the sponsored programs has created the disconcerting feeling that the place of worthwhile programs is not only secondary, but insecure."[49] An ACUBS member wrote that the networks' educational programs served merely as "bait to a trap": once the "big broadcasters" gained control, they would "offer no programs that are not paid for at the most exorbitant prices" and "certainly none will then be offered unless they can be used to sell cigars, cigarettes, toothpastes, patent medicines, etc."[50]

While commercial broadcasters influenced and used NACRE, they also felt the need for an organization of their own to promote commercial radio. The National Association of Broadcasters (NAB), founded in 1922, became an effective lobbying and public relations agent. Its activities ranged from officials speaking in favor of commercially sponsored educational radio programs to the publication of a 200-page book "presenting arguments in support of the system of broadcasting in the United States" for use by high-school debaters.[51] It adopted a "Code of Ethics" in 1925 and strengthened it in 1929, in an effort to curb criticism through self-regulation of fraudulent advertising and the advertising of harmful products.[52] Its members were kept informed of the alliances and activities of the *Ventura Free Press*, and excerpts from Davis's newspaper stories and letters appeared in the NAB newsletter.[53] The association's most effective work came as it interacted with the federal government on behalf of its members. NAB leaders believed they had "fathered" the 1927 Radio Act by helping shepherd the bill through Congress. One historian noted the "many informal services" the NAB "rendered" to the new Federal Radio Commission during its first months after passage of the act.[54]

The networks found pressure on Congress and the Federal Radio Commission (later the Federal

Communications Commission) to be their most effective strategy in resisting the reformers. Even CBS, only rarely visible on the national scene during its rarely years, presented its side of the ongoing argument to the regulatory agency and to the public. William Paley, founder and president of CBS, testified before the commission in 1934, and CBS published his talk as a pamphlet, *Radio as a Cultural Force*. Paley equated the commercial and educational missions of broadcasting when he described radio as "a new force in the distribution of goods as well as in the dissemination of ideas." Speaking directly to the arguments of the reformers, Paley discussed the importance of audience, asserted that CBS gave the public what it wanted to hear, listed the many "educational, informational, and generally cultural programs" presented by CBS, and denied that the network practiced censorship in any form.[55]

The inquiry at which Paley testified marked the next step in the reform campaign, as the foes of commercial radio proposed that Congress reserve channels for the use of nonprofit stations. The protesters hoped to turn the frequency reallocation process (once used to harass them) against the power of the networks. In this next stage of the war, both sides focused on the federal government as it prepared the 1934 Communications Act. The attempt to set aside certain frequencies for education and religious programming became a crucial battle.

Congressional Attempts to Reform Commercial Radio

Congress had first asserted the federal right to regulate radio in the 1912 Radio Act, but the beginning of broadcasting in 1920 brought new problems with which it was ill-equipped to deal.[56] Few members of Congress even knew at that point how radio worked. As late as 1929, during a discussion of the installation of broadcasting equipment in the chamber, one senator asked "if that radio is put back in the corner of the chamber here close to my seat whether it would be possible for one of those anarchists to send something through it and blow us all out of here."[57] Congress thus depended on the radio industry for information on technical matters

and on every other subject having to do with broadcasting.

Despite Congress's ignorance, both the detractors and defenders of commercialized broadcasting turned to the federal government for help in their efforts to influence broadcast radio's form and content. Throughout the 1920s and early 1930s Congress considered radio regulation and, while both sides sought to influence that legislation, the forces for commercialization clearly won. Although the Senate commissioned a study of commercial radio, Congress avoided outright regulation of either broadcast advertising or the radio networks. Instead, congressional attempts at reform fell into two categories – efforts to strengthen the ability of local stations to resist network domination, and attempts to guarantee nonprofit groups access to the airwaves – neither of which had much effect. By not pressing for more fundamental changes, the networks' opponents reinforced the congressional inclination to leave the commercialized system intact. Lobbyists for both sides emphasized legislation that regulated the results of the commercial system but left untouched the basis of that system.

During the years between the beginning of broadcasting and 1927, Congress had debated the question of where regulatory power should reside. The establishment of the Federal Radio Commission (FRC) grew out of a conference committee compromise on the 1927 Radio Act. The House bill called for the FRC to act in a purely advisory capacity, but the Senate gave the FRC authority over radio regulation. The compromise empowered the FRC to issue licenses for only one year, after which the Secretary of Commerce would take over that authority with the expert advice of the FRC.[58] Congress supposed that one year would give the FRC time to create a basic license allocation plan that the Secretary of Commerce could implement. Extension in 1928 of the FRC's power for another year seemed sensible, because the commission had made little headway in sorting out the license problem.[59]

The 1928 extension of the Radio Act contained the Davis amendment, which called for a geographic equalization of license grants and was one of Congress's first attempts to support alternatives to network radio.[60] Representatives of rural areas, concerned about a network monopoly of the airwaves, sponsored this and several other legislative initiatives to strengthen local stations. One Oklahoma representative noted that "so much power has been granted to the... chain stations, that they are absolutely crowding the small independent stations off the air." The legislation under consideration would keep the commission from doing what "it has done in the past," ignoring "all the rest of the country" and letting "a few stations in New York and Chicago dominate."[61] Members of Congress believed that each listener deserved to hear programs originating from an independent local station, rather than over a network affiliate or a faraway, powerful channel.

Both the House and the Senate debated several provisions in the early 1930s to ease the financial and managerial burdens of smaller stations and thus to improve their competitive position. Station owners, the sponsoring members of Congress argued, should be able to appeal FRC decisions in local courts, in order to promote local autonomy and to save money on travel expenses. One bill even proposed a complex formula for radio cases, with some disputes to be heard in local courts, others in three judge district courts, and the rest in the D.C. Circuit Court of Appeals.[62] Another attempt to allow the conduct of more business locally involved the use of examiners, instead of commissioners, to hold hearings. Proponents believed that this change would permit hearings in different communities with greater ease and speed. The scheme failed to win approval, partly because examiners appointed by the FRC, unlike the commissioners themselves, would not have been responsible to Congress.[63]

Representative Davis and his colleagues sought to preserve alternatives to homogeneous programming from big-city sources. But the Davis amendment forced the FRC to spend its time devising a complex reallocation plan that, in practice, often discriminated against nonprofit and non-network stations.[64] As it worked out, the amendment also helped ensure the survival of the networks by creating a system of widely scattered but strong local outlets, a system the networks found particularly convenient. Local stations not affiliated with a network – primarily those sponsored by colleges and universities – actually faced more difficulties because of the

new legislation, while other bills designed to help them failed to pass.

Despite the failure of early congressional radio reform, network opponents who had had little luck attracting support with their under-financed public relations campaigns continued to turn to the federal government for help. *Broadcast Advertising* magazine scorned such lobbying, as radio critics "unable to make an impression on the public, who seemed well pleased with things as they are... changed their tactics and went after the FRC and Congress in whose hands the control of radio lies."[65] The defenders of commercial broadcasting often portrayed their opponents as advocating complete government ownership and operation of the American radio system.[66] In fact, however, the protesters were asking that the government only act to preserve a mixed system of commercial and non-profit stations.

The protests against commercial radio did help to change the nature of proposed radio legislation. Early congressional efforts at reform of the radio industry had concentrated on structure rather than content. As broadcast advertising grew, and as its critics began to complain, Congress took notice. In 1932 Sen. James Couzens, a businessman with little experience in radio legislation, introduced a resolution "calling for a report from the FRC on the use of radio facilities for commercial advertising purposes." The resolution, directly critical of the commercialism of American broadcasting, noted "there is growing dissatisfaction with the present use of radio facilities for the purposes of commercial advertising."[67] Couzens's original resolution included seven questions about "the feasibility of government ownership and operation of broadcasting facilities"; the extent to which broadcasting stations were "used for commercial advertising purposes"; the power available to commercial stations; possible plans "to reduce, to limit, to control, and perhaps to eliminate the use of radio facilities for advertising purposes"; methods used by other nations to control broadcast advertising; whether announcements of sponsorship alone would be "practicable and satisfactory."; and financial information concerning representative broadcasting stations. Sen. Clarence Dill, sponsor of the 1927 Radio Act and now the object of fierce lobbying, saw a chance to placate educators clamoring for action and added eight questions to those of Senator Couzens, all of which dealt with educational radio stations and with educational programming on commercial stations.[68]

In public, both the radio industry and its detractors welcomed the FRC survey. The president of NBC believed the investigation would highlight "the splendid public service that most broadcasters are performing today" and he awaited "the result of this investigation with the greatest optimism."[69] The National Association of Broadcasters (NAB) adopted a resolution calling the Senate request "an opportunity to demonstrate to the American people the superiority of our system of broadcasting."[70] *Broadcast Advertising* agreed that a report to the Senate would find the "American" system "the only plan possible for a democracy," and called the survey "a showdown, with all the cards on the table. . . . a chance to drive home the fact . . . that too much advertising is not radio's only fault, nor its worst one."[71]

The behind-the-scenes maneuverings of the broadcasting industry, however, belied its public confidence. The NAB began a secret emergency fund-raising program to cover the cost of "providing the broadcasting stations with materials designed to present to the American public the real facts."[72] NBC scrambled to give its affiliates information "with which to answer questions regarding network programs," as it "is to our best advantage" that the answers given to the FRC survey be "uniform."[73]

Reformers saw the survey as a chance to show "the commercial radio monopoly" that "the American people are disgusted with the glaring evils which have been allowed to grow up in American radio by a negligent and commercially-minded Federal Radio Commission."[74] As usual, they relied on volunteers to present their case to the FRC and the public, and never marshaled the same level of pressure as did the commercial broadcasters. One member of the National Committee on Education by Radio (NCER) wrote to another that the matter "will require some pretty clever handling and I do not feel equal to the task." The educators did complain, after the fact, about the unfairness of the survey, noting that the FRC had chosen National Education Week, when networks broadcast more educational programs, as the sample period. Further, they argued that the FRC

ignored the NCER and other educational organizations, while it did talk to advertisers' organizations.[75]

The FRC's commitment to commercial radio pervaded its report, *Commerical Radio Advertising*, delivered and printed in 1932.[76] To answer the Senate's questions, the FRC solicited information from stations about their programs and practices, particularly during the week of November 8–14, 1931. It also corresponded with individual advertising agencies, the American Association of Advertising Agencies, the Secretary of State, and with others who had knowledge of broadcasting in foreign countries.[77] The report took the simple form of answers to the previously specified congressional questions, with the FRC presenting itself as a neutral purveyor of information. The responses to the questions about educational broadcasting were extremely detailed and quoted extensively from FRC dockets, but the FRC relied on opinion in its discussion of commercial radio. The commission contended that, at most, one-third of all radio broadcasts were commercial, while other programs, termed "sustaining," were "presented by the station without compensation and at its expense."[78] The FRC explained this apparent altruism by noting that sustaining programs helped stations serve the public interest as mandated by the 1927 Radio Act, enlarging and holding an audience and thereby increasing the value of time available for commercial programs.[79]

The report's concluding statements on the relationship between sustaining and commercial programming observed that "a radio broadcast station can present sustaining programs that are of great educational value and rich in entertainment only in a degree measured by the revenue derived from the sale of time for purposes of commercial advertising." The FRC reminded Congress that if it restricted radio sponsorship to announcements only, advertisers might stop using radio and "such non-use would immediately and inevitably be reflected in a decrease both in quantity and quality of programs made available to the public."[80] The report thus clearly outlined the perils to broadcasting if advertising disappeared, but it never addressed the other contingency: what would happen if sustaining programs vanished, victims to the growing demand by sponsors for airtime?

The report's conclusion emphasized the commission's own competence to regulate broadcasting. "The proper solution," the FRC wrote, "would seem to lie in legislation authorizing the commission to enact certain regulations... rather than specific legislation on the subject by Congress."[81] The FRC existed from year to year, dependent on yearly legislation for its continuance. Yet by 1932 it had accumulated a staff and bureaucracy that used the Senate's questions to make a case for their own jobs. Throughout the report, the FRC presented solutions to radio's problems that maintained or increased the commission's power.

Despite the FRC's dislike of "specific legislation," Congress exhibited a growing interest in regulating broadcast advertising, especially during the election year of 1932. Fiorello La Guardia, a progressive Republican from New York City, probably intended to protect political advertisers when he introduced a bill to establish reasonable fees for radio advertising. Another proposal prohibited commercials on Sunday. Both bills died in committee.[82] Organized labor and agricultural groups also sought legislation to change frequency allocations. Early in 1931 Sen. Otis F. Glenn of Illinois introduced an amendment to a House radio bill calling for the assignment of a cleared channel frequency to labor.[83] A year later the Chicago Federation of Labor lobbied for a clear channel for their station WCFL, got bills introduced in the House and Senate, and testified at hearings before the Senate Committee on Interstate Commerce, worrying the NAB.[84] The United Farm Federation of America suggested in 1932 that Congress set aside a clear radio channel for the "exclusive use of radio stations that may be erected by or devoted to the independent farm organizations only" and saw their resolution printed in the Congressional Record.[85]

The opponents of commercial radio soon moved from advocating individual channels set aside for particular nonprofit groups, to calling for a percentage of frequencies to be reserved for nonprofit stations. This new strategy rallied and brought together diverse groups. As early as 1931 Sen. Simon D. Fess, a Republican from Ohio, had introduced an amendment to the 1927 Radio Act to reserve 15 percent of all radio licenses for educational broadcasting. Despite the backing of various educators and re-

formers, Senator Fess had been unable to win congressional support for the proposal. "I never could get any reaction in favor of it," he told Education by Radio. "As soon as it was offered, the stations began a propaganda against it; just why I do not know."[86] The commercial radio magazines had raised a hue and cry against the Fess amendment. One editorial in Radio Digest had begun, "it seems incredible that so many of our great army of teachers should permit themselves to fall into the hands of schemers." The editor had considered the passage of the Fess bill "one of the most telling blows imaginable to the American Plan" and "the opening wedge to the complete dissolution of the system."[87]

It fell to Father John Harney, the father superior of the Paulist Fathers in New York City, to try to unite the nation's nonprofit groups and their congressional supporters behind a proposal to reserve 25 percent of all frequencies for "human welfare" organizations. A Roman Catholic religious order, the Paulist Fathers had founded a radio station in 1924. After being switched from frequency to frequency, and then forced to share time with other stations over the congested New York airwaves, WLWL found itself, despite appeals to the FRC, allotted only $15\frac{1}{2}$ hours weekly to broadcast. Father Harney decided to "attack on a wider front." In March 1934 educational, labor, and agricultural groups rushed to Harney's support after he presented an amendment to the Senate Committee on Interstate Commerce calling for certain frequencies to be reserved for nonprofit stations. Harney organized Catholic organizations and Catholic members of Congress to support his proposal and enlisted senators Robert Wagner of New York and Henry Hatfield of West Virginia to serve as cosponsors of his amendment.[88]

Consideration of the Wagner-Hatfield amendment became part of the continuing congressional debate that preceded the 1934 Communications Act. Lack of information and imagination about radio's potential power had short-circuited the 1927 congressional attempt at long-lasting, comprehensive radio legislation. In an effort to correct the oversights of the 1927 Radio Act, many representatives and senators had considered consolidating the regulation of all forms of communications.[89] Yet radio's growing political importance, FRC susceptibility to congressional pressure, and industry opposition to most proposed legislation had made Congress reluctant to take action. Amendments to the 1927 Radio Act had enabled the FRC to continue functioning and had given further shape to both the regulatory framework and the radio industry itself.

By early 1933 the lack of a coherent federal radio policy had become woefully apparent, and Congress passed a comprehensive radio bill only to see it blocked by lame-duck President Herbert Hoover's pocket veto. The 1927 Radio Act had essentially been created through the series of national radio conferences called by Hoover as Secretary of Commerce. Proud of his handiwork, Hoover apparently wanted no changes in what he considered "his" act.[90]

In March 1933, however, Franklin D. Roosevelt was sworn in as president, and the obstacles that had plagued earlier legislation receded. Members of Congress felt confident that they now knew how and where to place regulatory power, and which problems to face and which to ignore. (Most members placed both radio advertising and the network system in the category of issues best ignored.) The New Deal added to the push for new legislation. Congressional actions during the first months of Roosevelt's administration established several new administrative agencies, much like the FRC, vested with large discretionary powers and subject only to narrow judicial review. The New Deal Congress also moved away from a concern for small business toward attempts to regulate existing corporate combinations, in the same way earlier Congresses had approached the radio industry. Perhaps most significantly, Roosevelt broadcast six fireside chats in 1933 and 1934, seizing on "radio as a revolutionary new medium of person-to-person communications" and teaching members of Congress an unforgettable lesson about the political importance of broadcasting.[91]

In a 1934 message to Congress, Roosevelt called for a new "communications" bill, proposing a commission charged with regulating all forms of communications. Congress had discussed the possibility of a communications commission as early as 1929, and although many observers expressed surprise when the 1934 Communications Act, with its grant of large discretionary power to the newly created Federal Communications Commission, easily passed Congress, earlier debates, especially in 1933, had paved the way for its approval.[92]

The new bill also resolved several pressing regulatory problems. In 1934 the question of antitrust violations in the radio industry remained a major issue in Congress. The emphasis of the 1934 Communications Act on public service proved a basis for accepting the status quo of both the equipment "trust" (the manufacturers of receivers and transmitters) and the network system of chain broadcasting, thus pleasing both the general public and the radio industry. The act stated its purpose as "regulating interstate and foreign commerce by wire and radio so as to make available...a rapid, efficient, nation-wide and world-wide wire and communication service with adequate facilities at reasonable charges."[93] Accepting at long last the necessity for some regulation of radio, Congress now found its models in public utility and railroad legislation. The public utility model had appeared tangentially in the 1927 Radio Act, with the phrase that licenses should be granted to those serving "the public interest, convenience, or necessity"; this phrase had been developed in the public utilities field and was carried over into the 1934 Act.[94] The continuing congressional analogies between radio and railroad were incorporated as well, so that the language of the legislation designed to regulate radio mirrored the language of railroad regulation.[95] Congress thus consciously based its approach to the new technology of radio on those familiar regulatory forms that had earlier – as far as it was concerned – proved successful.

The few restrictions found in the 1927 Radio Act regarding monopoly within the radio industry were repeated in the 1934 Communications Act. With a statement forbidding interlocking directorates – a direct result of experience with the radio industry – Congress augmented provisions applying antitrust statutes to the manufacture of radio equipment and refusing licenses to any group found guilty of monopoly.[96] The 1934 act also continued the policy of the Davis amendment of insuring equal geographic distribution of radio licenses.[97] Proponents of a strong Federal Communications Commission lobbied against proposed provisions that would have strengthened local stations, including opportunities for local review and the use of examiners rather than commissioners. An amendment, introduced by Senator Dill but not part of the final bill, forbade monopoly in local station ownership. Senator Dill accepted consolidation at the national level, putting his efforts into an attempt to preserve competition at the local level.[98] On the whole, Congress in 1934 seemed content to regard radio manufacturing and broadcasting as interwoven parts of a natural monopoly. The networks, which in all their publicity had sought to appear as natural monopolies, thus escaped regulation.

The introduction of the Wagner–Hatfield amendment was the only challenge to congressional unanimity about the 1934 Communications Act. Much of the debate on the bill concerned this amendment, which had been reported out of committee with only its sponsors voting for approval. The original amendment called for the revocation of broadcasting licenses within ninety days and the reallocation of 25 percent of all frequencies to nonprofit groups. The provision that aroused the greatest controversy would have permitted nonprofit stations to sell time to defray their expenses. Senators Wagner and Hatfield spoke at length on the economic hardships of educational radio and on the importance of adult education in the United States. They willingly changed the ninety-day grace period before license reallocation to six months, the length of time for which broadcast licenses traditionally had been granted. But neither Wagner nor Hatfield could deny that the reallocation of all stations would be a huge job, nor were they willing to compromise on allowing nonprofit stations to sell some portion of their airtime. Senator Dill attacked the amendment on the grounds that, given the opportunity to sell time, the newly protected stations would be no different than commercial stations.

Members of Congress eventually defeated the amendment without having to vote on it by requesting that the new Federal Communications Commission make a study of the issue.[99] The reasons for the defeat were many. One historian faults Wagner and Hatfield's "stubborn reluctance" to change the provision that would have allowed educational stations to sell time, believing that they weakened their case by not considering other means of financial support.[100] But the promoters of the amendment had contended that without some means of support, educational stations would be as bad off as ever. Erik Barnouw blames the divisions within the ranks of the educators, as compared with the unity of the commercial broadcasters.[101] As always, the broadcasting industry had drawn together to oppose the amendment, since it represented both a cut in revenue of up to 25 percent and an extension of regulation. The National Association of Broadcasters had objected to the new category of stations as appealing only to special interests, maintaining that "the sole test of fitness for a broadcasting license is service to the public as a whole, as distinguished from service to any particular class, group or denomination."[102]

Congressional attitudes and preconceptions also worked against the amendment, which ran counter in some respects to the New Deal's faith in the delegation of broad powers to strong federal regulatory commissions. Sam Rayburn, a leading Democrat representative from Texas, believed that if Congress were to tell the FRC how to allocate frequencies "we would be in the same position that Congress would be in if, after giving to the Interstate Commerce Commission its function of regulating railroads and fixing the rates, we would then start out to introduce and pass measures to revise the rate structure."[103] In the end, the 1934 Communications Act gave the Federal Communications Commission unrestricted discretionary powers in the matter of license granting.[104] Left to the mercy of the new FCC, educational and other nonprofit stations faced continuing discrimination.

The FRC thus emerged strengthened by its transformation into the FCC. Its own bureaucratic momentum, combined with congressional knowledge of administrative agencies' susceptibility to pressure, made its inclusion in the new regulatory framework practically a foregone conclusion. Additionally, radio's growing use as a political tool and its importance in everyday life made administrative regulation, usually little noticed outside the industry, more appealing to Congress than prescriptive legislation. In its only attempt to influence programming, Congress left intact the 1927 provision mandating equal time for political candidates and forbidding censorship of political broadcasts.[105]

In many ways, Congress's attitude toward commercial broadcasting reflected what Ellis Hawley has called "the New Deal and the problem of monopoly." Hawley outlines two streams of economic thought operating during the New Deal, tracing them back to the New Nationalism and New Freedom first discussed in the 1912 presidential election: antimonopolists who believed in breaking up trusts to improve competition faced off against those who found monopolies inevitable and thus in need of control.[106] Just as in the rest of the New Deal era's legislation, a dialectic between regulation and competition can be found in the federal response to radio. At once concerned about the "radio trust" in manufacturing and the control of broadcasting by only a few companies, all three branches of the federal government also saw the need for a rationalization of the "natural monopoly" enjoyed by the networks. Federal planning and regulation, they hoped, might mitigate the drawbacks of a monopolistic system and increase competition. In the end, however, governmental regulation only strengthened the largest and commercialized broadcasting companies at the expense of the smaller and nonprofit broadcasters, and lessened competition, outcomes that mirrored most other interactions between the New Deal government and the economy.

Notes

1 Frank Hill, *Tune in for Education: Eleven Years of Education by Radio* (New York: National Committee for Education by Radio, 1942), 22; James Rorty, *Our Master's Voice: Advertising* (New York: John Day, 1934), 271.

2 Charles Culver and J. C. Jensen to Wallace White, 5 May 1926, White Papers.

3 Evan Carroon, "Financial Report for 1929," March 1930, NAEB Papers.

4 B. B. Brackett to R. C. Higgy, 29 May 1930, NAEB Papers. See also B. B. Brackett to E. E. Ross, 29 June 1933, 25 February 1932, and 29 June 1933, NAEB Papers.

5 Charles Culver to Wallace White, 5 May 1926 and 17 May 1926, White Papers.

6 Charles Culver to Wallace White, 19 May 1926, White Papers; J. C. Jensen to Wallace White, 21 March 1927 and 5 April 1927, White Papers.

7 T. M. Baird to H. J. Baldwin, 1 February 1934; B. B. Brackett to I. D. Weeks, 9 February 1933; C. C. Dill to B. B. Brackett, 13 February 1933; Joseph F. Wright to B. B. Brackett, 13 February 1933; A. M. Harding to B. B. Brackett, 18 March 1930; Carl Menzer to Harold G. Ingham, 22 August 1934. All with NAEB Papers.

8 Hill, *Tune in for Education*, 21–2.

9 Ibid., 52.

10 "National Committee on Education by Radio," *Education by Radio* 1 (25 June 1931): 80; "Child's Reaction to Movies Shown: Youthful Emotions More Stirred Than Adults' Payne Fund Study Reveals," *New York Times*, 25 May 1933, section 4, p. 7.

11 Tracy F. Tyler, *An Appraisal of Radio Broadcasting in the Land-Grant Colleges and State Universities* (Washington, D.C.: National Committee on Education by Radio, 1933).

12 Tracy F. Tyler, *Radio as a Cultural Agency: Proceedings of a National Conference on the Use of Radio as a Cultural Agency in a Democracy* (Washington, D.C.: National Committee on Education by Radio, 1934).

13 Hill, *Tune in for Education*, 13–14.

14 Armstrong Perry, *Radio in Education: The Ohio School of the Air and Other Experiments* (New York: Payne Fund, 1929), 13, 18; Joy Elmer Morgan, "Radio in Education," in Martin Codel, ed., *Radio and Its Future* (New York: Harper and Brothers, 1930), 78. For a similar experiment in New York, see Fred Siegel, "Teaching School by Radio," *Popular Radio* 5 (February 1924): 146–51.

15 *For a Genuine Radio University*, 26–7, 49–55, 58. For another view of the possibilities of using radio in education, see Percy Mackaye, "The University of the Ether," *Popular Radio* 5 (January 1924): 37–40.

16 On the "practical solution," see F. H. Lumley, "Introduction," *Education on the Air: Fifth Yearbook of the Institute for Education by Radio* (Columbus: Ohio State University, 1934), vii–viii. On the connection between the institute and the Ohio school system, see B. H. Darrow, "The Purpose of the Ohio School of the Air," in *Education on the Air: First Yearbook of the Institute for Education by Radio* (Columbus: Ohio State University, 1930), 197–203; R. C. Higgy, "Educational Broadcasting from Ohio State University," in *Education on the Air: First Yearbook of the Institute for Education by Radio* (Columbus: Ohio State University, 1930), 257–8.

17 Jerome Kerwin, *The Control of Radio* (Chicago: University of Chicago Press, 1934), 20–3.

18 Ibid., 24.

19 Ibid., 26–7.

20 For "education must come from above," see Kerwin, *The Control of Radio*, 11. For "all the evidence is not in," see ibid., 24. For the futility of complaints, see ibid., 25.

21 "James Rorty, 82, A Radical Editor," *New York Times*, 26 February 1973, 34.

22 Daniel Pope, "His Master's Voice: James Rorty and the Critique of Advertising," *Maryland Historian* 19 (Spring/Summer 1988): 12.

23 Rorty, *Our Master's Voice*, 266–7.

24 Rorty, "The Impending Radio War," 714–15.

25 Rorty, "Free Air," 282; Rorty, *Order on the Air*, 28–30.

26 On NCER, see Rorty, *Our Master's Voice*, 273; on publishers, see Rorty, *Our Master's Voice*, 267.

27 Giraud Chester, "The Press–Radio War: 1933–1935," *Public Opinion Quarterly* 13 (Summer 1949): 257; George E. Lott, Jr., "The Press–Radio War of the 1930s," *Journal of Broadcasting* 14 (Summer 1970): 275; Paul White, *News on the Air* (New York: Harcourt, Brace and Company, 1947), 30–49; A. A. Shecter with Edward Anthony, *I Live on the Air* (New York: Frederick A. Stokes, 1941), 1–16; "Broadcasters and Newspapers Make Peace," *Newsweek* 2 (23 December 1933): 18; "Controversy between Radio and Press," *Literary Digest* (29 September 1934): 5.

28 For a look at one aspect of radio news in the 1930s, see David Culbert, *News for Everyman: Radio and Foreign Affairs in Thirties America* (Westport, Conn.: Greenwood Press, 1976).

29 "Free Press Radio Campaign Backed by 726 Newspapers," undated newspaper clipping, Box 4, NBC Papers.

30 H. O. Davis, *The Empire of the Air* (Ventura, Calif.: Ventura Free Press, 1932), 91–2. See also 90–106.

31 H. O. Davis to Charles A. Webb, 5 January 1932, Folder 5, Box 15, NBC Papers.

32 H. O. Davis to H. L. Williamson, 25 September 1931, Box 4, NBC Papers.

33 H. O. Davis to Gene Huse, 8 August 1931, Folder 5, Box 15, NBC Papers.

34 H. O. Davis to "Publisher," 1 December 1931, Folder 5, Box 15, NBC Papers.

35 On his suggestions to publishers, see H. O. Davis, "The Radio Advertising Problem: Suggestions for the Conduct of Local Campaigns by Individual Publishers," 2 November 1931, Box 4, NBC Papers. On coordinating educators and publishers, see H. O. Davis to Thomas F. Clark, 21 January 1932, Folder 5, Box 15, NBC Papers.

36 H. O. Davis to Gene Huse, 8 August 1931, Folder 5, Box 5; H. O. Davis to L. Lea, 8 August 1931, Box 4; H. O. Davis to A. R. Williamson, 21 October 1931, Box 4; H. O. Davis to "Editor," 11 December 1931, Box 4; H. O. Davis to "Editor," 24 December 1931, Box 4. All with NBC Papers.

37 Lloyd Yoder to Don Gilman, "Your letter of introduction to Walter Woehlke," 30 September 1931, Box 4; Don Gilman to M. H. Aylesworth, "Walter Woehlke–Ventura Free Press," 1 October 1931, Box 4; David Sarnoff to M. H. Aylesworth, 21 October 1931, Box 4; Glenn Tucker "Confidential Memorandum," 20 October 1931, Box 4; M. H. Aylesworth to David Sarnoff, 23 October 1931, Box 4; Gene Huse to J. B. Maylard, 1 February 1932, Box 4; J. B. Maylard to Gene Huse, 19 February 1932, Folder 5, Box 15; Gene Huse to Frank Mason, 23 February 1932, Folder 5, Box 15. All with NBC Papers.

38 Owen D. Young, Statement, "The First Meeting of the Advisory Council of the National Broadcasting Company," 1927, Broadcast Pioneers Library (hereafter cited as BPL), Washington, D.C.

39 Report of the Chairman, Committee on Education, "Committee Reports, Advisory Council of the National Broadcasting Company," Fourth Meeting, 1930, 27–31; Report for the Committee on Education, "Committee Reports, Advisory Council of the National Broadcasting Company," Sixth Meeting, 16 February 1932, 23–30; Report of the Chairman, Committee on Education, "Committee Reports, Advisory Council of the National Broadcasting Company," Seventh Meeting, February 1933, 34–9. All with BPL.

40 Herman S. Hettinger, *A Decade of Radio Advertising* (Chicago: University of Chicago Press, 1933), 291. On CBS and for a network view in general, see Stanley Kaufman, "Radio and Its Present Relation to Education," *Radio News* 15 (November 1933): 265–6, 312.

41 Report of the Chairman, Committee on Education, "Committee Reports, Advisory Council of the National Broadcasting Company," Fifth Meeting, 1931, 23, BPL.

42 Ibid.

43 "NACRE Devotes Session to Advertising on Air," *Broadcast Advertising* 5 (June 1932): 28–29; Rosen, *The Modern Stentors*, 166. See also Report for the Committee on Education, "Committee Reports, Advisory Council of the National Broadcasting Company," Sixth Meeting, 16 February 1932, 24–5, BPL; Report of the Chairman, Committee on Education, "Committee Reports, Advisory Council of the National Broadcasting Company," Seventh Meeting, February 1933, 35–6, BPL; "Dr. Nicholas Murray Butler Heads New Educational Series," *Radio Digest* 27 (November 1931): 19.

44 Henry Adams Bellows, "Commercial Broadcasting and Education," NACRE press release, 22 May 1931, Box 4, Folder 49, NBC Papers; "NACRE Assembly," *National Association of Broadcasters News Bulletin*, 9 April 1932, BPL; "Proposes National Radio Institute," *National*

Association of Broadcasters Reports 1 (27 May 1933): 54, BPL.

45 Bellows, "Commercial Broadcasting and Education," 3.

46 "NACRE Devotes Session to Advertising on the Air," *Broadcast Advertising* 5 (June 1932): 129. See also Merle S. Cummings, "The Schoolmaster's Radio Voice," *Radio News* 13 (September 1931): 194–5, 240–1.

47 "Second Annual Assembly NACRE Closes," *National Association of Broadcasters News Bulletin*, 21 May 1932, BPL; Bellows, "Commercial Broadcasting and Education"; "NACRE Devotes Session to Advertising on the Air," *Broadcast Advertising*.

48 Rorty, "Free Air," 281.

49 Kerwin, *The Control of Radio*, 25.

50 B. B. Brackett to W. H. Bateson, 6 November 1931, NAEB Papers. See also B. B. Brackett to T. M. Beaird, 2 February 1932, NAEB Papers.

51 William Hedges, "Broadcast Education Should Be Commercially Sponsored," *Broadcast Advertising* 3 (September 1930): 33–4; "Debate Handbook Soon Ready," *NAB Reports* 1 (25 November 1933): 229, BPL.

52 Friedrich and Sayre, *The Development and Control of Advertising*, 8–9. See also "Commission Warns Broadcasters to Eliminate Offensive Advertising," *Broadcast Advertising* 4 (January 1932): 18, 20; David R. Mackey, "The National Association of Broadcasters: Its First 20 Years," vol. 1, 104–20, unpublished manuscript, BPL.

53 For example, "The Empire of the Air," *National Association of Broadcasters News Bulletin*, 16 January 1932, BPL; "The Campaign Goes On," *National Association of Broadcasters News Bulletin*, 14 May 1932, BPL.

54 David R. Mackey, "The Development of the National Association of Broadcasters," *Journal of Broadcasting* 1 (Fall 1957): 321.

55 William S. Paley, *Radio as a Cultural Force* (New York: Columbia Broadcasting System, 1934), 1. See also 5, 9, and 17.

56 Radio Act of 1912, Public Law 64, 62d Cong., 13 August 1912.

57 *Congressional Record*, 70th Cong., 2d sess., 1 March 1929, 4865.

58 H. Rept. 1886, 69th Cong., 1st sess., 27 January 1927; S. Doc. 200, 69th Cong., 1st sess., 31 January 1927.

59 Lawrence Lichty, "The Impact of FRC and FCC Commissioners' Backgrounds on the Regulation of Broadcasting," *Journal of Broadcasting* 6 (Spring 1962): 99.

60 Act of 28 March 1928, Statute Law 373.

61 *Congressional Record*, 70th Cong., 1st sess., 10 March 1928, 4488–9; see also 3373–4, 4486–500, 4508–9, 4562–90, 5155–75.

62 H. Rept. 2106, 72d Cong., 2d sess., 25 February 1933.

63 S. Rept. 1045, 72d Cong., 2d sess., 11 January 1933.

64 Schmeckebier, *The Federal Radio Commission*, 47ff.

65 "Broadcasting Is Subject of Senatorial Investigation," *Broadcast Advertising* 4 (February 1932): 160.

66 "Commission Warns Broadcasters To Eliminate Offensive Advertising," *Broadcast Advertising* 4 (January 1932): 18.

67 S. Res. 129, 72d Cong., 1st sess., 12 January 1932.

68 *Congressional Record*, 72d Cong., 1st sess., 12 January 1932, 37.

69 Report of the President of the National Broadcasting Company, "Reports of the Advisory Council of the National Broadcasting Company," Sixth Meeting, 16 February 1932, 15, BPL.

70 "Investigation Begins," *National Association of Broadcasters News Bulletin*, 16 January 1932, BPL.

71 "Broadcasting Is Subject of Senatorial Investigation," 18.

72 "Commercial Broadcasters To Intensify Lobby," *Education by Radio* 2 (10 March 1932): 38.

73 Paul F. Peter to Donald Withycomb, "FRC Questionnaire to All Stations," 20 January 1932, Folder 82, Box 9, NBC Papers; Paul F. Peter to Howard Milholland, "Program Bulletin to Stations: Federal Radio Commission's Questionnaire," 21 January 1932, Folder 82, Box 9, NBC Papers.

74 "Commercial Broadcasters To Intensify Lobby," 38.

75 Joseph Wright to B. B. Brackett, 29 November 1932, NAEB Papers; "To Members of the Association of College and University Broadcasting Stations," 1 March 1932, NAEB Papers.

76 S. Res. 270, 72d Cong., 1st sess., 1 June 1932.

77 "Broadcasting Is Subject of Senatorial Investigation," 16; Federal Radio Commission, *Commercial Radio Broadcasting: Report of the FRC in reply to Senate Resolution 129, Seventy-Second Congress, First Session*, (Washington, D.C.: Government Printing Office, 1932), 38–9.

78 FRC, *Commercial Radio Broadcasting*, 33.

79 Ibid., 14.

80 Ibid., 36–7.

81 Ibid., 37.

82 H.R. 12845, 72d Cong., 1st sess., 8 June 1932; "Bill To Fix Advertising Rates," *National Association of Broadcasters News Bulletin*, 2 July 1932, BPL; H.R. 8759, 72d Cong., 1st sess., 2 February 1932.

83   *Congressional Record*, 71st Cong., 3d sess., 17 February 1931, H.R. 11635, 5205–6.

84   *Congressional Record*, 72d Cong., 1st sess., 8 January 1932, H.R. 7253, 1555; *Congressional Record*, 72d Cong., 1st sess., 15 January 1932, S. 3047, 1997; "Labor Seeks a Clear Channel," *Education by Radio* 2 (April 1932): 57–60; "Labor Fighting for Channel," *National Association of Broadcasters News Bulletin*, 19 March 1932, BPL.

85   *Congressional Record*, 72d Cong., 1st sess., 25 January 1932, 2598.

86   John H. MacCracken, "The Fess Bill for Education by Radio," *Education by Radio* 1 (19 March 1931): 21–2; *Congressional Record*, 71st Cong., 3d sess., S. 5589, 8 January 1931, 1614; Rosen, *Modern Stentors*, 170; Rorty, "Free Air," 280–3; Bernard Schwartz, *The Economic Regulation of Business and Industry: A Legislative History of U.S. Regulatory Agencies*, vol. 4 (New York: Chelsea House, 1973), 2464.

87   "Broadcasting from the Editor's Chair," *Radio Digest* 27 (September 1931): 54; "Lawyers Attack Wave Grab! Standing Committee of Bar Association Vigorously Assails Fess Bill and Calls Attention to Menace in Setting Aside Channels for Special Interests," *Radio Digest* 27 (September 1931): 19–21, 96; H. A. Bellows, "Chaos," *Radio Digest* 27 (November 1931): 18, 95.

88   Sol Taishoff, "Powerful Lobby Threatens Radio Structure," *Broadcasting* 6 (15 May 1934): 5; Pusateri, *Enterprise in Radio*, 167–9; R. Franklin Smith, "A Look at the Wagner–Hatfield Amendment," in Harry Skornia and Jack William Kitson, eds., *Problems and Controversies in Television and Radio* (Palo Alto, Calif.: Pacific Books, 1968), 171; Robert McChesney, "Crusade against Mammon: Father Harney and the Debate over Radio in the 1930s" *Journalism History* 14 (Winter 1987): 118–30.

89   Rosen, *Modern Stentors*, 168.

90   For the bill that Hoover vetoed, see H.R. 7716, 72d Cong., 2d sess., 1 March 1933, 5397. On Hoover's role in radio regulation, see Edward F. Sarno, Jr., "The National Radio Conferences," *Journal of Broadcasting* 13 (Spring 1969): 189–202; C. M. Jansky, "The Contribution of Herbert Hoover to Broadcasting," *Journal of Broadcasting* 1 (Summer 1957): 241–9.

91   Arthur Schlesinger, *The Coming of the New Deal* (Boston: Houghton Mifflin, 1958), 558–9.

For a view of Roosevelt that portrays him as a more active participant in the passage of the Communications Act, see Robert McChesney, "Franklin Roosevelt: His Administration and the Communications Act of 1934," *American Journalism* 5 (1988): 204–29.

92   For Roosevelt's call for a new communications bill, see S. Doc. 144, 73d Cong., 2d sess., 26 February 1934. For early debate on a combined communications commission, see *Congressional Record*, 70th Cong., 2d sess., 1 March 1929, 4859. For surprise over the easy passage of the Communications Act of 1934, see Schwartz, *Economic Regulation*, 2373–6.

93   Communications Act of 1934, Public Law 416, 73d Cong., 19 June 1934, section 1.

94   Radio Act of 1927, Public Law 632, 69th Cong., 23 February 1927, section 9; Communications Act of 1934, section 303f. See also "Administrative Control of Radio," *Harvard Law Review* 49 (June 1936): 1333; Keith Masters, "The Present Status of Radio Law: A Survey," *John Marshall Law Review* 1 (1936): 211; P. M. Segal and Harry P. Warner, "Ownership of the Broadcasting Frequencies: A Review," *Rocky Mountain Law Review* 19 (February 1947): 111–22.

95   Schwartz, *Economic Regulation*, 2429.

96   Communications Act of 1934, sections 311, 313, 314.

97   Ibid., sections 302, 307.

98   Schwartz, *Economic Regulation*, 2488.

99   Erik Barnouw, *The Golden Web: A History of Broadcasting in the United States* (New York: Oxford University Press, 1968), 26.

100 Smith, "A Look at the Wagner–Hatfield Amendment," 176.

101 Barnouw, *The Golden Web*, 25–8.

102 "Supplementary statement by the National Association of Broadcasters regarding the amendment to H.R. 8301, to the Committee on Interstate and Foreign Commerce of the United States House of Representatives," Box 4, William Hedges Papers, Mass Communications History Center, Wisconsin State Historical Society, Madison.

103 Schwartz, *Economic Regulation*, 2504.

104 Communications Act of 1934, sections 302, 307.

105 Communications Act of 1934, section 315.

106 Hawley, *The New Deal and the Problem of Monopoly*, passim.

Chapter 5

The Effects of Telecommunication Reform on US Commercial Radio

Nina Huntemann

On February 8, 1996 US President Bill Clinton signed the Telecommunication Act. The policy was heralded for promoting competition and diversity in a new era of communication service. In the late '80s and early '90s, telecommunications and broadcast industries pressured Congress to enact new legislation that responded to emerging new technologies, specifically wireless communications and the Internet. Prior to 1996, communication regulation had not undergone major reform since the 1934 Communications Act. Spearheaded by Vice President Al Gore, a long-time advocate of new technologies as a senator, the Clinton Administration proposed legislation to eliminate cross-ownership restrictions between telephone and cable companies, lift national ownership caps on radio and television broadcasters, and further open telecommunication services to private investment. The bill moved through the US House Subcommittee on Telecommunications and Finance and the US Senate Committee on Commerce, Science, and Transportation with little to no public comment. Hearings and back-room committee meetings were largely attended by industry spokespeople, the National Association of Broadcasters (NAB) and National Cable Television Association (NCTA); representatives from long-distance and local telephone companies; and information technology service providers, AOL and Microsoft.

Congressional members, academics, and consumer advocates have since remarked that the 1996 Telecommunications Act was last century's most important legislation. However, public discourse about the bill was confined to questions of competition and technological progress, not public service. The assumption on Capitol Hill, well paid for by corporate media interests, insisted that any public service needs would be met by a deregulated market.

Instead of promoting competition and diversity however, the 1996 Telecommunications Act opened the flood gates for massive consolidation, particularly in the broadcast radio industry. The Act lifted all national ownership restrictions, permitting one company to own hundreds of radio stations across the country, with local ownership caps set at eight stations in the largest markets. The result of four years of mergers and acquisitions has brought about the most tightly knit and homogeneous group of owners the radio industry has seen since Westinghouse and RCA dominated the airwaves prior to World War II.

Merger Mania

Media brokers and broadcast station owners described 1996 as the "busiest and most lucrative" year ever ("Radio/TV Ownership," 1997). The Federal Communications Commission (FCC) reports that in the first year of the Act, 2066 radio stations changed owners, about 20 percent of the total number of commercial radio stations in the country. Whereas, from March

1995 to February 1996, twelve months prior to the Act, only 988 stations changed owners (FCC, 1997b, p. 2). According to broadcasting analysts, radio mergers in 1996 totaled $13.4 billion, compared to $1.5 billion in 1995 ("Radio Mergers," 1997). Even though acquisitions slowed in 1997 as the most lucrative stations were snatched up the year before and consolidation was reaching a plateau, the industry maintained record levels of activity with $12.7 billion in station trading (Brown, 1998, p. 32). Due to passage of the Telecommunications Act, the last years of the millennium experienced more station trading than the industry had seen in decades. Between 1987 and 1992 only 6,570 stations changed hands. From 1993 to 1998 station trading increased 53.3 percent, for a total of 10,071 stations changing owners. Of the $63 billion dollars spent purchasing radio stations from 1987 to 1998, two-thirds was spent after the 1996 regulation changes (BIA Companies, 1999).

Who Owns Radio?

We're down to where you could have a meeting of this industry in a closet today. Gary Stevens, broadcasting broker for Gary Stevens and Co.[1]

Since the Telecommunication Act lifted national ownership caps, the number of radio station owners has decreased 18.8 percent. In 1995 there were 10,246 commercial stations and 5,222 owners. By November 1997, only 4,507 owners held 10,475 stations (FCC, 1997b, p. 22). By the end of 1998, the numbers continued to decrease, with only 4,241 owners for 10,636 stations (BIA Companies, 1999). So even while the number of commercially-licensed stations increased by 390, new owners rarely entered the industry, and more than 981 owners – most of them small and local – have left radio since 1995.

With the decrease in owners and lifted national ownership restrictions, there are a growing number of large group owners. In 1997, the FCC observed that more than 30 owners controlled 20 or more stations each, with the top five radio group owners controlling 100 to 200 stations each (FCC, 1997b, p. 3). By the end of 1999 one radio conglomerate, Clear Channel Communications, controlled 973 stations with annual

revenues over $3 billion, nearly a quarter of total commercial radio revenues. In terms of national coverage, stations owned by Clear Channel broadcast in 153, or 55 percent of, radio markets.

The majority of large radio group owners are white males with highly educated backgrounds, several from Ivy League universities, schooled in business and law, not broadcasting, with annual salaries and compensation well into the millions. The demographic composition of radio executives has always been dismally homogeneous, but recently the state of ownership came under fire again when the National Telecommunications and Information Administration (NTIA) of the US Commerce Department (1997) reported that minority-owned stations in 1997 had decreased to 2.8 percent, from 3.1 percent in 1996. This decrease of 350 to 322 minority-owned stations occurred while the total number of radio stations increased.[2] Much of this decrease was attributed to the purchase of US Radio, the largest black-owned broadcast company in the nation, by Clear Channel Communications; a merger that was made possible by the 1996 Telecommunications Act.

In his first address to the NAB, FCC Chairman William Kennard stressed the link between station owners and radio programming: "The person who owns the station has the ultimate power to shape public opinion" (McConnell, 1998, p. 53). He urged the NAB to encourage minority ownership by implementing, for example, minority training and investment programs. However, the possibility of any significant increase in minority-ownership is remote given the concentration trend, which continues to squeeze out owners with less than 20 stations. Most minority owners control less than eight stations (US Department of Commerce, 1997).

Large radio groups are also reluctant to search out minority owners when selling or trading radio stations. Typically, stations are traded in groups across markets. Most minority owners control at most a few stations in one market, and thus are not attractive buyers in the giant merger and acquisition trend controlling radio sales. During the summer of 1997 the above scenario resulted in the loss of two potential minority-owned stations in a top ten Arbitron market.

In 1994 Viacom International purchased four radio stations in Washington, DC and then filed a temporary waiver with the FCC in order to sell off two of the stations to minority-owners and meet the 1994 ownership regulations (one TV, AM, and FM station per market). Before the temporary waiver expired, Viacom entered into an agreement with Evergreen Media (now part of Clear Channel) to sell, among others, the four Viacom DC stations. In response to the pending transaction the Rainbow–PUSH Coalition, headed by Reverend Jesse Jackson, filed a petition against the sale, claiming Viacom misrepresented itself to the FCC by selling the DC stations to a non-minority-owned radio group (FCC, 1997a). The petition, which threatened to hold up a $1.075 billion sale, was eventually dropped when the Coalition settled with Viacom and Evergreen for $2 million. The money was earmarked for research, scholarships, and public education about minority broadcast ownership. Evergreen was released from any promise to find minority buyers for the DC stations.

The threat of a buy-out or going under is particularly salient for black-owned broadcasters since most of these stations broadcast to urban, less affluent communities, where advertising revenue is among the lowest in the industry (US Department of Commerce, 1997). However, despite the financial difficulties faced by many minority owners, radio audiences continue to tune in, claiming that minority-owned stations tend to provide more community-based programming than local conglomerates (Fisher, 1998). Dissatisfied listeners are also tuning into unlicensed ("pirate") radio, Internet-based radio (Feit, 1997) and bypassing the conglomerate-controlled record industry altogether by swapping street-produced recordings (Miller, 1997) and trading digital (MP3) music files on the Internet. These tactics, although empowering on a small scale, relinquish radio, a medium once defined by its community character, to national corporate hands with a handful of white, MBA-educated men at the helm. Yet another outlet for public expression is in danger, if it is not too late, of becoming solely a media space, defined by market demographics and listener consumption habits.

The broader problem that community-radio advocates must face, as Larry Irving, NTIA Assistant Secretary for Communications and Information noted, is retrieving the importance of "diversity of ownership and diversity of view-point," which was a fundamental premise of broadcast regulation and public expectations of radio in the 1970s and '80s (Irving, 1997). A reinvigorated public debate about diversity in the media and a thorough examination of media owner activities would be a first step toward reclaiming radio.

Scanning the Dial for Diversity

There are multiple approaches to measuring the diversity of radio. Ownership diversity, discussed above, examines the number of owners to number of stations (i.e. 4,241 owners for 10,636 stations) and their market share – how much of the audience an owner captures (Napoli, 1999, p. 12). Recent data indicates that, for the industry as a whole, 53.4 percent of all US commercial radio stations are part of consolidated radio groups. These stations capture 67.3 percent of the total listening market. In terms of individual radio groups, 24 companies capture 82 percent of the listening audience in 20 markets and more than 90 percent of audiences in four markets (BIA Companies, 1999). Thus, concentrated ownership is wide and consolidated stations dominate the available listening audience.

For the most part minority-owner and radio diversity advocates agree with the Department of Commerce's call for investment and training programs for minority broadcasters, but they also argue that the question of who owns the media is only half of the problem. Defining diversity by numbers of minority-owners leaves questions of programming diversity and universal service unexamined (Americans for Radio Diversity, 1998). This concern is shared by political economy of communication scholar Vincent Mosco (1996) who states that policy studies, such as the Department of Commerce's report, make the mistake of "equat(ing) diversity with multiplicity." There is a "fundamental difference between the sheer number of voices (multiplicity) and the number of different voices (diversity)" (p. 258). A competitive and diverse media environment requires not only multiple outlets but a wide range of viewpoints as well. An 80 percent consolidated radio industry will look (and sound) quite different if the content of radio is diverse despite concentration, or relatively homogeneous. So far, however, the results of a profit-driven, conglomerated media environment indicate that diversity of viewpoints suffers at the hands of controlling advertising interests (Herman and McChesney, 1997, p. 7). This holds true across TV, radio, film and publishing, despite industry claims such as the following remarks by regional radio programming director for Jacor Broadcasting, Gabe Hobbs:

> As to the argument that if you concentrate the media in the hands of the few, the flow of information is too constricted, I don't buy that at all. We're not in the business of being pre-occupied with an agenda to advance a certain type of music or a political bent; that's just folly. We're here to return profits to our shareholders. (Reece, 1998)

In his comments, Hobbs provides the answer as to why commercial radio tends to represent narrow musical tastes and conservative political perspectives – shareholder profits. In order for Hobbs and his colleagues to maintain a high profit return, they must capture the maximum amount, in volume and price, of advertising revenues. Ad revenue pays for station equipment, staff salaries, and programming. Ad revenue surplus is the profit return shareholders receive. Given this relationship, if a DJ, news staff or recording artist offends an advertiser, Hobbs and programming directors across the country know to pull the offending material and make any concessions to please advertisers. Similarly, advertisers want to reach as many consumers as possible who are able to buy the advertised products. Gerry Boehme, ad placement buyer for Katz Media (a subsidiary of Clear Channel) explains this interest in specific consumer habits was made possible by improvements in marketing technology. "Traditionally, (radio stations) would define their target maybe in terms of age and sex, but now they're starting to talk about lifestyle and consumer habits and particular product consumption" (Tucker, 1997). This expectation requires programming and marketing directors to constantly survey audience spending and tailor their music and radio shows to the lowest common denominator. But how exactly has the profit-motive influenced radio programming and lead to a decline in content diversity?

Another approach to measuring diversity is to investigate radio formats and playlists – the content of radio programming. For marketing purposes, radio programming is broken up into musical genres, or format categories. These format categories are used across commercial radio to attract advertisers. Typical categories include Adult Contemporary, Country, Talk, News, Sports, Album Oriented Rock, and Middle of the Road (MOR). These format categories describe the type of music or radio programming broadcast the majority of station time and are associated with a particular demographic. Stations use this combined format and demographic information to lure advertisers. For example Contemporary Hits Radio (top-40) attracts 50 percent of its audience between the ages of 18 and 34 and MOR attracts 86 percent of its audience from ages 55 and up (Arbitron, 1999).

Based on the interest of attracting large audiences for advertisers, it is no surprise that Country is commercial radio's most popular station format, covering 22.4 percent of stations in the US (BIA Companies, 1999). According to Arbitron, Country enjoys the widest, and advertisers' most sought-after, audience: Adults age 25–34, 19.0 percent; age 35–44, 21.4 percent; and age 45–54, 18.4 percent (Arbitron, 1999, p. 26). In addition, 93 percent of Country radio's audience is white (Arbitron, 1998, p. 10).[3] The next most frequent radio format, Adult Contemporary (AC), covers 12.2 percent of all commercial stations (BIA Companies, 1999), and typically attracts 50 percent of its audience from the 25 to 44 age demographic (Arbitron, 1999, p. 18). Eighty-seven percent of AC listeners are white (Arbitron, 1998, p. 10). News/Talk/Sports is the third most popular format, covering 10.8 percent of all commercial stations (BIA Companies, 1999), with a 94 percent white audience (Arbitron, 1998, p. 10). In addition, News and Talk radio audiences are typically better educated and more affluent than the average American (Head, Sterling, Schofield, Spann, and McGregor, 1998, p. 262). On the other hand, the most popular black audience formats, Urban, also known as Rhythm & Blues with an 80 percent black audience and Urban AC with an 87 percent black audience (Arbitron, 1998, p. 10), account for only 186 and 126 stations respectively (Arbitron, 1999, p. 44–6). This data indicates that current radio station format options are overwhelmingly geared toward white audiences, and the music apparently of wide interest to black audiences is barely finding broadcast outlets.

In 1997 the FCC concluded that consolidation of the radio industry did not result in major station format changes. Overall, the diversity of radio programming available to audiences remained the same (FCC, 1997b). However, data for this survey was collected from March 1996 to November 1997, a year and a half directly following the 1996 Telecommunications Act. During this time radio conglomerates purchased successful radio stations in the highest ranked, metro markets such as New York, Los Angeles, Chicago and San Francisco, and typically did not mess with success by changing station formats. By the end of 1997 the radio industry was 80 percent consolidated, and the most successful radio stations were purchased by major radio conglomerates. The industry strategy has now turned to either purchasing stations in smaller markets, or buying less popular stations in the Metro markets and changing station formats to "round out" the radio holdings of a broadcast conglomerate, and thus be able to offer several demographic profiles to advertisers ("Chancellor Media Corporation forms national radio network," 1997).

The station formats offered by Clear Channel, the largest radio group, exemplify this current trend in radio programming. Clear Channel operates at most two stations in any one market in the same format, thus reducing station-to-station competition for a particular demographic. However, the diversity of formats this radio conglomerate provides nationally is quite narrow. The top station formats held by Clear Channel are: Adult Contemporary, 145 stations;[4] Talk, 133 stations;[5] and Country, 119 stations.[6] Nearly every radio market in Clear Channel's portfolio has at least one each of these formats. Combined, these three formats account for 41 percent (15 percent, 14 percent, 12 percent respectively) of Clear Channel's stations. Based on this programming strategy, pro-consolidation analysts and radio conglomerates claim radio consolidation is better for the listener because it decreases redundant station formats in a given area (Reece, 1998). However, as the Clear Channel format strategy suggest, al-

though station format choice per region may have increased post the Telecommunications Act, station formats nationwide are narrowing.

Station format is a partial indicator of content diversity. Formats tied to audience demographics suggest who is served by radio, but in terms of specific programming, formats only reveal the general type of music, news or talk shows broadcast. Within each type, it is possible for a range of music or talk show hosts to reach audiences. However, by examining another trend in radio programming influenced by the high rate of concentration – radio networks – it is possible to see the decrease of content diversity in consolidated radio markets.

Technological advances in satellite broadcasting have enabled large radio group owners to consolidate station operations, particular content development and distribution. It is increasingly common for playlists to be developed by regional program directors. Some playlists, like CHR (top-40), are restricted to about a hundred of the most recent popular recordings (Head et al., 1998, p. 265). Music from these lists is prerecorded at corporate headquarters. The "canned" music, complete with national advertising spots, is then distributed to individual stations via satellite (Dizard, 1997, p. 19). Local disc jockeys need only interrupt the satellite stream for weather and time updates, and local advertising spots. For example, Capstar Broadcasting, now part of Clear Channel, operates 313 stations from six regional operators: Atlantic Star (69 stations), Central Star (25 stations), Gulfstar (83 stations), Pacific Star (42 stations), Sea Star (28 stations) and Southern Star (66 stations). The radio conglomerate uses a network link called the StarSystem to develop and deliver a majority of its station programming (Capstar, 1998). Chancellor Media, purchased by Clear Channel in 1999, established a similar system, AM–FM Radio Networks, to distribute programming to its 108 stations ("Chancellor Media Corporation forms national radio network," 1997).

The distribution of syndicated programming has also increased with the concentration in radio ownership. Large radio groups are purchasing syndication rights and then piping out to their radio network music programs such as Casey Kasem's American Top-40, music call-in shows like Rockline, and, the fastest-growing syndicated programs, talk radio with the likes of Rush Limbaugh, Howard Stern, and Dr. Laura (Head et al., 1998, 262). The result of syndicated programming and corporate-developed playlists is a marked decrease in air play for local talent and community tastes.

In a review of black-formatted, non-minority owned radio stations, the Black Rock Coalition, a nonprofit organization promoting progressive and alternative black music, stated that these stations typically do not support new black artists or reflect the needs or interests of the local community (Ofori, Edwards, Thomas, and Flateau 1997, 129). Instead, stations tend to play mainstream, established artists supported by the conglomerated record industry. The relationship between large radio groups and the record industry is no surprise to independent and small group radio station disc jockeys who witness their conglomerate-owned colleagues accepting a new form of payola, called pay-for-play, to spin industry records.

Strapped for cash after the flurry of mergers and acquisitions following ownership deregulation, large group owners were searching for new revenue streams. Payola, the exchange of money or gifts from record promoters to DJs for playing certain artists, was outlawed by the federal government over thirty years ago. But pay-for-play is technically legal as long as DJs announce at the time of broadcast if a song was paid for by a record promoter, and the station, not the DJs, receives the money. In 1998, Chancellor Media (now owned by Clear Channel) signed $25 million in pay-for-play contracts for their 465 stations (Taylor and Schiffman, 1998). Although independent record labels have used pay-for-play to get their artists on the airwaves, conglomerate-owned record labels have a distinct advantage. They can afford to pay higher pay-for-play fees and sign contracts with large supergroup radio networks, like Chancellor Media, for airplay on stations across the country. This revised form of payola makes it even more difficult for independent record labels and unsigned artists to get their music onto station playlists.

Downsizing Radio

New forms of content programming, such as satellite broadcasting and network-wide play-lists also have serious implications for labor at conglomerate-owned stations. The immediate fallout of radio consolidation at the local level has been a flurry of pink slips. BIA Companies (1999) estimates that unemployment rates in broadcasting are "among the highest levels in the country and that current consolidation has reduced employment opportunities by 10%." Job opportunities thrive within the sales operations of conglomerated stations pushing to maximize cash flow. However, creative positions (on-air staff) and technical and clerical support staff are down. When a station is purchased by a conglomerate, local disc jockeys are replaced by satellite-beamed disc jockeys, station programmers are replaced by network programmers housed at corporate headquarters, teams of technical engineers are replaced by one engineer servicing many stations, and news staffs are replaced by wire service news, and regional weather and traffic syndicates. Since the round of staff firing increases the more local stations a conglomerate operates, radio personnel in larger metro markets where one company can operate up to eight stations are in greater danger of losing their jobs.

The effects of this trend rippled through the industry within months after radio merger-mania struck. At the NAB's Radio Show in October 1996, barely nine months after the Telecommunication Act was signed into law, radio personnel confronted station owners about the rash of staff cuts that followed consolidation. Wayne Brown, general manager of WPEG-FM in Charlotte, NC, stated, "With all the changes going on in the industry, my biggest concern is what happens to the people. The talent and staff ask: 'What does this all mean to me?' and the biggest challenge is reassuring the talent that they still have a place in the company" (Petrozzello, 1996, p. 46). At the time of the NAB Radio Show, Brown's station had recently been acquired by American Radio Systems as part of a six-station buy in the Charlotte market.

Reassuring his talent staff in the midst of merger-mania is a tall order considering Brown's own job as general manager was most likely in peril as well. Eliminating overlapping positions when multiple stations are owned in a market includes consolidating general and station managers as well as technical and talent staff. Individual station mangers are quickly replaced by regional managers in charge of two or more stations. For example, for its thirteen stations in the Albany/Schenectady/Troy, New York market, Clear Channel employs two general managers. One oversees seven stations, the other oversees six. In Raleigh/Durham, North Carolina, two general managers oversee nine stations (four to five stations), and in Dayton, Ohio one general manager supervises all eight stations.[7]

(Low) Power to the People

The mega-media corporations coming in and buying up stations have destroyed radio localism and the community it used to bring. Not to mention that it has really made radio bland. Jeremy Wilker, co-founder of Americans for Radio Diversity[8]

The obvious implication of consolidating radio personnel is the loss of jobs, but audiences lose too. As radio increasingly becomes a remote operation, the possibility for community radio, radio with a local focus, seems just as remote. Local radio journalists are some of the first to lose their jobs. Radio historian Robert McChesney (1997) writes, "To do effective journalism is expensive, and corporate managers realize that the surest way to fatten profits is to fire editors and reporters and fill the news hole with inexpensive syndicated material and fluff (p. 24).

Without local news staffs devoted to reporting small-town issues as well as national briefs, audiences receive canned regional news that may only occasionally cover issues reflecting the listener's immediate geographical area. Regional or wire news staffs are harder to hold accountable simply because they are more difficult to reach. With a larger area to cover, regional staffs cannot be in touch with community happenings, have time to interview local citizens, or devote in-depth coverage to local news events.

In 1998 the FCC expressed concern over the loss of community-focused radio and invited proposals to establish low-power radio service. At the time, low-wattage radio stations, often referred to as micro-broadcasting or pirate radio, were illegal. But the FCC, particularly Chairman Kennard and Commissioners Michael

Powell and Gloria Tristani, believed the decrease in community radio created by a conglomerated radio industry may be remedied by low-power stations.

For nearly a year the FCC gathered industry and consumer advocate opinion about the low-power radio proposal. The NAB and National Public Radio loudly opposed the idea, claiming that low-power stations would cause frequency interference for both other radio broadcasters and air traffic control signals. Other reasons the NAB and NPR cited included the unforeseen effects low-power radio would have on digital radio;[9] the current 12,000 commercial and non-commercial radio stations already fulfilled community needs; and low-power stations would be unable to serve mobile audiences and guarantee consistent and reliable service (NAB, 1998). Proponents of low-power broadcasting charged the NAB and the conglomerate radio interests it represented of being "greedy, mendacious" and unconcerned with serving the public interest (Dunifer, 1997).

On January 21, 2000 the FCC voted to authorize two new classes of radio licenses, a 50 to 100 watt station license with a three and a half mile coverage radius, and a one to 100 watt station with a one to two mile coverage radius. In order to encourage multiple owners, the FCC ruled that current radio station owners and other media property owners were ineligible for low-power licenses, and set national ownership caps at ten stations. Perhaps more significant than the ownership restrictions is the requirement that low-power radio licenses are issued for non-commercial use. Thus, advertising dollars and profit margins will not drive content, as in commercial radio. However, without public funding and ample community donations, these stations may feel pressure to tailor content, as have the national public radio and television stations, in order to please underwriters. The advantage of low-power licenses, which do not require large antennas and high-tech equipment for programming, is that operating costs are fairly inexpensive.

It is too early to predict what remedy for consolidation low-power radio will provide. Months before the FCC vote, members of Congress, financially supported by the broadcast industry, proposed legislation to block low-power licensing and the NAB intends to file a law suit against the ruling (Anderson, 2000). The FCC's attempt to restore the ideals of public service and community broadcasting stripped away by the 1996 Telecommunication Act by implementing low-power licensing is a telling sign of the times. In the conglomerated media environment, controlled by fewer and fewer corporations, citizens and public-service-minded regulators are left to scrounge for morsels on the broadcast spectrum. It is taken for granted that broadcasting today is overwhelmingly a commercial medium, and that broadcast owners have wide latitude to use the spectrum to maximize corporate profits. But the airwaves are a *public* resource. Low-power licensing, as a strategy to serve local communities and diversify the content of radio broadcast, in effect gives up the legal right of the public to shape the broadcast spectrum.

The response to conglomeration needs to be a national public debate about how the media, particularly the public-owned broadcast airwaves, should be distributed and for what purpose. The need for this discussion is pressing, as the possibilities for a national public forum are waning as media owners, whose power is highly invested in conglomerate, commercialized media, continue to subsume into their subsidiary holdings what's left of public space.

Notes

1 Quoted in Brown (1998).
2 The breakdown of minority ownership was as follows: Black-owned, 1.7%; Hispanic-owned, 1.05%; Asian-owned, .03%; and Native American-owned, .04%. Numbers for women-owned stations were not available (US Department of Commerce, 1997).
3 Arbitron measures the race/ethnicity of radio audiences by percentage of black, Hispanic and Other. I assume that "Other" includes all other race/ethnicity populations in the US, the majority of which are white.
4 Adult contemporary includes all formats with an AC-focus, such as Hot AC, Lite AC, Mix AC, Soft AC, Modern AC and NAC.
5 Talk stations includes formats listed as News/Talk, News/Talk/Sports, Talk/Sports, and Talk.
6 Data on Clear Channel's radio holdings was gathered in February 2000 from BIA Companies Media Access Pro radio database, available at http://www.biacompanies.com

7 Analysis based on BIA Companies Media Access Pro radio database as of February 2000. Available at http://www.biacompanies.com
8 Quoted in Reece (1998).
9 The radio industry and FCC are currently debating what and how digital audio broadcasting (DAB) will be implemented (Head et al., 1998, p. 145).

References

Americans for Radio Diversity. 1998. *ARD's guide to fighting a radio station sale*. <http://redparker.com/radio/ard/ fightguide.html>
Anderson, Rachel. 2000, February 1. "Low-Power Radio." Digital Beat Extra. <http://www.benton.org/News/Extra/ broad020100.html>
Arbitron. 1999. *Radio Today: How America listens to radio*, 1998 ed. New York: Arbitron. <http://www.arbitron.com/studies/radiotdy.pdf>
Arbitron. 1998. *America's top stations: A format profile*. New York: Arbitron. <http://www.arbitron.com/studies/topstns.pdf>
BIA Companies. 1999. *State of the radio industry, 1999*. Chantilly, VA: BIA Companies. <http://www.biacompanies.state_radio.htm>
Brown, Sara. 1998. Living large in 1997: TV, radio post records for multiples, broker involvement. *Broadcasting & Cable*, February 3, 32–4.
Capstar. 1998. *Company Profile*. <http://www.capstarbroadcasting.com>
Chancellor Media Corporation forms national radio network. 1997. Business Wire: Chancellor Media Corporation press release. September 24. <http://biz.yahoo.com/97/09/24/ amfm_y000_1.html>
Dizard, Wilson. 1997. *Old media, new media: Mass communications in the information age*, second edn. New York: Longman.
Dunifer, Stephen. 1997. *Stephen Dunifer responds to NAB & FCC*. <http://www.radio4all.org/news/dunifer-response.html>
Farhi, Paul. 1997. Dallas company crafts biggest U.S. radio firm. *Washington Post*, August 26, D1.
Federal Communications Commission. 1997a. FCC order regarding: Applications of Viacom International, Inc. and Evergreen Media Corporation. (DA Docket No. 97-1354). Washington, DC: Mass Media Bureau, Policy and Rules Division. <http://www.fcc.gov/Bureaus/Mass_Media/ Orders/1997/da971354.txt>
Federal Communications Commission. 1997b. *Review of the radio industry, 1997*. (MM Docket No. 98–35). Washington, DC: Mass Media Bureau, Policy and Rules Division. <http://www.fcc.gov/mmb/prd/radio.html>

Feit, Josh. 1997. High noon: Lars Larson and KXL make a last stand for Portland's independent radio. *Willamete Week*, September 24. <http://www.wweek.com/html/cobver092497.html>

Fisher, Marc. 1998. The great radio rebellion: The turned off fight back. *Washington Post*. June 2, D1.

Head, Sydney W., Sterling, Christopher H., Schofiel, Lemuel B., Spann, Thomas, and McGregor, Michael A. 1998. *Broadcasting in America: A survey of electronic media*, eighth edn. Boston: Houghton Mifflin Company.

Herman, Edward and McChesney, Robert. 1997. *Global media: The new missionaries of global capitalism*. London: Cassell.

Irving, Larry, 1997. The Big Chill: Has Minority Ownership Been Put on Ice? Remarks made at the annual meeting of the National Association of Black Owned Broadcasters, Washington, DC. September 11 1997. <http://www.ntia.doc.gov/nitahme/speeches/91197NABOB.htm>

McChesney, Robert. 1997. *Corporate media and the threat to democracy. An Open Media pamphlet series*. New York: Seven Stories Press.

McConnell, Chris. 1998. Kennard pushes for women, minorities: Tells broadcasters to come with a plan to encourage more participation. *Broadcasting & Cable*, April 8, 53–4.

Miller, Marc Crispin. 1997. Who Controls the Music? *The Nation*, August 25/September 1, 11–16.

Mosco, Vincent. 1996. *The political economy of communication: Rethinking and renewal*. London: Sage.

Napoli, Philip M. 1999. Deconstructing the diversity principle. *Journal of Communication*, 49: 7–34.

National Association of Broadcasters. 1998. *Microradio is a bad idea*. Washington, DC: NAB, April 27. <http://www.nab.org/PressRel/Releases/1698.htm>

Ofori, Kofi, Edwards, Karen, Thomas, Vincent and Flateau, John. 1997. *Blackout: Media ownership concentration and the future of black radio*. Brooklyn, New York: Dubois Bunche Center for Public Policy.

Petrozzello, Donna. 1996. Sales, personnel new challenges of consolidation: Radio owners suggest different approaches to business. *Broadcasting & Cable*, October 14, 46.

Radio mergers total $13.4 billion. 1997. *Broadcasting & Cable*, April 14, 52.

Radio/TV ownership. 1997. *Broadcasting & Cable*, April 4, 43.

Reece, Doug. 1998. KREV fans rally for radio diversity. *Billboard Magazine*, April 4.

Taylor, Chuck and Schiffman Mark. 1998. Chancellor pegs $25 mil. from pay-for-play. *Billboard Magazine*, May 2, 3–4.

Tucker, Bill. 1997. One company, many tunes. *CNNfn*, August 27. <http://cnnfn.com/hotstories/bizbuzz/9708/27/tunes_pkg/>

US Department of Commerce, National Telecommunications and Information Administration. 1997. *Minority commercial broadcast ownership in the United States*. Washington, DC: US Department of Commerce. <http://www.ntia.doc.gov/reports/97minority>

Part III

Television and Film

Introduction to Part III

Justin Lewis and Toby Miller

Television is, perhaps, the most ubiquitous of the cultural industries, not only because ownership of television sets has become almost universal in industrialized nations, but because of its dominating presence in leisure time. Because of its cultural significance, there is an extensive policy literature dealing with broadcasting in general and television in particular. Much of this work comes from what Tom Streeter refers to, in the US context, as "inside the beltway" approaches – namely, policy analysis that fits neatly into existing frameworks and structures, and which thereby accepts rather than interrogates the assumptions that inform these frameworks (Streeter, 1996).

There are those, of course, who would prefer to simply wish television away, and to argue that, by its very nature, television impoverishes public discourse and individual imagination. Television, in short, is seen by some as a bad technology that we would be better off without. It is easy to respond to such criticism by stressing its impracticality (to suggest that, as is often argued in relation to nuclear weapons, we cannot "un-invent" such a technology). But to resort to such a dismissal is to avoid the fundamental question of how television can add to cultural life and possibility. Whatever else it might be, television is miraculous in its range, economy, and simplicity. Rather than merely hanker after a mythic, print-based utopia of rational public discourse, it is surely possible to conceive of ways in which such a technology might be used to *expand* public discourse and imagination. In short: what is television good for?

Sadly, even to ask such a question, especially in the US, places us so far "outside the beltway" as to be almost inadmissible in mainstream policy circles. This is partly because, amongst political elites, the question of television's cultural potential is often seen as secondary to the demands of commercial broadcasters. And yet to fail to ask this question is to submit to an induced myopia, and to limit all policy deliberations thereafter. In short, if we are to seriously deal with the topical or day to day questions of contemporary television policy, we must begin by thinking about the ways which television might be (or is already being) used to make our cultures and societies happier, cleverer, more democratic, more understanding or more compassionate.

And yet the question of television's cultural value is difficult to pose because, to a greater or lesser extent (greater in the US, lesser in Europe) television is there to fulfil a banal economic function. As an industrial process, commercial broadcasting is unusual in the sense that it is difficult to sell programs – especially if they are transmitted through the air. In revenue terms, in most cases, commercial television's "products" – the things that get sold – are audiences. The more affluent the audience, the more profitable the airtime. Program-making is a secondary process, whose aim is not to inspire, move or inform, but to entice us to the store in a buying mood. In so doing, it *may* even be necessary to lure audiences with programs that are inspirational, moving or informative, but this is, from the industry's point of view, incidental to the main business. While this logic operates for other media, commercial television is unusual in that it is generally completely dependent on advertising revenue.

As a consequence, even on its own terms, the market-based logic of the system fails to address the needs or desires of television audiences, since television audiences are *not* the market but the *product*. So, for example, the desire to watch programs commercial free is antithetical to a system whose only revenue source is advertising. The emergence of pay-per-view cable or satellite channels would seem to be an advance in this respect, since they are able to sell commercial free programs directly to audiences. And yet the viability of these channels depends upon high levels of capital investment which, in many instances, is used to limit access to that which was, hitherto, cheaply and widely available. The most conspicuous instance of this strategy is sport, as media moguls like Rupert Murdoch buy the right to the most popular sports events, thereby removing them from the airwaves and raising the price of viewing.

In the United States, questions of cultural use or benefit, insofar as they were asked at all, came as something of an afterthought. As Robert McChesney documents, in the 1940s and '50s, television was slotted into the corporate structure that had been established for radio, and the broadcasting companies were simply told to go forth and multiply their profits (McChesney, 2000). The ad-based corporate approach to the production and delivery of television is policed by government agencies (which protect corporate airspace) and subsidized by tax relief on advertising expenditure. This is not a *laissez-faire* approach to television, but one in which government policy structures the market to favor certain interests (namely, broadcasters and advertisers).

Amongst US political elites, the cultural role and purpose of television was not seriously debated until the 1960s, when public television was created to provide a safe haven from the "vast wasteland" of commercial television. Even then, prominent television reformers rarely questioned the idea that television was primarily a technology to be used to generate profits from advertising revenue. As Laurie Ouellette describes, in a bid for cultural distinction (in Bourdieu's sense of the term) many of those involved in the creation of US public television ceded the

terrain of popular adult programming to the commercial networks. For many public television advocates, then and now, the whole notion of the *popular* was linked to ideas of laziness, ignorance, and vulgarity – with popular television, almost by definition, seen as offering nothing more than a series of tempting but unwholesome fast fictions. Thus while the rhetoric surrounding public television was full of platitudes about enhancing democracy, many of its aesthetic sensibilities were based on a contempt for the popular.

The British broadcasting system, under the guidance of Lord Reith, may have been conceived in a similarly contemptuous spirit, but its history forced it in different directions. Because British television was *not* initially regarded as a way of making money, the question of television was more broadly debated on its cultural as well as its economic merits (Scannell, 1996). In particular, the centrality of the BBC to the system as a whole (in contrast to the marginal status of PBS) required broadcasters to *deal with* the popular in the context of a public service model. Even when commercial television was allowed into the mix, it was under certain "public service" conditions. Indeed the creation of Channel 4 was an instance in which the *raison d'être* of the new channel was defined, at least in part, by the limits of the public service system to fulfil public service goals (such as appealing to diverse audiences and producing innovative programs).

Because the British model is widely regarded as the exemplar of a public service television system – a system in which the *cultural* question of television was regularly posed – it has received a great deal of attention in the policy literature. Unfortunately, eighteen years of Conservative government in Britain between 1979 and 1997 tended to move discussions away from the potential of a public service system onto a more defensive terrain. The chipping away of public service commitments and the introduction of new commercial channels – along with other attacks (such as the Peacock Inquiry's unsuccessful attempts to introduce advertising on the BBC), shifted the terms of discussion. Many of those who might have argued for more radical visions of public service became preoccupied with rearguard defenses of the status quo. In this sense, the debate over the creation of Channel 4 was, perhaps, the high moment of mainstream policy discussion in Britain, since it took place at a time before imagining television's cultural possibilities was overshadowed by the need to defend the very idea that television could be something other than an audience delivery system for consumer goods.

The increasing dominance of what Caroline Pauwels describes as the "consumer sovereignty" model of television (Pauwels, 1999) since the 1980s and the growing power of transnational media corporations – two linked but not inseparable developments – have taken place at a critical time. In the last two decades we have seen a growth in distribution possibilities (chiefly via cable and satellite), the development of more versatile digital technologies, and the medium's rapid spread throughout the developing world. In marked contrast to the era of deliberation and debate in countries with public service broadcasting, these three developments have often been subsumed by the unthinking tide of corporate neo-liberalism.

This has also changed our understanding of the spread of global media into rich and poor countries alike. The notion of cultural imperialism – powered by dominant, colonialist, national cultures – remains relevant but complicated by the transnational aesthetics of consumerism. Global media may be required to "go local" (especially in large markets like India), while their loyalties are no longer *necessarily* tied to national identities or even to a broader sense of "Western values." Thus the "liberalization" of economies around the world has not merely ushered in Western programs – or variations thereof – but TV systems that are merely licensed to sell, and whose function is to manufacture people into markets. Production, meanwhile, with everything from TV sets to TV programs, is increasingly subject to the "race to the bottom" logic of free trade agreements.

For its part film has always been part of cultural policy, from the silent era's faith in "the moving picture man as a local social force...the mere formula of [whose] activities" keeps the public well-tempered (Lindsay, 1970, p. 243); through 1930s research into the impact of cinema on American youth via the Payne Studies (Blumer, 1933; Blumer and Hauser, 1933); to post-World War II concerns about Hollywood's

intrication of education and entertainment and the need for counter-knowledge among the public (Powdermaker, 1950, pp. 12–15; Mayer, 1946, p. 24). As a governmental and business technology that spread with urbanization and colonialism, the cinema was one of many attempts to comprehend the very modernity that it brought into vision (Shohat and Stam, 1994, pp. 100–36). The medium's promiscuity points every day and in every way towards the social. It is three things, all at once: a *recorder* of reality (the unstaged pro-filmic event); a *manufacturer* of reality (the staged and edited event); and *part of* reality (watching film as a social event on a Saturday night, or a protest event over sexual, racial, or religious stereotyping). Film is a marker of culture that touches on consciousness and systems of value and either bind society together or illuminate its fissures. Film attained its majority as one of the principal new forms of inter-war communication. Along with the popular press and radio, it was designated as ideal for propaganda and social uplift.

Many discussions of film are signs of governmental anxiety: laments for civic culture in the US correlate an increase in violence and a decline in membership of Parent–Teacher Associations with heavy film viewing – as true today as it was when the Payne Fund Studies of the '30s inaugurated mass social-science panic about young people, driven by academic, religious, and familial iconophobia and the sense that large groups of people were engaged with popular culture beyond the control of the state and ruling classes. At the same time, social reformers looked to the cinema as a potential forum for moral uplift; if film could drive the young to madness, it might also provoke a sense of social responsibility.

But the cultural audience is not so much a specifiable group *within* the social order as the principal site *of* that order. Audiences participate in the most global (but local), communal (yet individual), and time-consuming practice of making meaning in the history of the world. The concept and the occasion of being an audience link society to person through screen texts, for at the same time as viewing involves solitary interpretation as well as collective behavior. Production executives invoke the audience to measure success and claim knowledge of what people want. But this focus on the audience is not theirs alone. Regulators do it to organize administration, psychologists to produce proofs, and lobby-groups to change content. Hence the link to panics about education, violence, and apathy supposedly engendered by the screen and routinely investigated by the state, psychology, Marxism, neoconservatism, the church, liberal feminism, and others. The audience as consumer, student, felon, voter, and idiot engages such groups. This is Harold Garfinkel's notion of the "cultural dope," a mythic figure "who produces the stable features of the society by acting in compliance with preestablished and legitimate alternatives of action that the common culture provides." The "common sense rationalities... of here and now situations" used by people are obscured by this condescending categorization (Garfinkel, 1992, p. 68). When the audience is invoked as a category of cultural policy by the industry, critics, and regulators, it immediately becomes such a "dope". Much non-Hollywood film wants to turn such supposed dopes into a public of thinkers beyond the home – civic-minded participants in a political and social system as well as an economy of purchasing. National cinemas in Europe, Asia, the Pacific, Latin America, and Africa are expected to win viewers and train them in a way that complements the profit-driven sector. The entertainment function is secondary to providing programs the commercial market would not deliver. Audiences are encouraged not just to watch and consume, but to act, to be better people.

Much of this anxiety has surrounded unequal international trade in film. In 1926, the League of Nations sponsored an International Film Congress to discuss the issue of US dominance of the market, but attempts to act in concert as particular trading blocs against Hollywood failed. The British Cabinet Office issued a paper to participants at the Imperial Economic Conference that year warning of the perils implicit in the fact that "so very large a proportion of the films shown throughout the Empire should present modes of life and forms of conduct which are not typically British." By the following year, the *Daily Express* newspaper worried that the exposure of British youth to US entertainment was making them "temporary American citizens" (quoted in de Grazia, 1989, p. 53). This has been an enduring complaint. Nearly sixty years later, the Commission of the European Communities was prescribing a common market

for TV production to counter the dominance of US media corporations.

National cinemas are generally conceived, announced, produced, and archived in reaction to Hollywood or former colonial powers that have ongoing "special relationships." They tend to be, in that sense, "anti-" cinemas, even as they demonstrate a familiar set of oppositions internal to their own discourse and practice (cultural versus commercial, local versus international, critical versus celebratory, personal versus generic). The anti-US rubric goes back a long way, and to many of us for whom Hollywood's sexual and commodity transcendence were promising signs in repressive or phantasmatic cultures, that rubric is as deeply flawed in its provincialism, moralism, and mediocrity as are local claims for "American exceptionalism."

We need to view national cinemas through twin theoretical prisms. On the one hand, they can be understood as the newest component of sovereignty, a twentieth-century cultural addition to ideas of patrimony and rights that sits alongside such traditional topics as territory, language, history, and schooling. On the other hand, national cinemas are sectors of the culture industries. As such, they are subject to exactly the rent-seeking practices and exclusionary representational protocols that characterize liaisons between state and capital in the name of the public good. Is the impulse toward having a national cinema crucial to the project of modernity, expanding the vision and availability of the good life to include the ability of a people to control its representation on screen? Or is this impulse merely a free ride for the culturalist fraction of a national *bourgeoisie*? We need to examine the relationship of nation to state – which agencies are responsible for enunciating the supposed spirit-in-dwelling of a site, and what basis do they use for doing so? The political audit we make of a national audiovisual space should focus on the extent to which it is open, both on-camera and off-, to the demographics of those inhabiting it. No cinema that claims resistance to Hollywood in the name of national specificity is worthy of endorsement if it does not actually attend to sexual and racial minorities and women, along with class politics. In other words, as per many other cultural-policy issues, is there a representation of the fullness of the population in the industry and on the screen?

And is state assistance predicated on an ideological identification of loyalty?

References

Blumer, Herbert. *Movies and Conduct*. New York: Macmillan, 1933.

Blumer, Herbert and Philip M. Hauser. *Movies, Delinquency and Crime*. New York: Macmillan, 1933.

de Grazia, Victoria. "Mass Culture and Sovereignty: The American Challenge to European Cinemas, 1920–1960." *Journal of Modern History* 61, no. 1 (1989): 53–87.

Garfinkel, Harold. *Studies in Ethnomethodology*. Cambridge: Polity Press, 1992.

Lindsay, Vachel. *The Art of the Moving Picture*. New York: Liveright, 1970.

Mayer, J. P. *Sociology of Film: Studies and Documents*. London: Faber and Faber, 1946.

McChesney, Robert. *Rich Media, Poor Democracy*. Chicago: University of Illinois Press, 2000.

Pauwels, Caroline. "From Citizenship to Consumer Sovereignty: The Paradigm Shift in European Audiovisual Policy." *Communication, Citizenship, and Social Policy: Rethinking the Limits of the Welfare State*. Ed. Andrew Calabrese and Jean-Claude Burgelman. Lanham: Rowman & Littlefield, 1999.

Powdermaker, Hortense. *Hollywood: The Dream Factory*. Boston: Little, Brown, 1950.

Scannell, Paddy. *Radio, Television and Modern Life*. London: Blackwell, 1996.

Shohat, Ella and Robert Stam. *Unthinking Eurocentrism: Multiculturalism and the Media*. London: Routledge, 1994.

Streeter, Thomas. *Selling The Air: A Critique of the Policy of Commercial Broadcasting in the United States*. Chicago: University of Chicago Press, 1996.

Chapter 6

Embedded Aesthetics: Creating a Discursive Space for Indigenous Media

Faye Ginsburg

The closing years of the twentieth century are witnessing a radical re-orientation of thought in the human sciences which defies conventional disciplinary boundaries and demands a new 'turning': away from the rationalising modes of modernity and towards a different grasp of the nature of knowing itself.... The power of visual media as a means of knowledge-creation is only hesitantly grasped by many in public life.... But, from the viewpoint of the emergent visual-aural culture of the twenty-first century, "what's on" creates the context for what is known and hence finally for what "is."

Annette Hamilton

Since the late 1970s, Aboriginal Australians (and other indigenous people) have been engaged in developing new visual media forms by adapting the technologies of video, film, and television to a range of expressive and political purposes. Their efforts to develop new forms of indigenous media are motivated by a desire to envision and strengthen a "cultural future" (Michaels 1987a) for themselves in their own communities and in the dominant society. Aboriginal cultures, of course, are extremely diverse, as Aboriginal cultural critic and anthropologist Marcia Langton has pointed out in her recent book on indigenous media production. "There is no one kind of Aboriginal person or community," she writes:

There are [two] regions which can be characterised, however, with reference to history, politics, culture and demography.... The first region is "settled" Australia... where most provincial towns and all the major cities and institutions are located, and where a

myriad of small Aboriginal communities and populations reside with a range of histories and cultures....

The second region is "remote" Australia where most of the tradition-oriented Aboriginal cultures are located. They likewise have responded to particular frontiers and now contend with various types of Australian settlement. (Langton 1993: 12–13)

Aboriginal media productions are as various as Aboriginal life itself, ranging from low-budget videos made by community-based media associations for both traditional people in remote settlements and groups in urban centers; to regional television and radio programming for Aboriginal groups throughout Central Australia made by organizations such as the Central Australian Aboriginal Media Association (CAAMA); to legal or instructional videos (often quite creative) made by land councils as well as health and other service groups; to documentaries and current affairs for national broad-casting; to independent features directed by cosmopolitan Aboriginal artists such as Tracey Moffatt whose first feature film, *Bedevil*, pre-miered at Cannes in 1993. Such works are inher-ently complex cultural objects, as they cross multiple cultural boundaries in their production, distribution, and consumption. For example, Aboriginal producers often collaborate with non-Aboriginal media workers, be they media advisers to remote settlements or staff at Austra-lia's national television stations. Works them-selves are often hybrid, combining traditional ritual knowledge and/or performance with MTV-style special effects. In terms of circulation and reception, these productions are seen by multiple audiences, including other Aboriginal and non-Aboriginal viewers in Australia, via cir-culation of video letters as well as local, regional, or national broadcasts, or by diverse overseas audiences through film festivals and conferences.

With an interest in enlarging analyses of film texts to account for broader contexts of social relations,[1] I have found it helpful to think of Aboriginal media as part of a *mediascape*, a term created by Arjun Appadurai to account for the different kinds of global cultural flows created by new media technologies and the images created with them in the late 20th century. Appadurai argues for situated analyses that take account of the interdependence of media practices with the local, national, and transnational circumstances that surround them (Appadurai 1990: 7). Using such a model for indigenous media helps to estab-lish a more generative discursive space for this work which breaks what one might call the fet-ishizing of the local, without losing a sense of the specific situatedness of any production. The com-plex mediascape of Aboriginal media, for example, must account for a range of circum-stances, beginning with the perspectives of Abo-riginal producers, for whom new media forms are seen as a powerful means of (collective) self-ex-pression that can have a culturally revitalizing effect. Their vision coexists uneasily, however, with the fact that their work is also a product of relations with governing bodies that are respon-sible for the dire political circumstances that often motivated the Aboriginal mastery of new com-munication forms as a means of cultural interven-tion.[2] Such contradictions are inherent to the ongoing social construction of *Aboriginality*.

Cultural critic Fiona Nicoll offers a helpful expli-cation of the term that has been the subject of considerable debate.[3] As she writes:

> "Aboriginality" ... [is] a colonial field of power relations within which Aborigines struggle with the dominant settler culture over the representation of things such as "identity," "his-tory," "land," and "culture." In contrast to the category "Aboriginal culture," which is always defined in opposition to a dominant "non-Abo-riginal culture," the concept of "Aboriginality" must be thought in *relation* to "non-Aborigin-ality." For it was the white settlers who lumped the various indigenous peoples under the hom-ogenizing name of "Aborigines," then brought into being the categories of "Aboriginal his-tory," "Aboriginal culture," "Aboriginal ex-perience" and "Aboriginal conditions." (1993: 709)

Thus, not only are Aboriginal film and video important to Aboriginal Australians, but they cannot be understood apart from the contempor-ary construction of Aboriginality. As nation-states like Australia increasingly constitute their "imagined communities" (Anderson 1983) through the circulation of televisual and cine-matic images of the people they govern, Abori-ginal media have become part of the mediascape of the Australian *national imaginary*.[4] Put in con-crete terms:

> "Aboriginality" arises from the subjective ex-perience of both Aboriginal people and non-Aboriginal people who engage in any intercul-tural dialogue, whether in actual lived experi-ence or through a mediated experience such as a white person watching a program about Abori-ginal people on television or reading a book. (Langton 1993: 31)

Discursive Spaces/Social Action

This essay is an extension of a larger effort initi-ated by Aboriginal cultural activists to develop a "discursive practice" – both for Aboriginal makers and for others who make and study media – that respects and understands this work in terms relevant to contemporary indigenous people living in a variety of settings (Langton 1993). Specifically, it examines how Aboriginal media makers understand their own work. How, one might ask, do people understand indigenous media works as they move through the complex circuits sketched above? What are the aesthetic standards – the discourses and practices of evaluation – that are applied to indigenous productions as they are positioned differently in various exhibition contexts? Are Aboriginal ideas about their "beauty/value" able to cross over cultural borders? I am concerned in particular with how notions of the value of indigenous media are being negotiated at different levels of Aboriginal media production.[5] While there are multiple arenas of Aboriginal production (local, regional, urban, etc.), in this essay I will focus on three sites of Aboriginal media work: remote communities; national television; and transnational networks of indigenous media producers that form around events such as film festivals or coproductions.

In these different arenas, Aboriginal producers from very different backgrounds use a language of evaluation that stresses the *activities* of the production and circulation of such work in specific communities as the basis for judging its value. In communities where traditional Aboriginal cultural practices are still relatively intact, such evaluation is culturally very specific, corresponding to notions of appropriate social and formal organization of performance in ceremonial or ritual domains. In her analysis of Aboriginal media production, Marcia Langton argues that such media from remote areas are "community-authored" (1993: 13). Summarizing studies in the 1980s of the organization of video production at the remote Warlpiri settlement of Yuendumu (Michaels and Kelly 1984), Langton writes that "the camera and camera person are attributed with the ritual role of *kurdungurlu* (ritual managers) . . . because they are witnesses to events and affirm their truth," while those in front of the camera are *kirda* (ritual owners) with acknowledged rights and obligations to tell and perform certain stories and ceremonies (1993: 65). Based on my own contact with Yuendumu in 1992, it is unclear whether these specific arrangements still endure in the 1990s. However, the general principle of kin-based rights to tell certain kinds of stories and ceremonial knowledge continue to shape production practices. More generally, then, "[t]here are rules, which are somewhat flexible, for the production, distribution and ownership of any image, just as

there are under traditional law for sacred designs which . . . refer to ancestors and ancestral mythology" (Langton 1993: 65).

In ways that are both similar and different, urban Aboriginal mediamakers are also concerned with their media productions as a form of social action. While their works are more typically understood as authored by individuals (Langton 1993: 13), many urban Aboriginal producers nonetheless see themselves as responsible to a community of origin (for example kin and friends in the urban neighborhood of Redfern in Sydney), although it is a sense of community less bound by specific cultural rules than that of people in remote settlements. This is especially true of those working for Australian state television who shoulder the specific burden of creating an "authentic" Aboriginal presence in the mass media and, more broadly, in Australia's national imaginary.[6] This tendency to evaluate work in terms of social action is striking to an observer schooled in Western aesthetics. With few exceptions, questions of narrative or visual form are not primary issues for discussion per se, despite the obvious concern for it in individual works. Rather, for many Aboriginal producers, the quality of work is judged by its capacity to embody, sustain, and even revive or create certain social relations, although the social bases for coming to this position may be very different for remote and urban people.[7] For the sake of discussion, I will call this orientation *embedded aesthetics*, to draw attention to a system of evaluation that refuses a separation of textual production and circulation from broader arenas of social relations.[8] For example, Eric Michaels, an American researcher who helped develop Aboriginal media production with Warlpiri people at Yuendumu in Central Australia, noted that for the people he worked with:

[Aboriginal] art or video objects become difficult to isolate for analysis because the producer's intention is the opposite. Warlpiri artists demonstrate their own invisibility in order to assert the work's authority and continuity with tradition. They do not draw attention to themselves or to their creativity. (Michaels 1987a: 34)

My argument, then, is that this new and complex object – Aboriginal media – is understood by its producers to be operating in multiple domains as an extension of their collective (vs. individual) self-production. However, it is important to recognize that Aboriginal producers from various locales and backgrounds – remote, urban, rural – come to their positions through quite different cultural and social processes. In the case of urban Aboriginal mediamakers, their embrace of *embedded aesthetics* may be an extremely self-conscious choice, produced out of contact with a variety of discourses. In the cases below, I will sketch the multiple ways that this kind of positioning of indigenous media emerges from very different social bases for the understanding of Aboriginality and its representation, especially as it passes across cultural and national borders.

Remote Control: Media in Traditional Communities

My first examples are drawn from two successful community-based Aboriginal media associations developed at relatively traditional remote settlements in the Central Desert area of Australia. The first is Ernabella on Pitjantjatjarra lands in South Australia, just south of Uluru (Ayers Rock). The second settlement is Yuendumu on Warlpiri lands in Central Australia, northwest of Alice Springs, home to the Warlpiri Media Association since 1982. Both are Aboriginal settlements with highly mobile populations that can vary from 500 to 1500 over the course of a year. Founded by missionaries in the 1940s, they became self-governing by the 1970s and retain infrastructures consisting of a community store, a town office, a police station, a primary school, a health clinic, a church, an art association, and local broadcast facilities (Langton 1993).

In 1983, people at Ernabella began producing video programs with the encouragement of white schoolteachers and advisers, in particular Neil Turner, who settled in the community, learned the language, and facilitated the development of Ernabella Video Televison (EVTV) from its inception to the present. Established in 1985, EVTV operates from a small video production, editing, and playback facility and an inexpensive satellite dish that provides local broadcasts of work produced by EVTV as well as items selected from national television feeds. Determined to be as independent as possible from government subsidies, EVTV has sup-

ported itself successfully through a self-imposed tax on cold drinks in the community store, the sales of EVTV videos, and occasional public and private grants (Batty 1993; Molnar 1989; N. Turner 1990).

Over the first decade of its existence, EVTV has produced over eighty edited pieces as well as thousands of hours of community television under the direction of a respected couple, Simon and Pantjiti Tjiyangu, and a local media committee made up of male and female elders. Their concerns range from monitoring the content of work shown – so that images are not circulated that violate cultural rules regulating what can be seen (e.g. tapes of women's sacred ceremonies are not edited and are only accessible to appropriate senior women) – and the timing of viewing so that television transmission, whether locally produced or the national satellite feed, does not interfere with other cultural activities.

Perhaps because the supervision of EVTV is largely in the hands of elders, the video work of Ernabella is distinguished by its emphasis on ceremonies, in particular the stories, dances, and sand designs that are associated with the Kungkarangkalpa (Seven Sisters Dreaming) (which explains the origins of the Pleiades constellation). In adapting such forms to video, EVTV producers include in their tapes the production process itself, which can involve the whole community, including children, dancers, storytellers, and video crew. For example, in tapes such as *Seven Sisters Dreaming: Tjukurpa Kungkarangkalpa Tjara* (made in 1985) one sees not just a performance as we understand it in the West. Dances and enactments of the story of the Seven Sisters are preceded by extensive preparation and participation by those members of the Pitjantjatjara community who are responsible for ritual knowledge and ceremony. This aspect of Pitjantjatjara ritual performance has been reconfigured to accommodate video production: the tape includes not only ritual preparation but also other participants offering their comments on the ritual as they sit at night by the campfire to view the day's rushes (Leigh 1992: 3). Such reflexivity is not a Brechtian innovation; rather, it authorizes the reconfiguring of traditional practices for video as "true" and properly done.

In addition to such framing of the production process, the value or beauty of such videos for the Pitjantjatjara videomakers is extratextual, created by the cultural and social processes they mediate, embody, create, and extend. The tapes underscore the cosmological power of ceremonies to invigorate sacred aspects of the landscape; they reinforce the social relations that are fundamental to ritual production; and they enhance the place of Pitjantjatjara among Aboriginal groups in the area, as well as for the dominant Australian regional culture. Over the last decade, people from Ernabella frequently have been invited to "perform" in nearby cultural centers such as Adelaide. Knowledge of these issues is important to understanding the value of EVTV tapes as texts that cross over cultural borders, reaching other Aboriginal and non-Aboriginal audiences. As media activist Philip Batty commented:

> the work of EVTV had the effect of engendering a kind of local renaissance in traditional dance, performance and singing. The various video programmes depicting the actual land where the dreaming lines were located gave renewed strength to traditional beliefs and values within the communities. (Batty 1993: 113)

As another example of indigenous media work emerging from remote Aboriginal settlements, the Warlpiri Media Association (WMA) began producing tapes in 1982 and established their own unlicensed local television station similar to that of EVTV, in April 1985. Frances Jupurrurla Kelly, a young Warlpiri man, became a key videomaker and central figure in developing WMA. Much of what has been written about that group for outsiders came out of the work of Eric Michaels, for the (then) Australian Institute of Aboriginal Studies, which commissioned him to research the impact of Western media on traditional Aboriginal people in Central Australia. When he arrived at Yuendumu, he discovered that:

> [t]here was, in the early 1980s, a considerable creative interest among Aborigines in the new entertainment technology becoming available to remote communities. There was equally a motivated, articulate, and general concern about the possible unwanted consequences of television, especially among senior Aborigines and local indigenous educators. In particular, the absence of local Aboriginal languages from

any proposed service was a major issue. [Michaels 1987a: 11]

As a result, Michaels also brought an interventionist approach to his research, encouraging people to produce their own videos without imposing Western conventions of shooting and editing. The broader concern that Michaels shared with Yuendumu videomakers was that, if people could make videos based on Aboriginal concerns, they might escape the more deleterious effects of broadcast television by substituting their own work for mainstream satellite television signals. While they had not tried video production before, Yuendumu residents were familiar with mainstream cinema, as well as the active production of Aboriginal popular music, as well as radio programs in Central Australia.[9] Since 1982, Warlpiri videomakers have produced hundreds of hours of tapes, on a range of subjects including sports events, health issues, traditional rituals, and their own history, as in *Coniston Story*, a tape in which the Aboriginal descendants of a revenge massacre of Warlpiri people by whites go to the site of the tragedy and tell their version of this "killing time." In an analysis of *Coniston Story*, Michaels notes that "one is struck by the recurrent camera movement, [and] the subtle shifts in focus and attention during the otherwise even, long pans across the landscape," shifts that Western interpreters might see as "naive" camerawork (1987a: 51). Rather, Frances Jupurrurla Kelly (the Warlpiri producer/director and camera operator) explains that the camera is following

> the movement . . . of unseen characters – both Dreamtime [ancestral] and historical – which converge on this landscape. . . . Shifts in focus and interruptions in panning pick out important things in the landscape, like a tree where spirits live or a flower with symbolic value. (Cited in Michaels 1987a: 52)

Jupurrurla's explanation suggests that in developing a new mode of telling Warlpiri history through video, his concerns were consistent with traditional Aboriginal cosmology in which the particular geographic features of the areas they inhabit (and the kin-based rights and responsibilities attached to them) are central to authorizing myths and ceremonies. Michaels argued that this emphasis on the meaning of landscape is apparent in many Warlpiri tapes and accounts for the value and beauty of such sequences for Warlpiri viewers (Michaels 1987b).

What is not immediately visible in the tapes themselves is that people organize themselves around media production in terms of the responsibilities of specific groups for knowledge and practices associated with certain geographic areas, similar to the case of Ernabella discussed above. In other words, the ways in which tapes are made and used reflect Warlpiri understandings of kin-based obligations for ceremonial production and control of traditional knowledge, as these index cosmological relationships to particular features in regional geography (Michaels and Kelly 1984). "The credibility of the resulting tape for the Warlpiri audience is dependent upon knowing that these people were all participating in the event, even though the taped record provides no direct evidence of their presence" (Michaels 1987a: 46). Thus, for Warlpiri videomakers, cultural production – if it is of any value – is understood as part of a broader effort of collective self-production always associated with the *jukurrpa*, the ontological system of kin- and land-based ritual knowledge, translated into English originally as "the dreaming" (Stanner 1956) and now also as "the law." Notions of value embedded in jukurrpa run contrary to Western notions of the social relations of aesthetic production that emphasize the creative "self-expression" of individuals who are assigned responsibility as authors. Rather:

> stories are always true, and invention even when it requires an individual agent to "dream" or "receive" a text, remains social in a complex and important sense that assures truth. Rights to receive, know, perform, or teach a story (through dance, song, narrative, and graphic design) are determined by any identified individual's structural position and social/ritual history within an elaborately reckoned system of kin. Novelty can only enter this system as a social, not an individual invention. Not only is one's right to invent ultimately constrained, it is particularly constrained with respect to the kinship role for it is the geneaology of an item – not its individual creation – which authorises it. (Michaels 1987b: 65)

These principles through which some Aboriginal videos from remote settlements are medi-

ated within and across cultural borders are consistent with the evaluative processes used for other "hybrid" Aboriginal media such as acrylic painting. As Fred Myers writes regarding the evaluations Pintupi painters from the Central Desert area make of their work, "the painters themselves have been unforthcoming about such aesthetic considerations." (Myers 1994: 15). Indeed

> The[ir] principal discourse... emphasizes their works as vehicles of self-production and collective empowerment... these are not necessarily interpretations that are outside the processes of representation themselves. (Myers 1994: 35)

In addition to providing a means for enhancing forms such as ritual performance, Aboriginal film and video offer innovative possibilities for collective self-production. As novel forms, these media provide sites for the re-visioning of social relations with the encompassing society, an exploration that more traditional indigenous forms cannot so easily accommodate. In media production, Aboriginal skills at constituting both individual and group identities through narrative and ritual are engaged in innovative ways that are often simultaneously indigenous and intercultural, from production to reception. For example, Yuendumu residents have produced a series of children's programs designed to teach literacy in Warlpiri. The series was invented by elders and schoolteachers, both white and Aboriginal. With grants written with the help of a media adviser, they received funding from the Australian government and hired a local Anglo-Australian filmmaker, David Batty (with whom they had worked before), to create the series *Manyu Wana* ("Just for Fun"). The result has been an ongoing series of collaborative community-based productions where kids, teachers, and filmmaker work together to improvise and then enact humorous short sketches to illustrate both written and spoken Warlpiri words in ways that seem to engage multiple audiences. Immensely popular in Yuendumu and neighboring Aboriginal communities, *Manyu Wana*, despite its very local origin and monolingual use of local language, has also been seen and appreciated all over the world.

National Imaginaries

Since the early 1980s, the demand for more Aboriginal participation and visibility in the Australian mediascape has been increasing, not only for local access to video in remote areas, but also for more Aboriginal representation on mainstream national television. This concern is not simply about equal access but a recognition that distortion and/or invisibility of Aboriginal realities for the wider Australian public can have a direct effect on political culture. Continuing exclusion of work by Aboriginal people from Australia's media institutions has sharpened Aboriginal awareness of the connections between political enfranchisement and the need to control their own images in the public sphere.

Aboriginal people – in terms of content and staffing – are still virtually absent from Australia's three commercial television networks (Langton 1993: 21).[10] However, two important efforts to increase an Aboriginal presence on public television were initiated in 1989. These were (1) the Aboriginal Programs Unit (APU) of the Australian Broadcasting Corporation (ABC), the stateowned national television station that reaches all of Australia; and (2) the Aboriginal Television Unit of the Special Broadcast Service (SBS),[11] Australia's state-funded station set up to provide culturally and linguistically appropriate programming, both imported as well as locally produced, for Australia's many ethnic communities.

In April 1989, the Special Broadcast Service initiated a 13-part television series devoted to Aboriginal issues, called *First in Line*, the first prime-time current affairs show in Australia to be hosted by two Aboriginal people. This was a border crossing of considerable significance to Aboriginal cultural activists.[12] The producers and crew were primarily Aboriginal, and they consulted with communities throughout Australia for items stressing the positive achievements of Aborigines (Molnar 1989: 38–9). Eventually, *First in Line* was discontinued, and an Aboriginal unit was established with Rachel Perkins at the head, a young Aboriginal woman who had trained at the Central Australian Aboriginal Media Association (CAAMA). She has been creating programming through the use of work such as *Manyu Wana* from regional and local Aboriginal media associations. In 1992, she commissioned and produced a series, *Blood Brothers*, comprised of four documentaries on different aspects of Aboriginal history and culture (Rachel Perkins, interview, May 2, 1992). While these efforts are important, the SBS has a relatively small audience and budget.

By contrast, the state-controlled and -funded Australian Broadcasting Corporation (ABC) has a much greater resource base and reaches a national audience. In 1987, the ABC set up the Aboriginal Programs Unit (APU),[13] but it was not until 1989 that their first Aboriginally produced and presented program, *Blackout*, began broadcasting on a Friday-evening time slot. This series, a weekly magazine show on Aboriginal issues, is still being produced. (In 1992, it was awarded the United Nations Human Rights Media Award.) Additionally, APU programs occasional series such as *The First Australians*, an eight-part series of independent documentaries on Aboriginal topics broadcast on Thursday nights in 1992.[14]

Unlike the producers from remote settlements, Aboriginal producers at APU grew up in urban or "settled" areas, are bicultural, often hold university degrees, and are sophisticated about the ins and outs of national television vis-à-vis their interests as indigenous makers. People like Frances Peters and Rachel Perkins are new kinds of cultural activists who are regular *border crossers*, a position they occupy as part of their own background (from Aboriginal families educated in the dominant culture's pedagogical system) and out of a recognition that they must speak effectively to (at least) two kinds of Australians. Like the more remote-living Aboriginal media makers discussed above, they are concerned with their work as part of a range of activities engaged in cultural revival, identity formation, and political assertion. Through their work in televisual media production, they have been able to assert the multiple realities of contemporary urban Aboriginal life, not just for their own communities but also in the national public culture where Aboriginal activism and political claims are generally effaced from the official histories.

For example, in 1991, Peters worked with fellow APU producer David Sandy to produce the first documentary special of APU for broadcast in 1992. The title, *Tent Embassy*, refers to the event that galvanized the beginning of what some have called the "Aboriginal civil rights movement." On Australia Day (January 26) 1972, four young Aboriginal men erected a small tent on the lawns of the Parliament House in Canberra and declared themselves a sovereign nation. The action succinctly dramatized the issue of Aboriginal land rights in the Australian imagination and helped catalyze a broader social movement. The return, in 1992, of some of the original activists, now in their forties, to the site of the original protest to reassert their claims and to occupy Parliament House as well becomes the occasion for the film to explore the last 20 years of Aboriginal politics. The history moves from the confrontational activism of the Aboriginal Black Power and the Black Panther movements in the 1970s, to the establishment in the 1980s of the Aboriginal and Torres Straits Islanders Commission (ATSIC), a five-billion-dollar bureaucracy that has been criticized by some activists as co-opting Aboriginal political power. *Tent Embassy* is built out of the stories of key activists – lawyer Paul Coe, scholar and activist Roberta Sykes, public figure Charles Perkins – as we see them in archival footage, in extended contemporary interviews. It opens with a wonderfully humorous dramatic recreation that suggests the spontaneous origins of the first protest and holds fast to the principle of making people primary over issues. Other events are tracked through archival footage, not only of the embassy protest, but also of crucial events leading up to it, such as the discovery of bauxite on Aboriginal lands in the 1960s, which helped put land claims on the national political agenda.

For productions like *Tent Embassy* to be effective in reaching large, mixed audiences, they require aesthetic considerations that negotiate multiple cultural perspectives. The challenge for producers is to create visions of Aboriginal culture and history that simultaneously address the realities of Aboriginal communities and intervene in representations of Australian national histories in ways that will attract both Aboriginal and non-Aboriginal audiences. Frances Peters (and a number of other Aboriginal producers) are exploring how to reposition cultural authority in their works by using satire, humor, and drama. These provide complex commentaries on their own identities

and on their relationships with the dominant society, without simplifying or reducing the Aboriginal experience for what are still predominantly white audiences. In Peters's words:

> Aboriginal people in Australia are not one nation; the differences are there, but we're all Aboriginal....I [am] trying to break a lot of image stereotypes. I think those stereotoypes may have something to do with why many indigenous artists are moving away from documentary and into fiction or drama films. We are sick of the documentary format; we've seen so many of them about us...so unfortunately what we've done is associate documentary with just another form of stereotyping. We've got the opportunity as aboriginal filmmakers to change that. (Peters 1993: 102)

Producers at APU are engaged in more than the creation of media images of themselves that alter their place in the world of representations. In considering this kind of work in relation to questions of indigenous aesthetics, one must recognize the value they place on media production as a form of social action. Frances Peters articulated this position clearly to me in discussing her position as an Aboriginal producer:

> Unlike you, we can't remove ourselves from the programs we're making because they're about us as well. And because they are about us, we always have that responsibility to our Aboriginal culture and country...we can't walk away and just make a program on a different theme next time....Ultimately you're not really answerable to a hell of a lot of people....But with us, with every program that we make, we are ultimately responsible to a larger Aboriginal community. And we can't remove ourselves from that responsibility. (Frances Peters, interview, April 30, 1992)

Peters's comments speak to the complex and embedded sense that indigenous producers bring to their work, never seeing it as existing apart from the mediation of social relationships, especially with communities of origin, whether urban or remote. However, *community* is not, for her, some romantic notion of a unified social position. It is, rather, a complex and unstable social construct, implicated in the changing understandings of Aboriginality in Australia today, as bureaucratic structures for the administration of

Aboriginal funding and policies have proliferated. As much as she feels accountable to a broader Aboriginal world, she queries the concept:

> Which community? Our communities have become bureaucratized and class-stratified. Accountability is riddled with fear of being made to feel guilty, or that you aren't Aboriginal enough. (Peters 1993: 105)

Her positioning (along with that of other producers) intersects and is influenced by emerging Western theoretical discourses in the arts, built on frameworks of multiculturalism, which emphasize "cultural diversity as a basis for challenging, revising, and relativizing basic notions and principles common to dominant and minority cultures alike, so as to construct a more vital, open, and democratic common culture" (T. Turner 1993: 413). In the world of Aboriginal media making, an approach built out of contemporary identity politics (which has influenced many urban-based Aboriginal producers) intersects with concerns that shape the work of more traditional Aboriginal producers from remote communities, thereby creating a sense (or even illusion) of coherence in the ways that a broad range of Aboriginal makers evaluate their work. Regardless of this outcome, it is important to recognize that urban Aboriginal producers working in bicultural settings have embraced an *embedded aesthetic* as a strategic *choice*. Their efforts to develop an alternative approach to their work, while emerging from their experiences as Aboriginal Australians, are nonetheless self-conscious; the Western aesthetic conventions of the dominant society are culturally available to them as well. This sense of self-conscious positioning is evident in Frances Peters's description of coming to consciousness in her days as a student and Aboriginal radio producer:

> So, I was going to university, getting a formal education, and then spending my Saturday afternoons having great fun at an Aboriginal radio station [Radio Redfern], breaking all the rules. We were creating our own sounds, basically, we were promoting our music, and we were telling our own news in ways and forms that we chose. All that raised a lot of questions for me about the media and how I was going to see myself working in it. It was hard; it was a

> battle, and I used to fight in every one of those classes at University. (Peters 1993: 99)

Transnational Mediations

For most producers, their sense of community is very local. However, new and more expanded communities of identity are emerging through collaborative activities that transcend the boundaries of the nation-states that encompass them. Over the last five years, indigenous media productions have increasingly become part of *global cultural flows*. Connections are being built by indigenous producers who have been organizing a transnational indigenous network via film festivals and conferences, as well as joint productions such as the Pac Rim initiative, a documentary series being made jointly by indigenous filmmakers from Australia, New Zealand, the United States, and Canada. These events are becoming the basis for constituting an emergent organization of indigenous media producers. For example, the First Nations Film and Video Makers World Alliance (FNFVWA) was formed at the September 1992 Dreamspeakers Festival in Edmonton, Canada, itself the first indigenously organized international Aboriginal film and video festival. In such exhibition venues organized by and for indigenous people, media workers frame their work with a discourse of self-determination, clearly placing collective and political interests over those of individual expression. Such positioning is evident, for example, in the following statement of aims of the FNFVWA drawn up in 1992:

  a. to raise awareness of First Nations issues
  b. to establish a film and video communication network
  c. to ensure that traditional lands, language, and culture are protected
  d. to implement work and training exchanges
  e. to establish a world conference
  f. to ensure environmental protection and management
  g. to promote our teachings of history and culture
  h. to distribute and market our own films.

A major concern of all those indigenous filmmakers who attended Dreamspeakers was the need for our works to be distributed amongst other indigenous groups in other countries, that we are our own international market. The problem we felt was that our works are almost always received [more positively] by overseas audiences than by those in our own countries.

This statement of principles developed by a group of indigenous attendees (and the weeklong Dreamspeakers Festival itself) was striking in the lack of discussion of themselves as artists concerned primarily with formal issues or even freedom of expression. The indigenous media makers in the alliance, who came from all over the world, were all engaged in asserting the relationship of their work to broader arenas of social action. Such positions complicate structures of distribution and public culture in which the (media) artist's position is valued as being outside or critical of society, as in Adorno's view of art as an "intrinsic movement against society," a social realm set apart from the means–end rationality of daily bourgeois existence (Adorno 1970: 336, quoted in Bürger 1984: 10).

Recent shows of indigenous film/video that have been organized by dominant cultural institutions situate them as new forms of aesthetic/political production yet continue to look for aesthetic innovation in the text itself, rather than in the relations of production and reception that shape the evaluation and mediation of the text in unexpected ways. Mainstream showcases, for example, continue to focus on "individual makers" in places associated with "auteurship" in the arts, such as programs of The Museum of Modern Art (1990, 1993), The New Museum (1990), or the Walter Reade Theater at Lincoln Center (1992), all sites of exhibition of indigenous media in New York City. In such venues, indigenous work is in tension with Western discourses that valorize the individual as a political or artistic agent in opposition to a broader polity. Although this has been changing as the broader zeitgeist in the West embraces multicultural and identity-based politics as frames for the exhibition of various expressive media, the structures for showing work in most cases still put forward "the artist," repressing the embeddedness of individual artistic production in broader social and political processes. For the most part, indigenous producers reject this dominant model of the media text as the expression of an individuated self and continue to stress their work as on a continuum of social action authorizing Aboriginal cultural empowerment.

In conclusion, I want to emphasize that the social relations built out of indigenous media practices are helping to develop support and sensibilities for indigenous actions for self-determination. Self-representation in media is seen as a crucial part of this process. Indigenous media productions and the activities around them are rendering visible indigenous cultural and historical realities to themselves and the broader societies that have stereotyped or denied them. The transnational social relations built out of these media practices are creating new arenas of cooperation, locally, nationally, and internationally. Like the indigenous producers themselves, I suggest a model that stresses not only the text but also the *activities* and social organization of media work as arenas of cultural production. Only by understanding indigenous media work as part of a broader mediascape of social relations can we appreciate them fully as complex cultural objects. In the imaginative, narrative, social, and political spaces opened up by film, video, and television lie possibilities for Aboriginal mediamakers and their communities to reenvision their current realities and possible futures, from the revival of local cultural practices, to the insertion of their histories into national imaginaries, to the creation of new transnational arenas that link indigenous makers around the globe in a common effort to make their concerns visible to the world.

Notes

1 For a fuller development of this position, see Ginsburg 1994a.
2 These contradictions, some have argued, are typical of liberal welfare states and their indigenous populations, a system that Jeremy Beckett calls welfare colonialism (1988).
3 For examples of debates on Aboriginality, see Beckett 1988, Thiele 1991, Lattas 1991, and others in a special issue of *The Australian Journal of Anthropology* entitled Reconsidering Aboriginality.
4 I follow Annette Hamilton's use of the term *national imaginary*. Drawing on ideas from Benedict Anderson, Edward Said, and Jacques Lacan, Hamilton uses the term to describe how contemporary nation-states use visual mass media to constitute *imagined communities*. She uses Lacan's idea of

the imaginary as the mirror-phase in human development when the child sees its own reflection as an "other": "Imaginary relations at the social, collective level can thus be seen as ourselves looking at ourselves while we think we are seeing others" (Hamilton 1990: 17). As examples, she cites the current popularity of Aboriginal art and popular music, as well as films such as *Crocodile Dundee*, in which the outback and Aboriginal knowledge play a critical role, as if Australian appropriation of Aboriginal culture can justify "the settler presence in the country, and indeed…the presence of Australia as part of a world cultural scene" (Hamilton 1990: 18). Given current world conditions, representations of the Australian nation must take account of what Hamilton calls an increasingly "internationalised image-environment," in which images of indigenous peoples now carry a heavy semiotic load (1990). Aboriginal media have become implicated in the circulation of commodified images of Aboriginality, including "hi-tech primitives" engaged in their own televisual production. For a fuller discussion of this position, see Ginsburg 1993a.

5   For a discussion of the origins and use of the term *indigenous media*, see Ginsburg 1993a.

6   While the opportunities of such positions are obvious, there is some concern on the part of Aboriginal filmmakers that they are expected to confine their work to conventional or romanticized representations of Aboriginality, what Haitian anthropologist Michel-Rolph Trouillot calls "the savage slot" (Trouillot 1991).

7   Urban-based filmmakers such as Tracey Moffatt may be more oriented toward formal issues, although they, too, often couch their interests in terms of their social possibilities as *interventions* into dominant conventions of representation regarding Aboriginal men and women in popular culture, as was the case with both *Night Cries* (1990) and *Nice Coloured Girls* (1987). In the case of markers such as Moffatt, this language may be less a product of Aboriginal categories and more a reworking of available discourses in the independent cinema movement, of which she is a part.

8   For an interesting discussion of similar issues in relation to Aboriginal writing, see Muecke 1992.

9   For a fuller discussion of the development of Australian Aboriginal media in different locales, see Batty 1993, Ginsburg 1991 and 1993a, Michaels 1987a, Molnar 1989, and O'Regan 1993.

10 Langton notes:

    One network was even broadcasting a drama series featuring a European acting in place of the original Aboriginal Character, Bony, from the novels of Arthur Upfield….A new and welcome twist…was the appointment of Stan Grant, an Aboriginal journalist, to the position of anchor on *Real Life* [a nightly current affairs program]. [1993:21]

11 In 1978, the government established a separate Special Broadcast Service (SBS) initially to serve immigrant minorities. By the mid-1980s, the SBS altered its policy to include the presentation of Aboriginal radio and television programs and to take as its mandate the correction of popular misconceptions about Aboriginal history and culture.

12 Michael Johnson and Rhoda Roberts were the hosts for 38 programs that aired Tuesday nights at 7:30.

13 While the state-controlled and -funded Australian Broadcasting Corporation (ABC) had been training Aborigines since 1980, by 1987 only seven Aborigines were employed there. That same year, the prime minister established the Aboriginal Employment and Development Policy (AEDP), which requires all industries to have 2 percent Aboriginal employment by 1991 (Molnar 1989: 36–8).

14 As of 1993, APU had six Aboriginal staff who produce *Blackout*, a weekly late-night program on Aboriginal affairs, as well as occasional documentaries and dramatic works. As such, it is a precedent-setting model for including indigenous people and their concerns in the imaginary of the nation-state and beyond.

References

Adorno, Theodor W. 1970. *Ästhetische Theorie*. Gesammelte Schriften, 7. Frankfurt: Suhrkamp.

Anderson, Benedict. 1983. *Imagined Communities*. Verso: London.

Appadurai, Arjun. 1990. Disjuncture and Difference in the Global Cultural Economy. *Public Culture* 2(2):1–24.

Batty, Philip. 1993. Singing the Electric: Aboriginal Television in Australia. In *Channels of Resistance*. Tony Downmunt, ed. Pp. 106–25. London: British Film Institute.

Beckett, Jeremy. 1988. The Past in the Present; The Present in the Past: Constructing a National Aboriginality. In *Past and Present: The Construction of Aboriginality*. Jeremy Beckett, ed. Pp. 191–217. Canberra: Aboriginal Studies Press.

Bürger, Peter. 1984. Theory of the Avant-Garde. *Theory and History of Literature*, 4. Minneapolis: University of Minnesota Press.

Dutchak, Philip. 1992. Black Screens. *Cinema Papers* (March–April) 87:48–52.

Ginsburg, Faye. 1991. Indigenous Media: Faustian Contract or Global Village? *Cultural Anthropology* 6(1):92–112.

——. 1993a. Aboriginal Media and the Aboriginal Imaginary. *Public Culture* 5(3):557–78.

——. 1993b. Station Identification: The Aboriginal Programs Unit of the Australian Broadcasting Corporation. In *Visual Anthropology Review* 9(2):92–6.

——. 1994a. Culture and Media: A (Mild) Polemic. *Anthropology Today* (April):5–15.

——. 1994b. Production Values: Indigenous Media and the Rhetoric of Self-Determination. In *The Rhetoric of Self-Making*. Deborah Battaglia, ed 1995. Pp. 121–37. University of California Press.

Hamilton, Annette. 1990. Fear and Desire: Aborigines, Asians, and the National Imaginary. *Australian Cultural History* 9:14–35.

——.1993. Foreword. In *Well, I Heard It on the Radio and I Saw It on the Television*. By Marcia Langton. Pp. 5–7. Sydney: Australian Film Commission.

Langton, Marcia. 1993. *Well, I Heard It on the Radio and I Saw It on the Television*. Sydney: Australian Film Commission.

Lattas, Andrew. 1991. Nationalism, Aesthetic Redemption, and Aboriginality. *The Australian Journal of Anthropology* 2(2):307–24.

Leigh, Michael. 1992. Fade to Black: An Introductory Essay. In *Cultural Focus, Cultural Futures*. (Film festival catologue.) Pp. 1–3. Canberra: Department of Foreign Affairs and Trade.

Michaels, Eric. 1986. Hollywood Iconography: A Warlpiri Reading. Paper presented at the International Television Studies Conference, British Film Institute, London.

——. 1987a. *For a Cultural Future: Francis Jupurrurla Makes TV at Yuendumu*. Melbourne: Art and Criticism Monograph Series.

——. 1987b. Aboriginal Content: Who's Got It – Who Needs It? *Art and Text* 23–4:58–79.

——. 1988. Bad Aboriginal Art. *Art and Text* 28 (March–May):59–73.

Michaels, Eric, and Francis Jupurrula Kelly 1984. The Social Organization of an Aboriginal Video Workplace. *Australian Aboriginal Studies* 1:26–34.

Molnar, Helen. 1989. Aboriginal Broadcasting in Australia: Challenges and Promises. Paper presented at the International Communication Association Conference, March.

Muecke, Steven. 1992. *Textual Spaces: Aboriginality and Cultural Studies*. Kensington: New South Wales University Press.

Myers, Fred. 1994. Beyond the Intentional Fallacy: Art Criticism and the Ethnography of Aboriginal Acrylic Painting. *Visual Anthropology Review* 10(1):10–43.

Nicoll, Fiona. 1993. The Art of Reconciliation: Art, Aboriginality and the State. *Meanjin* 52(4):705–18.

O'Regan, Tom (with Philip Batty). 1993. An Aboriginal Television Culture: Issues, Strategies, Politics. In *Australian Television Culture*. Pp. 169–92. St. Leonards, Australia: Allen and Unwin.

Peters, Frances. 1993. Breaking All the Rules. (Interview with Jacqueline Urla.) *Visual Anthropology Review* 9(2):98–106.

Stanner, W. E. H. 1956. The Dreaming. In *Australian Signpost*. T. A. G. Hungerford, ed. Pp. 51–65. Melbourne: F. W. Cheshire.

Thiele, Steve. 1991. Taking a Sociological Approach to Europeanness (Whiteness) and Aboriginality (Blackness). *The Australian Journal of Anthropology* 2(2):179–201.

Trouillot, Michel-Rolph. 1991. Anthropology and the Savage Slot: The Poetics and Politics of Otherness. In *Recapturing Anthropology*. Richard Fox, ed. Pp. 17–44. Santa Fe: School of American Research Press.

Turner, Neil. 1990. Pitchat and Beyond. *Artlink* 10(1–2):43–5.

Turner, Terence. 1993. Anthropology and Multiculturalism: What Is Anthropology That Multiculuralists Should Be Mindful of It? *Cultural Anthropology* 8(4):411–29.

Chapter 7

Doing it My Way – Broadcasting Regulation in Capitalist Cultures: The Case of "Fairness" and "Impartiality"

Sylvia Harvey

Speech concerning public affairs is more than self-expression; it is the essence of self-government. US Supreme Court, 1969, cited in Kahn, 1984: 287

The press, designed for freedom's best defence,
And learning, morals, wisdom to dispense,
Perverted, poisoned, lost to honor's rules,
Is made the sport of knaves, to govern fools.
Philadelphia, *Public Ledger*, 1839, cited in Kellner, 1990: vii

Introduction

This article suggests the need for a longer-term historical perspective to be brought to bear on our studies of a changing media world. It explores two instances of state intervention in broadcasting regulation and suggests, on the basis of these limited examples, that there are a number of different capitalist 'roads', rooted in different histories and different cultures, that these deeply affect the organization and content of the media and that it matters very much which one we travel down at the present time.

Two events in particular, one on each side of the North Atlantic, have triggered these observations: first, the decision taken by the American Federal Communications Commission (FCC) in 1987 to suspend the regulation known as the 'Fairness Doctrine' and, second, the decision by a British Conservative government in 1990 to provide a new statutory force for the long-standing requirements for 'impartiality' in broadcasting. The North American decision derives, as we shall see, from new interpretations of old First Amendment free speech rights, in the context of a Reaganite revolution which mobilized the philosophy of individualism increasingly in the interests of large corporations. The British regulation, requiring a continuation and strengthening of a regulatory practice so recently discarded in America, derived partly and merely from existing 'custom and practice' in British broadcasting and, more specifically, from a fear expressed by Conservative politicians that broadcasting was dominated by a 'Left-wing establishment' (Wyatt, 1990).

These differences of approach to the regulation of broadcasting from two governments which, under the leadership of President Reagan and Prime Minister Thatcher, had seemed so united on key aspects of economic and social policy, are arguably remarkable and call for some further exploration and analysis. However, this exploration itself takes place within a changed political and intellectual climate. The old goalposts of difference between 'West' and 'East', capitalist and communist have moved or become obscured, and the old paradigms which allowed for instant intellectual identification have begun an uneasy process of reconfiguration. Media analysts continue to sign up to the verities and values of democracy, community and pluralism and media investors continue to pursue the primary objective of profitability, albeit within a shifting political landscape that requires constant surveillance and feedback. However, neither commentators nor investors (nor, as importantly, consumers) can continue comfortably to inhabit the Cold War antinomies of 'free society' versus 'communist dictatorship', 'capitalist exploitation' versus 'equality and emancipation'.

Capitalism Since the Cold War: Why Regulate?

Since the fall of the Berlin Wall in 1989, a host of other boundaries have been challenged and eroded. In the northern hemisphere the two great armed and antagonistic blocs, the capitalist West and the communist East, have rustled and shifted from an age of Star Wars, distinctive values and the threat of mutual annihilation to a new era of confusing quasi-identity and even merger. A better word to use for this new period of accommodation might be 'take-over', as the advocates of capitalist free markets and individual freedom of expression have claimed victory over the exponents of proletarian power, a socially managed economy and the goals of human emancipation and equality. Communism as the spectre haunting Europe, seeking a political voice for workers, for the producers dependent upon capital, has been replaced by the ghosts of eighteenth-century philosophers claiming again an absolute virtue for the invisible hand of the market.

The advocacy of market dynamism and market imperatives has gone hand in hand with calls for a lessening of the power of the state (lower taxes, less state control) and a shift of emphasis from the rights of workers as producers of wealth to a focus on their new identity as consumers. Those with little power as consumers have found themselves, despite the modern factor of universal suffrage, increasingly marginalized in social and political terms. This is the so-called 'one-third–two-thirds society' where the very mechanisms of democracy itself reproduce the comfort of a majority and the poverty and desperation of a minority. In the language of ghosts, this has been one of the effects of the spectre of Adam Smith banishing the spectre of Karl Marx.

And yet, as we examine the actual as opposed to the imaginary landscape we find, dotted all over the land in the wealthier parts of the globe, the institutions of welfare capitalism. These institutions, responding to various political currents and effective to a greater or lesser degree (food stamps but not public housing, social security but not universal health care) constitute an in-practice recognition of the limitations of free market arguments. Whether in North America or in Europe these institutions, and their ever increasing social security budgets, serve as silent testimony to the proposition that, left to itself, the capitalist market cannot provide in key areas of human need, and that the capitalist state in the era of universal suffrage must find ways of responding to these needs.

Even from a quite radical free market perspective there has been a growing recognition in this century that the state must intervene, where necessary, to ensure more perfect competition. And the exponents of this form of intervention have found themselves increasingly caught up and crowded by the company of their political enemies, namely, the Rooseveltian 'New Dealers' in America and the social democratic reformers in Europe. By the end of the twentieth century New Dealers and social democrats have, in their turn, come under severe pressure, shivering in the icy and ideologically purposeful blasts of Reagan-economics and the Thatcherite advocacy of individualism and the values of free enterprise. State intervention and regulation have become philosophically and practically marginalized even while that proportion of the population that continues to participate in electoral democracy expects the state to manage risk and to provide at least minimal forms of security. It is in this broader context of welfare capitalism on the one hand, and of anti-statism on the other, that we must situate our current debates about the nature and extent of government involvement in the organization and content of systems of public communication, while recognizing that this issue has not up to now been in the front rank of concerns either for politicians or for their electorates.

A late twentieth-century audit of public policy offers us a landscape of wild and fruitful contradictions: the inability of free market societies to deliver on their promises of human happiness without considerable state intervention; the failure of 'actually existing socialism' (albeit deformed since 1917 into the shadow of an aggressive capitalism) to deliver political freedom and economic advancement. These complexities suggest a new starting point for analysis, one involving three key elements: first, a recognition both of the importance of the market and of its limitations as an allocative mechanism; second a rejection of the powers of a political or economic elite to control media output (the Stalinist nomenclatura, the capitalist ruling class and their various descendants) and, third, a new audit of public service broadcasting and a sceptical investigation of the consequences of increasing concentrations in media ownership. In respect of this last point it is worth noting that journalists and scholars in reaching for a vocabulary to describe the new giant media corporations have come up with a metaphorical language of 'princes' and 'moguls' seen to be achieving a possibly unhealthy dominance in the realm of ideas and of entertainment. These metaphors offer an ironic pointer for any critical and historical approach to the analysis of contemporary media, for they suggest the possibility of a return to a pre-democratic age – the feudal era which preceded the aggressive and creative transformations wrought by the bourgeois revolution.

Here we encounter some of the strange unpredictabilities and reversals of historical development. For the new centurions of multinational capital have donned the garb of eighteenth-century free market philosophers, not to challenge the economic and political dysfunctionalism of feudalism but to inhibit or destroy those broadcasting institutions that were (particularly in Britain) the product of state intervention in the early period of universal suffrage. State provision has had to be dismantled, disabled or limited in order to create a new set of market relationships where citizens become consumers, providers become investors and profitability becomes the motivating force in the economic cycle.

This, however, is a system in flux with different capitalist states providing very different examples. In the USA, public sector or not-for-profit broadcasting was always too small and insignificant to provide any serious challenge to private sector interests while in Britain, by contrast, not-for-profit broadcasting has retained considerable prestige and popularity. So the interesting question for the future, in the realm of public communication, may be not so much whether capitalist theory and practice has wiped out its communist adversary, but whether private sector provision can coexist with not-for-profit provision and how amenable both sectors are to regulation by the state acting, or claiming to act, in the larger public interest. Early and arguably utopian theorists of capitalism believed that the general interest and the greater good would be served by the benign and invisible hand of the market; communists argued that a system rooted in the economic exploitation and political disempowerment of workers, the producers of wealth, could never meet the general interest or represent the general good. It is these disagreements about the nature and effects of capitalism as an economic and social system that, of course, underlie debates about discovering and instating the public interest in broadcasting.

The American Supreme Court, one of the great institutions of a successful bourgeois revolution, has reflected in its judgements over the years some of the tensions in capitalist culture which stem from any attempt at operationalizing the concept of public interest. In a 1973 judgement, reflecting upon the scope and propriety of actions taken by the Federal Communications Commission on behalf of Congress, it noted the imperative of maintaining a balance between the conflicting demands of private ownership and of public accountability:

> Congress, and the Commission as its agent, must remain in a posture of flexibility to chart a workable 'middle course' in its quest to preserve a balance between essential public accountability and desirable private control of the media. (Ramberg, 1986: 21)

Just how difficult such a 'posture of flexibility' becomes depends very much on the balance of competing social interests in capitalist democracies. But the questions implied here: 'just how desirable is private control?' and 'just how possible is public accountability?' remain in play, and very much at the heart of any public policy agenda for the twenty-first century.

That these arguments are still in play suggests that the legacy of the bourgeois revolution with its emphasis on the imperatives of economic and social change and on the free exchange of ideas is not yet exhausted. It may be useful here to recall that, in the wake of the anti-bourgeois revolutions in Russia and in China, Mao Tse Tung was asked what he thought had been the result of the French Revolution. His answer was that it was 'too soon to tell'. Likewise, and notwithstanding the trenchant critiques of the failure of capitalist *societies* to deliver liberty, equality and social solidarity, and of the failure of the global capitalist *system* to facilitate the creation of democratic states in many parts of the world, it is almost certainly too soon to tell what are the results of the bourgeois revolution. For the different tendencies within this revolution suggest different pathways, different roads to the future, different degrees of accommodation with the ideas of communism, socialism and social democracy and with the concept of the public interest.

And while the press whose birth is almost coincidental with the bourgeois revolution has remained largely unregulated in capitalist democracies (at least as regards content), broadcasting – influential child of the century of universal suffrage – has been widely seen to require some measure of regulation in the public interest.

Back to the Future: Republican and Aristocratic Versions of Public Interest

The concept of a public sphere and arguments for its maintenance and development as a space for locating the general good and articulating the public interest can be traced back to the polities of classical Greece and Rome, as Hannah Arendt has demonstrated (Arendt, 1958). In the writings of Jürgen Habermas the idea can be linked to the Marxist view that the objectives of capitalism as an economic system and of democracy as a political system are mutually incompatible. However, many of the formulations of the idea are also compatible with liberal theories of society. Indeed, as an ideal to be discovered or con-

structed it is arguably one of the key categories in the passionate defence of democracy proposed by people who inhabit a range of different ideological camps and political parties. Habermas's own formulation is open to such pluralistic use:

> By 'the public sphere' we mean first of all a realm of our social life in which something approaching public opinion can be formed. Access is guaranteed to all citizens. A portion of the public sphere comes into being in every conversation in which private individuals assemble to form a public body. (Habermas, 1979: 198)

Thus we can take the concept of the public sphere to indicate that set of cultural practices and institutions which, taken together, provide the means for the sort of public communication that is required for the development and maintenance of democratic societies.[1] In Britain, in the context of a long history of public service broadcasting, a number of scholars have argued that this method of broadcasting, despite its deficiencies, provides an actually existing model for the constitution of the public sphere (Garnham, 1986; Scannell, 1989a, 1989b; Smith, 1993).

However, much subsequent exegesis of Habermas's theory in both Europe and America has concentrated on his sense of the loss or decline of the public sphere since the time of its first creation in the eighteenth century by a new and vigorous bourgeois 'public'. Habermas regrets, in the modern age of mass communications and mass democracy, a kind of 're-feudalization' of the public sphere involving a degradation of the space for rational and effective debate on matters of public policy among equal and equally participating citizens. In the sphere of public communication the exchange of ideas has, he argues, given way to the exchange of commodities. American critics in particular, gathering the fruits of 70 years of commercially driven broadcasting, have been keen to emphasize this pessimistic view (Entman, 1989; Kellner, 1990; Blumler and Gurevitch, 1995; Fallows, 1996a; Schiller, 1996).

If the bourgeois revolution remains very much our active and operational legacy, now directing the tides of economic change on a global basis, the legacy of the communist revolution has been challenged and even 'cancelled', or perhaps gone underground where its effects become difficult to trace and identify.

The energetic expansion of capitalism remains, on the contrary, very much 'above ground' propelled into all the corners of the world by the new centurions of the multinational corporations. The relative unaccountability of its power holders and their ambiguous and even threatening relationship to the institutions of democracy has been noted by a number of commentators. The language of such critics echoes Habermas's suggestion of a process of 'refeudalization', reaching back into the past for a description of the abuses of power which seem also to characterize aspects of the present. Thus the British social historian Harold Perkin identifies the danger of a society in which:

> the feudal lords of the giant corporations manipulate their multi-national estates with scant regard to national governments or the interests of the local inhabitants...(Perkin, 1989: 518)

while the American theorist of corporate communications, Stanley Deetz, draws from the language of colonization to describe corporate power in contemporary America. In his view 'corporate colonization' is 'the most effective system of control in human history' and one that reaches into every area of life:

> Everything from personal identity and use of natural resources to definitions of value and distribution of goods and services has increasingly come under corporate control.... Commercial organizations make decisions for the public, but rarely are these decisons grounded in democratic processes. (Deetz, 1992: ix)

However, despite its current globalizing and even homogenizing reach, there remain some still operationally significant differences between the capitalist cultures of different countries. It will be argued here that some of these differences are especially significant for the analysis of broadcasting and for any assessment of its role and future prospects as an agent of democratization.

Within the long history of the bourgeois revolution and the gradual establishment of mature capitalist economies and societies, broadcasting is itself a relatively recent arrival, as recent in fact as the birth of universal suffrage (women only obtained the vote in the USA and Britain in the course of the 1920s). In respect of this relatively short history of democracy and of broadcasting, it has become a commonplace observation that the latter has developed in very different ways in Britain and America, and these differences have been traced in terms of finance, programme content, programming philosophy, control and regulation.

But the history of developments in public communication in this century, and the potential for change and development in the next, may be better understood in the context of older debates. Reaching back to the period of the American revolution and the war of independence against the rule of a British king, these debates involve questions about the nature of the good society, the relationship between people and government and the means required to ensure freedom of expression and the free circulation of ideas. Only the most schematic and selective account of these debates is possible here.

If the British case involves a slow overlaying of the principles and practices of meritocracy (and democracy) across the ancient framework of aristocracy and monarchy, the American case involves a much more radical and explicit process of self-recognition and self-designation. It is this still radical republican vision that was outlined, in 1776, in the American Declaration of Independence:

> We hold these truths to be self-evident, that all men are created equal, that they are endowed by their Creator with certain inalienable rights, that among these are life, liberty and the pursuit of happiness. That to secure these rights, governments are instituted among men, deriving their just powers from the consent of the governed. That whenever any form of government becomes destructive of these ends, it is the right of the people to alter or abolish it. (Wilson, 1967)

It is clear from this statement that the rights and liberties of individuals are taken as paramount and that government, far from being an absolute source of power and authority, is justified primarily in terms of its ability to secure these primary rights. By 1791 a First Amendment to the Consitution had been framed which re-stated this scepticism, placing particular limits on the power of government:

> Congress shall make no law...abridging the freedom of speech or of the press; or the right of the people peaceably to assemble. (Wilson, 1967)

Interpretations of this First Amendment, not least with respect to modern systems of mass communication, the press and broadcasting, have been the subject of innumerable and fierce debates up to the present time. Indeed, as we shall see, interpretations of this amendment favouring the rights of broadcasting *corporations*, and not only individuals, to enjoy freedom of speech, were a key factor in the 1987 suspension of the 'Fairness Doctrine'. Until that time the Federal Communications Commission (FCC) had applied the 'doctrine' of fairness in the regulation of American broadcasting. Among other things this had involved the allocation of free airtime to individuals and groups who could not afford paid advertisements but who wished to counter the arguments put forward in political advertising. It is important to note, however, that the First Amendment itself had severely restricted the forms of regulation that the federal government, acting through its 'agent' the FCC, felt able to apply. Thus, for example, while the British state had no qualms about prohibiting both political editorializing by broadcasters and political advertising on the airwaves, the American state, bound by the stern directives of the Constitution felt obliged to allow both.

The Declaration of Independence signalled not just a rejection of the authority of the English king but a positive substitution of the rights of individuals for the traditional duties of a hierarchically organized society. As the principle of equality defied the norms of aristocratic culture a new type of social organization was brought into being. The historian Joyce Appleby notes some of the consequences of this process in her study of the founding of a new capitalist social order in America. In this respect she cites the observations of a European outsider, Alexis de Tocqueville, author of the influential mid-nineteenth-century study, *Democracy in America*:

> Aristocracy had made a chain of all the members of the community, from the peasant to the king: democracy breaks that chain, and severs every link of it. (Appleby, 1984: 52)

De Tocqueville offers here a pessimistic view of the consequences of the democratic experiment, indicating some of the features of a culture of radical individualism which was to give rise, in a later era, to a particular philosophy of public communication. Contrasted with this view, the conservatism of British culture offered a more organic sense of the links between individuals of different classes, and proferred a more positive, even interventionist, view of the role of government in maintaining the unity of society. It is this positive view, conferring legitimacy on a wide range of governmental activities, that is expressed in the late eighteenth century by the British political philosopher Edmund Burke:

> Government is a contrivance of human wisdom to provide for human wants. Men have a right that these wants should be provided for by this wisdom. (Perkin, 1989: 519)

This notion of the enabling (as opposed to restrictive or interfering) role of government can be seen to inform the traditions of public administration in Britain in the early twentieth century, creating a framework for what came to be called 'public service' broadcasting (Thomas, 1978; Owen, 1996). If British broadcasting in the 1920s reflected a world in which the servants remained silently 'downstairs', and where working-class voices were not permitted to approach the microphone, it equally embodied a commitment to the principle of public trusteeship and to the creation of a cadre of (at least theoretically) neutral and expert civil servants acting in the national interest and for the common good. The negative and positive features of this benevolent paternalism can be unravelled from the rich fabric of public policy on broadcasting as this has been woven in Britain through to the last decade of the twentieth century.

In the Reagan–Bush period aspects of the older republican vision with its emphasis on individual liberties and the role of the courts in protecting these, together with a scepticism about the role of government, were effectively mobilized in the interests of large corporations, while the collectivist elements of the American revolution, 'the right of the people peaceably to assemble' were downgraded and lacked political resonance. This partly explains the suspension of the Fairness Doctrine, seen as an instance of what British free marketeers, agreeing with the Reaganite FCC, might have dismissed as the unwelcome attentions of the nannying state.[2] Meanwhile, in Britain itself, one of the historical ironies of the Thatcherite public policy corpus was the establishment of a legally supported prohibition on broadcaster advocacy, a development that was arguably the fruit of a rapprochement between aristocratic one-nation Tories and social democrats.

Regulation in the Public Interest: 'Fairness' and 'Impartiality'

Unlike the British system, the development of broadcasting regulation in the USA has been much affected by court rulings, both at state and at Supreme Court level. From the earliest days there was deep uncertainty both at the FCC and among lawyers as to the interpretation of the wording in the 1934 Communications Act that required broadcasters to promote the 'public interest, convenience and necessity'. The very vagueness of the phrase, taken in conjunction with the apparent precision of the First Amendment and the militant vigilance of the industry (McChesney, 1993), led many commentators to the view that only the Supreme Court would be able to adjudicate not just on its meaning, but also on the proper scope of its policy implications and attendant regulatory practice. Bennett Ramberg's review of some 32 Supreme Court rulings between 1930 and 1983 reveals, as we might expect, that interpretations have varied according to the changing composition of the Court and the changing economic, political and social environment (Ramberg, 1986).

Within the FCC and the industry itself the tides also flowed with different intensities and in different directions. One of the high points of New Deal interventionism may be found in the 1941 FCC ruling in the Mayflower case. Freedom of speech was linked not to the corporate freedom of the broadcaster considered as a First Amendment subject but rather to the varied information needs of the listeners:

Freedom of speech on the radio must be broad enough to provide full and equal opportunity for the presentation to the public of all sides of public issues... the licensee has assumed the obligation of presenting all sides of important public questions, fairly, objectively and without bias. (Kahn, 1984: 122)

The FCC took the view that the public interest could not be served by a broadcasting system in which broadcasters were themselves allowed to advocate particular causes and interests. The judgement was succinct: 'the broadcaster cannot be an advocate... the public interest – not the private – is paramount', and the function of broadcasting was explicitly linked to the objectives of democracy:

the public interest can never be served by a dedication of any broadcast facility to the support of his own partisan ends. Radio can serve as an instrument of democracy only when devoted to the communication of information and the exchange of ideas fairly and objectively presented. A truly free radio cannot be used to advocate the causes of the licensee. (Kahn, 1984: 122)

This view of broadcasting as an 'instrument' of democracy was one which – while it remained current in certain intellectual quarters – was largely rejected in American government thinking and in regulatory practice by the 1980s. In Britain, by contrast, the probibition on broadcaster advocacy remains one of the cornerstones of public policy, receiving legal recognition and support in the 1990 Broadcasting Act.

In the USA the period immediately after the Second World War saw, if briefly, a 'high tide' in positive regulation with the appearance of the FCC's 'Blue Book' (1946). This document outlined the need for a 'well-rounded program service' and the importance of meeting 'the tastes, needs and desires of all substantial groups among the listening public'. However, the FCC's additional proposal that a 'reasonable proportion of time' should be devoted to unsponsored programmes was seen by the industry to be too much of a threat to its profitability, and the Blue Book was never enforced (Kahn, 1984: 148–64).

Taken in context the FCC's 1949 Fairness Doctrine ('In the Matter of Editorializing by

Broadcast Licensees', in Kahn, 1984) might also be seen as a sign of accommodation to an industry vigorously fighting to maintain its own control over the organization and content of broadcasting. Fearful that the 1941 Mayflower judgement might be taken to be a contravention of First Amendment free speech rights, the FCC's 1949 ruling endorsed the broadcasters' rights both to editorialize (in other words, to advocate their own causes) and to carry political advertising. However, in attempting to achieve some kind of balance between the rights of broadcasters and those of listeners, the Commission introduced some new procedures to govern the treatment of controversial issues of public importance, and issued guidelines for the public on how to file complaints (Corner and Harvey, 1996: 260–2). Broadcasters were required both to 'devote a reasonable percentage of their broadcasting time to the discussion of public issues' and to ensure that listeners had 'a reasonable opportunity to hear different opposing positions on the public issues of interest and importance in the community' (Rowan, 1984: 32).

One illuminating example of the Fairness Doctrine in practice concerns cigarette advertising. In 1967, in response to a complaint, the FCC ruled that a station carrying cigarette commercials 'has the duty of informing its audience of the other side of this controversial issue of public importance – that however enjoyable, such smoking may be a hazard to the smoker's health' (Kahn, 1984: 257). Despite the Commission's attempt to rule the exceptional nature of cigarette advertising, a subsequent court hearing found in favour of a complainant who argued that the Doctrine should also allow the case against atmospheric pollution to be made in response to advertisements for large cars. The court followed a clear logic of argument in making this ruling, but it nonetheless, arguably, struck at the economic foundations of the American broadcasting system. If 'free' airtime was to be found by the broadcaster to counter the claims made in a range of advertments, the system might soon find itself in crisis. The FCC was to resolve the issue, but not before widespread anxiety had been generated in the broadcasting and advertising industries. In 1974 it rescinded its earlier judgement, arguing now that advertisements should not normally be seen as 'presenting a meaningful discussion of a controversial issue of public importance'. Henceforth the Doctrine would be reserved for 'those "commercials" which are devoted in an obvious and meaningful way to the discussion of public issues', that is, to political advertising (Ray, 1990: 101–2).

Despite the ups and downs of its implementation, the Fairness Doctrine was eloquently supported by a Supreme Court ruling in the Red Lion case of 1969. The Court's judgement provides what is probably still the clearest explanation and the most persuasive endorsement of the Doctrine, arguing that its objective was to 'enhance rather than abridge the freedoms of speech and press protected by the First Amendment' and that it involved 'a legitimate exercise of congressionally delegated authority'. The Court considered the special characteristics of broadcast media in arriving at its judgement and presented a key comparison with the right of government to 'limit the use of sound-amplifying equipment potentially so noisy that it drowns out civilized private speech' nothing that 'the right to free speech of a broadcaster... does not embrace a right to snuff out the free speech of others' (Kahn, 1984: 278, 284–5). In the Court's view a licensee has no constitutional right to hold a licence or to 'monopolize a radio frequency to the exclusion of his fellow citizens' since, no matter how many new channels might become available for allocation, there were still more applicants than frequencies. The licensee had 'no right to an unconditional monopoly of a scarce resource which the Government has denied others the right to use' and there is 'no sanctuary in the First Amendment for unlimited private censorship operating in a medium not open to all' (Kahn, 1984: 286–7, 288). The interests of the listeners should be paramount and the Court's emphasis was on:

> the right of the public to receive suitable access to social, political, esthetic, moral, and other ideas and experiences. (Kahn, 1984: 287)

By 1987 the attitude of public authorities towards broadcasting had radically changed. Mark Fowler, appointed Chair of a Reagan-influenced FCC, had suggested that television was 'just an appliance, like the toaster' (Kellner, 1990: 92). Fowler had seen the further development of a free market in broadcasting and the progressive removal of forms of state regulation as a primary objective, relaxing, among other things, the requirements for public affairs programming and for public access to industry documentation. Meanwhile the industry itself continued to demand the minimum of regulation, seeing any talk of quality and standards, and of the rights of the public, as an unacceptable infringment of their right to broadcast what they chose. In this context, with presidential support for deregulation and despite opposition from Congress, the suspension of the Fairness Doctrine was not surprising (Stein, 1996). In June 1987 President Reagan vetoed a bill that had been designed by the Senate to include the Doctrine in the provisions of the Communications Act; in August the FCC declared the Doctrine unconstitutional. Their judgement was based on two main claims: that the Doctrine's procedures placed unacceptable limits on broadcasters, violating their First Amendment rights, and that it had a 'chilling effect' on the reporting of controversies, as editors sought to avoid being drawn into the complexities of expressing balanced views.

In Britain, the approach to the representation of controversial issues in the broadcast media was very different. In respect of both the BBC and commercial broadcasting the observance of impartiality was regarded as, effectively, a necessary condition of the right to broadcast. In 1923 John Reith, Chief Executive of the British Broadcasting Company and subsequently first Director General of the BBC, noted:

> Great discretion has to be exercised in such matters, but if on any controversial matter the opposing views were stated with equal emphasis and lucidity then at least there can be no charge of bias. (Briggs, 1961: 171)

Two years later the Crawford Committee, in its Report to Parliament, cautiously recommended that 'a moderate amount of controversial material should be broadcast, provided the material is of high quality and distributed with scrupulous fairness' (Smith, 1974: 55). By the mid-1960s the BBC's Governors had formally recorded their views on this matter and included them as an 'Annex' to the Corporation's Licence:

> The Board recall that it has always been their object to treat controversial subjects with due

impartiality, and they intend to continue this policy both in the Corporation's news services and in the more general field of programmes dealing with matters of public policy. (BBC, 1984: 191)

These agreed conventions on impartiality were generally effective, though for a long time they operated within a framework that was culturally and often politically conservative and not inclusive of the full range of beliefs and values in British society (Philo and Hewitt et al., 1982). Moreover, throughout its history, the BBC has been amenable to direct and indirect pressure from government.[3]

Historically, the production of the BBC's broadcasting conventions had relied upon the ethos of a gentleman's club and (at least up to the 1980s) on the consensual framework of British politics. However, the introduction of commercial television saw the beginnings of a more formal, more transparent and arguably more democratic relationship between Parliament and broadcasting, exemplified in the passing of the 1954 Television Act. The BBC had always operated under Royal Charter, even though its licence had to be approved by Parliament; the 1954 Act provided the first major legal codification of what was expected of (commercial) television. Interestingly the wording on 'due impartiality' used by the BBC Governors appeared earlier in the 1954 Act which also established the first legally authorized regulatory body, the Independent Television Authority (ITA). The ITA was required to ensure:

> that due impartiality is preserved on the part of the persons providing the programmes as respects matters of political or industrial controversy or relating to current public policy. (Smith, 1974: 110)

It is also important to note that while the new law introduced the possibility of privately owned and advertiser-financed broadcasting, it did not permit the introduction of directly sponsored programmes or of political advertising. In this way it was believed that advertisers and their clients would be kept at a distance, away from the arena of programme making and of editorial decision making. Moreover, the transmission of programmes was to be in the hands of a public corporation (the ITA) and not directly controlled by the new television companies. Thus a framework for commercial broadcasting was created which differed in many key respects from the American model.[4]

Apart from the 'due impartiality' requirement, broadcasters were not permitted to editorialize and this was enshrined in the licence granted to the BBC:

> The Corporation shall at all times refrain from sending any broadcast matter expressing the opinion of the Corporation on current affairs or on matters of public policy, other than broadcasting. (BBC, 1984: 188)

A similar prohibition was built into the regulatory Code governing commercial broadcasting: 'the avoidance of editorializing on the part of the licensees is integral to the preservation of due impartiality in the service they provide'. Moreover compliance with the Code was a condition of holding the licence (ITC, 1995: 14, 13).

As has already been noted, the prohibition on broadcaster advocacy was in the USA regarded as a violation of First Amendment rights. In Britain it was regarded as the necessary institutional basis for impartiality. Thus a British equivalent of the Mayflower ruling remains in force up to the present time.

Unlike the commercial television companies (ITV) which were subject to legally prescribed forms of regulation, the BBC was subject only to self-regulation; though by the 1980s it was not at all complacent on the subject. In the course of Margaret Thatcher's premiership a number of serious attacks were made upon the BBC both by the Conservative Party and by the Conservative government. These attacks related to a variety of issues, including the coverage of the Falklands War, the American bombing of Libya and programmes about internal security matters (Milne, 1988). Some Conservatives objected to the Corporation's evidently critical attitude towards the apartheid government of South Africa, and it may have been in response to this situation that the BBC published its 'footnote' to the impartiality policy. The 1985 *Annual Report* noted:

> impartiality is not absolute neutrality.... For example, the BBC does not feel obliged to be neutral as between truth and untruth, justice and injustice, freedom and slavery, compassion

and cruelty, tolerance and intolerance (including racial intolerance). (BBC, 1984: 171)

In November 1988, coincidentally in the same month in which the government published its proposals for broadcasting legislation, the BBC had held a prestigious and well-prepared seminar on the subject of impartiality and published the proceedings early in the following year (BBC, 1989). A summary of the findings – which dealt with both factual and fictional programming – was included in the Corporation's 'Producers' Guidelines' and the whole exercise seems to have worked well as part of an astute programme of political self-defence. In a preface to the document the Chairman of the Governors (himself appointed by the Prime Minister) endorsed the view that:

> impartiality is the core of the contract between the BBC and the national audience. The BBC is funded by the entire community and must report and reflect the full range of opinions, experience and aspirations within the community.... Only as long as the nation as a whole believes the BBC is impartial and has no axe to grind will it give it the support which guarantees its independence, and therefore its ability when necessary to transmit challenging and uncomfortable programmes. (BBC, 1989: 5)

A year later, and after a flurry of concern that 'impartiality' was becoming a stick with which to beat and silence awkward journalists, the Conservative government included a section on impartiality in the Broadcasting Act (Broadcasting Act, 1990: 6; Mathias, 1993; Willis, 1993; Harvey, 1994: 121). It was left to the new regulatory body, the Independent Television Commission (ITC), to work out the detail.

The ITC shared with BBC broadcasters and Governors a concern that the impartiality rule might result in the production of bland, 'safe' and uncontroversial programmes. The law required 'that due impartiality is preserved ... as respects matters of political or industrial controversy or relating to current public policy' (ITC, 1995: 14). However, the ITC ruled that this:

> does not mean that 'balance' is required in any simple mathematical sense or that equal time must be given to each opposing point of view, nor does it require absolute neutrality on every

issue. Judgement will always be called for. (ITC, 1995: 14)

In addition 'personal view' programmes were allowed, as long as these did not purport to be the view of the broadcaster and allowed appropriate opportunities for response. Opinionated programmes could be produced but only in the context of a clearly defined series of programmes which covered a full range of views. Dramatized documentaries which claimed to be based on fact were to be 'bound by the same standards of fairness and impartiality as those that apply to factual programmes in general' though the role of the 'creative imagination' in introducing a fictional dimension was recognized (ITC, 1995: 17).

Thus under a British Conservative government the principle of impartiality and the prohibition on broadcaster advocacy were enshrined in law. The implementation of these principles was monitored through the application of a code which, by and large, reflected the consensus of a professional community which recognized, though it was not always committed to, the ethos of public service broadcasting.

Conclusion

In his 1989 book, *Democracy without Citizens*, Robert Entman offers a careful assessment of the Fairness Doctrine and some informed speculation on the likely consequences of its suspension:

> The Fairness Doctrine provided some limited ability for the poor side in a referendum to answer the organized interests on such issues as smoking bans or nuclear power safety; that lever is no longer available.... Those who have the wealth to own stations or buy time on them will dominate television's contributions to issue discussion. (Entman, 1989: 123)

He also notes that some of the broadcasters themselves seemed sceptical about the consequences of the 'free market place of ideas' argument advocated by Reaganite Republicans and the FCC. In the late 1980s the three major television networks declined to take advocacy advertisements feeling that this practice 'allows the fellow with the biggest pockets to set the agenda'; it was however, common among smaller stations to take such commercials (Entman, 1989: 195).

If the suspension of the Doctrine made it easier for richer people and harder for poorer people to influence the public agenda, Patricia Aufderheide's research into the post-1987 record of the broadcasters seems to have demonstrated that, at least among the journalists, most had not perceived the Doctrine, during the period of its enforcement, to have a chilling effect on coverage. Moreover, there seemed to have been no significant increase in the coverage of controversial issues since the suspension, and the resources for such coverage had been reduced – all major networks had experienced cutbacks in the three areas of news, standards and minority affairs (Aufderheide, 1990: 51).

In 1996, some seven years after Entman's scholarly assessment of the value of the Doctrine and the limitations of the theory of a marketplace of ideas, the Washington editor of the *Atlantic Monthly* launched an attack on American journalists. The American public, he argued, had become deeply sceptical about their media, believing them to be: 'arrogant, cynical, scandalminded, and destructive':

> We have a system of news that tells people constantly that the world is out of control, that they will always be governed by crooks, that their fellow citizens are out to kill them. (Fallows, 1996b)

This state of affairs was causing, he suggested, 'a quiet consumer boycott of the press', and if journalists were to win back the respect and even the attention of their audiences their work should help people to 'understand, even control, events that will affect them' (Fallows, 1996b). This would involve journalists in less opinionated punditry and more detailed research into events, issues and policies:

> if journalists should choose to engage the public, they will begin a long series of experiments and decisions to see how journalism might better serve its fundamental purpose, that of making democratic self-government possible. (Fallows, 1996b)

Fallows's claim that the media have become a negative force in 'undermining' American democracy is striking, and may be accurate. At the very least it should be considered in conjunction with the significant rates of voter abstention from the political process; in Britain some 30 percent of the electorate do not participate in national elections, in America the figure is more like 60 percent.

However, the limitations of Fallows's approach stem from his concentration on the work of individual journalists. These journalists work within a system of largely privately owned media, and media owners must inevitably put first their duty to their shareholders, and therefore to profitability. Moreover, their target markets are by no means coextensive with the whole of society. Business interests, together with the long history of debates about the First Amendment and the establishment in the courts of a corporate right to freedom of speech, have made these owners hostile to public regulation. Nonetheless, at least in the area of broadcasting (though not in the case of the paper press), both legislation and a series of Supreme Court judgements have established the legitimacy of the activity of regulation in the public interest. It is this sort of regulation that probably alone can provide a stable framework for public interest journalism.

While the Fairness Doctrine remains suspended, the ideas behind it will not go away; they are too powerful and too deeply embedded in debates about the nature of a democratic society to disappear in a puff of free market smoke. But these ideas have been under sustained attack. Powerful and internationalized private interests have sought to persuade politicians and publics that regulation of this kind is unnecessary both because of the expansion of available broadcasting channels and because consumer choice and the use of the on/off button are taken to provide a sufficient regulatory mechanism for both quality and content. Thoughtful bystanders, sympathetic to the idea that democratic government requires an informed electorate, may conclude that private and monopoly control of the information content of broadcasting could be the best thing for advocates of the one-party state since the death of Stalin.

It may be useful to consider the future prospects of the Fairness Doctrine in relation to the unfolding of public policy in another but related area of American life: the issue of freedom of expression on private property. A number of court rulings have confirmed free speech rights in the context of privately-owned shopping malls. In 1963, for example, the Michigan Supreme Court found in favour of a trade union wishing to distribute leaflets urging a consumer boycott of non-union shirts within a shopping centre, on the grounds that this space had become 'public or quasi-public' in character. A 1980 ruling in California supported the right of a group of high school students to collect signatures on a petition in the common area of a privately-owned shopping mall. In his commentary on these cases Warren Freedman noted:

> Private property is said to reflect the social fabric of society, and the absoluteness of ownership has long been modified to serve the collective needs of society at large. (Freedman, 1988: 38–9)

It seems inconceivable, in the long run, that militant individualism could affirm free speech rights for visitors on private property while denying them to visitors on the airwaves.

Capitalist democracy in Britain has taken a different path as regards the presentation of controversial public affairs in the media, with the insistence on broadcaster impartiality and the banning of political advertising. The paradox here is that while such policies flow from the traditions of an organic, paternalistic and pre-democratic society, their effect is almost certainly to provide strong and durable legal safeguards for freedom and diversity of expression within a democracy. The two traditions of paternalism and of militant individualism both arise out of and help to constitute the different capitalist cultures of Britain and the USA. Their different patterns, models and methods offer examples, and to some extent choices, to those countries currently on the fast track to the creation of democratic states and concerned with the regulation of public communication in the public interest.

No one is blowing the trumpet at the walls of capitalist Jericho, but the tension between the priorities of privately owned broadcasting and the information needs of an electorate remain unresolved. The still extraordinary project of democracy – the concept of self-government through a process of political representation – continues to speak quietly within the heart of the capitalist citadel. This 'still, small voice' was perhaps already there, at the beginnings of the bourgeois revolution and even one of its motivating forces. Making this speech more public, more shared and more effective is the great and achievable task for citizens of the twenty-first century.

Notes

1　Recent debates about 'the public sphere' have considered whether it is to be thought of as singular or plural. The notion of alternative or oppositional public spheres is explored in Jakubowicz (1991) and Negt and Kluge (1993); the argument for 'a plurality of competing publics' and for the existence of 'subaltern counterpublics' is developed in Frazer (1990); several accounts of the black public sphere are developed in a special issue of *Public Culture*, (1994).

2　A more complex and detailed account of regulatory theory and of the often unexpected consequences of deregulatory practice in the field of telecommunications is given in Horwitz, (1989).

3　In the 1930s government pressure resulted in a BBC decision not to invite the leader of the Communist Party to broadcast a contribution to a series of current affairs talks (Scannell and Cardiff, 1991: 75). In the 1980s a controversial programme about Northern Ireland, *Real Lives*, was prevented by the Governors from being screened, following government pressure (Milne, 1988: 189–93).

4　The ITV companies became responsible for their own programme transmissions and scheduling after the 1990 Broadcasting Act.

References

Appleby, J. (1984) *Capitalism and the New Social Order: The Republican Vision of the 1790s.* New York: New York University Press.

Arendt, H. (1958) *The Human Condition.* Chicago, IL: University of Chicago Press.

Aufderheide, P. (1990) 'After the Fairness Doctrine: Controversial Broadcast Programming and the Public Interest', *Journal of Communication*, 40(3): 47–72.

BBC (1984) *Annual Report and Handbook* 1985. London: BBC.

BBC (1989) *Impartiality: Representing Reality.* London: BBC.

Blumler, H. and M. Gurevitch (1995) *The Crisis of Public Communication.* London and New York: Routledge.

Briggs, A. (1961) *The History of Broadcasting in the United Kingdom.* Vol. I, *The Birth of Broadcasting.* Oxford: Oxford University Press.

Broadcasting Act (1990). London: HMSO.

Corner, J. and S. Harvey (eds) (1996) *Television Times: A Reader.* London: Arnold.

Deetz, S. (1992) *Democracy in an Age of Corporate Colonization: Developments in Communication and the Politics of Everyday Life.* Albany: State University of New York Press.

Entman, R. (1989) *Democracy without Citizens: Media and the Decay of American Politics.* New York and Oxford: Oxford University Press.

Fallows, J. (1996a) *Breaking the News: How the Media Undermine American Democracy.* New York: Pantheon Books.

Fallows, J. (1996b) 'News You Can't Use', *The Guardian*, 1 April.

Frazer, N. (1990) 'Rethinking the Public Sphere: A Contribution to the Critique of Actually Existing Democracy', *Social Text*, 25–6: 56–80. Reprinted in C. Calhoun (ed.) (1992) *Habermas and the Public Sphere*, pp. 109–42. Cambridge, MA: MIT Press.

Freedman, W. (1988) *Freedom of Speech on Private Property.* New York: Quorum Books.

Garnham, N. (1986) 'The Media and the Public Sphere', in P. Golding, G. Murdock and P. Schlesinger (eds) *Communicating Politics.* Leicester: University of Leicester Press. Reprinted in N. Garnham (1990) *Capitalism and Communication: Global Culture and the Economics of Information.* London: Sage.

Habermas, J. (1979) 'The Public Sphere', pp. 198–201 in A. Mattelart and S. Sieglab (eds) *Communication and Class Struggle*, volume 1. New York: International General. First published as an encyclopaedia article in German in 1964; published in English translation by Sara Lennox and Frank Lennox in *New German Critique* 3 (Fall), 1974.

Habermas, J. (1989) *The Structural Transformation of the Public Sphere: An Inquiry into a Category of Bourgeois Society*, trans. Thomas Burger with the assistance of Frederick Lawrence. Cambridge: Polity Press. (First published in German in 1962).

Harvey, S. (1994) 'Channel 4 Television: From Annan to Grade', pp. 102–32 in S. Hood (ed.) *Behind the Screens: The Structure of British Television in the Nineties.* London: Lawrence and Wishart.

Horwitz, R. B. (1989) *The Irony of Regulatory Reform. The Deregulation of American Telecommunications.* New York and Oxford: Oxford University Press.

Independent Television Commission (1995) *The ITC Programme Code.* London: ITC.

Jakubowicz, K. (1991) 'Musical Chairs? The Three Public Spheres in Poland', pp. 155–75 in P. Dahlgren and C. Sparks (eds) *Communication and Citizenship: Journalism and the Public Sphere*. London and New York: Routledge.

Kahn, F. J. (ed.) (1984) *Documents of American Broadcasting*. Englewood Cliffs, NJ: Prentice-Hall.

Kellner, D. (1990) *Television and the Crisis of Democracy*. Boulder, CO: Westview Press.

Mathias, G. (1993) 'Competing with Impartiality', *British Journalism Review* 4(1).

McChesney, R. (1993) *Telecommunications, Mass Media and Democracy: The Battle for the Control of U.S. Broadcasting, 1928–1935*. New York and Oxford: Oxford University Press.

Milne, A. (1988) *DG: The Memoirs of a British Broadcaster*. London: Hodder and Stoughton.

Negt, O. and A. Kluge (1993) *The Public Sphere and Experience: Analyses of the Bourgeois and Proletarian Public Spheres*, trans. by P. Labanyi et al. Minneapolis: University of Minnesota Press.

Owen, J. (1996) 'Crisis or Renewal? The Origins, Evolution and Future of Public Service Broadcasting 1922–1996; unpublished doctoral dissertation, University of Westminister, London

Perkin, H. (1989) *The Rise of Professional Society: England since 1880*. London: Routledge.

Philo, G. and J. Hewitt et al. (1982) *Really Bad News*. London: Writers and Readers Publishing Cooperative.

Public Culture (1994), 7(1). Special Issue on the Black Public Sphere.

Ramberg, B. (1986) 'The Supreme Court and Public Interest in Broadcasting', *Communications and the Law*, 8(6): 11–30.

Ray, W. B. (1990) *FCC: The Ups and Downs of Radio–TV Regulation*. Ames: Iowa State University Press.

Rowan, F. (1984) *Broadcast Fairness. Doctrine, Practice, Prospects*. New York and London: Longman.

Scannell, P. (1989a) 'Public Service Broadcasting and Modern Public Life', *Media Culture & Society*, 11: 135–66.

Scannell, P. (1989b) 'Public Service Broadcasting: The History of a Concept', in A. Goodwin and G. Whannel (eds) *Understanding Television*. London: Routledge.

Scannell, P. and D. Cardiff (1991) *A Social History of British Broadcasting*, Volume 1: *1922–1939: Serving the Nation*. Oxford: Blackwell.

Schiller, H. (1996) *Information Inequality. The Deepening Social Crisis in America*. New York and London: Routledge.

Smith, A. (ed.) (1974) *British Broadcasting*. Newton Abbot: David and Charles.

Smith, A. (1993) 'Public Service Broadcasting Meets the Social Market', *Books to Bytes. Knowledge and Information in the Postmodern Era*. London: British Film Institute.

Stein, L. (1996) 'The Battle over the Fairness Doctrine: Deregulation and the Shifting Balance of Power in the Regulatory Process', unpublished paper, Radio–Television–Film Department, University of Texas at Austin.

Thomas, R. M. (1978) *The British Philosophy of Administration: A Comparison of British and American Ideas 1900–1939*. London and New York: Longman.

Willis, J. (1993) 'Vague Sense of Unease', *The Guardian* 25 January.

Wilson, V. (ed.) (1967) *The Book of Great American Documents*, Brookeville, MD: American History Research Associates

Wyatt, Lord (1990) Speech, col. 369, *Hansard, House of Lords*, 11 July. London: HMSO.

Chapter 8

TV Viewing as Good Citizenship? Political Rationality, Enlightened Democracy and PBS

Laurie Ouellette

The 'Media and Democracy' Debate

As Stanley Aronowitz argues, twentieth-century American democratic ideals are rooted in the contradictory ideas of Thomas Jefferson and John Dewey. According to Jefferson, democracy required a universal public education system designed to effectively train the franchised populace for proper citizenship. Dewey, on the other hand, believed that the roots of democracy were in the face-to-face interactions of the agrarian town hall. Both visions were thought to be seriously compromised by industrialization, urbanization and the growth of consumer culture and mass media (Aronowitz, 1993: 75–83) – shifts that, as John and Barbara Ehrenreich (1979) argue, coincided with the rise of a professional-managerial class (PMC) in the US. According to their account, the concentration of wealth in the late 1880s could accommodate and indeed required an expanded class of managers, technocrats and professionals to run corporations and state bureaucracies, produce and circulate legitimate knowledge, mediate the conflicts between capital and labour and produce a 'rational, reproducible social order'. The PMC assisted with the rationalization of industrial capitalism and the promotion of a national consumer culture – but it also produced fierce objections to some of the 'degenerative' symptoms of these transformations (Ehrenreich and Ehrenreich, 1979: 9–14).

Out of the PMC, progressive reformers emerged seeking to soften the harshest blows of monopoly capitalism, counter the seductive appeal of mass amusements and bring order to a nation that had outgrown its previous system of 'loose laws and regulations' (Ehrenreich and Ehrenreich, 1979; Jowett, 1982: 218). When the surplus accumulated by industrial capitalists (Carnegie, Rockefeller) became a 'force for the regulation and management of civil society' and the expansion of the public sector, the PMC carried out the management of these operations, note the Ehrenreichs (1979: 15). PMC reformers believed that with the 'careful and logical application of scientific principles to the management of government they could bring about opportunity, progress, order and community' (Jowett, 1982: 212). Their aims were often contradictory, in that they hoped to uplift the immigrant working class through rational science and create a 'progressive version of the old community ideal' of *gemeinschaft*, but they hinged on the ideals (rationality, objectivity) that legitimated the PMC's authority (Ehrenreich and Ehrenreich, 1979: 17; Jowett, 1982: 212). In this sense, the PMC was pivotal to the 'show and tell' mode of governing which Bennett describes (1995: 98). Its call for public service culture as an alternative to mass amusements, for example, can be seen as a move to fuse citizenship with self-shaping strategies. As John Kasson argues, the progressive demand for rational recreation was fuelled by hopes that under 'enlightened municipal auspices' and expert supervision, culture could be deployed as a more 'constructive force in social integration and moral development'. The impetus was not to democratize public access to cultural resources, but to train citizens loyal to a particular model of democracy. 'Safe and sane Fourth of July celebrations would rekindle a sense of common faith', public parks would instil 'habits of discipline and cooperation' in the unruly poor and community centres would 'supplant poolrooms and saloons as agents in the acculturation of recent immigrants' (Kasson, 1978: 101–2).

A related logic can be seen operating in the 'media and democracy' debate as articulated within social science and broadcast reform discourse. Here again, the rational thinking, expertise and cultural guidance of the PMC were considered essential to the smooth operation of democracy. By the early 1920s, Walter Lippmann was arguing that the banalities, fragmentations and distortions of modern life had subverted the basis of popular democracy (Aronowitz, 1993: 80). In his classic work *Public Opinion* (1922), Lippmann called for a bureaucracy of 'objective' experts who could restore reason to politics, thus relieving the mass public from the 'impossible' task of forming a competent opinion. Cultural reformers, on the other hand, pushed for public service alternatives to commercial radio that could transform the masses into better, more discriminating citizens – although many also believed that 'quality' programmes would be lost on the 'moronic mob' (McChesney, 1994: 95–6). Like the promise of democratic education for all noted by Bennett, the early critics of radio hinged their discontents on the claim that a potentially uplifting mass medium had fallen into the hands of capitalist barbarians ill suited to such a task (Douglas, 1987: 313). By the early 1930s, 'educational radio' had become the leading rationale for reform because, in the words of Joy Elmer Morgan of the National Committee on Education by Radio, the majority of listeners would find themselves 'entrapped in a paradise of medioc-

rities' without the 'guidance of an educated minority' (quoted in Rubin, 1992: 272). Morgan also saw educational radio as a solution to unemployment and a safeguard against the collapse of civilization (Hoke, 1932). While major reform was blunted by corporate lobbying campaigns and a lack of popular support, professional educators did eventually secure limited space on the ether, whereas labour unions and other 'special interest' groups were denied direct access (McChesney, 1994). The 'enlightenment' priorities of PBS can be traced to this precedent.

The dismal ratings of the public service programming that was broadcast on commercial radio (and later television) were often cited by network executives as evidence that the masses preferred entertainment to public affairs (Sarnoff, 1955; see also Boddy, 1990). This rationale obscured the contradictions that eventually necessitated PBS as well as the class coding of 'serious' alternatives. The suggestion that commercial television was a 'cultural democracy' gave credence to reform arguments calling for the preservation of political democracy with educational channels – but it also cast doubt on their ability to instil better habits and 'choices' in the mass citizenry. Paul Lazarsfeld and his colleagues at the Bureau of Applied Social Research solved this dilemma by rationalizing the paradox of the enlightenment rationale. Since the 1940s, the researchers had reported with dismay that college-educated professionals were the core audience for public affairs programming. In the influential *Personal Influence* study, they explained this skew with the concept of the 'two-step flow', proposing that information trickles down from 'experts who can be trusted to know what is really going on' to the 'less active sections of the population' (Katz and Lazarsfeld, 1955: 276). Males with college degrees were said to be the nation's 'opinion leaders', while public affairs leadership among women was said to increase 'with each step up the status ladder'. While more than half the wage earners surveyed reported turning to their peers for guidance on political matters, only 6 per cent of business leaders and professionals reported seeking advice from wage earners. To explain this lopsided exchange, the researchers proposed 'vertical influence'. The assumption was that ideas flowed from 'primary influentials' to certain wage earners, who then became 'informed' opinion leaders in their communities. The prospect of working-class autonomy was negated with the assertion that 'primary opinion shapers' were the males of the 'higher strata' who read more newspapers and magazines and 'possessed education and social prestige' (Katz and Lazarsfeld, 1955: 273, 285–6). With this theory, the researchers were able to reaffirm the liberal pluralist logic that oriented US media research (Hall, 1982).

The concept of the two-step flow obscured the relationship between class, cultural capital and the consumption of socially legitimated public affairs, representing the males of the PMC as model citizens and natural leaders. It also figured in reform discourse, in that programming oriented to an educated habitus, in Bourdieu's formulation (1984), was considered a national priority. By the 1950s, television had been installed in living rooms, the cold war was escalating and the decline of citizenship was regarded as a pressing problem. While some critics scorned early experiments in televised debates and panel discussions, believing that the new medium posed an inherent threat to democracy because it catered to 'popularity and emotion' over 'intelligence and reason' (Cherne, 1952: 14), others saw a chance to cultivate 'first class educational citizenship' (Hunter, 1961: 19). But commercial television, like radio, developed as an advertising-sponsored entertainment medium designed to pitch consumer goods to the widest possible audience. Under the banner of public service, reformers soon mobilized to create an educational alternative. Private benefactors like the Ford Foundation invested millions in the ETV infrastructure with the purpose of combating political apathy and a perceived lack of a 'realistic and meaningful sense of values' in the public (Ford, 1980: 2). Appalled by the 'vast wasteland', FCC Chairman Newton Minow was also a vocal supporter. Noting that the Russians and Chinese were using television to 'educate as well as propagandize', he promoted ETV as a way to bring 'to a mass audience the knowledge needed to keep our society growing, the cultural heritage to keep our society rich, and the information needed by our citizens to keep our society free' (Minow, 1962: 9). Quoting Aristotle, the manager of a local ETV station expressed this goal in more apocalyptic terms, arguing that in a democracy it was 'particularly necessary for people

to be educated and informed,' because if they were not 'their bad judgments would plunge the state into disaster' (Schwarzwalder, 1959: 9).

By the 1960s, the enlightenment rationale for broadcasting reform was joined by a focus on the unmet informational requirements of opinion leaders. TV critics, reformers, social scientists and policy-makers believed that the college-educated 'minority' was especially poorly served by commercial television's lowest common denominator approach, particularly in the area of public affairs. Many believed an expanded, nationalized ETV system was needed to get vital information to such people ('A Panel', 1966). The skewed allocation of resources inherent to this focus was rationalized by the trickle-down benefits of the two-step flow. Harold Lasswell called for 'civil enlightenment' at a level of discourse that presumed a 'common audience framework of knowledge to which it is possible to add information and interpretive detail' (Lasswell, 1962: 102). The audience of informed opinion leaders envisioned by Lasswell was confirmed by Wilbur Schramm's (1963) social scientific study of the ETV audience. Rather than uplifitng the masses, ETV was found to attract already influential and educated people. ETV viewers were better informed and more apt to read 'better' newspapers and 'talk and think about the news more'. They were also more active in professional, political and PTA organizations. Schramm attributed these findings to the 'strong achievement norm' shared by ETV viewers, an explanation that represented the model citizenship of the PMC as emanating from its greater self-discipline, intelligence and leadership skills. Still, the results of a current events quiz administered with the study suggested that the underfunded, localized ETV stations were not fully informing the nation's opinion leaders. As Schramm reported, it was 'easy to be shocked that two-thirds of our WGBH viewers had forgotten who Robert Oppenheimer was, if they ever knew' (Schramm et al., 1963: 67–70).

The cancellation of network public affairs programmes such as Edward R. Murrow's See It Now coupled with perceptions of declining news standards and programme mediocrity in commercial television sparked demands for federal intervention. This moment marked the beginning of what Daniel Hallin describes as the decline of 'high modernism' in commercial television's journalism (1994). As James Baughman argues, it also signalled a crack in liberal 'idealism about the possibilities of the American system of broadcasting', which once expected capitalist owners to serve a mass market *and* a higher mission, or 'to be good entrepreneurs and good citizens' (1985: 173). While critics confused quality with their own educated tastes, their argument hinged on the alternating claims that commercial television was failing to produce an informed citizenry, and that the mass public had chosen triviality and 'instant gratification' to the detriment of the nation's opinion leaders (see e.g. Robinson, 1960; 'Public Taste', 1961; Ratner, 1969). The expertise and cultural guidance of the intelligentsia were seen as pivotal to the correction of these dilemmas. At a summit to discuss the problem of mass culture, former Kennedy adviser Arthur Schlesinger argued that it was the duty of the government to 'rescue' television because 'soap opera and give-away' shows make more money for the stockholders than 'news and Shakespeare' (1961: 149). Conceding that 'if horse opera sells more autos than Ed Murrow then the advertiser has to go for horse opera', the editor of *Harper's* magazine called for a tax on private broadcasters to fund a public service-oriented National Broadcasting Authority. Run by a board of directors that 'might include the president of Harvard, the heads of the Carnegie and Rockefeller foundations, and the director of the Metropolitan Museum', it would produce in-depth news, top-quality music and theatre, documentaries, the arts and public affairs. Under the arrangement, which drew praise from governmental officials, civic leaders and the mass culture critic David Reisman, the viewer who was 'not interested' in better television could simply turn to a western on CBS or a song-and-dance number on ABC (Fischer, 1959).

The revelation of quiz show fraud in the late 1950s gave reform discourse additional credibility. While the scandal placed commercial television's profit motives in the spotlight, the 'TV problem' was defined as a matter of discipline and taste, producing a cultural template for enlightened democracy on PBS. A classic example was Walter Lippmann's declaration: 'there is something radically wrong with the fundamental national policy under which television operates.'

Writing in his *New York Herald Tribune* column, Lippmann cast commercial television as a 'prostitute of merchandising', but his main complaint was that a 'superb scientific achievement' had been misused at the cost of 'effective news reporting, good art, and civilized entertainment'. Conceding that the best way to produce wealth was through private enterprise, he argued that the reverse was true for ideas, and proposed that the people at 'Harvard and Yale and Princeton and Columbia and Dartmouth' find a way to run a public service network that would show 'not what was popular but what was good'. Presuming the network would not be popular, he argued: 'it might well attract an audience that made up in influence what it lacked in numbers' (1959: 26).

In his memoir (1967), Fred Friendly, the former president of CBS News who resigned when his network broadcast a rerun of *I Love Lucy* over hearings on the Vietnam war, articulated the TV problem through a more politicized, but no less hierarchical framework. Friendly did not question television's relationship to the consumer economy but he did attribute commercials and ratings for the decline of 'first-rate' news and public affairs. Friendly became a consultant to the Ford Foundation, and with its president, former National Security Adviser McGeorge Bundy, he advocated a fully-fledged public service system to operate in opposition to both principles. Under Friendly's guidance, Ford remained a benefactor in the transition from ETV to PBS and helped fund early programmes, including *The Advocates*. By this point, the rationale for producing a 'better public' via television was bound up with a call to reach out to unruly and disenfranchised citizens. The uprisings of the era, coupled with worries that 'earlier American achievements in community-building' had been overrun by the automobile (Heckscher, 1968: 127–8), positioned PBS as a way to restore participatory democracy. This discourse promised gains for marginalized citizens – but its political rationality was rooted in an effort to restore social control by channelling dissent into legitimate behaviours and official channels.

In the minds of reformers, participation hinged on enlightenment and ongoing guidance – conditions that required PMC leadership. When the Report of the National Advisory Commission on Civil Disorders reported that the typical ghetto rioter was a high school drop-out ('Breeding', 1968: 66), this became para-mount. With Ford's support, influential business and cultural leaders formed the National Citizens for Public Television, taking solving the 'nation's racial ills' as a priority (National Citizens, 1968). This was not a call for the reallocation of cultural resources. Within policy discourse it was explicitly linked to citizen training strategies. According to US Commissioner of Education Howard Howe, the goal was to provide the sort of education that would prevent America's 'market places from becoming riot places' (1967: 13). With 'patient counseling and advice', explained liberal Senator Hubert Humphrey, helpless and disenfranchised groups could be moved 'into the mainstream of American life' (1966: 49). In an influential report, the Carnegie Commission summed up this reform logic succinctly, calling on public television to be a 'civilized voice in a civilized community' (1967: 18).

As the Ehrenreichs note, the upsurge of middle-class activism in the late 1960s challenged the traditional leadership role of the PMC. PBS was also perceived as a way to return student and anti-war protesters to reason and official procedures for expressing and remedying grievances. This aim was governmental rather than hegemonic, in that its purpose was to instil a logic of good citizenship that suited the capitalist state. As one supporter stated, public television's purpose was not to promote any particular ideology, but to make sure that 'those who govern will respond to fair and reasonable arguments' and 'those who are governed will respect the authority of the government and limit their protests to ways that do not wreck society' (Blakely, 1969: 57). Transforming 'discontents into proposals', 'high-decibel talk into high level discourse' and 'problems and issues into orderly procedures', it would revitalize the decision-making process (Blakely, 1969: 175).

Opinion Leaders and PBS

PBS began operating in 1969 as the most visible entity of the national public television bureaucracy. In a 1970 speech before the National Press Club, John W. Macy, President of the Corporation for Public Broadcasting (CPB), articulated

the new service's public affairs priorities. These included: (1) providing an alternative to the 'sensationalist' and 'distorted' news that commercial television was locked into due to its pursuit of ratings; (2) returning the public to the idea that through rational debate reasonable men could work to solve public issues; and (3) providing the viewer citizen with an opportunity for making judgements and opinions known on these issues. The move to create an electronic public sphere where citizens could look, learn and actively participate in proscribed ways was bound up in the corporate rationalization of the 'TV problem', the visibility of protesting in the network news and the need to differentiate and socialize opinion leaders. It was envisioned as a cultural corrective, not a cultural transformation. As Macy (1970: 286–8) explained,

> none of this should be interpreted as criticism of the commercial networks or stations. By and large, they are doing – and doing very well indeed – what they must do under a system which measures survival and success in terms of mass-audience ratings that respond more to the stimulus of entertainment and excitement than to information.

The representation of commercial television as the consequence of audience demands for emotion, triviality, distortion and conflict – and the positioning of PBS as a cultural technology to reform these desires – fostered an emphasis on subdued aesthetics and educated ways of thinking and behaving. This meant that the public interest value of PBS was defined against the perils of unenlightened participation and popular reception. Most of the public affairs formats developed emphasized reason over passion, professionalism over advocacy, tedium over drama, expert over personality, civility over rudeness and officialdom over human interest and dramatic events. The view that 'too zealous an intent to entertain can lead to the falsification of what should be presented as unadorned as possible' (Blakely, 1969: 115) led to an emphasis on 'cross-talk' programmes based on print-oriented prototypes like *Newspaper of the Air* and *Newsroom*. These Ford-funded local ETV programmes were developed to offer serious alternatives to the 'trivial and meaningless' stories presented by 'plastic, deep-voiced readers of another's copy'. Featuring lengthy news reports and commentary from print journalists, and little visual or human interest material, *Newsroom* was 'an oasis of news in a television desert' distinguished by the adjectives 'authoritative', 'serious' and 'professional'. While its purpose was to 'provide the kind of coverage not available elsewhere' for all television viewers, an audience study turned up a rating of less than 1 per cent in every city surveyed. According to researchers, the programme was 'too written' and demanding for the average person to follow (CPB, 1969; Ford, 1970).

When the National Public Affairs Center for Television (NPACT) was created to produce programmes for PBS, it also stressed cross-talk formats like *Washington Week in Review*, a national version of *Newsroom* which focused on the doings of the Washington Beltway. NPACT's *A Public Affair*, intended to counterpose commercial television's horse-race approach to electoral politics, was similarly 'long on interviews, filled with visiting experts, marked by discussions', observed the *Washington Post* (Laruent, 1972: n.p.). In a democracy the 'quality of information you consume' is at least as important as the 'quality of the automobile you buy', said correspondent Robert MacNeil of its distinction (quoted in 'Public Television', 1973: E653). That the viewership for NPACT programming was 'of course, small' was officially explained by displacing class differences on to differences in 'selectivity' and the motivation to seek out quality information and analysis. The gap between public and commercial television mirrored that between ordinary daily newspapers and the 'selective, focused journalism provided by the *Wall Street Journal*', explained NPACT President Jim Karayn. The gendered dimensions of the parallel were acknowledged when Karayn proposed that the loss of public affairs on PBS would mean a 'castrated system' (Karayn, 1972: n.p.).

Within the public television bureaucracy, discussions of the audience drew from the logic of the two-step flow. The PMC was seen as the natural viewership on the basis of its governing abilities, exemplary citizenship and discriminating tastes. Before Nixon accused public television of liberal elitism, supporters were arguing that public television must develop constituencies that would provide strong financial, political, social, intellectual and moral support

(Blakely, 1969: 123). There was, however, also an institutional imperative to bring 'others' into the audience, especially when the news media began reporting PBS's minuscule ratings and that most people perceived the service as one for the higher educated segment of the population. But the political rationality that gave rise to PBS meant that the impetus to gear programming to the habitus of the PMC could not be questioned. Thus, the promise of democratic enlightenment for all existed in perpetual tension with a move to differentiate television viewers according to knowledge–power relations. Articulating the latter purpose, an unpublished study of the public television audience commissioned by Ford argued that

> The commercial networks aim primarily for the blue-collar class, and are grateful for white-collar viewers. Blue-collar households prefer the sitcoms and action series that are the staple of commercial television. The skew toward the better educated is a strength, not a weakness... if the skews were toward middle and lower-income, public broadcasting would be competing directly with the three large networks, who are already adequately serving those groups. Public television has to be an effective way to reach opinion leaders. (Statistical Research, 1974: 15)

Governmentality and Social Control

Beyond the creation of an informed citizenry, Macy also presented expanded opportunities for citizen involvement in the democratic process as a public affairs priority. However, such gains were contingent on discursive requirements and behavioural rules considered essential to enlightened democracy but threatened by the 'vast wasteland'. PBS was called on to manage the contradictory requirements of the consumer culture and the state theorized by Miller – which meant reconstituting citizen subjects loyal to a particular form of dialogue (1993: 136). The impetus to return television viewers to rational debate drew from the discourse of the Enlightenment, which saw reasoned deliberation as the foundation of Western democracy. While reason has historically been associated with educated white men and the written word, traits said to be irrational (such as emotion) have been associated with popular culture, including television, and are thought to be the legacy of women and the lower classes. The importance of 'unfiltered' objectivity on PBS as a counterpoint to 1960s demands for 'group access' to television and the 'maze of complexities' (the Fairness Doctrine, the Equal Time Provision) they produced for commercial broadcasters (Blakely, 1969: 165) drew on the claim that only professional experts were equipped to distinguish reality from the distortions that troubled Lippmann. However, as Michael Schudson argues, objectivity is not just a claim about what kind of knowledge is reliable. It is 'also a moral philosophy, a declaration of what kind of thinking one should engage in' as well as a logic that insulates and rationalizes professional authority, which can then serve as a mode of social control (Schudson, 1978: 7–8).

The promotion of rational thinking on PBS was more than an effort to enlist viewers in the productive, non-violent resolution of conflicts. It was also a cultural template for proper citizenship that hinged on knowledge–power relations that excluded emotionally and bodily-invested political participation, such as women's consciousness-raising groups, boisterous union meetings and bar-room debates, consumer boycotts and mass protests. The requirement of civility worked in complementary ways. As Kasson argues, the 'established codes of behavior' ascribed to civility have historically functioned as a social classification system 'against a fully democratic order and in support of special interests, institutions of privilege, and structures of domination' (1990: 3). The idealization of public television as a Habermasian public sphere orienting critical defences does not problematize its rules of conduct – rules that were ascribed to PBS at the historical moment when commercial television was thought to have undermined political democracy. The differentiation of opinion leaders was also a way to make proper citizenship – cerebral discussions of state affairs, calm and guided deliberation, voting – visible. Participation in these processes hinged on decorum, in terms of who could appear on the programmes and how they addressed viewers at home. Drawing from the work of Peter Stallybrass and Allon White (1986), Bennett (1995: 27) traces similar proscriptions to the exclusion of codes of behaviour associated with fairs and other places of popular assembly:

> No swearing, no spitting, no brawling, no eating or drinking, no dirty footwear, no gambling: These rules which, with variations, characterized literary and debating societies, museums and coffee houses, also, as Stallybrass and White put it, 'formed part of an overall strategy of explusion' which clears a space for polite, cosmopolitan discourses by the construction of popular culture as the 'low-Other,' the dirty and crude outside to the emergent public sphere.

For most television viewers, adopting the subject position of a good citizen as constructed by PBS meant accepting an aesthetic and political order governed by a higher authority. It required either access or acquiescence to communicative 'codes' (Aronowitz, 1993: 90) rooted in the education, cultural capital and social habitus of the PMC. This requirement functioned as a form of social control, promoting the idea that 'action without knowledge and understanding, sooner or later, is wrong action' (Blakely, 1969: 90–3). While hegemony theory has illuminated how the conflicts of the late 1960s were negotiated and partially recuperated by commercial television (Gitlin, 1980; Spigel and Curtin, 1997), which had an economic motive to 'win' popularity, PBS's response was governmental in the Foucauldian sense. This is especially evident in the simulated and live official government activities that were broadcast. Based on ETV prototypes that televised students role-playing state procedures, these initiatives functioned as a display of official power. These initiatives were less about holding politicians accountable to the mass citizenry than about affirming the rationality of the existing decision-making process.

Live coverage of Congressional activities like the Senate Foreign Relations Committee's hearings on the resumption of bombing in North Vietnam was perceived not as an expansion of democracy, but as citizen education. The purpose, said Macy, was to demonstrate that 'laws are not made in a vacuum' and that those 'responsible for making them must consider many factors before recording a vote' (1970: 286). The purpose of NPACT's 'gavel-to-gavel' coverage of the 1972 Republican convention was to counter the 'stage-managed circus atmosphere' of commercial news by 'focusing exclusively on official business'. While commercial television played up the protesting but framed it as youthful deviance (Gitlin, 1980), PBS could not recuperate dissent in a similar way. The mandate to produce a 'better' and more enlightened public could not justify dwelling on civil disobedience. Conceding that 'nobody pretends this will be the most exciting program' on TV, a PBS spokesperson explained that if 'Gerry Ford is giving a very dull speech and a riot is going on outside, we will stay with Gerry Ford' ('Farewell', 1972: 61).

PBS formats based on the electronic simulation of the New England town hall were rooted in the democratic ideals championed by Dewey. However, they were also perceived institutionally as mechanisms for instilling active citizenship in the interests of the capitalist state. The formats were promoted as a way to restore community cooperation lost massification of society, but there was also concern about the 'kind of training' that was necessary to prepare television viewers for such roles. The solution proposed by one consultant was to balance the invitation for all 'citizens to exercise intelligent decision making' with an emphasis on 'the leadership segment of society', to ensure the quality of the town halls and their outcomes (Kettering, 1969: 35). That the PMC would mediate the initiatives went without saying. Referencing a situation at WJCT-TV in Jacksonville, Mississippi, where the public affiliate managed a potentially antagonistic encounter by placing some citizens in an expensive club and others in a community hall in a poor district while the 'experts held forth in the studio', Macy naturalized the power dynamics of this arrangement with the promise – rooted in the historical reforms of the PMC – of smooth reconciliation. Confrontations, he explained, do not 'lead to action' (1970: 286).

National town halls broadcast on PBS spoke of a similar tension between participatory democracy and social control. Co-funded by the CPB, government agencies and corporations, these initiatives, which were extensively publicized and encompassed programming as well as telephone advice hotlines, community outreach, study guides and the appearance of 'countless authorities', addressed the problem of deviant and disenfranchised citizens – particularly the student counterculture and the urban poor. While progressive in some respects, they were also a move to reform behaviours deemed degenerative or amoral by coupling 'problem-solving' with self-shaping rehabilitation strategies. The discursive framing of the ventures suggests how they sought to make power visible. For example, *The Turned On Crisis* was billed as an effort to 'detect, educate and rehabilitate drug users' funded in part by the National Institute of Mental Health. *VD Blues*, hailed as 'one of the most significant events in the history of television as a medium for education, enlightenment, and raised consciousness' (Resnik, 1972: 33), exposed the medical consequences of the 1960s sexual revolution, prompting a rush of visits to clinics, according to PBS publicity.

The Advocates: TV Viewing as Good Citizenship?

Not all PBS public affairs programmes were wedded to a model of enlightened democracy. The nod towards cultural pluralism demanded by the tensions of the era created space for innovative but marginalized alternatives. *Black Journal*, one of the few PBS programmes to feature black critics and journalists, subverted the philosophy outlined by Macy by collapsing its regulated boundaries (high versus low, reason versus emotion, politics versus pleasure) and by presenting 'experts' as representatives of popular movements who were invested in their outcome. Envisioned as a way to 'bring television back to the people' rather than citizen training, it featured discussions among reporters, professors, celebrities and leaders of the Black Panthers and the All-African People's Revolutionary Party as well as music and cultural performances. It refused the decorum of most PBS public affairs programmes and challenged their definition of legitimate knowledge by setting up call-in opportunities for viewers at home and featuring a black clairvoyant named Lillian Cosby, who successfully predicted the Nixon resignation. As one critic observed, the difficulty was that *Black Journal* appeared on PBS, because its aura was a barrier to attracting a large black following (Gray, 1972). Still, the programme's transgressions were duly noted by the guardians of enlightened democracy, defined not as ideological deviance but as a failure of conduct and control. According to the *New York Times*, the problem with *Black Journal* was that it opted for 'fast pace' and 'bridges of song' over reason and objective reporting (Gould, 1970: n.p.).

Within PBS publicity, *Black Journal* was positioned as evidence of cultural pluralism as opposed to a model of citizenship. The flagship public affairs programme, and the clearest example of the philosophy of 'enlightened democracy', was *The Advocates*, which debuted in 1969 with the goal of recasting 'the passive TV viewer in an active role, working and voting to make democracy a reality'. Created by a Harvard law professor and co-funded by Ford and the CPB, the weekly debate epitomized the move to return reason to America's living-rooms by 'combining the vivid communication of television with the cool analytical power of experts'. The advocates, who were also lawyers, made their cases by calling witnesses and advancing arguments in a 'logical, orderly fashion'. Their presentations and cross-examinations culminated in a studio audience vote and the judgement of a 'decision-maker', usually a public official involved in the issue. Later episodes extended the final decision to viewers at home, whose votes were tallied and sent to Congress and other governmental agencies. For this service to democracy, PBS drew bipartisan praise from scores of commentators and the *Congressional Record*. While described as the closest television had come to a contribution to participatory democracy, the mail-in vote was the only participation offered. Similar to other PBS public affairs offerings, the purpose was to differentiate opinion leaders and demonstrate the ins and outs of proper citizenship.

The Advocates took up controversial issues ranging from the withdrawal of troops in Vietnam to school desegregation to whether to impeach Richard Nixon. But its governmental aim was to display legitimate ways to express and resolve conflicts. The intention was not to 'wade through the muck and mire of the past, viewing with alarm and advising us all to understand the social, political and economic forces that contributed to the mess.' It was to empower citizens to 'do something' about problems. This invitation was guided and controlled by the model of democracy constructed by the programme. According to *The Advocates*, this meant that there were only two positions on any issue, that experts were best equipped to define the issues, that both sides were equally defensible within the rational debate format, that mass participation was limited to the ritual of voting and that consensus could be achieved within the existing institutions of self-government. The programme's long and medium shots, lengthy unedited sequences, harsh lighting and minimal use of visuals constructed an educational aesthetic, relaying the idea that democracy was both a lesson and a solemn affair above the social world of popular culture and its audience.

The emphasis on rational science conveyed a similar message in a different way. The fairness of the debate format was stressed above the significance of any given issue, and the professional orchestration of balance was emphasized over the rightness or wrongness of the positions offered. PBS insisted that the 'two committed halves equal one balanced whole', a message that was emblematized by the programme's logo, which featured arrows pointed in opposite directions coming together as a unified symbol. On the one hand, the focus on rational debate among amiable opponents was a way to please funders (such as Congress) concerned with balance. But, similar to the dissonance between addressing an 'undifferentiated public of political equals' and screening out behaviours associated with popular assemblies which Bennett observes of the museum (1995: 90), it also facilitated the 'self-display' of bourgeois democracy and screened out 'unenlightened' popular participation. *The Advocates* epitomized the call for PBS to balance 'understanding and skills' with the upsurge of angry citizens who were demanding a 'piece of the action', the 'right to have a say', a share of the 'power' (Blakely, 1969: 171).

It was assumed, in the representation of 'balance', that everyone who appeared on the programme possessed the training and pedigree to articulate a position. According to PBS, it was essential to have professional advocates, because 'commitment alone may lead to gross errors of judgment'. Class differences were obscured by defining preferred dispositions as essentially democratic. The most important qualification for being an advocate was the disposition to avoid 'the temptation of making a highly emotional but fallacious argument'. To prevent this, the advocate was to present 'not his personal opinion, but responsible arguments for each side of the case'. On the first season they took arbitrary positions, and liberals often ended up 'playing' conservatives. In later episodes it was assumed that the advocates would be committed but able to adhere to requirements of professionalism and decorum. The two who appeared most regularly were Howard Miller, a University of Chicago law school graduate who was said to balance his arguments with 'lessons in philosophy, history, and the morality of Western man', and Harvard Law School graduate William Rushner, a former Wall Street lawyer and publisher of the *National Review*. While they 'disagreed about the issues', the men described themselves as close friends who shared a commitment to a process of dealing with conflicts. It was the televised display of this *process*, not the content of the debates or their role in informing the public, that defined the programme's governmental logic. As Rushner explained,

> I think our common ground comes mostly in having the same kind of job to do and the same kind of attitude towards it. I've said to people who've asked whether I get along with Howard, that I do. The reason is, we have a great many more things in common, in terms of the problems we face, than we have separating us ... remember we're both trained lawyers, and lawyers tend to think in much the same way. So even if we have different or diametrically opposed points of view on a topic, the way we will go about 'slicing up' the topic and analyzing it will be a lawyer's way. ... For two men, speaking calmly and intelligently, to disagree profoundly about an issue may be polarization; but to have people yelling 'pig!' at each other, or shouting 'burn, baby, burn!' is a different kind of polarization – it is non-communicative polarization. I don't think *The Advocates* contributes to it; I think quite the reverse. ('Advocates', 1971: n.p.)

Suggesting how the aim described by Rushner may have been perceived by the PBS audience, one viewer sent the following comment: 'this is the best one I have ever seen and it was so fair and dignified that at the end I liked the lawyers and witnesses for both sides equally well and could have voted either way.'

The individuals who 'put such a show together' included a roster of journalists, lawyers and political scientists that would have pleased Lippmann. The people who appeared as moderators, decision-makers and witnesses also formed a 'guest list that reads like Who's Who'. The primary moderator, Victor Palmieri, was the president of an investment company who had served as deputy executive director of Lyndon Johnson's National Advisory Commission on Urban Problems, commonly known as the Riot Commission. Nearly everyone who testified as a witness was college educated, often male and frequently a government official, politician, author, professor or other type of professional ('top men, well informed', said *Daily Variety*). The studio audience, which was not permitted to question or comment, was also almost exclusively white and middle class. If this was not the case, audience members were required to accept middle-class dress codes and rules of appropriate behaviour, such as 'behaving with reasonable calm' and avoiding heckling. On the few occasions when people outside of these categories were invited to play a role, they were positioned by the logic of the programme in ways that undermined their knowledge and credibility. For example, in an episode about the Princeton Plan, a proposal to allow students time off from school to volunteer for electoral campaigns, a construction worker was called to testify as a 'hard hat' with 'no particular purpose except he was against special favors to college kids'.

Working-class guests who appeared on *The Advocates* were also a source of fodder in the popular press. In an episode dealing with a welfare reform bill, a San Francisco fish worker was called to testify that he earned less from his job than mothers who received welfare, and took the opportunity to elaborate on his views beyond the proscribed line of questioning. Later in the programme, a welfare mother who was in the studio audience shouted out opinions and stormed out of the building in protest. Contrary to the enthusiastic press coverage *The Advocates* generally received, the TV critic for the *Boston Globe* reported that the welfare episode was 'not particularly illuminating'. He conceded it provided 'some laughs' when a 'belligerent witness told how he felt in earthy terms, including a swear word here and there' and a woman became unruly and 'shouted epithets that reached the microphone', but 'the cause of enlightenment wasn't served much until an assistant secretary of labor ... showed up near the end and explained the provisions and implications of the measure in voluminous detail' (Shain, 1969: n.p.).

While the testimony of people with lived knowledge directly relevant to the legislation was discredited as uncivilized and unenlightened, the Congressman who served as the decision-maker was praised for his efforts in welfare reform, which included 'simulating' the lifestyle of welfare recipients to see if changes in the system were justified. Quoting a PBS publicity item, many TV critics who reviewed the episode noted that the Democrat and his wife 'ate for a week on foods available for the welfare-budget of 66 cents per day and found that with ingenuity a healthful menu was possible'. Qualifying this finding with another PBS quote, they explained that of course, 'Mrs. Bingham is a nutrition expert with knowledge unknown to the majority of the welfare recipients'. The knowledge–power relations set up by *The Advocates* divorced politics from the experiences and emotions of subordinated classes – and in so doing cast democracy as a high affair properly managed by professionals.

According to the Ehrenreichs, the middle-class radicalism of the late 1960s signalled a crisis for the capitalist state at the point when students began questioning their privilege and authority and identifying with the adversary positions of the black revolutionary movements and, eventually, the economic conditions of the white working class. *The Advocates* spoke to this crisis in an attempt to return campus activists to rational debate as the proper way to handle disputes, and an effort to instil dispositions and behaviours suitable for opinion leaders. PBS encouraged local stations to actively promote the programme on campuses, seeking out 'student representatives' who could help build an audience by word of mouth. Issues that were of interest to student protesters, such as Vietnam, amnesty for draft dodgers and FBI surveillance of the New Left were debated, and students were often called to testify on these episodes. The legalization of countercultural activities like marijuana smoking was also debated, as was the institutionalization of legitimate opportunities for political participation epitomized by the Princeton Plan. There were counterhegemonic gains, in that the outcomes of the debates sometimes challenged government policies, but the knowledge–power relations embedded in the

format of the programme reconstituted dissent as professional reform logic. For example, following the debate on Vietnam culminating in a decision to withdraw US troops, PBS issued a press release suggesting that the public opinion produced in a reasoned, orderly way on *The Advocates* was credible – which implied that the unruly demands of the anti-war movement were not.

A similar effacement of agency was evidenced in episodes addressing the demands of the women's movement. *The Advocates* debated a number of issues relevant to women, including the Equal Rights Amendment, work schedules to accommodate parenting, no-fault divorce and access to birth control. These episodes offered a higher profile for female experts, and one exceptional pre-Roe *vs.* Wade debate over the legalization of abortion featured a female lawyer defined as a 'women's liberation activist' as the advocate. However, democracy was still contingent on the codes of thinking, behaving and governing required by *The Advocates*. This meant that modes of political expression associated with women, such as sharing personal, often painful and emotional experiences, had to be incorporated within the logic of rational debate, if included at all. It meant that the non-hierarchical models of decision-making idealized by the women's movement could not be implemented. And it meant that grassroots organizing was largely irrelevant. If change was the sole consequence of an expert debate followed by a vote and an official procedure, it followed that active struggles were not really necessary. Therefore, PBS could issue a press release crediting *The Advocates* with the passage of liberalized abortion legislation in several states without even mentioning the women's movement.

The Advocates made an effort to reach a broad, presumably male audience by using sports figures in promotional campaigns describing *The Advocates* as 'The PBS Fight of the Week'. But research showed its audience to be comprised mainly of PMC males, as *TV Guide* suggested when it called the programme 'The thinking man's fight of the week' (Gunther, 1973: 10). PBS proudly admitted the skew in publicity aimed at opinion leaders, noting that 'In a medium that has bred the sixty-second attention span, *The Advocates* requires thoughtful attention for an entire hour. And it's getting it.' This discourse placed the impetus for resisting commercial television's seductive appeals, and for becoming a good citizen, solely on the viewer. In broader terms, it obscured the tension between the demands of the consumer economy and the political order with the logic of individual responsibility. The binary between good and bad citizenship was echoed in the popular press, where reviewers constructed hierarchies between the responsible citizens who watched *The Advocates* and the hedonistic, apathetic masses who preferred 'the movies on ABC and the second half of Hee Haw' ('Television Review', 1970: n.p.). Viewer letters excerpted by PBS in the debate tallies forwarded to public officials and the news media often drew from the discourse of the 'TV problem' to construct similar binaries. The following comments, for example, suggest that *The Advocates* offered the symbolic material for middle-class viewers to assert their rational thinking, self-discipline and good taste:

> Friends – and you are my friends when you present such thought provoking programs, implying that some of us out here in the Vast Wasteland can and do think. Not many TV programs pay us this compliment.

> A truly splendid program. Of all the myriad and generally spiritually demeaning offerings on television only your broadcasts are consistently interesting and civilized. Keep up the good work.

This construction of good citizenship affirmed a hierarchical model of democracy congruent with the social scientific logic of the two-step flow. According to *TV Guide*, *The Advocates* was hardly a success by 'mass' standards, but it attracted 'influential people' and had 'an impact where it counts' (Gunther, 1973: 7). While political participation did not extend beyond the ritual of voting, the 22,000 plus votes received each month were taken as public opinion that mattered. Neither the sociodemographic profile of the PBS audience nor the fact that pre-addressed postcard ballots were available only to public television's contributing viewer-members were seen as reason to qualify the results of the debates. What was emphasized was the bipartisan nature of the voting audience – a pattern that was then evoked to affirm PBS's ability to produce political balance and liberal pluralist consensus. The 'vote swings heavily from conservative to liberal and occasionally perches in the middle of the fence,' explained a PBS press release, and the majority of 'liberal positions on social issues' were balanced by some 'very conservative thinking on the subjects of law and order and the economy.' As the Ehrenreichs argue, such 'balance' is precisely what one would expect from the reformist faction of the PMC.

The Advocates rationalized a model of government that stabilized the capitalist political structure by affirming the necessity of dominant institutions and the leadership abilities of white male PMC elites. Television viewers who refused to take part in the programme were positioned as hedonistic and apathetic citizens unworthy of active participation in self-government. Viewers who didn't play by the rules were not good citizens but deviants, as epitomized by an incident where the 'pot cigarettes' sent in following the debate over marijuana were 'promptly turned over to the police because under existing federal and most state laws, the possession of marijuana is a crime'. In 1973, PBS was partially restructured by policies established by the Nixon administration intended to curb its perception of 'East coast liberal bias'. To the dismay of many TV critics and viewers, public affairs programmes were among the first casualties. While some were rescued by viewer contributions and corporate sponsorship, *The Advocates* was cancelled in 1974, when it failed to secure a benefactor and the local station support necessary for public subsidies. By this point, civil disobedience had subsided and Ford had moved on to other projects. Cable was also being developed to reach niche markets, alleviating the problem of differentiating 'news junkies' and opinion leaders with 'lowest common denominator' television programming. Ironically, before it was dropped, *The Advocates* pondered whether Congress should initiate impeachment hearings on Richard Nixon, resulting in a forty/sixty split in favour of the procedure. As with an earlier episode debating whether Spiro Agnew's tax evasion plea bargain should be accepted, the purpose was not to promote ideological reconciliation, but to affirm the rationality of democratic institutions during a moment of crisis.

Summing up this logic, one viewer letter pro-claimed, 'Your program was fantastic...once this corruption is eliminated our government will be the better for it and faith in the process will be restored.'

The campaign to instil good citizenship is not as explicit on PBS today, but we can see traces in the subdued officialdom of *The News Hour*, the 'enlightened democracy' of *Washington Week in Review*, the periodic effort to educate the public with campaign specials and the audience of opinion leaders drawn to these programmes, and to PBS as a whole. At a time when debates about the future of public television are dominated by a free market conservative discourse seeking to stamp out the enterprise, a cultural studies approach to policy can unpack the political rationality of PBS, with an eye towards equalizing the allocation of its cultural resources. Here, I have shown how the idealization of citizenship as an em-powered subject position glosses over the dis-tinct but complementary knowledge–power relations constructed under the banner of dem-ocracy and 'public service'. In an era when the governmental aims ascribed to PBS are no longer as contingent on public television, it is harder to sustain the rationale for public media, and easier for conservatives to cast PBS as a dated service whose functions are now met by channels like CNN and C-SPAN. The reconstitution of public television will require new rationales that go beyond the focus on anti-commercialism and whether programmes have or have not 'provoca-tively challenged' the status quo (Ledbetter, 1997: 217). As Bennett argues, the design of equitable cultural policy necessitates a change in the *relations* between cultural institutions and the public. 'The ultimate referent of mass society,' notes Aronowitz, 'is the historical moment when the masses make the (still) con-tested demand for the full privileges of citizen-ship, despite the fact that they are obliged to work at mundane tasks, are typically untrained for the specific functions of governance, and are ensconced in the routines of everyday life' (1993: 77). In light of my research, I am suggesting that demands for participation that subvert estab-lished binaries between mass and political cul-ture, and for access that is not predicated on educated, masculine and Eurocentric ways of thinking and behaving, are necessary to move beyond a marketplace construction of 'cultural

democracy' and a liberal ideal rooted in enlight-enment and social control.

References

'A Panel Speaks on Public Affairs Programming' (1966) *NEAB Journal*, January–February: 54–66.

'Advocates Define Their Terms' (1971) *Image*, WNET-TV, New York, 2 May: n.p. NPBA, WNET Collection, Program Guides, Box 4.

Aronowitz, Stanley (1993) 'Is a democracy possible? The decline of the public in the American debate', in Bruce Robbins (ed.) *The Phantom Public Sphere*, Minneapolis: University of Minnesota Press.

Baughman, James (1985) *Television's Guardians: The FCC and the Politics of Programming, 1958–1967*, Knoxville: University of Tennessee Press.

Bennett, Tony (1992b) 'Useful culture', *Cultural Studies*, 6(3): 395–408.

—— (1995) *The Birth of the Museum*, London: Rou-tledge.

Blakely, Robert (1969) *The People's Instrument: A Philosophy of Programming for Public Television*, Washington DC: Public Affairs Press.

Boddy, William (1990) *Fifties Television*, Urbana, IL: University of Chicago Press.

Bourdieu, Pierre (1984) *Distinction: A Social Critique of the Judgment of Taste*, trans. Richard Nice, Cam-bridge, MA: Harvard University Press.

'Breeding Ground for Riots' (1968) *Saturday Review*, 20 April: 66.

Carnegie Commission (1967) *Public Television: A Program for Action, The Report of the Carnegie Commission on Educational Television*, New York: Bantam.

Cherne, L. (1952) 'Biggest question on TV debates', *New York Times Magazine*, 2 March: 14.

Clark, Charles S. (1992) 'Public broadcasting', *Con-gressional Quarterly Researcher*, 18 September: 812.

Corporation for Public Broadcasting (CPB) (1969) *Newsroom: An Audience Evaluation for KQED-TV*, unpublished report, NPBA, reference shelf.

Douglas, Susan (1987) *Inventing American Broad-casting 1899–1922*, Baltimore, MD: Johns Hopkins University Press.

Ehrenreich, John and Ehrenreich, Barbara (1979) 'The professional-managerial class', in Pat Walker (ed.) *Between Labor and Capital*, Boston, MA: South End Press.

'Farewell to Razzmatazz' (1972) *Newsweek*, 21 August: 61.

Fischer, John (1959) 'TV and its critics', *Harper's*, July: 12–18.

Fletcher, James E. (1977) 'Commercial versus public television audiences: public activities and the Watergate hearings', *Communication Quarterly*, 25(4): 13–16.

Ford Foundation (1970) *Newsroom: A Report*, unpublished report, NPBA, reference shelf.

——(1980) *Ford Foundation Activities in Noncommercial Broadcasting*, New York: Ford Foundation.

Friendly, Fred (1967) *Due to Circumstances Beyond Our Control*, New York: Vintage Books

Gitlin, Todd (1980) *The Whole World Is Watching*, Berkeley: University of California Press.

Gould, Jack (1970) 'A black critic for a black show?', *New York Times*, 11 October: n.p., NPBA, PBS Collection, Program Files, *Black Journal*, Box 13.

Gray, Karen (1972) 'Black journal: an overview', *Educational Broadcasting Review*, 6(4): 231–2.

Gunther, Max (1973) 'The thinking man's fight of the week', *TV Guide*, 14 April: 7–10.

Hall, Stuart (1982) 'The rediscovery of "ideology": the return of the repressed in media studies', in Michael Curevitch, Tony Bennett, James Curran and Janet Woollacott (eds) *Culture, Society and the Media*, London: Methuen.

Hallin, Daniel (1994) 'The passing of the "high modernism" of American journalism', in Casey Ripley, jun. (ed.) *The Media & The Public*, New York: H. W. Wilson Co.

Heckscher, August (1968) 'The quality of American culture', in President's Commission on National Goals, *Goals for Americans*, New York: Prentice Hall.

Hoke, Travis (1932) 'Radio goes educational', *Harper's*, September: 473.

Howe, Harold (1967) 'Tenth anniversary program of KTCA-TV', 17 September, unpublished transcript, NPBA, reference shelf.

Humphrey, Hubert (1966) 'Remarks to the convention', *NAEB Journal*, January–February: 49.

Hunter, Armand L. (1961) 'The way to 1st-class educational citizenship', *NPBA Journal*, July–August: 19–23.

Jowett, Garth (1982) 'The emergence of the mass society: the standardization of American culture, 1830–1920', in Jack Salzman (ed.) *Prospects: The Annual of American Cultural Studies*, New York: Burt Franklin & Co. Inc.

Karayn, Jim (1972) 'In defense of public television', *Wall Street Journal*, 15 November: n.p., NPBA, PBS Collection, NPACT, Box 2.

Kasson, John (1978) *Amusing the Million: Coney Island at the Turn of the Century*, New York: Hill & Wang.

——(1990) *Rudeness & Civility*, New York: Hill & Wang.

Katz, Elihu and Lazarsfeld, Paul (1955) *Personal Influence*, Glencoe, IL: The Free Press.

Kettering Conference on Public Television Programming (1969) 'Transcript of proceedings', 25–28 June, unpublished report, NPBA, CPB Collection, Box 34.

Laruent, Lawrence (1972) 'Vanoucur-MacNeil start a new kind of news', *The Washington Post*, 3 September: n.p., NPBA, PBS Collection, NPACT, Box 2.

Lasswell, Harold (1962) 'The future of public affairs programs', in Institute for Communication Research (ed.) (1962) *Educational Television: The Next Ten Years*, Stanford, CT: Institute for Communication Research.

Ledbetter, James (1997) *Made Possible By... The Death of Public Broadcasting in the United States*, New York: Verso.

Lippmann, Walter (1922/1954) *Public Opinion*, New York: Macmillan.

——(1959) 'The TV problem', *New York Herald Tribune*, 27 October: 26.

McChesney, Robert (1994) *Telecommunications, Mass Media & Democracy: The Battle for Control of U.S. Broadcasting, 1928–1935*, New York: Oxford University Press.

Macy, John (1970) 'The critics of television: a positive answer', speech before the National Press Club, 15 January, rpt in *Vital Speeches of the Day*, 15 February: 286–8.

Miller, Toby (1993) *The Well-Tempered Self: Citizenship, Culture and the Postmodern Subject*, Baltimore, MD: Johns Hopkins University Press.

Minow, Newton (1962) 'Our common goal: a nationwide ETV system', *NAEB Journal*, January–February: 1–9.

National Citizens for Public Broadcasting (1968) *The State of Public Broadcasting: A Report to the American People*, New York: National Citizens for Public Broadcasting, NPBA, reference shelf.

'Public Taste Molds TV' (1961) *Broadcasting*, 18 September: 26.

'Public Television: In the Balance' (1973) *Congressional Record*, 5 February: E653.

Ratner, Victor (1969). 'The freedom of taste', *Television Magazine*, November: 54.

Resnik, Henry S. (1972) 'Putting VD on public TV', *Saturday Review of Education*, 14 October: 33–8.

Robinson, Hubbel (1960) 'You, the public, are to blame', *TV Guide*, 26 November: 14.

Rubin, Joan Shelley (1992) *The Making of Middlebrow Culture*, Chapel Hill: University of North Carolina Press.

Sarnoff, David (1955) 'The moral crisis of our age', *Vital Speeches of the Day*, 1 December: 118–19.

Schlesinger, Arthur (1961) 'Notes on a cultural policy', in Normin Jacobs (ed.) *Culture for the Millions?*, Princeton, NJ: D. Van Nostrand Company, Inc.

Schramm, Wilbur, Lyle, Jack and de Sola Pool, Ithiel (1963) *The People Look at Educational Television*, Stanford, CT: Stanford University Press.

Schudson, Michael (1978) *Discovering the News*, New York: Basic Books.

Schwarzwalder, John (1959) 'Educational television and the sense of urgency', mimeographed commencement address presented to the University of Minnesota, 16 July, NPBA, reference shelf.

Shain, Percy (1969) 'Hot TV debate on Advocates debut', *Boston Globe*, 13 October: n.p. NPBA, PBS Collection, Program Guides, *The Advocates*, Box 1.

Spigel, Lynn and Curtin, Michael (eds) (1997) *The Revolution Wasn't Televised: Sixties Television and Social Conflict*, New York: Routledge.

Statistical Research Inc (1974) 'Public broadcasting audience analysis', unpublished report, 31 May 1974, NPBA, reference shelf.

Stallybrass, Peter and White, Allon (1986) *The Politics and Poetics of Transgression*, London: Methuen.

'Television Review' (1970) *Alhambra California Post*, 5 October: n.p., in 'The critics respond to *The Advocates*', unpublished report, NPBA, PBS Collection, Program Guides, *The Advocates*, Box 1.

Chapter 9

Burning Rubber's Perfume

Isaac Julien

Ten years ago I made my first film, *Who Killed Colin Roach?*, for The Roach Family Support Committee. Colin Roach was a young British black man who died under mysterious circumstances in the foyer of Stoke Newington police station. The documentary dealt with questions of police accountability to the black communities in North London. My later film *The Attendant*, which opened at the Institute of Contemporary Arts in March 1993, deals with questions of black gay representations. I now find myself in the ironic position of testing the liberal parameters of black and gay audiences.

During the 1980s black British cinema became the cutting edge of independent British film culture because we, some of the black people working in film, wanted to make oppositional work. In the 1990s I wonder how many black programme-makers are committed to a film cultural practice that comes out of a political interest? A more critical debate needs to take place to assess such a cultural shift. New interventions for black independent film-making have to be made if we want to witness continuity in the tradition of black fiction film and drama production in Britain. This paper, which explores the restrictions in the development of a critical black British cinema, along with the *Black and White in Colour* documentaries, is my attempt at ensuring such a debate takes place.

Relocating Memory

At a seminar I attended on 9 November 1992, organised by the Institute for Fiscal Studies and

entitled 'The British Film Industry: A Role for Government?', Mark Shivas, Head of Drama for BBC Television, spoke about how the BBC was and still is a training ground for directors. He said that some of Britain's best-known directors had made their first films at the BBC – Stephen Frears, Mike Leigh, Ken Loach, to name only a few. He went on to describe how his department had managed to make British films successful both here and abroad, using *Truly, Madly, Deeply* (Dir: Anthony Minghella 1990 BBC) as an example of that success. He then quoted Truffaut on how British cinema doesn't exist. Britain, Truffaut maintained, was unable to make movies. As Shivas spoke, I knew that his grand narrative of what effectively constituted white film-makers' biographies would be different from 'others'.

A further example of that difference is illustrated by the career trajectory of Lloyd Reckord, who made the first black fiction films in Britain. He said:

I remember going to the BBC and talking to a young director who had come in as a trainee. Originally he had been a young actor in the theatre and had worked with me as a walk-on at the Old Vic. Now, here he was, one of the BBC's latest recruits on a directors' programme. This sort of thing made me a little unhappy because I thought, 'I haven't heard that so-and-so directed anything, or showed initiative by going out to make a film with his own money, which I have done twice.' And I had also produced a number of plays around town, some commercially. Yet nobody, at any time, offered me a break as a trainee director in television. Talking to people today, they tell me that it isn't much better... I eventually left Britain for good in the late 60s because I'd had enough.[1]

This statement also makes me feel unhappy, but it is the 'black fact of life'. A necessary, abject reflection, a counter-narrative to Mark Shivas's statement on training in the BBC. I wish this post-colonial situation would end, but it hasn't and that's why some of us are still here today and some of us are not. As James Baldwin stated:

If we – and now I mean the relatively conscious whites and the relatively conscious blacks, who must, like lovers, insist on, or create, the consciousness of the others – do not falter in our duty now, we may be able, handful that we are, to end the racial nightmare... If we do not now dare everything, the fulfilment of that prophecy, recreated from the Bible in a song by a slave, is upon us: 'God gave Noah the rainbow sign, No more water, the fire next time!'[2]

As we know Channel 4 was born in such a fire – the fire of burning cars, wheels and tires that were the 1981 riots. And as we know when rubber burns it smells and part of that odour lingers even now with us in this room.

The Limits of Cultural Difference in the Field of Vision

In the *Variety Europe Focus* on Channel 4 Television, I read with some nostalgia how the BBC Oxbridge route had been upstaged by the independent producers and that, however marginalised, contributions had been made by ghetto programming, in the scheduling of black producers' and film-makers' work on Channel 4. That black independent film-making had at least had some small, limited form of continuity was due to a critical commitment made by the Independent Film and Video Department in Channel 4. But now ten years on I feel somewhat sceptical when I read Andrea Wonfor, Channel 4's Controller of Arts and Entertainment, claim, 'There's a limit to how many programmes people can take on the Third World, environment or racial issues.' She continues, 'They're all extremely important parts of the mix, but the channel is beginning to have a broader brief, which is healthy.'[3]

Could this be a hint at the demise of the Multicultural Department at Channel 4 and if that happened, do you think we would smell any rubber burning outside Channel 4 windows today? I doubt it. There is a case to be made, however, that although the inauguration of the Multicultural Department at Channel 4 was originally an important gesture in securing representations of ethnic minority programming in Channel 4 and its initial output was successfully received, it has always been felt by black independents to have failed to establish a black independent production base in Britain. By its very existence it has tended to absolve other commissioning departments (except the Independent Film and Video Department) in Channel 4 from seriously accepting proposals from black producers.

The usual pattern is that black programme ideas have too often been referred back to the Multicultural Department. I continue to scan *Variety* and I come across an advert rightly congratulating Channel 4. The ad reads:

We've financed 43 features films together so far... *American Roulette, Bad Behaviour, Bearskin, The Belly of an Architect, Blue Black Permanent, The Bridge, Child from the South, The Crying Game, Dakota Road, December Bride, Diamond Skulls, The Dressmaker, Dust Devil, Eat the Rich, Empire State, Friends, Hear My Song, High Hopes, High Season, Hush-a-bye-Baby, Into the West, The Kitchen Toto, Ladder of Swords, Last of England, Life is Sweet, Mike Leigh Untitled 92, The Miracle, The Nature of the Beast, No Worries, On the Black Hill, Paper Mask, Prick Up Your Ears, Resurrected, Rita, Sue and Bob Too, Sammy and Rosie Get Laid, Secret Rupture, Stormy Monday, Sour Sweet, Venus Peter, Vroom, Waterland, We Think the World of You, Wild West.*

It ends with the words, 'And it's been a pleasure. Let's do many more Channel 4!!'[4] This ad is from British Screen.

Now we would all agree that this is a highly commendable list, something to be proud of in fact, but nevertheless I smell the scent of rubber burning here, can you?

One only has to watch a film like *The Crying Game* (Dir: Neil Jordan, Palace Productions, 1992) to recognise that an undeniable shift has taken place. In this film, questions of ethnicity, nationalism and violence have a central place in the narrative, while the subplot utilises racial and sexual gender-bending twists, transgressing the boy meets girl/boy romance – straight queer cinema for hets, blackness and queerness in the performance of Jaye Davidson, whose 'otherness' gives the film that extra kick when s/he reveals his/her secret by showing 'a bit of the other' (a black cock).

In an essay entitled 'What is this "Black" in Black Popular Culture?', Stuart Hall has warned us: 'There's nothing that global postmodernism loves better than a certain kind of difference, a touch of ethnicity, a taste of the exotic as we say in England "a bit of the other".'[5]

If we translate that racial 'difference' to feature film production in Britain, then who is going to be in the relative positions of power to visually portray 'difference' and 'otherness' in the cinema? The cinematic commodification of the 'Other' does not necessarily mean that black directors will have opportunities to tell our own stories. The movement of black directors from 'de-margin to de-centre' in film and television production into the so-called mainstream will be met by the personal and institutional essentialist practices of white supremacy. This is precisely where we/I will witness the resistance, evident from the list of films mentioned above, where the film-makers are almost always white, middle class, predominately male and heterosexual.

But this is not the only domain of film culture that is resistant to change. The letters page of *Sight and Sound* recently published a homophobic letter, as if to signal that the time had come to swallow the dogma of commonsensical definitions of cultural, racial and sexual difference in the form of a critique around political correctness. Similar patterns are evident in the so-called liberal press. In a *Guardian* interview, in Cannes last years,[6] Ben Gibson, an Executive Producer of *Young Soul Rebels*, effectively endorsed the statement made by the author, Deborah Orr, that my sexuality and racial identity were the basic reasons for me being allowed to make *Young Soul Rebels* for the BFI. Gibson replied that his predecessor Colin MacCabe's aim was to 'go and find people who were interesting within the culture, and then address them with the issue of culture'. Although he claims his own policy and taste will do the opposite, he also suggested that, 'By its nature art film culture attracts women, gays and blacks', effectively endorsing MacCabe's so-called sociological policy that he would wish to criticise. Could this presumed change in 'taste' not in fact be a rejection of 'difference' pathologised as 'sociology' in the name of a return to the 'sameness' of old-fashioned (white) modernism? Even Derek Malcolm in his otherwise supportive review of last year's Carthage film festival in the *Guardian*, reporting that black British film-makers had been refused support from the British Foreign Office and that *Young Soul Rebels* had then been censored by the Carthage film festival itself, in the opening of his review said

> It isn't easy being a black British film-maker since, if you do get some money to make a movie in Britain, you aren't likely to be able to show it widely at home. *Abroad is a different matter. There they tend to give you prizes, sometimes just for turning up at all.* (my emphasis)[7]

I could not help but ask myself whether the tone of the introduction of this review would be warranted if he were writing about white British film-makers winning prizes for their films in an international festival? The politics of envy around 'difference' in British cinema makes for interesting kinds of cultural policing in the writing of film journalism. Alas, these 'structures of feeling' do not belong exclusively to critics. I eventually felt it in being forced to leave my own workshop, Sankofa, and in my dealings with British Screen.

The British Screen Experience

A recent experience I had at British Screen with two white producers and a white scriptwriter on a feature film script which I hoped to direct on the life of Roger Casement illustrates why there have not been any feature films directed by blacks in collaboration with that organisation.

My name had been used to raise initial script development from the European Script Fund. My agent and I thought there should be a new scriptwriter. Together with the producers I approached British Screen for further development funding and in the meantime was approached by a well-known screenwriter who was then engaged to rewrite the script. I was eventually given the new draft, which I thought was great, but it had by then been decided by the producers' scriptwriter and British Screen that they would be looking at other directors. Of course, a more famous, white director was chosen.

At the same time other well-known black directors and black writers were submitting treatments which were getting rejected by British Screen. The board that decides on such proposals had at that time only one black producer among its members.

During this same period a series of meetings took place to set up a working party to discuss the creation of a Black Film Production Fund, where, in collaboration with other broadcasting institutions and film bodies, scripts would be developed for television, TV drama and feature films and thus encourage a black production base, where black producers, writers and directors would work together. I believe the desire to change things at British Screen is there and spoken in good faith, but in terms of the production decisions made by the British Screen board I sense a lack of objectivity towards black film projects. Many black filmmakers and writers who apply to be funded but dare not speak up for fear of being penalised in some way, I believe have the same suspicions. One black producer on the board or a special black film fund does not solve the problems that these institutions of whiteness produce. I for one no longer feel comfortable with the sort of multiculturalism which would practise a segregationist policy of whites through this door and blacks through that.

The Problem of Form in Black Film and TV Practice

Racially speaking, there are two kinds of modernism in British film culture. The restrictions of modernism in black culture's translation to the screen goes something like this. High Culture equals Art Cinema, which really means white cinema, whereas black cinema is almost exclusively meant to be restricted to the domains of popular culture. This is true of black sitcoms, which are no longer content to use racial difference just as entertainment for whites; instead the genre uses its own black epistemology to transform itself. For example, the brilliant thing about *Chef*, Lenny Henry's sitcom, is that it carnivalises both high and popular culture in true Bakhtinian style.

Television has helped to smash the old high culture/popular culture divide. It could also transform the forms and genres of British cinema if we could see a possibility for a series like *Chef* to be developed into a fully-fledged feature. But confusion lies in what we think black film/drama/cinema should be, both in terms of 'institutional functions and desires' and black audiences' drives and wish fulfilment fantasies. The 'demands and practices' of black filmmakers are seldom considered beyond political expediency. 'When are we going to have our own British Spike Lee?' is the simplistic question lingering on everybody's lips. There still remains some tension in the debate on black representation in the cinema between representation as 'depicting' and representation as 'delegation'. We are in fact trapped within the confines of hetero-populist black culture in the cinema and comedy in television, while white 'drama' and white British cinema – those uniformly high-cultural modernist occupations – continue to define who can enter its canon and who cannot.

The debate revolves essentially around national identity. The Foreign Office let it be known, when they refused to cover the cost of black British films to be shown in Tunisia, that they considered them 'not likely to be representative of British cinema' (they hadn't even seen the films!) and would 'possibly give a bad image of Britain... After all, they're not exactly *Howards End*.'[9]

Too many of the views mentioned above manage to repress what has been taking place in Britain over the last twenty-five years, namely the formation of a black European cinema. I would hope that any advertisements celebrating Channel 4's twentieth anniversary would more accurately reflect Britain's racial and cultural diversity at the end of the twentieth century. If that happens, I won't feel such a celebration to be as premature as I have felt it to be this time round.

Notes

1 Lloyd Reckord, *Black and White in Colour*, BFI, London, 1992, p. 55.

2 James Baldwin, 'The Fire Next Time', *The Price of the Ticket* (Michael Joseph, London, 1985) p. 379.

3 *Variety Europe*, 2 November, 1992.

4 *Variety Europe*, 2 November, 1992.

5 Stuart Hall, 'What is This "Black" in Black Popular Culture', in *Black Popular Culture*, Bay Press, Seattle, 1992.

6 Deborah Orr, 'In a time warp or out ahead?', *Guardian*, 18 May, 1992.

7 Derek Malcolm, 'Not quite Howards End', *Guardian*, 21 October 1992, review section, p.5.

9 Derek Malcolm, 'Not quite Howards End'.

Chapter 10

The Film Industry and the Government: "Endless Mr Beans and Mr Bonds"?

Toby Miller

A cinematograph film represents something more than a mere commodity to be bartered against others.

Palache Report, 1944[1]

When we talk about government film policy, we are referring to a network of practices and institutions intended to sustain and regenerate production, distribution and exhibition. These include technical training, tax breaks, local government assistance, copyright legislation, co-production treaties, European Community programmes, media education, archiving, ambassadorial services and censorship. Such practices are planned and executed through networks of institutions and discourses. In the domain of film, public debate over policy is minimal in comparison with arguments over whether television rots your brain, or videos turn you into a mass murderer. For Colin MacCabe, 'almost all appeals to "policy", like its repellent semantic cousin "management", are appeals away from a reality which is too various and too demanding'.[2] But getting to know film policy and intervening in it is an important part of participating in film culture.[3] Resistance goes nowhere unless it takes hold institutionally. For example, the gains made in British film by women and people of colour have come about through harnessing the work of social move-

ments to a critique of state policies and programmes in actionable ways.

During the 1980s, the Conservative government unravelled a gradually accreted system of subvention which had protected and stimulated the British film industry since the 1927 Cinematograph Films Act. The system had operated under twin imperatives – to deal with the cultural impact of *le défi américain* (in 1926, the *Daily Express* suggested Hollywood was turning British youth into 'temporary American citizens'); and to shore up the domestic industry.[4] The Tories under Margaret Thatcher, however, were not interested in the screen as a site either of cultural diversity, or industrial development through state participation.[5]

Seventy years on from that first legislation, identical imperatives apply. The 1990s opened with the British film industry in a period of extreme fragility and uncertainty and a Tory government indifferent to its fate. But the news was not all bad. As one critic put it, the 'lumpen-monetarist approach to this industry has swept away some of the humbug', though he warned that 'the effect will be purely negative if the elimination of an industrial policy for the cinema is not used as an opportunity to promote a cultural policy in its place'.[6]

Has this happened? Or are public subsidies being given to support unspecified claims about cultural maintenance, diversity, and development? Was the commerce-culture demon of film policy under any sort of control in 1990s Britain? Absolute answers depend on textual and audience studies, but there are suggestive signs in the debates signalled and thrown up by government action. This chapter goes looking for them under three broad headings: the New International Division of Cultural Labour; Institutions; and Facing the Millennium.

The New International Division of Cultural Labour

I want to . . . ensure that film making in the UK remains a pleasurable and profitable experience for overseas companies.

Chris Smith, 1997[7]

In reviewing foreign films made in the UK, the *Independent* newspaper refers to Britain as 'Our green and profitable land', while David Bruce notes of Scotland that it 'has tended to be regarded more as a film location and source of stories than as a film culture'.[8] The same might be said for much of Britain. For apart from some efforts in support of a local film culture, the period under review saw bald attempts at a purely industrial policy to exploit the New International Division of Cultural Labour (NICL).

The NICL derives from reworkings of economic dependency theory that followed the inflationary chaos of the 1970s. Developing markets for labour and sales and a shift from the spatial *sen*sitivities of electrics to the spatial *in*sensitivities of electronics, pushed businesses beyond treating Third World countries as suppliers of raw materials, to look on them as shadow-setters of the price of work, competing among themselves and with the First and Second Worlds for employment. Just as manufacturing fled the First World, cultural production has also relocated, though largely within the industrialised market economies. This is happening at the level of film production, marketing and information. Across the screen industries, labour market slackness and developments in global transportation and communications technology have diminished the need for film industries to be concentrated in one place. Fragmentation reduces labour costs and allows multinational companies to take advantage of tax incentives, exchange rates and other factors of production, moving on when they are offered more favourable terms elsewhere. Communications technology permits electronic off-line editing across the world, but also facilitates increasingly sophisticated digital effects, problematising the very need for location shooting. The trend is clearly towards horizontal connections to other media and a break-up of public-private distinctions in ownership, control, and programming philosophy.[9]

Britain has been a major player in the NICL, as both foreign investor and recipient of off-shore production funds. In one sense none of this is new, since Hollywood has long tapped the UK for people, locations, settings and stories. But from the 1980s, it became impossible to recoup the cost of most British feature films domestically, and the industry was forced to look outside. The necessity of finding employment for skilled workers and their employers turned the industry into a welcome mat for foreign, particularly US, filmmakers. In 1991 a British Film Commission (BFC) was formed to market UK production expertise and locations by providing overseas producers with a free service articulating local talent, locations and subsidies, and generating a national network of urban and regional film commissions. In 1997, seven Hollywood movies accounted for fifty-four per cent of the £465 million spent on feature film production in the UK. But Britain faces increasing competition to capture Hollywood production finance. Between 1990 and 1998, thirty-one film commissions were set up across the globe and many of them, such as the British Virgin Islands Film Commission, are solely concerned with attracting foreign capital. In 1998, the Government opened a British Film Office in Los Angeles in an attempt to facilitate traffic between Hollywood and Britain by offering liaison services to the industry and promoting British locations and talent. The BFC announced the new government's outlook on cinema: 'set firmly at the top of the agenda is the desire to attract more overseas filmmakers'.[10]

One key agency, the London Film Commission (LFC), was formed in 1995 with a £100,000 grant from the Department of National Heritage to attract off-shore film production. It subsequently obtained funding from United International Pictures and the Corporation of the City of London, but needed a bail-out from the government of £95,000 in 1998 when it failed to attract sufficient private-sector money to continue operations. The LFC promotes the capital to overseas film-makers, arranges police permits, and liaises with local residents and businesses. Its defining moment was *Mission: Impossible*. According to the Commissioner, the film's Hollywood producers: 'came up with all these demands and I just went on insisting that, as long as they gave us notice, we could schedule it'.[11]

The hold on foreign capital is always tenuous, however, and depends heavily on foreign exchange rates. Of course, this too relates to state activity – the government's decision to float the pound and free the Bank of England from democratic consultation contributed to a situation in 1998 where a strengthening currency raised costs for overseas investors and encouraged locals to spend elsewhere, with severe implications for off-shore film funds.

In order to keep British studios going, regulations were promulgated under John Major that meant films entirely made in Britain counted as British, regardless of theme, setting, or stars. So *Judge Dredd* with Sylvester Stallone is 'British', but *The English Patient*, which did too much of its post-production work abroad to qualify, is not. Until 1998, ninety-two and a half per cent of a film had to be created in the UK. At the end of that year, the government reduced this requirement to seventy-five per cent to encourage those American companies unwilling to relinquish the right to use sophisticated Hollywood special effects and post-production facilities to make their films in Britain.[12]

Britain was a late starter as a co-production partner, although an intergovernmental treaty of 1965 spawned some Anglo-French productions. This agreement specified films of high cultural quality, but assistance was routinely granted to money-spinners when the local industries were in trouble (financing was made available for the James Bond film, *Moonraker*, for example). Increasing European co-operation in the early 90s stimulated new projects, though few

of them were commercially successful. Ken Loach, Mike Leigh and Peter Greenaway have all made use of European co-production partners, but more money has been lavished on expensive costume pictures such as *Nostradamus* (Roger Christian, 1993), *Victory* (Mark Peploe, 1998) and *The Serpent's Kiss* (Philippe Rousselot, 1997) which have conspicuously failed to find an audience capable of recuperating their £6–8 million budgets. In 1993 Britain joined Eurimages, the continental film fund of the Council of Europe, which supports documentary, exhibition, distribution and marketing through interest-free loans, but the Conservative government thought it poor value for money and quickly withdrew.[13] During this period, the European Commission's MEDIA programme was launched, with the aim of pushing European film production towards responsiveness to local cultures while keeping a close eye on profitability – an attempt to blend culture and commerce.

What do film industry mavens make of this situation? Michael Kuhn, managing director of PolyGram Filmed Entertainment (PFE), the company which dominated the British film industry in the 90s, considers that 'Europe (when you talk about mainstream movies) is almost a vassal state to that Hollywood business' and argues that only 'supra-national government institutions' can turn this around, because of the lack of a firm financial base to compete with Hollywood's mix of production and distribution and the United States' cartel-like discrimination against European producers.[14] Ironically, PFE has now been taken over by the North American drinks conglomerate, Seagram, and will merge in some form with another of Seagram's subsidiaries, the Hollywood major, Universal.

In contrast to Kuhn, Rupert Murdoch welcomes 'new joint ventures between the Hollywood majors and both public and private broadcasting' in Europe, citing the numbers of European workers invisibly employed in the making of *Titanic*: 'this cross-border cultural co-operation is not the result of regulation, but market forces. It's the freedom to move capital, technology and talent around the world that adds value, invigorates ailing markets, creates new ones'.[15] This view finds support in the upper echelons of the EC, which has offered US film marketers unhindered access to the European marketplace – a new turn for the Commission, driven by the same neoliberalism that has characterised Tony Blair's Labour government and its predecessor.

The other side to British film and the state is its work as a plenipotentiary. The preferred image of Britain is one of heritage and tranquillity. The Foreign Office declined to fund black British films at the 1992 Carthage film festival because they were deemed 'not likely to be representative of British cinema' and might 'give a bad image of Britain.... After all, they're not exactly *Howard's End*'.[16] And for the first British-Bangla Film Festival, held in Dhaka in 1998, the British Council selected films with colonial echoes such as *Mrs Brown*, *Chariots of Fire*, *The English Patient* and *A Night to Remember*, to show alongside Bangla movies.

Institutions

Television has more or less become the film industry.

John Hill and Martin McLoone, 1997[17]

The divide between television and cinema is barely sustainable other than in very limited exhibitionary terms. When it comes to personnel, ideas, genres, funds, companies and the state, the lines are very blurred indeed. The 1990s saw the BBC cling to a vision of itself as a groundbreaker, but some critics saw it as stuck in a mentality of white domination, a world of colonialism *manqué* that still views diversity as an add-on. Isaac Julien notes how many black directors have felt unwelcome there, and don't fit into the Corporation's usual narrative for its successful employees.[18] Channel Four's Multicultural Department, initially hailed as an important intervention into Britain's screen whiteness, did not succeed in stabilising independent black film production and served as a token that let the mainstream of the station carry on with business as ever.

The BBC has worked with an annual budget for film production of approximately £5 million through the 90s. This is a tiny sum in film industry terms, though the BBC also buys TV rights to independently produced pictures.[19] BSkyB has invested small amounts in British films and has participated in film pre-sales from 1994 in order to fulfil obligations for European content.[20]

Toward the end of the decade Channel Four purged its programming staff and started a film company, Film Four Ltd, with funds freed up by the belated opportunity to reinvest profits rather than remit them to ITV. The new firm was envisaged as a movie studio, but it had much work to do – in 1998, Channel Four films accounted for just one per cent of UK box-office revenues. In February 1999, Film Four announced a London-based partnership for production and global distribution with Arnon Milchan and TF1, primarily designed to make and sell UK films.[21] It would be odd to rhapsodise Film Four's success as a commercial bridgehead, but it did at least stave off privatisation. Nonetheless, increasing commercialisation does not bode well for the independent and minority sector's access to the channel or its charter obligation of multiculturalism.[22]

The commerce–culture divide of British film can be seen at work in the British Film Institute during the decade. At the start of the 1990s, the Institute produced a number of documents arising from a meeting with Margaret Thatcher to discuss the future industry. The plan that emerged was commercial rather than cultural. It attempted to address the shortfall between outgoings and incomings by encouraging industry restructuring, fiscal incentives to invest and additional co-productions, as well as establishing a firm to sell British films internationally.[23] At the same time, Colin MacCabe, BFI Head of Research, claimed that the Institute had demonstrated a 'long-term commitment to a national television and cinema which fully articulates the multitude of cultures that now constitute modern Britain' and claimed Britain as the only European country that had been 'genuinely harnessing the talents of a whole range of communities'.[24] So culturecrat MacCabe claimed a continuing and impressive role for an inclusive film culture, while his commercecrat colleagues proposed a new agenda.

Of course, the dividing line between them is not so great as this might imply, as both were concerned with cinematic specificity and commercial viability. This is clear from the breadth and overlap of their work, from UK Film Initiative pamphlets like *The View From Downing Street*, to the Museum of the Moving Image and *BFI 2000*.[25] The crisis of the left in the 1990s has seen an embrace of the market, while the triumph of the right has seen it needing to heed the demands of minorities, even if it is as niche target consumers rather than as workers and migrants.

Views vary greatly on the merits of British Screen Finance, a quasi-autonomous non-government organisation formed in 1986 to assist commercially oriented films. It has operated through state funds, BSkyB deals, left-over National Film Finance Corporation money, Channel Four and the European Co-production Fund. David Puttnam claims that it has managed to link well with Europe, bring on new talent, and assist unusual projects to secure funding (he lists *Orlando, Scandal* and *The Crying Game* as examples).[26] By contrast, Isaac Julien details instances that suggest black film-makers consistently fail to obtain support.[27]

In addition to London-focused bodies, there is vibrant but under-resourced life elsewhere in the UK in the work of production agencies for Wales, Northern Ireland and Scotland, and in cities such as Sheffield and Glasgow, interested in boosting their cultural credentials (or not: the Liverpool Film Commission elects to advertise itself internationally as 'a lookalike for... Nazi Germany, and cities of the Eastern bloc'). This work is funded by the BFI, local councils, arts agencies and the Scottish and Welsh Offices.[28] The Scottish Film Council and Scottish Film Production Fund, founded in the 80s, established a Glasgow Film Fund in 1993 with financial input from the Glasgow Development Agency, Glasgow City Council, the European Regional Development Fund and Strathclyde Business Development. This patchwork of sources is typical, as is the decision to combine funds in high-end conventional narrative film-making rather than locally textured, independent, 'edge' cinema.[29] According to David Bruce,

> Location shooting by overseas companies in 1995... [was] at a record level and Scotland would be appearing on screen in its own right, or doubling for somewhere else, all over the world. (Someone said that had there been a 1996 Oscar for 'best supporting country' Scotland would have won).[30]

When the various bodies were amalgamated into Scottish Screen in the late 90s, there were accusations that locally-derived Lottery funds were lining the pockets of the English, and outrage

when the board, comprised of TV executives and the London Scottish, voted to finance a project by their own Chair.[31]

A Northern Ireland Film Council began in 1989 on a volunteer basis as a forum dedicated to 'the development and understanding of film, television and video in the region'. The Department of Education funded the Council from 1992 and it became a local site for disbursing screen-related Arts Council money and combining disparate funding streams, as well as a public sphere for debating the need to regionalise BBC production.[32] In 1997 it became the Northern Ireland Film Commission, with the task of attracting outside production. Andrew Reid, the Commission's locations officer, reported that: 'Producers come here expecting the place to be rubble.... Instead they end up having a great time. And I can show them mountains, beaches and great scenery. They can't quite believe it'.[33] Five features were shot in Northern Ireland in 1997 – a considerable increase on earlier years.[34]

Much of the money now available to these bodies, both directly and indirectly, comes from the National Lottery, launched in 1995 and now a major source of funds for film production. One idea floated under the Major government was to take £100 million from Lottery funds and match it with £200 million from the City to start a major film studio, complete with share offering. This was rejected by Labour in favour of a franchise system and in 1998 the Arts Council of England nominated DNA, Pathé and the Film Consortium for Lottery franchises and encouraged them to unify production, distribution and sales. The decision was by no means universally popular. One critic complained that underachieving 'whingeing cultural tsars' had turned into 'greedy moguls' via a system that discouraged diversity and innovation.[35] In December 1998, the government announced that £27 million would be allocated to film from the Lottery, along with £20.8 million in annual direct grants.[36]

Besides measures designed to stimulate film-making, there are other policies which affect the industry. The deregulatory verve of the Conservative government did not apply to questions of public morality in quite the same way that it did to economics. Censorship was increased through the Video Recordings Act in 1984 as part of the moral panic surrounding young people and popular genres, and the Criminal Justice Act of 1994 required censors to address issues of horror, drug use, criminal conduct and violence following the James Bulger murder case.[37] On other fronts, copyright, company incorporation and industrial relations machinery are also parts of state policy that affect film-making, along with general measures designed to stimulate industry, such as the Enterprise Investment Scheme.[38]

Facing the Millennium

There are catastrophic cycles in the history of British film. This is how they run: British movies suddenly become internationally popular; the Americans arrive and buy up everything they can; some years later they pull out; our industry collapses in the wake.

Sally Hibbin, 1998[39]

Each new wave of acclamation for British cinema in the 90s was followed by regretful decline, to the point where the triumphs of 1997 and 1998 came to be seen not so much as vital signs but as harbingers of cyclical failure.[40] When it came to power, the Blair government announced its intention of doubling the share of UK box-office for British films. Within its first hundred days the new administration had appointed the country's first official Minister for Film, announced the three Lottery recipients, permitted Channel Four to spend more on film-making, and introduced a hundred per cent tax rebate scheme for production (later problematised by European rules). This was done in the name of 'helping the film industry to develop from a series of small craft businesses into a properly integrated modern industry'.[41] Plans included raising US $24 million annually for development, production and distribution via a voluntary levy on UK film companies, including subsidiaries of US firms, to form an 'All-Industry Fund'. But the idea was ditched toward the end of 1998, when it became clear that both television companies and Hollywood studios were loath to pay for it.[42] The government announced a restructuring of film funding under the umbrella of a new institution to be born from the amalgamation of the BFI, the BFC, and the film section of the Arts Council of England (which administers the Lot-

tery).[43] Meanwhile, four areas of weakness in the local industry were identified by the government's Advisory Committee on Film Policy – training, generic marketing, distribution and development – and industry-government committees were set up to address such matters and provide points of liaison with sources of private finance.[44] Critics of these plans saw them as adding bureaucracy to already strapped institutions; supporters claimed the new arrangements would streamline and co-ordinate the industry. Meanwhile, training had moved toward a corporatist model via Skillset, a tripartite body with David Puttnam as its titular head.[45]

The rhetoric of modernisation was in keeping with the government's broader industrial policy. The move toward import substitution and export-oriented cultural industrialisation showed a preference for large, consolidated entities that work in competition with one another. In the cinema, this has seen a populist, big-budget, apolitical model preferred to an artisanal 'poor' cinema articulated around social issues. According to Puttnam, 'strong cultural resistance can best be built on the basis of a firm understanding of the realities of the marketplace'. He insists on the need to 'get away from relying on cultural defence, and concentrate our energies on industrial success'.[46] Film Minister Tom Clarke argued for films that were 'Made with passion, fuelled by cash', and expressed his enthusiasm for 'large, vertically integrated companies with deep pockets'.[47] But the aim of increasing the proportion of UK film receipts going to British cinema has proved difficult to achieve: market share fell by half in 1998.[48] Outsiders wondered whether direct state intervention via quotas and levies might be the way forward.[49]

Conclusion

Film policy in Britain shares a dilemma in common with that for most other national cinemas – the commerce–culture relationship. There is always a struggle between the desire to build a viable sector of the economy that provides employment, foreign exchange and multiplier effects; and the desire for a representative and local cinema that reflects seriously upon society through drama (as in the work of directors like Derek Jarman, Isaac Julien, Mike Leigh, Peter

Greenaway and Sally Potter). Future research and political action by the left into film must avoid cultural reductionism just as keenly as we used to avoid economic reductionism, beware falling for the rhetorics of consumerism and citizenship and require each part of the commerce–culture divide to illustrate the relationship between multinational capital and diversity, the role of the state in consumption, and the place of corporations in culture. Lastly, we must look to minority and migrant interests. Colin McArthur's requirements of Scottish film could well be read out to whatever remains of the 'sceptred isle': 'a historically specific grappling with the contradictions of the . . . past and present, a set of recurrent themes and styles discernibly amounting to a *collectivity*'.[50] The burden of government to address a population in all its life-forms must animate policy. If it does not, we shall see either 'rootless *Titanic*-style movies, free of geography, culture or humour, that play as well in Prague as in Peoria'. That means 'endless Mr Beans and Mr Bonds', but very few Ms Potters or Mr Juliens.[51]

Acknowledgements

My thanks to Talitha Espiritu for securing materials and to Robert Murphy for editorial comments.

Notes

1   Quoted in Political & Economic Planning, *The British Film Industry* (London: PEP, 1952), p. 12.
2   Colin MacCabe, 'A Post-National European Cinema: A Consideration of Derek Jarman's *The Tempest* and *Edward II*', in Andrew Higson (ed.), *Dissolving Views: Key Writings on British Cinema* (London: Cassell, 1996), p. 192.
3   Toby Miller, *Technologies of Truth: Cultural Citizenship and the Popular Media* (Minneapolis: University of Minnesota Press, 1998), pp. 71–90, 265.
4   Quoted in Victoria de Grazia, 'Mass Culture and Sovereignty: The American Challenge to European Cinemas, 1920–1960', *Journal of Modern History*, vol. 61, no. 1, 1989, p. 53.
5   John Hill, 'British Film Policy', in Albert Moran (ed.), *Film Policy* (London: Routledge, 1996), pp. 101–5.
6   Geoffrey Nowell-Smith, prefatory statement, in Lester Friedman (ed.), *Fires Were Started: British Cinema and Thatcherism* (Minneapolis: University of Minnesota Press, 1993), p. vi.
7   Department for Culture, Media and Sport, 'Chris Smith goes to Hollywood', *M2 PressWIRE*, 27 October 1997.
8   Peter Guttridge, 'Our green and profitable land', *Independent*, 11 July 1996, pp. 8–9; David Bruce, *Scotland the Movie* (Edinburgh: Polygon, 1996), p. vii.
9   Miller, *Technologies*, pp. 171–81; Toby Miller, 'The Crime of Monsieur Lang: GATT, the Screen, and the New International Division of Cultural Labour', in Moran (ed.), *Film Policy*, pp. 72–84.
10 Peter Guttridge, 'Our green and profitable land', pp. 8–9; Paul McCann, 'Hollywood film-makers desert UK', *Independent*, 14 August 1998, p. 7; John Hiscock, 'Hollywood backs British film drive', *Daily Telegraph*, 24 July 1998, p. 19; http://www.britfilmcom.co.uk/content/filming/site.asp.
11 Louise Jury, 'Mission possible: red tape cut to boost film industry', *Independent*, 4 July 1996, p. 3.
12 Marie Woolf, 'Why the next English Patient will be British', *Independent on Sunday*, 20 December 1998, p. 9.
13 Anne Jäckel, 'European Co-Production Strategies: The Case of France and Britain', in Moran (ed.), *Film Policy*, pp. 85–97.
14 Michael Kuhn, 'How can Europe benefit from the digital revolution?', presentation to the European Audiovisual Conference, Birmingham, 6–8 April 1998. Kuhn severed his links with PolyGram at the beginning of 1999.
15 Rupert Murdoch, presentation prepared for the European Audiovisual Conference, Birmingham, 6–8 April 1998.
16 Quoted in Isaac Julien, 'Burning Rubber's Perfume', in June Givanni (ed.), *Remote Control: Dilemmas of Black Intervention in British Film & TV* (London: BFI, 1995), p. 61.
17 John Hill and Martin McLoone, 'Introduction', in John Hill and Martin McLoone (eds), *Big Picture Small Screen: The Relations Between Film and Television* (Luton: John Libby Media, University of Luton Press, 1996), p. 1.
18 Isaac Julien, 'Burning Rubber's Perfume', in Givanni (ed.), *Remote Control*, pp. 56–7.
19 Sarah Street, *British National Cinema* (London and New York: Routledge, 1997), p. 22.
20 John Hill, 'British Television and Film: The Making of a Relationship', in Hill and McLoone (eds), *Big Picture Small Screen*, pp. 160–1.
21 Adam Dawtrey, and Benedict Carver, 'Power trio ink int'l deal', *Daily Variety Gotham*, 1 March 1999, pp. 1, 34.

22 Adam Dawtrey, 'New strategy comes to the 4', *Variety*, 8–14 February 1999, pp. 33, 40.

23 Steve McIntyre, 'Vanishing Point: Feature Film Production in a Small Country', in John Hill, Martin McLoone, and Paul Hainsworth (eds), *Border Crossing: Film in Ireland, Britain and Europe* (Belfast: Institute of Irish Studies/BFI, 1994), p. 103.

24 Colin MacCabe, 'Preface', in Givanni (ed.), *Remote Control*, pp. ix, x.

25 Jane Headland and Simon Relph, *The View From Downing Street* (London: BFI, 1991) was one of a series of pamphlets published under the rubric 'UK Film Initiatives' by the BFI.

26 David Puttnam, with Neil Watson, *Movies and Money* (New York: Alfred A. Knopf, 1998), p. 250.

27 Isaac Julien, 'Burning Rubber's Perfume', in Givanni (ed.), *Remote Control*, p. 60.

28 Stephen Goodwin, 'Screen revival for Scotland's forgotten film collection', the *Independent*, 13 August 1998, p. 6; Steve McIntyre, 'Art and Industry: Regional Film and Video Policy in the UK', in Moran (ed.), *Film Policy*, pp. 215–33; http://www.afilm.com/2/01/03/.

29 Colin McArthur, 'The Cultural Necessity of a Poor Celtic Cinema', in Hill, McLoone and Hainsworth (eds), *Border Crossing*, p. 113.

30 David Bruce, *Scotland the Movie*, p. 4.

31 Don Boyd, 'Cowards, liars, cultural despots and subsidized cronies: a portrait of Britain's film industry – from the inside, naturally…', *New Statesman*, 126, 31 October 1997, p. 34.

32 Geraldine Wilkins, 'Film Production in Northern Ireland', in Hill, McLoone and Hainsworth (eds), *Border Crossing*, pp. 141, 143.

33 David Gritten, 'The other Ireland unreels: after watching the Republic become a movie mecca, the Northern Ireland film industry is growing under today's relatively tranquil conditions', *Los Angeles Times*, 1 February 1998, p. 4.

34 Matt Cowan, and Linda Wertheimer, 'Northern Ireland Film Commission', *All Things Considered*, National Public Radio programme, 18 May 1998, transcript; David Gritten, 'The other Ireland unreels', p. 4. See also John Hill, 'Filming in the north', *Cineaste*, vol. xxiv, nos 2/3, 1999, pp. 26–7.

35 Tim Adler, 'A new script to save British film', *Daily Telegraph*, 26 February 1999; Boyd, 'Cowards, liars, cultural despots and subsidized cronies', p. 34.

36 Marie Woolf, 'Why the next English Patient will be British', *Independent on Sunday*, 20 December 1998, p. 9.

37 Jeffrey Richards, 'British Film Censorship', in Robert Murphy (ed.), *The British Cinema Book* (London: BFI, 1997), p. 176; Miller, *Technologies*, pp. 62, 199–200.

38 KPMG, *Film Financing and Television Programming: A Taxation Guide* (Amsterdam: KPMG, 1996), pp. 225–53; Hilary Clarke, 'Hidden tax rises: the making of the movies', *Independent on Sunday*, 7 March 1999, p. 3.

39 Sally Hibbin, 'Britain has a new film establishment and it is leading us towards disaster', *New Statesman*, 127, 27 March 1998, p. 40.

40 Sheila Johnston, 'Was 'British invasion' boon or bane for foreign?', *Variety*, 22–8 February 1999, p. A10.

41 Department for Culture, Media and Sport, 'Chris Smith goes to Hollywood', *M2 PressWIRE*, 27 October 1997.

42 Tim Adler, 'A new script to save British film', *Daily Telegraph*, 26 February 1999.

43 Eric Boehm, 'Mixed reviews on Brit pic fund revise', *Variety*, 15 December 1998, pp. 5, 24.

44 Adam Dawtrey, 'U.K. pols give up plan for film levy', *Daily Variety Gotham*, 1 December 1998, p. 10.

45 'Northern Ireland Film Commission received Skillset training Kitemark from Lord Puttnam', *M2 PressWIRE*, 22 February 1999.

46 Quoted in Boyd Tonkin, 'Will Lottery funding help Mike Leigh or Ken Loach make more and better films? Not if David Puttnam and his friends have anything to do with it', *New Statesman*, 126, 23 May 1997, p. 38 and Angus Finney, *The State of European Cinema: A New Dose of Reality* (London: Cassell, 1996), p. 8.

47 Tom Clarke, 'Made with passion, fuelled by cash', *New Statesman*, 127, 17 April 1998, p. 23. In July 1998 Clarke was replaced as Films Minister by Janet Anderson.

48 *The Economist*, 'European film industry: worrying statistix', 350, 6 February 1999.

49 Ian Christie, 'Will Lottery money assure the British film industry? or should Chris Smith be rediscovering the virtues of state intervention?', *New Statesman*, 126, 20 June 1997, p. 38.

50 Colin McArthur, 'The Cultural Necessity of a Poor Celtic Cinema', in Hill, McLoone and Hainsworth (eds), *Border Crossing*, p. 115. For a contradictory view, see Alan Lovell, 'The British Cinema: The Known Cinema?', in Murphy (ed.), *The British Cinema Book*, p. 241.

51 Sally Hibbin, 'Britain has a new film establishment and it is leading us towards disaster', p. 40.

Part IV

The Internet

Introduction to Part IV

Toby Miller

Who invented the Internet? When he's not busy claiming the status of a role model for *Love Story*, Al Gore sometimes includes this achievement in his CV. He is not alone – chain bookstores feature memoirs by all manner of white entrepreneurial men making similar assertions. The truth is out there, though, and it lies in the realm of government action – with major cultural ramifications.

For while Al, his girlfriend Tipper, and his roommate Tommy Lee Jones were padding around Ivy-League dorms during late-night ice-cream feasts, the US Air Force's RAND Corporation was busily devising means of waging the Vietnam War. Its consultancy services didn't end there, of course. Our friends over at the Corporation also addressed the question: what if the Soviet Union managed to strike at the heart of the domestic US communications system? A successful attack would leave the country disabled, unless a devolved network could be introduced. The packet system of today originated with that desire to decentralize computing through nodal, semi-autonomous sites. In keeping with those origins – state-driven Cold War consultancies – the Internet, as we all know, grew up nested within public institutions of government and education, and the associated warfare–welfare para-bureaucracy of publicly-funded but ostensibly independent research by private universities and firms. How, then, did what I'll call "cybertarianism" emerge as an origin myth of individual inventors/investors working to free communication from states and corporations?

Libertarian individualists of the US Electronic Frontier Foundation and many other sites, both corporate and not (libertarians need to organize?), today view the Internet as a technologically entrepreneurial zone. It is said to permit human ventriloquism, autonomous subjectivity, and a break-up of state power – all thanks to the "innate" properties of cyberspace. Hence my coining the term "cybertarian." Cybertarian mythology rests not only on a flawed, albeit touching, account of the person as a ratiocinative, atomistic individual who can exist outside politics and society. It equally assumes that what was: (i) born of warfare consultancies and "big science"; (ii) spread through large institutions; (iii) was commodified for a tiny fraction of computer users; and (iv) is moving towards comprehensive corporate control, can be claimed, now or ever, for the wild boys of geekdom. A touching foundation myth, typical of US fantasies about the autonomous subject breathing life into the world – this simply isn't credible, as an account of past, present, or future. Even hackers happily turn up at FBI conventions on Internet security, aiding the state and business to uncover errors and openness in operating systems. The expansion of entertainment conglomerates into the Internet will not, of course, end the technical capacity of web users to make their own sites. But it *will* minimize their significance. Crucial portals take up the traditional corporate role of policing zones and charging tolls. The fastest, easiest, most accessible search systems linked to browsers will direct folks to the "best" sites – which will not be those of cybertarians. Or not quite. Because there is a far older subject lurking here – older than the cybertarian, older even than the libertarian. This is, of course, the citizen. Whereas the cybertarian is a monad, happily sitting at the controls of his life, the citizen is intersubjective, keen to link her life with others in solidarity as well as conflict.

In Internet terms, cultural citizenship encompasses discussion groups, ventriloquism, physical space and hardware for collaboration, and access to and by *non*-citizens, such as temporary workers and refugees. The New International Division of Cultural Labor (NICL) and the Internet will interact in ways we can only imagine, as cultural labor is internationalized on an uneven basis that favors North over South and capital over labor. Already, we are seeing signs in the US of a new drive towards unionization, as lapsing cybertarians find an end to vested shares, salaries, and health care if they got on board too late, or with global competition for their jobs. As film and television production goes global in search of locations, skills, and docile labor, post-production and distribution centralize, thanks to armchair management by computer. Meanwhile, away from the salariat, those affected by the division of labor in manufacturing and agriculture need rights to communication in the new media.

What should be done? We need to theorize the Internet in terms not just of individual access, but political rights, economic development, cultural norms, and tastes. The NICL must be centered in deliberations that look to those who are disenfranchised from citizenship and consumption, via a global statement of worker and citizen rights. Cybertarians? Look under "corporate" in your phone book in a few years. They will either be there, or jabbering away with radio hams at conventions for oddities of the twentieth century.

Meanwhile, of course, the Internet continues to be a site for playing out key tropes of policy discourse. The ideology of civil society is founded on the liberal individual, but not just in the guise of the sovereign consumer who deploys means–ends rationality to maximize his or her utility. For that craven figure ultimately dies alone, surrounded by rotting goods and spent services: *anomie* is the fate of such isolates, in the truly lonely hour of the last instance. To avoid such an end, the liberal individual must also learn sociability and collaboration. In our media-thick era, this desire for a double-sided subject has produced a litany of binary judgments: solo TV-viewing is bad, whereas team bowling is good; gambling on-line is bad, but church attendance is good.

In early 2000, 55 percent of the US population was estimated to have access to the Internet – by far the highest absolute numbers of any country in the world. But depression and loneliness are disproportionately represented amongst these denizens of the Internet, so much so that US cultural critics, functionalist sociologists, and media mavens have become concerned that the liberal individual is unbalanced, with the selfish utilitarian outweighing the pro-social volunteer. Put another way, the corollary of the Internet's spread across the nation is said to be the rise of solitude and a diminution in social activity – the loss, in short, of civil society. Again, the litany of binary judgments applies: less time shopping in stores, but also less time spent with the family; more time in the house, but more of that time working (Markoff, A1). The other side to these numbers is that e-mail, not web purchase or other financial transactions, is dominant – just 25 percent of users buy on line and less than 10 percent bank that way, accounting for expenditure of almost US $15 billion in 1999 (Markoff, 2000, A18; Vogel, Jr. and Druckerman, 2000). Such figures suggest the Internet is a *source* of sociality, not its scourge. But let's not bother the mavens with such facts.

This anxiety over how private life is being transformed (not, we are told, by shifts in the structure of capitalism, but courtesy of the innately freewheeling logic of this technology and its double-edged force of freedom and responsibility) is a luxury open to few. Just as most of us in the world do not eat meat, so the vast majority (80%) have never made a telephone call, let alone logged on. Across Africa, only Zimbabwe, Egypt, and South Africa have Internet services in each major city. One million of the continent's 900 million people are on-line (Everard, 2000, pp. 29, 33).

So what relevance does the liberal individual have for such contexts? Simple. This individual is taken as a model for economic and social policy throughout the world. Economic models are based on the desire to maximize utility in a selfish way – the consumer as a desiring machine.

Social models are based on the preparedness to think beyond oneself, to contribute to social cohesiveness via forms of voluntary association that sidestep the pitfalls of both business and government.

The anomic subject of the North may be lost in a world of consumption, and not involved in enough volunteerism to keep the domestic underclass out of the welfare rolls, but is nevertheless a good-object model for development economists in their prescriptions for the Third World: away from import subsitution industrialization (ISI) and toward export-oriented industrialization (EOI). The various theorists and agencies of development have rejected their 1960s faith that Third World countries could develop economically by mirroring the primary, secondary, and tertiary industries of the North, via ISI. Now, the plan is to identify industries where these nations have a potential competitive edge in the global market through such factor endowments as natural resources, capital formation, or knowledge, emphasizing EOI. So where the World Bank once concentrated on modernizing civil services and supporting new investment, today it takes competition and corporate participation as its lodestone – don't give money to the people's representatives, hand it to their bosses (Nulens and Van Audenhove, 1999, pp. 458–9).

This focus on actually existing factor endowments will supposedly enable Third World countries to catch the eye of entrepreneurial industrialists, who in turn are looking for comparative advantage, in order to deliver a product to our equally rational subject, the liberal individual hunkered down in front of the computer screen. Each phase of calculation and transaction is, therefore, modeled on the putatively innate proclivity of economic "man" to maximize utility.

How does this relate to the Internet and to models of civil society? Telecommunications across the globe have long been a complex ISI amalgam of private and public investment and management, as states with large populations have sought to balance national security and delivery of services to their populations with the desire for cost-effectiveness. But relevant international lending and aid organizations and the International Telecommunications Union (ITU) have moved into an EOI era of structural adjustment, in keeping with the prevailing

neoliberal "Washington Consensus" of economic management (a.k.a. pressure from US business interests). Whilst the World Bank trots out shibboleths about the need for nationally specific telecom strategies, it will not budge on two meta-policies that trump all others: commodification and competition, based on a borderless model of corporate control. Such significantly different economies and polities as Thailand, Vietnam, and India are increasingly "encouraged" to select multinational corporations to establish their Internet systems. The idea of wealthy urban users subsidizing other areas is scotched. So Bangalore may be a central site for world computer work, but many rural regions of South Asia have no telephone service (Everard, 2000, p. 40; Nulens and Van Audenhove, 1999, pp. 463, 459).

In concert with the Bank and the ITU, the United Nations' Economic Commission for Africa adopted an African Information Society Initiative (AISI) in 1996. AISI envisages a continental network founded on classical liberal principles: the rule of law and *laissez-faire* internationalist investment (cut your tariffs and we'll come visit!). Out of this will flow the magic elixir of development: a globally competitive, yet supposedly self-reliant population of liberal individuals. Right, now just clarify something for me: will that be like the Green Revolution, or Project Camelot, or dam-building, or population control – name your "triumph" of Western-exported modeling?

There can be no doubt that these policies, both across economies and specifically in the communications industries, have helped create and/or sustain capitalist classes. The corporate world, within as well as outside Third World countries, adores those nations with nascent or fully-formed *bourgeoisies* and *petites bourgeoisies*. So we read that Internet Gratis signed up 450,000 Brazilian subscribers in the first four weeks of the new century (every 2.5 seconds at one point) as if this signaled open access to the entire population. The 95 percent of Latin Americans without access are virtually absent from this discourse, other than in their putative role as consumers (Helft, 2000; Vogel, Jr. and Druckerman, 2000).

The precept of the liberal subject, as both sovereign consumer and civil-society participant, has real material impact, regardless of its respectively selfish and folksy reputations. That liberal subject is a crucial target if we are to win the debate over the allocation of resources in this area. So let's spend some time interrogating the anomic US figure staring out at the screen, pondering where to go today. Such travel is at some cost – to others.

References

Everard, Jerry. *Virtual States: The Internet and the Boundaries of the Nation-State*. London: Routledge, 2000.

Helft, Daniel. "Free Access Takes Brazil by Storm." *Industry Standard*, February 21, 2000: 143.

Markoff, John. "A Newer, Lonelier Crowd Emerges in Internet Study." *New York Times*, February 16, 2000: Al, A18.

Nulens, Gert and Leo Van Audenhove. "An Information Society in Africa? An Analysis of the Information Society Policy of the World Bank, ITU and ECA." *Gazette* 61, no. 6 (1999): 451–71.

Vogel, Thomas T., Jr. and Pamela Druckerman. "Latin Internet Craze Sets Off Alarm Bells." *Wall Street Journal*, February 16, 2000: A23.

Chapter 11

The Marketplace Citizen and the Political Economy of Data Trade in the European Union

Richard Maxwell

Recently in the courts, there appeared before the magistrates an unfortunate fellow, upon whose forehead was inscribed a strange and singular tattoo: *Born to Lose!* Thus above his eyes he bore the epigraphy of his life like the title of a book, and subsequent interrogation proved this bizarre inscription to be cruelly true.

Charles Baudelaire, *Edgar Poe: His Life and Works*, 1856

Introduction: The Inscription on the Rue de la Loi

There once was a billboard within sight of the European Commission offices scattered along the Rue de la Loi in Brussels. It depicted a young woman whose eyes rolled to look up at someone just beyond the frame. Her mouth was frozen in a peevish simper, while her chin rested slightly cocked on her hands in a rehearsed look of virtue betraying a secret vice. Her upward glance directed attention to a bar code stamped on her forehead. Over this image a caption asked: 'Don't you want to be a number?' The woman's expression mirrored what every cynical onlooker must have thought about such an interrogation. Yet her apparent hostility to the question was framed not as a judicious response

to the proposed diminishment of her freedom but rather as an infantile and brazen reaction to a legitimate business request.

This advertisement invited a particular kind of consumer to identify with it, one who could make sense of the contradictory image of the defiant youth emblazoned with a machine-readable ID tag. The woman was studiously indifferent to the inscription on her forehead and to the gaze of the camera: her image signified unconstrained cool, a connotation of extroversion, mobility and individuality. The figure shrugged off the weight of being a numbered subject while endorsing the injunction to accept surveillance as a minor nuisance in marketplace relations. 'Of course', she seemed to say, 'I don't want to be a number; nobody *wants* to be a number. It's merely a state we all suffer.'

This figure of the marketplace citizen symbolises the emerging political economy of data trade in the European Union. In one breath, merchants and lawmakers have acknowledged that no-one worth their individuality actually wants to be numbered and tracked. In the next, this charitable rhetoric becomes condescending, telling consumers that in the real world everybody has become a number anyway. Consider the views of Bernard Siouffi, Director of the Union Française de Marketing Direct and leading figure in the French and European trade organisations of direct marketing, mail order and distance sell-ing. 'I'm a marketing man, okay, so I like to be transparent to consumers', Siouffi explained. 'I like consumers to express free will, and if they don't want to be on a marketing list I ask them to write a letter telling me they want out'. In the end, said Siouffi, 'it's a choice people make. They don't want TV, they don't want Internet, they want to be on an island. So I put them on an island' (Interview, 27 February 1996). For Siouffi, we are objects of surveillance by virtue of our location within the informational market-place; that's life in the marketer's world. We are also free to seek shelter from surveillance, an option that is meant to be comforting, though it resonates, in Siouffi's words, with a sense of exile and isolation.

This article focuses on two joined but oppos-ing principles of personal data protection affecting citizens of the European Union in the global informational marketplace. One is the legal standard determining the legitimate busi-ness purposes of surveillance, in particular that form of consumer surveillance associated with marketing research. The other concerns the meaning and scope of personal privacy as it changes under such surveillance. The article is organised into four parts. The first part argues that the extension of personal data protection from national to supranational levels is an effect of the consolidation of global information markets. This provides the context for discussion of the European Parliament and Council's 1995 Directive 'on the protection of individuals with regard to the processing of personal data and on the free movement of such data' ('the Directive'). The second part discusses how persistent im-provements of surveillance techniques and com-munication technology make it feasible to delocalise and recombine data virtually with the speed of light, pushing the available legal defence of privacy rights from *a priori* to *a posteriori* oversight. The third part offers a critique of the political economy that underpins an ideology embodied in the Directive which elevates the commercial right to use and trade personal data over the individual right to privacy. The fourth part discusses the ethical dilemmas that policy-makers must take into account for meaningful reform of structured inequalities of privacy and surveillance, and the conclusion considers what it means for citizenship and identity when peo-

ple's lives are wired into the global informational marketplace.

Big Brother Born Again in Legal Harmony and Corporate Synchrony

For businesses involved in transborder collec-tion and trade of personal data the only good data protection is the one that does not bar the extraction, handling and trade of the data com-ponents that constitute a consumer profile. At least that's the way it must seem to transnational operators like Eric Gerritsen, General Manager of the Rome office of Burson-Marsteller, the largest public relations firm in the world. According to Gerritsen, 'probably 85 percent of Burson-Marsteller's communication is com-puter-to-computer mail linked by an intercom-munication system stretching across 55 countries and five continents'. Burson-Marstel-ler uses this vast network whenever they 'need to know more about how people perceive a product in different countries'. For such research, Bur-son-Marsteller's agents can request information from one of three 'knowledge centres' based in Asia, America or Europe. These knowledge centres are databases containing the records of projects that Burson-Marsteller has presented to their clients over the last 20 years. 'All 15 EU countries contribute to keeping our knowledge centre in London alive and updated', said Ger-ritsen. 'They have tons and tons of documents about anything you want to know. We have someone in every European Union country who's in charge of collecting local knowledge and sending it to London' (Interview, 21 Febru-ary 1996). As Gerritsen's description of Burson-Marsteller's network suggests, data trade regula-tion affects transnational corporate operations on three territorial scales: the nation, the globe and the supranational region.

Originally, most data protection laws were aimed at limiting the intrusions of national gov-ernment authorities into the lives of citizens, but today many of these laws apply to private cor-porate uses of personal data as well. Where they exist, national privacy protection laws generally instruct domestic and foreign companies to act fairly with publicly available data sources and to disclose when business-related data processing takes place. Data protection has found expression on a global scale too, with recommendations and binding agreements encompassing planetary data trade. Two decades ago, for example, the Organization for Economic Co-operation and Development issued voluntary guidelines that proposed to standardise national policies on data protection with the goal of reconciling 'fundamental but competing values such as privacy and the free flow of information' (1980, p. 1). Also, more recently, the World Trade Organization developed its own 'Agreement on Trade-Related Aspects of Intellectual Property Rights' (1996), which set up rules for worldwide data commerce that affect the global flows of personal information.

In contrast, the EU Directive is an example of regulation working at the level of the supranational region. The Directive requires Member State governments to 'harmonise' hitherto incommensurate national regulations and to create national data protection laws where there were previously none. Before the Directive, the Council of Europe's 'Convention on Data Protection' (1981) was the 'most important Europe-wide agreement' on data privacy (Schwartz 1995a, p. 477). The more complicated and detailed EU Directive expanded on the Council of Europe's, as well as the OECD's, general principles, but allowed EU Member States more latitude to accommodate their laws to national legal and political traditions. The Directive is, however, binding. It was the first of its kind to instruct national governments to protect privacy rights while fomenting the free transborder flow of personal information within a supranational information marketplace.

To the extent that the Directive acknowledged the right of privacy, it did so only to sanction privacy protection as the single most effective inducement for consumer and citizen participation in information markets. Prior to the Directive, several of the national laws and recommendations that served as templates for the Directive already articulated this strategic function for privacy. For example, authors of one influential report prepared for the European Council clearly envisioned supranational data protection as a condition for free trade. The report, nicknamed for Martin Bangemann, the European Commissioner for Industrial Affairs who headed the Council's task force, stated that

without legal security of a Union-wide approach, lack of consumer confidence will certainly undermine the rapid development of the information society. Disparities in the level of protection of such privacy rules create the risk that national authorities might restrict free circulation of a wide range of new services between Member States in order to protect personal data ('Europe and the Global Information Society' 1994, p. 18)

This summarised the views of 'experts' from 20 top European telecommunication, industrial and media conglomerates. Among the firms represented in the Bangemann group were Olivetti, IBM-Europe, Alcatel, Reed Elsevier, Deutsche Telekom, Siemens, Philips, Telefónica of Spain, and the largest publicly owned conglomerate in Italy, the IRI. With the ostensible motivation to make recommendations on how best to create employment and competitiveness in the European Union, the Bangemann Report concluded that the EU should 'put its faith in market mechanisms as the motive power to carry us into the Information Age' ('Europe and the Global Information Society' 1994, p. 3).[1]

Thus the Directive's call to harmonise Member States' data protection laws clearly aimed to protect commercial freedom within the framework of liberalised trade of personal data and to synchronise transnational data commerce within the EU. An underlying assumption of the Directive was that there were no remaining personal information sources left to be annexed to the commercial market system; everyone was presumably wired in to the marketplace and, with proper protections, so would their private lives. This was an idea shared by official, corporate and scholarly commentary on data protection in the EU. From the point of view of market researchers in particular, the only problem with existing markets was that they lacked categorical definition. The goals for such business firms were therefore to consolidate data on what people think and desire and then to use that knowledge to cultivate universal devotion to the marketplace while securing niche market allegiances.

The Directive's framework for assessing harm caused by planned, ongoing or completed processing of personal information nevertheless stands as a guideline for fair and proper use of

stored and circulating data. It instructs commercial users of personal data to act responsibly in
the eyes of their customers and relevant public
authorities. Data merchants must declare,
among other things, what the data will be used
for, how people can access the data, and whether
the data will be used again for new purposes. For
those under surveillance, this means we can find
out who keeps tabs on us and for what reasons,
and we can challenge the accuracy of the information about us, upgrade it, or have it destroyed.
It would therefore seem that the Directive's call
for Europe-wide data privacy laws represents a
major advance for people who have no defence
against, or awareness of, the measures of marketing research and other corporate uses of personal data. Upon closer inspection, however,
these laws can be shown to compromise
privacy in favour of corporate data commerce.
The basic question is not whether details
of a person's life story ought to be seized and
processed, but how to do it without abating
either consumer loyalty or the free circulation
of commercial information.

Law, Territory, Speed and the TNC Advantage

The Directive's Article 4 endows each Member
State with the authority to inspect data processing taking place within their national territory
and to ensure compliance with the Directive's
provisions. Following the Directive, data protection agencies also have the general power to interpret the adequacy of commercial data security
and instruct commercial operators on legitimate
uses of personal data they want to process. Further, most national data protection agencies can
inhibit a private company from putting personal
data they've already plucked from a citizen into
wider circulation. Any bit of personal data ex-
tracted or handled under territorial jurisdiction
of a Member State is thereby protected, but only
as far as the law can legitimately and practically
monitor network locations and data destinations.

An important concern for data protection
agencies is the potential harm caused when publicly accessible sources of personal information,
such as phone or professional directories, are
tapped by third parties for trade purposes other
than those originally intended by the phone

company or professional organisation. However, the most egregious harm identified by the
Directive is the unauthorised use of 'sensitive
data' which reveal a person's health, religion,
race, political or philosophical beliefs, ethnic
origin, sex life, or trade union membership (Article 8, Paragraph 1). Marketers are required, for
example, to halt surveillance of individuals if the
information requested falls into the category of
sensitive data. Exemptions to this rule exist –
evidence that the data subject has consented,
for example.

The adequacy of sensitive data protection is
one of the three key standards, apart from data
quality and procedural rules, used to interpret
the lawfulness of transborder data trade in the
EU. Before the Directive was approved, this
standard could be found in multilateral agreements between Germany, France and Britain
where national authorities facilitated international data trade. Without such agreements,
'it was a problem for multinational companies
to comply with different data protection laws in
each European country', according to Anne
Carblanc, executive secretary of France's National Commission on Informatics and Freedom
(CNIL) (Interview, 26 February 1996). Despite
their agreements, French, German or British
businesses wishing to export personal data to
EU countries without data protection, like
Greece or, until recently, Italy, confronted
more numerous obstacles. Compliance with
the Directive will supposedly eliminate this
problem. But until Member States completely
transpose the Directive into their national laws,
each business exchange will have to be closely
inspected and will risk getting slapped with a
data embargo order (Schwartz 1995a, p. 488).

Schwartz (pp. 491–2) cites a well-known
example of a data embargo which involved a
disputed transfer of employee records from
Fiat-France to Fiat headquarters in Italy,
a country which had no data protection law at
the time. The French data protection agency,
CNIL, issued an embargo order that remained
in force until a contract was signed in which the
Italian multinational agreed to offer French Fiat
workers protection of their personnel files in
Italy equivalent to French law. In Germany, the
relevant authorities cannot impose a pretransfer
embargo, though they may implement one after
they have proven that a commercial operator has

failed to correct procedural, technical or organisational shortcomings in data processing. In any case, the Directive empowers all supervisory authorities to block data transfers should they seek to do so. For example, Danish, British, French and Dutch data protection agencies can now recommend a pre-transfer blockade on a transnational exchange of personal data (Schwartz, pp. 488–91). The Danish, French and British agencies can also directly issue the embargo, while the Minister of Justice holds such authority in the Netherlands.

Such a case-by-case 'contractual solution' became one option for dealing with transnational corporation (TNC) data transfers to countries lacking data protection standards like those set forth in the Directive. But, as Carblanc argues, 'the fact is that even if contracts are made it's very hard to know if they will be respected. We have no possibility to investigate in the US, for example.'

Here it is worth thinking briefly about how far the harmonisation of national policies in Europe will affect US businesses and US data regulation. Global marketers operating in the US, where protections covering sensitive data are virtually non-existent, generate lists as diverse as those profiling 'political conservatives, liberals, women who buy wigs, impotent middle-aged men, gamblers, male buyers of fashion underwear, and buyers of "skimpy swimwear and related items such as clingy short dresses and skirts"' (Reidenberg 1995, pp. 519–20). In the US, everything from hospital records and voter registration lists to liquor purchases and gay magazine subscriptions can be bought and sold. There are market research firms specialising in the whereabouts and tastes of Hispanic, Jewish and African-American communities, as well as companies monitoring the shopping patterns of Catholics and lesbians.

The US business culture and politics of data regulation alarms most European data protectors. 'No-one in Europe believes anyone should know about religious or ideological beliefs', said Miguel Orea of the Spanish data protection agency (Interview, 11 January 1995). According to Orea, 'people still remember the way the census was used to persecute Jews during the Nazi regime. So no-one here is obligated to declare their religion or political party.' If the US situation horrifies many European regulators, it

delights many European marketers. 'We'd love to have access to that kind of personal information', said Mattia Camellini upon hearing of available source lists of sensitive data. Camellini, the manager of sales and publicity for the Italian direct marketer, SEAT, added wistfully: 'The United States is a marketer's paradise' (Interview, 21 February 1996).[2]

In addition to the complications arising from having a major trading partner with an incompatible regulatory regime, European supervisory authorities face another, increasingly intractable, problem. One of the inherent disadvantages for data protection in the global information economy comes from the spatial dislocation and temporal discontinuity of computerised information flows. Consider first how the Directive's general provisions define stages of data processing in a linear order from collection to destruction. In theory, data protection can be applied at any of these recognised processing stations, which are treated as confinable zones of data handling. The first stage is collection, the point at which data fragments or files are brought together from such primary sources as surveys, polls and consumer focus groups and panels. Data are put into circulation at this point and remain in circulation through another dozen stages of data processing, including the recording of collected data, organising and storing data, altering or adapting, retrieval, consultation, use, and disclosure of data 'by transmission', dissemination, 'or otherwise making available', and so on until data are destroyed (Directive, Article 2). Although drafters of the Directive eliminated the rhetorical emphasis on 'the file', the substitute term 'processing' could not bury the sense that data are stationed within discrete physical spaces where they can be inspected.

In practice, however, data rush across the planet through telecommunication infrastructures made up of a mixture of privately owned local and long-distance networks, public and private monopolies operating national and regional networks, and global enterprises owning or leasing combinations of networks which tie their far-flung operations into one system. The lumbering legal process is a slow match for such stealthy and instantaneous data commerce. Because of telematic velocity and network dispersal, supervisory authority loses the political muscle needed to slow down personal data processing for inspection by regulators. As Charlotte Marie Pitrat, the French government's commissioner to the CNIL, put it, 'How can I use a right of data privacy if the future of data processing will be characterised by increased speed of data flows and greater delocalisation of data?' (Interview, 28 February 1996).

Speed and dispersion of data flows turned the problem of locating discrete files into a dilemma of locating and monitoring actions of businesses (data controllers) which operate processing equipment within national territories directly or through a surrogate. However, the Directive (Article 4) stopped short of giving Member States the authority to obstruct the flow of personal data which are simply in transit through EU-based equipment (say, from the US to Singapore). Moreover, it said nothing of the impossibility of tracking data after the elusive third and fourth transactions. In this context, data protection authorities, no matter how their rules compare, were forced to take a back seat to telematic technology. Today, data commerce not only outranks data privacy but outflanks any serious oversight of data processing. And, as Pitrat argued, 'because multinational companies can always transfer files from country to country, it will be something of a shell game to find out where the data have gone'.

Transnational corporations have already adjusted themselves to a range of data protection laws, some stricter than others. As Carblanc notes, 'Big firms have much more facility to comply with the laws than the smaller ones'. The TNC advantage has been helped along by legal consultants who specialise in helping companies engage in transborder data trade or trade within national markets where personal data protection exists. Otherwise, internal codes of conduct promulgated by international trade organisations or within individual firms have encouraged TNCs to fit their data processing activities to suit data protection regimes. 'Being a multinational corporation we interact with all the different legal practices within all the fifteen different European countries', said Burson-Marsteller's Gerritsen. 'So we go by whatever standard presents the worst condition for us. We know the law is coming down the line, so we have to be ready for it.'

In contrast, small- to medium-sized national firms are not typically positioned as well to take advantage of the new regulations. For instance, the costs of case-by-case contractual solutions for transborder data trade would alone be prohibitive, limiting the territorial expansion of smaller firms. Invariably it's the smaller firms that violate sectoral codes or fail to write internal codes of conduct. Moreover, according to Alain Tessier-Flohic of the French Ministry of Justice, 'most of the small companies don't even declare their files' (Interview, 27 February 1996).

The question for the 'experts' reverts once again to how to treat personal data with a minimum of harm to the individual and still maintain commercial freedoms. Meanwhile, databases fatten, networks spread wide and far, and data grow from a trickle to a flood, making it harder to know where data are at any given moment.

Who Owns their Own Privacy?

The Directive defines personal data as 'any information relating to an identified or identifiable natural person ('data subject')'. The 'personal' comprises every data fragment that might possibly constitute an individual's identity, from the artifice of identification numbers to the nose on a face. In theory, anything specific to 'physical, physiological, mental, economic, cultural or social identity' falls under the category of personal data deserving of protection (Article 2). Nevertheless, in practice, personal traits of identity can be defended legally only on condition that they constitute part of a legal property (Maxeiner 1995, pp. 624–6).

In the US, for example, the right of publicity is a misappropriation tort (Reidenberg 1995, p. 504) prohibiting 'the use of a person's name, likeness, or other indicia of identity, by a third person for purposes of trade, without consent' (Maxeiner 1995, p. 624). A right of publicity does not confer absolute ownership of 'indicia of identity' upon the data subject, but it does protect the 'commercial value of an individual's identity' when such identity circulates as audiovisual merchandise (Reindenberg 1995, p. 504; Gross et al. 1988). In French civil code, the 'right of image' functions similarly. In the Directive's Article 41, the property standard recognises people's rights to access and to verify processing of their personal data, including the 'right to know the logic involved in the automatic processing of data concerning' them, but it nullifies this right when its application will 'adversely affect trade secrets or intellectual property and in particular the copyright protecting the software'. Likewise in the 1996 US Telecommunications Act a property standard held that telecommunications carriers must protect 'customer proprietary network information' (Section 702, Article 1) and that 'Every telecommunications carrier has a duty to protect the confidentiality of proprietary information' (Section 702, Amendment of Title II). Similar language is repeated in Section 7 of the WTO's TRIPS document, which privileges copyrightable expression over any personal claims to the component parts of that expression.

In all these definitions, personal 'factors of identity' specific to body, mind, beliefs and culture have political and economic protections when they circulate as intellectual property, including significantly when they are somebody else's property. Indeed, people can defend their secrets only if they represent them in the form of private property. This paradoxical bond of surveillance, property and privacy flows from the classical liberal notion that equates individual self-determination within the realm of personal privacy with a commercial business's self-determination within the public realm of the marketplace. This rivalry of two freedoms is, in theory, a contest of equals so long as both sides – the personal space and the marketplace – produce income-generating property. According to Curry (1997, p. 695), such is the view informing 'the two main traditions in intellectual property regulation, the Anglo-American labor-based tradition and the Hegelian-based personality theory, or theory of moral right'. In the labour-based tradition, we author ourselves, make our private realms productive, and claim our labour as our property. In the moral rights tradition, property expresses personality: 'one becomes fully human only by owning property, just because only in that way can one show the world who one is' (Curry 1997, p. 695).

Thus if ordinary people interpret their private activities as marketable goods, then a balance between the rival freedoms of person and market can be struck. This was the lesson that Linda Tripp taught Monica Lewinsky, that talk show hosts are still teaching American television audiences, and that publishers of tell-all memoirists learned with renewed zeal in the last decade. Informational equality rests on the universal presumption that everyone will treat events in the personal realm as productive of informational commodities or properties.

In the practice of everyday life, however, most of us do not display our personal lives to make money or build assets. Indeed, such an idea is extremely foreign. Yet today a business that extracts details from individual life stories can turn personal data into information that serves a commercial purpose. This could be data drawn from credit card transactions, product warranty cards, or newfangled 'relationship marketing' which records tastes, sizes and hatreds in order to speed up repeat purchasing. Even if we refuse or fail to see in a manner that is congenial with the capitalist interpretation of private life, there are scores of businesses that persist in treating the effects and products of our private actions as raw material for the production of intellectual properties.

This conflict between popular and commercial interpretations of privacy's usefulness and meaning disrupts the harmonious discourse of the rival freedoms of personal space and market place and forces liberal thought to make a crucial ideological modification. If the way we value stories elaborated in private space is incommensurable with values generated in the marketplace, then personal privacy rights are downgraded. Ironically, the same liberal paradigm of sovereignty that protects a person's private life enables this denigration of private space. Ashley defines the 'paradigm of sovereignty' as 'an unquestioned condition of empowerment of all those sovereign subjects who are recognized as competent and free to reflect upon questions of law, prohibition, and constraint' (1989, p. 270). The Directive upholds this paradigm by defining privacy as a human or personal right bestowed upon an individual within a territorial democracy. Citizens of the Member State or the European Community are thereby empowered to withhold personal information from the marketplace. Yet under these very same terms, a person, a corporation or the Community itself can also be defined as competent, free and empowered to peek behind the veil of personal secrecy on grounds that they have a legitimate business or vital public interest in doing so. In this modified representation of rival freedoms, then, personal privacy attains merely semi-sovereign status in relation to the master sovereignty accorded to commercial uses and trade of personal data.

To understand the force of this ideology, compare the private realm of personal information to the inhabited territories of North America that were conquered under the banner of European civilisation. English common law deployed the sovereignty paradigm in order to uphold white colonisers' proprietary claims to lands occupied by 'wandering' native American tribes. English law guided American jurists to rename the discovery of land as a conquest and to transform this 'conquered' land into a space controlled by property rights. In this way, the US Supreme Court justified the expropriation of native lands and the denial of property rights to the original inhabitants. By this imperialist logic the European settlers could 'discover' the land in a natural, or unproductive, state and take it, cultivate it, and make it intelligible to European minds through its representation as property.

In 1823, Chief Justice Marshall ruled in Johnson v. M'Intosh that while the conversion of 'discovery of an inhabited country into conquest' appeared as an 'extravagant pretension', it was nevertheless the law, for the conquest had been asserted in principle, sustained over time, enforced across the territory, and became the source of income-generating property for the settlers (Harr and Liebman 1977, p. 13). As Marshall wrote in his opinion, 'if the principle has been asserted in the first instance, and afterward sustained; if a country has been acquired and held under it; if the property of the great mass of the community originates in it, it becomes the law of the land, and cannot be questioned'. The native Americans who lived on this conquered land were defined as mere occupants, demoted to the status of semi-sovereign people. 'So, too, with respect to the concomitant principle', wrote Marshall, 'that the Indian inhabitants are to be considered merely as occupants, to be protected, indeed, while in peace, in the possession of their lands, but to be deemed incapable of transferring the absolute title to others.'

Similarly, present-day legal opinion regards as legitimate the annexation of personal data 'discovered' under circumstances in which such data are found in an unproductive state – that is, when

they are not yet represented as intellectual property. Like the native lands, the space inhabited by personal identity stories is denigrated as an uncultivated wasteland, rendered semi-sovereign, and thereafter conquered in the name of progress. Surveillance and progress have long been united under the sign of property in modern, bureaucratic societies. An American legal scholar notes, for instance, how the 'activist state and service economy depend on an increased and intensified knowledge of the citizen in such roles as taxpayer, employee, consumer, or recipient of the state's benefits'. He goes on to assert that 'when gathering personal information is the objective, good, perhaps even excellent, reasons will often exist *not* to leave someone alone' (Schwartz 1995b, p. 558).

It is precisely under such imperial definitions that data merchants take charge of life-world details. After all, their authoritative self-representation makes them 'productive' of property within the informational marketplace. This semantics of power sustains the semi-sovereignty of data privacy and perpetuates the master sovereignty of business surveillance. The belief that the life-world of the indigenous people was inherently symbolic, non-material, and susceptible to conquest not only denied their identity stories any self-determined economic and political value but defined out of existence the very people with whom these stories originated.

The perception of this imperial legacy can be further sharpened by considering the patriarchal interpretation of intimacy's value. The elevation of commercial secrecy over personal secrecy, even within the realm of undisclosed intimacies, flows from the patriarchal preference for interpreting privacy as a place of merely symbolic development, the nurturing zone. A severe inequality migrates from European conquest to welfare handling of women's lives and to market-oriented treatments of intimate details – that is, the devaluation and depoliticisation of personal stories and secrets which are outside of the circle of income-generating property. This disparity stems from the normative separation of material production in a structured society of work, state and economy from so-called non-material, non-productive aspects of life in unstructured realms of domestic consumption, leisure and culture.

In other words, the belief that private life is inherently symbolic, non-material and feminine generates a chain of signifiers which expels economic and political value from the intimate spaces of life (Fraser 1989, pp. 132–3, 161–87). Such a distinction not only erases domestic labour and masks micro-political problems behind 'the quiet bliss of homeyness', as Habermas has written (Habermas 1989, p. 159; cf. Fraser 1989, pp. 161–87). It also underwrites the data merchant's authority to oversee the infrastructure of consumption. Think in this light again of marketing research's institutional power to snoop on consumers, of Linda Tripp's conquest of her 'friend's' intimate concerns, of so-called trash talk shows, and behind them of the commercial compulsion to convert marginal, 'unproductive' personal trivia into something valuable inside the 'productive' informational marketplace.

The Ethical Dilemma of Automated Encounters

The global data trade and the ensuing reterritorialisation of personal data protection intensifies a social process that Frank Webster (1995, pp. 1, 217–18) calls 'the informatisation of life'. One aspect of this process concerns the consolidation of markets through automatic data processing at a distance. Such delocalised data handling eliminates the possibility of engaging the decision-makers who label and differentiate us within the informational marketplace. As a consequence, both customer and business are barred from the full range of sources which are vital for the development of an ethical regard for private concerns and a critical awareness of the structured inequality of surveillance and privacy. In place of ethical sources there are technical assurances that the moral standards of proper data handling can be structured not only into the national laws of Member States but into the wiring and computer programs themselves. Like the legal instruments which are designed to ensure that corporations comply with the law, these mechanical standards supposedly defend people against the misuse of personal information while it is in circulation.

There are at least three problems with these technical and legal assurances that must be confronted in order to make meaningful reforms of personal data protection. First, machines and laws cannot substitute for the kind of moral pressure that can be brought to bear in face-to-face disputes over the use of personal information. While there is no reason to believe a local firm would act any more respectfully around personal privacy than a transnational firm, their proximity and even inclusion in the narrative spaces in which personal identity stories are elaborated makes them susceptible to popular interpretations of life's value. Rethinking data protection from the perspective of such an ethics of encounter could perhaps begin with what Barbara Ehrenreich calls 'the effort to make moral reflection a habit again' (1998, p. 12). Enactments of this effort to make moral reflection a habit in daily negotiations of privacy and publicity might start in anonymity and respect for the unknown in each other and engender more situational definitions of privacy's boundaries and surveillance's propriety. In other words, policy could do more to accommodate a greater variety of forms and modes of mutual respect by issuing a lasting challenge to the faceless automation of personal data commerce and its regulation.

The second problem flows from the first: the very language through which ethical sources serve to help us cultivate a sense of the harm and security pertaining to privacy/surveillance comes up silent in automated informational marketplaces. Perhaps this linguistic component of the face-to-face encounter is the most important, for it is everyday language, not the law, which carries the burden of representing the boundary defining where the personal secret ends and the publicity of private concerns begins. Such an ethics of encounter is thrown over for a prescripted standard of interpretation and judgement that follows from the social construction of privacy's semi-sovereignty. This moral standard, which is inscribed in the design of both information technology and its regulation, instructs us to value those personal stories that fall within the productive circle of the marketplace and to abase our appreciation of those that wander unproductively outside of it. In short, policy-makers could do more to foment national debates, discussions and, above all, the conditions for the elaboration of a language in which privacy and surveillance are not just represented in restatements of the sovereignty paradigm and the corollary property standard of self-worth.

This leads directly to the third problem. The morality of arguments about technical and legal assurances is ironic and cruel in the sense that the deployment of relevant laws and technologies also simultaneously insinuates surveillance deeper into our lives. For example, consumer surveillance like credit checks automatically judge and interpret an individual's value based on a data image of his or her financial worth. Were the relevant data treated responsibly and in full accordance with the law, automatic processing of a credit rating can easily occur without the data subject ever knowing what's happening. The moral standard remains intact, but within its own discourse lowers the reasonable expectation of privacy. Extending this logic further, market segmentation discriminates against selected groups of people by mechanically jettisoning them outside the market for certain goods and services, destroying their anonymity in the process. It may be too much to ask policymakers to break free of liberal discourse that unites surveillance and progress, but it's time they became more alert to the ways in which the articulation of policy invests commercial surveillance with greater legitimacy.

The residual effects of automated encounters in the informational marketplace include both increasing social stratification and the diminishment of personal autonomy. As Reidenberg (1995, p. 539) argues:

> Individuals perceive transactions in public places, such as the purchase of groceries at the supermarket or books at the bookstore, as anonymous activities, yet information records collected and maintained by store computer systems enable these activities to be personalised. Stores and other third parties can link specific transactions to individuals. Citizens no longer have the freedom to choose the terms of personal information disclosure and consequently have lost the capacity to participate in decisions about societal information flows. This denial of participation inherently manipulates citizens; liberty for the control of personal information reverts back in time.

The denial of participation, of the face-to-face encounter, creates a situation in which social change depends on categorical definitions and probabilistic accounts of what the consumer wants or what that person is worth. The possibility of an ethical regard for privacy and publicity is buried. Automation carries conveniences, but the conditions for challenging marketplace inequalities are impoverished when machines reconcile the ever-difficult relation between who we are and who the data merchants think we are.

Conclusion: Citizenship and Identity in the Informational Marketplace

Anecdotes abound concerning governmental bureaucrats enthusing over the potential to create permanent identification numbers of citizens and a national data bank in which all the disparate files on individuals can be stored and accessed for matching at will. We witness how surveillance cameras and other kinds of electronic eavesdropping cover the streets of major cities. Private corporations everywhere are notorious for mistreating credit information, for obnoxious, personalised direct marketing campaigns, and for the disruption of home life by survey researchers. At work, bosses and bootlickers watch and listen to ensure compliance with rules or to insert a little hearsay into a personnel file about such things as someone's willingness to work overtime or their propensity to socialise while on the job. In Europe, it's not unheard of to have personality tests, based on vulgar predictive models of behaviour and attitude, form part of such employment records. Tales like these can be found repeated throughout the world, some exaggerated while others underestimate the truth. In Rome, for example, there's private company called Sogei which was designed to catch Italy's tax evaders. From within its high-security building and surrounding grounds, Sogei projects and enacts the master sovereignty of data commerce. Sogei controls, for the Ministry of Finance, a gigantic processing centre which matches citizen files drawn from such sources as utilities bills, health histories, credit card accounts and bank records – all of this linked by national identification numbers.

All these stories share a common thread: personal information provides raw material for rendering people into data images. The coherency and accuracy of a data image, which has also been called a virtual individual, digital individual or digital puppet (Curry 1997), is not measured against the contradictory and complex lives of ordinary people; it is rather a function of the purpose for which it was created. For government, that might mean discerning the good taxpayer. For the police, the data image is a function of knowing the criminal type. For marketers, it's the target consumer. For employers, the model worker. In this sense, data images are always narrow interpretations of a person's identity, caricatures which are variously interpreted and judged by disparate institutions. No computerised file is expansive or smart enough to contain the full extent of details comprising personal and collective stories, and no cross-matching of files can possibly make up for this weakness. Thus, upon reflection, such fragmentary images would appear as strangers to those whom they supposedly identify. Yet these are images which circulate as authoritative markers of our identity, not only among institutions, friends and strangers, but sometimes in personal estimations of our own lives as well.

In this article I've argued that the mainstream discussion of data privacy and surveillance rests on imperialist and patriarchal assumptions about 'unproductive', 'worthless' or 'uncultivated' personal space. The imperious view of privacy's vulnerability issues from the sovereignty paradigm which legitimates the annexation of semi-sovereign possession – from this property-based principle, discovery converts to lawful conquest. The patriarchal view recapitulates the sovereignty paradigm in personal, intimate spaces to sustain the interpretation of personal data as non-economic, symbolic and unprocessed stuff. In these terms, information merchants like those working in marketing research take meaningless intimacies and transform them into 'productive' exchange values, as processed personal data flowing securely within the regulated networks of the informational marketplace.

The type of citizen best fit to this political economy is someone who can exercise their autonomy within the marketplace without making a childish fuss over the number stamped on their body. The good citizens of the marketplace suit this ideology because they participate in the information society knowing full well that their digital lives are being tracked. If you conceive of your privacy within this economics of display regulated by intellectual property, then you can begin to make peace with yourself as a market-place citizen. This means seeing data profiles as real features of our postmodern society and of ourselves (Curry 1997, p. 695).

To someone like Eric Gerritsen, there is no question about the good character of the marketplace citizen. They give marketers better data, because they 'are aware of how the data will be used'. Gerritsen acknowledged that Burson-Marsteller could 'get higher response rates if we fool people instead of telling them the straight story'. But in his experience, 'when people know the story and they sign up anyway, they'll probably be a good contact'. As Gerritsen knows, 'it's more cost-effective to have fewer people who are ready to talk rather than going to ten people and have eight who aren't even going to open the door'. Nobody who values their individuality wants to be a number; but in a corporate-dominated culture, the only valued individuality is one that bears that bizarre inscription.

Notes

1 The insertion of privacy protection into tracts promoting free data trade can also be found in US reports on telecommunication reform. Like the Bangemann group, the US National Information Infrastructure Advisory Council was dominated by a corporate-presence, including Disney, NYNEX, the National Newspaper Association, Bellcore, Corning, AT&T, MPAA, CBS, MCA and various other media and utilities operators. Also like Bangemann, the US Department of Commerce's second 'Report of the Information Infrastructure Task Force' cited people's fears of surveillance as a potentially intractable barrier to efficient and profitable use of the information infrastructure, arguing that 'Citizen control over private information' was a necessary condition for workable information markets ('The Information Infrastructure' 1994, p. 3).

2 The traditional difference in definition between US and EU regulation of personal data processing has to do with accountability and enforcement of rules guiding data privacy. In the US, sectoral laws put the burden upon individual customers to seek amends from individual companies in the courts while privacy torts set out guidelines for civil behaviour among citizens, including rules regarding each individual's right to exploit the commercial value of their name and image (Reidenberg 1995, pp. 505–6). Joel Reidenberg, who along with Paul Schwartz has written a comprehensive study of American data protection laws,

cited several trade association reports to summarise the US business reaction to the Directive. Reidenberg (1995, p. 541) wrote that it was 'loud and negative, but the need to respond galvanised American companies to evaluate their information practice policies'. He adds that 'Both legislative and executive branch officials began to evaluate US standards in light of the more comprehensive European principles'.

References

Ashley, Richard, 1989, 'Living on border lines: Man, poststructuralism, and war', in James Der Derian and Michael J. Shapiro (eds), *Intertextual/International Relations: Postmodern Readings of World Politics*, New York: Lexington Books/Macmillan, Inc, pp. 259–321.

Baudelaire, Charles, 1856, 'Edgar Poe: His Life and Works' in Raymond Foye (ed), *The Unknown Poe: An Anthology of Fugitive Writings by Edgar Allen Poe with Appreciations by Charles Baudelaire, Stéphane Mallarmé, Paul Valéry, J. K. Huysmans and André Breton* (trans. Raymond Foye), San Francisco: City Lights, 1980, pp. 79–92.

Council of Europe, 1981, *Convention for the Protection of Individuals with Regard to Automatic Processing of Personal Data*, January 28, No. 108.

Curry, Michael, 1997, 'The digital individual and the private realm', *Annals of the Association of American Geographers*, 87:4, pp. 681–99.

'Directive 95/46/EC of the European Parliament and of the Council, of 24 October 1995, on the protection of individuals with regard to the processing of personal data and on the free movement of such data', 1995, *Official Journal of the European Communities*, November 23: No. L 281/31–50.

'Europe and the Global Information Society: Recommendation to the European Council', 1994 (The Bangemann Report), May 26, Brussels.

Ehrenreich, Barbara, 1998, 'Conscience on campus', *The Progressive*, 63:12 December, pp. 11–12.

Fraser, Nancy, 1989, *Unruly Practices: Power, Discourse and Gender in Contemporary Social Theory*, Minneapolis: University of Minnesota Press.

Gross, Larry, John S. Katz and Jay Ruby, 1988, *Image Ethics: The Moral Rights of Subjects in Photography, Film, and Television*, New York: Oxford University Press.

Habermas, Jürgen, 1989, *The Structural Transformation of the Public Sphere: An Inquiry into a Category of Bourgeois Society* (trans. Thomas Burger with Frederick Lawrence), Cambridge, MA: The MIT Press.

Harr, Charles M. and Lance Liebman, 1977, *Property and Law*, Boston: Little, Brown and Company.

Maxeiner, James R., 1995, 'Business information and "personal data": Some common law observations about the EU Draft Data Protection Directive', *Iowa Law Review*, 80:3, pp. 619–38.

Organization for Economic Cooperation and Development 1980 *Recommendation of the Council Concerning Guidelines Governing the Protection of Privacy and Transborder Flows of Personal Data*, September 23.

Reidenberg, Joel R., 1995, 'Setting standards for fair information practice in the US private sector', *Iowa Law Review*, 80:3, pp. 497–552.

Schwartz, Paul M., 1995a, 'European data protection law and restrictions on international data flows', *Iowa Law Review*, 80:3, pp. 471–95.

Schwartz, Paul M., 1995b, 'Privacy and participation: Personal information and public sector regulation in the United States', *Iowa Law Review*, 80:3, pp. 553–618.

US Department of Commerce, 1994, The Information Infrastructure: Reaching Society's Goals, Report of the Information Infrastructure Task Force Committee on Applications and Technology, DOC, Technology Administration, National Institute of Standards and Technology.

Webster, Frank, 1995, *Theories of the Information Society*, London/New York: Routledge.

World Trade Organization, 1996, *Agreement on Trade-Related Aspects of Intellectual Property Rights, Including Trade in Counterfeit Goods*, May 14.

Chapter 12

"That Deep Romantic Chasm": Libertarianism, Neoliberalism, and the Computer Culture

Thomas Streeter

One step in the process of constructing a viable alternative to the neoliberal paradigm in communication policy is developing an understanding of why neoliberalism is so popular. It is important to counter the neoclassical economist's answer – "it's rational" by pointing to the many contradictions, irrationalities, and failures of neoclassically-based policies (e.g., Streeter, 1996). But as with most or all successful political movements, the power of neoliberalism does not seem to be purely a matter of scholarly argument. Furthermore, although it is true that part of neoliberalism's success can be explained in terms of the corporate interests it serves, this is not always the case. As Robert Horwitz (1989) and others have pointed out, some forms of market-oriented policy have been instituted despite the opposition of industry. And in any case, the broad political legitimacy of reforms undertaken on behalf of businesses needs to be explained. So the question remains: Why is the current quasi-religious faith in markets as the solution to all problems so compelling to so many? What makes it seem reasonable, forward-thinking, even a little bit thrilling?

The answer may well lie not just in economic or technological logics, but also in cultural ones. This chapter focuses on the careers and styles of two key figures in the development of today's "net culture," Stewart Brand and Theodor Nelson, and explores some elements of the pol-

itics of the culture of computers. On the one hand, this chapter confirms and elaborates an argument made or suggested by others, notably by Richard Barbrook and Andy Cameron in "The Californian Ideology" (1996) and Thomas Frank (1997) in *The Conquest of Cool*, that the computer culture can be understood as a deeply contradictory but politically powerful fusion of 1960s countercultural attitudes with a revived form of political libertarianism. Exploring the history and structure of that fusion, I believe, helps explain both neoliberalism's success and how it might be undone.

On the other hand, this chapter elaborates on aspects of the "structure of feeling" (Williams, 1961, pp. 48–71) of that fusion. The "deep romantic chasm" of my title is a line from Coleridge's poem *Kubla Khan;* I use it not just as an echo of one of the first visions of a world wide web, Theodor Nelson's *Xanadu* project, but also to suggest that an important component of net libertarianism rests more on a romantic notion of individualism, based on an expressive, exploring, transfiguring idea of the individual, than the calculating, pleasure-maximizing utilitarian individual characteristic of conservative economic theory. There are positive lessons to be learned from this romantic individualism, both in its compelling, popular character and in the key role it has played in technological and social innovation. But, as the word chasm suggests, this romantic individualism is limited: it is ultimately based on a pathological and illusory vision of isolation and escape from history and social context, which becomes evident in the expressive styles of net culture, the particularly obsessive fascination with interaction through the computer screen, and also in some of the policy directions advocated by culture, especially those involving intellectual property.

Why the Computer Culture Matters

It is easy to dismiss the computer culture as merely an adolescent subculture, as many do, whose values and principles hardly matter beyond the video game market. But the computer culture, although certainly not at the center of today's power structures, can be understood as standing in complex relation to the hegemonic bloc in the Gramscian sense. Members of the culture are fond of pointing out how the corporate and government worlds have been repeatedly wrong about or slow to catch on to developments that the computer culture pioneered, such as microcomputers, networking, user-friendly interfaces, multimedia, and the internet. So most obviously, "netizens" function as sources of innovation, as inventors and pioneers serving as a useful corrective to corporate myopia. Furthermore, among policymakers, both the products of the computer culture and to a lesser degree the culture itself often serve as archetypal examples of the marketplace in action. The new computer culture has become a political icon or ideogram: in many a policymaking mind today, the rapid global dissemination of microcomputers and the internet stand as models of what is good about the market. And these days, the computer culture itself has produced quite a few prominent cheerleaders for marketplace policies.

A full accounting of the impact of the computer culture on industrial and political decision making is far beyond the scope of this chapter. But as an illustration of its effect, it seems likely that the computer culture has played an important role in one of the more important communication-policy issues of our time: the headlong rush to privatize the internet. The explosion of the internet in the early 1990s left the mainstream corporate world surprised and bewildered; they had spent the previous decade investing in proprietary commercial on-line services like Prodigy, and yet suddenly here was a superior system they neither controlled nor understood. One might have explained the internet's success in terms of its nonprofit origins and nonproprietary organizing principles; the principles of open cooperation that are to some degree built into its design and that have encouraged its rapid global spread arguably reflect the ethic of sharing and collective inquiry common to the research universities that fostered the internet's development in the 1980s. Instead, at roughly the same time that Mosaic (the "killer app" of the internet) appeared, *Wired* magazine, the libertarian Electronic Frontier Foundation, and similar organs of the computer counterculture offered us another interpretation: the internet was a triumph not of nonprofit principles or of cooperation between government and the private sector but of a kind of romantic marketplace entrepreneurialism – a "frontier." As this interpretation seeped into policymaking circles and eventually became the "common sense" of the day, any policy lessons that might have been learned from the internet's nonprofit origins thus have been roundly ignored. Since the early 1990s, the only question has been how to completely commercialize the system, not whether or not to do it.

Cybernetics and the Countercultural Roots of the Computer Culture

Many of the computer culture's more prominent proponents came to political awareness while protesting the Vietnam war, and much of the culture's style and attitude has clear roots in the 1960s. Stewart Brand, for example, created and edited the countercultural compendium, the *Whole Earth Catalog*, and his *Coevolution Quarterly* was guest-edited by the Black Panthers in 1974 (Kleiner, 1986, p. 331). Yet *Coevolution Quarterly* eventually evolved into a computer software catalog, and today Brand is known as a technology booster, a fellow traveler with the editorial staff of *Wired* magazine, which not long ago featured Newt Gingrich on its cover. As a group, Brand and his cohort have become important promoters of contemporary economic conservatism.[1]

The term *cybernetics*, coined by Norbert Weiner in the late 1940s, came out of a set of interactions among intellectuals that included Gregory Bateson and Margaret Mead. Bateson, who to my knowledge never cared much about computers, went on to develop both a set of ideas about systems theory, ecology, and the human mind and a particularly effective pop writing style for presenting those ideas. In the 1970s, Stewart Brand went on to elevate Bateson to the status of guru, particularly in the pages of *Coevolution Quarterly*. And then in the early 1980s, *Coevolution Quarterly* evolved into the *Whole Earth Software Review*, essays about solar power were replaced by reviews of the latest computer software, and *Coevolution*'s nonprofit egalitarian principles (e.g., all employees received the same pay) were replaced by a for-profit inegalitarian salary structure;[2] several of the key figures in this 1980s evolution, like Art Kleiner and Kevin Kelly, went on to become founders and contributors to *Wired* magazine. Throughout this kaleidoscopic four-decade process the term cybernetics has remained a constant.

The role in all this of Gregory Bateson (and Stewart Brand's interpretation of him) is instructive. Bateson's books from the late 1960s, the most famous of which was *Steps to an Ecology of Mind* (1972), were written in a highly accessible, engaging way that eschewed academic jargon and reference; and in a style that was a kind of hip, charming version of the voice of the British gentleman amateur. Highly abstract ideas about systems theory, for example, are put in the mouth of a six-year-old girl chatting with her father. Hence, college students and literate hippies across the land, and even some precocious high school students, could curl up in a bean bag with one of Bateson's books and make some sense of it without the guidance of professors. Bateson was an anti-Derrida.

In the *Whole Earth Catalog*, Brand added to this accessible but thoughtful style a nonlinear, playful form of presentation that mixed descriptions of nonflush toilets with political tracts, a novel, and iconoclastic journalism – it was in the *Catalog* that most of the United States finally learned how astronauts went to the bathroom. On the one hand, the style expressed the "everything is related" holism of Batesonian systems theory. But it was also the case that the *Catalog*

was made for browsing. Certainly, the accessible, cluttered style of the *Catalog* shared something with the general style of the consumer culture; reading the *Whole Earth Catalog* in the early 1970s was probably fun in much the same way that reading the Sears catalog was in the 1890s. But the *Whole Earth Catalog* stood apart from the rest of the consumer culture in important ways: it was information rich, deliberately lacked glitz, and was not about consuming products for leisure time activities but – in its own mind at least – about understanding and building things for everyday life. To a whole generation of readers, and I think still to some extent today, this kind of writing is a breath of fresh air; its frankness and thoughtfulness was an antidote to the breezy, sugar-coated, condescending, anti-intellectual tone of much of the pop media, whereas its accessibility contrasted with the jargon-ridden, mystified styles that permeate our academic, government, and corporate bureaucracies.

Until the mid-1970s, one of the icons of those bureaucracies was the computer: for most of the culture, mainframe computers seemed to exemplify the mysterious, technological unfriendliness of our modern institutions. It was in the fusion of computer technical communities with features of countercultural practice and belief that this view of the computer began to change. Some of the origins of the shift in the character of the computer are probably familiar to many because of their mythologizing in the press: the computer-hobbyist community, in which Bill Gates and Steven Jobs both got their start, and the Xerox Palo Alto Research Center (PARC), which did much to invent or first implement the windows, mice, networks, and graphic interfaces that now grace our desks. But fewer (outside the computer culture) are familiar with the work of Theodor Nelson, the man who coined the term hypertext and claims to have invented the concept of linked electronic texts that led to the World Wide Web and the explosion in popularity of the internet.

Nelson clearly played a pioneering role in fostering the intellectual environment that made possible subsequent industrial developments; his intellectual influence on both the microcomputer revolution and the surprising success of the internet is arguably much greater than that of any of the computer impresarios that are in every technology reporter's Rolodex, like Nicholas Negroponte. Nelson's magnum opus was a book first published in 1974 called *Computer Lib*. It was essentially a transposition of the style, format, and countercultural iconoclasm of the *Whole Earth Catalog* into the world of computers.[3] It is impossible to establish exactly how widely read *Computer Lib* was, but it seems likely that most of those in attendance at the West Coast Computer Faire and similar now-legendary venues had at least some familiarity with Nelson and his work, and Nelson himself reports glowingly on a visit to Xerox PARC in the mid-1970s (Nelson, 1974b).[4] (I know at least one computer professional who told me, "*Computer Lib* changed my life"; Nelson claims to have encountered at least fifty such individuals [1987, p. 9]) And Nelson did frequently publish essays in science and computer journals and served for a time as editor of one of the first pop computer magazines, *Creative Computing* (Anderson, 1984, p. 74).

Computer Lib is full of concepts and approaches to computer use that were then unusual but have since become commonplace.[5] User-friendly interfaces, small personal-sized computers, mice, graphic interfaces, and non-computational uses of computers, like word-processing, e-mail, multimedia, and hypertext are all elaborately explained and advocated. He even anticipates contemporary buzz words: eighteen years before "web surfing" spread throughout the culture, Nelson wrote, "If computers are the wave of the future, displays are the surfboards" (1974b, p. 22).[6] And Nelson articulates grandiose notions about computers' liberatory potential that are now standard fare among netizens, claiming that "knowledge, understanding and freedom can all be advanced by the promotion and deployment of computer display consoles (with the right programs behind them)" (p. 58).

The style of *Computer Lib* is resonant with that of both Bateson and the *Whole Earth Catalog*.[7] The book criticizes and pokes fun at the mystifying jargon in which computers were then typically described. "I believe in calling a spade a spade – not a personalized earth-moving equipment module," Nelson quipped (1974b, p. 58). The language is deliberately playful and non-Latinate: computers are described as "wind-up crossword puzzles." And a loose sympathy with

countercultural politics and iconoclasm is also present: Nelson boasts of having been at Woodstock (1974b, p. 2), associates his critique of the computer profession with the feminist critique of the medical profession in *Our Bodies, Ourselves* (Nelson, 1974a, p. 2), inserts a solemn paean to nogrowth economics (p. 63), and puts a Black-Power-style raised fist on the cover. And the book's hand-drawn graphics, paste-up style, and self-published origin – Nelson brags about eschewing mainstream publishers – all bespeak an antiestablishment sentiment (albeit an undertheorized one).

"That Deep Romantic Chasm": *Xanadu* and Nelson's Dream of Perfect Intellectual Property

How did all this countercultural iconoclasm applied to computers metamorphose into a hotbed of neoliberalism? In a brief passage, almost as an afterthought, Nelson raised the problem of funding a universally available hypertext computer system:

> Can it be done? I dunno.... My assumption is that the way to this is *not* through big business (since all these corporations see is other corporations); *not* through government (hypertext is not committee-oriented, but individualistic – and grants can only be gotten through sesquipedalian and obfuscatory pompizzazz); but through the byways of the private enterprise system. I think the same spirit that gave us McDonald's and kandy kolor hot rod accessories may pull us through here. (1974b, p. 45)

In keeping with the pop-Marxism common in the early 1970s counterculture, Nelson thus sees both corporations and government as similarly suspect. But the allusion to Tom Wolfe is telling: his solution is not the Marxist but the libertarian one of free markets, imagined as if they could exist without supporting institutional structures like government and corporations.

Nelson's faith in the marketplace was by no means unique within the computer community. In the mid-1970s, the young Bill Gates was also trying to convince his fellow computer hobbyists in venues like early computer magazines that they should stop sharing software and start paying each other for it (Cringely, 1996, p. 55). But Gates clearly had a straightforward business model in mind. However sound his arguments may have seemed to many, they had no counter-cultural cachet.

Nelson's vision, in contrast, is rooted in a romantic, not utilitarian, form of individualism. He was not envisioning himself as simply a prag-matic, self-interested businessman. He never mentioned markets, profitability, or business in-centives. His writings bespeak a passion for in-quiry and experimentation for their own sake and a disdain for traditional business practices and shallow economic self-interest. And, in any case, by most accounts his major efforts to launch or participate in business ventures have been disasters (Wolf, 1995, p. 137).

The romantic character of Nelson's individu-alism is most evident in his proposals for a hypertext system called Xanadu, which helped inspire the World Wide Web and which, appro-priately enough, is named after the exotic "pleas-ure palace" in Coleridge's opium-induced poem *Kubla Khan*. Xanadu was described in *Com-puter Lib* and has apparently been Nelson's life's work ever since; as of this writing, after one major failed attempt to develop the system under a corporate umbrella, a small group in Australia seems to be carrying the flame for the project (Nelson, 1997a).

Xanadu, according to Nelson, is supposed to be a computer-based system of "connected litera-ture" that is easily accessible worldwide, much like today's World Wide Web. But with an im-portant difference: "The system," Nelson says, "must guarantee that the owner of any informa-tion will be paid their chosen royalties on any portions of their documents, no matter how small, whenever they are most used" (Nelson, 1997b). Nelson thus has always been opposed to those, like Richard Stallman, who argue that computer software should be freely distributed (Nelson, 1974b, p. 158).[8] His argument is on the surface a recapitulation of the (highly question-able) common sense of intellectual-property law in the US: "Copyright," he argues, "makes pub-lishing, and the better computer software, pos-sible" (Nelson, 1974a, p. 3).

It is crucial, however, that Nelson's desire to uphold an intellectual property system seems to have been fostering not an industry but a certain vision of fairness: "You publish something, anyone can use it, you always get a royalty auto-matically. Fair." The vision is of an isolated, "free" individual who communicates without the mediation of publishers, libraries, or educa-tional institutions. This economic fairness, moreover, is of a piece with intellectual fairness: "You can create new published documents out of old ones indefinitely, making whatever changes seem appropriate – without damaging the ori-ginals. This means a whole new pluralistic pub-lishing form. If anything that is already published can be included in anything newly published, any new viewpoint can be fairly pre-sented" (Nelson, 1983, ch. 2, p. 38). With Xanadu, each individual contribution to the system is perfectly preserved and perfectly rewarded: the computer system itself is sup-posed to prevent the possibility of unattributed theft of ideas because each "quotation" is pre-served by an unalterable link that not only allows readers to instantly call up intellectual sources but also ensures direct payment for each "use."[9] It's a vision of a mathematically perfect property system, of Lockean abstractions made manifest by computer technology.

By standard measures, Nelson has had a checkered career on the margins of the same commercial and educational computing com-munities that have been so deeply influenced by his ideas. Thus, there is something poignant about his vision: it is the vision of an outsider, never entirely secure or well rewarded by insti-tutions, who has never been treated "fairly," who imagines a utopia in which those "unfair" insti-tutions are supplanted altogether by commu-nities of free individuals working at computer consoles. It is a utopia where there are no arbi-trary powers, like IBM's monopoly, or arbitrar-ily powerful authorities with careers built on glad-handing or hot air; a utopia where no ten-ured journal editor can prevent one's article from reaching publication and no short-sighted cor-porate executive can arbitrarily deep-six a be-loved project on behalf of cost-cutting. Nor can any of these people claim an underling's idea as their own.

By most accounts (though not by Nelson's), Xanadu itself has been a failure; it is the mother of all vaporware. Nelson's writings for the last quarter-century are full of unfulfilled predic-tions of the system's imminent completion and publication; to this day Nelson insists that a viable working system is just around the corner (Nelson, 1997a). *Wired* magazine published a lengthy history of Xanadu, titled "A Hacker Tragedy," which depicts the effort as a quixotic and fundamentally impractical effort driven more by neurosis than by programming ability or vision (Wolf, 1995). I am not competent to evaluate the specifics of the software (which in any case remain largely proprietary), but I would hazard a guess that part of the impossibility of the effort may be of a piece with Nelson's vision of property. The logarithmically increasing demands on computing resources that such a perfect system would demand (each alteration recorded, each reading generating compensation for each author, a complete record or all such transactions accessible to all throughout the system) may have been its technological Waterloo; in conventional economic language, the system would probably drown in its own "transaction costs."

The tragic impossibility of Xanadu may be of a piece with the dream that motivates it, a dream of community unmediated by the complex burdens of history and institutions, of individual creativity without the ties of social context. What is missing from Nelson's view of the world, of course, is a sense of the determining character of history, politics, and social complexity; his dream, in fact, is precisely to overcome the arbitrary hierarchies and messy interconnectedness of our imperfect world, not by struggling with that interconnectedness but by escaping from it into the computer screen. That is why, in all the countless computer utopias we have seen depicted over the last fifteen years, no one changes any diapers. In Nelson's visions of cyberspace, as in so many others, there is no particular sense of people eating, growing food, getting old or sick, or building roads, houses, and factories. There is generally an absence of, even a disdain for, bodies: actual human bodies are often cavalierly dismissed as mere "meat" in net culture, and the real world described as "meat space" (Dery, 1997).

The entire problem of transaction cost in neoclassical economic theory is itself an effort to account for economic "externalities"; all that messy political and social stuff that does not fit the conventional economic models of isolated individuals competing in a marketplace. In Nelson's computer utopia, as in most such visions, there is little sense of any of the constitutive character of even the most immediate of those "externalities": the expensive educational systems and the massive government funding of science and defense that provided the context for all the computer-oriented experimentation, speculation, and reflection like Nelson's. The fact that computer experts are overwhelmingly well-educated middle- and upper-class white males working in cozy research campuses of universities and corporations is studiously ignored. The social conditions that formed the background conditions for the computer culture and its accomplishments of the 1970s and 1980s – patriarchy, class relations, the wide availability of higher education in the 1950s and 1960s through government programs like the GI bill – are rendered invisible. The oft-told story of Bill Gates learning about computers in high school and then dropping out of Harvard to found Microsoft is treated as an example of classic entrepreneurial pluck, as if Gates were some modern day Robinson Crusoe operating in isolation from social support; the profound difference in social power available to the young man from a wealthy family who drops out of Harvard compared with, say, one who drops out of an inner city high school, or with a woman who drops out of college to have a baby, disappears from the computer libertarian scenarios. The expensive computer that Gates learned on in high school is treated like a fact of nature, not the product of the well-funded school system of the type increasingly available only to the privileged.

Law as Computer Code: The Fantasy of Escape from History into the Computer Screen

The means by which the eventual marriage of the computer counterculture's libertarianism with today's conservative movement were accomplished are well illustrated by Stewart Brand's (1987) celebratory book about MIT's Media Lab. Brand opens with an epigraph that dedicates the book to the "drafters and defenders of the First Amendment" and that describes the amendment as an "elegant code by witty programmers." Here in a nutshell are the characteristic tropes of the computer culture: wry wit, iconoclasm, and a breathtakingly naïve denial of history and social process. For as any legal historian and most lawyers know, the first amendment, whatever its merits, is not at all like computer code. It has never functioned with the automatic, mechanical certainty of a computer program. Its contemporary meanings in American law are barely half a century old; in the nineteenth century, for example, it was frequently interpreted to mean that censorship was discouraged at the federal level but completely legitimate at the local and state levels. A computer program executes itself in the same way each time, regardless of who is operating the computer; a legal principle, in contrast, is interpreted differently depending on its social and historical context. The current strong interpretation of the First Amendment in the United States is a political accomplishment, a result of complex social and ideological struggles, not a result of feeding the Bill of Rights into a neutral legal machine (Kairys, 1990; Streeter, 1995).

Yet the fantasy that laws do work that way is a key commonality between the current rising conservative tide and the otherwise disparate computer culture. A radical distinction between law and politics is central to the libertarian faith; law, the theory goes, underpins a system of individual liberties neutrally and mechanically, whereas government involves the arbitrary and subjective political interference with those rights. Clever and elegant legal codes by witty legal programmers allow us to be self-interested, unattached, free individuals, monads in a marketplace, whereas government coerces us into repressive collectives. That is why conservatives can imagine that there is no contradiction between their frequent calls for law and order and their criticisms of government intrusion into our lives. The fantasy that law works like a computer code, in sum, undergirds the denial of history, social structure, and political struggle that is central to the libertarian faith in markets, at least in its more naïve forms. The habits of thought that metamorphosed from 1960s countercultural social libertarianism into technology-based economic libertarianism, and eventually lent credibility to today's dominant neoliberalism, thus rely on a metaphorical interfusion of law with computers, in which each is imagined to function like the other.

Ted Nelson's faith in the ahistorical formalist understanding of law becomes clear when he defends his insistence on copyright protection:

> I've heard ... arguments, like "Copyright means getting the lawyers involved." This has it approximately backwards. The law is ALWAYS involved; it is CLEAN ARRANGEMENTS of law that keep the lawyers away.... If the rights are clear and exact, they are less likely to get stepped on, and it takes less to straighten matters out if they are. Believe it or not, lawyers LIKE clean arrangements. "Hard cases make bad law," goes the saying. (Nelson, 1997b)

Most of those familiar with the historical details of intellectual-property law would probably be more than a little skeptical of the idea that intellectual-property can be rendered into such "clean arrangements." Based as it is on such nebulous notions as "originality" and the distinction between an idea and its expression, intellectual property is a famously shifting and murky area of the law, replete with qualifying complications like fair use, copyright collectives, and compulsory licensing. Intellectual property is a classic example of a form of property where, as one famous essay on property law put it, "crystals turn to mud" (Rose, 1988). With *Xanadu*, of course, Nelson promises a technological fix to all this murkiness. But historical experience and a little common sense would suggest that the fit between technologies and intellectual property has only grown murkier as technologies have grown more sophisticated. The internet and the World Wide Web, in particular, though they do embody much of Nelson's utopian fantasy, blur rather than clarify the boundaries of authorship and intellectual property that were central to his vision; it is easier than ever before to copy someone else's work without attribution, and uncertainty in the realm of intellectual property is one of the major legal and policy issues of the day.

Both the passionate attachment to the formalist vision of law and its naiveté became abundantly clear when Congress added the pornography-prohibiting Communications Decency Act (CDA) to the 1996 Telecommunications Act, and the computer culture flew into a libertarian high dudgeon over the CDA. Computer pundit Brock Meeks, for example, flooded the internet with outraged diatribes, frequently repeating the query "Which part of NO LAW don't you understand?" – as if no one could read the amendment and interpret it differently. (The fact that for 150 years the best-trained jurists in the land *did* read the First Amendment quite differently seemed to have escaped Meeks' consciousness.) Similarly, the Electronic Frontier Foundation's John Perry Barlow distributed an outraged "Declaration of Independence of Cyberspace," as if the CDA were the last straw that would precipitate a popular rebellion against governments worldwide. As the First Amendment is a favorite topic of reporters, the flap over the CDA became the primary focus of press coverage of the 1996 act, the only element of the Act that had any controversy associated with it.

In fact, the CDA takes up less than a page of the nearly hundred-page Telecommunications Act, and was correctly understood by many at the outset as unenforceable and unconstitutional. The bulk of the act, by contrast, is a rather typical piece of corporate welfare, handing out various favors to corporate interests and creating some behavioral ground rules that provide industry overall with stability and protection from cutthroat competition during a period of organizational and technological change. The key progressive component of the act, one with important implications for fostering the open, public debate that is the goal of free-speech law, was arguably the creation of a universal service fund for schools and libraries. Yet all this was accomplished by elaborate inside-the-beltway maneuvering, and the universal service issue escaped any widespread public debate, even on the internet. In retrospect, it seems probable that the computer culture's loud objections to the CDA, rather than promoting the cause of freedom, in fact served to deflect attention from the much more important, and in the long term, more freedom-restricting procorporate components of the 1996 Telecommunications Act. One of the more enduring legacies of computer libertarianism may be the way it served to distract attention from the core of the 1996 Act, thus ensuring its easy passage.

Conclusion

There is much of value in the computer culture and its legacy. People like Ted Nelson were more right about the future of computers than the bulk of the managers who controlled decision making in the electronics industry; the computer culture was on to something. And its success has helped keep alive a respect for iconoclasm. Although I think the dominant impact of *Wired* was conservative and co-optive, it is an intriguing fact that, for a few years during the height of its popularity, business managers across the land were thumbing through a magazine that would routinely include observations like, "One of the dirty secrets of capitalism is that the harder you work the less you get paid."

The most important lesson of the computer counterculture is that the dramatic success of the internet, small computers, user-friendliness, open systems, and hypermedia is evidence of a widespread desire for connection and cooperation in a context free of the private and public hierarchies that so often dominate our lives. Unlike the standard conservative marketplace fables in which we are told that all will be well if we dedicate ourselves to the selfish, calculating pursuit of the profit motive, computer utopians like Ted Nelson and Stewart Brand celebrate pleasures of unrestricted communication, of connection with others, pleasures that are both aesthetically and intellectually creative and social and that cannot be reduced to the calculating self-interest of *homo economicus*. Nelson's vision of computers was always one in which computers are interlinked and are used creatively in liberatory ways, in which they are tools for social interaction, not merely tools for controlling people and machines in the name of enhancing the efficiency of profit-driven enterprises. Ted Nelson may have been an outlier, but he spoke to real resentments and dissatisfaction with the hierarchical worlds of managers and bureaucrats that characterize so much of modern life.

As a political formula, the romantic libertarianism that the computer culture offers as an alternative is as powerful as it is wrongheaded. True, in the hands of political hacks like George Gilder, the formula may be just an after-the-fact rhetorical trick to justify broader conservative social policies. But what the cases of Theodor Nelson and Stewart Brand suggest is that, for many, the formula can be deeply compelling. In a warped way, it articulates genuine dissatisfaction with existing power structures and genuine desires for forms of social life that are less hierarchical and more liberating than those offered by the current corporate-dominated welfare–warfare state.

Any politically progressive use of the insights, styles, and dissatisfactions that gave birth to the computer culture would have to bring out its hidden histories and social constituents. One of the liabilities of the colloquial, accessible writing style of the computer culture is that it obscures intellectual legacies and context; you have to read Gregory Bateson very carefully to notice his debts to Freud and social and anthropological theory. It needs to be made clear that the pleasant anarchy of the internet is not just the product of an absence of control but that it was built upon a foundation of support from nonprofit research universities and their costly and fragile culture of open intellectual exploration. The inanities of corporate managerialism that are so deftly criticized by both Ted Nelson and "Dilbert" need to be put in the historical context of the modern corporate form of organization and its supports in the legal system, such as the fiction of the corporate individual.

More abstractly, I think a compelling alternative form of individualism needs to be developed. Nelson's dream of freedom in computer screens in practice devolves into a desire for *disconnection*, freedom *from* relations with others through illusions like legal neutrality or the "technical fix" of the computer itself. This articulates with the conventional conservative notion of freedom as purely negative, as freedom *from*, not freedom *to*. And like that conventional conservative idea of freedom, it too easily works to support the corporate hierarchies it imagines it will overthrow. For a certain kind of person (primarily white, male, educated, and middle- or upper-middle class), playing with a computer in fact *feels* like an escape into another world, into a kind of freedom. Computer obsession bespeaks, I think, a fear of the political, of interconnectedness, a distorted wish to escape the unpredictability and unknowability of relations with others that comes from being social creatures. That obsession is understandable, perhaps, given the limitations of contemporary life; but it is a shallow and ultimately illusory form of freedom. Over the long term, any successful politics of the Left will have to address the genuine dissatisfactions and desires that make the computer seem like a form of freedom, like an escape; but it must do so in a way that leads beyond them in the direction of something more situated: a mature version of freedom.

Notes

1 The political full circle of Brand and his cohort can be seen in the fact that, while in 1969 arch Vietnam war-supporter Ithiel de Sola Pool and Brand were on opposite sides of the barricades, by 1987 Brand was explicitly basing his political analysis on de Sola Pool's *Technologies of Freedom* (Brand, 1987, p. 214).

2 Stewart Brand set out to create a *Whole Earth Software Catalog* and a *Software Review* in the summer of 1983. Editors for these projects were offered salaries competitive with other computer-writing jobs, and the policy of equal-pay-for-all-staffers that had been in place at *Coevolution Quarterly* since 1976 came to an end. The same year, *Coevolution Quarterly* raised its subscription prices without, as had been done in the past, discussing it or mentioning it in the magazine. In the fall of 1984, the *Whole Earth Software Review* and *Coevolution Quarterly* were combined and the joint publication was named *Whole Earth Review*. See Kleiner (1986, pp. 336–7).

3 *Computer Lib* resists conventional citation. It has two halves, printed back-to-back in the same volume with each half inverted to the other, so that it essentially has two front covers, one titled *Computer Lib* and the flip side titled *Dream Machines*. As each half has separate page numbers, citations below refer to page numbers in *Computer Lib* or *Dream Machines*, as appropriate. The copy used here is described as the First Edition, "Ninth Printing, Sept. 1983," and thus, though the copyright listed on both first pages is 1974, a description of events of 1975 like the appearance of the MITS Altair are described, and in Nelson's own biography (p. 3) of *Computer Lib* he describes activities through 1977. A heavily revised and re-typeset edition was published in 1987 by Tempus Books of Microsoft Press; as some of the more interesting historical material was removed in this revision, citations below are to the First Edition unless otherwise noted.

4 *Dream Machines*, p. "X" (the second page of a lettered, unnumbered "Special Supplement to the Third Printing, August 1975" that starts *Dream Machines*). The passage predicts that Xerox PARC's innovations – those that would lead to the creation of the Macintosh less than a decade later – will lead Xerox to dominate the computer field. But Nelson concluded with the following prescient

parenthetical statement: "The above predictions are based, of course, on the assumption of Xerox management knowing what it's doing. Assumptions of this type in the computer field all too often turn out to be without basis. But we can hope."

5 In one of many prescient passages, Nelson critiques a June 30, 1975, *Business Week* article, "The Office of the Future," which foretells computerized offices staffed by centrally located, specially trained word-processing technicians and predicts that the only companies that will succeed in this field will be IBM and Xerox. Nelson continues: "Well, this is hogwash. . . . The office of the future, in the opinion of the author, will have nothing to do with the silly complexities of automatic typing. It will have screens, and keyboards, and possibly a printer for outgoing letters. All your business information will be callable to the screen instantly. An all-embracing data structure will hold every form of information – numerical and textual – in a cats'-cradle of linkages; and you, the user, whatever your job title, may quickly rove your screen through the entire information-space you are entitled to see. You will have to do no programming" (1974b, p. x).

6 Robert Hobbes Zakonís "Hobbes Internet Timeline v3.1" (<http://www.info.isoc.org/guest/zakon/Internet/History/HIT.html>) attributes the first use of the term *web surfing* to Jean Armour Polly in 1992.

7 Lest there be any doubt that Nelson was familiar with the *Catalog*, in *Dream Machines*, (p. 3) he writes, "Of course I'm blatantly imitating, in a way, the wonderful *Whole Earth Catalog* of Stewart Brand." He also cites the *Domebook*, a popular instruction manual on geodesic domes, as inspiration. And *Computer Lib* visually quotes *The Whole Earth Catalog's* cover (and most famous image) with a full-page computer-generated image of earth from space, captioned "The Hole Earth Catalog" (p. 69).

8 These ideas are more explicitly elaborated in Nelson's self-published *Literary Machines* (1983), chap. 2, pp. 35–8. (Each chapter has separate page numbers.)

9 The Xanadu Australia web page (<http://www.xanadu.net/the.project.html/>), describes the project thusly: "We need a way for people to store information not as individual 'files' but as a connected literature. It must be possible to create, access, and manipulate this literature of richly formatted and connected information cheaply, reliably, and securely from anywhere in the world. Documents must remain accessible indefinitely, safe from any kind of loss, damage, modification, censorship, or removal except by the owner. It

must be impossible to falsify ownership or track individual readers of any document. This system of literature (the "Xanadu Docuverse") must allow people to create virtual copies ("transclusions") of any existing collection of information in the system regardless of ownership. In order to make this possible, the system must guarantee that the owner of any information will be paid their chosen royalties on any portions of their documents, no matter how small, whenever and wherever they are used."

References

Anderson, J. (1984, November). Dave tells Ahl: The history of creative computing. *Creative Computing*, pp. 67–74.

Barbrook, R., and Cameron, A. (1996). The Californian ideology. *Science as Culture*, 26, 44–72.

Bateson, G. (1972). *Steps to an ecology of mind*. New York: Ballantine Books.

Brand, S. (1987). *The Media Lab: Inventing the future at MIT*. New York: Viking Penguin.

Cringely, R. X. (1996). *Accidental empires: How the boys of Silicon Valley make their millions, battle foreign competition, and still can't get a date* (2nd edn.). New York: Harper Business.

Dery, M. (1997, September 28). The cult of the mind. *New York Times Sunday Magazine*, pp. 94–6.

Frank, T. (1997). *The conquest of cool: Business culture, counterculture, and the rise of hip consumerism*. Chicago: University of Chicago Press.

Horwitz, R. (1989). *The irony of regulatory reform: The deregulation of American telecommunications*. New York: Oxford University Press.

Kairys, D. (1990). Freedom of speech. In D. Kairys (Ed.), *The politics of law: A progressive critique* (rev. edn.) (pp. 237–72). New York: Pantheon.

Kleiner, A. (1986). A history of *Coevolution Quarterly*. In A. Kleiner and S. Brand (eds.), *News that stayed news: Ten years of Coevolution Quarterly 1974–1984*. San Francisco: North Point Press.

Nelson, T. (1974a). *Computer Lib*. (Flip side of *Dream Machines*). Self-published.

——. (1974b). *Dream Machines*. (Flip side of *Computer Lib*). Self-published.

——. (1983). *Literary Machines* (5th edn.). Self-published.

——. (1987). *Computer Lib/Dream Machines* (rev. edn.). Redmond Washington: Tempus Books of Microsoft Press.

——. (1997a). The Xanadu Australia web page. <http://www.xanadu.net/the.project/>.

——. (1997b). <www.hyperstand.com/Sound/Ted Report2.html>.

Rose, C. (1988). Crystals and mud in property law. *Stanford Law Review*, 40, 577–610.

Streeter, T. (1995). Some thoughts on free speech, language, and the rule of law. In R. Jensen and D. S. Allen (Eds.), *Freeing the First Amendment: Critical perspectives on freedom of expression* (pp. 31–53). New York: New York University Press.

——. (1996). *Selling the air: A critique of the policy of commercial broadcasting in the United States*. Chicago: University of Chicago Press.

Williams, R. (1961). *The long revolution*. Westport, Conn.: Greenwood Press.

Wolf, G. (June, 1995). The curse of Xanadu. *Wired*.

Part V

The Arts and Museums

Introduction to Part V

Justin Lewis and Toby Miller

Many areas of cultural life involve struggles over definition, and none more so than the notions of art and artistry. For many, the term "the arts" signifies a range of activities heavily appropriated by notions of excellence and tradition – notably classical music, ballet, contemporary dance, opera, the theater, literature, painting and sculpture. It is not simply that this is what most people think of when they use or hear the term, it is an understanding deeply inscribed within cultural policy: these, after all, are the activities that generally get funded in the name of art. How we define art therefore has a very real currency, since this definition demarcates those cultural activities regarded worthy of state support from those that are not.

To use the term "art" is often a way of establishing distinctions between certain kinds of cultural practice, distinctions policed by experts, scholars, and artists who advise funding agencies or bestow critical legitimacy on various artforms and artists. If newer art forms – such as film or jazz – are admitted into the category there is an implication of a certain elevation acquired through scholarly legitimacy. These distinctions are generally grounded in aesthetic judgments about what is good or bad, and while these aesthetic deliberations have a certain degree of autonomy, they are also – as Bourdieu has argued – implicated in social as well as artistic hierarchies of taste and preference. Both class distinction and what we might politely call "art appreciation" are strongly related to educational and class background – a background through which one acquires what he refers to as the "cultural competence" to appreciate art (Bourdieu, 1984). The audiences for the arts *thus defined* tend to be more upscale in class terms.

Indeed, the arts have long been considered a signifier of class distinction, whether by working-class people who see the arts as only "for posh people" (Lewis, 1990, p. 20), by the aspiring middle classes, or by elites desiring of ways to legitimate their position in cultural terms (DiMaggio, 1982). This is not to reduce arts appreciation to a mere pose – the enjoyment of art may be deeply felt – but to recognize the way it is implicated in class relations. Thus advocates for public funding of the arts are caught up in a profound contradiction between a democratic spirit (the desire to make art economically accessible and to place it in the public rather than the private realm) and a class-bound aesthetics. Admission to galleries or concert halls is subsidized so that all may enter, while the act of admission is simultaneously a marker of class distinction. If the sentiments behind arts subsidies are sometimes egalitarian, the consequences are not.

So it is, for example, that free admission to the Tate Modern art gallery in London is financed by profits from the National Lottery. Although there is no doubt that free admission broadens the generally esoteric appeal of modern art, this arrangement effectively taxes one cultural activity (the cheaper forms of gambling) whose participants tend to be poorer than average, and uses it to reduce the cost of a cultural activity generally frequented by a more affluent clientele (or, in the case of students, the potentially more affluent). What is justified in the name of universal access thus ends up being a regressive redistribution of resources. It follows that political debates about the public funding of art are full of curious alliances – conservatives sometimes speaking on behalf of popular taste against what is portrayed as aesthetic excess, and progressives defending the judgments of cultural elites to decide what is worthy of public support.

The contradiction between a democratic urge and the desire to adhere to certain forms of aesthetic hierarchy often takes the form of a kind of cultural evangelism – once the vulgar masses get a taste of great art, it is supposed, they will lose their vulgarity. If this was self-evidently the motivation behind late nineteenth-century philanthropic gestures such as the "People's Palace" in London's East End, it remains lurking behind many defenses of contemporary arts subsidies. Few arts funding agencies, in their more platitudinous moments, have been able to resist intonations of this kind. Art is good for the human spirit, we are told, and we will all be better if we are exposed to its elevating influence.

It is not enough to deny – as many arts advocates do – the class distinctions attached to artistic or cultural tastes as if they were some form of coincidence (these denials usually involve reference to artists with working-class backgrounds or the kinds of meritocratic anecdotes that sustain myths of equality of opportunity like the "American Dream"). Since the twentieth century, the custodians of elite culture have rarely justified their evaluations in straightforwardly social class terms, preferring to envision an aesthetically distinct class of artists and evaluators. As F. R. Leavis – one of the most famous advocates of cultural hierarchies – put it: "In any period it is upon a small minority that the appreciation of art and literature depends: it is only a few who are capable of unprompted first-hand judgment – the minority capable of not only appreciating Dante, Shakespeare, Donne, Baudelaire, Hardy, but of recognising (that) their latest successors constitute the consciousness of the race at a given time.... Upon this minority depends our power of profiting from the finest human experience of the past.... Upon them depend the implicit standards of that order the finer living of an age, the sense that this is worth

more than that, that the centre is here rather than there... without which distinction of spirit is thwarted and incoherent" (Leavis, 1930, pp. 3–5). To his credit, Leavis (unlike many artists or arts advocates who rely on ineffable notions of genius) attempted as clearly as he could to define *the means* by which these distinctions could be made, by which we could judge what is great, good or merely ordinary, and to thereby detach the ability to make artistic judgments from "the small minority" who could hitherto make them. And yet, as Raymond Williams pointed out, it was a notion of culture and art defined specifically in opposition to the popular (Williams, 1976), and it is the *antithesis between the popular and the artistic* that resounds throughout discussion of "the arts." It is therefore an elitist aesthetic *by definition*, and while there is no necessary overlap between an arts elite and class privilege, it is not surprising if the two become connected in the institutional hierarchies that shape contemporary social life.

These notions of art have been challenged for some time by sections of the community arts movement. For some, the community arts have been guided by a cultural evangelism that fails to dislodge art as a predefined set of categories and approaches, but simply undertakes to deliver it to the community. Other community artists have taken a more radical approach, and have challenged conventional definitions of art head on. Community artists like Owen Kelly redefined art as culture, finding creativity and expression in the popular and everyday, and building upon it. The goal was not to change, elevate or convert, but to provide resources and training to develop what was already there (Lewis, 1990). Art, in other words, was no longer conceived in antithesis to the popular, but as something that might exist alongside and through it. The most fundamental problem with the redefinition proposed by radical community artists is that by undercutting the value system that designated art as worthy or unworthy of public support, we are forced to conceive of entirely new criteria for public policy. If we no longer fund something because it is deemed worthy by experts and practitioners in the know, then on what basis *do* we fund it? Since the answers to this question are neither univocal nor obvious, a traditional system that, for all its contradictions, has a clear rationale about the attribution of value is difficult to dis-place.

The question remains nonetheless, and its importance for the development of a progressive arts policy is undiminished. Many debates about public arts funding – notably in the US where arts funding, as meager as it is, has long been under a sustained attack from free market libertarians and moral conservatives – tend to skirt around the issue. As George Yúdice points out, when Republicans launched their attack on the National Endowment for the Arts via complaints about the homoerotic photography of Robert Mapplethorpe, the notion that art be conservatively defined and subject to a set of standards was something upon which both Jesse Helms and the Endowment's liberal defenders agreed. The argument was simply about the nature of those standards. Similarly, defending public arts funding by attacking privatization provides an easy target, but begs the question of why progressives should support a subsidy for the edification and amusement of the educated classes.

A critical cultural policy is thereby faced with two choices. It can either work with existing definitions of arts and struggle to find ways to make those practices more democratic, or it can begin with a redefinition that avoids class-based aesthetic hierarchies. The second course is necessarily a difficult one: if we use broad, more inclusive definitions of artistic or creative practices, we need also to establish principles by which one practice is worthy of subsidy and another less so.

Public policy for museums faces the same questions, as well as some particular to the museum as an institution. The museum is to the arts as the documentary is to cinema: stolid, serious, and indomitable. But it is also a peda-gogic tool of some dynamism. The nineteenth century's proliferation of public art museums in Western nations is directly related to a new duty for the visual arts – to be agents of civilizing discipline. The public museum embodied a crit-ical shift of focus away from the intramural world of the princely museum. Prior to the En-lightenment, royal collections were meant to express monarchical grandeur and induce a sense of insignificance in the viewer. But mod-ernity called out for identification and a mutual, municipal ownership that hailed visitors as par-ticipants in the collective exercise of power

(Turner, 1993, pp. 60–2, 74–5, 98; Bennett, 1995, p. 166).

The same is true today: the implied visitor is given a "proper" perspective on the site's his-tory and the visitor's place in it. And a prior age is made known. This past time once occupied our own physical space. As such, it is part of our transcended and either admirable or regret-table heritage. We can learn from it, but it is definitely over. The visitor is expected to under-stand that we now live in a moment of increased knowledge and perspective. This understand-ing activates a historical form of cultural citizen-ship. It emerges in the here and now, but in reaction to the past. The past's commemor-ation in museum form is a strictly delimited ethical zone, a space in which "proper" and "im-proper" conduct are divided. This ethical zone of the historical citizen sifts out the good, the bad, and the sublime in past treatment of people, noting discontinuities and linearities in a movement towards present, enlightened, standards.

This style of historical narrative is teleological – the latest epoch is always the most advanced. And its heritage dates to the very origins of public culture: successive French coups after 1789 saw the Louvre provided with at least one additional ceiling with each change of regime, a renovation that explained past glories as leading to present power and gave a revisionist account of previous regimes (Duncan, 1995, p. 29).

The genre of the museum calls upon a demo-cratic rhetoric associated with access, as an open space for the artifactually occasioned site of public discussion. But as a pedagogic site, it functions in a disciplinary way to forge public manners. It is an opportunity for the public to deliberate on some aspect of cultural history is opposed to an opportunity for museum magis-trates to give an ethically incomplete citizenry a course of instruction. This binary can itself be made more subtle. Consider the varied histories that underpin Holocaust memorials in the US: to remember the dead or the self, as survivor or liberator; to constitute the US as the preserve *par excellence* of freedom; to draw tourists; to be a community center; to stress religious or ideological affiliations; and to obtain votes. All these decisions are made "in political time, contingent on political realities" (Young, 1992, p. 58). Yet this "political time" is rarely made explicit to visitors. Germain Bazin, an early curator at the Louvre, thought of the museum as "a temple where Time seems suspended" and quasi-religious individual epiphanies would be experienced; of course, these moments were directed from on-high via lectures on the value of the arts that positioned the state as the key point of articulation between work and subject (quoted in Duncan, 1995, p. 11; also see p. 27).

Tony Bennett argues that critical cultural policy must address the contradictions inscribed in the institutional form of the public museum. The first is the contradiction between the museum as an instrument for universalizing claims of collective ownership of cultural property and the museum as an instrument for differentiating populations. The resulting tension between a museum in theory (collectively owned) and in practice (designed and managed to exclude certain kinds of people) leads to an unendable demand for access and use, as social movements pressure for a democratizing expansion of the collective. A politics of representational proportionality emanates from the contradiction between the space of representation associated with the premise of universality inherent in the institution of the public museum and the fact that this injunction is impossible due to the gendered, racist, classist, or nationalist patterns of its exclusions and biases.

Exclusions are brought about not so much by prohibiting entry, or confining visitors, but by education. In both its arrangement of things and its instructions to the public on how to approach collections, the museum hails its audience as respectful trainees. Visitors are induced by example, exhortation, and even the physical layout of the space, to adopt certain manners and relinquish others. They learn to look and not touch, to walk about calmly and gently, and to distinguish the graceful from the riotous. These are modes of conduct related to behavior in a space, rather than internal reactions to art on a wall or in a display case (Bennett, 1995, pp. 1, 7, 90–1, 97, 102–3). That *ur*-teen movie of rebellion, *Ferris Bueller's Day Off* (John Hughes, 1986) features a high-art diegetic insert, as otherwise unruly funsters move respectfully around the Chicago Art Institute's collection, finding themselves to be maturing subjects, ready for

college – all part of the museum's mission as an ethical workplace.

Museums are charged with bringing public attention to what has previously been concealed, to take the secrets of an elite into the populace at large. Instead of objectifying that population, as per the public executions of eighteenth-century Europe, the museum subjectifies people, offering them a position *in* history and a relationship *to* history. By the end of the nineteenth century, Western Europe had created public art museums as "signs of politically virtuous states," and a series of American cities (Boston, Cleveland, New York, Chicago, Buenos Aires, Lima, Rio de Janeiro, and Mexico City) followed suit. When the English Parliament debated public art museums, discussion centered on how to prepare the people to appreciate the grandeur of art, and an imposing form of architecture was deemed the best method of instilling awe (Duncan, 1995, pp. 11, 32, 21). The public museum's universal address has characteristically obliterated difference or, more often, caricatured it via racist and imperialist appropriation and scientism, sexist exclusion or mystification, and class-based narratives of progress. The entire project of "discovery" has also infantilized the visitor. The principal characteristic of the museum era is mastery over the physical environment and other countries. Scientific and imperial triumphs target more than the visitor, for they also infantilize those beyond such discourses or subject to them. This rhetoric of universal uplift runs into trouble when it encounters "excellence"-inflected definitions of heritage and the aura of leading museums as prestigious clubs (Bennett, 1995, p. 97; Jordanova, 1991, pp. 22, 32; Price, 1994, pp. 25, 30). This promise of the modern has produced complications ever since.

References

Bennett, Tony. *The Birth of the Museum: History, Theory, and Politics*. London: Routledge, 1995.

Bourdieu, Pierre. *Distinction: A Social Critique of the Judgment of Taste*. Trans. Richard Nice. Cambridge, Mass.: Harvard University Press, 1984.

DiMaggio, Paul. "Cultural entrepreneurship in 19th century Boston: the creation of an organizational base for high culture," *Media, Culture and Society*, vol. 4, no. 1, 1982.

Duncan, Carol. *Civilizing Rituals: Inside Public Art Museums*. London: Routledge, 1995.

Jordanova, Ludmilla. "Objects of Knowledge: A Historical Perspective on Museums." *The New Museology*. Ed. Peter Vergo. London: Reaktion, 1991, 22–40.

Leavis, F. R. *Mass Civilization and Minority Culture*. Cambridge, 1930.

Lewis, Justin. *Art, Culture and Enterprise: The Politics of the Cultural Industries*. London: Routledge, 1990.

Price, Clement Alexander. *Many Voices Many Opportunities: Cultural Pluralism and American Arts Policy*. New York: American Council for the Arts/Allworth Press, 1994.

Turner, Graeme. *National Fictions: Literature, Film and the Construction of Australian Narrative*, 2nd edn. Sydney: Allen and Unwin, 1993.

Williams. Raymond. *Culture and Society*. New York, Columbia University, 1976.

Young, James E. "Holocaust Memorials in America: Public Art as Process." *Critical Issues in Public Art: Content, Context, and Controversy*. Ed. Harriet F. Senie and Sally Webster. New York: Iconeditions, 1992, 57–70.

Chapter 13

The Political Rationality of the Museum

Tony Bennett

In her essay 'The Museum in the Disciplinary Society', Eilean Hooper-Greenhill argues that the ruptures of the French Revolution 'created the conditions of emergence for a new "truth", a new rationality, out of which came a new functionality for a new institution, the public museum' (Hooper-Greenhill 1989: 63). Established as a means of sharing what had previously been private, of exposing what had been concealed, the public museum 'exposed both the decadence and tyranny of the old forms of control, the *ancien régime*, and the democracy and utility of the new, the Republic' (ibid.: 68). Appropriating royal, aristocratic and church collections in the name of the people, destroying those items whose royal or feudal associations threatened the Republic with contagion and arranging for the display of the remainder in accordance with rationalist principles of classification, the Revolution transformed the museum from a symbol of arbitrary power into an instrument which, through the education of its citizens, was to serve the collective good of the state.

Yet, and from the very beginning, Hooper-Greenhill argues, (Hooper-Greenhill 1989) the public museum was shaped into being as an apparatus with two deeply contradictory functions: 'that of the elite temple of the arts, and that of a utilitarian instrument for democratic education' (Hooper-Greenhill 1989: 63). To which, she contends, there was later added a third function as the museum was shaped into

an instrument of the disciplinary society. Through the institution of a division between the producers and consumers of knowledge – a division which assumed an architectural form in the relations between the hidden spaces of the museum, where knowledge was produced and organized in camera, and its public spaces, where knowledge was offered for passive consumption – the museum became a site where bodies, constantly under surveillance, were to be rendered docile.

In taking my bearings from these remarks, my purpose in what follows is to offer an account of the birth of the museum which can serve to illuminate its political rationality, a term I borrow from Foucault. The development of modern forms of government, Foucault argues, is traced in the emergence of new technologies which aim at regulating the conduct of individuals and populations – the prison, the hospital and the asylum, for example. As such, Foucault contends, these technologies are characterized by their own specific rationalities: they constitute distinct and specific modalities for the exercise of power, generating their own specific fields of political problems and relations, rather than comprising instances for the exercise of a general form of power. There is, Foucault further suggests, frequently a mismatch between the rhetorics which seemingly govern the aims of such technologies and the political rationalities embodied in the actual modes of their functioning. Where this is so, the space produced by this mismatch supplies the conditions for a discourse of reform which proves unending because it mistakes the nature of its object. The prison, Foucault thus argues, has been endlessly subject to calls for reform to allow it to live up to its rehabilitative rhetoric. Yet, however ineffective such reforms prove, the viability of the prison is rarely put into question. Why? Because, Foucault argues, the political rationality of the prison lies elsewhere – less in its ability to genuinely reform behaviour than in its capacity to separate a manageable criminal sub-class from the rest of the population.

The museum too, of course, has been constantly subject to demands for reform. Moreover, although its specific inflections have varied with time and place as have the specific political constituencies which have been caught up in its advocacy, the discourse of reform which motivates these demands has remained identifiably the same over the last century. It is, in the main, characterized by two principles: first the principle of public rights sustaining the demand that museums should be equally open and accessible to all; and second, the principle of representational adequacy sustaining the demand that museums should adequately represent the cultures and values of different sections of the public. While it might be tempting to see these as alien demands imposed on museums by their external political environments, I shall suggest that they are ones which flow out of, are generated by and only make sense in relation to the internal dynamics of the museum form. Or, more exactly, I shall argue that they are fuelled by the mismatch between, on the one hand, the rhetorics which govern the stated aims of museums and, on the other, the political rationality embodied in the actual modes of their functioning – a mismatch which guarantees that the demands it generates are insatiable.

Thus, to briefly anticipate my argument, the public rights demand is produced and sustained by the dissonance between, on the one hand, the democratic rhetoric governing the conception of public museums as vehicles for popular education and, on the other, their actual functioning as instruments for the reform of public manners. While the former requires that they should address an undifferentiated public made up of free and formal equals, the latter, in giving rise to the development of various technologies for regu-

lating or screening out the forms of behaviour associated with popular assemblies, has meant that they have functioned as a powerful means for differentiating populations. Similarly, demands based on the principle of representational adequacy are produced and sustained by the fact that, in purporting to tell the story of Man, the space of representation shaped into being in association with the formation of the public museum embodies a principle of general human universality in relation to which, whether on the basis of the gendered, racial, class or other social patterns of its exclusions and biases, any particular museum display can be held to be inadequate and therefore in need of supplementation.

To argue that this discourse of reform is insatiable, however, is not to argue against the political demands that have been, still are and, for the foreseeable future, will continue to be brought to bear on museums. To the contrary, in arguing the respects in which these demands grow out of the museum's contradictory political rationality, my purpose is to suggest ways in which questions of museum politics might be more productively pursued if posed in the light of those cultural dynamics and relations peculiar to the museum which they must take account of and negotiate. In this respect, apart from looking to his work for methodological guidance, I shall draw on Foucault politically in suggesting that a consideration of the 'politics of truth' peculiar to the museum allows the development of more focused forms of politics than might flow from other perspectives.

Let me mention one such alternative here. For the birth of the museum could certainly be approached, from a Gramscian perspective, as forming a part of a new set of relations between state and people that is best understood as pedagogic in the sense defined by Gramsci when he argued the state 'must be conceived of as an "educator", in as much as it tends precisely to create a new type or level of civilisation' (Gramsci 1971: 247). Nor would such an account be implausible. Indeed, a Gramscian perspective is essential to an adequate theorization of the museum's relations to bourgeois-democratic polities. In allowing an appreciation of the respects in which the museum involved a rhetorical incorporation of the people within the processes of power, it serves – in ways I shall outline – as a useful antidote to the one-eyed focus which results if museums are viewed, solely through a Foucaultian lens, as instruments of discipline. However, I want, here, to bend the stick in the other direction. For once, as in the Gramscian paradigm they generally are, museums are represented as instruments of ruling-class hegemony, then so museums tend to be thought of as amenable to a general form of cultural politics – one which, in criticizing those hegemonic ideological articulations governing the thematics of museum displays, seeks to forge new articulations capable of organizing a counter-hegemony. The difficulty with such formulations is that they take scant account of the distinctive field of political relations constituted by the museum's specific institutional properties. Gramscian politics, in other words, are institutionally indifferent in ways which a Foucaultian perspective can usefully temper and qualify.

The Birth of the Museum

Let me now turn, in the light of these considerations, to the origins and early history of the public museum, an institution whose distinguishing characteristics crystallized during the first half of the nineteenth century. In doing so I shall foreground three principles which highlight the distinctiveness of the public museum with respect to, first, its relations to the publics it helped to organize and constitute, second, its internal organization, and, third, its placement in relation both to kindred institutions as well as to those – both ancient and modern – to which it might most usefully be juxtaposed.

Douglas Crimp's account of the birth of the modern art museum offers an instructive route into the first set of questions (Crimp 1987). Crimp regards the Altes Museum in Berlin as the paradigmatic instance of the early art museum, seeing in it the first institutional expression of the modern idea of art whose initial formulation he attributes to Hegel. Constructed by Karl August Schinkel, a close friend of Hegel's, over the period 1823 to 1829 when Hegel delivered his lectures on aesthetics at the University of Berlin, the conception of the Altes Museum's function, Crimp argues, was governed by Hegel's philosophy of art in which art, having ceded its place to philosophy as the

supreme mode of our knowledge of the Absolute, becomes a mere object of philosophical contemplation. The space of the museum, as this analysis unfolds, thus becomes one in which art, in being abstracted from real life contexts, is depoliticized. The museum, in sum, constitutes a specific form of art's enclosure which, in Crimp's postmodernist perspective, art must break with in order to become once more socially and politically relevant.

The argument is hardly new. The stress Crimp places on the Hegelian lineage of the art museum is reminiscent of Adorno's conception of museums as 'like family sepulchres of works of art' (Adorno 1967: 175), while his postmodernist credo echoes to the tune of Malraux's 'museum without walls' (Malraux 1967). Yet while it may make good sense, as part of a political polemic, to view art museums as institutions of enclosure from the point of view of the possible alternative contexts in which works of art might be exhibited, Crimp is led astray when he proposes 'an archaeology of the museum on the model of Foucault's analysis of the asylum, the clinic and the prison' on the grounds that, like these, it is 'equally a space of exclusion and confinement' (Crimp 1987: 62). Quite apart from the fact that it's difficult to see in what sense works of art, once placed in an art museum, might be likened to the inmate of the penitentiary whose confinement results in subjection to a normalizing scrutiny directed at the modification of behaviour, Crimp's thesis would require that the context for art's display provided by the art museum be regarded as more enclosed than the contexts provided by the variety of institutions within which works of art, together with other valued objects, had been housed from the Renaissance through to the Enlightenment.

This is patently not so. While such collections (whether of works of art, curiosities or objects of scientific interest) had gone under a variety of names (museums, *studioli, cabinets des curieux, Wunderkammern, Kunstkammern*) and fulfilled a variety of functions (demonstrations of royal power, symbols of aristocratic or mercantile status, instruments of learning), they all constituted socially enclosed spaces to which access was remarkably restricted. So much so that, in the most extreme cases, access was available to only one person: the prince. As we trace, over the course of the late eighteenth and early nineteenth centuries, the dispersal of these collections and their reconstitution in public museums, we trace a process in which not just works of art but collections of all kinds come to be placed in contexts which were considerably less enclosed than their antecedents. The closed walls of museums, in other words, should not blind us to the fact that they progressively opened their doors to permit free access to the population at large. The timing of these developments varied: what was accomplished in France, violently and dramatically, in the course of the Revolution was, elsewhere, more typically the product of a history of gradual and piecemeal reforms. Nevertheless, by roughly the mid-nineteenth century, the principles of the new form were everywhere apparent: everyone, at least in theory, was welcome. David Blackbourn and Geoff Eley, in tracing these developments in the German context, thus stress the respects in which the advocacy of museums – along with that of adjacent institutions embodying similar principles, such as public parks and zoos – was premised on a bourgeois critique of earlier absolutist forms of display, such as the royal menagerie. In doing so, they counterpose its formative principle – that of addressing 'a general public made up of formal equals' – to the formally differentiated forms of sociability and edification that had characterized the *ancien régime* (Blackbourn and Eley 1984: 198).

In these respects, then, and contrary to Crimp's suggestion, the trajectory embodied in the museum's development is the reverse of that embodied in the roughly contemporary emergence of the prison, the asylum and the clinic. Whereas these effected the sequestration and institutional enclosure of indigent and other populations, which had previously mixed and intermingled in establishments whose boundaries proved relatively permeable or, as in the scene of punishment or the ships of fools, had formed parts of elaborate public dramaturgies, the museum placed objects which had previously been concealed from public view into new open and public contexts. Moreover, unlike the carceral institutions whose birth coincided with its own, the museum – in its conception if not in all aspects of its practice – aimed not at the sequestration of populations but, precisely, at the mixing and intermingling of publics – elite and popular – which had hitherto tended towards separate forms of assembly.

I make these points not merely to score off Crimp but rather to stress the respects in which the public museum occupied a cultural space that was radically distinct from those occupied by its various predecessors just as it was distinct in its function. This, in turn, serves to underscore a methodological limitation of those accounts which tell the story of the museum's development in the form of a linear history of its emergence from earlier collecting institutions. For it is by no means clear that these provide the most appropriate historical co-ordinates for theorizing the museum's distinctiveness as a vehicle for the display of power. Depending on the period and the country, many candidates might be suggested for this role – the royal entry, the court masque, the tournament, the *ballet de cour* and, of course, the various precursors of the public museum itself. However, while, in the early Renaissance period, many of these had formed vehicles for the display of royal power to the populace, they ceased to have this function from the sixteenth century as, with the emergence of absolutism and the associated refeudalization of courtly society, they came to function mainly as court festivals or institutions designed to display monarchical power within the limited circles of the aristocracy.

So far as the public display of power to the general population was concerned, this increasingly took the form, especially in the eighteenth century, of the public enactment of the scene of punishment. Yet if the museum took over this function, it also transformed it in embodying a new rhetoric of power which enlisted the general public it addressed as its subject rather than its object. The logic of this transformation is best seen in the respects in which the development of the museum and the prison criss-cross one another in the early nineteenth century – but as histories running in opposing rather than, as Crimp suggests, parallel directions. Thus, if in the eighteenth century the prison is a relatively permeable institution effecting an incomplete enclosure of its inhabitants, its nineteenth-century development takes the form of its increasing separation from society as punishment – now severed from the function of making power publicly manifest – is secreted within the closed walls of the penitentiary. The course of the museum's development, by contrast, is one of its increasing permeability as the variety of restrictions placed on access (when granted at all) – people with clean shoes, those who came by carriage, persons able to present their credentials for inspection – are removed to produce, by the mid-nineteenth century, an institution which had migrated from a variety of private and exclusive spheres into the public domain.

The place of the two institutions in the history of architecture underlines this inverse symmetry of their respective trajectories. Robin Evans has shown how, while there was no distinctive prison architecture before 1750, the next century witnessed a flurry of architectural initiatives oriented to the production of the prison as an enclosed space within which behaviour could be constantly monitored; an architecture that was causal in its focus on the organization of power relations within the interior space of the prison rather than emblematic in the sense of being concerned with the external display of power (Evans 1982). Museum architecture was comparably innovative over the same period, witnessing a spate of architectural competitions for the design of museums in which the emphasis moved progressively away from organizing enclosed spaces of display for the private pleasure of the prince, aristocrat or scholar and towards an organization of space and vision that would allow museums to function as instruments of public instruction (Seling 1967).

Nor, in thus passing one another like ships in the night, are the museum and the penitentiary oblivious of the fact. When Millbank Penitentiary opened in 1817, a room festooned with chains, whips and instruments of torture was set aside as a museum. The same period witnessed an addition to London's array of exhibitionary institutions when, in 1835, Madame Tussaud set up permanent shop featuring, as a major attraction, the Chamber of Horrors where the barbarous excesses of past practices of punishment were displayed in all their gory detail. As the century developed, the dungeons of old castles were opened to public inspection, often as the centrepieces of museums. In brief, although often little remarked, the exhibition of past regimes of punishment became, and remains, a major museological trope.[1] While the functioning of such exhibitions in relation to Whiggish accounts of the history of penality is clear, this trope has also served as a means whereby the museum, in instituting a public

critique of the forms for the display of power associated with the *ancien régime*, has simultaneously declared its own democratic status. Thus, if the museum supplanted the scene of punishment in taking on the function of displaying power to the populace, the rhetorical economy of the power that was displayed was significantly altered. Rather than embodying an alien and coercive principle of power which aimed to cow the people into submission, the museum – addressing the people as a public, as citizens – aimed to inveigle the general populace into complicity with power by placing them on this side of a power which it represented to it as its own.

An Order of Things and Peoples

This was not, however, merely a matter of the state claiming ownership of cultural property on behalf of the public or of the museum opening its doors. It was an effect of the new organizational principles governing the arrangement of objects within museum displays and of the subject position these produced for that new public of free and formal equals which museums constituted and addressed. In Hooper-Greenhill's account, the function of princely collections during the Renaissance was 'to recreate the world in miniature around the central figure of the prince who thus claimed dominion over the world symbolically as he did in reality' (Hooper-Greenhill 1989: 64). Based on the interpretative logic of what Foucault has characterized as the Renaissance *episteme*, which read beneath the surface of things to discover hidden connections of meaning and significance, such collections were 'organised to demonstrate the ancient hierarchies of the world and the resemblances that drew the things of the world together' (ibid.: 64). As, in the course of the eighteenth century, the force of the Renaissance *episteme* weakened under the weight of, again in Foucault's terms, the principles of classification governing the classical *episteme*, museum displays came to be governed in accordance with a new programme. Governed by the new principles of scientific taxonomy, the stress was placed on the observable differences between things rather than their hidden resemblances; the common or ordinary object, accorded a representative function, was accorded priority over the exotic or unusual; and things were arranged as parts of series rather than as unique items.

It is odd, however, that Hooper-Greenhill should leave off her account at this point. For the epistemic shift that most matters so far as the public museum is concerned is not that from the Renaissance to the classical *episteme* but that from the latter to the modern *episteme*. As a consequence of this shift, as Foucault describes it in tracing the emergence of the modern sciences of Man, things ceased to be arranged as parts of taxonomic tables and came, instead, in being inserted within the flow of time, to be differentiated in terms of the positions accorded them within evolutionary series. It is this shift, I suggest, which can best account for the discursive space of the public museum. The birth of the museum is coincident with, and supplied a primary institutional condition for, the emergence of a new set of knowledges – geology, biology, archaeology, anthropology, history and art history – each of which, in its museological deployment, arranged objects as parts of evolutionary sequences (the history of the earth, of life, of man, and of civilization) which, in their interrelations, formed a totalizing order of things and peoples that was historicized through and through.

The conceptual shifts which made this possible did not, of course, occur evenly or at the same time across all these knowledges. In the case of history and art history, Stephen Bann (1984) attributes the development of the two principles governing the poetics of the modern history museum – the *galleria progressiva* and the period room – to the Musée des monuments français (1795) and Alexandre du Sommerard's collection at the Hôtel de Cluny (1832), although Pevsner (1976) traces elements of the former to Christian von Michel's display at the Dusseldorf gallery in 1755. In the case of anthropology, while Jomard, curator at the Bibliothèque Royale, had argued, as early as the 1820s, for an ethnographic museum that would illustrate 'the degree of civilisation of peoples/who are/ but slightly advanced' (cited in Williams 1985: 140), it was not until Pitt Rivers developed his typological system that display principles appropriate to this objective were devised. Nor was it until towards the end of the century that these principles were widely diffused, largely due to the influence of Otis Mason of the Smith-

sonian. Similarly, the theoretical triumph of Darwinism had little effect on museum practices in Britain until Richard Owen, a defender of Cuvier's principle of the fixity of species, was succeeded, towards the end of the century, by William Henry Flower.

When all these caveats are entered, however, the artefacts – such as geological specimens, works of art, curiosities and anatomical remains – which had been displayed cheek by jowl in the museum's early precursors in testimony to the rich diversity of the chain of universal being, or which had later been laid out on a table in accordance with the principles of classification, had, by roughly the mid-nineteenth century, been wrenched from both these spaces of representation and were in the process of being ushered into the new one constituted by the relations between the evolutionary series organized by each of these knowledges. In these respects, and like their predecessors, museums produced a position of power and knowledge in relation to a microcosmic reconstruction of a totalized order of things and peoples. Yet, and as a genuinely new principle, these power–knowledge relations were democratic in their structure to the degree that they constituted the public they addressed – the newly formed, undifferentiated public brought into being by the museum's openness – as both the culmination of the evolutionary series laid out before it and as the apex of development from which the direction of those series, leading to modern man as their accomplishment, was discernible. Just as, in the festivals of the absolutist court, an ideal and ordered world unfolds before and emanates from the privileged and controlling perspective of the prince, so, in the museum, an ideal and ordered world unfolds before and emanates from a controlling position of knowledge and vision: one, however, which has been democratized in that, at least in principle, occupancy of that position – the position of Man – is openly and freely available to all.

It is, however, around that phrase 'at least in principle' that the key issues lie. For in practice, of course, the space of representation shaped into being by the public museum was hijacked by all sorts of particular social ideologies: it was sexist in the gendered patterns of its exclusions, racist in its assignation of the aboriginal populations of conquered territories to the lowest rungs of human evolution, and bourgeois in the respect that it was clearly articulated to bourgeois rhetorics of progress. For all that, it was an order of things and peoples that could be opened up to criticism from within inasmuch as, in purporting to tell the story of Man, it incorporated a principle of generality in relation to which any particular museum display could be held to be partial, incomplete, inadequate. When contrasted with earlier absolutist or theocratic spaces of representation – spaces constructed in relation to a singular controlling point of reference, human or divine, which does not claim a representative generality – the space of representation associated with the museum rests on a principle of general human universality which renders it inherently volatile, opening it up to a constant discourse of reform as hitherto excluded constituencies seek inclusion – and inclusion on equal terms – within that space.

I shall return to these considerations later. Meanwhile, let me return to the question of the relations between the prison and the museum in order to clarify their respective positions within the power–knowledge relations of nineteenth-century societies. In examining the formation of the new social disciplines associated with the development of the carceral archipelago and, more generally, the development of modern forms of governmentality, Foucault stresses the respects in which these knowledges, in mapping the body with their individualizing and particularizing gaze, render the populace visible to power and, hence, to regulation. While the various exhibitionary knowledges associated with the rise of the museum similarly form part of a set of power–knowledge relations, these differ in both their organization and functioning from those Foucault is concerned with. If the orientation of the prison is to discipline and punish with a view to effecting a modification of behaviour, that of the museum is to show and tell so that the people might look and learn. The purpose, here, is not to know the populace but to allow the people, addressed as subjects of knowledge rather than as objects of administration, to know; not to render the populace visible to power but to render power visible to the people and, at the same time, to represent to them that power as their own.

In thus rhetorically incorporating an undifferentiated citizenry into a set of power–knowledge relations which are represented to it as emanating from itself, the museum emerged as an important instrument for the self-display of bourgeois-democratic societies. Indeed, if, in Foucault's account, the prison emblematizes a new set of relations through which the populace is constituted as the object of governmental regulation, so the museum might serve as the emblem for the emergence of an equally important new set of relations – best summarized in Gramsci's conception of the ethical state – through which a democratic citizenry was rhetorically incorporated into the processes of the state. If so, it is important to recall that Gramsci viewed this as a distinguishing feature of the modern bourgeois state rather than a defining attribute of the state as such. Whereas, he argues, previous ruling classes 'did not tend to construct an organic passage from the other classes into their own, i.e. to enlarge their class sphere "technically" and ideologically,' the bourgeoisie 'poses itself as an organism in continuous movement, capable of absorbing the entire society, assimilating it to its own cultural and moral level' (Gramsci 1971: 260). It is in this respect, he contends, that the entire function of the state is transformed as it becomes an educator. The migration of the display of power from, on the one hand, the public scene of punishment and, on the other, from the enclosed sphere of court festivals to the public museum played a crucial role in this transformation precisely to the degree that it fashioned a space in which these two differentiated functions – the display of power to the populace and its display within the ruling classes – coalesced.

References

Adorno, Theodor W. (1967) *Prisms*, London: Neville Spearman.

Bann, Stephen (1984) *The Clothing of Clio: A Study of the Representation of History in Nineteenth-Century Britain and France*, Cambridge: Cambridge University Press.

Bennett, Tony (1988) 'Convict chic', *Australian Left Review*, no. 106.

Blackbourn, David and Eley, Geoff (1984) *The Peculiarities of German History: Bourgeois Society and Politics in Nineteenth Century Germany*, Oxford: Oxford University Press.

Crimp, Douglas (1987) 'The postmodern museum', *Parachute*, March–May.

Evans, Robin (1982) *The Fabrication of Virtue: English Prison Architecture 1750–1840*, Cambridge: Cambridge University Press.

Gramsci, Antonio (1971) *Selections from the Prison Notebooks*, London: Lawrence & Wishart.

Hooper-Greenhill, E. (1989) 'The museum in the disciplinary society', in J. Pearce, *Museum Studies in Material Culture*, Leicester: Leicester University Press.

Malraux, André (1967) *Museum without Walls*, London: Secker & Warburg.

Pevsner, Nikolaus (1976) *A History of Building Types*, New Jersey: Princeton University Press.

Seling, H. (1967) 'The genesis of the museum', *Architectural Review*, no. 131.

Note

1 I have, however, touched on this matter with particular reference to Australian museums. See Bennett (1988).

Chapter 14

Art

Owen Kelly

If the community arts movement has been un-clear about the nature of *community*, and the way in which community relates to the agencies and processes of the state, then it has been equally unclear about the nature of *art*, and the way in which it is defined in our society and the methods by which it is produced and distrib-uted. Instead, community artists have often dodged the issues by claiming that such a discus-sion would be diversionary, or unhelpfully obtuse, and they have thus been forced, by de-fault, to rely on a loose set of entirely unargued 'common sense' definitions of what art is.

This confusion has had a number of calami-tous consequences, not least of which has been a prevalent tendency to concentrate on the mech-anical techniques of the various art forms, to the exclusion of any consideration of the necessary mental techniques of thought, planning, style and aesthetic decision which govern them; or the wider social forces which shape and direct those mental techniques. This has occurred be-cause of the community arts movement's inabil-ity to deal with questions of style, due to the movement's lack of any common theoretical understanding; and through the resulting (and erroneous) assumption that the material means of artistic production are somehow neutral, and therefore capable of being used without any questions being asked.

At its most simplistic, this has resulted in the sort of community printshop where 'clients' are shown the minutiae of screen-printing (how to wash the screen, how to apply green film, how to use a light box) as a neutralised technical subject,

and then given no assistance at all in the process of designing the poster they are going to print. In a confused bid to avoid imposing style or visual language on the users, this type of practice actu-ally undermines the aims and purposes of those people wanting to produce the poster. For example, if the poster is for an AGM or a fund-raising dance then it will have served its purpose if it contributes to a well-attended AGM or dance, and will have failed if nobody turns up. The fact that this purpose may be impeded more by bad design than by bad reproduction is often never discussed, even if it is understood. Instead there is contented talk about the way in which learning to use a silkscreen 'demystifies' the pro-cess of printing; a benefit which is at best a secondary consideration for most of the users.

In refusing to develop a theoretical frame-work, it becomes easy to imagine that a full and effective knowledge of visual language will spring whole from any group of people as soon as their blindfolds have been removed; and to imagine that their blindfolds can be removed by showing them the mechanics of a silkscreen or a 35mm darkroom. To believe this is to fall into the very 'naive romanticism' which Lord Gibson accused politically motivated community artists of exhibiting. Ironically, however, the way out of this dilemma is not, as he would have it, less theory and more 'common sense', but the re-verse: a well argued theoretical framework which provides a basis for questioning lazy 'common sense' assumptions.

Art is an ideological construction; a general-isation which has a complex history through which its meaning has both shifted and narrowed. In its current usage its chief purpose is to bestow an apparently inherent value onto certain activities and the products resulting from these activities, while witholding this value from certain other similar activities. In this respect the term 'art' functions as one of a series of categories whose purpose is to assist in the construction and maintenance of a hierarchy of values which, having been constructed, can be made to appear as both natural and inevitable. Thus there are activities which may be interesting and rewarding in their own right, and which may be pursued as hobbies, leisure activities or even careers, but which will never, no matter what standard they reach, be accorded the status of art. The process by which this happens is profoundly political: it is not in any sense a consequence of impersonal market forces, nor is it the unfortunate outcome of a series of historical accidents. It is the result of some groups being more powerful than others; of some groups being in the position to gain access to the levers of power which is denied others.

The process of persuasion, or trickery, through which sculpting in bronze is designated a living art form and model aeroplane making is relegated to the status of an adolescent hobby, is almost entirely concerned with an ability to engage the interest and approval of those agencies which have achieved a *de facto* power to license activities, or classes of objects, as art; and almost nothing at all to do with any specific 'value' in the activity itself. A visit to a large model railway exhibition will readily confirm this, for many of the more ambitious layouts are self-evidently the result of vision, planning, craftsmanship and tenacity. They could legitimately be described as an evocative, and peculiarly British, form of social realist sculpture, and indeed, if they had happened to be built by an accredited 'artist' as part of a private and 'artistic' obsession, and if they had happened to be located in an accredited gallery, that is how they would be described. As it is they are seen, if they are seen at all, as a kind of wilful infantilism.

What we refer to as 'the arts' amounts to a selection of activities within a much wider area, which we could refer to as *pleasure*. Moreover, the arts are a class specific subdivision of pleasure, since they coincide with the habits of enjoyment of a metropolitan ruling class. Historically,

they are the descendants of the *court arts*, through the patronage of which the royalty and nobility amused themselves and demonstrated their prestige and power. The claim these 'arts' make to moral or intellectual superiority comes from their lineage, and from the powerful positions of those advancing these claims on their behalf, and not from any inherent qualities that they possess.

Ed Berman has asserted that the tradition initiated by Lord Keynes in CEMA (and later in the Arts Council of Great Britain) of funding a narrow spectrum of cultural activities, which produce pleasure for the participants and possibly for the spectators, while ignoring the rest of the population, is 'an upper class, cultural imperialist trick'. He argues that 'the reason we give money to opera and not to, say, tiddleywinks or model aeroplane making is that a small group of people have, over the years, been able to persuade, or trick, an even smaller number of people who have their hands on the levers that an eighteenth century folk art is somehow normal or normative for twentieth century British society. That smaller group of people, through a host of agencies of governmental processes have then also managed to persuade, or trick, the whole of the rest of society into believing that this folk art is normal for our society and deserving of subsidy, whereas it really is not.' This process of 'persuasion' has not just involved the extolling of the operatic virtues, and their inflation into an alleged cornerstone of civilisation, but a powerful and systematic downgrading of other activities, which have been shunted into categories which are treated as though they were automatically, and self-evidently, of a lower order. To be near the top of the category *country and western* is still to be ranked as less 'serious', less worthy, than almost anything in the category *operatic aria* in the eyes of those controlling the institutions that together determine the dominant cultural agenda; the group of activities that we mean when we talk, as Sir Roy Shaw has, about 'serious art'.

This is not a new argument. As long ago as 1843 Jeremy Bentham argued that 'prejudice apart, the game of push-pin is of equal value with the arts and science of music and poetry. If the game of push-pin furnish more pleasure, it is more valuable than either.' Bentham was arguing here for a strictly utilitarian form of populism in which, in modern terms, *The Sun* would have to be seen as a better newspaper than *The Times* because more people buy it. He was arguing that there are *no* possible criteria in matters of judgement and value, other than simple numerical criteria. What I am arguing (and what, I believe, Ed Berman is arguing) is related to Bentham's argument, but it is not the same, and it is more complex in both its premises and conclusions.

I am arguing that what we refer to as *art* is but one facet of a range of social practices in which communities engage, and through which they derive meaning and pleasure; and that we must understand this, and understand its consequences, before we can begin to categorise one thing as better artistically than another. We cannot do this by simply referring to the works of art, or the art practices, as though they contained some innate qualities missing from pushpin. Instead, in trying to gauge the value of a work of art, we must make our judgement specific rather than generalised, material rather than abstracted. Rather than trying to deduce a single universal value from a work of art, we must be prepared for an infinite series of different specific values in answer to the question: to whom is this art of value and for what purposes is it valued? From this perspective we can see how opera relates to the wider social practices of one social group while leaving other groups untouched. We can also see that, for another social group, the same is true of country and western music; and that this difference provides no basis whatsoever for ranking either the activities, or the groups who participate in them, in some wider cultural hierarchy.

As with the term *community*, we must use the term *art* in a dynamic way, recognising that if it describes anything useful at all it is a set of social relationships, and the social practices that result from them. Such a way of looking at art is suggested by Raymond Williams:

'The distinction between art and non-art, or between aesthetic and other intentions and responses, as well as those more flexible distinctions by which elements of a process, or intentions and responses, are seen, in real cases, as predominant or subordinate, can ... be seen as they historically are: as variable social forms within which the relevant practices are perceived and organised. Thus the distinctions are not eternal verities, or supra-historical categories, but actual elements of social organisation ...'

The term 'art', then, does not describe a set of activities, but a framework within which certain activities are placed, and the distinctions which are maintained between 'art and non-art' are part of the dominant structures of our 'social organisation'.

For our purposes, art can best be seen as a term used to describe a network of interrelated activities, of cultural practices, and not as a label to be wielded in a limiting or excluding way. The more usual use of the term, in which it is contrasted with an existing category of 'non-art', can only amount, at best, to a self-conscious claim to be part of a particular heritage. This is a claim which, in the end, amounts to an attempt to legitimise a pleasure through analogy; through the assertion that a pleasure is important because it resembles a previous activity which is now considered to have been important. Thus drab, serialist composers today claim their 'art' to be worthy of attention because they assert that it is the direct descendant of Beethoven, Mahler and Schoenberg, and attack the public for remaining resolutely uninterested in it, for refusing to 'make the effort'.

If we see art as a similar kind of term to community, we can see that it too describes a goal to be attained, not an abstraction which must be seized or captured. This goal differs from the goal of community, though, in that it cannot *itself* be pursued. It is a generalised *effect* which will arise from within specific work practices, which will themselves necessarily take particular material forms. These practices might be photography, or mural painting or printing or cookery or writing or drama or gardening. We will be too self-conscious if we habitually claim that we are doing these things *as artists*, even though the creation of an art may be a part of our goal. We are, in fact, doing these things as photographers, muralists, printers, cooks, writers, actors or directors, and gardeners. These are the roles which, in one way or another, we actually occupy; and our eagerness to designate ourselves as 'artists' or 'community artists' is often a way of demystifying our actual practice to the disadvantage of the people with whom we work.

This can be easily demonstrated. If I announce myself as a community artist, the people to whom I am talking are likely to have no way of deciding what their expectations of my skills should be, since the title does not relate directly to any specific skills or practice. If, on the other hand, I announce myself as a photographer, the people to whom I am talking *will* have a set of criteria which they can adopt in order to form an opinion of my skills. They will have opinions about photographs, they will be able to ask to see some photographs that I have taken previously, and they will be able to relate the two in a way which will enable them to decide how seriously to take what I tell them. They might ask questions that they feel a photographer should be able to answer, or they might watch me load a camera to see how competent I am. In announcing myself as a community artist I run the risk of revealing so little about myself, in terms which people can understand, that I can never be challenged by the group with whom I am working. Where this occurs I will forever be the externally validated teacher imposing my will on the class, and never a participant in a democratic group.

If we can see, then, that *community* and *art* are both descriptions of processes which are, for our purposes, aims and goals, then we can see that the term *community artist*, while being a convenient label to use in some circumstances (most of which are concerned with funding), does not, in fact, describe *what* we do, but only *why* we do it. We can see, too, that it is entirely possible to pursue the goal of creating an art, or of creating a community art, without the need to designate some people as 'artists', with the implicit assumption that there is a larger group of people who are not artists. The term 'art' must therefore be removed, in our practice, from any imagined relationship with a polar opposite called 'non-art'; and recognised instead as a different kind of category altogether. It is a category which cannot be approached like a kidnapped heirloom, and somehow seized back, but must instead be analysed and acted upon dynamically. If we do this we can begin to imagine a community arts movement without any 'artists', but with a variable set of producers and authors, working in partnership. We can begin, then, to look at the processes of creativity and authorship which are supposed to fuel the production of art, and in which, in one way or another, we all participate.

Chapter 15

Object Lessons: Fred Wilson Reinstalls Museum Collections to Highlight Sins of Omission

Pamela Newkirk

Fred Wilson's childhood in an upper-middle-class, white New York suburb can be glimpsed in a grade-school self-portrait in which he encased his curly-topped, caramel-toned body in a suit of armor. The protective shield evolved after a snowball attack on Wilson by a pack of white boys, but the underlying isolation defines his youth.

As the only African American child in his Westchester County school, Wilson coped by sequestering himself in the basement of his home, crafting three-dimensional scenes from cardboard boxes. In time, his cityscapes and scenes from the Vietnam War, replete with body parts and exploded bridges, transformed the basement into his private fantasy world. His solitary pursuit was nurtured by his mother, a Carib-French-British painter who taught art in New York City public schools, and his father, an African American civil engineer.

"I felt like an outsider," Wilson recalls, sitting in his expansive East Village loft. "It was me against everyone," he says quietly above the jazz filling the air. "I was very alone. It helped my imagination. There was plenty of room to develop an inner life. It was very good training." Now 45 and the recipient of a 1999 MacArthur Award, he has achieved worldwide recognition for his museum installations, which address the way hallowed cultural institutions tend to marginalize or ignore nonwhite cultures.

With a touch of humor and piercing irony, Wilson characteristically rearranges and juxtaposes pieces from the permanent collections of museums in order to reinterpret their meaning. In his 1992 exhibition "Mining the Museum," at the Maryland Historical Society, for example, alongside busts of famous white men like Henry Clay, Napoleon Bonaparte, and Andrew Jackson he set up pedestals bearing only labels naming famous black Americans, such as Frederick Douglass and Harriet Tubman. The obvious exclusion of the portrait heads themselves highlighted the figures' absence from the museum's collection. Wilson's approach vividly spotlights practices that have long evaded public scrutiny.

"You feel you've been coaxed and cajoled into seeing your own foibles," says Harry S. Parker III, director of the Fine Arts Museums of San Francisco, describing the impact of Wilson's work. "It literally turned things upside down," he explains, referring to Wilson's show "Speaking in Tongues: A Look at the Language of Display," at the M. H. de Young Memorial Museum last January. Wilson took objects from the de Young collection and placed them in new contexts. A 19th-century marble bust of a man Wilson titled *Ancestor Figure* was accompanied by text that did not identify the artist or subject. In other words, it was displayed the way non-Western art typically is. The text read: "The importance of this ancestor is symbolized by the folds of cloth draped around his shoulders. Though his cloth or drapery would have been worn in many other cultures, here it is borrowed from the costume traditions of the ancient Greeks. To the Euro-American peoples, the ancient Greek architecture and costume symbolizes their democracy and enlightened philosophy, rather than the slavery and patriarchy that characterized both ancient Greece and the United States in the 19th century."

In the same show, the text accompanying an exhibit of Impressionist paintings described the artists as "a renegade French tribe of the 19th century which broke away from mainstream society."

Wilson, his youthful, bearded face framed by gray-flecked dreadlocks, is contemplative and candid as he recalls the experiences that inform his art. He measures his words during long pauses and only occasionally reveals traces of the humor evident in his work. "A lot of my work comes from my early experiences," he says. "Having had some experience with racism made me aware of people's plight."

Other times, Wilson is open and breezy, as when explaining his collection of globes displayed atop an imposing antique armoire in his loft. "I'm a world kind of guy," he quips. "I could have made art that attacked corporate greed, but this is my world," he says, his almond-shaped eyes tightening.

Wilson's experience at Manhattan's Music and Art High School cemented his plans to pursue a career in art. Surrounded by musicians, painters, dancers, and actors from widely diverse backgrounds, he began to feel part of a community. After high school, he reentered a predominantly white world, first as a fine-arts major at the State University of New York at Purchase, and then as a freelance teacher and preparator at New York's Museum of Modern Art, the American Crafts Museum, the American Museum of Natural History, and the Metropolitan Museum of Art.

Working in these institutions not only made him more comfortable handling rare items, but also honed his sense of irony. What was not collected and venerated became as important to Wilson as what was. At the Museum of Modern Art, for instance, he wondered why works by Jacob Lawrence were not exhibited and why a Wifredo Lam painting was hung near the coat check rather than in a gallery. At the American Museum of Natural History, he questioned the message conveyed by placing large sculptures of a Senegalese man and woman at the entrance to the Hall of Mammals. "This mixing of animals and humans – these things are really subtle," he says. "You wonder what kind of stereotypes they foster."

In 1977, fresh out of school, Wilson retreated to East Harlem, where he ran three nonprofit community centers. The experience reinforced his need to belong, as did the time he spent with other artists of color whose work was being largely ignored by mainstream museums and galleries. "We were not being shown in galleries," he says of the 1970s and 1980s. "We were really developing ideas as a community. We were all kind of annoyed, but we had each other." He counts among his longtime artist friends Albert Chong, Lorna Simpson, Renée Green, Jimmy Durham, and James Luna, and the painter Whitfield Lovell, with whom he shares his loft.

In the 1980s Wilson was constructing large indoor and outdoor platform sculptures, featuring paintings of such popular-culture icons as Lucille Ball, Muhammad Ali, and the pope. "These were people who were extremely well known in the world," Wilson explains, "particularly the Third World. I was trying to create vertical monuments that relate to the culture." But he encountered an unexpected obstacle. In 1983 his sculpture bearing the pope's image was to be exhibited at Columbus Circle, outside the city's cultural affairs offices. While the project proposal had cleared the requisite hurdles, several days before the unveiling the work was eliminated from the show. New York's then-cultural commissioner Bess Myerson told Wilson that the Catholic Archdiocese objected to the appropriation of the pope's image. "I was a young artist and really wanted to be in the show," says Wilson. So he instead displayed a sculpture of Lucille Ball, and the work was accepted.

Wilson next began depicting figures, such as Gauguin and James Audubon, who had complex relationships with Third World cultures. "My interest in culture and history entered prominently in those sculptures," he says. "I realized my true calling wasn't constructing things. When the museum projects started to happen, they said everything I wanted to say."

By the late 1980s, publicly funded institutions seemed to be including more minority artists, and by 1990, galleries were recognizing the underground multicultural art world. "The Decade Show: Frameworks of Identity in the 1980s," a collaboration between the Studio Museum in Harlem, the Museum of Contemporary Hispanic Art, and the New Museum of Contemporary Art, marked a watershed event for nonmainstream artists. The show featured a broad sampling of artists from different racial, ethnic, and gender backgrounds – from Jean Michael Basquiat to Tom Nakashima. the Guerilla Girls, and Kay WalkingStick, and even white males Eric Fischl and Bruce Nauman.

That same year, 1990, Wilson presented a show at New York's White Columns gallery called 'The Other Museum,' which included African masks bound and gagged with French or British flags. A vitrine beneath them displayed boxes of insects marked with the name of an African country. Labeled "French and British Collection, 1914," the boxes commented on the way African nations have been collected. He continued his critique of institutional culture in his 1992 show "Mining the Museum," at the Maryland Historical Society. There, in addition to the portrait busts on pedestals, Wilson juxtaposed ornate Victorian chairs with a crude whipping post from the museum's furniture-storage room. In a period metalwork display, repoussé silver vessels were exhibited alongside slave shackles. He changed the label on an 1806 Benjamin H. Latrobe watercolor that had been titled *View of Welch Point and the Mouth of Backcreek* to "Jack Alexander in a Canoe" to acknowledge and dignify the anonymous black figure. The simple adjustment underscored the way slaves were depersonalized in early American paintings. The show, which broke attendance records for the museum and was cited by the American Association of Museums as the exhibition of the year, provoked museum directors to question not only what they exhibited but what they did not show. Some critics began to characterize the softspoken Wilson as extreme or angry. He was described as a "radical black New York artist" and a "political activist." In a generally favorable review of "Mining the Museum," *New York Times* art critic Michael Kimmelman nonetheless criticized Wilson for being a "didact."

According to Kimmelman, "He aims to convey certain messages. Those messages may be packaged in more or less clever ways, they may be ennobling and enduring. But the packaging is ultimately a means to an end and largely forgettable once the message has been revealed." Marcia Tucker, founding director of New York's New Museum, disagrees. It is precisely because Wilson's work is not "that didactic wagging finger" that she finds it so compelling. "He makes things visible that are present but that are rarely acknowledged," she explains. "He's very forceful about what he says, but he doesn't do it with a heavy hand."

Wilson himself comments, "I think in America if you're a black person and you say something on your mind, no matter how mildly you say it, you're being radical."

His demanding schedule since 1992 is a testament to the resonance of his work. Wilson has been invited to sift through museum collections worldwide and filter them through his own lens. At the University of Melbourne's Ian Potter Museum, he placed the religious objects of the region's indigenous people in a glass-enclosed gallery where aborigines could go to handle the pieces after hours. A similar installation at the de Young in San Francisco made museum officials consider building a permanent viewing gallery for art by various ethnic groups. "It's a humane way to venerate their work and a way for the public to see they have a spiritual life," says Wilson. "These things are not just dead cultural relics."

In Winston-Salem, North Carolina, in 1994, Wilson removed the floorboards in one of the city's historic black churches and replaced them with Plexiglas to reveal the tombstones of slaves that had been removed from a nearby cemetery and stacked in the foundation.

Susan Lubowski Talbott, current director of the Des Moines Arts Center and former director of the Southeastern Center for Contemporary Art in Winston-Salem, which curated the installation, says it was the most important exhibition she has ever done. "What was so remarkable to me is that black people, white people, the descendants of the Moravians, art critics, tourists, and newspaper people from all over the country came and had the same reaction, no matter their level of sophistication. It elicited emotion to the point of tears. Much of Fred's work is very level and even, and before you know it, it punches you in the stomach." Furthermore, she notes, "I think, based on his popularity, his work has an impact on the way museums look at issues. He's sought after."

San Francisco's Parker agrees. "It got us all thinking about our collection, some of the meanings we might be telegraphing without even knowing it." Describing Wilson's approach, Lubowski Talbott says, "It's a gentle poke with a very fine, rather than blunt, instrument." She points out that Wilson's show at the Southeastern Center for Contemporary Art exploring Winston-Salem's African American history not only drew the unsolicited support of foundations and individuals but was also incorporated into the community's school curriculum.

Nevertheless, some museum directors who invite Wilson to mine their collections have implied their wish to disassociate themselves from his examination. One nervously suggested calling a Wilson show "Museum Held Hostage," an idea the artist rejected. Asked whether he's an activist, as critics have intimated, Wilson replies, "Maybe I'm in denial, but I don't see myself that way."

Neither does Parker. "After all of the implied criticism, you'd think museums would not like Fred Wilson," says Parker. "But in addition to poking everyone in the ribs, he became everyone's good friend. There's a lot of seriousness, but he does not seem angry or hostile. So much of what he's saying and pointing out he does with humor, and he has such a light touch that you don't feel offended or chastised."

Last fall Wilson was completing a commission for the New Jersey Transit light-rail system, in which he capitalizes on the site of the underground railroad and the existence of a medical center currently under construction to create a theme of healing. Slave narratives etched on columns in braille reflect on an overhead canvas at night. The project, which he has been working on for four years, opens in March. He has also received a commission from the University of California in San Francisco to create a work centering on diversity. Wilson is represented in New York by Metro Pictures, where prices for his work range from $2,000 to $6,000 for photographs and from $20,000 to $30,000 for larger installations.

The MacArthur Award, amounting to $315,000 over five years, will provide Wilson with some real financial relief. But the artist remains cautious about the recognition. He recalls receiving news of it in a Los Angeles hotel room. "I jumped up and down on the bed. I couldn't have guessed it," he says, "the kind of respect I get from museum professionals. They respect my opinion. I have conversations with Philippe de Montebello," he notes, carefully pronouncing the name of the Metropolitan Museum of Art's director. "The MacArthur is almost hard for me to fathom." Now, he adds wryly, "I say something and it gets quiet."

The grant also allows him to say no to some engagements, cancel others, and consider projects that are not lucrative. "I had overcommitted myself," he says, ticking off commissions across the country that have left him little time for friends, family, visiting jazz clubs, and attending avant-garde theater performances. With many projects nearing completion, Wilson says he would like to travel to places he's never been, including his maternal grandparents' native St. Vincent, India, and Brazil. He also looks forward to meeting other MacArthur fellows. "I've been on this carousel and didn't know how to get off. Now I'd rather spend a long time on pieces," he says. Parker, like others, believes Wilson's work will have a long-term impact on museum culture.

"A lot of artists may please you, but they don't change your way of thinking," Parker says. "Once you see one of his shows you have some Fred Wilson in you. You're looking for ironies. It's more than an intellectual interest. It changes the way you think about art."

Part VI

Sport

Introduction to Part VI

Toby Miller

Some readers may be surprised to see sport alongside film, music, and art in a book about cultural policy. But these areas are linked in their connection to issues of national ideology and the state's aim of training its population via government. For with the advent of modernity, wealth, health, and a sense of belonging became goals, to be attained through the disposition of capacities across the population: "biological existence was reflected in political existence" through the work of "bio-power." Just as bio-power brought "life and its mechanisms into the realm of explicit calculations and made knowledge-power an agent of transformation of human life," (Foucault, 1991) so these calculations became of interest to processes of governance. Bodies were identified with politics, because managing them was part of running the country. For Foucault, "a society's 'threshold of modernity' is reached when the life of the species is wagered on its own political strategies" (ibid. pp. 97, 92–5 and 1984, p. 143). Governmentality is destined for a place beyond sovereignty, in the social field. Its target is the whole population, and sport is a key symbolic and material method for turning leisure into practice, and pleasure into fitness.

The unusual relationship between sport and nation, with the former more clearly part of popular civil society than, say, national museums, obscures both its history of colonialism and its somewhat more recent *étatisation*. A trend towards ruling-class control of sport is structurally homologous with, and historically connected to, state monopolies on legitimate violence. The work of governments in normalizing sports has been crucial: first, policing holidays to normalize vacations and regularize recreation as play and spectatorship; second, securing the conditions of existence for a partial commodification that still make sport governed rather than classically competitive (*viz.* antitrust exemptions and the like); third, supporting the generation of a media-sports-culture complex by putting up the risk capital for a new genre over many years; fourth, allocating resources to sport as both a diplomatic symbol and a domestic training mechanism; and fifth, being the site of appeal by activists opposed to global capital as well as others using the courts to secure financial advantage. This is the citizenship-access side to sport.

Governments are usually concerned about sport as a route to improved urban public health, military fitness, and the diversion of rebellious class politics. Modern leaders from Hitler and Pétain to Carter initiated physical fitness tests to invigorate and ideologize the young. As commodities, television, and international competitiveness have upped the ante, the state has stepped in on behalf of nationalist ideology (consider the Malaysian government's takeover of the 1998 Commonwealth Games from a quasi-private concern). This trend hints that sport may be an early-warning sign of transformations in the nature and relationships of government – that whereas the state formerly focused its search for and exercise of power internally, now it looks beyond. A concentration on territorialization as a site of control and the generation of wealth has been supplemented, and perhaps supplanted, by a deterritorialized contest over resources and market share.

This sporting governmentality initially manifested itself through compulsory schooling, moral uplift, and "Britishness" from the former Empire. Until late in the nineteenth century, government intervention in sport generally took the form of protecting ruling-class interests in hunting from other classes, or ensuring social control of pastimes such as gambling; but at that point, numerous voluntary associations formed to codify and rule pastimes that had previously been organic forms of recreation. As these bodies extended their local hegemony, and a series of international sporting events came to parallel First-World economic and political engagements, their relationship to "legitimate" expressions of national interest and representation intensified – a rare case of relative autonomy from the nation-state combined with the "right" to stand for the nation.

The Mexican Revolution moved quickly to institutionalize sport in the 1910s as a sign and source of national unity, and the same moment saw the British Government encouraging the National Rifle Association to use human-figure targets as military preparation. When the Argentine Olympic Committee was founded in 1922, it promised to work for "the perfection of the race and the glory of conquering what is noble, worthy, and beautiful." The successes of physical-education movements and Western European fascism inspired the British to institutionalize gymnasium curricula in order to meet any armed challenge. The US Peace Corps argued in *Sports Illustrated* in 1963 that sports were a more productive terrain for its mission than teaching because they were "least vulnerable to charges of 'neo-colonialism' and 'cultural imperialism.'" John F Kennedy established the President's Council on Youth Fitness to counter a "growing softness, our increasing lack of physical fitness," which constituted "a threat to our security." From a very different angle, the Sandinistas abolished professional sport in Nicaragua, focusing instead on nation-building through a large-scale sport-for-all policy.

Colonel Gadhafi's *Green Book*, which lays out the basis for Libyan revolution, is opposed to sports spectatorship, calling instead for sport to be "practiced by all and not left to anyone else

to practice on their behalf." A recent Aotearoa/New Zealand Minister of Recreation and Sport referred to his portfolio as a route to "social and economic prosperity" through the promotion of "active, physical lifestyles." He identified an additional benefit: "being *into* sport" ensured being "out of court." This longstanding criminological obsession deems familially-based and formal sporting activities to be worthy, integrative norms, whilst informal leisure is demonized. Even the former Jamaican Socialist Prime Minister, Michael Manley, also a distinguished historian of cricket, pushed such a line: male violence is a danger that can be pacified and redirected into an appropriate sphere – literally, national fitness. Sovietism saw sport as a means of socializing the people into new values and away from capitalistic self-indulgence. The German Democratic Republic sought to integrate sport and its cultural history into the everyday of the citizenry, a means of writing socialist physicality over Nazi brutality. For colonial powers in the Anglo-Caribbean, it marked the power of the English over the locals – something successfully protested against in Africa and later used as a site of resistance to repressive post-colonial rulers, notably in Cameroon. So if nineteenth-century colonialism took it as the "white man's burden" to utilize "games" to "civilize" and control populations, this had some unintended consequences. C. L. R. James points to the appropriation of cricket from the master:

we were a motley crew. The children of some white officials and white business men, middle class blacks and mulatto's, Chinese boys ... Indian boys ... and some poor black boys who had won exhibitions or whose parents had starved and toiled on plots of agricultural land ... yet rapidly we learned to obey the umpire's decision without question, however irrational it was. We learned to play with the team, which meant subordinating your personal inclination, and even interests, to the good of the whole. We kept a stiff upper lip in that we did not complain about ill fortune. We did not denounce our failures, but "well done" or "hard luck" came easily to our lips. We were generous to opponents and congratulated them on victories, even when we knew they did not deserve it. ... Eton or Harrow had nothing on us. (1963, p. 34)

Inevitably, sport's codification and expansion also encounters critique and engagement from those who have slowly been granted full citizen rights. Consider the US version of governmentality. The northeastern Puritans devoted great efforts towards quelling seventeenth-century pleasures of the lower orders, such as cockfighting and horseracing. This spread to the classically modern abhorrence of cruelty to animals across the country in the nineteenth century, with associated state intervention. The push towards Americanization of new immigrants in the late nineteenth and early twentieth centuries was embodied in the formation of voluntary sporting associations. In the two decades from 1881, the US birthed national bodies to regulate tennis, golf, and college sports. Over the next twenty years, baseball, hockey, and football professionalized. The First World War saw a major articulation of sporting values with militarism and citizenship – an internal Americanization equating national sports with patriotism. The American Legion sponsored baseball to counter working-class radicalism and to encourage social and migrant integration. When feminist criticisms of sport emerged in the 1960s, part of their force concerned the claim to equitable public funding promised by the modern. Hence the Title IX Educational Amendments discussed here, which forced US colleges that were in receipt of Federal funds to allocate them across campus in proportion to the number of men and women they enrolled. These were among the first women's legislative gains of the contemporary era, and they addressed the expenditure of state money on the body as a source of fitness. Governmentality and cultural policy are revealed in this instance as exemplary opportunities for social-movement activism. At the same time, the state-capital relation can lead to exploitation of taxpayers, as per the corporate welfare provided by countless US cities to sports team owners, also detailed in this volume.

References

Foucault, Michel. "Governmentality." Trans. Pasquale Pasquino. *The Foucault Effect: Studies in Governmentality*. Ed. Graham Burchell, Colin Gordon, and Peter Miller. London: Harvester Wheatsheaf, 1991, 87–104.

Foucault, Michel. *The History of Sexuality: An Introduction*. Trans. Robert Hurley. Harmondsworth: Penguin, 1984.

James, C. L. R. *Beyond a Boundary*. London: Stanley Paul, 1963.

Chapter 16

Hegemonic Masculinity, the State, and the Politics of Gender Equity Policy Research

Jim McKay

Introduction

A sometimes acrimonious controversy has emerged over the appropriate role of intellectuals working in the areas of cultural studies and cultural policy.[1] To date, much of the debate has focused on abstract issues like the advantages and disadvantages of 'putting policy into cultural studies' – to use Bennett's phrase – or if academics should be facilitators or critics of cultural policy. However, there has been a dearth of concrete accounts of tensions between the academics who conduct policy research and the organisations which fund and implement it. In this article I examine the response of the Australian Sports Commission (ASC) to two academic studies it funded on gender equity policy (GEP). I also illustrate the crucial function of the media in articulating masculine definitions of GEP in sport.

Managing Gender

Achieving equity for women in sport will not be an easy process, but will involve a need to change social attitudes as well as long established practices. I am, however, determined to do all in my power to provide a special focus on the issue of women's involvement in sport and am confident that government

and sporting organisations together, can play a vital role in stimulating desired change. Ros Kelly, Federal Minister for Sport[2]

I can assure you that the Commission is fully committed to addressing the issues that face women in sport through research, programs, promotion, action to seek more female administrators, coaches, officials and through identifying and seeking to remove any impediments that we might find which are placed in the way of full participation by women. Jim Ferguson, Executive Director of the ASC[3]

In 1990, the ASC, the Federal statutory authority responsible for sport, designated gender equity (GE) as a priority research area and funded three academic studies through its Applied Sports Research Program (ASRP). All grant proposals were appraised by an expert research committee, which comprised ASRP administrators and independent academics. I was funded to identify why there were so few women administrators in sporting organisations, with specific emphasis on the barriers to women's access and advancement. The project replicated and extended similar studies conducted in Britain, Canada, Scandinavia and the USA (Acosta and Carpenter 1992; Fasting 1987; Fasting and Sisjord 1986; Hall et al 1989, 1990; Kane 1990; Kane and Stangl 1991; Knoppers 1992; Macintosh and Beamish 1988;

Raivio 1986; Theberge 1984, 1987; West and Brackenridge 1990; White and Brackenridge 1985; White et al 1991; Whitson and Macintosh 1989). I also drew on theories and methodologies used in other well-known academic and policy studies of gender and organisations (*Beneath the Veneer*, 1990; Collinson and Knights 1990; Marshall 1984; Morgan 1986; Morrison et al. 1987; Powell 1988; Reskin and Roos 1990; Spencer and Podmore 1987).

In 1991 and 1992 I conducted in-depth interviews with 46 men and 45 women in middle and senior management positions involved in sports administration in all States and Territories. Potential respondents were sent a form letter then telephoned to see if they would participate in the study. With the exception of one person who had to go overseas urgently, everyone agreed to take part. All interviewees were sent a standardised, detailed questionnaire that was completed and returned by 40 (87%) of the men and 43 (96%) of the women. Each participant was interviewed for about an hour and all but two conversations were recorded on audio cassettes. The interviews covered the following topics: career paths and plans; perceptions of why there were so few women administrators; instances of sexual prejudice and discrimination; suggestions for recruiting and retaining more women administrators; and perceptions of GE initiatives. Compared to women, men were less talkative about issues related to barriers, GEP, sexual prejudice and discrimination, and wrote fewer responses to open-ended questions. Consequently, less in-depth information was elicited from them on these topics. The interview tapes were transcribed, analysed and compared with responses to the dozens of close-ended questions. A purposive sample was used in order to include voluntary and private organisations, Federal and State departments, a wide variety of sports, a broad range of managerial responsibilities, and as many senior women managers as possible. The study was not designed to reveal characteristics of individuals, but to examine the perceptions of men and women occupying some of the most powerful positions in Australian sport. For this reason and to maintain confidentiality, pseudonyms were used and all organisations were disguised.

The findings were consistent with previous sport-related studies and the general literature on gender and management. Most women believed that both perceptions and overt actions by men created organisational cultures in which *women in general* were devalued, isolated and excluded.[4] Many male managers had views of family and work that were consonant with their own marital relationships – wives stayed at home to raise children and perform unpaid domestic labour. Male managers tended to perceive GE as 'a women's issue' and saw that the recipe for implementing it simply was to 'add women and stir'. None of the few organisations that did have GE plans had placed issues of men, masculinity and leadership on the agenda. To paraphrase Ruth (1989), most managers saw organisational 'change' related to GE as something that men did *to* or *for* women, rather than a process that involved modifications for both sexes (Bluckert 1989; Drake 1985; Hearn 1989, 1992a; Simmons 1989).

Thus, it was hardly surprising that men's and women's perceptions of their organisations were highly polarised. Whereas most men perceived their organisations to be gender-neutral and governed by merit, most women believed that they were systematically disadvantaged by the following factors: sexual harassment; physical intimidation; having to balance work and family responsibilities; informal male networks; patronage; masculine biases in recruitment, interviewing, selection, development and promotion; inadequate grievance procedures; gender stereotyping; glass ceilings; lack of women role models and mentors; exclusion and isolation; lesbian-baiting; executive inaction regarding GE issues; and the particularly masculine ambience of sport. I concluded that current GEP in Australian sport would do little to counter the organisational cultures of sporting organisations, because they were governed by regimes of masculinity and managerialism that made women's position in them peripheral.

One of the unintended outcomes of the study was the number of unsolicited negative perceptions about the ASC's handling of GEP. Criticisms of the Commission had been aired publicly in February 1991, when the House of Representatives Standing Committee on Legal and Constitutional Affairs and the ASC jointly held the *Equity for Women in Sport Seminar* at Parliament House in Canberra. The Seminar was one of a series conducted by the Committee in the course of its 'Inquiry Into Equal Status and Equal Opportunity for Australian Women'. One keynote speaker (Timpson 1991) noted that the Commission's own GEP was wanting – a point that was not lost on many interviewees. Some respondents believed that the Commission was hastily instituting its GE plan mainly because of the pressure brought to bear on it by the Inquiry. Numerous respondents observed that although the Commission was supposed to be promoting GE in Australian sport, none of its 6 SES level managers and only 3 of its 12 Board members were women. Some interviewees also were aware that senior women in the Commission had formed an informal support group to address what they believed was the Commission's recalcitrance in implementing its own equity and justice policies. Moreover, the Australian Institute of Sport, which comes under the purview of the Commission, had allowed its facilities to be used for a photographic session involving a female model which appeared in an issue of *Inside Sport*, a glossy, glamorous monthly magazine ostensibly concerned with sport.

My report to the Commission included a sample of such negative comments. One of my main recommendations was that the Commission should have important educative, funding and steering functions in ensuring that GE principles were comprehensively integrated into its own organisation and all ASC-funded organisations. The recommendations were compatible with those contained in the recent national agendas for women, the Public Service Commission's Strategic Plan for Equal Employment Opportunity for the 1990s and the Report of the Inquiry Into Equal Status and Equal Opportunity for Women in Australia.[5] I also discussed the appropriateness of my recommendations during an extended interview with Mr Michael Lavarch, who chaired the Inquiry into Equal Status and Equal Opportunity for Australian Women.

The Commission's Response to the Report

The history of men's opposition to women's emancipation is more interesting perhaps than the story of that emancipation itself. (Virginia Woolf 1933)

Those who have power never give it up without a long and intense struggle. (Margaret Timpson, during her keynote speech to the Parliamentary inquiry into gender equity in Australian sport, 1991)

In August 1992 I submitted my report (*Why so Few? Women Executives in Australian Sport*) to the Commission's National Coordinator of Sports Research, who, in turn, sent it to two independent academics for assessment. After both assessors fully endorsed it, the Coordinator issued invitations for a media launch of the report by the Minister of Sport at Sports House in Sydney. A few days before the scheduled launch, the National Coordinator informed me that the Commission's Executive Director, Jim Ferguson, had cancelled the launch because the report was 'factually incorrect'.

In a subsequent phone call, Ferguson and Bob Hobson, Director of Corporate Services said they were concerned about how the report could be interpreted. Their 'concern' was based on the following aspects of the report: it was not objective or valid because it only dealt with people's perceptions of barriers; it contained unfounded criticisms of the Commission; and the above two issues could have embarrassed the Minister, who recently had been embarrassed by the release of an environmental kit. After some discussion, Ferguson agreed to send me a summary of his and Hobson's comments for possible incorporation in a modified version of the report.

The subsequent fax reiterated and extended the items raised in our conversation and included additional criticisms that the report: (1) seemed to have 'a heavy weighting towards the views of women rather than those of the men', and, therefore, could be criticised as a 'put up job'; (2) was based on 'selective quotations to support a preconceived view'; (3) seemed to suggest that men had been 'written off'; (4) contained illustrations that were 'offensive and possibly even libellous'; (5) was 'heavily biased towards US research'; and (6) suggested recommendations that were either inconsistent, impractical or outdated. Regarding the last item, I was told that given the cost of childcare, the Commission was unsure how to implement my recommendation that it should play a pivotal role in coordinating efforts to make affordable, flexible and quality childcare available to employees, volunteers and members of sporting organisations. Furthermore, I was informed that there had been a change in some figures I used in an Appendix which came from one of the Commission's own publications. The number of women Board members in the Commission had increased from 3 to 4, and there now were 35 males (instead of 40) and 8 females (instead of 6) as either executives, section managers or program coordinators. I also was advised that if 'we were to restrict the numbers to executive/ administrative positions, the ratio would be 20 male to 11 female'.

It was stated that I accepted 'uncritically all the things said' [by respondents] when there was 'no argument to support [my] thesis'. Ferguson elaborated that 'some assessment would normally be required of the raw information', then asked: 'Are the [respondents'] perceptions correct'? Despite reservations, I decided to reply. First, there seemed to be a possibility that the report would be suppressed. Second, I had interviewed past and present Board members and managers of the ASC and knew that some held opinions which diverged from those of Ferguson and Hobson. Third, had the report not been released, I would have been complicit in the inability and unwillingness of men to listen to women's perceptions of gender issues in their organisations.

My response indicated that I had shielded the Commission from extensive criticism and had made recommendations designed to enable it to counter this disapproval effectively. I also took on board some of the Commission's advice. For instance, given the Commission's perception of the expense of childcare, I modified my recommendation significantly: 'The ASC should be allocated the funds necessary to assist sporting organisations plan for GE in sport'.

Shortly afterwards I received a call from Sue Baker-Finch, Coordinator of the Commission's Women and Sport Unit, who asked me to provide some 'hard, quantitative data' and to reinstate the original recommendations, as the Commission 'would look foolish if it backed away from them now'. I replied that I would be happy to include statistical information and naturally agreed to reinstitute the original recommendations.

Just before I completed the alterations, I received a telephone call from Roy Masters, a former Rugby League coach and journalist with

The Sydney Morning Herald. He wanted my comments on a story he was filing based on criticisms of the report that allegedly had been made by Ferguson and Kelly, the Federal Minister for Sport. I told Masters that all of the accusations were untrue. In his column Masters stated that Ferguson:

> cancelled the launch and returned the study to McKay, requesting that he resubmit the document, including the analysis on which his conclusions were based ... Ferguson's complaint is that only about five pages of the report represent McKay's own thoughts.

The Minister was cited as being:

> pleased that a senior officer in her portfolio had read the report thoroughly before it was launched.

> It is important to get the facts right, otherwise it can destroy your case ... I don't want to discourage academic independence, but it is crucial that the methodology be correct if we are to implement recommendations based on university works.

According to Masters:

> Most responses quoted in the study are made by women, the overwhelming impression ... being that if a woman sport administrator made a comment, it was accepted as a truism by McKay.

> A detailed examination of the report demonstrates it is littered with perceptions and ignores analysis, making no attempt to quantify results

> In my opinion, many of the recommendations are vague or out-dated ... it appears McKay sees what he wants to see.

Masters noted that I endorsed the recommendation of the Parliamentary inquiry regarding access to affordable, flexible and quality childcare 'without making any input on the costs or practicalities of this'. What Masters did not disclose was his membership of the Board of the Commission, and of its Women and Sport Unit.

Despite this incident, I submitted a revised report that contained the following minor changes: (1) placing more emphasis on the importance of perceptions in organisations; (2) mentioning some sport-related studies from overseas; (3) using more Australian examples in one of the tables; (4) detailing the advantages of qualitative research; (5) fine-tuning aspects of some of the recommendations; (6) including three complex tables of statistics; (7) listing the Commission's major GE initiatives; and (8) recommending that the Commission develop and promote its own human resource management program as an example of sound GE practice in sporting organisations.

I also replaced the statement: 'There was a widespread perception among both the men and women in this study that the ASC was at best contradictory and at worst hypocritical in its own GE action', with: 'Although the Commission has implemented a variety of GE programs, many respondents were concerned about the absence of women in senior, decision-making positions who could serve as role models. The Commission currently is addressing this issue in its own GE plan.' I further enclosed a dozen anonymous interview excerpts which reflected the strong views held by some interviewees. I stressed that I had made no changes to the data that appeared in the original document, as they constituted the backbone of the report.

The Commission accepted the revised report and invited me to attend a low-key media launch at the NSW Academy of Sport in Narrabeen on 24 February 1993. After returning from the launch I received a call from Charles Miranda of the *Canberra Times*, who inquired why the first launch was cancelled, why there had been two reports, and why had the launch been held at such short notice in Narrabeen instead of a more accessible venue. He then raised virtually the same allegations as Masters. I reiterated that the statements were incorrect and emphasised that if executives were making such statements, then they were contradicting the fact that the report had just been launched by an executive, who publicly stated that it would be fully discussed at the next Board meeting. Miranda's subsequent column also resembled that of Masters. For instance, it focused on my Canadian background, my use of some American references, asserted that the study was out-of-date, and claimed that 'there is no evidence to support the author's con-

clusions'. In our telephone conversation Miranda alleged that male executives he had interviewed were 'extremely unhappy with the emotional tone of the report'. He claimed that my purportedly 'emotive descriptions' were evident in the following statement in the document:

> If we think of the world of work as a pyramid, then most women are concentrated at the bottom in dirty, unsafe, tedious, insecure and low paying jobs. Regardless of their occupation, women usually are paid less than men even when they perform identical tasks.

> Although some men are taking greater responsibility for domestic labour, women perform most tasks during the 'second shift'. Studies have shown that husbands of working wives do almost as little in the way of domestic labour as husbands with spouses not in the workforce. (McKay 1992a:4).

The Commission's reaction to my report was not an isolated incident. Another academic submitted a grant proposal to investigate the experiences of women who facilitate and service sport played by others (Thompson 1991). As a condition of receiving funds, the ASRP insisted that men had to be included in her study, when there was no precedent for ASRP projects to include both sexes. In fact, most ASRP studies have dealt almost exclusively with men. This focus is so taken for granted that reports are frequently published without noting that all participants are male. The rationale given to the investigator was that her study, based on qualitative data, would be strengthened by including men.

'Talking to the ISAs'? Or 'Speaking in Tongues'?

In a controversial essay, Bennett (1989) has queried the received wisdom toward cultural studies and cultural policy by intellectuals. He argues that both the American and British versions of cultural studies have limited potential – the former is excessively aesthetic, while the latter subscribes to monolithic images of the state and/ or capitalism and populist political strategies. In place of intellectual grand-standing, Bennett (1989: 7–8) offers 'a third course for cultural studies' producing knowledge that:

can be effectively used within actual existing spheres of cultural policy formation as constituted in the relations between governmentally constituted spheres of cultural management and the agencies and constituencies operative within those spheres.

Elsewhere, Bennett (1992:32) states that 'putting policy into cultural studies' will entail:

> talking to and working with what used to be called the ISAs [Ideological State Apparatuses], rather than writing them off from the outset and, then, in a self-fulfilling prophecy, criticizing them again when they seem not to affirm one's direst functionalist predictions.

Although I have reservations about some of the implications of Bennett's position, his remarks are extremely apposite to sport in Australia. Neglect of sport by critical policy analysts has meant that policy and research have been dictated by physical educators and sport scientists. Their awkward combination of liberal-humanism and instrumental rationality has legitimised state funding of programs like exercise management, corporate health, talent identification, elite sporting performance and random drug testing (McKay 1991a).

However, intellectuals wishing to 'talk to the ISAs' should be aware that the latter tend to communicate from an uncompromising male point of view. The tenacity of what Pateman (1988) calls the 'fraternal social contract' is vividly illustrated by the above reactions. The Commission's response to my findings and Thompson's research – especially when both studies were specifically targeted and funded by the Commission itself to investigate gender inequalities – are sober reminders of some men's formidable capacity to contain and resist women's experiences of gender. The attempts to silence and rebuff women administrators' voices is another clear example of the potent role sport plays in both reinforcing and constituting masculine hegemony in Australia (McKay 1991a, 1991b, 1992b).

Conclusion

According to Yeatman (1990:16), within the current managerial discourse of the 'administrative state', equal opportunity has been 'reframed in terms of what it can do to improve management, not what it can do to develop the conditions of social justice and democratic citizenship in Australian society'. The Commission's reaction is both symptomatic and constitutive of the mutually reinforcing hegemonic discourses of masculinity and corporate managerialism that pervade the organisational culture of the Australian state (Bryson 1986, 1987; Kenway 1992). Thus, it is difficult to see how GEP in sport can escape being framed by the logic of 'masculine managerialism' that suffuses both the state and sport in Australia.

Epilogue

> I give an extra special vote of thanks to the women of Australia who voted for us believing in the policies of this Government. Prime Minister Paul Keating during his 1993 election victory speech

In 1992 Roy Masters was reappointed to the ASC Board by Ros Kelly and Bob Hobson was nominated as the ASC's Senior Officer responsible for EEO. In 1993 Jim Ferguson was reappointed by Ros Kelly as the ASC's Executive Director and Ros Kelly was reappointed Minister for Sport.

Notes

I would like to thank Rhonda Bushby, Geoff Lawrence and Shona Thompson for their constructive comments on an earlier draft of this manuscript.

1   For some commentaries on the cultural policy/ cultural studies debate in Australia see Bennett (1989, 1992), Cunningham (1992), Flew (1992), Wark (1992), and the special issue on this topic in *Meanjin*, 51(3), 1992. For a discussion of intellectuals as 'cultural workers' see Connell (1983).
2   Australian Sports Commission (1992:iii).
3   House of Representatives Standing Committee on Legal and Constitutional Affairs (1991:1).
4   For more on gender, power and organisational cultures see Cockburn (1991), Hearn (1992b), Hearn and Parkin (1987), Hearn et al. (1991) and Mills and Tancred (1992).
5   See Margaret Timpson's address to the Parliamentary Committee in *Equity for Women in Sport* (1991).

References

Acosta, V. and Carpenter, L. J. (1992) 'As the years go by – coaching opportunities in the 1990s', *Journal of Physical Education, Recreation and Dance*, March: 36–41.

Australian Public Service (1992) *Equal Employment Opportunity. A Strategic Plan for the Australian Public Service for the 1990s*, Canberra: EEO Policy and Programs Unit of the Public Service Commission.

Australian Sports Commission (1992) *Towards Equity in Sport*, Belconnen: Australian Sports Commission.

Beneath the Veneer: The Report of the Task Force on Barriers to Women in the Public Service. (1990) Ottawa: Canadian Government Publishing Service, (4 volumes).

Bennett, T. (1989) 'Culture: theory and policy', *Culture and Policy* 1: 5–8.

——(1992) 'Putting policy into cultural studies', in L. Grossberg, C. Nelson, and P. Treichler (eds), *Cultural Studies*, London: Routledge.

Bluckert, P. (1989) 'Courage and spark: discovering new meanings and expressions of leadership by men', *Equal Opportunities International*, 8 (1): 21–4.

Bryson, L. (1986) 'A new iron cage? A view from within', *Canberra Bulletin of Public Administration*, 50: 362–70.

——(1987) 'Women and management', *Australian Journal of Public Administration*, 46: 259–73.

Cockburn, C. (1991) *In the Way of Women: Men's Resistance to Sex Equality in Organisations*, London: Macmillan.

Collinson, M. and Knights, D. (1990) *Managing to Discriminate*, London: Routledge.

Connell, R. W. (1983) 'Democratising culture', *Meanjin*, 42: 295–307.

Cunningham, S. (1992) *Framing Culture: Criticism and Policy in Australia*, Sydney: Allen & Unwin.

Drake, P. (1985) 'Of course we have women managers in our business, but...', *Management Education and Development*, 16 (2): 120–7.

Fasting, K. (1987) 'The promotion of women's involvement in Norwegian sports organizations' in T. Slack and R. Hinings (eds), *The Organization and Administration of Sport*, London: Sports Dynamics Publishers.

Fasting, K. and Sisjord, M. K. (1986) 'Gender, verbal behaviour and power in sports organisations', *Scandinavian Journal of Sports Science*, 8 (2): 81–5.

Flew, T. (1992) 'Policy pitfalls: reply to Stuart Cunningham', *Media Information Australia*, 65: 87–90.

Hall, A., Cullen, D. and Slack, T. (1989) 'Organizational elites recreating themselves: the gender structure of national sports organizations', *Quest*, 41: 28–45.

——(1990) 'The gender structure of national sport organisations', *Sport Canada Occasional Papers*, 2 (1).

Hearn, J. (1989) 'Leading questions for men's leadership, feminist challenges, and men's responses', *Equal Opportunities International*, 8 (1): 3–11.

——(1992a) 'Changing men and changing managements: a review of issues and actions', *Women in Management Review*, 7 (1): 38.

——(1992b) *Men in the Public Eye*, London: Routledge.

Hearn, J. and Parkin, W. (1987) *Sex at Work*, Brighton: Wheatsheaf.

Hearn, J., Sheppard, D, Tancred-Sheriff, P., and Burrell, G. (eds) (1990) *The Sexuality of Organisation*, London: Sage.

House of Representatives Standing Committee on Legal and Constitutional Affairs (1991) *Equity for Women in Sport*, Canberra: House of Representatives Standing Committee on Legal and Constitutional Affairs.

——(1992) *Half Way to Equal* (Report of the Inquiry Into Equal Status and Equal Opportunity for Women in Australia), Canberra: House of Representatives Standing Committee on Legal and Constitutional Affairs.

Kane, M. J. (1990) 'Structural variables that offer explanatory power for the underrepresentation of women coaches since Title IX: the case of homologous reproduction', *Sociology of Sport Journal*, 8 (1): 47–60.

Kane, M. J. and Stangl, J. M. (1991) 'Employment patterns of female coaches in men's athletics: tokenism and marginalization as reflections of occupational sex-segregation', *Journal of Sport and Social Issues*, 15 (1): 21–43.

Kenway, J. (1992) 'Feminist theories of the state: to be or not to be?' in M. Muetzelfeldt (ed.), *Society, State and Politics in Australia*, Sydney: Pluto Press.

Knoppers, A. (1992) 'Explaining male dominance and sex segregation in coaching: three approaches', *Quest*, 44: 210–27.

Macintosh, D. and Beamish, R. (1988) 'Socioeconomic and demographic characteristics of national sports administrators', *Canadian Journal of Sport Science*, 13 (1): 66–72.

McKay, J. (1991a) *No Pain, No Gain? Sport and Australian Culture*, Sydney: Prentice Hall.

——(1991b) 'Sporting women and hysterical men', *Australian Society*, 10 (9): 49–50.

——(1992a) *Why so Few? Women Executives in Australian Sport*, Belconnen: Australian Sports Commission.

——(1992b) 'Exercising hegemonic masculinity: sport and the social construction of gender' in G. Lupton, T. Short and R. Whip (eds), *Society and Gender: An Introduction to Sociology*, Sydney: Macmillan.

Marshall, J. (1984) *Women Managers: Travellers in a Male World*, Chichester: John Wiley and Sons.

Mills, A. and Tancred, P. (eds) (1992) *Gendering Organisational Theory*, London: Sage.

Morgan, G. (1986) *Images of Organizations*, New York: Sage.

Morrison, A., White, R. and Van Velsor, E. (1987) *Breaking the Glass Ceiling*, New York: Addison-Wesley.

Office of the Status of Women (1989) *A Say, a Choice, a Fair Go: The Government's National Agenda for Women*, Canberra: AGPS.

——(1993) *WOMEN – Shaping and Sharing the Future. The New National Agenda for Women*, (2nd edn), Canberra: AGPS.

Pateman, C. (1988) 'The patriarchal welfare state' in A. Gutmann (ed.), *Democracy and the Welfare State*, Princeton: Princeton University Press.

Powell, G. (1988) *Women and Men in Management*, London: Sage.

Raivio, M. R. (1986) 'The life and careers of women in leading positions in Finnish sports organisations' in J. Morgan and R. Small (eds), *Sport, Culture, Society: International Perspectives*, London: E. & F. Spon.

Reskin, B. and Roos, P. (1990) *Job Queues, Gender Queues: Women's Inroads Into Male Occupations*, Philadelphia: Temple University Press.

Ruth, S. (1989) 'Leadership, men and equality', *Equal Opportunities International*, 8 (1): 25–8.

Simmons, M. (1989) 'Creating a new men's leadership: developing a theory and practice', *Equal Opportunities International*, 8 (1): 16–20.

Spencer, A. and Podmore, D. (eds) (1987) *In a Man's World: Essays on Women in Male-Dominated Professions*, London: Tavistock.

Theberge, N. (1987) 'A preliminary analysis of the careers of women coaches in Canada' in T. Slack and R. Hinings (eds), *The Organization and Administration of Sport*, London: Sports Dynamics Publishers.

——(1984) 'Some evidence of the existence of a sexual double standard in mobility to leadership positions in sport', *International Review for the Sociology of Sport*, 19 (2): 185–95.

Thompson, S. (1991) 'Mum's taxi: gendered servicing of sport', paper presented at The Australian Sociological Association Annual Conference, Murdoch University, 10–14 December.

Timpson, M. (1991) 'Public policy and funding of women's sport' in *Equity for Women in Sport*, Canberra: House of Representatives Standing Committee on Legal and Constitutional Affairs.

Wark, M. (1992) 'After literature: culture, policy, theory and beyond', *Meanjin*, 51 (4): 677–90.

West, A. and Brackenridge, C. (1990) *Wot! No Women Sports Coaches? A Report on the Issues Relating to Women's Lives as Sports Coaches in the United Kingdom: 1989/1990*, Sheffield City Polytechnic: PAVIC Publications.

White, A. and Brackenridge, C. (1985) 'Who rules sport? Gender divisions in the power structure of British sports organisations from 1960', *International Review for the Sociology of Sport*, 20: 96–107.

White, A., Mayglothing, R. and Carr, C. (1991) *The Dedicated Few – The Social World of Women Coaches in Britain in the 1990s*, West Sussex Institute of Higher Education, Centre for the Study and Promotion of Sport and Recreation for Women and Girls.

Whitson, D. and Macintosh, D. (1989) 'Gender and power: explanations of gender inequalities in Canadian national sport organizations', *International Review for the Sociology of Sport*, 24: 132–50.

Yeatman, A. (1990) *Bureaucrats, Technocrats, Femocrats: Essays on the Contemporary Australian State*, Sydney: Allen & Unwin.

Postscript

Shortly after I completed this study, the Women and Sport Unit lost its semi-autonomous status in the ASC. While recent studies have shown that immense disparities exist between males and females in virtually every aspect of Australian sport, millions of dollars of public money has been spent on high-performance sport as an investment in the anticipated 'gold medal rush' at the 2000 summer Olympics in Sydney. The succession of Labor governments (1983–96) expressed more enthusiasm for gender equity initiatives than the two Coalition governments that replaced them. The latter have pursued socially conservative and economically radical policies that are at best indifferent and at worst antagonistic toward women's rights (Beeson and Firth, 1998). Their neoliberal measures have included: cutting staff in the Office of the Status of Women by 40 percent; preventing the Affirmative Action Agency from naming publicly companies that refuse to indicate how they are promoting gender equity in the workplace; abolishing job training programs specifically for women; slashing funds for legal aid and childcare; and mounting an 'anti-PC' campaign in general. The government has also made it clear that policy work by academics should have demonstrable benefits to the private sector. At the same time, there also has been an increase in reactionary anti-feminist and pro-masculinist discourses in education, health and the popular media (McKay and Ogilvie, 1999).

References

Beeson, M. and Firth, A. (1998) Neoliberalism as a political rationality: Australian public policy in the 1980s. *Journal of Sociology* 34: 215–31.

McKay, J. and Ogilvie, E. (1999) New Age – Same Old Men: Constructing the 'New Man' in the Australian Media. *Mattoid* 54: 18–35.

Chapter 17

Sports Wars: Suburbs and Center Cities in a Zero-Sum Game

Samuel Nunn and Mark S. Rosentraub

During the next week, Arlington will be discovered for all the reasons that it ought to already be known. Having the All-Stars here will establish a national identity we otherwise could never have achieved.

Richard Greene, Mayor of Arlington, Texas,
site of the 1995 Major League All-Star game
and home of the American League's Texas Rangers

The [Dallas/Fort Worth] metroplex is so intertwined that there is no one city that really stands independently any more, whether you're talking about Dallas or Fort Worth or Arlington. The All-Stars are a good thing for all of us.

Terry Ryan, Executive Director,
Fort Worth Chamber of Commerce

For the past 150 years, U.S. cities have fought with one another to cultivate and capture economic development opportunities. For at least 50 years, major league sports teams (Major League Baseball, the National Football League, the National Basketball Association, and the National Hockey League) have been a part of this new "civil war" as intense competition for scarce franchises (each league controls the number of teams that can exist) has emerged between cities (Burstein and Rolnick, 1995). In the past 25 years, the tension has been more pronounced as interurban rivalries have developed within metropolitan areas. Smaller suburban cities have sought to achieve "major league" status by attracting teams from their neighboring central city (J. E. Miller, 1990; L. Miller, 1994).

Cities use various inducements to attract teams, hoping that the presence of a major league franchise will stimulate economic development or civic pride and reputation. Although there is considerable debate over the economic value of teams, even if one were to accept the most optimistic estimates (Bale, 1989; Zimbalist, 1992), the benefit of new jobs, a higher quality of life, increased tourism, and more spending would seem to affect all cities in a region. If the available benefits or returns from a team accrue to a region, then providing incentives to encourage moves within a region (from center cities to suburbs or from suburbs to center cities) will only result in increased profits for teams and higher salaries for players. Further, if teams do not generate a concentration of benefits for an investor city, then all cities in a region would be well served by treating professional sports teams as regional assets that require regional cooperation to minimize public expense. The purpose of this article is to explore these issues through a review of the reasons clubs move, the importance of sports for local and regional growth, and the impact of professional sports teams on the economies of cities in the Dallas/Fort Worth region, an area with extensive intraregional competition for teams.

Why Teams Move

Although teams enjoy substantial benefits from the fan loyalty that comes from playing in the same area year after year, they always have sought larger fan markets and more profitable playing facilities. There were a number of franchise moves in the formative years of most leagues. In later years, however, teams still moved. In Major League Baseball (MLB), three teams left markets that seemed large enough to support only one club. The St. Louis Browns were nearly bankrupt when they became the Baltimore Orioles in 1954, the Boston Braves moved to Atlanta in 1953, and the Philadelphia Athletics moved to Kansas City in 1955. Those were the first moves of major league baseball teams since 1903 and were a precursor of things to come. In subsequent years, the Dodgers, Giants, Braves, Pilots, Athletics, Senators, and Senators II each moved to other regions. In the National Basketball Association's (NBA) early years, teams went from smaller to larger cities (Rochester Royals to Cincinnati, Tri-City Blackhawks to Milwaukee and St. Louis as the Hawks, Fort Wayne Pistons to Detroit). Several National Football League teams (NFL) also moved during the league's formative years, with the Chicago Cardinals landing in St. Louis (1960) before heading to Phoenix (1988) and the Rams moving to Los Angeles (1946) from Cleveland before going to Anaheim (1980) and then St. Louis (1995). The Baltimore Colts of the All-America Football Conference played one season as the Miami Seahawks and, after joining the NFL in 1950, folded in 1951. The new Baltimore Colts, reborn in 1953, moved to Indianapolis in 1984. When the American Football League began play in 1960, it needed to move the Dallas Texans to Kansas City (Chiefs) and the Los

Angeles Chargers to San Diego. In later years, the Raiders moved to Los Angeles (1982) before returning to Oakland (1995).

There has also been a spate of moves within metropolitan regions. The Buffalo Bills, Kansas City Chiefs, Los Angeles Rams, Miami Dolphins, New England Patriots, New York Jets, New York Giants, Dallas Cowboys, Detroit Lions, Kansas City Royals, Cleveland Cavaliers, and the Detroit Pistons each have moved from center city locations to suburban locations in their metropolitan regions. The Cavaliers returned to downtown Cleveland in 1994, and the Minnesota Vikings and Minnesota Twins both left suburban locations for a new home in downtown Minneapolis. Currently, there are at least seven franchises considering moves within their metropolitan areas, and most of these would entail a move from a central city to the suburbs: the Dallas Mavericks, the Dallas Stars, the New York Yankees, the New York Mets, the Florida Panthers, the Miami Heat, and the Arizona Cardinals (suburb to suburb move). An eighth team, the Chicago Bears, recently ended their flirtation with two different suburban locations. Although interregional moves of teams are more numerous and receive more publicity, intraregional moves are a substantial part of the economics and management of professional sports.

Sports and Local Economies

Providing subsidies to attract a team would not be an issue of concern if substantial benefits resulted. For the most part, although sports are immensely popular and important as a cultural icon, they remain a small business with a modest ability to affect economic development.

Teams as local businesses

Using average ticket prices, attendance levels, typical food and beverage sales, local media revenues, and luxury seating revenues, it is likely that only two teams in 1994, the Toronto Blue Jays and the New York Yankees, had annual revenues of more than $100 million. Several baseball teams had gross revenues that exceeded $60 million, including the Chicago White Sox, the Chicago Cubs, the Atlanta Braves, the Colorado Rockies, the Los Angeles Dodgers, and the Cali-

Table 17.1   Private sector employment and payroll levels in all United States counties with 300,000 residents, 1992

Standard industrial code classification	Employment as a percentage of total	Payroll as a percentage of total
Eating and drinking places	6.56	2.16
Hotels and other lodging places	1.55	.82
Amusement and recreation services	1.26	.94
Commercial sports	.12	.18
Professional sports, managers	.06	.10
Remaining retail trade	13.05	8.21
Remaining services	32.76	31.49
Manufacturing	16.66	21.42
Wholesale trade	7.33	9.35
Transportation	6.34	7.90
Finance, insurance, and real estate	8.88	11.59
Agriculture	.59	.39
Mining	.32	.55
Construction	4.64	5.12
Unclassified	.05	.07
Total for all counties	55,662,194	$1,502,221,516,000

Source: U.S. Department of Commerce (1985, 1990).

fornia Angels. Firms with annual budgets of $60 million or $100 million are certainly vital, vibrant, and valued in terms of the development of any region's economy. But businesses of this size are quite small compared to other organizations in urban areas. The most successful sports franchise has gross revenues that are less than half of a typical urban campus of a state university, and most teams have budgets that are equal to about 20% of the budget of an urban campus of a state university (Klacik and Rosentraub, 1993).

Professional sports in a region's economy

With these figures in perspective, it is probably not surprising that professional sports are a very small part of the economy of any county or region. Table 17.1 summarizes private sector employment and payment levels across all counties with at least 300,000 residents. Of the 55,662,194 private sector jobs across these 161 counties, .06% or 33,397 were associated with either professional sports teams or managers. In terms of total payroll dollars, these jobs accounted for one tenth of 1% of the $1.5 trillion in annual private sector payrolls reported for these 161 counties. This tiny percentage, however, still amounted to more than $1.5 billion. Moreover, sports employ-

ment is not concentrated in larger counties, as shown in table 17.2. Professional sports never accounted for more than .08% of the jobs in counties of different sizes and only accounted for about one half of 1% of the private sector's total payroll. When we changed the focus of the analysis to each of the 161 counties, in no county did the number of jobs with professional teams or sport managers account for more than four tenths of 1% of all jobs. The counties with the largest concentration of sports jobs as a proportion of their local economies are identified in table 17.3. It is important to note, however, that in three of the counties the salaries from the professional sports sector accounted for more than one half of 1% of all private sector payrolls, but in no county did sports salaries account for more than three quarters of 1% of private sector payrolls (see table 17.3).

In percentage terms, sports are a very small part of any county's private sector economy, but this does not mean sports payrolls are trivial or even small numbers of dollars. In Cook County (Illinois) the payroll for professional teams was more than $112 million, and the annual payroll in Hennepin County (Minnesota) was $100 million. In St. Louis City, the annual payroll was more than $52 million. Sports can generate large payroll numbers, even when those figures represent a tiny percentage of total payroll dollars (see table 17.3).

Professional sports and related spending

One of the justifications frequently used to support public investments in professional sports is the related spending for food, beverages, hotel rooms, and souvenirs. Assume, for the moment, that there is a direct relationship between all amusement and recreation services and purchases at restaurants and hotels. In other words, to establish a "high-end estimate" for spending associated with sports, we assumed that everyone engaged in any form of recreation also ate a meal at a restaurant or stayed at a hotel.

Amusement and recreation spending accounted for 1.26% of all private sector jobs in counties with more than 300,000 residents (see table 17.1) and .94% of all private sector payrolls. If that represented the portion of restaurant and hotel jobs and payrolls associated with amusements and recreation services, then 701,334 jobs with an annual payroll of $14.1 billion were created in hotels and restaurants from all recreational activities. That would mean commercial (which includes racing) and professional sports accounted for .18% of all jobs or 14.3% of the amusement and recreational service jobs. This would also mean that of the 701,334 jobs in restaurants and hotels created by amusement and recreational jobs, 100,192 jobs across America were created in restaurants and hotels as a result of sports. In payroll terms, this would amount to $4.2 billion for the entire country. But that was for all sports, not just professional sports. If we looked at just professional team sports, the corresponding numbers

are 233,781 jobs with an average annual payroll of $1.5 billion across America. (These numbers were calculated by assuming that the proportion of recreation jobs in the economy produced a similar proportion of jobs in the hotel and restaurant sectors of the economy.) Because the total private sector payroll was $1.5 trillion, the figure of $1.5 billion amounts to one tenth of 1% of the private sector payroll reported for counties with more than 300,000 residents in 1992. Again, this is not a small number, but in percentage terms it is virtually negligible. Others also have found that the amount of restaurant and hotel trade related to sports facilities, in percentage terms, is quite small (Baade, 1994). In summary, sports teams are not economic engines that can drive an economy; they are small businesses with very modest and almost inconsequential effects on a region's wealth. But is that all there is?

Professional sports, image, and economic development

At a minimum, sports clearly add to the perception that a city is "a nice place to live." Teams will not reduce pollution levels, reduce crime, improve learning in schools, or make people better workers, parents, or spouses, but they do create entertainment and help define the quality of life in any city. Other things also define the quality of life, including public schools that produce highly educated children, safe streets, museums, the performing arts, libraries, colleges, and universities. Corporations carefully evaluate all these factors as indicators of the quality of life in a community when making locational decisions, and because professional team sports

Table 17.2   The percentage of employment and private sector payrolls by county populations, 1992

	Population of county			
Industry	300,000 to 500,000 (n = 66)	500,001 to 1,000,000 (n = 65)	1,000,001 to 2,000,000 (n = 22)	More than 2,000,000 (n = 8)
Professional sports employment as a percentage of total employment	.03	.06	.08	.06
Professional sports payrolls as a percentage of private sector payrolls	.14	.13	.24	.52

Table 17.3   U.S. counties with the largest concentrations of direct employment in professional sports: jobs and annual payrolls, 1992

County (state)	Pro sports employment as a percentage of all jobs	Pro-sports payrolls as a percentage of all payrolls	Total pro-sports jobs	Total pro-sports payroll (in thousands)
Summit (OH)	.35	NA	760	
Fulton (GA)	.32	NA	1,727	
Baltimore (city)	.26	NA	760	
Oakland (MI)	.24	.39	1,419	$68,171
Bronx (NY)	.19	NA	378	
Erie (NY)	.19	NA	742	
Queens (NY)	.18	NA	758	
Cook (IL)	.16	.17	3,696	$112,423
Marion (IN)	.16	.51	762	$62,025
St. Louis (city)	.16	.74	422	$52,574
Suffolk (MA)	.16	NA	761	
Philadelphia (PA)	.13	NA	748	
Salt Lake City	.11	NA	382	
Hennepin (MN)	.10	.51	690	$100,634

Note: NA = data not available due to confidentiality issues.
Source: U.S. Department of Commerce (1992).

make an important contribution to the definition of that quality, the level and quality of professional sports can contribute to or help define a city or region's image and its attractiveness. But can sports or any single factor affect locational decisions or economic development?

Robert Ady, President of PHH Fantus Consulting, a company that specializes in corporate relocations, probably best summarized the importance of the image sports convey to a city. In June 1993, he was speaking to a group of business and community leaders at Arrowhead Stadium in Kansas City. Asked to describe why companies move to certain areas, he noted,

In fact, the single-most important location criteria today is grouped under operating conditions. No, I must tell you now that it is not the presence of a professional sports team; it is in fact the availability of a qualified workforce. In today's competitive and ever-changing environment, companies are locating where they feel assured of securing such a workforce. Not only the availability of managerial talent but, more importantly, the availability of skilled and technical talent. Other typical operating condition criteria might include proximity to an international airport, tranquil labor-management relations, sophisticated telecommunications availability, and dual-feed utility systems.

Ady also noted some of the positive dimensions of sports for economic development. Sporting events represent a great opportunity to bring prospective companies to a city and highlight things the city has accomplished with the private sector. Because bringing a prospect to town is essential to any relocation process, sports can be a great tool when making the deal. Further, sports seem to be a force that generates tremendous civic pride and an enhanced reputation, which can generate an "image" that sets one community apart from another (Rosentraub, 1996). It is hard not to acknowledge the benefits generated from the positive feelings and excitement created when a team wins (Verducci, 1996).

Sports and intraregional competition

Movement of teams within a region does not provide increased access to a larger media market, and intraregional moves are unlikely to attract new fans. In some isolated instances, concerns with security may deter some spectators, but successful teams playing in areas that have reputations (founded or unfounded) for crime have not had problems attracting fans (e.g., Chicago Bulls, New York Yankees) to attend day or night games. Cities usually seek teams to enhance their reputations or stimulate economic growth. Yet if a team already exists within a region, will its movement generate benefits that can be captured by the suburban city that offers an incentive package? Suburban cities seek teams for many of the same reasons larger central cities have: identity, economic development related to recreation and tourism, and the establishment of a quality of life that can attract firms with higher-income employees (Wilson, 1994). Armed with reports that indicate that quality of life issues are central to the locational choices of businesses with the highest-income employees, suburban cities continue to express interest in attracting teams to enhance the quality of life within their borders.

Sports and the Dallas/Fort Worth Region

The Dallas/Fort Worth region's history with major league professional teams began in 1960. The upstart American Football League, eager to challenge the more established NFL, targeted rapidly growing areas that did not have teams and placed one of its charter franchises, the Texans, in Dallas in 1960. The NFL, in an effort to protect potential markets, quickly responded with its own expansion and awarded the Dallas Cowboys a franchise in the same year. The older league, with more prestige and the ability to attract more fans as a result of its established and popular teams with many star athletes (e.g., Chicago Bears, Green Bay Packers, New York Giants, etc.), was far more successful in this new market, resulting in the Texans' move to Missouri in 1963, where they became the Kansas City Chiefs.

Major league baseball came to the region in 1972. The Dallas/Fort Worth area had been a long-standing site for minor league baseball. However, in 1971, in Arlington, a suburb between Dallas and Fort Worth, the mayor convinced Bob Short to move his floundering Washington Senators to the center of the Dallas/Fort Worth region. Arlington had a stadium on the main interstate highway that connects the two larger center cities. In 1972, the

Texas Rangers began play in Arlington Stadium, a facility initially developed for a minor league team but adjacent to Interstate 30 and at the geographic and transportation center of the region.

The National Basketball Association (NBA) made its appearance in the Dallas/Fort Worth area with the awarding of the Dallas Mavericks team franchise in 1980. The team has played in Reunion Arena in downtown Dallas since its inception. Reunion Arena was opened in 1980, providing the city with its initial "first-class" enclosed facility capable of competing with Fort Worth's Tarrant County Convention Center (located approximately 40 miles west of Reunion Arena, at the opposite end of Interstate 30 in downtown Fort Worth).

The NHL did not come to the Dallas/Fort Worth region until the 1990s. In 1994, the Minnesota North Stars moved to Reunion Arena and began play as the Dallas Stars. Two minor league hockey teams, however, have remained active in the region. The Fort Worth Fire still plays at the Will Rogers Auditorium, a small venue on Fort Worth's westside. The Dallas Freeze plays its home games approximately five miles east of Reunion Arena. In several markets, minor league hockey with its lower ticket prices remains economically viable and even a complement to NHL teams that typically charge far more for tickets.

The attraction of the Dallas Cowboys, Texas Rangers, Dallas Mavericks, and the Dallas Stars was seen as a major image and economic development coup for the Dallas/Fort Worth region. Sports provided a conduit in which a new image could be shaped, and the success of the Cowboys certainly helped to create other perspectives on Dallas. The relocation of the Washington Senators, at about the same time that the region opened the Dallas/Fort Worth Regional International Airport, continued the process of changing the region's image.

When the region was attempting to attract its first teams, there was virtual harmony and cooperation among all cities; the goal was to bring major league sports to the area and enhance the region's reputation, image, and quality of life. However, as soon as any of the teams began to discuss their preferences for new playing facilities, this harmony quickly dissipated. In the same order they appeared in the region, the teams began to seek improved stadia and arenas. The Cowboys initially played their home games at Dallas's historic but aging Cotton Bowl, which lacked many of the modern amenities teams and fans sought in the late 1960s. In addition, the Cotton Bowl was and is located in a predominantly minority, declining neighborhood that continues to suffer from high crime levels and economic disinvestment. In the late 1960s, the Cowboys and the city of Dallas exchanged ideas and plans for a new downtown facility or a facility north of downtown. Four separate plans were developed, but none could be supported by all parties. The team also initiated negotiations with the city of Irving, a suburb adjacent to Dallas, which borders the Dallas/Fort Worth Regional International Airport. The team and the city of Irving reached an agreement for the building of Texas Stadium, where the Cowboys have played since 1971.

The Texas Rangers and the city of Arlington had a long history of problems with Arlington Stadium. Designed to serve a minor league franchise, it was not only too small, but a large proportion of its seats were outfield bleachers. The city made two major sets of innovations, including a new upper deck, but the facility could never seat the promised 50,000 fans. With only 42,500 seats, more than one third of these outfield bleachers, the revenue potential for the team was extremely limited. In the early 1990s, the Rangers began to explore their options, which included a new facility in Arlington, a stadium in Dallas, a stadium in one of Dallas's northern suburbs, or a possible move to St. Petersburg and its Sun Coast Dome. The Florida city had built the dome stadium without a commitment from any team. The Rangers and the Chicago White Sox both used the threat of a move to the Sun Coast Dome to secure new facilities (Mier, 1993). However, the Rangers were unlikely to want to leave the nation's eighth largest media market, and so the team's attention was focused on Arlington, Dallas, and Dallas's northern suburbs. The team and the city of Arlington eventually developed the plans that led to "The Ballpark in Arlington," a facility widely proclaimed as one of the finest in America.

The competition between cities in the region for the Rangers set the stage for another round of sports wars involving the Mavericks and Stars. Reunion Arena, although relatively new, does not have the luxury suites and club seating that have increased the profitability of several NBA and NHL teams. In addition, the arena's capacity is less than the newer facilities that several cities have developed. Indeed, indoor arenas now frequently have more than 20,000 seats or are at least 15% larger than Reunion Arena. In 1993, the Mavericks' owners began to explore the possibility of a new arena with the city of Dallas. At the same time the team was negotiating with Dallas, the team's owner purchased land in a northeast suburb in an effort to consider a move from Dallas to the city of Lewisville. Lewisville's voters narrowly defeated a proposition to implement a local sales tax to support their investment in the arena, but then Arlington signaled its interest in building a new arena for the Mavericks and Stars by hiring a consulting firm to develop a feasibility study. The favorable results of this assessment were released to the media and discussed at a city council meeting. Although the city of Arlington's official position was that it would not make a proposal to the Mavericks and Stars until such time as a deal was not feasible in Dallas, Arlington's officials did nothing to conceal their excitement in attracting both teams. In the first half of 1995, then, a sports war had broken out in the Dallas/Fort Worth region for the Dallas Mavericks and Stars.

Sports Franchises and the Intraregional Distribution of Benefits

We have argued earlier that interurban competition for sports franchises occurs for several reasons: economic effects and presumed fiscal returns, image and prestige benefits, and improvements to the quality of life. These same reasons have been cited by suburban officials in the Dallas/Fort Worth metropolitan region when competing with central cities to attract wandering franchises. In this latest round of competition, the Dallas/Fort Worth suburbs have sought to lure away the Dallas central city's teams. In the context of these actions, the suburban cities must believe that any additional public investments needed to attract the Mavericks or the Stars will create special benefits for the host suburban community. Thus, as either existing or potential "investor cities" in the sports clubs,

suburban cities behave as if there is a clear prospect of capturing larger shares of the benefits
presumed to come from being home to a sports
franchise. However, interurban competition for
teams within a metropolitan region may not be
the same as interregional competition between,
for example, St. Petersburg and Chicago for
a sports franchise. Therefore, in considering the
intraregional competition for sports teams, at
least three critical questions emerge:

1   Do the implied image, prestige, and quality
    of life effects of "being home" to a sports
    franchise in Dallas/Fort Worth result in in-
    vestor cities reflecting comparatively larger
    or faster metropolitan population growth?
2   Are the investor cities within the Dallas/Fort
    Worth metropolitan area recognizing in-
    creased fiscal benefits when compared to
    other noninvestor cities?
3   Are the investor cities exhibiting a larger
    proportion of the high-income and high-
    skill occupations that seek an impro-
    ved quality of life when compared to other
    noninvestor cities in the Dallas/Fort Worth
    metropolitan area?

Population growth

As noted earlier, three Dallas/Fort Worth cities
(Dallas, Arlington, and Irving) have been the
prime municipal investors in the region's professional sports teams. Characterized as a key element in the "quality of life" of a city, the presence
of a sports franchise is seen as a potential lure for
more population. Has this in fact occurred at a
higher rate in the Dallas/Fort Worth investor
cities when compared to other noninvestor cities
in the region?

The answer to this question is no: A variety of
other cities in the Dallas/Fort Worth region grew
at considerably higher rates in the two decades
since sports suburbanization became active in and
around Dallas/Fort Worth. Table 17.4 denotes
population change in three investor cities and in
14 noninvestor cities within the region. In terms of
both nominal percentage changes and net local
growth (i.e., nominal growth less the national
growth of cities of the same size class), the region's
noninvestor cities are doing better on average than
the investor cities. From 1970 to 1980, Arlington
grew considerably, but four other suburbs grew at

a higher rate; from 1980 to 1990, five noninvestor
suburbs grew at a higher rate than Arlington.
From 1970 to 1980, Irving ranked 13th among all
17 cities examined here but did manage to exceed
the rate of growth in six of the noninvestor cities in
the 1980s. Overall, however, these population
data do not support the proposition that sports
franchises attract people to the "host" investor
city faster than to other noninvestor cities within
the same region.

Comparative fiscal benefits

Investment in sports franchises is expected to
have several effects on a city's finances. Because
sports-related facilities are often fixed capital investments, city officials anticipate higher property values around such sites, which in turn are
expected to generate more property taxes for the
municipality. However, city officials voice less
attention to the debt effects of sports facilities.
Fixed sports investments require the use of public
debt to finance these facilities, so we would also
speculate that investor cities may exhibit higher
levels of debt. On the other hand, because these
fixed investments bring in fans and presumably
create entertainment complexes around stadia,
more sales tax among investor cities also might
be expected. Finally, investment in sports facilities is expected to affect the operating expenditures of investor cities; that is, if higher property
taxes and sales tax revenues are being generated,
there may be more revenues to support higher
levels of public municipal spending. Conversely,
if revenues are not increased, the expenditure
requirements of sports franchises and their fixed
investments may detract from expenditures available for general government services. Either way,
we expect to see different spending patterns by
investor versus noninvestor cities. Thus an examination of investor and noninvestor cities can tell
us whether intrametropolitan competition for
sports teams has created in the Dallas/Fort
Worth region comparatively larger fiscal benefits
for the investor cities or, alternatively, whether
the fiscal boundaries of metropolitan jurisdic-
tions are too porous to keep the preponderance
of benefits.

In a previous study of the 1970 to 1978 period
in Dallas/Fort Worth, we demonstrated that, in
general, Arlington and Irving were not able to
capture a larger share of fiscal benefits than other

Table 17.4 Population change, by city and sports investor class, Dallas/Fort Worth metropolitan area, 1970–1990 and 1980–1990

	Population (1970)	Population (1980)	Change (1970–1980)	National percentage of change	National growth by city size	Net local growth	Population (1990)	Change (1980–1990)	Nominal percentage of change	National growth by city size	Net local growth
Investor cities											
Arlington	90,229	160,113	69,884	77.5	8.6	68.9	261,717	101,604	63.5	15.1	48.4
Dallas	844,401	904,078	59,677	7.1	-16.1	23.2	1,007,618	103,540	11.5	-7.3	18.8
Irving	97,260	109,943	12,683	13.0	8.6	4.4	155,037	45,094	41.0	15.1	25.9
Average growth				32.5		32.2			38.6		31.0
Noninvestor cities											
Bedford	10,049	20,821	10,772	107.2	12.5	94.7	43,762	22,941	110.2	2.6	107.6
Euless	19,316	24,002	4,686	24.3	12.5	11.8	38,149	14,147	58.9	8.9	50.0
Farmers Branch	27,492	24,863	(2,629)	-9.6	17.2	-26.8	24,250	(613)	-2.5	2.6	-5.1
Fort Worth	393,455	385,164	(8,291)	-2.1	12.4	-14.5	447,619	62,455	16.2	20.3	-4.1
Garland	81,437	138,857	57,420	70.5	8.6	61.9	180,635	41,778	30.1	15.1	15.0
Grand Prairie	50,904	71,462	20,558	40.4	8.6	31.8	99,606	28,144	39.4	20.5	18.9
Grapevine	7,049	11,801	4,752	67.4	9.0	58.4	29,198	17,397	147.4	2.6	144.8
Hurst	27,215	31,420	4,205	15.5	17.2	-1.7	33,574	2,154	6.9	8.9	-2.0
Lewisville	9,264	24,273	15,009	162.0	9.0	153.0	46,521	22,248	91.7	8.9	82.8
Mesquite	55,131	67,053	11,922	21.6	8.6	13.0	101,484	34,431	51.3	20.5	30.8
North Richland Hills	16,514	30,592	14,078	85.2	12.5	72.7	45,895	15,303	50.0	8.9	41.1
Plano	17,872	72,331	54,459	304.7	12.5	292.2	127,885	55,554	76.8	20.5	56.3
Richardson	48,405	72,496	24,091	49.8	17.2	32.6	74,840	2,344	3.2	20.5	-17.3
Southlake	2,031	2,808	777	38.3	9.0	29.3	7,082	4,274	152.2	.7	151.5
Average growth				69.7		57.7			59.4		47.9

Note: National growth by city size (columns 5 and 10) is total population growth in all U.S. cities of this size class during the period.
Source: North Central Texas Council of Governments (1970–1991); U.S. Department of Commerce (1980–1990).

Table 17.5 Mean per capita city finances, by city and sports investment class, Dallas/Fort Worth metropolitan area, 1980–1991

	Assessed Property Value	Property Taxes	Sales Taxes	Total Debt	Total Expenditure
All cities	51,162	196	152	1,083	818
Investor cities	43,445	207	160	1,246	806
Arlington	32,341	162	127	1,479	726
Dallas	50,804	266	200	1,449	1,009
Irving	47,190	194	155	811	683
Noninvestor cities	53,119	193	150	1,042	821
Euless	24,806	120	79	484	389
Farmers Branch	106,790	432	400	1,201	1,362
Fort Worth	28,705	226	133	1,325	1,001
Garland	31,649	149	74	1,323	1,278
Grand Prairie	35,778	164	101	875	671
Grapevine	57,853	219	214	1,435	1,317
Hurst	31,695	155	184	463	542
Lewisville	36,723	168	110	1,195	501
Mesquite	29,491	142	116	643	638
North Richland Hills	28,873	122	108	846	574
Plano	77,256	219	111	1,171	785
Richardson	144,917	201	173	1,545	794
F-score	1.69	.75	.41	3.97	.04
Probability	n.s.	n.s.	n.s.	.05	n.s.

Note: All figures expressed in constant 1992 dollars and represent 12-year averages for each city, except for Grand Prairie, which reflects a 10-year average. *F*-score and probability refer to differences between investor and noninvestor city groups. n.s. = not significant.
Source: U.S. Department of Commerce (1980–1991); Moody's Investors' Services (1980–1992).

Dallas/Fort Worth cities after the movement of the Rangers and Cowboys in the early 1970s (Rosentraub and Nunn, 1978). As the new suburban franchise locations matured during the 1980s, however, new entertainment and business complexes may have evolved that gave the two suburban cities comparatively better fiscal performance. The same may be hypothesized for the city of Dallas because of the Dallas Mavericks franchise beginning in 1981.

As shown in table 17.5, differences in fiscal performance from 1980 to 1991 do indeed exist but not always in the direction expected for the investor cities. Investor cities do have statistically higher levels of per capita debt than noninvestor cities: Per capita debt is nearly 20% higher on average among Dallas, Arlington, and Irving than in noninvestor cities. Arlington's per capita debt is exceeded by only the city of Richardson. Because Dallas, Arlington, and Irving were not the fastest-growing cities in the region (see table

17.4), these higher debt levels are not driven completely by population growth; other factors that are likely to include the fixed asset financing and service requirements of professional sports facilities also must underlie these debt figures.

Otherwise, although no other statistically significant differences exist, the nominal per capita differences are still intriguing. First, noninvestor cities on average have higher per capita assessed property valuations than investor cities. From the perspective of metropolitan fiscal policy, this is critical insofar as a combination of high per capita debt and lower assessed value per capita in the investor cities creates the potential for fiscal stress as a result of investments that are not present in the noninvestor cities, which generally exhibited lower debt and higher assessed valuation. Second, in terms of property and sales tax revenue per capita, the investor cities on average are doing somewhat better than noninvestors, although the differences are not statis-

Table 17.6 Changes in high skill occupations, by city and sports investment class, Dallas/Fort Worth metropolitan area, 1970–1990

	Number in high-skill occupations (1970)	As percentage of city's employment	Number in high-skill occupations (1980)	As percentage of city's employment	Number in high-skill occupations (1990)	As percentage of city's employment	1970–1980	1980–1990
Investor cities								
M		29.8		26.9		32.9		
Arlington	15,689	39.1	27,149	31.2	51,805	35.4	73.0	90.8
Dallas	91,431	24.4	122,570	26.4	162,567	31.8	34.1	32.6
Irving	11,047	25.8	14,190	23.3	28,668	31.4	28.5	102.0
Noninvestor cities								
M		26.6		27.8		35.3		
Euless	1,908	24.4	3,156	23.4	7,631	33.0	65.4	141.8
Farmers Branch	2,767	23.9	3,981	27.7	4,274	32.2	43.9	7.4
Fort Worth	29,524	18.4	41,616	23.2	60,644	29.3	41.0	45.7
Garland	8,865	25.8	20,418	27.9	31,451	32.0	130.3	54.0
Grand Prairie	4,599	21.5	6,730	19.3	14,107	27.8	46.3	109.6
Grapevine	645	22.8	1,753	26.8	6,942	41.6	171.8	296.0
Lewisville	879	21.6	3,081	24.6	9,451	34.2	250.5	206.8
Mesquite	4,301	19.5	6,294	18.2	16,163	29.7	46.3	156.8
North Richland Hills	2,036	29.7	4,594	28.5	8,493	33.3	125.6	84.9
Plano	2,777	37.4	15,026	42.3	34,688	48.2	441.1	130.9
Richardson	9,280	47.8	17,019	44.2	19,269	46.7	83.4	13.2

Note: High-skill occupations include executive, administrative, managerial, professional, and technical occupations. "City's employment" refers to employment of the individual city only.
Source: U.S. Department of Commerce (1970–1990).

tically significant. Furthermore, seven noninvestor cities exhibited a higher average annual property tax per capita than Arlington, and five noninvestor cities collected more sales tax per capita on average. Irving did somewhat better in these two revenue categories, but a number of cities without franchises still exceeded its 12-year averages.

Overall, this fiscal comparison lends additional empirical support to the proposition that investor cities cannot prevent the leakage of public tax and revenue benefits of sports investment to other cities in the metropolitan region. In terms of these fiscal indicators, there is not a great deal of differentiation between investor and noninvestor cities, or at least very little that is statistically significant. This suggests that if the presumed fiscal largesse of the sports franchises is real, the region as a whole appears to share in it, even though costs of the sports investments are localized within the three investor cities.

Comparative attraction of high-skill employment

We argued earlier that the image and prestige effects of sports franchises are important to city officials. However, it is not just quality of life per se that cities seek when competing for professional sports teams. On the contrary, the quality of life arguments used to invoke public incentives to attract or keep sports teams are frequently underpinned by the hope that the quality of life aspects of professional sports teams will in turn lure high-skilled, highly paid employees to the host (investor) cities. This proposition can be tested by examining the proportion of each Dallas/Fort Worth city's occupational workforce that is classified as executive, administrative, managerial, professional, or technical. Of all the standard labor force occupational classifications, these reflect the "high-skill" occupations (executive, administrative, managerial, professional specialty, and technicians) in which people presumably seek the high quality of life to which professional sports are believed to contribute.

Changes in high-skill occupations in the Dallas/Fort Worth region, classified by city and sports investment class, are shown in table 17.6. Once again, several noninvestor cities in the Dallas/Fort Worth area fared as well as and often better than Dallas, Arlington, and Irving. Looking at the average proportion of high-skill employment, the investor cities exceeded noninvestors in 1970 only, and by 1990 noninvestor cities averaged a 35% high-skill workforce, compared to 33% in the investor cities. On an individual basis, noninvestor cities such as Plano, Richardson, Garland, and Farmers Branch have consistently had proportions of high-skill occupations similar to the investor cities. Of the investor cities, however, Arlington has maintained the proportion of high-skill occupations at approximately one third of its labor force, exceeding both Dallas and Irving in 1970, 1980, and 1990. In 1990, Arlington ranked third behind Plano and Richardson. Similar findings are exhibited in terms of the decade-by-decade growth of high-skill employment. Several noninvestors (e.g., Plano, Lewisville, Grapevine, Euless) indicate more growth than the investor cities. This was certainly true from 1970 to 1980 and from 1980 to 1990 when comparing the average growth in high-skill occupations between the investor and noninvestor cities as two separate groups. Moreover, individual noninvestor cities had 10-year growth rates far exceeding the investor cities. With respect to attracting and keeping high-skill occupational classes, then, the investor cities in the Dallas/Fort Worth region do not show clear evidence of doing a better job than many noninvestor cities.

Conclusion: Sports and the Regional Citistate

It comes as no surprise that sports teams produce important image, civic pride, and quality of life benefits for all communities in a region. There is also a very small economic impact from a team that enhances a region's economy. However, the decentralized and integrated nature of America's urban economies makes it impossible for any single city to capture a disproportionate share of these benefits, regardless of their size or their tangible and intangible nature. As a result, it is very unlikely that any single city that invests in sports will be able to capture a substantial portion of the benefits generated. At the regional level, however, image and quality of life benefits may make a shared investment by all cities in professional sports a prudent addition to the region's asset base. For any individual city, however, there are insufficient economic, quality of life, or image benefits to warrant a large investment. Indeed, given the dispersion of benefits, there is an incentive for other cities in a region to encourage another community to make an investment and then become a "free rider," enjoying the relatively small gains without supporting the risks taken. With the returns from sports spread across the entire metropolitan region, any investments also should be supported by the entire region.

If a region is to invest in professional sports, where should facilities be located? There is obvious attraction to two possible sites. First, successful arenas and stadia are those that can be easily reached by large numbers of people. Central locations with access to public transportation are clearly advantageous. For example, Toronto's Skydome with only 500 parking spaces has attracted more than 4,000,000 fans for baseball. Cleveland and St. Louis have also integrated mass transportation systems with their sporting venues. Second, cities within all regions need to consider the very important benefits generated when central cities retain their role and image as centers for recreation and culture. Baltimore, Boston, Cleveland, Indianapolis, and Toronto are but five examples of cities that have used sports to enhance the image of their downtown regions. St. Louis is making a similar effort, as is Detroit after losing two of its franchises to the suburbs.

Sports teams will not pave streets, improve schools, enhance the environment, or establish the needed infrastructure for economic development. Sports teams also will not lead economic growth or revitalization (Rosentraub, Swindell, Przybylski, and Mullins, 1994). In addition, subsidizing sports teams will lead to a situation in which economically privileged owners and players disproportionately profit from the public sector's largesse. However, teams that attract millions of people to downtown areas can offer some balance to the decentralizing forces that define urban economies and provide a balance of roles for center cities and their suburbs in metropolitan development. But if you enter sports wars, it is better to do it as a unified region that does not exacerbate the already excessive subsidies sports teams receive from interregional competition.

References

Baade, R. A. (1994). *Stadiums, professional sports, and economic development: Assessing the reality* (Heartland Policy Study, No. 68). Chicago: Heartland Institute.

Bale, J. (1989). *Sports geography.* London: E. & F. N. Spon.

Burstein, M. L., and Rolnick, A. J. (1995). Congress should end the economic war among the states. In *Federal reserve bank of Minneapolis, 1994 annual report.* Minneapolis, MN: Federal Reserve Bank.

Klacik, D., and Rosentraub, M. S. (1993). *The economic importance and impact of IUPUI as a major urban university for Indianapolis and central Indiana.* Indianapolis: Indiana University–Purdue University, Center for Urban Policy and the Environment, School of Public and Environmental Affairs.

Mier, R. (1993). *Social justice and local development policy.* Newbury Park, CA: Sage.

Miller, J. E. (1990). *The business of baseball.* Chapel Hill: University of North Carolina Press.

Miller, L. (1994, October 20–6). Why Dallas shouldn't replace Reunion Arena. *The Dallas Observer,* pp. 17–29.

Moody's Investors' Services. (1980–92). *Moody's municipal and government manual.* New York: Author.

North Central Texas Council of Governments. (1970–91). [Annual population estimates]. Unpublished staff reports.

Rosentraub, M. S. (1996). Does the emperor have new clothes? Sports and economic development. *Journal of Urban Affairs,* 18(1), 23–32.

Rosentraub, M. S., and Nunn, S. (1978). Suburban city investment in professional sports. *American Behavioral Scientist,* 21, 393–414.

Rosentraub, M. S., Swindell, D., Przybylski, M., and Mullins, D. R. (1994). Sport and downtown development strategy: If you build it will jobs come? *Journal of Urban Affairs,* 16(3), 221–39.

U.S. Department of Commerce. (1970–90). *General social and economic characteristics, Texas.* Washington, DC: U.S. Bureau of the Census.

U.S. Department of Commerce. (1980–90). *Statistical abstracts.* Washington, DC: U.S. Bureau of the Census.

U.S. Department of Commerce. (1980–91). *City government finances.* Washington, DC: U.S. Bureau of the Census.

U.S. Department of Commerce. (1985). *County business patterns* [CD-ROM]. Washington, DC: U.S. Bureau of the Census.

U.S. Department of Commerce. (1990). *County business patterns* [CD-ROM]. Washington, DC: U.S. Bureau of the Census.

U.S. Department of Commerce. (1992). *County business patterns* [CD-ROM]. Washington, DC: U.S. Bureau of the Census.

Verducci, T. (1996). Marinermania: How a tottering team's bid for a wild-card birth turned into a late-season frenzy. *Sports Illustrated*, 84(5), 78–90.

Wilson, J. (1994). *Playing by the rules: Sport, society, and the state*. Detroit: Wayne State University Press.

Zimbalist, A. (1992). *Baseball and billions*. New York: Basic Books.

Part VII

Music

Introduction to Part VII

Justin Lewis

Popular music is often regarded as something beyond the reaches of state policy – and, some would say, just as well for being so. When policy is invoked or discussed, it is usually in regard to various moments of censorship (or attempts thereof), whether it be the banning of songs from the playlists of public or private radio stations or the inclusion of "advisory warning labels" on potentially offensive records, tapes or CDs. The problem with this view – and this point could be made in relation to all discussions of censorship – is that it suggests a rather naïve view of production. It implies that there is a vast world of music (or literature, or art) that is simply *there*, to be celebrated, ignored or suppressed as people or governments see fit. The music industry, however, is, like all cultural industries, deeply implicated in policy regimes, regimes that influence aesthetic patterns of production and distribution.

Some of these regimes are part of broader political economies. This was made apparent by Peterson and Berger's 1975 study of concentration and diversity of production in the postwar US pop music industry. Their findings suggested that industry concentration appeared to be closely related to innovation and diversity – the more diverse the ownership structure, the more diverse the musical content. Peterson and Berger's conclusions have been complicated (although not refuted) by Paul Lopes's inclusion of more recent data, which suggest that the presence of a variety of labels is an important factor in maintaining creative dynamism – even if those labels have moved from being independent to

corporate owned. Industry concentration has moved apace since Lopes's study, and as we glide into an era in which (at the time of writing) most of the hundreds of music labels are owned by just four media giants with extensive links in other cultural industries as well as the electronic industry (AOL – Time Warner, Universal/Polygram, Sony and Bertelsmann), it remains to be seen how tolerant these corporate owners will be of the less profitable and more innovative labels in their recording empires.

Moreover, it could be argued that some of the measures used in the Peterson/Berger and Lopes analyses (such as the number of successful new artists in a given year) are indicators rather than guarantees of a diverse or innovative music culture. So, for example, pop music culture's need for a perpetual shock of the new can be satisfied in ways that are superficial or profound. A procession of new artists may signify an explosion of new styles and sounds (as it did, say in the late 1970s and early 1980s) or little more than a formulaic freshness of face. And since most early innovators – whether in the early days of rock'n'roll, punk/new wave, or rap/hip hop – have begun their careers on genuinely independent labels, the freedom of labels like the "Alternative Distribution Alliance" to promote innovation when they operate under the auspices of a giant media corporation like AOL – Time Warner remains unclear.

The ability of the independent sector to produce more innovative artists than corporate empires is not a mysterious, abstract correlation. The corporate sector is intrinsically wary of risk and intolerant of unprofitable subsidiaries. While independent labels *may* be similarly motivated, in the music industry they are often populated by people who are not in it for the money but for the pursuit of more ambitious, cultural goals. As economic units, some of the smaller, musically bolder independents make no sense in the rather limited terms of neo-liberal rationalism, because their inspiration is not simply pecuniary. They're in it for the music. As a consequence, the independents tend to have their ears closer to the ground – figuratively if not literally. Most of the boundaries in pop music history – whether aesthetic, racial or lyrical – have been busted open from the margins. And whether the corporate sector that has always controlled most of the industry has followed lamely and belatedly – in the case of rock'n'roll – or with avaricious opportunism, it has followed nonetheless. Perhaps more visibly than in any other sector, the major corporations are one step behind.

Writing in the early 1980s, Mulgan and Worpole characterized the independent sector (revitalized in the UK by the punk new wave era) as the research and development wing of the industry, albeit one subsidized by the independent's capacity for self-exploitation (in economic terms). In practice, this meant that independent labels were in no position to prevent their successful artists being enticed away by the majors – a relationship that was iniquitous for the independents but, apparently, healthy for the industry as a whole. Even if we accept the terms of these inequities, how might a cultural policy seek to maintain its democratic vitality when the "independents" are no longer independent? One of Mulgan and Worpole's answers, through their work at the Greater London Enterprise Board in the 1980s, was to push public investment to key parts of the independent sector (in this case, to the *distribution* of material through Rough Trade and the Cartel) in order to free those outside the mainstream from dependence on the generally more conservative corporate labels.

In a similar spirit, other local authorities and public funding agencies in the UK (and elsewhere) have subsidized performance venues, rehearsal space and even recording facilities, while the long since departed Greater London Council became a regular promoter of free performances and festivals in parks and other public spaces. The Netherlands Pop Music Foundation is another example of state intervention to support pop music at a grass roots level. The aim of these investments is within the philosophy of *enabling* development at the grass roots or the margins as well as sustaining local music culture. And yet most of the public investment in the pop music industry to date has been inadvertent, whether in the form of dole payments to unemployed youth (allowing, for example, aspiring British musicians to eke out a living by combining dole checks with cash-in-hand earnings from small gigs), or in the form of subsidies to US college radio stations, whose play-lists tend to be more innovative and diverse than commercial stations. While it may be antithetical to free market logic, the dole has helped to give British pop music culture its energy and diversity, since the market will not, on its own, sustain the hundreds and thousands of British musicians whose presence keeps the industry vibrant. And without college radio in the US, there are few outlets within the higher formulaic structure of commercial radio to promote anything that sounds new or different. This is not to reduce the success of the British and US music industries to a kind of Marxist political economy (there are, after all, other countries with similar forms of subsidy but without vibrant pop music traditions), merely to suggest ways in which the political economy of pop relies on more than marketplace mechanisms.

In an era of global production and distribution, policy initiatives in pop music, like other fields of culture, are often about preservation or support for the local rather than the global. The cultural imperialism thesis would seem to apply well to an industry so dominated by Anglo-American musicians, with countries like Canada and Australia introducing quota provisions for radio airplay to encourage the promotion of their own industry. And yet there is no doubt that the mixing of Anglo-American music with other musical traditions (notably from Africa and Latin America) has been productive as well as repressive, as musicians fuse musical traditions to create new styles and forms. The notion of cultural imperialism is also complicated by the absorption of local styles into the global corporate mix. So, for example, MTV and MTV-style formats in India are required to co-opt Indian film music traditions rather than supplant them. This is not to say that the role of the transnational corporations is healthy and benign, simply that it is not necessarily a matter of one culture dominating another or of global competing with local.

In a global corporate culture, one can imagine all sorts of policy interventions that might promote diversity and innovation, although some of these imaginings may be harder to sell than others. There is no reason, for example, that Arts Councils or Endowments could not use their resources to promote, produce or distribute innovative pop music (*without* encumbering it with certain art house requirements). Regulation against trusts or monopoly holdings is also long overdue – particularly when the same few companies not only control most production and distribution, but are horizontally integrated with a range of related cultural industries (notably electronics, film, and magazines). If vertical integration allows a degree of market control, horizontal integration gives them a huge promotional advantage (movies promote soundtracks promote movies etc.). Thus the rapid shift from vinyl to CD was not market-driven, but pushed by the music corporations, acting in consort, to make vinyl more difficult for retailers to sell and more difficult for people to buy. Those labels linked to the electronics industry were thus able to sell a new range of hardware CD players as well as many of the same old recordings in a new format.

Another regulatory area requiring serious consideration is intellectual property law. The days when folk music traditions – such as the blues – operated under collective, public traditions of ownership are long gone. Songs emerging from folk traditions are now enshrined within a regime of individual property holdings. So, for example, the song "Happy Birthday to You" now belongs to AOL – Time Warner, which is, like most corporate property owners, assiduous in policing (and benefiting from) its use, (which is why many restaurant chains no longer allow it to be sung on their premises). While the "Fair Use" provisions in US copyright law do allow a degree of appropriation in the public domain, the costs of defending "Fair Use" is prohibitive enough to allow companies to quash unauthorized use by forms of legal intimidation (issuing strongly

worded "cease and desist" warnings from well-funded legal departments).

As Kembrew McLeod writes, in an era when "sampling" has become part of the state of the art, copyright law has no less than changed the sound of contemporary music. The cost of obtaining permissions has put pressure on many hip-hop artists to reduce the number or range of samples they use, forcing greater reliance on fewer hooks and stemming creativity. When one of the central artistic genres consists of a form of musical collage (hip-hop as well as more avant-garde artists), tightly enforced codes of copyright significantly limit the raw material available.

There are broader issues of cultural policy here, particularly with the increasing use of trademark law as a form of corporate policing of critical speech. There are also no easy solutions: if copyright law – even with fair use provisions – has had a deleterious effect on contemporary pop, intellectual property law also offers a degree of protection against corporate appropriation of musical material. What is undeniable is that a cultural policy for pop must begin by facing the limits and consequences of living in a musical oligarchy. In such conditions, any return to folk traditions of collective ownership would be transformed by iniquitous displays of naked market power.

And yet progressive policy debates about pop music are few and far between. This is, perhaps, more conspicuously true of pop music than with any other area covered in this volume. The alternative is to simply entrust the industry to an oligarchy and the fragile network of inadvertent exceptions to the general drift towards neo-liberal policy frameworks.

References

Lopes, Paul D. "Innovation and Diversity in the Popular Music Industry, 1969 to 1990." *American Sociological Review* 57, no. 1, 1992: pp. 56–71.

Mulgan, G. and Worpole, K. *Saturday Night or Sunday Morning*, London: Comedia, 1986.

Peterson, R. and Berger, D. "Cycles in Symbolic Production: The Case of Popular Music," *American Sociological Review* 40, 1975.

Chapter 18

Radio Space and Industrial Time: The Case of Music Formats

Jody Berland

Radio as a 'Secondary Medium'

In the broadcasting industry, radio is commonly referred to as a 'secondary medium'. The phrase conveys the pragmatic view that no one cares whether you listen to radio so long as you do not turn it off. Since it was displaced by television, radio has been expected to accommodate itself technologically and discursively to every situation. Are you brushing your teeth, turning a corner, buying or selling jeans, or entering inventory into the computer? So much the better. Your broadcaster respects the fact that these important activities must come first. Radio is humble and friendly, it follows you everywhere. In any event, television makes more money.

This denigration of radio's potential in the guise of demographic pragmatism arouses my suspicions and my sympathy. Canadian history has long been shaped by a perceived affinity between the politics of radio and the possibilities of culture. They are bound up together by debates about the media and the nation-state, which originated with radio in the 1920s and continue unabated to the present; by influential critical analysis of the role of technologically and spatially mediated communication in the building of empires; and by continuous political and legislative crises, mainly focused on the broadcast media, concerning the possibility of lasting cultural difference in North American culture. In addition, and perhaps in response to all this, there is a popular myth that Canadian radio is

the best in the world. I ascribe to it myself on most days.

But as the airwaves fall victim to the politics of privatization, radio is becoming progressively more 'popular'. Programming is defined by more and more sophisticated processes of audience research; it is increasingly framed by cross-media corporate strategies designed to cut costs, and to reach across ever-expanding space; and it is increasingly built around music formats. This 'popular' radio hopes that more people will listen, but not really. Format radio depends on distraction for its existence. Its primary goal is to accompany us through breakfast, travel and work without stimulating either too much attention or any thought of turning it off. In this respect it is mutually interdependent on the daily life for which it provides the soundtrack; more specifically, it is designed to harmonize all the contradictions of domestic and working life that radio could illuminate and transform.

The radio text is heard across all the institutional, social, solitary and mobile corners of urban and rural experience. It leaves no one untouched. During an average week, 94 per cent of Canadians listen to radio at least once, and on average for nineteen hours; 95 per cent of this listening takes place as a secondary activity (Statistics Canada 1990: 1). This is fewer hours than we devote to television, but the more time we spend in cars (a salient issue, given recent cuts to rail service and public transport), the more time radio may be able to claim from us. (But will it? As new cars come equipped with increasingly sophisticated stereo cassette and portable CD players, and as teens opt for tapes over radio, is this radio making itself obsolete? This is more than a technological issue, as the following discussion suggests.) Almost 90 per cent of radio listening time in Canada is now claimed by commercial radio. This cumulative success of commercial radio would have been inconceivable without music; music is indispensable for its schedule, its income and its listeners.

The assumption that more or less continuous music is the ideal programme content for radio rests on the equally convenient assumption that radio listeners are mainly not listening very closely and that this is the 'natural' condition for radio communication. Thus the flow of music/commercials/talk offered by format radio has become inseparable from the mental image of wallpaper which shadows the concept of 'secondary medium'. This concept distinguishes radio from television on the basis of its mobility, ubiquitousness and habitual presence in work and other social contexts. The phrase 'secondary medium' forces us to remember that radio programmers, industry analysts and government researchers know very well where we are and what we are doing while we are listening to a particular station. It usefully reminds us that radio's role as carrier of recorded music is not determined solely by radio's (non-visual) technological capacities, but is equally a product of the radio apparatus as a social, institutional and economic entity that depends on the music industry for its own reproduction. At the same time, it should remind us – appropriately, perhaps, since this role is now declining – that the critical emphasis on radio as a promotional vehicle for records has tended to simplify our understanding of its complex nature.

The close identification of music and radio arose in the 1950s, when, in response to TV's dethroning of radio in the living room, records came to form the principal raw material of radio programming. Since TV took over not only radio's domestic space but also many of its entertainment conventions, the industry had to devise new programming and commercial functions (as well as more mobile technologies) for radio. The record/DJ format arose partly because it was cheaper (no scriptwriters, union fees, sound effects, etc.) and partly because it attracted a new market of listeners – teens – who could be delivered to advertisers through radio rather than television. Music now provides well over 50 per cent of all radio airtime. Even the partial usurpation of music marketing by videos has not challenged radio's reliance on recorded music, whatever the genre. In effect radio has become a dependent medium, constrained by television on one side and the music industry on the other; its 'secondary' status is rooted historically and institutionally in that position.

The proportion of music in the radio schedule is much higher on FM, whose share of listeners has increased steadily since the mid-1970s. FM now claims over 40 per cent of listening time in Canada, and around 60 per cent among young listeners (BBM 1986; Mietkiewicz 1985). FM carries more music because of its superior transmitting technology and because its music formats help to construct and define the group most attractive to radio's advertisers: younger adults in urban areas. Recently FM stations have led the market in a number of Canadian cities. FM's success has corresponded with an increase in the number of available frequencies, an increase in the proportion of listening time devoted to music, the growth of corporate integration in the radio industry, the re-emergence of programme syndication, the introduction of satellite programme distribution and a decline in the airtime quota of Canadian music, which is gradually being shifted to the domain of marginal campus/community stations and the increasingly impoverished Canadian Broadcasting Corporation (CBC). The rise of FM is thus part of a larger change in which, as a result of technical, economic and administrative development, music has become the primary instrument of commercial radio's delocalization.

Yet radio continues to represent itself as the local medium, placing this theme at the centre of its commercial and regulative strategies, its daily schedule and its programming rhetoric. Rather than taking this rhetoric at its word, the following explores the 'work' of the music/radio text as part of a productive apparatus reconstructing both space and time.

Format

Radio is a medium which constructs and presents its own identity through its production.

Radio has no reality, write Hennion and Meadel (1986), except to produce the reality that it records; it is nothing but intermediary, and its reconstruction of the music catalogue is its way of constructing its own identity, or discursive context, and its audience. If radio exists 'only to make others present, an invisible machine for making the world visible to itself' (ibid.: 286), the community which speaks and is spoken through that medium is also constituted by it, and is formed by its structures, selections and strategies. It is for this reason that radio comprises an ideal instrument for collective self-construction, for the enactment of a community's oral and musical history. Brecht (1990) argued that this role would be realized only when radio became a means of communication, rather than one of distribution. Contemporary radio functions as the latter, but it represents itself as the former. This rhetorical achievement is accomplished through music.

In North America, commercial radio is dominated by format stations in which the organization of music-programming mediates and differentiates station and listener identities. Formats were introduced because they could deliver relatively cheap programme/listener revenues to radio after the arrival of television. Their commercial consolidation was dependent on the development of transistor technologies, which allowed greater mobility and fragmentation among listeners, and of market research, which allowed broadcasters to be more specific about the listeners they were selling to advertisers. Today, the term 'format' has two related meanings; it describes 'the type of programming done by a station, such as Top-40 or all-news. It also refers to the routine, or the list of specific ingredients, found in a programme hour. This includes specific phrases to be spoken, programme content, and the order and manner of placement' (Johnson and Jones 1978: 112). Formatting ensures that a station is clearly distinguishable from other stations (unlike TV, which distinguishes programmes and times), through a clear musical identity constructed in harmony with the precise demographics and researched common tastes of the targeted audience. Formats have tended to become more specialized, largely because research methods have grown more sophisticated; listeners' loyalties are an effect, as much as cause, of this specialization process.

Format music programming styles thus appear to spring from and articulate a neutral marriage of musics (country and western, Top 40, etc.) and demographics, and to correspond opportunistically to already established listener tastes, whose profiles are discovered through the neutral science of market research. For broadcasters and regulators, the division of a given broadcasting area according to demographic typologies reflects a division in the needs and listening expectations of 'targeted' listeners, who have already been defined (and researched) as members of demographically discrete groups, who are conceived as firmly established in their musical tastes and listening habits, and who should be served, therefore, according to this line of thought, by an appropriately diversified and rationalized radio spectrum.

Every format follows a complex set of rules for programming, including the style and range of music selections, size and origin of playlist, quotas for musical repetition, relative numbers of current and past hits and their usual sequence, conventional relationships between music and speech, and so forth. A major change in any one of these is inconceivable without a subsequent change in all of them and in the relationships amongst them. For instance, a switch from Middle of the Road (MOR) to contemporary hit radio (CHR) would demand (besides a new music director) a new on-air style, different news, a smaller playlist with higher weekly rotation and faster turnover of hits, and above all, a successful transition to new sources of advertising revenue for the less affluent but presumably larger market. Urban markets support an increasing number of pop-music format stations which compete for listeners and advertisers on the basis of finely researched distinctions notwithstanding some considerable crossover of music selections. An increased number of stations in a particular city certainly does not guarantee a wider range or diversity of music selections.

In Canada, FM formats are closely regulated. Broadcasters seeking a licence or renewal must commit themselves to a general format and prove both the viability and need for the chosen format in that particular city. Their 'Promise of Performance' must detail the type and range of popular music to be programmed, as well as the intended percentage of Canadian content, maximum repeat quotas for hits, proportions of hits to other musical selections (regulation prohibits more than 50 per cent, though as with most restrictions there are exemptions for Canadian selections), total commercial time, amount of 'foreground' programming, and so on. This regulation is intended to maintain musical diversity in FM programming, given an increasingly competitive market and the well-documented tendency for broadcasters to duplicate successful formats as long as they can draw sufficient advertising revenue (Glasser 1984). Through format regulation, commercial radio is supposed to be balanced between viable market conditions on the one hand, and non-market cultural objectives like musical diversity and Canadian content on the other. Such scrupulous management of the market offers a bureaucratically dense trace of the government's ostensible defence of 'public interest', which used to be represented by the public system.

Given format radio's tendency towards duplication, and the pressures on programmers to prefer mainstream and crossover hits whatever the format, the rationale for FM regulation is more evident than its success. Actual musical diversity is doing less well than the radio market which, while more or less stable in terms of total revenues, is heavily imbalanced (like the programming itself) between centre and margins, with major stations drawing huge revenues and many others continuing without reported profits for years at a time. New stations are still being licensed, though this does little to increase the range of music programming available; it merely intensifies the competition for advertising revenue and refines radio's production of audiences as more specialized commodities. In sum, the post-TV proliferation of stations and the refinement of research-based formats have contributed more to the expansion and rationalization of commercial revenues gained by the radio market as a whole than to the substantive diversity of tastes that is claimed to warrant such proliferation, and which, in any case, tends to be created as much (or as little) as indulged by radio practices.

The organization of audiences by music format does rationalize the radio market, but this is not the same as diversifying or enriching radio programming. This would entail diversifying musical production itself, and diversifying

the exposure of musics to specific audiences – the opposite of what has actually occurred in the evolution of music formats. Diversifying the production of music is achieved by diversifying the site of its production; that is, by making music recording and broadcasting more widely accessible to a range of musical practices and styles. These objectives are not the intention or the effect of contemporary radio music formats, whether or not they are addressed to listening markets who buy records.

The Market

In recent years, radio production has been transformed by music television and other changes in the production and circulation of records; by more sophisticated methods of audience-testing and market research; by satellite and computer technology, and subsequent programme services; by concentration of ownership structures; and by the re-emergence of networks. In other words, the process of mediation between station and listener is itself the subject of economic and technical modernization, which has a direct influence on the radio 'text' itself. As this process is rationalized, so too is the text. What is important about the music, in that context, may be not so much what it says, but what it displaces, not so much whom it draws together, but how, and on what terms, and of course what it leaves out.

In 1989, the most successful formats were Adult Contemporary/Gold, MOR and, well behind these, Country, Album-oriented rock and Contemporary Hit Radio. The consolidation of Adult Contemporary on AM, and of Album-oriented rock on FM, as leading formats (following a gender distinction – women listen more to AM, men to FM), plus the slight decline of MOR on both AM and FM bands, and the relatively low standing of country and dance music formats on FM, in combination confirm the relative strength of formats featuring current singles, though this tendency – mainly a response to the influence of videos – is less marked than in the mid-1980s because of the resurgence of 'Gold' formats.

The rise of video as a marketing tool reduced the supply of new recordings, while video's emphasis on singles tended to marginalize the rest of the album in terms of radio airplay. In conjunction with the relative ageing of the population (and the consequent relative decline of record consumption), this has changed the role of radio in the distribution of records, especially Canadian-content records, which has further added to a decline in their supply (Hahn 1985: 17). After music television went on the air, the number of records in circulation declined; by 1985, releases by new artists were down 45 per cent internationally compared with five years previously (Bergeron et al. 1986: 42). In Canada, the multinationals release current recordings selectively, following their commercial success in Britain or the US; this leads to further reduction of the number of records in circulation. While the number of records being released has decreased internationally, the proportion of national and international hits has risen in relation to local releases; this trend is exacerbated in Canada, where the music industry earns about 14 per cent of its revenues from Canadian record and tape sales.

There are several issues worth considering in relation to these developments. First, the size of the radio market as a whole has remained stable; people are not tuning in to FM from television or magazines, but from AM stations, which have been subject to a strict 30 per cent Canadian-content quota since 1971. FM stations (depending on format) tend to be subject to lower Canadian-content quotas, and are frequently criticized for unloading Canadian content into off-peak listening hours. The relative decline of AM radio means less airtime for Canadian music, which spells trouble for the already marginal Canadian recording industry (ibid.: 127). Competition from US stations also contributes to lower Canadian-content quotas, and probably reduced sales, in the border cities. Second, and in relation to this, formats that succeed in major markets affect listening patterns more widely. In addition to the dissemination of playlists from *Billboard*, or from major urban markets to smaller stations, and the rise of syndicated programmes distributed by satellite, people tune into stations in large metropolitan centres even when they do not live there themselves (BBM 1986; *Report of the Task Force on Broadcasting Policy* 1986: 24). The bigger the urban market, the more its stations function as magnets to listeners in surrounding areas, developing listening patterns from the centre out-

wards that are disproportionate in terms of the spatial distribution of the population. Because of this 'spill' effect, residents of smaller towns tend not to listen to their own stations.

This is not because urban stations play more regional music, or even a wider range of music selections. Since a large city is more fragmented, or, to put it another way, since urban stations are competing for a larger revenue base and draw on more precise audience research, radio-programming is more specialized. CHR, AC and AOR formats are more popular in big cities, where listeners (or perhaps their employers and shop-owners) seem to prefer more contemporary formats with a higher turnover and a smaller range, that is, tighter and faster playlists (CRTC 1987: sec. 8.3.3). Urban format specialization is also tied to a greater emphasis on nationally distributed records, which have international promotion in television, magazines and other contexts.

Stations in smaller towns are more open to, and more reliant on, locally or regionally produced recordings (Hahn 1985: 23–4). But they are being culturally and economically marginalized by the urban specialization process and its attraction to small-town listeners. The growth of FM may be encouraging this process, because the revenue for FM stations increases commensurately with the expansion of audience reach. In contrast, AM stations experience a declining rate of revenue increase as audience size increases (Babe 1985: 95–100). The marginalization of local music production (and other programme sources) is also being intensified by the erosion of the public broadcasting system, which, ironically, is invariably accompanied by rhetorical flourishes about the greater local sensitivity of commercial broadcasting. As everyone knows, private broadcasters produce far less local programming. The only tangible proof of commercial radio's local allegiance lies in the high proportion of advertising revenue drawn from local businesses – the direct reversal of television revenue, which is three-quarters nationally based (*Report of the Task Force on Broadcasting Policy* 1986: 396). The proportion of radio revenue derived from local advertisers has risen substantially, from 60 per cent in 1969, to over 73 per cent in 1984 (Babe 1985: 27).

The effect of all this is that urban stations are attracting a higher proportion of listeners, while programming a decreasing number of music selections. This means that more and more listeners are listening to fewer and fewer songs. This reflects, and helps to legitimate, the general trend towards spatial and economic centralization which characterizes radio in Canada and music production internationally.

Space and Time

If the hit parade had emerged by the time Harold Innis wrote *Empire and Communications* (1950), perhaps he would have offered some specific hypotheses about its spatial–temporal impact. In his work, media-produced relations between time and space have direct consequence for the growth of geopolitical formations and monopolies. Time-binding communications ensure continuity across time, and preserve memory, identity and hierarchy; space-binding media, such as telegraphs, roads and electronic media, permit more rapid dissemination of information across space, but erode local memory and the self-determination of peripheral groups. Commercial radio seems to follow this latter pattern through its hyperactive restructuring of the spatial soundscape, its impact on changing patterns of consumer-communities, and its role in the creation of international distribution systems, in much the same way that, in Innis's prognosis, the rise of print created the material-political foundations for the present era.

In fact format radio and the current changes in music radio occupy an interesting but paradoxical position in this picture. Radio was developed to transmit across space, to overcome physical barriers and to make transitory messages broadly available; in this respect, it is a space-binding medium, ensuring the rapid, broad distribution of changing texts without restriction to an originary space or a cultural elite. On the other hand, it is aural, vernacular, immediate, transitory; its composite stream of music and speech, including local (if usually one-way) communication, has the capacity to nourish local identity and oral history, and to render these dynamic through contact with other spaces and cultures. This capacity for mediating the local with the new defines its styles of talk and construction of station identity. But format radio is thoroughly industrialized both in its temporal language and in its relations of produc-

tion, which are increasingly technologically rationalized, and less and less local in origin or scale. This paradox allows format-based music radio to be omnisciently 'local' without arising from or contributing to local cultures.

Radio, like other media, is constituted (and constitutes us) spatially as much as by genre, signification, or mode of address. This thought is already half accomplished by the common emphasis on radio's resilient portability since the invention of transistors. Doesn't the birth of the hit parade form a homologous whole with cars, highways and scenic pull-offs, drive-in movies, blue jeans, and Coke? But the point can be taken further. In the radiophonic production of sound texts and local, if not locally autonomous audiences, it is possible to identify more precisely how 'spatial form and spatial strategy can be an active element of accumulation', as Doreen Massey (1984) argues in more general terms.

A number of elements in the production process spring to mind. Most broadly, radio provides an international distribution system for records. Music recording has become a globally integrated process within a centralized economic structure which shapes the conditions and locations of manufacture and distribution. The demand for currency in sound values produces an incentive for technological innovation that ensures, among other things, a process of continuous rationalization in studio production facilities and strategies. Recording, touring and the music press can all be mapped out in relation to a construct of centres and peripheries; you could argue that this map is materialized semiotically every time a musician displays his or her commercial success by moving to more sophisticated recording facilities, which almost invariably follows the move to a major label.

But here we are concerned with radio, which, on the surface at least, is a more dynamically local medium. Shifts in recording and listening technology and music marketing have reinforced commercial radio's dependency on the organizational rationalization of music programming, even where record promotion is not part of the station's demographic mandate. Responding to a competitive, media-saturated and increasingly deregulated environment, radio programmers are more inclined to turn to computer programmes for music selection to cut programming costs, than to flex the boundaries of musical taste. Across Canada, over one hundred stations now relay rock or country music programmes by satellite from St Catherine, Ontario (south of Toronto), produced by Canadian Radio Networks (CRN). CRN claims four minutes an hour for national advertising sales, and formats six and a half minutes into each programme hour for local spots (Careless 1990). Otherwise the programmes are live, DJ-hosted, delivered cheaply and all night long, from what is often the other side of the country. 'In essence', writes a radio columnist for *Broadcaster*, 'it's a local station gone national. This illusion exists because CRN jocks steadfastly refuse to identify their location. As well, the service offers toll-free 1–800 request lines, so listeners can call in and talk to a jock, wherever they may be' (ibid.). The only drawback, for this columnist, is unemployment for hundreds of DJs. Two more CRN networks – CHR and oldies – are in the works.

Such mechanisms rationalize radio production across vast distances, in effect restricting local communication to advertisers. They also facilitate the economic security and spatial diffusion of monopolies, in the recording and electronic industries, which are more interested in opening up markets for new cultural hardware and its accompanying software than in the recording and marketing of a wide range of musics, or the potential contribution of such musics to patterns of urban communication. If ensuing radio practices assure listeners of their right to a certain powerful habitual pleasure, they also suppress equally fundamental rights: Lefebvre (1976: 35) speaks of *the right to the town* (how often do you hear DJs – aural icons of local culture – encouraging debates or actions on urban development, racism, pollution, daycare, land rights, public transport?) and *the right to be different* ('the right not to be classified forcibly into categories which have been determined by the necessarily homogenizing powers') which, he argues, are endangered by the economic and political management of urban space.

As we have seen, radio produces difference through format competition, but only that which is demographically and administratively profitable. More clearly evident is radio's management of urban space, perhaps its chief accomplishment, in its promotion of local business, its management of traffic, time and temperament in relation to rhythms of the working week.

Radio Space and Temporal Narratives

Like the radio schedule itself, with its strict markers of the hour, its subtly clocked rotation of current and past hits, its advance promotion of a new release, the music playlist functions as a kind of metalanguage of time. The playlist offers a grammar of temporality which draws in the listener and produces him or her (economically, as a commodity; experientially, as a listener) as a member of a stylistic community defined, more and more, in inexorably temporal terms, rather than in relation to geographic or more explicitly substantive identification – assembled that is, in terms of the preferred speed and rate of musical consumption (cf. Straw 1988). The music playlist continuously (but variously) demarcates the present from the immediate or distant past. With its new hits, its repetitions and recyclings, its rising and falling stars, the playlist reinforces the space-bias of commercial radio by making diverse communities as listeners more and more the same, by spreading processes, values and decisions outwards from a technical and administrative centre, and by defining value in terms of rapid temporal change, competency in terms of knowledge of that change. The playlist is a central functional element within the radiophonic narrative which, paradoxically, constantly posits the local as its subject.

Radio's textual interaction of music and speech can be analysed as a type of narrative, one which simultaneously addresses and represents the specific targeted community. This makes the DJ or host a kind of narrator, and suggests that the combined elements of old and new songs, advertisements, news and weather on the hour, and so on, can be analysed as structural functions within the narrative, which is constructed through their specific combination. Where traditional tales are analysed as a structural combination of narrative elements condensed across time, we might consider contemporary radio narratives as the condensation of structural relations in and across space, in an interdependent relation of reverse proportionality to time. Space is collapsed because access to it (at least imaginatively) is expanded; time is speeded up and broken into contemporaneous moments within the still-tangible discipline of the working week. The construction of radio audiences is not then simply an abstract (if quantifiable) assemblage of listeners with similar tastes, but also a ritualized transformation of people's relationships to (and in) space and time. Radio creates a new sense of time, not directly parallel to previous kinds, an overt disciplining of the hours of the day which also permits a non-spatial movement in and out of its compulsions with the simultaneous suspension/intensification of marked time through music, and the return/casual proliferation of social time through talk.

Radio is often described as a surrogate or 'portable friend' (Dominick 1979: 99). Early psychological and market research established the truism that radio's functions are 'to "involve" the listener in the great and small events of the day; the provision of commonly shared experiences that can facilitate interpersonal experiences and also that can cement the solidarity of various subcultures... within a mass audience' (Mendelsohn 1979: 96). This companionable set of functions is attributed to radio's technical mobility, its mix of music and talk and the ways this 'represents' the collective choices and desires of its listeners, and its mode of address, which establishes a simulated intimacy that is specific to the medium. Radio announcers are instructed to address their audience in the singular, never as a mass, and to establish a mood of friendly companionship for their listeners, often assumed to be women.

Popular radio offers a sense of accessibility to and interaction within its own community, distinguishing itself from television through highly conventional and elaborated strategies of representation. Such conventions work to establish and draw attention to the radio station as a live and local context. They include signposting ('Later we'll be talking to... Coming up: the new release from... You can hear it right here on...'), styles of interviewing, spontaneous patter, informal commentary on music selections and music-related gossip, station identifications (Montreal's CHOM-FM, member of the nationwide CHUM chain which also owns MuchMusic Television, calls itself 'the spirit of Montreal'), and so forth, all of which contribute to a sense of localness, immediacy and accessibility.

Radio's localness is emphasized in all textbooks and industry commentaries on on-air practice. Successful DJs account for their popularity by claiming special contact with the local scene. 'Radio is very much a local medium', advise Johnson and Jones (1978: 118), authors of a leading American textbook on modern radio station practices. In the same paragraph, they note that 'in fact, no local station really originates all of its programming material. Phonograph records are nationally distributed, as is the news from wire services. Most ideas are borrowed, not originated'. Stephen Barnard (1989: 92) observes that 'radio stations throughout the world use records as a major source of programme material for reasons of tradition, convenience, and economics', and notes the current trend among record companies to play down local talents and to encourage national trends at the local level. Thus broadcasters become what Babe (1985: 24) calls 'localizers' of international content.

If radio is local, most of what we hear – other than the weather forecast – is not. Nor is the sum of technological relations upon which contemporary radio depends. Some stations produce their own commercials, but the soundtrack for them is as often as not imported (in the case of CHOM, from California in a boxed CD set). We think of radio as a low-tech medium, but it is not an autonomous one. Its dependencies follow the same patterns of more advanced technologies wherein the cycle of technical innovation/democratization does not democratize access to production, but only to (some) information, which can thereby be disseminated more centrally. To put it with complete cynicism (meaning only partial truth), radio's atmosphere of local involvement is designed to attract the highest possible proportion of listening hours for sale to local advertisers, and thus to maintain and promote the particular local 'feel' that can attract both listeners and advertisers. Local relevance becomes the shorthand for radio's competition with television, its dependency on advertising revenue from local sources, and its promotion of music sales at the local level.

In this context the DJ serves to personalize and thus to locate the station as more than an abstract mediation of records, advertisers and listeners. DJs are increasingly disempowered in terms of programming, and make fewer and fewer

decisions about music and other content. But it
falls to the DJ's voice to provide an index of radio
as a live and local medium, to provide immediate
evidence of the efficacy of its listeners' desires. It
is through that voice that the community hears
itself constituted, through that voice that radio
assumes authorship of the community, woven
into itself through its jokes, its advertisements,
its gossip, all represented, recurringly and powerfully, as the map of local life.

Conclusion

In Canada, as elsewhere, privatization, networking and intensified competition in the broadcasting sphere contribute to what Carey (1975: 33)
calls 'pervasive recentralization': a general shift
of the location of authority to 'more distant,
diffuse and abstract centres', thus eroding the
'effective capacity of proximate relations'. Commercial radio is constrained by an increasingly
monopolized (and televisualized) distribution
system for recorded music, and its programming
is shaped by increasingly centralized hierarchical technical processes which it helps to valorize
and reproduce. It posits listeners' desire as the
engine of that set of social and technical relations. Through its mediation, it makes that account true.

Radio has unique capacities to map our symbolic and social environment. These capacities
are considerably constrained by the national and
international nature of music distribution and by
radio's impetus towards technological rationalization. Radio mediates between local listeners
and musical selections, but its forms of mediation, defined by the music format, can be
heard as a naturalizing of technological change
and the ongoing, sometimes violent displacement of its listeners. Its narrative depends on
(though it also helps to diffuse) people's feelings
about community, about territory, work and
weekends, roads and traffic, memory and play,
and what might be happening across town. Its
special resource is the psychic investment of
listeners in local space, whether they are isolated
within it or driving across it; the displacement of
this space in the radio airwaves has direct semiotic and structural implications in the shifting
strategies of empire.

Notes

An earlier version of this paper was published in
Popular Music 9/2, 1990.

References

Attali, Jacques (1985) *Noise: The Political Economy of Music*, Minneapolis, MN: University of Minnesota Press.
Babe, Robert (1985) *A Study of Radio: Economic/ Financial Profile of Private Sector Radio Broadcasting in Canada*, prepared for the Task Force on Broadcasting Policy, Department of Communications, Ottawa.
Barnard, Stephen (1989) *On the Radio: Music Radio in Britain*, Milton Keynes: Open University Press.
Barnes, Ken (1988) 'Top 40: a fragment of the imagination', in Simon Frith (ed.), *Facing the Music*, New York: Pantheon.
Barthes, Roland (1977) *Image–Music–Text*, ed. and trans. Stephen Heath, Glasgow: Fontana/William Collins & Co.
BBM (Bureau of Broadcast Measurement) (1986) *A Review of Trends in Canadian Radio Listening 1976–1985*, Ottawa.
Bergeron, Denis, Chater, Brian and Roberts, John (1986) *Music and the Electronic Media in Canada*, Study for the Task Force on Broadcasting Policy, Ottawa.
Berland, Jody (1988) 'Locating listening: popular music, technological space, Canadian mediation', *Cultural Studies* 2(3): 343–58.
——(1991) 'Towards a creative anachronism: radio, the state, and sound government', *Public* 4(5): 9–21. Reprinted in D. Augartus and D. Lander (eds) (1993) *Radio Rethink*, Banff: Walter Phillips.
Brecht, Bertolt (1990) 'Radio as an apparatus of communication', in Simon Frith and Andrew Goodwin (eds), *On Record*, New York: Pantheon.
Canadian Broadcasting Corporation (1989) *Radio Format Report*, Colleen Cronin: Toronto, CBC Research Office.
Careless, James (1990) 'Canadian radio networks: a service for budget-conscious broadcasters', *Broadcaster* November: 6–7.
Carey, James (1975) 'Canadian communication theory: extensions and interpretations of Harold Innis', in G. J. Robinson and D. F. Theall (eds), *Studies in Canadian Communications*, Montreal: McGill Programme in Communications.
——(1989) *Communication as Culture*, Boston: Unwin and Hyman.

Crane, Jonathon (1986) 'Mainstream music and the masses', *Journal of Communication Inquiry* 10(3): 66–70.

Crisell, Andrew (1986) *Understanding Radio*, London: Methuen.

CRTC (Canadian Radio Television and Telecommunications Commission) (1987) *Listening Trends 1976–1986*, Ottawa: Mary Giordano, Broadcasting Directorate, Radio Policy Planning and Analysis Branch.

Dominick, Joseph R. (1979) 'The portable friend: peer group membership and radio usage', in Gary Gumpert and Robert Cathcart (eds), *Intermedia: Interpersonal Communication in a Media World*, New York: Oxford University Press.

Fornatale, P. and Mills, J. (1980) *Radio in the Television Age*, Woodstock, NY: Overlook.

Glasser, Theodor (1984) 'Competition and diversity among radio formats: legal and structural issues', *Journal of Broadcasting* 28: 122–42.

Hahn, Richard (1985) *A Study of the Supply of English Language Sound Recordings to Canadian Private Radio Stations*, Study for the Task Force on Broadcasting Policy, Ottawa.

Hennion, Antoine and Meadel, Cecile (1986) 'Programming music: radio as mediator', *Media Culture & Society* 8(3): 281–303.

Innis, Harold (1950) *Empire and Communications*, Oxford: Oxford University Press.

Johnson, J. S. and Jones, K. (1978) *Modern Radio Station Practices*, Belmont, CA: Wadsworth.

Lefebvre, Henri (1976) *The Survival of Capitalism: Reproductions of the Relations of Production*, London: Allison & Busby.

Liska, Peter (1988) 'Digital broadcast radio', *Broadcaster*, July.

Massey, Doreen (1984) *Spatial Divisions of Labour: Social Structures and the Geography of Production*, London: Macmillan.

Mendelsohn, Harold (1979) 'Listening to Radio', in Gary Gumpert and Robert Cathcart (eds), *Intermedia: Interpersonal Communication in a Media World*, New York: Oxford University Press.

Mietkiewicz, Henry (1985) 'Radio a gamble for all except high rollers', *Toronto Star*, 18 February.

Report of the Task Force on Broadcasting Policy (1986), Ottawa: Minister of Supply and Services.

Rothenbuhler, Eric (1987) 'Commercial radio and popular music: processes of selection and factors of influence,' in James Lull (ed.) *Popular Music and Communication*, Beverly Hills: Sage.

Statistics Canada (1990) 'Who listens to radio?', *Focus on Culture* 2(4): 1–3.

Straw, Will (1988) 'Music video in its contexts: popular music and post-modernism in the 1980s', *Popular Music* 7(3): 247–66.

Toronto Star (1988) 'Spinning too much Top 40 lands CKFM in hot water', *Toronto Star*, 14 April: b1.

Toushek, Gary and Unger, M. (1988) 'Helping radio programmers: a computer system to handle the routine but vital tasks', *Broadcaster*, September.

Chapter 19

Musical Production, Copyright, and the Private Ownership of Culture

Kembrew McLeod

While this chapter focuses on a particular form of cultural production, music, its conclusions can be applied to many other areas of cultural production beyond the scope of this study. First, I examine the ways in which United States copyright law affects musical production and, second, how the culturally situated notions of authorship and ownership that ground copyright work to reinforce existing power relations within economies of musical distribution (and world economies, more generally). Folk, blues, and hip-hop are three musical genres used to concretely ground an analysis of what happens when an area of cultural production that had been previously (relatively) untouched by intellectual property law becomes immersed in that sphere of social relations.

The immersion of one sphere of social relations into another is framed within articulation theory, which allows us to carefully map those interconnections within a field of power relations. I demonstrate how this field of power relations (which helps define the process of articulation) is heavily balanced against those modes of cultural production that conceive of authorship and ownership in ways that conflict with the assumptions that ground intellectual property law. Because the idea of private property has gained a long-standing hegemony in the West, intellectual property owners have the ability to bring the power of the state against cultural producers who incorporate preexisting, privately owned musical and textual elements into

their compositions. Further, the ideas about what constitutes authorship work to define who is an owner and, therefore, who stands in a position of power.

Articulation Theory

Articulation carries with it two dominant meanings. The first – to speak, to be articulate – is that which is more well-known in the United States, but it is the second meaning – the joining (the articulation) of two parts – that is of primary concern here. Articulation, within the writings of Hall (1980; 1985; 1996), Laclau (1977), Grossberg (1992) and Slack (1996), has primarily been concerned with questions of ideology and political/cultural formations – how particular ideologies become fixed to certain cultural practices, political movements or the like. This is the primary way it has been developed within cultural studies for the past twenty years. Hall (1996, p. 140) states, "a theory of articulation is both a way of understanding how ideological elements come, under certain conditions, to cohere together within a discourse, and a way of asking how they do or do not become articulated, at conjunctures, to certain political subjects." Articulation theory can trace its origins to Gramsci, particularly to his theory of hegemony. Hegemony is the process whereby a particular class or group exercises power over shaping the ways in which a subordinate group makes sense of the world, therefore eliminating the need for a constant exercise of violent coercion. Slack (1996) states, "The vehicle of this subordination, its 'cement', so to speak, is ideology, which is conceived of as an articulation of disparate elements, that is, common sense...Gramsci offers a way of understanding hegemony as the struggle to construct (articulate and re-articulate) common sense out of an ensemble of interests, beliefs and practices" (p. 117).

In my use of articulation theory, I take a different tack by connecting the form it has taken in the past twenty years with Laclau's initial conceptualization of articulation theory as a way of analyzing the encroachment of a capitalist mode of production into a pre-capitalist, Third World mode of production. Frank (1970), another scholar who was dealing with the same issues, rejected the notion of a "dualist thesis" that conceived of Latin America as co-existing in both capitalist and feudalist sectors. Instead, he posited that once it initially encountered mercantile capitalism, Latin America became almost instantly integrated into the capitalist world system. This did not sit well with Laclau (1971), who engaged Frank in an extended debate about economic development in Latin America, helping to define issues that were later taken up by Alavi (1973), Rey and Dupre (1973), and Jhally (1979). Jhally characterizes the different positions of those who have engaged in this debate.

> For Frank the issue of contradiction does not arise because we are dealing with a single mode of production. For Laclau contradiction is negated by "indissoluble unity." For Rey, contradiction and coexistence are not seen as total opposites but as conflicting features of a historical *process* in which the Althusserian notion of "articulation" is vital to his work.... What Rey and his colleagues have done is to apply this internal articulation between different levels of a mode of production to the articulation *between* modes of production. So the central notion of contradiction becomes a much more theoretically useful concept because articulation can define and specify the nature of that contradiction. (p. 74)

By recovering this earlier formulation of articulation that has gone underdeveloped for the past twenty years, I hope to expand the kinds of subject matter and analysis to which articulation

theory may be applied. I use articulation to map the interconnections between an area of cultural production and the sphere of intellectual property law, and in doing so I make three moves. First, I use articulation theory to understand why intellectual property law is used in the singular when it is in fact comprised of a number of different property laws that have quite different histories (for instance, copyright law evolved out of seventeenth-century British common law whereas trademark law developed from nineteenth-century unfair trade law). Rather than simply being all included in the same chapter of law text books, copyright, patent, trademark and right of publicity law all share a basic common characteristic: a historically and culturally situated notion of authorship and ownership that is rooted in Western Enlightenment philosophies that emphasize individualism, originality and property rights (Geller, 1994; Ong, 1982; Rose, 1994a). Therefore, these various laws are articulated with each other through a common conception of authorship and ownership, and they can be referred to as a more general, singular law without creating much intellectual slippage.

The second move I make is to map the articulations of certain areas of cultural production and the sphere of intellectual property law by paying attention to how differing conceptions of authorship and ownership are negotiated, as well as examining the specific social, political, and economic circumstances that characterize an area of cultural production. The third and final theoretical move I make is to demonstrate how a number of very different areas of cultural production are connected to *each other* – how they are articulated with the others *through* intellectual property law. This allows us to demonstrate how the contradictions that occur when hip-hop and folk music become immersed in copyright law are linked to, for instance, the patenting of human genes and crop seeds, or any number of other seemingly disparate areas of cultural production affected by intellectual property law.

Folk Music

Folk music differs in sound and composition in different regions throughout the world, but one defining feature of this mode of cultural production is that it is based on the borrowing of preexisting lyrics, melodies and rhythms. Toelken (1986) states that a folk song is seldom memorized word-for-word, but instead it is recalled and continually recomposed in varying ways that suit the context of the place, performer and audience. In an illustration of the ethic that is at the core of the folk music tradition, Bess Lomax Hawes – the former director of the Folk Arts Program at the National Endowment for the Arts – recalled a conversation with the famous folk singer Woody Guthrie, the composer of "This Land is Your Land." She stated, "I told Woody that I thought that the chorus of [his song] 'Union Maid' had gone so completely into oral tradition that no one knew where it came from...It was part of the cultural landscape, no longer even associated with him. He answered, 'If that were true, it would be the greatest honor of my life'" (Zeitlin, 1998, p. A15).

Folk music, in all its variations, is a mode of cultural production that is intertextual in nature. Literary theorist Julia Kristeva is credited with coining the term "intertextuality," which is grounded in the proposition that "every text builds itself as a mosaic of quotations, every text is an absorption and transformation of another text" (quoted in Newman, 1995). The intertextual borrowing of preexisting cultural texts (whether they be musical, visual or oral in nature) has been at the core of cultural production in societies where orality was a dominant form of communication, and intertextuality continues to be important in print-based societies (Ong, 1982). While folk music still exists in print cultures, it originated in oral cultures – cultures that rely heavily on structure and formula to aid the transmission of oral poems and folk songs from singer to singer, generation to generation. Ong (1982) writes, "In an oral culture, knowledge, once acquired, had to be constantly repeated or it would be lost: fixed, formulaic thought patterns were essential for wisdom and effective administration" (p. 24).

The situated notions of originality and authorship that arose in the West during the rise of capitalism, the printing press and the Enlightenment (histories that are very much interconnected) are alien to oral cultures that cultivated folk music. Ong (1982) states, "Print culture gave birth to the romantic notions of 'originality' and

'creativity,' which set apart an individual work from other works even more, seeing its origins and meaning as independent of outside influence, at least ideally" (p. 133). Print culture attempts to close off intertextuality by emphasizing the importance of a pure text untainted by the influence of other texts, of others' ideas. The anxiety that lies in many modern writers, an anxiety that they are actually creating nothing new under the sun, is something that oral cultures did not share (Ong, 1982). Folk singers within oral cultures also did not share this uneasiness surrounding the so-called "originality" of their compositions; in fact, there was no framework within which they could even conceive of such a concept.

Rather than this more traditional understanding of cultural production – that of cultural texts being part of a shared commons – becoming dominant in contemporary Western society, it is the conception of the "original," individual author that has informed copyright law and other intellectual property laws. Authorship and ownership are deeply interconnected – one cannot exist without the other – so, therefore, *how* an author is defined heavily influences *who* is designated as an owner. An example of how the economic and cultural power that is granted by this definition of authorship disempowers populations that do not share the tenets that underlie copyright law is the "world music" sector.

"World music" involves the distribution of a large number of non-Western recordings by the multinational record companies that dominate the world's music distribution, and the term is a commercial label for what is largely comprised of various indigenous folk musics. Because of the way Western intellectual property law is structured, individuals and record companies can copyright the music of other cultures, even though they may have done nothing more than press the "record" button. Seeger (1996) argues that, while copyright law is complex and varies from country to country, by and large, "copyright laws recognize only individual invention or composition (or that by a small group). In general, they do not recognize oral traditions or folk music as copyrightable, and do not establish enduring rights to an invention or idea" (p. 90).

The intellectual property laws and treaties that the US and other Western nations have pressured non-Western and Southern Hemisphere countries to adopt are biased against the mode of cultural production used to create many non-Western musics. Mills (1996) writes that many non-Western musics do not meet the criteria for copyright protection (there must be an "original," identifiable author), a requirement that puts an undue burden on traditional cultures. This functions to relegate the music of traditional cultures "to the public domain where it may be freely used without legal restraints. Conversely, recorders may copyright their recordings of traditional music and obtain *de facto* control over its use and dissemination" (Mills, p. 60).

North American and European countries, particularly the US, have waged an unrelenting battle against developing countries to adopt an intellectual property system that is advantageous to these already wealthy countries. The Trade-Related Aspects of Intellectual Property Rights (TRIPS), which is part of the General Agreement on Tariffs and Trade (GATT), has been an instrumental element in forcing World Trade Organization (WTO) member countries to adopt US-backed intellectual property laws (Emmott, 1994; TRIPS, 1999). TRIPS imposes minimum standards on copyright, patent, trademarks and trade secrets, standards that are much more stringent than the legislation in developing countries, and which often run counter to their national interests (Shiva, 1997; TRIPS, 1999).

The logical extension of the consequences of the increasing private ownership of culture can be felt in less developed countries, which typically bear the brunt of innovations within the capitalist system. In a parallel case, it is not uncommon for United States-based multinational companies to take out patents on the products based on knowledge of local plants that indigenous people have cultivated. These multinationals can then both profit from any of its medicinal values in developed countries, and – in countries that become TRIPS compliant – gain a legal monopoly on the production of that particular commodity in the native country. This monopoly legally restricts those who had previously created the product and potentially forces them to be consumers of the patent owner's product. As is the case with world music and authorship, collective cultivation of knowledge about biological matter is not recognized as a legally protectable form of authorship. However, the companies or researchers with the capital to isolate and identify genetic structures are recognized as an author (and owner), even if they were merely led to the valuable plants by the indigenous people who already knew about their uses. The articulations between copyright law and non-Western folk music are similar to the articulations between patent law and the cultivation of indigenous knowledge about plants and other biological matter. In short, the way in which intellectual property law defines authorship advantages the West, and it increases (and creates new ways to facilitate) the redistribution of resources from poorer countries to rich countries.

To pull back and focus more closely on folk music-making, one of the most striking contradictions that arises when copyright law governs this area of cultural production is the fact that this practice comes to be redefined as *plagiarism* and, therefore, copyright infringement. The expansion of the sphere of intellectual property law into this domain of cultural activity changes the practices folk musicians engage in to the point that today's folk music is considered more of a musical style or genre, a section of a record store, than a cultural activity with a rich, lengthy historical tradition. Granted, in more small-scale economies, such as bluegrass music festivals, this practice of borrowing from earlier songs is still alive and well. But if those same bluegrass artists were to release and distribute a recording of their live performances, they would have to assign songwriting credit, gain permission from the songwriter and/or publisher (especially if any changes were made), and pay royalties or else risk being sued.

Another major way in which the expansion of copyright affects folk music production is the fact that copyright makes possible the legal appropriation of folk songs or melodies by individual or corporate owners. This relates to the discussion of the "world music" sector, but this practice has also occurred in North America and Western Europe. The copyrighting of folk music occurs primarily in two ways. First, a musician or folk song collector can either copyright a traditional folk song outright, or copyright the arrangement of a song. Second, artists can incorporate elements that are heavily based on the melody or lyrics (or both) of an earlier folk song and copyright the "new" song under their own names. In the first case, the classic English folk song "Greensleeves" has been copyrighted and, further, Paul Simon copyrighted the most well-known and ensconced arrangement of the traditional song "Scarborough Fair" after it was recorded by his duo Simon and Garfunkel (Mirapaul, 1996). An example of the second case of folk song appropriation lies in the prototypical heavy metal band, Led Zeppelin, who – like many other rock bands – borrowed heavily from the songs of blues artists in their own copyrighted songs. After copyrighting their appropriations, Led Zeppelin have turned around and licensed those songs when artists sampled the group, as the Beastie Boys did on their album *Licensed to Ill* (Glenn, 1996). Nevertheless, there are far too many individual cases to begin to cite, so – to conclude this section – I will briefly focus on one particular example to provide a model.

The song "Happy Birthday to You" is the most sung song in the English language, and it surely fits one definition of being a folk song in that it is a widely shared musical text that is deeply ingrained in everyday life and, in the minds of many, the song belongs to the "folk," the people (Birthday song, 1988; Hawes, 1970). It meets another definition of a folk song because of its borrowed origins. "Happy Birthday to You" is not a folk song that can, for instance, be traced back to eighteenth-century England, but the compositional history of the song indicates that its melody and lyrics cannot be traced to one single author. The song was originally composed by Mildred J. Hill and her sister Patty, and was published in 1893 within their book *Song Stories for the Kindergarten* as "Good Morning to All" (Fuld, 1985). According to Grattan (1993), children liked the song so much that they began singing it at birthday parties, changing the words to "Happy Birthday to You," a spontaneous form of lyrical parody or alteration that is commonly employed in the folk song creation process. This song's origins date back beyond the Hill sisters' version; it is documented that a very similar song was published by Horace Waters in 1858 as "Happy Greetings to All" (Claghorn, 1996). "Happy Birthday to You" also bears a substantial similarity to two other previously published songs, "A Happy New Year" and "Happy Greeting to All" (Fuld, 1985).

Although it is widely perceived to be in the public domain, and is sung in many different languages throughout the world, its copyright is now strictly enforced by Warner-Chappell, a subsidiary of AOL – Time-Warner which currently holds worldwide rights to the song (with the exception of Japan) (Birthday song, 1988; Sold, 1989). Over the course of the twentieth century, there have been numerous legal battles that transpired between members of a public that believes the song is part of a public domain and a company that needs to protect its investment by restricting its use. Everyone from the famous popular music composer Irving Berlin to Stravinsky have met with legal trouble when they incorporated elements of "Happy Birthday to You" into their musicals or symphonies – as have restaurants and singing telegram companies (Ball, 1988; Ewen, 1969; Lebrecht, 1996). Restaurants whose servers sing "Happy Birthday to You" must buy a permit and, consequently, many chain restaurants do not allow the song to be sung on the premises. Other larger chain restaurants like ShowBiz Pizza Place and Bennigan's have developed their own versions of the birthday song so as to avoid costly licensing fees or potential lawsuits (Hayes, 1993; Shepard, 1992).

Even though the melody that was appropriated by the Hill sisters had already been floating around for a number of years and the Hills did not even invent the lyrics, they were nevertheless able to "capture" the melodic and lyrical elements that make up the song and claim them as their own. Such appropriations become more critical when unequal power relations are at play, such as the case with the African-American blues tradition, which operates within the folk mode of musical production.

Blues

The blues was a significant target of appropriation by whites, especially in its early recorded history within the music industry. For instance, W. C. Handy derived many of his copyrighted "original" songs (such as "Saint Louis Blues," "Yellow Dog Blues," and "Joe Turner Blues") from direct exposure to African-American folk songs in his frequent visits to the South (Barlow, 1990). According to Barlow, Handy often "reconstructed the melodies and the lyrics of commonly known folk blues from memory, and published them under his own name; this was not an uncommon practice in the record industry during the heyday of the blues" (p. 18).

The British heavy metal band Led Zeppelin borrowed heavily from blues artists and, on their debut album, they used significant elements of blues artist Willie Dixon's "You Shook Me," "I Can't Quit You Baby" and "You Need Love" without credit, assigning themselves the copyright. Dixon successfully sued the group because his songs were copyrighted, but other songs in the Zeppelin catalog are comprised of lyrical themes, melodies and riffs culled from blues artists in a manner that is not as blatantly derivative, but in a way that significantly appropriated nonetheless (Hochman, 1994; Catlin, 1992). Even after Led Zeppelin's career came to a halt, Zeppelin guitarist Jimmy Page continued to borrow from Dixon. In a post-Zeppelin collaboration with David Coverdale, Varga (1993) points out that Page's "Shake My Tree" bears a striking resemblance to Dixon's classic "I Just Want To Make Love To You."

It is important to note that Dixon and virtually all other blues artists engaged in the same type of borrowing that Zeppelin did. For instance, many of Dixon's copyrights incorporate material from the folk-blues public domain, such as the song "My Babe," which was part of the Southern folk tradition long before he claimed them (Catlin, 1992). It is doubtful that blues artists such as Leadbelly "wrote" every single song for which he was assigned a copyright. For instance Leadbelly's song "In the Pines," which Nirvana reworked as "Where Did You Sleep Last Night," has obvious antecedents in the nineteenth century (Nirvana, incidentally, share a copyright license with Leadbelly for their cover version on their *Unplugged* album) (Moss, 1997). Also, John Lee Hooker's "Crawlin' King Snake" was based on a 1941 recording by Tony Hollins, which was in turn rooted in a song that Blind Lemon Jefferson recorded in 1926, "That Black Snake Moan" (Catlin, 1992).

Despite the fact that Led Zeppelin and other rock groups engaged in the same type of borrowing that these early blues artists did, the power dynamics within the two cases are quite different. There is an obvious contrast between African-Americans borrowing from common cultural texts developed by other African-Americans and a white English group (backed by a powerful record label and its lawyers) slightly reworking a rural black man's song without giving credit or financial compensation. And the complexities surrounding the fact that Nirvana share a copyright license with Leadbelly for that band's reworking of his "In the Pines" – a song that was itself based on a nineteenth-century folk song – illustrate contradictions that occur when intellectual property law is applied to the blues and other types of folk music. While it is true that artists within the blues tradition from which Dixon comes engage in the intertextual practice of borrowing other existing melodies, lyrics, song structures and the like, this existed *within* a community of musicians who came from relatively similar backgrounds.

Blues artists, if they are to potentially make a living from their music, are pulled into the logic of intellectual property law-fostered relations. When Willie Dixon sued Led Zeppelin for making thousands of dollars from his songs, he implicitly had to buy into notions of originality and creativity that are relatively foreign to the blues folk tradition that enabled and structured the creation of his songs. Many early blues artists could not read or write, and existed primarily within an oral culture, so the emphasis on the system of copyright (which, by its very name, requires literacy and a familiarity with print culture) put these artists at a distinct disadvantage. For instance, by the time Willie Dixon's daughter, Shirley Dixon, was eight years old, she said, "I had filled in many copyright forms and typed his lyrics out and mailed contracts" (Hochman, 1994, p. F10). So, to survive within the mainstream record industry, blues and folk artists must disengage themselves from an intertextual mode of cultural production and buy into a conception of authorship and ownership based in Western Enlightenment thought.

Artists like Deep Forest and Enigma do not procure entire songs in the way that Led Zeppelin did, but they sometimes take recognizable chunks from the "world music" they sample (just as Led Zeppelin also borrowed riffs and melodies from blues artists, but not whole songs). With their cut-and-pasting of found sounds captured with samplers, these mostly dance-oriented artists sample indigenous music from around the world and fuse it to a beat. These samples can provide the entire hook for a song like Enigma's "Return to Innocence," which appropriated a recording of a folk song performed by two members of an indigenous Taiwanese tribe. As was discussed in the previous section, copyright law only recognizes particular types of authorship as legitimate. Therefore, the organization that had the capital to record this music was recognized as the owner, not the couple that performed the song, or the tribe that maintained the song as part of a cultural commons. The song was a huge European hit that was later licensed to be the theme song of the 1996 Atlanta Olympics, and the song made massive amounts of money for Enigma and the record company but no money for the members of the Taiwanese tribe whose performance was sampled in the Enigma song (Huang, 1996; Sandburg, 1998).

By looking at this form of cultural appropriation purely from an economic vantage point – that of Western companies taking resources from other cultures – one can miss an important point. For some cultures, music is extremely important and bound up in daily life, with songs having the power to bring life or death, rain or drought, food or starvation. Therefore, keeping their songs tightly controlled is a vitally important element of their culture, something that transcends issues of money and property. As I mentioned much earlier in this chapter, the same logic operates in the way that Western copyright and patent law, respectively, facilitate the appropriation of "world music" and the indigenous knowledge of plants. Trying to find an equitable way of balancing the needs of various oppressed people (blues artists, "world music" artists, and others) within a particular intellectual property regime is difficult. It becomes even more complicated when we examine the case of hip-hop music – a form of African-American music that, at its core, is founded on the need to freely appropriate the musical and textual elements that surround hip-hop artists.

Hip-Hop

Hip-hop, popularly known as rap music, emerged during the 1970s within the postindustrial landscape of the South Bronx, New York, and was largely developed by African-Americans, Latinos, and Jamaican immigrants. Hip-hop's primary mode of musical production was intertextual in nature and, in its embryonic form in the early 1970s, it simply consisted of a DJ collaging the "best" (i.e. most danceable) parts of songs for hip-shaking partygoers. The length of the song fragments became shorter as increasingly skilled DJs began isolating what are called "breakbeats" – the rhythmic percussion breaks on songs. Sometimes playing the same breakbeat one after another on two turntables, DJs learned to extend the length of particular parts of songs and, as they developed their craft even more, DJs essentially began to compose new music with old records. MCs initially were used to give the party more of an energetic feel, and they soon developed their style from simple catch phrases ("yes yes y'all" or "on and on till the break of dawn") to lengthier, rhymed story fragments – a style that became known as rapping. In the early days of hip-hop, before the first hip-hop recording was released, the way in which hip-hop was heard was either in live venues or on taped recordings of those performances played on portable stereos. These performances consisted of MCs rapping on top of an instrumental bed of collaged beats arranged by the DJ (Toop, 1991).

"Rapper's Delight," by the Sugarhill Gang, was the first hip-hop recording, and when it was released in 1979, it became a huge hit. The Sugarhill Gang consisted of a group of MCs who had no connection to the original South Bronx hip-hop scene and were put together by the owners of the New Jersey-based Sugarhill Records to capitalize on this local trend. In part because they were outsiders, they attempted to use more traditional means to create the instrumentation, so the Sugarhill Gang used studio musicians instead. Because "Rapper's Delight" was a major hit, it influenced the way hip-hop was heard on record in its early years of recorded existence, but many felt that it did not stay true to the original sound of hip-hop as it was performed in local clubs and in the parks (Adler, 1991). With the help of drum machines and digital samplers, by the mid-1980s, hip-hop artists were able to use these tools to make easier the collaging of beats and sounds that used to be the job of the DJ. Sampling was an extension of the intertextual practices that were developed by hip-hop DJs, practices which are deeply rooted in aspects of African-American cultural production.

After a decade of existing on the margins of mainstream popular culture, hip-hop music began to sell more than before and, in 1988, the annual record sales of hip-hop music reached $100 million, which accounted for 2 percent of the music industry's sales. The next year, the magazine *Billboard* included rap charts and music video outlet MTV debuted *Yo! MTV Raps*, which quickly became the network's highest rated show (Samuels, 1991; Silverman, 1989). By 1992, rap was generating $400 million annually, roughly 5 percent of the music industry's annual income (Vaughn, 1992). These estimates climbed to $700 million in annual revenues for rap in 1993 (Rose, 1994b). In 1998, hip-hop music sales continued to outpace music industry gains in general (a 31% increase over the previous year, compared to the music industry's 9%), and hip-hop outsold what had previously been the top-selling format, country music (Farley, 1999).

This dramatic change in the profile of hip-hop brought many changes, one of the most significant of which was the proliferation of copyright lawsuits that were prompted by the un*author*ized use of music that was incorporated into new hip-hop recordings. It is symbolic that the first sampling-related copyright infringement lawsuit was brought against the Beastie Boys, hip-hop artists who were the first to earn a number one record on the charts of *Billboard*, the US music industry's trade magazine. This provoked a flurry of legal activity that made record companies wary of the potential lawsuits that could occur if they released records that contained unauthorized samples.

From the simple breakbeats created by DJs with two turntables in the mid-1970s to the dense and edgy sound collages of Public Enemy in the late-1980s and early-1990s, it is clear that preexisting, but reconfigured, recordings have provided the backbone of hip-hop music. But when hip-hop became a multi-million dollar industry, numerous lawsuits were filed and, as a result of this, hip-hop artists found it increasingly difficult to operate the way their predecessors did (Buchsbaum, 1993; Garber, Garber and Spizman, 1992). A major obstacle that limits hip-hop artists' ability to freely sample is the perpetual threat of legal action that may result from the use of an unauthorized sample. As a result, labels reacted

by creating a complex system of business and legal networks that include the sample clearance houses, which are businesses that specialize in licensing samples for hip-hop and pop music artists. The sample clearance practices that arose in the wake of industry-wide copyright infringement lawsuits are often very expensive, and the financial burden is completely absorbed by the hip-hop artist, producer, or both, who pay for the cost out of their future royalties ("Documents," 1995; Pedroso, 1994).

To clear a sample taken from a record, two types of fees must be paid: *publishing* fees and *master recording* (or *mechanical*) fees. The publishing fee, which is paid to the company or individual that owns a particular song, often consists of a flexible and somewhat arbitrary formula that calculates a statutory royalty rate set by Congress (Fernando, 1994). This formula takes into account the sampled artist's popularity, the popularity of the artist that is sampling, and the time length of the sample that is used ("A New Spin," 1992; Finell, 1992). To license an original song's master recording (for example, a bass line from Chic's "Good Times" or James Brown's well-known scream), many times, one must pay a one-time flat fee, which can often be very expensive – ranging from an estimated $100 to $10,000, averaging $2,000 to $3,000, and sometimes reaching as high as $100,000 for a single sample, if it is allowed to be used at all (Fernando, 1994; Soocher, 1992; Browne, 1992).

A director of a sample clearance house estimated that the clearance fees for the average hip-hop album totaled about $30,000 in the early 1990s, and those rates have significantly risen throughout the 1990s (Fernando, 1994). Often the cost can be much more. For instance, after De La Soul was sued for copyright infringement, they took pains to clear the fifty-plus samples that appeared on their follow-up album, *De La Soul is Dead*, which cost over $100,000 in clearance and legal fees (Browne, 1992). Sometimes it can cost that much for a single sample, as is the case with 2 Live Crew, who had to pay roughly $100,000 to lift a section of dialogue from Stanley Kubrick's *Full Metal Jacket* (Browne, 1992). This is an extremely large amount of money, especially when it is added to the cost of recording, promotion, music videos, etc. (Spero, 1992). The peril in paying such high flat fees is that often times a great amount of money is spent on records that achieve relatively little success (the vast majority of all records released in a given year fail commercially) ("A New Spin," 1992).

States Tommy Boy record executive Daniel Hoffman, "It's a legal and administrative hassle and it costs us a lot of money" (Browne, 1992, p. 54). Chris Lighty, a hip-hop management company executive, states, "It's very hard to find these [copyright owners] and very expensive legally. You can spend between $5,000 and $10,000 just trying to obtain a license and still come up dry" (Russell, 1992, p. 1). In reference to Lighty's comments about "coming up dry," he discusses a case in which a production team assumed that the licensing of a sample was imminent, so they completed and mastered the album only to find that the license was rejected. The production team had to re-enter the studio to remaster the album, deleting the song with the unauthorized sample in the process because, Lighty states, "We decided it was expensive to remaster, but not as expensive as getting sued" (Russell, 1992, p. 1). The Beastie Boys' album, *Paul's Boutique*, contains a dizzying array of hundreds of samples from 1960s, 1970s and 1980s songs woven together, some that are extremely obscure and brief, and some slightly longer and more recognizable. Alan Light, an editor at *SPIN* and *Vibe*, discusses this album in relation to the current cost of sampling, "You could never make that record today. It would be *way* too expensive. You could still use recognizable samples in 1989 and not have to pay millions and millions of dollars for them" (Hofmann, 1999).

In the early-to-mid-1990s, a large number of popular hip-hop artists who dominated the rap and pop charts used live musicians on their records – something that was virtually unheard of at the second half of the 1980s (Hunt, 1993; George, 1993; Hill, 1995; Gettelman, 1994; Guilliatt, 1993). Even when these artists were using recognizable instrumental phrases, interestingly, they were often played by hired studio musicians who were instructed to make it sound like the original recording. This seemingly odd and circuitous music-making process is, in actuality, a rational course of action for a producer who wants to sidestep the often-expensive *mechanical* royalty fee (though he or she still has to pay for the *publishing* fee). For example, Treach of Naughty By Nature states that while samples were used on their debut album, over half of the album consisted of live instrumentation (Landis, 1992). Treach (personal communication, January 30, 1998) told me that the use of live instrumentation was partially a stylistic decision, but it also had a lot to do with the cost of mechanical royalty licensing fees, especially in light of the cost of securing the right to use a Jackson 5 sample for their hit, "OPP."

Leading hip-hop magazine *The Source* reported that Redman's 1996 album, *Muddy Waters*, was a stylistic departure from his previous funky, sample-heavy outings. "With the soaring price of samples," *The Source* states, "Redman says he made a deliberate decision to do less sampling" (Brodeur, 1996, p. 88). During an interview with me, Redman (personal communication, December 5, 1997) complained, "They was taking me to the cleaners, fuckin' publishers. They wanted me to pay, like twenty G's [$20,000] for one sample, on top of all the other samples, and the video budget and the promotion. That means I won't see a fucking paycheck and my kids don't eat, you know what I'm saying?" Fugees member Wyclef says that his use of live instrumentation is primarily an aesthetic choice, because, in addition to being a hip-hop producer and MC, he is a multi-instrumentalist. Wyclef, who has both sampled other people's records and used live instruments to closely mimic records, told me that copyright has played a part in his use of instruments, on a subconscious level, at least. He stated, "Yeah, it's a way of getting around that mechanical fee, so that has something to do with it. Licensing is expensive" (Wyclef, personal communication, February 27, 1998).

The legal and bureaucratic restrictions that have emerged around copyright have helped turn, essentially, hip-hop's primary mode of cultural production on its head by pressuring hip-hop artists to avoid directly sampling from records and, instead, recreate sounds with live instruments. Sampling still exists, but it does so in more limited forms, in which one or two prominent samples are typically featured rather than the dense collages that hip-hop promised, and generated, before sampling-provoked copyright lawsuits permanently altered the way hip-hop was produced and distributed. I would argue (as have others) that copyright restrictions have limited hip-hop's aesthetic potential, and they have done so to the detriment of this cultural form.

Conclusion

The way intellectual property law is deployed and enforced by Western countries works to shape and limit the products of mass-produced and distributed musical forms that are based on the intertextual borrowing of existing musical texts. From hip-hop artists and folk musicians to avant-garde sound collage artists and composers included in the "classical" cannon, intertextuality has been a central component in cultural production for centuries. But intellectual property law carves out little space for intertextual cultural practices, even when one takes into account the existence of the US copyright law "fair use" provision, which allows for the limited use of parts of copyrighted texts, in particular circumstances. Just as patent law is used to prevent farmers from replanting patented seeds from a previous season (something farmers have done since humans stopped being nomadic), copyright law places very real restrictions on the compositional methods used to produce folk music, which is also something that dates back many centuries. Just as is the case with patent-owning agricultural and pharmaceutical companies, these restrictions on musical production place copyright owners at an advantage, and the existence of these centuries-old cultural practices means little more to owners than something that interferes with their profit margins.

The best and most realistic place to begin fixing some of the problems that intellectual property law poses for cultural production is the "fair use" statute. In determining whether a work is fair use, the US Congress outlined the following four factors:

(1) the purpose and character of the use, including whether such use is of a commercial nature or is for nonprofit educational purposes;
(2) the nature of the copyrighted work;
(3) the amount and substantiality of the portion used in relation to the copyrighted work as a whole; and

(4) the effect of the use upon the potential market for or value of the copyrighted work. (Elias, 1996, p. 169)

In 1994 the Supreme Court handed down its most explicit ruling on fair use. In this case, the controversial hip-hop group 2 Live Crew sampled the bass line and drum beat from Roy Orbison's hit "Pretty Woman," and interpolated the original's melody to rewrite the lyrics to refer to an "ugly woman" (Biskupic, 1994). The 2 Live Crew version of Roy Orbison's "Pretty Woman" was unambiguously a parody of the original song, and the Supreme Court's loosening of the commercial presumption within the "fair use" statute was limited to works that explicitly convey a purpose of parody. It did not have much effect within the hip-hop industry because it dealt with sampling only within the context of parody; it did not deal with the larger issues of what constitutes fair use in sampling practices. Nevertheless, this ruling did establish a way of conceiving of "fair use" *not* as a simple checklist where if all requirements are not met, it constitutes infringement. Instead, all four dimensions can be weighed in relation to each other when determining fair use. For instance, even if a work is distributed commercially and contains a substantial element of a copyrighted work, if it does not attempt to replace the original's place within the market, it can still be a "fair use." A good place to begin opening up copyright law to recognizing the legitimacy of intertextual practices is the fair use statute, by more heavily weighing the question of whether or not a work that appropriates interferes with the original cultural text's value. (For instance, would the existence of a parody by 2 Live Crew dissuade those who liked Orbison's version from buying the original version? The answer is, most likely, not.)

But there are other considerations to contemplate, because the issues I have raised in this chapter are complicated. Opening up copyright law to more openly allow for appropriation may work to the benefit of hip-hop producers, but not to the benefit of – for instance – blues musicians who have dealt with a long history of white musicians "borrowing" and claiming authorship of work that was produced by African-Americans. The same is true for "world music" musicians, though there is the other consideration of respecting the significance music has for many traditional cultures. In this case, the question is not how we can equitably compensate traditional cultures for the use of their music, but how we can respect their right to not have such crucial practices tampered with and appropriated.

For these contradictions, there is no simple solution (or even a complex but logistically possible one) that can fairly balance, for instance, the needs of African-American hip-hop producers with the needs of blues musicians and, further, the rights of similarly oppressed dark-skinned people outside of the West. By loosening the legislative restrictions on the appropriation of intellectual property, one is potentially creating a more fair system for one marginalized group while putting at a disadvantage another marginalized group. But this is often what happens when cultural systems collide, and sometimes the differences cannot be resolved in a way that is not problematic for one or more cultures. Significantly, Western intellectual property laws work to the advantage of wealthy owners by, first, legally enforcing a construction of authorship that legally allows for the appropriation of traditional cultural resources and, second, legally protecting from appropriation that which they "own." Without having to make intellectual property laws any more flexible by expanding the scope of the "fair use" statute, intellectual property owners get to have their cake and eat it too by keeping others from borrowing elements of their property while at the same time taking from others and making it their property.

References

A new spin on music sampling: A case for fair play. (1992). *Harvard Law Review*, 105, pp. 726–39.

Adler, B. (1991). Run-D.M.C. Liner notes on *Run-D.M.C. Greatest Hits* [CD]. New York: Profile Records.

Alavi, H. (1973). The state in post-colonial society. In K. Gough and H. P. Sharma (eds.) *Imperialism and revolution in South East Asia*, (pp. 145–73). New York: Monthly Review Press.

Ball, I. (1988, December 21). Beware if you sing happy birthday. *The Daily Telegraph*, p. 6.

Barlow, W. (1990). "Fattening frogs for snakes": Blues and the music industry. *Popular Music and Society* 14, 2, 7–36.

Birthday song rights for sale. (1988, October 20). *The Chicago Tribune*, p. C15.

Biskupic, J. (1994, March 8). Court hands parody. *The Washington Post*, A1.

Brodeur, S. (1996, December). Seeing red: The funkadelic Redman continues to bring the outer limits back to the underground. *The Source*, pp. 85–8.

Browne, D. (1992, January 24). Settling the bill: Digital sampling in the music industry. *Entertainment Weekly*, 102, p. 54.

Buchsbaum, H. (1993, September 17). The law in your life: Hip-hop musicians and copyright law. *Scholastic Update*, p. 12.

Catlin, R. (1992, July 29). Blues greats guilty of "borrowing," too. *Chicago Sun-Times*, p. B41.

Claghorn, G. (1996). *Women Composers and Songwriters: A Concise Biographical Dictionary*. Lanham: Scarecrow Press.

Documents that accompany sound masters. (1995, September). *Entertainment Law & Finance*, 10, 6, p. 7.

Elias, S. (1996). *Patent, copyright & trademark: a desk reference to intellectual property law*. Berkeley: Nolo Press.

Emmott, S. (1994, September 17). Genes, share them or lose them. *New Scientist*, p. 41.

Ewen, D. (1969, January 8). Yanks sing this song most often. *Variety*, p. 4.

Farley, J. (1999, February 8). Hip-hop nation. *Time*, 153, 54–64.

Fernando, S. H. Jr. (1994). *The new beats: Exploring the music, culture, and attitudes of hip-hop*. New York: Doubleday.

Finell, J. G. (1992, May 22). How a musicologist views digital sampling issue. *New York Law Journal*, p. 5.

Frank, A. G. (1970). Latin America: Underdevelopment or revolution. New York: Monthly Review Press.

Fuld, J. J. (1985). *The Book of World Famous Music*. Toronto: General Publishing Company.

Garber, M. D., Garber, S. W. and Spizman, R. F. (1992, April 22). The rap on "sampling." *The Atlanta Journal and Constitution*, p. C3.

Geller, P. E. (1994). Must copyright be for ever caught between marketplace and authorship norms? In B. Sherman and A. Strowel (eds.) *Of authors and origins* (pp. 158–201). Oxford: Clarendon Press.

George, N. (1993, February). The chronic. sound recording reviews. *Playboy*, p. 22.

Gettelman, P. (1994, March 4). US3 breaks the sound barrier; the group's blend of hip-hop and jazz takes the blue note label to new heights. *Billboard*, p. 6.

Glenn, J. (1996, January 14). Americana. *The Observer*, p. 46.

Grattan, V. L. (1993). *American Women Songwriters: A Biographical Dictionary*. Westport: Greenwood Press.

Grossberg, L. (1992). *We gotta get out of this place: Popular conservatism and postmodern culture*. New York: Routledge.

Guilliatt, R. (1993, January 31). Pop music: Jazz and hip-hop take the plunge. *Los Angeles Times*, Calendar, p. 3.

Hall, S. (1980). Race, articulation and societies structured in dominance. In UNESCO *Sociological theories: Race and colonialism* (pp. 305–45). Paris: UNESCO.

Hall, S. (1985). "Signification, Representation, Ideology: Althusser and the Post-Structuralist Debates." *Critical Studies in Mass Communication* 2, 2, pp. 91–114.

Hall, S. (1996). On postmodernism and articulation: An interview with Stuart Hall. In D. Morley and K. Chen (eds.) *Stuart Hall: Critical dialogues in cultural studies* (pp. 131–51). New York: Routledge.

Hawes, B. L. (1970). The Birthday: An American Ritual. Unpublished master's thesis, University of California–Berkeley, Berkeley.

Hayes, E. (1993, April 10). "Happy birthday to you" tune can't copyright good memories. *Orlando Sentinel Tribune*, p. E1.

Hill, B. (1995, March 26). A grass-roots movement: Live performances build Philly band's support. *The Washington Post*, p. G1.

Hochman, S. (1994, October 8). Willie Dixon's daughter makes sure legacy lives on. *Los Angeles Times*, p. F10.

Hofmann, J. G. (Producer). (1999, March 12). *Beastiography*. New York: MTV.

Huang, R. (1996, August 29). Imperfect harmony: Age-old chants strike a discordant note. *Far Eastern Economic Review*, 159, 35, p. 50.

Hunt, D. (1993, June 29). Liberating hip-hop with jazz sound: Freestyle Fellowship adds riffs to rhymes. *Los Angeles Times*, Calendar, p. 1.

Jhally, S. (1979). Marxism and underdevelopment: The modes of production debate. *Alternate Routes*, 3, pp. 63–93.

Laclau, E. (1971, May/June). Feudalism and capitalism in Latin America. *New Left Review*, 67, pp. 19–38.

Laclau, E. (1977). *Politics and ideology in Marxist theory*. London: New Left Books.

Landis, D. (1992, January 16). Court Rights over hip-hop music. *USA Today*, 20.

Lebrecht, N. (1996, May 11). Echoes Strike a Chord. *The Daily Telegraph*, p. 7.

Mills, S. (1996). Indigenous music and the law: An analysis of national and international legislation. *Yearbook for Traditional Music*, 28, pp. 57–86.

Mirapaul, M. (1996, September 12). When it comes to folk music, rights get murky. *New York Times CyberTimes*: http://search.nytimes.com/web/docsroot/library/cyber/digicom/1216digicom.htm.

Moss, M. D. (1997, May–July). Who owns the songs the whole world sings? *Sing Out! Folk Song Magazine*, 42, 1, p. 3.

Newman, J. (1995). *The ballistic bard: Postcolonial fictions*. New York: Arnold.

Ong, W. (1982). *Orality and literacy*. New York: Routledge.

Pedroso, A. I. (1994, April). Tips for music producer agreements. *Entertainment Law & Finance*, 11, 1, p. 3.

Rey, P. and Dupre, G. (1973). Reflections on the pertinence of a theory for the history of exchange. *Economy and Society*, 2, 1.

Rose, M. (1994a). The author as proprietor: Donaldson v. Becket and the genealogy of modern authorship. In B. Sherman and A. Strowel (eds.), *Of authors and origins* (pp. 158–201). Oxford: Clarendon Press.

Rose, T. (1994b). *Black Noise: Hip-hop Music and Black Culture in Contemporary America*. Hanover: Wesleyan University Press.

Russell, D. (1992, January 4). Judge clips Biz Markie on sampling issue. *Billboard*, 104, 1, p. 1.

Samuels, D. (1991, November 11). The hip-hop on hip-hop: The "black music" that isn't either. *The New Republic*, p. 24.

Sandburg, B. (1998, December 11). Copyright wilderness. *Broward Daily Business Review*, p. B1.

Seeger, C. (1996). Ethnomusicologists, archives, professional organizations, and the shifting ethics of intellectual property. *Yearbook for Traditional Music*, 28, pp. 87–105.

Shepard, S. (1992, January 6). Name that tune. *Memphis Business Journal*, p. 3.

Shiva, V. (1997). Biopiracy: The plunder of nature and knowledge. Boston: South End Press.

Silverman, E. R. (1989, May 29). Hip-hop goes the way of rock 'n' roll: Record moguls snap up labels. *Crain's New York Business*, p. 3.

Slack, J. D. (1996). The theory and method of articulation in cultural studies. In D. Morley and K. Chen (eds.) *Stuart Hall: Critical dialogues in cultural studies* (pp. 112–27). New York: Routledge.

Sold. (1989, January 2). *Time*, p. 88.

Soocher, S. (1992, May 1). As sampling suits proliferate, legal guidelines are emerging. *New York Law Journal*, p. 5.

Spero, F. (1992, December 5). Sample greed is hurting hip-hop business. *Billboard*, p. 7.

Toelken, B. (1986). Ballads and folksongs. In E. Oring (ed.), *Folk groups and folklore genres: An Introduction* (pp. 147–74). Logan, UT: Utah State University Press.

Toop, D. (1991). *Rap Attack 2: African Hip-hop To Global Hip-hop*. London: Serpent's Tail.

TRIPS & its negative consequences. (1999, July 20). [Online] *The Hindu*. Available: Lexis-Nexis.

Varga, G. (1993, March 18). Coverdale is no Plant for another Zeppelin. *The San Diego Union-Tribune*, Night and Day, p. 11.

Vaughn, C. (1992, December). Simmons' rush for profits. *Black Enterprise*, p. 67.

Zeitlin, S. (1998, April 25). Strangling Culture With a Copyright Law. *The New York Times*, p. A15.

Chapter 20

"We Are the World": State Music Policy, Cultural Imperialism, and Globalization

Roy Shuker

State attitudes and policies towards popular culture are a significant factor in determining the construction of meaning in popular music. At the level of attitudes, State cultural policies are indicative of the various views held about the very concept of culture itself, debates over government economic intervention in the marketplace versus the operation of the 'free market', the operation of cultural imperialism, and the role of the State in fostering national cultural identity. As the Task Force Report on *The Future of the Canadian Music Industry* (1996) put it:

> Most industrialized states believe that cultural products must not be treated as commodities. The cultural exemption contained in international trade agreements reflects a recognition that it is in their diversity that the richness of human cultures is to be found and that the distinctive characteristics of each culture should be preserved.

The internationalisation of the music industry has historically been equated with 'cultural imperialism', with local cultures dominated and to varying degrees invaded, displaced and challenged by imported 'foreign' cultures. The solution to this situation is usually seen as some combination of restrictions upon media imports and the deliberate fostering of the local cultural industries, including sound recording. These are illustrated here by Canada's MAPLE test and Federal policies supporting local music; and New Zealand's quota debate and subsequent operation of NZ On Air. (For a further instructive example, see Breen 1999 on Australia. Fuller considerations of popular music and cultural policy, and a broad range of international examples, can be found in Wallis and Malm 1992; Robinson et al. 1991; Bennett et al. 1993; Ewbank and Papageorgiou 1997).

There are also examples of both the central and local State attempting to use popular music as one way to regenerate local communities, and stimulate community support for local music (see, for example, Cohen 1991, on Liverpool; Elderen 1989, on the Netherlands Pop Music Foundation; and Street 1993, on Norwich). For reasons of space, however, I have chosen to concentrate here on cultural policy at the national level.

Culture and the State

State cultural policies have been largely based on the idealist tradition of culture as a realm separate from, and often in opposition to, the realm of material production and economic activity. This means that government intervention in its various forms – subsidy, licensing arrangements, protectionism through quotas, etc. – is justified by the argument which has been clearly elaborated by Garnham:

> 1. that culture possesses inherent values, of life enhancement or whatever, which are fundamentally opposed to and in danger of damage by commercial forces; 2. that the need for these values is universal, uncontaminated by questions of class, gender and ethnic origin; and 3. that the market cannot satisfy this need. (Garnham 1987: 24)

Drawing on the Romantic cultural tradition, a key part of this view is the concept of the individual creative artist:

> The result of placing artists at the centre of the cultural universe has not been to shower them with gold, for artistic poverty is itself an ideologically potent element in this view of culture, but to define the policy problem as one of finding audiences for their work rather than vice versa. (ibid.)

This ideology has been used by elites in government, administration, intellectual circles, and broadcasting to justify and represent sectional interests as general interests, thereby functioning as a form of cultural hegemony.

Seeing classical music, ballet, and the theatre as 'high culture' or 'the arts', legitimates both their largely middle-class consumption and their receipt of State subsidy. 'Popular culture' is then constructed in opposition to this, as commercial, inauthentic, and so unworthy of significant government support. A comic example of this view was provided by civil servant Sir Humphrey Appleby, giving advice to his ministerial 'boss' in the television comedy series *Yes Minister*:

> Subsidy is for Art. It is for Culture. It is not to be given to what the people want, it is for what the people don't want but ought to have. If they really want something they will pay for it themselves. The Government's duty is to subsidize education, enlightenment and spiritual uplift, not the vulgar pastimes of ordinary people. (Episode: 'The Middle-Class Rip Off', BBC Television)

Such a dichotomised high–low culture view is unsustainable, yet it nonetheless remains a widely held and still powerful ideology.

The assumptions and issues underpinning such a high–low culture distinction were also neatly illustrated by the contrasting attitudes of two former New Zealand Prime Ministers. In 1983, the then Prime Minister Robert Muldoon, heading a National (Conservative) administration, justified his continued rejection of arguments for a cut in the sales tax on records (such a tax did not apply to 'cultural' items like books), by claiming that pop music could not be considered cultural: 'If you use the word "culture" in its normal sense', he said, 'I don't think (leading local groups) Split Enz and Mi-Sex are cultural'. This view, of course, was a defensible consequence of the high culture position outlined above. In contrast to this, in 1986 Labour Prime Minister David Lange's objections to the Government being 'the inevitable funder' of the New Zealand Symphony Orchestra aroused considerable controversy. Mr Lange said he had nothing against what he was sure was an 'extraordinarily competent' group of musicians, but the example of the orchestra as a socially worthy purpose did not inspire him to reach for his cheque book! Asked if the Government would help foot the orchestra's costs, he noted that the local pop group Peking Man played to a wider audience while receiving no State assistance. When reporters observed that the orchestra was regarded as a national cultural treasure, Lange quipped that was because it lost money: 'Things are regarded as raving socialist or national cultural treasures if they lose a packet. I just happen to like Dire Straits more than I like Debussy', said Mr Lange, who took the British rock group to lunch during its 1986 New Zealand tour (Press Report, 4 November 1986).

Cultural Imperialism, Globalisation, and Music

The common preference of listeners and record buyers for foreign-originated sounds, rather than the product of their local artists and labels, is associated with the cultural imperialism thesis. Cultural imperialism developed as a concept analogous to the historical, political and economic subjugation of the Third World by the colonising powers in the nineteenth century, with consequent deleterious effects for the societies of the colonised. This gave rise to global relations of dominance, subordination and dependency between the affluence and power of the advanced capitalist nations, most notably the United States and Western Europe, and the relatively powerless underdeveloped countries. This economic and political imperialism was seen to have a cultural aspect:

the ways in which the transmission of certain products, fashions and styles from the dominant nations to the dependent markets leads to the creation of particular patterns of demand and consumption which are underpinned by and endorse the cultural values, ideals and practices of their dominant origin. In this manner the local cultures of developing nations become dominated and in varying degrees invaded, displaced and challenged by foreign, often western, cultures. (O'Sullivan et al. 1994: 62; see also Robinson et al. 1991)

In terms of mass media and popular culture, evidence for the cultural imperialism thesis, as it became known, was provided by the predominantly one-way international media flow, from a few international dominant sources of media production, notably the USA, to media systems in other national cultural contexts. Not only did this involve the market penetration and dominance of Anglo-American popular culture, more importantly, it established certain forms as the accepted ones, scarcely recognising that there were alternatives:

One major influence of American imported media lies in the styles and patterns which most other countries in the world have adopted and copied. This influence includes the very definition of what a newspaper, or a feature film, or a television set is. (Tunstall 1977: intro.)

The cultural imperialism thesis gained general currency in debates through the 1970s and 1980s about the significance of imported popular culture. Such debates were evident not only in the Third World, but in 'developed' countries such as France, Canada, Australia, and New Zealand, all subject to high market penetration by American popular culture. Adherents of the thesis tended to dichotomise local culture and its imported counterpart, regarding local culture as somehow more authentic, traditional, and supportive of a conception (however vaguely expressed it may be) of a distinctive national cultural identity. Set against this identity, and

threatening its continued existence and vitality, was the influx of large quantities of slick, highly commercialised media products, mainly from the United States. Upholders of the cultural imperialism view generally saw the solution to this situation as some combination of restrictions upon media imports and the deliberate fostering of the local cultural industries, including music.

The cultural imperialism thesis has generally been applied to film, television and publishing; with a few exceptions (Wallis and Malm 1984; Lealand 1988; Laing 1986; Robinson et al. 1991), it has not been examined in relation to popular music. At first sight, its application here appears warranted, given that the major record companies are the dominant institutions of the music industry, and local pressings of imported repertoire take the major share of national music markets. But to what extent can this situation be seen in terms of cultural invasion and the subjugation of local cultural identity? Such figures present only the bare bones of the structure of the music industry, and tell us little about the complex relationship of the majors to local record companies in marginalised national contexts such as Canada and New Zealand.

Although the existence of cultural imperialism became widely accepted at both a 'commonsense' level and in leftist academia, its validity at both a descriptive level and as an explanatory analytical concept came under increasing critical scrutiny in the 1980s. The validity of the local/authentic versus imported/commercial dichotomy is difficult to sustain with reference to specific examples, while media effects are assumed in a too one-dimensional fashion, underestimating the mediated nature of audience reception and use of media products. More importantly, the cultural imperialism thesis is predicated on accepting the 'national' as a given, with distinctive national musical identities its logical corollary. However, the globalisation of Western capitalism, particularly evident in its media conglomerates, and the increasing international nature of Western popular music bring these notions into question.

There are three significant points to be made here: first, Anglo-American popular culture has become established as the international preferred culture of the young since the 1950s. This is not to subscribe to any reductionist view of an international youth culture (cf.,

Reich 1967), but to make the point that American rock 'n' roll was 'an instance of the use of foreign music by a generation as a means to distance themselves from a parental "national" culture' (Laing 1986: 338). Second, local products cannot be straightforwardly equated with local national cultural identity, and conversely (arising from the first point) imported product is not to be necessarily equated with the alien. Indeed local product is often qualitatively indistinct from its overseas counterpart, though this in itself is frequently a target for criticism. Third, while specific national case studies demonstrate the immense influence of the transnational music industry on musical production and distribution everywhere, they 'just as clearly indicate that world musical homogenization is not occurring' (Robinson et al. 1991: 4). The process is rather one in which local musicians are immersed in overlapping and frequently reciprocal contexts of production, with a cross-fertilisation of local and international sounds. Mitchell (1996) provides an instructive analysis of this process, with reference to a range of national examples and musical genres. The global and the local cannot be considered binary categories, but exist in a complex interrelationship.

More recently, reflecting the internationalisation of capital – a trend particularly evident in its media conglomerates – the term 'globalisation' has replaced cultural imperialism. As an explanatory concept, however, globalisation is often used too loosely, and is open to similar criticisms to cultural imperialism. Currently, 'glocalisation' has emerged as a more useful concept, emphasising the complex and dynamic interrelationship of local music scenes and industries and the international marketplace (see Leyshon et al. 1998).

The major problem faced by record companies is the uncertainty of the music market. It is widely agreed that, at best, only one in eight (to ten) of the artists A & R sign and record will achieve sufficient sales to recoup the original investment and start to earn money for the artists and generate a profit for the company. This situation has led major record companies to look for acts that are already partially developed and which indicate commercial potential, especially in the international market (Hesmondhalgh 1996; Negus 1999). This is an approach with considerable implications for local artists operating primarily at a regional or national level.

Local branches of the majors (e.g. Sony Canada) find that it is more economic to concentrate on local pressings of imported repertoire, usually from the United States, given the costs of developing master recordings. There is an economic advantage in releasing recordings based on foreign master tapes: no production costs are involved when importing a foreign master, while producing a Canadian content master involves costs from $10,000 to $200,000, plus the cost of one or more promotional videos. Risks are high in originating master tapes since only one in ten is financially successful.

Attempts at the national level to foster local popular music production are primarily interventions at the level of the distribution and reception of the music. They attempt to secure greater access to the market, particularly for local products in the face of overseas music, notably from the United Kingdom and the United States. Such attempts, along with the issues surrounding cultural imperialism and globalisation and the status of the local, can be more fully addressed through two national examples: Canada and New Zealand.

Global Music, National Culture: Canada

Canadians value music: 70 per cent identify it as an important part of their lives, and 46 per cent buy music on a regular basis (DFSP 1999: 3). Reflecting this, the Canadian music industry is economically significant; in 1996, Canadians spent C$107 per person on recordings, compared with C$76 on books (ibid.). In addition, popular Canadian artists such as Celine Dion, Bryan Adams, Alanis Morissette, Shania Twain, and Robert Charlebois are the country's best-known cultural ambassadors abroad.

The history of the Canadian music industry has been shaped largely by its relationship to the international marketplace, especially its proximity to the dominant United States market for popular music. During the 1980s and into the 1990s, the Canadian music industry was dominated by the local branches of the majors.

The eight largest record companies in Canada are foreign-owned; 89 per cent of the revenues from the Canadian domestic market goes to multinationals. Their interest in Canadian music is restricted to those recordings which are marketed across the continent. This preference also shapes current government programs for subsidising domestic recording. All other recording remains economically, spatially, and discursively marginal. (Berland 1988; see also Robinson et al. 1991: chap. 5)

Economies of scale applied to production meant that indigenous product was far more costly to produce and frequently had inferior production values compared with imports (largely) from the United States. With record distribution also dominated by the majors, and commercial radio frequently tied to US programme formats and broadcast sound quality, the Canadian industry and musicians had only a small market share: in 1988 the independents received approximately 11 per cent of national revenues from record sales. One consequence of this situation was that only a small percentage of music bought in Canada originated there, even when it was made by Canadian artists (e.g. Bryan Adams). This economic situation sat uneasily with the historical Canadian concern to encourage nationhood and a cultural identity via communications technology, while at the same time resisting the intrusion of American media and messages. These concerns have pushed the State to the forefront in media and cultural policy (see Dorland 1996).

The Canadian music industry as a whole was considerably stronger by the mid-1990s. Recordings generated substantial economic activity: retail sales in Canada totalled C$1.3 billion in 1997, while the royalties paid to Canadian songwriters, composers and publishers (as public performance rights) totalled C$49 million in 1997, up from C$34 million in 1993 (DFSP 1999). While this overall picture is impressive, the historical dichotomy remained: Canadian firms earn about 90 per cent of their revenue from selling Canadian-content recordings, while 88 per cent of the revenues of foreign-controlled firms comes from selling recordings made from imported masters. Foreign firms have five times the revenue, eighteen times the profit, ten times the long-term assets, and sixteen times the contributed surplus and retained earnings of Canadian-controlled firms (Task Force 1996).

It should also be acknowledged, however, that the majors are not simply parasitic here. Brain Robertson, President of CRIA (Canadian Recording Industry Association), stresses the important investment in Canadian talent by the multinationals (majors), now around C$40 million a year in Canadian Content production. 'This has escalated tremendously in the last decade, and represents a huge investment per year in Canadian music and artists and their recordings' (author interview, July 1999). Canadian brewing giant Seagram's takeover of MCA in 1995 (and Polygram in 1998) meant that a major recording company was now based in Canada, but as yet this appears to have had little impact on the development of local repertoire.

Yet as Straw (1993, 1996) has observed, while the general picture of a marginalised local sound-recording industry remains valid, contradictions are now evident. On the one hand, there is the increased international visibility and success of Canadian artists/music within the global sound-recording industry, although these artists frequently record in the United States, for US-based companies; e.g. Bryan Adams, Alanis Morissette, Shania Twain. On the other hand, there is also an increased share of the local market for music of Canadian content, with commercially significant sales for several locally based performers, including Bare Naked Ladies, Our Lady Peace, Red Rodeo, and Sarah McLachlan. In 1998, Our Lady Peace's CD *Clumsy* sold over 800,000 copies in Canada, along with well over half a million copies in the USA; Bare Naked Ladies had a top ten *Billboard* single ('One Week'), and their album *Stunt* reached sales of three million (Chauncey 1999: 57). Artists working in non-pop or rock genres are also having a national impact: singer and jazz pianist Diana Krall attained platinum sales (100,000 in Canada) with her CD *Love Scenes*, and her latest CD, *When I Look in Your Eyes*, went gold (50,000) on the day of its release in June 1999; both releases also gained significant exposure and sales outside of Canada.

At the same time, the popular music market has changed dramatically, with the splintering of 'mainstream rock', once the dominant genre, into a wide range of genre styles and performers, along with the willingness of the major record companies to market/exploit these. These trends have created uncertainty as to the future role and status of Canada's small, locally based firms, which have traditionally nurtured and been economically dependent on new musical styles. In other words, reflecting glocalisation, the relative market positions and relationship of 'majors' and 'independents' in the Canadian market has changed (Straw 1996). The growth of foreign markets has made artist development in Canada more globally oriented. The Canadian branches of the majors, and Canadian owned independent labels such as Nettwerk Productions, Attic Music Group, True North, and Marquis Classics are increasingly looking to develop artists with international appeal. Randy Lennox, president of Universal Music Group (Canada) states: 'We're watching specific market trends worldwide when signing an artist today' (LeBlanc 1999).

In the midst of these shifts, positive Government policy toward the local music industry appeared to be more necessary than ever, a view shared by the comprehensive and influential Task Force Report, on *The Future of the Canadian Music Industry* (Task Force 1996). The Task Force was asked to develop proposals that would ensure that the industry could maintain its central role in promoting Canada's cultural identity by providing an increasing choice of Canadian music. Objectives set for the industry were to maintain its ability to compete in Canada and abroad; to be adequately compensated for use of its copyrighted material; and to benefit from new technologies. The Task Force concluded: 'While cultural objectives should provide the basis for music industry policy, measures that strengthen the creation, performance, production, distribution and marketing of Canadian music will also generate important economic benefits' (Task Force 1996). The Task Force report was a comprehensive document and here I concentrate on only two aspects of it: the operation and future of the 'Can Con' regulations, administered by the Canadian Radio and Telecommunications Commission (CRTC), and the Sound Recording Development Program (SRDP).

The CRTC and Can Con

The CRTC was established by Parliament in 1968. The Broadcasting Act requires the CRTC to ensure that each 'broadcasting undertaking...shall make maximum use, and in no case less than predominant use, of Canadian creative and other resources in the creation and presentation of programming' (unless the specialised nature of the service makes it impracticable). The CRTC has responsibility for establishing classes of broadcasting licences, the allocation of broadcast licences, making broadcasting regulations, and the holding of public hearings in respect of such matters.

In pursuit of this goal, a Canadian Content quota on AM radio was introduced in 1971, and extended to FM radio in 1976. These quotas took into account particular station airplay formats, and expected a reasonably even distribution of Canadian selections throughout the day and through the broadcast week. What constitutes 'Canadian' was established by the MAPLE test, in which at least two of the audio components of a recording must be:

'M' – music is composed by a Canadian
'A' – artist (principal performer) is a Canadian
'P' – performance/production is in Canada
'L' – lyrics are written by a Canadian
'E' –

Can Con, as the local content requirements came to be known, proved controversial, but had an undeniably positive impact on the Canadian recording industry:

> That simple regulation was a watershed. It was the expression of a protectionist policy designed to allow Canadian musicians to be heard in their own country, The overall effect of the regulations has been the creation of an active, vigorous, self-supporting, and surprisingly creative industry – one that hardly existed prior to the regulations. (Flohel 1990: 497)

It seems to be generally agreed that, while the current group of Canadian international stars would have 'made it' anyway, their early careers received a significant impetus from the airplay guaranteed by Can Con. Further, and perhaps more importantly, the quota allowed a 'middle' group of performers to make an impact – and a living – within the Canadian industry: 'there's a whole lot of middle ground Canadian artists who are fabulous acts and Can Con has helped to ensure that they get the airplay that allows them to become the stars that they have become in Canada and, in many cases, nowhere else in the world' (Doug Pringle, director of programming at Rawlco Communications, responsible for a number of newer radio stations, cited in Melhuish 1999: 73).

In early 1999, after a series of public hearings and a review of radio policy by the CRTC, the Canadian content requirement was increased to 35 per cent. This change did not indicate a 'failure' of the previous requirement, but was a recognition that the local industry was now in a strong enough position to provide sufficient acceptable recordings to meet such an increase.

The Sound Recording Development Program (SRDP)

The SRDP was created in 1986 to provide support to Canadian-owned companies for the production of Canadian audio and video music and radio programmes and to support marketing, international touring, and business development. This recognised that it was necessary to assist the industry to enable it to provide the local content required under the CRTC regulations. With the exception of the support provided to Specialized Music Production, which is administered by the Canada Council, SRDP support is the responsibility of two organisations, FACTOR and MusicAction, based on an agreement with the Department of Canadian Heritage.

The 1991 evaluation of the SRDP found that it had had a very positive effect on the sound recording industry, but that its resources (funding was initially C$5 million) were inadequate to significantly strengthen the independent sector of the industry and, in particular, that it provided too little support to marketing and distribution. This view was confirmed by the Task Force report, which regarded the scheme as now substantially under-funded: 'A major concern for both English and French language industries is the inadequacy of the resources available to support the marketing of recordings by Canadian artists' (Task Force 1996).

The Task Force (1996) recommended that the resources of the Sound Recording Development Program should be increased immediately to C$10 million annually and sustained at that level for a period of five years, but it was not until late 1999 that Government policy began to address this, and a comprehensive review of the programme was begun. Speaking in 1999, Brian

Chater, President of CIRPA (the Canadian Independent Record Producers Association) emphasised there remained a pressing need to get 'serious structural funding' in the local industry:

> The music business has become very much like the film business; you have to have a lot of bucks to play the game, and a lot of the time it won't work anyway. Now if you don't invest three or four hundred grand on each project, nobody thinks you're serious. Do five of those and you've spent a couple of million dollars. The reality with project funding is that you're always scrambling from A to B trying to pay the bills with the project money. What we want to see indies have access to is structural funding, so that you can operate a company rather than do projects. (Melhuish 1999: 79; also discussed in author interview, July 1999)

The Canadian case raises crucial questions about the role of music as a form of discourse actively engaged in the uniting of fragmenting of a community. It presupposes that listeners consciously identify – and identify with – specifically locally produced music. The frequent negative reaction local product provokes is an important reminder of how what counts as popular music has been identified with a particular imported form, the result of the dominance of American radio formats, music videos, and production values.

Further, it is misleading to automatically assume that local musicians embody and support a Canadian cultural nationalism in their work. Indeed, Canada itself is characterised by considerable cultural diversity, with strongly developed regional music scenes and idioms. Attempts to include more French language music on Canadian radio illustrate the difficulties of conflating 'the national' in multicultural/ bilingual settings. A 1989 hearing of the CRTC led to a 1990 regulation stipulating that at least 65 per cent of the vocal music played weekly by all Francophone AM and FM radio stations, irrespective of format or market, must be French-language. The tensions this created for an industry and artists wanting to remain 'culturally politically correct' but also needing to appeal to the larger, international market, illustrated the double-bind in which Quebec is caught. 'Like other small nations, it feels the need to protect its local products from multinational conglomerates but aims none the less at generating its own international hits... the debate under study goes to the very heart of this double bind' (Grenier 1993: 124).

New Zealand on Air

These questions of the relationship between popular music, local cultural identity, and the internationalisation of the music industry are also evident in New Zealand. The 1989–90 debate over a compulsory quota for NZ music on the radio traversed the arguments over the importance of supporting the local music industry, the constitution of the 'local', and the relationship between airplay and commercial success (see Shuker 1994). When a quota was not introduced, New Zealand On Air (NZOA) was established, to administer the funds collected by the broadcasting fee. Its brief included provision for subsidising local music – a kind of quota default option.

As in Canada, New Zealand's local recording companies and their products are largely marginalised by the dominant position of the international record companies (the 'majors'), and the sheer quantity of 'imported' material (mainly New Zealand pressings of international repertoire). Given the economic and cultural significance of recorded music, this situation has been the focus of considerable public debate and Government cultural policy. New Zealand can best be regarded as an example of a country with a small market for recorded music, with a small share for local music within the major-dominated turnover of the local phonogram market, and with a relatively unimportant role for local sounds within the international music market. This places New Zealand on a similar footing to Canada and the Netherlands. As Rutten observes, the fact that there is a very limited domestic market for local music in such countries 'poses important problems, given the skyrocketing costs of recording and marketing. It is necessary to look to larger markets in order to recoup investments in a band or an artist' (Rutten 1991: 300).

There are a number of established NZ independent labels, along with branches of the majors who dominate the global music industry.

According to industry sources, the subsidiaries of the multinational record companies continue to supply approximately 90 per cent of the domestic market. While any strict division between the majors and the 'indies' is no longer really tenable, with distribution deals tying the two sectors of the industry together, there remain interesting questions about the dynamics of their relationship. This is particularly the case with the operation of the majors with respect to local product.

The New Zealand popular music scene has experienced periodic highs and lows through the last decade. After a low period in the late 1980s (in terms of overall chart success), local artists made strong chart showings both at home and internationally during 1991–2, greatly assisted by the introduction of NZ On Air's music schemes. Flving Nun, the country's main independent label, saw continued sales growth, particularly in the United States. During the next few years, despite the continuation of NZ On Air's funding of videos and CD compilations of local artists, retail sales fluctuated and chart success failed to match the peak level achieved in 1992. This was followed in the mid-1990s by the international success of OMC ('How Bizzare'), Crowded House, and Neil Finn, and strong local showings by artists such as Bic Runca, Shihad, Che Fu, and The Feelers.

Despite occasional successes, the vital signs of the local recording industry remain mixed. The local scene remains insufficient to support full-time professional performers, there is still only limited radio and television exposure for local artists, and initiatives to support the industry remain limited. Several explanations have been offered for this: a general lack of effort on the part of the majors to sign and develop New Zealand artists; the general lack of an industry infrastructure, especially in terms of management and the opportunities for radio and television airplay; and the inadequacies of the local industry, which is seen to have failed to grasp the opportunities open to it.

Logically, given the economies of scale involved, the majors concentrate more on promoting their overseas artists, with their local performers treated as a lower priority. The majors also in a sense feed off local labels, treating them in the same fashion as North American professional sports franchises use their 'farm teams' to foster talent and provide local back-up as necessary. But this is as much a symbiotic relationship as it is a parasitic one. The independents need the distribution and marketing support the majors can provide, particularly in overseas markets, while NZ performers who outstrip the strictly local need the majors to move up a league. This was evident with the two main New Zealand independent record labels operating in the late 1980s: Flying Nun, and Pagan (Mitchell 1996), and continues to be the case.

New Zealand artists who remain 'at home' will always remain marginal to the international music industry, since the country lacks the population base to support a music industry on the scale of neighbouring Australia. The result is a tension between the support for the purely local, and the need to go offshore to follow up national success. Shihad, arguably New Zealand's premier band, in late 1998 relocated to Los Angeles:

> We're not turning our back on New Zealand. A lot of people are coming to the realisation that as a climate for making music New Zealand is tremendously wealthy in terms of what we have available to us and what people can produce here. But the actual platform for getting music out into the market place is absolutely shit. We're crippled in comparison to places like Australia where they have local content quotas. (Tom Larkin, drummer, Shihad, *Rip It Up*, October 1998: 14. Shihad is now based in Melbourne, Australia)

Given the marginal status of New Zealand's recording industry in the international arena, and the difficulties facing local artists, the initiatives taken by New Zealand On Air (NZOA) to foster New Zealand music, in operation since July 1991, are of crucial importance. NZOA's brief is not restricted to 'popular music', but in practice this is the case, with classical music having its own sources of funding and support. NZOA is charged with ensuring that 'New Zealanders have a diverse range of broadcasting services that would not otherwise be available on a commercial basis'. A key strategy in pursuit of this goal is 'To encourage broadcasters to maintain a sustained commitment to programmes reflecting New Zealand identity and culture'. Working towards achieving this includes 'funding programming on television and radio

about New Zealand and New Zealand interests, including the broadcasting of New Zealand music' (NZOA Annual Report 1995/96: Statement of purpose and goals).

NZOA's popular music programme has four main schemes related to radio and television. In addition, it has put out two major CD compilations: *Kiwi Gold Disc* (1996) and *Kiwi Gold Disc II* (1998), collections of 'classic' New Zealand hits from the past, which are sent to every radio station in the country to boost the amount of material they have available for airplay. The ongoing schemes are (from NZOA 1999: Annual Report).

1 Radio Hits, which provides incentives to record companies to produce records suitable for the commercial radio play list; and lessens the financial risk inherent in recording and releasing singles, by enabling partial recovery of recording costs.

2 The Hit Disc, which assists record companies to get airplay for new releases, and makes sure that 'every Programme Director in every NZ radio station has access to a broadcast quality copy of new singles which have commercial radio airplay potential'. The first of these, and still the most important, is the *Kiwi Hit Disc*, made up of 'new New Zealand music on release or about to be released by record companies'. The *Indie Hit Disc* and, most recently, the *Iwi Hit Disc*, are similar schemes with more of a niche market.

3 Music Video, 'funding NZ music videos as part of a compaign to get more NZ music on air', through subsidising production costs of selected videos.

4 New Zealand Music on Radio, which involves funding specialist radio programmes promoting NZ music, for commercial radio and student radio, aimed at the youth audience.

In each of the first three schemes the criteria for support is similar, or identical. First, 'It must be New Zealand music. The priority is original New Zealand music but we accept covers as well' (Music Video; Radio Hits; Kiwi Hit Disc). Second, there must be a confirmed record release: 'the video must back up the release of a single or EP in NZ either by an independent or a major label' (Music Video); and 'A record

company – either a major or one of the independents – must be involved in releasing the
record' (Radio Hits). Priority goes to projects
distributed nationally usually via one of the
major record companies. Third, a key consideration is broadcast potential: 'our priority is
videos which are likely to generate repeat
screenings on national network television'
(Music Video); 'To qualify for funding, the
record must attract significant airplay on commercial radio' (Radio Hits); and 'the record must
be a realistic contender for significant airplay on
commercial radio' (Kiwi Hit Disc). Seven radio
stations are used as barometers, and the schemes
use programmers from TV shows and radio as
consultants to identify broadcast potential.

A mix of cultural and commercial criteria are
being applied here, with an emphasis on the
latter. It is important to recognise that the
schemes in themselves do not guarantee exposure through local television and radio. What
they do is facilitate the production of local product, including an acceptable technical quality of
these videos and recordings; and make it more
available to local programmers. Recognising
this, in early 1998 NZOA began employing a
'song plugger', whose role was to push (promote) the forthcoming Hit Disc to key radio
station programmers. This represented a dramatic departure for NZOA, but was a necessary
move given that, despite six years of effort, there
appeared to have been only limited improvement in the levels of New Zealand music getting
airplay on commercial radio.

The NZOA music schemes are in a very real
sense the alternative to a local content quota.
A recent improvement in the proportion of
local content on radio suggests that NZOA
may be close to its breakthrough goal of 'double
digits'. Yet even with the more forceful presentation of the products of its various schemes, it
remains to be seen if this goal can be achieved,
thus making a quota unnecessary. In July 2000
the funding for the NZOA music schemes was
virtually doubled, from NZ$2 million to
NZ$3.78 million a year, to enable the implemen-
tation of strategies to get increased airplay for
local recordings.

The transformation of the global circulation
of cultural forms is creating new lines of influence and solidarity which are not bounded by
geographically defined cultures, and popular

music is not exempt from such processes. Accordingly, we need to be conscious of the danger
of too easily dichotomising the local and the
global, recognise the dynamism and intertextuality of at least the best of contemporary popular music, and avoid adopting a narrowly defined
cultural nationalist position. Nevertheless, there
remain important economic arguments for the
support of the local. The continued development
of the infrastructure of the Canadian and New
Zealand music industries is central to generating
opportunities for local musicians, and for providing a launching platform for access to the
international market.

Debates over cultural policy and popular
music embrace a volatile mix of the ideological
and the economic. At the ideological level, there
is the maintenance of an outmoded high–low
culture dichotomy, which partly serves to legitimate the general neglect of the popular, including popular music. At the same time, however,
the State is also concerned to respond to the
significant level of community support for local
culture, and the perceived necessity of defending
the local against the continued and increasing
dominance of international popular media.
This concern is mediated by the difficulty of
establishing the uniqueness of national 'sounds',
be they New Zealand or Canadian.

References

Bennett, T., Frith, S., Grossberg, L., Shepherd, J. and
    Turner, G. (1993) *Rock and Popular Music: Politics,
    Policies, Institutions*, London: Routledge.
Berkenstadt, J. and Cross, C. R. (1998) *Nevermind:
    Nirvana*, New York: Schirmer Books.
Berland, J. (1988) 'Locating Listening: Technological
    Space, Popular Music, Canadian Mediations', *Cul-
    tural Studies*, 2, 3, October.
Breen, M. (1999) *Rock Dogs*, London: Pluto Press.
Chauncey, Sarah (1999) 'The Artists', *Canadian Mu-
    sician*, 20th Anniversary Issue, 21, 2 (March/April):
    48–58.
Cohen, Sara (1991) *Rock Culture in Liverpool: Popu-
    lar Music in the Making*, Oxford: Clarendon Press.
DFSP (1999) 'The Canadian Recording Industry',
    Presentation prepared by DFSP, Ottawa: Depart-
    ment of Canadian Heritage, 5 January.
Dorland, M. (ed.) (1996) *The Cultural Industries in
    Canada: Problems, Policies and Prospects*, Toronto:
    James Lorimer & Company.

Elderen, P. L. van (1989) 'Pop and Government Policy in the Netherlands (1985)', in Frith, S. (ed.), *World Music, Politics and Social Change*, Manchester: Manchester University Press.

Ewbank, A. J. and Papageorgiou, F. T. (eds) (1997) *Whose Master's Voice? The Development of Popular Music in Thirteen Cultures*, Westport, CT: Greenwood Press.

Flohel, R. (1990) 'The Canadian Music Industry: A Quick Guide', in Baskerville, D. (ed.), *Music Business Handbook and Career Guide*, New York: Sherwood, pp. 495–503.

Garnham, N. (1987) 'Concepts of Culture: Public Policy and the Cultural Industries', in *Cultural Studies*, 1, 1 (January): 23–7.

Grenier, L. (1993) 'Policing French-Language Music on Canadian Radio', in Bennett, T. et al., *Rock and Popular Music*, pp. 119–41.

Hesmondhalgh, D. (1996) 'Flexibility, Post-Fordism and the Music Industries', *Media, Culture and Society*, 18, 3: 469–88.

Laing, D. (1986) 'The Music Industry and the "Cultural Imperialism" Thesis', *Media, Culture and Society*, 8: 331–41.

Lealand, G. (1988) *A Foreign Egg in Our Nest? American Popular Culture in New Zealand*, Wellington: Victoria University Press.

LeBlanc, L. (1999) 'CANADA: They're Never Home Anymore!', *Billboard*, 16 January: 49, 58.

Leyshon, A., Matless, D. and Revill, G. (eds) (1998) *The Place of Music*, New York and London: The Guilford Press.

Melhuish, Martin (1999) 'The Business', *Canadian Musician*, 20th anniversary issue, 21, 2 (March/April): 67–80.

Mitchell, T. (1996) *Popular Music and Local Identity*, London and New York: Leicester University Press.

Negus, K. (1999) *Music Genres and Corporate Cultures*, London and New York: Routledge.

O'Sullivan, T., Hartley, J., Saunders, D., Montgomery, M. and Fiske, J. (1994) *Key Concepts in Communications*, London: Methuen.

Reich, C. (1967) *The Greening of America*, New York: Penguin.

Robinson, D., Buck, E., Cuthbert, M., et al. (1991) *Music At The Margins: Popular Music and Global Diversity*, Newbury Park, CA: Sage.

Rutten, P. (1991) 'Local Popular Music on the National and International Markets', *Cultural Studies*, 5, 3 (October): 294–305.

Shuker, R. (1994) *Understanding Popular Music*, London and New York: Routledge.

Straw, W. (1993) 'The English-Canadian Recording Industry since 1970', in Bennett, T. et al. (eds), *Rock and Popular Music: Politics, Policies, Institutions*, London: Routledge.

——(1996) 'Sound Recording', in Dorland, M. (ed.), *The Cultural Industries in Canada: Problems, Policies and Prospects*, Toronto: Lorimer.

Street, J. (1993) 'Local Differences?: Popular Music and the Local State', *Popular Music*, 12, 1: 42–56.

Task Force (1996) *A Time for Action: Report of the Task Force on the Future of the Canadian Music Industry*, Ottawa: Department of Heritage, March.

Tunstall, J. (1977) *The Media are American*, London: Constable.

Wallis, R. and Malm, K. (1984) *Big Sounds from Small Countries*, London: Constable.

——(eds) (1992) *Media Policy and Music Activity*, London: Routledge.

Part VIII

International Organizations and National Cultures

Introduction to Part VIII

Toby Miller

Cultural policy is generally undertaken in a national frame, but the twentieth century saw the formation of numerous global and regional forms of political, economic, and cultural government, often with quite radical impacts. UNESCO (the United Nations Educational, Scientific, and Cultural Organisation) became the key site of Third World claims for cultural nationalism in the 1970s, as the poorer nations' numerical majority enabled them to gain control: a culturalist/Third World answer to First World capitalism. This in turn opened up the space to call for a New World Information and Communication Order (NWICO), the cultural version of the New International Economic Order that was being argued for in the United Nations Conference on Trade and Development. UNESCO sponsored a series of studies and conferences critical of multinational capital, arguing amongst other things for journalism that was sensitive to local issues rather than corporate news needs. This led to a backlash from First World journalists and media institutions, and then their governments, to the point where the reactionary Reagan and Thatcher régimes removed the US and Britain from UNESCO, battering its budget in the process. UNESCO retreated to a much less powerful position on cultural policy, weakened in turn by the neoliberal tide sweeping international organizations from the 1980s. Nevertheless, many agreements struck under UNESCO's auspices are of great importance.

In 1954, the Organisation had established its attitude to art and the state in *The Convention for the Protection of Cultural Property in the Event of Armed Conflict*. The *Convention* works from the assumption of a universal heritage in the form of art, such that its theft as a consequence of military action is a crime against humanity. Against this proposition stands a cultural–nationalist view that a people has a special relationship to art based on origin, not location or ownership. This is enshrined in UNESCO's 1970 *Convention on the Means of Prohibiting and Preventing the Illicit Import, Export and Transfer of Ownership of Cultural Property*, which focuses not on this global demesne but on the property laws of specific sovereign-states. At different moments, postcolonial nations have called on each of these logics in their struggles with First World theft of artifacts. The fruitful contradictions between these positions comes out in their incapacity to deal with emergent identities, where social change and hybridization bring into question either universalism or myths of origin (Coombe, 1998, pp. 220–3). In 1956, UNESCO put forward its "Recommendation on International Principles Applicable to Archaeological Excavations" and in 1972 a *Convention Concerning the Protection of the World Cultural and National Heritage*. These instruments have suffered from prolix prose that is difficult to articulate with national legislation, and the absence of any mechanism of enforcement, not to mention the arrogant departure by the Reagan and Thatcher Governments. Nevertheless, several museums have adopted similar codes (Whisnant, 1995, p. 310). The salient debates revolve around the relative merits of art forms and customary traditions, interest in cross-cultural knowledge and the desire to own artifacts of other cultures, and global economic inequality (McNaughton, 1995, p. 22).

The United States, for instance, followed UNESCO practice in a 1970 treaty with Mexico and a 1981 compact with Peru on the return of stolen cultural property, followed by the 1982 Cultural Property Law (Whisnant, 1995, pp. 310–11). In 1993, the US Government imposed emergency restrictions on the importation of antiquities from Mali, principally artifacts from the Tellem Caves and clay sculptures from the inland Niger delta. The limitations were in accord with the 1970 *Convention*, but they were the first instance of any First World art importer applying the ban to exports from an African country. Alpha Oumar Konaré, President of Mali at the time, once presided over the International Council of Museums. He emphasized the importance to the Republic of the struggle against illegal archaeology, appreciating the stand of the US given the prestige on the international museum circuit that goes with such holdings. In this instance, the very materials of a people, their customary and artistic heritage, are placed within a market system of value connected to the seemingly benign operation of aesthetic relativism, the outcome a blow to the artifactual history of a nation. Mali's sovereignty was then mobilized as a protocol by an international organization to prevent such losses. Prevailing museum policies in the US assisted this safeguarding. The cultural politics of the situation revolved around four material pressures: the desires of wealthy foreigners to own these objects, the poverty of traditional owners, a push towards global appreciation of cultural production, and the notion of cultural maintenance. It is telling that the US does not offer equivalent cultural protection to its own people, with the exception of Native Americans (McNaughton, 1995; Zolberg, 1995, p. 11).

In addition to UNESCO, there are also various regional economic organizations that adopt cultural policies. In South America, certain post-dictatorship states of the 1990s settled on a form of regional cultural integration that would unite the continent via the Mercado Común del Sur (MERCOSUR). It began in 1991 and has an annual Gross National Product across its membership of US $1 trillion (Burges, 1998; Galperin,

1999, p. 631). MERCOSUR is a response to the realization that an exclusively national approach may hinder the formation of appropriate counters to local and multinational cultural–commercial processes such as migration, textual piracy, and cross-national indigenous solidarity. Culture is more than a frosting to this economic community, because there are intense differences of culture, ethnicity, race, language, and experience of modernity across the region. The 1994 Colonia Protocol liberalizes cross-border investment within the organization, but largely excludes the culture industries, although Argentina permits much more foreign ownership than, for example, Brazil. In 1996, a Cultural Integration Protocol was adopted which sets out the legal infrastructure for cultural integration as a means of increasing economic integration by facilitating the circulation of goods for exhibitions and other cultural events, a writers' exchange, fellowships, and culture houses in poorer nations (Galperin, 1999, pp. 638–9). MERCOSUR's first Visual Arts Biennial in Brazil marked the advent of bilingualism in the south through texts produced in "portunhol," a mix of Spanish and Portuguese, which is regarded as part of the search for a continental unity that is a prerequisite for the legitimacy needed to push for monetary stabilization, regional free trade, and so on.

The European Union (EU) has expanded from its origins as a 1951 free-trade agreement towards political integration over the past forty years. After World War II, anything beyond an economic base would have been problematic, given the sorry story of fascism (Lopez, 1993, p. 143). The 1993 Treaty on European Union expressed the need for cultural policies to ensure both national diversity and continental identity ("Cultural Policy in the European Union"). Article 128 of the Community's charter commits to "the flowering of the cultures of the Member States" in the context of "national and regional diversity" and "common cultural heritage." The Community puts "culture and citizenship... hand in hand" ("'Citizens'").

Pan-nationalism has generally failed at political unification because of cultural difference and communication limitations. The latter problem does not confront Europe today, but the former does, and the period since the mid-1970s has seen the Community turn decisively in the direction of cultural programs, partly for political reasons and partly for economic. The dominant definition of the "new European" is organized via Judaeo-Christian religious beliefs, Hellenistic accounts of the polity, arts, and sciences, and Roman jurisprudence: they distinguish the World Wars started by capitalistic nationalism from transnational culture and seek to invent a heritage to counter Americanization (Borneman and Fowler, 1997, p. 488).

But there is much criticism of the fact that this is a top-down definition, with the running towards European integration undertaken by bureaucrats and politicians rather than local forces as they seek to prove to Europeans that cultural policies are adding to their shared heritage, not just inventing it. This challenge is itself articulated by the EU, which says it seeks to transform "the technocrats' Europe into a People's Europe." EU directives deploying such logics are increasingly under attack for the partiality of this amalgam and its connection to imperialist tropes and "othering" of Asia and Africa. Critics refer to the EU as "magisters of culture" (Pieterse, 1991, pp. 3, 5, 6). On the right, Thatcher always insisted that the EU eschew any fantasy of "some identikit European personality" on the one hand and a Leviathan-like "super-state" on the other (quoted in Schlesinger, 1991, p. 184). For cultural critics disappointed with the yearning for the authentic but equally dismissive of pragmatism, this raises the specter of being simultaneously "essentialist and instrumentalist" (Shore, 1996, p. 482). But is this the intention of European literature prizes, museum networks, TV channels, and so on? Would any resulting "leviathan" by that time have become organic? For some, there is a link to the Enlightenment that binds Europeans, and this has become part of the official ideology of the EU. Progress, reason, rationality, and humanism are exemplified in the choice of Schiller's "Ode to Joy" (the lyrics to Beethoven's Ninth Symphony) to be its anthem (Shore, 1996, p. 481; Lopez, 1993; "Culture/ Audiovisual").

Cultural issues within civil society but beyond business are left in the hands of the newly fetishized buffers between state, religion, population, and media – non-governmental organizations (NGOs), the prescription for third-sector change that can magically mediate between citizen, government, and corporation. The US has 2 million such institutions, almost all of them formed since 1970. Russia has gained 650,000 since the end of state socialism and Kenya births 240 a year.

Most NGOs associated with aid are effectively regranting institutions that utilize state moneys in ways designed to avoid accusations of neocolonialism from the Left and governmental waste from the Right. So the US gives US $700 million annually to Africa through surrogates, and Médecins Sans Frontières derives half its budget from state agencies. Everybody benefits by this neat sleight of hand. Or do they? Some bodies become captive of their real funders – so Congress's taste for good Christian souls holding the purse strings has led to the neologism RINGOs (religious NGOs), symbiotic relations with governments produce GRINGOs (governmental NGOs), and corporate self-modeling offers BINGOs (Business NGOs) (*Economist*). No wonder the World Bank's claim that NGOs guarantee a mixed-internet model for the Third World reads so spuriously (Nulens and Van Audenhove, 1999, p. 459). As per UNESCO, the history of MERCOSUR, the EU, and NGOs is one of intense utopianism (Enlightenment rhetoric) brokered and colored by economic self-interest, with cultural policy a key site for articulation.

Consider Europe. The abiding logic of the EU's audiovisual policy is really commercial: it clearly favors existing large concerns that can be built upon further. And the New International Division of Cultural Labor has served to bring into doubt the opposition US:entertainment::Europe:education, with art cinema effectively a "Euro-American" genre in terms of finance and management, and much of Hollywood itself owned by foreigners. In this sense, the seeming discontinuity with earlier concerns, when the EU had a primarily economic personality, is misleading: a notion of cultural sovereignty underpins concerns *vis-à-vis* the US, but so too does support for monopoly capital and the larger states inside its own walls. Meanwhile, the old notions of state cultural sovereignty that were so crucial to Europe's political traditions are being attenuated by the twin forces of "bruxellois centralization" from outside and separatist ethnicities from within.

The development of a cultural imperialism thesis, in Latin America in particular, argued that the US, as the world's leading producer and exporter of television, was transferring its dominant value system to others. There was said to be a corresponding diminution in the vitality and standing of local languages and traditions, and hence a threat to national identity. Latin America was the cradle of this research tradition, because it combined features which standard development theory deemed to be incommensurate: long-term independence of political sovereignty and perennially unequal economic exchange. The thesis regarded cultural imperialism as isomorphic to other forms of imperialism. As Herbert Schiller expresses it, "the media-cultural component in a developed, corporate economy supports the economic objectives of the decisive industrial–financial sectors (i.e. the creation and extension of the consumer society)."

This is just one illustration of the tendency in European debate to conflate the sign "mass culture" with the sign "American," denying in the process the power of the extraordinary heterogeneity of the domestic US audience and conflating source of supply with impact at point of consumption. At the Symposium International sur l'Identité Culturelle Européene in Paris in 1988, the *leit motif* was terror in the sight of "la déferlante américaine – the American wave." One is reminded here of Billy Wilder's 1948 film, *A Foreign Affair*. A US Congressperson is referring to postwar relief efforts in Europe: "If you give them food, it's democracy. If you leave the labels on, it's imperialism." Nevertheless, it is worth noting that Brazilian audiences watching customized versions of *Dallas* had their viewing of a supposedly local text punctuated by advertisements for Levi's, General Motors, Volkswagen, and Coca-Cola.

Of course, having identified this as a problem, the next move for the subordinated is to form themselves as distinctly different and able to represent that difference via the concept of a nation. There is little agreement over what nations are, what national identity is, or how to explain national movements. But culture is clearly important here at the level of the constitution of community, the performance of typical words and actions. Elements such as idiom and syntax are important means for the transmission of retraining at times of economic change as well, so that these matters quickly become of formal, instrumental concern in the governance of populations. A standard language – Parisian French – was, for example, an essential component in the emergence of the *bourgeoisie* after the French Revolution. And when considering what can go into a public's constitution of itself and its surroundings, it is hard to decry the presentation of facts such as that 87 percent of English-language Caribbean television was imported in 1988, up 10 percent in ten years, with most of it in the field of drama.

But to repeat, the point has been well made that the valorization of traditional cultural formations is frequently profoundly repressive of particular categories of person. The enunciation, disposition, and protection of a culture may be done by and for local elites in the name of a romanticized harking after authentic community spirit. Such practices stress differences and distinctions between one nation and another even as they suppress intra-national inequalities. The development of telecommunications systems in Nigeria, India, and the Philippines provides instances where a rhetoric of technology transfer and community access has essentially served the interests of multinational corporations and local elites whilst being publicly funded. And the notion of the redemptive powers of certain genres (drama, news, and sport, for instance) may also serve the interests of particular categories of person – most conceptions of cultural conservation are forwarded by a particular group which claims to possess a particular geopolitical space and goes guarantor of its cultural validity and authenticity.

References

Borneman, John and Nick Fowler. "Europeanization." *Annual Review of Anthropology*, no. 26 (1997): 487–514.

Burges, Sean W. "Strength in Numbers: Latin American Trade Blocs, a Free Trade Area of the Americas and the Problem of Economic Development." *Council on Hemispheric Affairs Occasional Paper*, no. 2 (April 1998).

"Citizens' Access to Culture." <http://europa.eu.int/en/comm/dg10/culture/en/citizens.html>.

Coombe, Rosemary. *The Cultural Life of Intellectual Properties: Authorship, Appropriation, and the Law*. Durham: Duke University Press, 1998.

"Cultural Policy in the European Union." <http://www.europa.eu.int/pol/cult/en/info.htm>.

"Culture/Audiovisual Council: Outcome of June 28 Session." *European Report*, June 30, 1999.

Galperin, Hernan. "Cultural Industries Policy in Regional Trade Agreements: The Cases of NAFTA, the European Union and MERCOSUR." *Media Culture & Society* 21, no. 5 (1999): 627–48.

Lopez, Susana. "The Cultural Policy of the European Community and its Influence on Museums." *Museum Management and Curatorship* 12, no. 2 (1993): 143–57.

McNaughton, Patrick R. "Malian Antiquities and Contemporary Desire." *African Arts* 28, no. 4 (1995): 22–7.

Nulens, Gert and Leo Van Audenhove. "An Information Society in Africa? An Analysis of the Information Society Policy of the World Bank, ITU and ECA." *Gazette* 61, no. 6 (1999): 451–71.

Pieterse, Jan Nederveen. "Fictions of Europe." *Race & Class* 32, no. 3 (1991): 3–10.

Schiller, Herbert I. "Not Yet the Post-Imperialist Era." *Critical Studies in Mass Communication* 8, no. 1 (1991): 14.

Schlesinger, Philip. *Media, State and Nation: Political Violence and Collective Identities*. London: Sage, 1991.

Shore, Chris. "Transcending the Nation-State?: The European Commission and the (Re)-Discovery of Europe." *Journal of Historical Sociology* 9, no. 4 (1996): 473–96.

"Sins of the Secular Missionaries." *Economist* 29 January 2000: 25–7.

Whisnant, David E. *Rascally Signs in Sacred Places: The Politics of Culture in Nicaragua*. Chapel Hill: University of North Carolina Press, 1995.

Zolberg, Vera L. "Museum Culture and the Threat to National Identity in the Age of the GATT." *Journal of Arts Management, Law and Society* 25, no. 1 (1995): 5–16.

Chapter 21

Television Set Production at the US–Mexico Border: Trade Policy and Advanced Electronics for the Global Market

Mari Castañeda Paredes

Electronics is the infrastructure. It is going to underpin and shape the world's economy, and potentially its political organizations, in the 21st century. It is not just an industrial segment. And it is our belief, after much study, that [advanced] technologies – not just television – will be at the hub of the information age's infrastructure. American Electronics Association, *Hearing before the Committee on Governmental Affairs*, August 1, 1989

This chapter is a discussion of television set production at the US–Mexico border and the political-economic policies that have transformed the borderlands into one of the most important export-processing enclaves for electronics. Indeed, Mexico's *maquiladoras* (also known as in-bond or twin-plants) are the biggest producers of television electronics intended for the global market. With the emergence of new media industries, such as advanced digital television, the *maquiladora* program is fast becoming a critical sector in the international division of advanced electronics labor, and a dominant feature of Mexico's political, economic and cultural domains.

In 1988 the US Congressional Budget Office announced that the worldwide electronics sector surpassed $500 billion in market sales (1989, p. 27). Ten years later, the division of electronic components alone – semiconductors, electronic tubes, printed circuit boards and cathode ray tubes – produces over $300 billion annually,

with the US dominating a third of the marketplace (US DOC, 1999, p. 8). The US International Trade Administration contends that "electronic components are the fundamental building blocks for the [advanced] electronics industry," with a wide array of enterprises – telecommunications, automotive, medical, armed forces, computers and television – increasingly using components in their products and/or services. Thirty years earlier, Herbert I. Schiller proclaimed that advanced communications and electronics were becoming critical sectors in the American and international economy (1992, p. 53). The Clinton Administration's strive in the 1990s to develop an integrated National Information Infrastructure (NII) and a "Framework for Global Electronic Commerce" confirmed Schiller's prophecy regarding the extension of the American capitalist system into new areas of cultural production, like the Internet (White House, 1997; see also US NTIA, 1997).

Lent and Sussman (1998), Miller (1998) and Dan Schiller (1999) have argued that these new digital industries are girded by traditional modes of economic production and by what Miller calls a "new international division of cultural labor" (p. 172). Like manufacturing, digital commerce creates seamless, inter-linked systems of production and distribution that camouflage the spatial division of "men and women who labor to make these commodities available for public and private use" (Mosco 1998, p. 5; see also Siegel, 1998; Barnet and Cavanagh, 1994). The transcendence of locational boundaries also requires the facilitation of the State, and its increasingly liberal behavior is a key shift in global political economy. Trade policies such as the North American Free Trade Agreement (NAFTA) for instance, are utilized as political-economic tools for creating and extending transnational centers of production while concurrently exerting pressure on the global economic system. The production of television equipment at the US–Mexico border is at the center of "this competitive struggle for global market shares" and the State's role in preserving free trade ideology (Sinclair, 1993, pp. 220–1).

The chapter is divided into three sections, in the first of which I discuss the economic policies that shaped the context for the development of the *maquiladora* program in Mexico. The second section provides a specific examination of television electronics *maquiladoras* and the system's specific relationship to the NAFTA. In the last part of this chapter I briefly discuss the labor and cultural implications of the *maquila* production system for border communities, a critical issue that I would like to examine further in future work.

The Transnationalization of Television Production

In order to understand the more recent history of *maquiladora* TV manufacturing, we need to step back to examine a little-known law passed sixty years ago, the same year as the 1934 Communications Act – the Foreign-Trade Zones (FTZ) Act. Whereas the Communications Act and its creation of the Federal Communications Commission received tremendous fanfare that year, the FTZ Act and its creation of the Foreign

Trade Zones Board went unnoticed (US DOC, 1997, p. 1). Yet the FTZ Act became an important statute in the manufacturing, repackaging, relabeling, repairing, and storing of television sets, radio receivers and telephones in the US. FTZ regulations permitted manufacturers within designated zones to import foreign merchandise, such as electronic components, on a tariff-free basis under the conditions that imported components were utilized in domestic production. By manufacturing and assembling products in a foreign-trade zone, corporations were granted preferential tariff treatment, thus decreasing overhead costs (National Association of FTZ, 2000, p. 1).

The FTZ policy supplemented the US Customs program at a time when the international political economy manifested "an important transformation in the [re]configuration of capital" (Van Der Pijl, 1998, p. 96). The FTZ Board claims that the primary purposes of the program centered on removing "certain disincentives associated with manufacturing in the United States" and encouraging businesses to retain some level of domestic residence (US CBO, 1999, p. 3). By reducing tariffs via FTZ the US government sought to "promote American competitiveness" in international trade (National Association of FTZ, 2000, p. 4). Accordingly, many FTZ sites came to reside along the 300-mile stretch of the US–Mexico border where ports of entry have twin cities or sister townships on both sides (like San Diego–Tijuana, El Paso–Cordova Juarez, Douglas–Agua Prieta) that conveniently host hundreds of export-oriented factories.[1] The US Department of Commerce (1997) stated that the $16 billion foreign-trade zones industry is an "important and enduring public policy which [is] part of the government's total efforts to maintain a level playing field for [US interests] in international trade" (p. 8).

Like the US government's effort to bolster an export economy, Mexico also experimented with developing its own version of free trade zones. The Mexican government's launch of the Border Industrialization Program (BIP) in the mid-1960s stabilized the border economic crisis at the end of the twenty-three year old *Bracero* (farmworker) Program in which cheap immigrant laborers were hired for various US businesses, most notably agriculture. However, pressure from American unions to dismantle the program resulted in the US Government's mass deportation of workers to the Mexican border (Fox, 1999, p. 100). The overabundance of laborers in addition to the growing demand for improved tariff structures for export manufacturing plants provided the fertile ground for transforming the border into a *zona libre*. BIP allowed "investors to temporarily import duty-free all the inputs, machinery, and parts needed for assembly," which formally established the *maquiladora* industry (Carroll, 1995, p. 161). Mexican policymakers regarded the *maquiladora* system as a "temporary economic solution" for the long-term problems of unemployment, limited foreign capital, and the area's deteriorating infrastructure with the hope that a more permanent model would later be established (Grunwald, 1989, p. 10).

Quintero Ramirez (1990) explains that the transformation of the border into a primarily (foreign-owned) free trade zone reinforced the historical, asymmetrical relationship between US capital and Mexican labor, and authorized "US companies to procure services, products, and labor that were too costly or illegal in America" (p. 22). The harmonization of Mexico's exports trade policy with the flourishing FTZ program in the United States in the mid-1960s created an interdependent system that became impossible to dismantle. An FTZ licensed company, for example, would export TV electronic components to a *maquiladora* in Mexico as interim or "in-bond" materials. Once the products were subassembled into partially or wholly finished commodities, the *maquiladora* would re-export the products, such as TV sets, back to the United States. Mexican Customs would at that point, impose a processing tariff but only on the value-added in Mexico, which for the most part consisted of labor. Next to Sri Lanka, where the average production worker earns 47 cents an hour, Mexican *maquiladoras* are one of the cheapest forms of production with an average wage of $1.83, seventeen dollars less than in the United States (US ITC, 1999, B-56). Lastly, the products were sent to a US-based plant for final assembly, repackaging, relabeling, or storage. If these activities occurred in an FTZ, the products qualified for "domestic content" treatment and reduced tariff processing. Consequently, FTZ and *maquiladora* policies created a cross-border

system of production that most benefited (and continues to benefit) US transnational interests. The synergistic relationship between American-based capital and Mexican labor transfigured the "temporary" *maquiladoras* into permanent fixtures across the borderlands.

Maquiladoras and TV Electronics

Currently, there are 4,500 *maquiladora* plants located along the US–Mexico border with a work force of over one million (Kraul and Smith, 1999, A1), and over 700,000 of those employees reside in either Tijuana or Mexicali, Baja California. The population in this limited geographic area is expected to swell beyond three million in this decade, more than any other export-processing zone in the world. With its growing pool of workers, *la frontera norte* (especially at the entry ports of Tijuana and Mexicali) is "the most advantageous global export platform" for manufacturing, and transnational trade (ibid., A11). The Institute for Policy Studies concurs that the leading corporations, for instance General Electric of Massachusetts, "have already established a sizable base in Mexico and [are using] NAFTA to expand that base" (Institute for Policy Studies, 1993, p. 5). The nullification of multilateral "obstacles," such as tariff-barriers and protective policies, further integrates commerce and trade policy on the North American continent. This integration process gained steam in the early 1970s with the rise of US foreign trade zones/subzones as well as the expansion of export production in newly developing countries (Bell, 1971, pp. 112–51). Increasingly, the US–Mexican border became central in the drive towards integration because of its low-cost labor force, sizable consumer market, favorable regulatory environment, and prime location as an export focal point between the US, Canada, the Pacific Rim, and the rest of the Americas.

Of all the manufacturing sectors, electronics-based *maquiladoras* constitute the largest percentage of "production-sharing" operations on the border, which corresponds with the market surge of electronics components and "global efforts to reduce manufacturing costs" (US ITC, 1999, pp. 1–2). Most studies examining electronics-based *maquiladoras* view the factories as support networks for the broader consumer market (automobiles, petroleum, apparels) but very little scholarship seriously examines the *maquiladora* program as a "global export platform" for television electronics (Eden and Molot, 1993; Dillon, 1998). Yet advanced electronics production in Mexican *maquila* enclaves is one of the most productive sectors, manufacturing more than "120 million TVs and 60 million desktop computers" annually (Hart, Lenway, and Linden, 1997, p. 3). From 1995 to 1998, the US imported from Mexico $14 billion worth of *completed* color television receivers, but exported $5 billion in TV components and parts – not completed sets (US ITC, 1999, B-47). These numbers correspond with the rise of employment in TV *maquiladoras*, approximately 4,000 per year since the mid-1990s (Romano, 1997, p. 12). The US International Trade Commission notes that the sum total employment in foreign TV manufacturing may actually be higher since the numbers currently available do not include the production of TV-related components, such as integrated circuit boards and wooden cabinetry; only the number of employees completing TV sets (ibid., C-4).

The labor-intensive operations required for building TV receivers and the "lower labor costs" in Mexico were the prime reasons why manufacturers moved color television set production, particularly for small screen sets, south of the border, and consequently propelled the "integration" of North American television set production (ibid., pp. 1–2). Initially, factories in Mexico supplied American manufacturers with subassembled components for color receiver assembly. By the end of the twentieth century every US-based TV transnational had significant operations in Mexico including the "stuffing" of printed circuit boards and electron rods in color picture tubes and sets. The high labor content required for TV receiver manufacturing motivated companies "to take advantage of the [low wage] *maquiladora* program, while design and R&D remained in the US" (ibid.). Statistics from the US Department of Commerce confirm that since NAFTA's ratification, transnational corporations have extended their capitalization of foreign assembly, production-sharing, and export processing programs such as *maquiladoras* in order to "enhance competitiveness" in the "fierce" global economy (US ITC, 1999, p. 3).

The history of television manufacturing in the United States is a rich tale of fierce foreign competition, the surge of new innovations such as large screen TVs, and political-economic policies that promoted "open markets." The failure of the US government to develop a stringent policy against what the Committee to Preserve American Color Television (COMPACT) called the "Japanese threat" resulted in vulnerability of the American market (US House of Representatives, 1989, p. 240). Between the US Treasury not actively enforcing anti-dumping duties intended to protect the domestic industry, and Japan's high import tariffs prohibiting American TV manufacturers from entering the Japanese market, COMPACT predicted that the American-owned TV manufacturing industry would eventually deteriorate. In addition, the final assembly operations permitted by the FTZ Act allowed many foreign manufacturers to assemble color televisions in the United States (with picture tube subassembly plants in Mexico), thus circumventing the Trade Commission's orders against "predatory pricing."

The lack of trade law enforcement by the US government interestingly paralleled the free trade mantra of GATT and the World Trade Organization: "world peace through world trade" (Barnet and Cavanagh, 1994, p. 250). Jefferson Cowie (1999) explains that the marketplace, once an actual place location for the exchange of goods and services, seems to have grown into a free-flowing torrent of capital and information that threatens to overwhelm workers' grasp on the pace of history. Pacts such as NAFTA place an official stamp on the idea that we live in a new era defined by the mobility of capital and the weakening of organized labor and the regulatory state. Symptomatic of the "reformation of capitalism," the "locational revolution" in production, and the "manic logic" of globalization, these new developments, it is often argued, have recast the world economic system at tremendous cost to workers and their communities (p. 3).

Indeed, the recent public protests against the WTO talks in Seattle, Washington and Washington, DC reflect an awareness and dawning intolerance towards labor exploitation, environmental putrescence, and free trade policies that further extend the "spatialization" of production on a global scale. International labor and human-rights organizations, like *Global Exchange*, argue that multinational organizations – with the help of government policies – are "marching humanity, along with the rest of the planet, into a toxic, money-maddened, repressive future" (Finnegan, 2000, p. 42). This may seem like an extreme judgment, but let us consider one example. The development of the digital television industry did not stem from the public's demand for a higher resolution TV set. Rather, its emergence is a direct result of the growing commercial and network convergences taking place between well-established sectors like television electronics and new media, like the Internet. Embodied in this convergence is the "transnationalization of economic activity," which Dan Schiller argues is "directly generalizing the social and cultural range of the capitalist economy as never before. That is why I refer to this new epoch as one of *digital capitalism*." The deployment of labor and capital at the level of manufacturing is one of the most apparent modes that reveal the dilemmas with global economic integration.

The broadening assembly of the world's television sets at *maquiladoras* on the US–Mexico border illustrates the magnitude and implications of this integration. According to John DaPonte, Executive Secretary of the Foreign-Trade Zones Board in the US Department of Commerce, "shipments across national borders have vastly multiplied in the past half century, and countries [such as Mexico] have become active participants in production and trade. Finished products are no longer simply shipped into or out of countries" (1995, pp. 8–12). The high-tech production of television equipment along the Tijuana–San Diego borderlands is a microcosm of a larger economic trend that encompasses the capitalization of less-industrialized border regions (helped along by government investment incentives and extensive telecommunication networks) in order to create "global export platforms" – often at the expense of mistreated laborers and squandered natural resources.

By exporting low-skill, low-cost, labor-intensive jobs to Mexico's *maquiladoras* while maintaining higher-end, knowledge-based assignments in the US, which in fact characterizes the historical industrial strategy of US-based television manufacturers, multinational corpor-

ations are able to create a system of "production-sharing." But as virtuous as this may sound, in reality the asymmetrical division of labor exploited by the *maquila* industry is related to what Sklair (1993) calls the "reformation of capitalism" (p. 156). Understanding the multidimensional characteristics of this change is critical because although capital is transformed and restructured within national and regional boundaries, it operates on a global scale. For many television equipment firms, "Mexican *maquiladoras* are in fact pivotal to their North American operations and expansion plans" (Choi and Kenney, 1995, p. 3). Since the mid-1980s, "it's been the major electronics firms who have dominated the television *maquila* industry in Tijuana, and have likewise propelled the new phase of high-tech *maquiladoras*" (Quintero Ramirez, 1990, p. 32).

Yet on the surface the *maquiladora* program appears innocuous and insignificant on account that the transborder system parcels assembly procedures into disconnected fragments. According to the San Diego Economic Development Corporation's twin-plant directory, there are only eighteen *maquiladoras* – out of six hundred – which manufacture entire television sets or television-related components in Tijuana (1993). If the directory is taken at face value, television production actually appears to be a minuscule part of the *maquiladora* industry. The San Diego EDC directory fails to mention, however, the countless television-related products manufactured by *maquiladoras*, such as harnesses, interrupters, connectors, inductors, transformers, coils, electronic sensors, printed circuits, cables, diode rectifiers, transistors, electromagnetic relays, channel converters, and metallic exhibitors. The failure to include these products although they are necessary for building television sets accommodates the "Made in the USA" project of multinational manufacturers. According to Sklair (1993), trade policies such as NAFTA grant the corporation "enormous power since it can now unite capital, technology, and labor in a historically restructured form" (p. 212).

NAFTA and Maquiladoras

The enactment of NAFTA further clears the way for all multinational corporations, especially those with high import taxes, to take advantage of the Mexican labor force residing along the US–Mexican border. The two-way trade between the US and Mexico currently generates over $34 billion dollars per year, and US trade representatives expect American exports to the rest of Latin America to reach well over "$232 billion by 2010, more than the European Union and Japan combined" (Kolbe, 1989, p. 49; Schrader, 1999, A1). The integration of North America is not a recent phenomenon but a historical trend in the "rationalization" of transborder industrial activity in which manufacturing is just one of a series of processes that also includes marketing and retail. As President Clinton declared, "multilateral trade agreements" are part of a long-term goal toward creating a global economic policy that transforms the Western Hemisphere "into the largest single market in the world, stretching from Alaska to Argentina" (Flanigan, 2000, C1). Policies promoting the elimination of trade and investment barriers as well as the elaboration of exportation strategies are central to Mexico's growth as an "exporters' hub" for global commerce.

Electronics alone is expected to grow 20 percent annually as a result of the NAFTA-based factory tax accord that will treat foreign multinationals who own *maquiladoras* as affiliate domestic firms (Kraul and Smith, 1999, A1). In addition to the low-tax treatment, the accord also makes headway towards eliminating, at least in Mexico, "domestic content" percentages and transportation regulations in production-sharing enterprises. This is important in the new era of television and multimedia equipment *maquiladoras* since many of the high-tech components – microprocessors, A/D converters, digital signal processors, compression circuitry, and image processors – can now be imported from other low-wage countries, thus cutting costs even further (Hart, 1989, p. 31). In addition to advanced digital television, these core technologies are also used in automobiles, aircraft, security systems, and automated machinery. Consequently, as advanced communication applications are broadened and merged with traditional sectors in the acceleration of "new international markets," the *maquiladora* industry acquires an increasingly critical role in the long-term growth of the US export economy (Schiller, 1999, p. 88).

The factories on the border are also central to Mexico's economic growth. They currently account for "46 percent of Mexico's $40 billion in exports," generating over $200 million in value-added revenue, and Mexican officials, especially those in Baja California, expect multinationals to continue investing in fixed capital (Kraul and Smith, 1999, A1). Politically and economically, Mexico is doing its part to insure that investors remain in the country indefinitely. In addition to NAFTA, Mexico revised its "Ley de Inversiones Extranjeras" (Foreign Investment Law) in an effort to create an unrestricted Mexico (Gobierno del Estado de Baja California 1994, p. 5; see also Easton, Grinspun and Paraskevopoulos, 1996). These policies highly impact the Mexican domestic market. From 2001, the sale of *maquiladora* export products was no longer restricted to the border regions (Baja California, Chihuahua, Coahuila, Nuevo Leon, Sonora, and Tamaulipas). Rather all *maquiladora*-produced goods will be sold without restraints throughout Mexico's national market. Under the rubric of free trade, the "open market" of capital and labor is touted as the global economic model of the twenty-first century. Unfortunately this hurts communities that are dependent on the small producer economy, but cannot compete with the economic resources of transnational firms. Yet the promotion of free trade policies is part of the larger objective to create a transnational environment in which products and capital flow freely between the US, Canada and Mexico, and in the future, to the rest of Latin America. As a result we will see not less but more dependence on low-wage *maquiladoras* as the production of next-generation consumer electronics products and services like DTV becomes an integral part of the global political economy.

The Case of Sony Electronics Corporation

Sony Electronics Corporation owns the largest Baja California border region television *maquiladora*/twin-plant assembly in the world, employing over 20,000 workers (Sony, 2000a). Along with the San Diego-based Sony Technology Design Center, which the city of San Diego licensed as a foreign-trade zone, the five *maquiladoras* in Tijuana and Mexicali manufacture approximately ten million color television sets annually, 80 percent of which are sold in the US and Latin America (Khosrow, 1990, p. 28). According to Sony, its North American operations "make up about one-third of the [company's] worldwide operations, and its US operations [concentrate] on engineering, design, sales, marketing, distribution and customer service" while its plants in Mexico focus on manufacturing (Sony, 2000b, pp. 1–2). In 1999, *Industry Week* magazine described Sony as "one of the world's largest publicly held manufacturing companies," and praised the Sony Technology Design Center for its "production-sharing" operations with the Mexican factories (ibid.). It also ranked Sony's Tijuana-based *Centro de Manufactura de Mexico* (the largest of all the factories employing 10,000 workers) the #1 *maquiladora* for its success in achieving "product synergy" between its border manufactories.

Yet "product synergy" and "production-sharing" are merely decorous labels for a transborder division of labor that employs low-wage, low-skilled factory workers in Tijuana, which they hire by the thousands, while concurrently hiring higher-skilled, knowledge workers in the US. The $46 million expansion of Sony's twin-plant operations on the border in 1997 accentuates their strategic plan to utilize cost-cutting tactics in order to dominate the digital era of consumer electronics (ibid.). According to the Sony Corporation of America, the expansion of its North American electronics operations will allow the company to "meet US market needs in a quickly evolving electronics market [as well as] export products and components to other worldwide markets" (ibid).

Sony announced that it plans to "evolve" households in the next decade with a menu of home entertainment and TV equipment choices. As a vertically integrated corporation it "has a unique vantage point as the only company involved in virtually every aspect of the digital television chain – from broadcasting and content creation to TV set manufacturing" (ibid.). Given DTV presents an opportunity for the convergence between television, telecommunications and computers, Sony Electronics is also currently forming strategic alliances with a medley of business enterprises (Microsoft, Intel, General Instrument, Philips, and Sun Microsystems) in attempt to take advantage of the metamorphosing

advanced communications industry. They're working with broadcasters to deliver the high-definition camera, editing and special effects equipment and monitors they need for digital TV programming; with computer server makers to develop MPEG-2 encoders and decoders needed to transmit DTV feeds; and with content providers to create high-definition programming and Internet software. In the new era of television, one company representative explained that "the best strategy is synergy. We are now becoming horizontally and vertically integrated with both our [manufacturing] plants and creative resources" (Interview, 1993). This puts Sony as well as other electronics corporations in a prime position to take advantage of the favorable tariff treatment provided by NAFTA as well as prepare for the shift towards digital television (Kraul, 1997, D1).

Labor and Culture at the US–Mexico Border

A discussion of *maquiladoras* cannot be complete without addressing the issues of labor and culture at the US–Mexico border, one of the most populated export-processing zones in the world.

Since the inauguration of NAFTA in 1994, the *maquiladora* industry has surpassed productivity levels in all sectors. With transnational companies manufacturing and exporting more products from Mexico's *zona libre*, then it is feasible to presume that wages, living standards and working conditions have improved for Mexican *maquila* laborers. On the contrary, wages have remained stagnant since the *maquiladora* program began in 1965 and many plants have not (voluntarily) stopped operation since first opening their doors; they literally manufacture products "24 hours a day, seven days a week, including holidays" (La Botz, 1992, pp. 163–4). In addition to 9–14 hour workdays, assembly line employees are exposed to hazardous and toxic industrial waste like zinc, lead, fiberglass, freon, nitric acid, and phosphate. A 1989 AFL–CIO study found that *maquiladora* corporate owners often ignored the serious environmental, health, and safety problems. "[Owners] frequently denied basic health and safety protections against occupational illness or disease, and [Mexican workers] risked the loss of their jobs if they protested these dangerous conditions" (ibid, p. 168). Young women workers are particularly put at-risk in *maquiladoras*. Perceived as "passive, healthy and impressionable," girls in their teens and twenties are believed to withstand oppressive working conditions and the sexual harassment of male supervisors. La Botz (1992) blames the situation in *maquiladoras* on the lack of independent, democratic labor unionism where rights would be protected and respected. Rather the unions currently in place are government-endorsed entities that are often utilized by corporate owners "as vehicles for employer intimidation and coercion" (p. 169).

This is not to say that unlike Mexico, union activism in US manufacturing plants has higher success rates. At one particular twin-plant in Southern California, where employee rosters are filled with the names of Mexican/Latino Spanish-speaking immigrants, union busting and union passivity are common, often silencing workers and/or limiting their access to labor rights information (Cordero, 2000). Fox (1999) asserts that the explicit operations on the US–Mexico border prove that labor issues are not "passé" but opportunities to investigate the implications and contradictions of North American economic integration (p. 2). In fact the economic, political and cultural transformations reinforced by NAFTA demonstrate the theoretical and empirical need to continue examining Mexico's *fronteras* as more than bounded geographic locales on a map, but as transborder centers of contestation and cooperation that link detached sites of production, consumption, and trade on a regional and global scale (Sassen, 1998, p. 74). In Los Angeles, a diverse group of Chicanos is joining forces with *frontera* academics, artists, writers, and musicians in an effort to develop a transborder dialogue that is long overdue (Sarabia, 2000). The goal is to historically explicate (through literature, music, and art) how *maquiladoras* and US public policy have impacted communities on both sides of the border. This is a new endeavor for a new millennium that hopes to integrate *el pueblo* on its own terms.

Conclusion

Trade policies are an important tool in the race to dominate the global market, especially in televi-sion electronics production. According to the US Department of State, the US–Mexico border is central to the long-term economic growth of the United States, and governments on the North American continent are developing economic ordinances that promote the utilization of tariff-free *maquiladoras* (Schrader, 1999, A1). With a work force of over one million, and a production capacity estimated to grow over $40 billion in this year alone, officials from the US, Canada, and Mexico are currently negotiating a new tax regime that would allow the "free flow" of trade to occur permanently. One Canadian government official asserted that by utilizing free trade accords as "levers," industrialized countries could influence the economic policies of developing countries, an "effective tool short of war" (Weston, 1994, p. 69).

Transborder government policies have historically played an important role in transforming the US–Mexico border into a site for high-tech production for the global market. The case of television *maquiladora* manufacturing is just one example of how political-economic policies are utilized to expand commerce regionally. More importantly, it illustrates how the rise of particular industries, such as electronic components, are transforming the US–Mexico border into a global export platform for North American production. Yet Mexico is paying a high price in its bid to become an international player. Free markets do not "level-the-playing-field," as policymakers claim, and the present-day battles in Mexico over social disparities and the degeneration of public interest objectives reflect a deepening divide between social classes. During a recent university strike where military officers attacked the demonstrators, Mexican students, professors, and social activists complained how "nobody is seeing the danger we face in the country. [The] state, in partnership with industry, wants to dismantle what is the essence of a public university and establish a system that only feeds the needs of big corporations in the private sector" (Smith, 2000, A1). The strike in Mexico exemplifies the ironic twist of trade policy. While government officials argue that multilateral tariff agreements are necessary in order to systematize long-term economic stability, they fail to describe how economic change will specifically develop social stability or the redistribution of resources. As President Clinton noted in the 2000 World

Economic Forum, "those who believe globalization is only about market economics are wrong. We simply cannot expect trade alone to carry the burden of lifting nations out of poverty" (Wright, 2000, A1). Conveniently President Clinton failed to detail how the US planned to achieve this righteous goal. For now, government is counting on globalization and free trade to bridge the gap between the world's rich and poor.

Notes

The author wishes to thank Professor Dan Schiller for guiding the dissertation chapter on which this article is based, and the editors for providing helpful comments.

1 Texas and California hold the number one and number two spots for the most foreign-trade zones in the US, with the former hosting 81 sites and the latter 31 respectively, and each of these sites has between one to fifty companies operating within the FTZ.

References

Barnet, Richard J. and Cavanagh, John. 1994. *Global Dreams: Imperial Corporations and the New World Order*. New York: Touchstone.

Bell, Harry A. 1971. *Tariff Profiles in Latin Amerca: Implications for Pricing Structures and Economic Integration*. New York: Praeger Publishers. pp. 112–51.

Carroll, Elsie L. Echeverri. 1995. "Flexible Production and NAFTA." *NAFTA and Trade Liberalization in the Americas*. Austin, Texas: Bureau of Business Research.

Choi, Dae Won and Kenney, Martin. June 27, 1995. *The Globalization of Korean Industry: Korean Maquiladoras in Mexico*. UC Davis: Institute of Governmental Affairs. No. 6.

Cordero, Maria. January 13, 2000. Interview. Twin-Plant employee.

Cowie, Jefferson. 1999. *Capital Moves: RCA's 70-Year Quest for Cheap Labor*. Ithaca: Cornell University Press.

Dillon, Sam. January 13, 1998. "Sex Bias at Border Plants in Mexico Reported by US." *The New York Times*.

Easton, George E., Grinspun, Ricardo and Paraskevopoulos, Christos C. 1996. *Economic Integration in the Americas*. Cheltenham, UK: Edward Elgar.

Eden, Lorraine and Molot, Maureen Appel. 1993. "Continentalizing the North American Auto Industry." Cameron, Maxwell A. and Grinspun, Ricardo. *The Political Economy of North American Free Trade Agreement*. New York: St. Martin's Press.

Finnegan, William. April 17, 2000. "After Seattle: Anarchists Get Organized." *The New Yorker*.

Flanigan, James. February 2, 2000. "US Outlines Bold New Global Economic Policy." *Los Angeles Times*.

Fox, Claire F. 1999. *The Fence and the River: Culture and Politics at the US–Mexico Border*. Minneapolis, MN: University of Minnesota Press.

Gobierno del Estado de Baja California. September 1994. *Oportunidades Que Ofrece el Tratado de Libre Comercio a las Empresas de Tecate, BC*. Baja California: Secretaria de Desarrollo Economico.

Grunwald, Joseph. 1989. "The Future of Maquiladoras." Hyde, Jaye, and Hyde, Julianne, eds. *The Mexican Maquiladora Guidebook*. San Diego: HPH Publications Inc.

Hart, Jeffrey A. 1989. *Strategic Impacts of High Definition Television for US Manufacturing*. Bloomington, IN: National Center for Manufacturing Sciences.

Hart, Jeffry, Lenway, Stephanie, and Linden, Greg. 1997. *Advanced Displays In Korea And Taiwan*. Berkeley, CA: Brie.

Institute for Policy Studies. July 1993. *NAFTA's Corporate Cadre: An Analysis of the USA-NAFTA State Captains*. Washington, DC: Institute for Policy Studies.

Interview. April 1993. Sony Electronics Booth, National Association of Broadcasters Convention. Las Vegas, Nevada.

Khosrow, Fateui. 1990. *The Maquiladora Industry: Economic Solution or Problem?* Praeger: New York.

Kolbe, Jim. 1989. "The Wharton Study: Maquiladoras Save US Jobs and A Lot More." Hyde, Jaye and Hyde, Julianne, eds. *The Mexican Maquiladora Guidebook*. San Diego: HPH Publications Inc.

Kraul, Chris. December 2, 1997. "Sharp will Build Assembly Plant in Rosarito Beach: The Factory, Producing TVs and Vacuum cleaners, would Create More than 1,000 Jobs." *The Los Angeles Times*.

Kraul, Chris. December 30, 1998. "Asian Companies Continue to Flock to Tijuana Area." *Los Angeles Times*.

Kraul, Chris and Smith, James F. 1999. "US, Mexico Reach Deal on Factory Tax." *The Los Angeles Times*.

La Botz, Dan. 1992. *Mask of Democracy: Labor Suppression in Mexico Today*. Boston, MA: South End Press.

Lent, John A. and Sussman, Gerald, eds. 1998. "Global Productions." *Global Productions*. Cresskill, NJ: Hampton Press Inc.

Miller, Toby. 1998. *Technologies of Truth*. Minneapolis, MN: University of Minnesota Press.

Mosco, Vincent. 1998. "Political Economy, Communication, and Labor." Lent and Sussman, eds. *Global Productions*. Cresskill, NJ: Hampton Press Inc.

National Association of Foreign-Trade Zones. (January 2000). "What is a Foreign-Trade Zone?" http://www.naftz.org/whatrftz.html

Quintero Ramirez, Cirila. 1990. *La Sindicalizacio en Las Maquiladoras Tijuanenses: 1970–1988*. Mexico City: Consejo Nacional Para la Cultura y las Artes Publicaciones.

Romano, Catherine. September 1997. "Mexico y El Mundo." *Management Review*. V86, N8.

San Diego Economic Development Corporation. October 1993. *San Diego–Baja California Twin Plant Directory*. San Diego, CA: EDC Publications.

Sarabia, Saul. April 5, 2000. I would like to thank Saul for bringing this group to my attention.

Sassen, Saskia. 1998. *Globalization and Its Discontents: Essays on the New Mobility of People and Money*. New York: The New Press.

Schiller, Dan. 1999. *Digital Capitalism: Networking the Global Market System*. Cambridge, MA: The MIT Press.

Schiller, Herbert I. 1992. *Mass Communications and American Empire*. Boulder, Colorado: Westview Press.

Schrader, Esther. September 14, 1999. "Mexico Learns Lesson Well in Pursuit of Trade Accords." *Los Angeles Times*.

Siegel, Lenny. 1998. "New Chips in Old Skins: Work and Labor in Silicon Valley." Lent and Sussman, eds. *Global Productions*. Cresskill, NJ: Hampton Press Inc.

Sinclair, Scott. "NAFTA and US Trade Policy." 1993. Cameron, Maxwell A. and Grinspun, Ricardo. *The Political Economy of North American Free Trade*. New York: St. Martin's Press.

Sklair, Leslie. 1993. *Assembling for Development: The Maquiladora Industry in Mexico and the United States*. San Diego: Center for US–Mexican Studies.

Smith, James F. February 6, 2000. "Mexico Strike Extends Beyond Academic." *The Los Angeles Times*.

Sony Corporation of America. 2000a. "Sony Electronics at a Glance." http://www.sel.sony.com/SEL/corpcomm/profile/businesses/SELataGlance.html

——(2000b). "Sony de Tijuana." http://www.sel.sony.com/SEL/corpcomm/profile/businesses/STE.html

US Census Bureau. Foreign Trade Division. October 13, 1999. Foreign-Trade Zone Statistics. Washington, DC: US Census.

US Congressional Budget Office. July 1989. *Staff Working Papers: The Scope of the High-Definition Television Market and Its Implications for Competitiveness*. Washington, DC: GPO.

US Congressional Budget Office. March 1999. *The Domestic Costs Of Sanctions On Foreign Commerce*. Washington, DC: Congress Of The US, GPO Digital Copies, http://www.cbo.gov/showdoc.cfm?index=1133&sequence=0&from=1

US Department of Commerce. October 8–12, 1995. "Variations on the Freeport Theme – A US Perspective." Conference Paper Presented by John Da Ponte, 23rd Annual NAFTA Conference, Kamuela, Hawaii. Washington, DC: FTZ Board, DOC.

US Department of Commerce. 1997. *The Foreign-Trade Zones Act: Keeping Up with the Changing Times*. Washington, DC: FTZ Board.

US Department of Commerce. 1999. *US Industrial Outlook: 1994–2000*. Washington, DC: US DOC.

US House Of Representatives. 1989. *High Definition Television: Hearing Before the Subcommittee on Telecommunications and Finance of the Committee on Energy and Commerce*. Washington: US GPO. March 8 and 9.

US International Trade Commission. December 1999. *Production Sharing: Use of Foreign Assembly Operations, 1995–1998*. Washington, DC: USITC Publication 3265.

US National Information and Trade Administration. 1997. *Advanced Digital Video and the National Information Infrastructure: Executive Summary*. Washington, DC: Government Printing Office.

US Senate. August 1, 1989. *Prospects of Development of a US HDTV Industry*, Hearing, Committee on Governmental Affairs. Washington, DC: Government Printing Office.

Van Der Pijl, Kees. 1998. *Transnational Classes and Transnational Relations*. London: Routledge.

Weston, Ann. 1994. *The NAFTA Papers: Implications for Canada, Mexico, and Developing Countries*. Ottawa, Canada: The North–South Institute.

White House. July 1, 1997. "Framework for Global Electronic Commerce." Washington, DC: White House Policy Paper. http://www.ecommerce.gov/framework.htm

Wright, Robin. January 30, 2000. "Clinton Urges Dialogue on Globalization." *The Los Angeles Times*.

Chapter 22

Trade and Information Policy

Sandra Braman

As society is transformed by the use of new technologies, information policy issues cross traditional boundaries to be found in a wide range of decision-making arenas. The New World Information Order (NWIO) debate lies relatively quiescent in Unesco, but surfaces in international trade negotiations in response to the US push to get trade in services, or international information flows, included under the General Agreements on Tariffs and Trade (GATT), a set of international trade agreements designed to deal with goods. The US move of the 1980s to extend the GATT to 'trade' in information has met great resistance from both developed and developing nations.[1]

From the beginning, proponents of a New World Information Order have referred to transborder data flows (TBDF) and a range of other types of international information flows in addition to news (Cruise O'Brien, 1980, 1983; Hamelink, 1979; Richstad and Anderson, 1981). Developing countries were in this sense ahead of the developed world in understanding that the key to distribution of the world's resources lay within the international information system.

The Uruguay Round of GATT talks is one venue in which the geopolitical shift of the late twentieth century away from a Cold War configuration towards a new bloc system is being crafted (Cline, 1983). The fact that these talks deal with international information flows during a period of such global structural change is in itself interesting, for those flows have a cybernetic effect on the nature of that change. Not only do the new telecommunications services make possible instantaneous and massive global information flows which have enabled the development of transnational corporations (TNCs) (Antonelli, 1981, 1984) and other new organizational forms; these flows also feed back information to be used in future rounds of decision-making, thus further shaping the mutating environment.

NWIO-type issues may well reach their denouement in trade negotiations. The dominance of the trade arena at a time when the nature of the international information policy regime[2] is just being established means that trade operational definitions, modes of argument and value hierarchies are likely to influence the information policy regime as well.

This discussion of the debate over trade in services in the GATT will explore the information policy dimensions of current trade issues of major geopolitical importance. Opening with background on the GATT and the trade in services issue, it continues through the problems of economic analysis that underlie trade treatment of information and an exploration of the range of policy options available, and concludes with recommendations regarding strategies for those promoting NWIO-type concerns.

Trade in Services and the GATT Agreements

History of the GATT and developing nations

The GATT agreements were created after the Second World War as part of the global reorganization which also involved international monetary and fiscal arrangements. They grew out of US/United Kingdom talks begun in 1941 and represented the first systematic attempt to deliberately structure a global economic environment.

The fundamental principle behind the provisions of the GATT is equal treatment for every nation. This seemingly democratic notion unfortunately works to the disadvantage of developing nations which need special treatment in order to survive and thrive. The theoretical force driving the agreements comes from classical trade theory as developed during the mid-nineteenth century by Ricardo and others. At that time the global economy was seen as ever-expanding and capable of providing prosperity for all according to two principles: (1) each nation has a comparative advantage, or specific economic niche within the world system, determined by its resources ('factor endowments'); and (2) national and global prosperity will emerge only when each country specializes in its area of comparative advantage and trades the resulting goods internationally. It is not coincidental that this economic theory provided a nice justification for imperial practices in the political realm.

The GATT – now a collection of over 100 multilateral and bilateral agreements signed by 96 nations – was originally created for temporary usage while the more subtle and complex Havana Charter, which included features sensitive to development issues, was discussed. After three years of debate about the Havana Charter and the related proposed International Trade Organization, in 1950 the US killed the plan and with it, in Spero's words, 'The potential integration of the concerns of less developed countries in the regulation of international trade...' (1981: 184).

Though developing countries had aired hundreds of proposals, ranging from a direct transfer of resources to flexibility in the assignment of legal responsibilities in order to meet their special needs, none were incorporated into the final agreements (Hudec, 1975, 1987). Nor did the realities of GATT implementation favor development needs. Basic provisions institutionalized arrangements that ignored significant differences among countries. The most favored nation principle eliminated the possibility of preferential trading arrangements, and the GATT rule of reciprocity was problematic for Southern countries with little to offer in exchange for concessions in their favor. Thus from the moment the trade regime was established, the concerns of developing countries were left out of the decision-making calculus. The elite-oriented power structure of GATT decision-making, revolving around a Secretariat composed of representatives from leading developed nations, similarly blocked developing countries from effective participation in decision-making processes (GATT, 1979, 1986a, 1986b, 1986c, 1986d, 1987a, 1987b, 1988a, 1988b).

The provisions of the GATT were challenged by developing countries from the start. Receptiveness seemed to increase in response to Soviet threats to form an alternative international trade organization oriented to Third World needs (Roeder, 1985), and to a rise in the price of oil (Bergen, 1987). Humanitarian motives, such as helping nations in need – what Ruggie (1982) calls the 'embedded liberalism' of the post-war trade regime – seem to have gained and lost force to match the power of the energy cartel. Actual development-oriented provisions of the GATT, such as those of the Tokyo Round of the 1970s, were viewed by developing nations as outmoded and/or insufficient (Cline et al., 1978; Preeg, 1973).

Frustration with the impact of existing trade rules on developing nations led to activity outside the GATT as well. Beginning in the early 1950s, Unesco began compiling lists of trade barriers to the international flow of information (see, for example, Unesco, 1955). The UN Conference on Trade and Development (UNCTAD) was finally formed specifically to further the trade interests of developing nations. UNCTAD has provided a forum for discussion of trade issues of concern to developing countries and encouraged research on trade in services in the Third World, but has been frustrated in its international effectiveness because of the difficulty of reaching the consensus among developing countries needed to establish unified positions (Cutajar, 1985; UNCTAD, 1984).

In the 1980s, developing nations continued to question the ability of the GATT to meet their needs in a time of transformation of the global economy (Damon, 1986; Lowenfeld, 1986). Traditional trade sanctions are still used despite research that shows their effects to be more symbolic than actual (Lindsay, 1986; Odell,

1985), and the use of non-tariff trade sanctions, made easier by the shift to an information economy, is increasing. Bilateral trade agreements, such as the US–Canada Free Trade Agreement, are on the rise, and many in both the developed and developing worlds are questioning the continued viability of multilateral fora such as the GATT (Destler, 1986; Roach, 1987; Schwab, 1987).

Trade in services in the GATT

The word 'services' is among many in the current trade environment with a myriad meanings (Bravender-Coyle, 1985; Bruce, 1985; Bruce et al., 1986). The 1983–4 national studies on trade in services generated in response to an agreement at the 1982 GATT Ministerial Meeting simply listed what industries each country included, demonstrating wide variations (see, for example, the submissions of Canada, the EEC, the United States, the Federal Republic of Germany, Japan, the Netherlands, and Sweden to the GATT). Services mentioned are as diverse as tourism, insurance, advertising, accounting and data processing. Most mass media activities, including news collection and distribution, are subsumed under other categories and have received shockingly little direct attention.

While not all of the services being discussed involve international information flows, Nusbaumer (1987) lists the International Standard Industrial Code (ISIC) numbers for those that do: financial services (81); business services, including advertising (8325), legal (8321) and accounting (8322) services; data processing and communication services (8323, 7200); recreational and cultural services (94), including motion picture production, distribution and projection (9411, 9412) and radio and television broadcasting (9413); domestic and personal services, like photography (9592); sanitary and social and related community services, including education (8130) and research and scientific institutes.

Cass and Noam, influential participants in the US regulatory process, define services as 'commercial activities that do not result in production of tangible goods' (1989: 4), but the definition offered by *The Economist* seems to be the most popular: 'Services are anything that can be bought and sold but cannot be dropped on your foot' (*The Economist*, 1985: 20).

Services can be final products, such as television programming or an advertising campaign. They can also be intermediate inputs in the production of other goods or services, as in automated control of a manufacturing line or flows of transaction data. The distinction is significant for policy-making, for while the former are most often interorganizational, the latter are generally intra-organizational and thus less accessible to decision-making in the public sector despite their enormous impact.

The US effort to develop trade rules to govern services began in 1974 when it established a services advisory committee as part of the Trade Act of that year (Rivers et al., 1987). Increasingly over the next few years services were mentioned in provisions of both bilateral and multilateral agreements, as information creation, processing, flows and use continued to rise in importance to the US economy (Bauer et al., 1963; Candilis, 1988; Cohen, 1981).

In 1982 the US forced trade in services onto the agenda of the GATT, using access to the US market and a threat to withdraw from the GATT as prods. Resistance to discussion in the area, however, contributed to the delay of the opening of the Uruguay Round by at least two years (Brazil, 1988; Shelp, 1987). Dozens of meetings on the subject between the ultimate opening of the Uruguay Round and the 1988 mid-term meeting yielded nothing but long lists of fundamental differences.

Services achieved equal status with goods in US law with the Omnibus Trade and Competitiveness Act of 1988, a major overhaul of trade legislation justified by reference to a new global economic system developed over the last decade and characterized by integration between trade, technological development, investment and services. It is the position of the US that extension of trade law to services is the logical and inevitable response to these shifts (Feketekuty, 1986; Feketekuty and Aronson, 1984; Feketekuty and Hausar, 1985). A more cynical view, shared by the developing countries (Atinc et al., 1984), points to the US budget deficit, balance of trade and potential for comparative advantage in many of the services industries. The GATT effort is certainly part of the overall US attempt to find a new equilibrium in a period of structural change in the global economy that includes a decline in its hegemonic position.

Sides in the debate over inclusion of trade in services under the GATT agreements have not broken down cleanly along developed/developing country lines. The countries of Western Europe for several years rejected the US initiative, based both on the kinds of defensive concerns expressed so effectively in the Nora/Minc report, and on a growing sensitivity to specific cultural concerns of their own (Becker, 1986, 1988a; Hamelink, 1979, 1983, 1984). While by the 1980s the EEC had expressed its intention to compete internationally in the services area and begun to shape policy that would lead it in that direction (Engel, 1989; Noam, 1986), alternatives to the GATT were also being considered. Many of the developing countries that have achieved NIC status did so through a shift of their economies to services.

Whether or not creating a trade regime for services serves anyone's self-interest, it has become necessary to develop some kind of international regime governing international flows of information of all kinds. Legal problems in this area have been the subject of discussion for at least two decades. These problems derive from two sources: (1) new types of activities, relationships and corporate structures made possible by technological development have generated their own, also in many cases new, legal issues; and (2) within every jurisdiction, clashes among concurrently applicable legal systems – a situation which has resulted from the convergence of technologies and therefore of legal systems developed to deal with each – generate additional legal difficulties.

Treatment of services as trade under the GATT is one extreme of a range of possible types of regimes to govern international information flows. Alternatives include creation of different trade-type arrangements, institutions outside the trade arena altogether, and the New World Information Order. Individual country commitments to attempt to maintain or initiate delinkage represent another extreme, but offer less in the way of suggestions for comprehensive global arrangements.

At the beginning of the 1990s, the trade in services issue is still open. International working groups are exploring exactly what the GATT rules would mean if applied to specific services, sector by sector. The agreement to conduct these studies before discussing general principles, and to do so on a sectoral basis, were seen as victories for those countries that oppose the inclusion of trade in services under the GATT agreements.

Arrangements in sectors such as financial services and insurance will have structural effects on communications activities. Delivery of such services so dominates the international telecommunications network that 'users' within telecommunications policy circles are considered to be entities such as Citibank and American Express rather than either individuals or the public in general. Decisions made to serve corporate interests determine the technological and legal environment in which the media and other cultural forces operate.

Those who oppose inclusion of trade in services under the GATT agreements from both developed and developing worlds do so based on a variety of theoretical positions. For some, dependency theory, with its emphasis on cultural as well as economic and political imperialism, is the engine. Others find their objections in traditional economic theory, but feel their countries are poorly positioned in the information economy as envisioned under US-proposed trade rules. Arguments in both cases focus on interrelationships among international information flows, the distribution of resources and decision-making control in the global economy, and the ability of social groups to exercise self-determination.

Those who support inclusion of trade in services under the GATT – and support also can be found in the developing world as well as the developed – depend upon notions of rationalization and harmonization of the global economy (Ochel and Wegner, 1987; Petersmann and Hilf, 1988; Rubin and Jones, 1989). From this perspective, notions of comparative advantage and the international division of labor are not only sensible but need to be extended.

While in some ways this split replays the NWIO debate in Unesco, in other ways the particularities of trade offer unique modes of action and opportunities for those who represent NWIO-type concerns.

Problems in Economic Analysis

Though Easterbrook argues that the shift of the study of communication to the center of analysis of economic history is a 'pronounced shift in vantage point', (1960: 559) and the post-Second World War period has seen a proliferation of studies dealing with the economics of information, a number of problems remain with the attempt to analyze information in economic terms that present genuine difficulties when dealing with services for the purposes of trade.

1   How are individual units of information to be identified? Information most often comes 'bundled', as part of a stream of messages or a compilation; by virtue of having been edited, synthesized, analyzed, organized, patterned, indexed or referenced; or because it is inextricably linked to some physical good. Because bits of information acquire value from their context, it is difficult to define or price individual units.

2   How can an economic value be placed on information when both utility and exchange value mutate over time? For many kinds of information, timeliness is crucial to value, which as a consequence can vary rapidly and dramatically over time depending on the type of information and the circumstance.

3   How is an economic value to be placed on information when both utility and exchange value vary according to the interests of the buyer? Information that is valuable to the news reporter or stock market participant may be useless to the welfare mother, novelist or geologist, and vice versa. How can such complex and variable functions be understood sufficiently to be described algorithmically and inserted into economists' quantitative models and calculations?

4   How is an economic value to be placed on information when it is seemingly impossible to control its shared ownership among increasing numbers of people, what Cleveland (1985) calls its 'leakiness'?

5   When is a flow of information across a border 'trade'? The question of how to identify trade in services is key (Sauvant, 1985, 1986). It is generally accepted that there are four ways trade in services *can* occur: (a) by resident activities across national borders to non-resident entities abroad; (b) through contractual relationships such as licensing, partnerships, sale of intellectual property, etc.; (c) within national boundaries to non-residents; and (d) through foreign affiliates.

Because many services are delivered via the international telecommunications network, issues of control over, ownership of and standards for that network intertwine with questions about services either produced or delivered via that network. Globalization of corporate activities confounds the attempt to identify specific geographic poles between which trade can be said to occur. Foreign direct investment (FDI) is sometimes considered trade, and sometimes not (UNCTC, 1989); Petit (1986) distinguishes between 'real' and 'fictional' trade along these lines.

6   How is the complexity of the information environment to be handled quantitatively? Ciotti-Revilla and Merritt criticize most NWIO-related discussions for ignoring the multi-actor, multi-component nature of the situation. They note, 'The sheer order of magnitude... of these large and complicated networks is a much-neglected aspect of the NWIO debate. The number of communication channels in the existing international system is in fact so large that it yields some of the largest numbers thus far encountered in the social universe' (1982: 243).

7   How is information labor to be valued? Caporaso wrote in 1986 that 'modern interpretations of the international division of labor are extremely confused', (1986: 1) and then went on to offer a definition of labor that for the first time doesn't *exclude* services: 'activity of a physical or mental sort intended to produce wealth' (1986: 5). Concepts used in the valuation of labor will have to come to terms with the importance of creativity and ideas in an information economy, yet most labor theorists who to date have dealt with the impacts of technological change have largely focused on the loss of employment or geographic relocation (Goldthorpe, 1982; Labovitz and Gibbs, 1964; Noyelle and Stanback, 1984; Perrolle, 1983; Shaiken, 1986; Urry, 1987). There are exceptions; Goldhaber (1983) suggests new labor classes may be forming, while Nusbaumer (1987) suggests qualitative measures will come into play under new theories of labor value that will be part of a general shift in economic paradigm forced by the need to understand trade in services.

8 How should the types of value that inhere in services but not in goods be treated? Again, the power of ideas is difficult to quantify, and there are other services-specific values, such as mobility, the efficiency gain from performance of a given activity at a particular site rather than another. The cultural, political, social, aesthetic and religious value of information flows are also irreducible to quantitative economic measures of the type used for boots and belt buckles.

Cass and Noam (1989) attempt to resolve these difficulties by denying any fundamental difference between information and physical goods. While this is certainly utilitarian from the regulators' point of view, the arguments depend largely upon assertion and refusal to acknowledge the existence of any non-commodity values. Gibbs and Mashayekhi responded to earlier such attempts by saying: 'Certain scholars have strained both their imaginations and credibility in this context...' (1988: 82).

Traditional trade theory is under attack for failing to take into account international structural change as well as gross differences among nations in terms of market and political power. A computerized analysis of alternative theories (Dixon, 1985) found that world system theory is a better predictor of actual trade concentration. Another simulation compared a moderate version of an alternative trade theory emphasizing concessionary tariffs popular among some developing countries with the more radical alternative of delinking. This study found the development objectives of the two approaches incompatible: partial delinking seems to reinforce the existing division of labor while greater engagement seems to lead to changes in the division of labor. The benefits to the South under either scenario are not equally distributed, and policies which benefit the South under either scenario have costs for the North (Pollins, 1985; Trimberger, 1979).

The Conjuncture: Trade and Information Policy

Different decision-making arenas that deal with the same subject matter are distinguishable by their modes of argument, value hierarchies and operational definitions. The specific configurations of the GATT in these areas both determine the receptivity of trade negotiators to NWIO-type concerns and outline a political space in which there is room for maneuvering in response to the trade in services gesture.

Modes of argument: technical and rhetorical

The trade arena is undergoing debate over the technical nature of its discourse, and is engaged in modes of argument rhetorically dominated by the notion of 'free flow'. Both will be discussed here.

Technical modes of argument. The field of communication policy in general is one in which discussion of negotiation patterns is on the rise. Several have examined this issue as it regards trade in services (Barton, 1986; Bhagwati and Ruggie, 1984; Cline, 1983), some even suggesting specific strategies (Gray, 1983; Noyelle and Dutka, 1986; US, 1988). This interest is raised by decreasing US effectiveness in international negotiations which reflect the combination of its declining hegemonic position and the build-up of resentment against the United States for consistent self-absorption in its policy-making in this area in the past.

The examination of negotiation techniques is also related to a questioning of the nature of regulation in general that cuts across policy issue areas. The nature, effects and utility of the regulatory process as well as of specific techniques are coming into question by traditional policy analysts (Harter and Eads, 1985; Knieps and Spiller, 1983; Pekelis, 1968; Schwartz, 1977; Stewart, 1983), while the critical legal studies movement presents a challenge on more philosophical grounds.

The intrusion of both of these questions – how to negotiate, and the nature of regulation – into the trade arenas offer political opportunities. Examination of the negotiation procedures and approaches opens the possibility of creating a decision-making process in which a wider range of players may effectively be involved and a greater range of values, including non-commodity values, incorporated. The range of potential alternatives to existing GATT arrangements is widened. Not only are alternative organizational settings made possible; there is also room for development of new regulatory techniques. This is a moment in which aggressive theoretical and conceptual work may find a receptive audience.

Rhetorical modes of argument: 'free flow'. 'Free flow' is a powerful rhetorical formation capable of great shifts in meaning. Its role as a metaphorical hinge linking information flows and trade in physical goods – as well as reactions to its use as a policy-making argument – derive from the histories of its use in both trade and information policy.

The nineteenth century saw 'free trade' as a key feature of colonial empires. The latter third of that century also saw the 'free flow' of information, ironically, entering international discourse with an NIWO-type complaint by the US, which felt maligned by biased news reports that showed a US dominated by racism, bizarre crimes and Indian wars. This early charge of what has come to be called 'coups and earthquakes' reporting stemmed from the complaint that the US had been dealt out of a European cartel of international news agencies formed shortly after the invention of the telegraph (Blanchard, 1986).

In the twentieth century, Wilsonian internationalism gave another spur to free flow that served both the rhetoric of free speech and the interests of big business. Attribution of the Depression to the protectionism of the 1920s offered another set of motivations for free trade (Bronze, 1961; Goldstein, 1988; Gowa, 1988; Haggard, 1988; Hauser, 1986).

Following the Second World War, the US promoted the free flow of information on the one hand, and an international trade regime based on the free flow of goods on the other. In both arenas, 'freedom' was meant to apply in the same ways to nation-states around the world, irrespective of their cultures, socio-economic conditions, or position within the world system. And in both arenas, developing countries found this type of freedom to their disadvantage. Socio-economic conditions of most Third World countries declined under the GATT's free trade provisions; the use of new information technologies appears to have aggravated the situation. At the same time, the international distribution of information seemed biased against developing countries, who found themselves inaccurately portrayed, unable to protect their own information resources, and unable to access the information needed to negotiate internationally.

The rhetoric of free flow currently being used to justify inclusion of trade in services under the GATT agreements thus carries a lot of baggage. It is clear that the phrase can be used to describe a wide range of policies with varying degrees of actual openness, and that many of those policies have acted to the disadvantage of the developing countries. There is fear that joining the notions of free flow of goods and of information may multiply the damaging consequences (Hepworth and Robins, 1988). As a consequence, use of this phrase is backfiring on those who assumed it would have persuasive, and therefore political, value in achieving their economic goals.

The notion of a free and balanced flow is difficult to establish as an alternative without an infrastructure that makes such a flow possible. Thus any agreement of this kind must entail a commitment on the part of developed nations, via international organizations or on their own, to assist in the development of the information infrastructure of developing countries. This in fact has been the foreign aid thrust of the Japanese for several years.

Operational definition: information as commodity

In order for information to be tradable, it must be conceived of as a commodity. While Wuthnow (1987) argues that international flows of science information were commodities critical to the world-economy as early as the seventeenth century in Europe, clearly over the last hundred years more and more types of information have come to be commoditized.

The idea that information should be seen as a commodity, however, competes with other definitional approaches (Braman, 1989; Carey, 1988; Machlup and Mansfield, 1983; Peters, 1988). For many, the value of information is political, social, religious, cultural or aesthetic, and economic valuations are at best irrelevant and at worst sacrilege. Cochran (1960), Eisenstadt (1980) and other historians have shown how differences in such matters yield differences in social, political and economic organization.

The suggestion that international information flows can and should be treated in exactly the same way as trade in tables and chairs offends many as the ultimate stage in a commoditization process that has been resisted all along the way, and objections to which are profound. On the other hand, societies that are comfortable with commoditization as a – or the – dominant feature of the landscape find the process logical. For those to whom extension of the international division of labor and accumulation of capital are reasonably the dominant goals, the harmonization of accounting, communication and legal systems that would result from the inclusion of trade in services under the GATT agreements is simply an efficient means of getting on with things (Hurwitz, 1983; Roth, 1989). The focus on information as a commodity by the US is part of an overall rejection of cultural, social or political valuation of international information flows that is embedded in background studies for policy-makers, congressional hearings and policy statements in a quite self-conscious way.

The trade arena differs from Unesco and other places where NWIO-type issues have been discussed by this operational definition of information. Use of an operational definition of information as a commodity makes the trade arena much less receptive to NWIO-type concerns, for the discourse itself denies the existence or importance of values represented by those who promote a New World Information Order.

Value hierarchies: the constitutional debate

On one level, the debate over trade in services is a conflict between values, with cultural, social or political concerns on the one hand and economic goals such as efficiency and profit on the other. On another level, the debate is about how to rank value hierarchies themselves. The discourse among nation-states as to which value hierarchies should dominate internationally, and how deviant systems may be accommodated, is responded to in the GATT context by the suggestion that the locus of constitutional responsibility be moved from the nation-state to the international level. This suggestion first arose during the post-Second World War talks, and has gained in power since. The theoretical environment surrounding the Uruguay Round has been filled with talk of the constitutional role to be played by trade agreements.

The argument starts by defining the constitutional act not as the positive act of constituting a community, but as the negative act of protecting against dangers (Cass, 1987). From this per-spective, the dangers of the 1990s come from the international trade environment, and so agreements that protect against those dangers are constitutional in nature. Other arguments include the efficiency of an international constitution, and the utility of such laws when maneuvering domestically (Hauser, 1986; Hills, 1988). For Simon and Waller (1986), economic sovereignty via international agreements is a way of resolving extra-territorial jurisdictional disputes. Jackson (1984, 1988) emphasizes the interactions between constitutional activities at the national and international levels.

The suggestion that the locus of constitutional power should be removed from the nation-state level to the international both reflects and stimulates a weakening of the nation-state and increased interdependence among nation-states and between them and the international system (Gasiorowski, 1985; Krasner, 1976; Krommenacker, 1986). What the US calls 'harmonization', others term the extra-territorial exercise of power. Inclusion of trade in services under the GATT would accelerate the shift of power from the national to the international level, while making it easier for US-based legal and regulatory approaches to extend their reach internationally.

While this interdependence, Bruce (1983) argues, heightens the responsibility as well as widening the opportunities of domestic policy-makers, it makes developing countries nervous. Already feeling their sovereignty under attack as a result of a variety of types of economic, political and cultural dependency, this aspect of the trade negotiations generates yet another reason to oppose inclusion of trade in services under the GATT agreements. Mosco calls the US–Canada Free Trade Agreement, the declared model for the GATT, the 'first constitution to guarantee that the fundamental rights of multinational business to pursue commerce and set social and public policy take precedence over the political rights of national citizens and their national governments' (1990).

Policy options

There is a range of options available to every country as it decides how to position itself generally within the international economy and, more specifically, where it stands on the question of including trade in services under the GATT or other trade agreements. Concerns about possible negative effects can be found within every nation, including the US, which has for years suffered from a lack of diversity in program content compared to what is available to television viewers in other nations for whom US programming is only one, instead of the, source. Each country's choices will depend upon cultural inclinations, level of education of the leadership, level of education of the population, existing information infrastructure, investment relationships and current position *vis-à-vis* the global information production chain[3] and the international division of labor.

The range of policy options

The key question is how a society balances its desired integration into the global economy against cultural, political and social concerns. For most nations, information policy is an aspect of, or tightly related to, industrial and economic planning (Neu et al., 1987). Nations that value successful trade relationships above all will be inclined to go along with the desires of the heaviest players, and so support the notion of including trade in services under the GATT agreements, or under whatever other trade agreements their major trading partners desire. Strategies for developed nations that seek a position of strength within the information economy will concentrate on staking out a niche and defending it from others; the high definition television (HDTV) debate is an example of a niche – production of broadband receivers – over which several nations are battling.

Developing nations that desire to integrate as completely as possible have a couple of choices. They can seek similarly to establish their own niche, as in the case of Cyprus and several of the group of NICs. They can alternatively focus on making themselves irreplaceably necessary to a stable, sizable and prosperous trading partner or partners, and be willing to do so irrespective of the social, cultural or political costs entailed. The data processing support offered by Korea and several Caribbean nations to the US are examples of this approach (Walsham, 1979; Yoffie, 1983). If, however, O'Donnell (1980) is correct that the later a state forms, the more important the state apparatus is to economic growth, there may be a con-

tradiction in following this policy in the realm of services, with its consequent state-weakening effects. It is clear that relationships with transnational corporations have different effects depending upon a state's location within the world system (Evans, 1985; Hveem, 1987; Mexico, 1988).

At the other extreme, the concept of complete delinkage from the international economy as the best solution for developing countries that seek to break their dependent relationships still holds power. Brazil, which has had a national information policy since the 1960s, is an example of a country which has attempted delinkage via self-sufficiency in its information economy; reports on the progress of this policy range from calling it a complete success, to attributing that success to support from a black market in information technologies, to claims that Brazil is two or three generations behind the rest of the world in its information industries. In general, attempts at delinkage have left nations or regions further behind according to economic criteria without providing the kind of sustenance on cultural and social grounds that would be needed to justify the cost. Becker (1988b) argues that the problem with dissociative strategies is not knowing when to start them, but in knowing when to stop. It is one of the consequences of the development of new information technologies that not even those nations that desire to do so can completely separate themselves from the global information economy, for at the very least the transistor radio and videocassettes have made their way everywhere.

Refusal to participate in GATT discussions over the legal treatment of the international flow of services has a disadvantage in that it cuts alternative voices out of the discussion altogether, ensuring that the needs of developing nations and others concerned with the cultural, social and political value of information will not be taken into account in determining the most significant body of rules governing international information flows. While this presence is not now strong, it is argued that things are better than they would have been without pressure from developing countries within the GATT system. The disadvantages of protectionism are also pointed out on theoretical grounds by traditional economists (Hauser, 1986).

There is a variety of positions in between the two extremes of complete acceptance or complete withdrawal. Ideally, a nation would seek some level of integration into the international information economy, but would find a way and level of doing so that would be culturally comfortable and permit sustained attention to other values deemed important. Some argue that such integration is critical to the future of developing nations (Bascur, 1985; Ewing, 1985). Within the trade in services discussion, both developed and developing nations which take such an intermediary position have supported research by nation and by sector (Patterson, 1986). These nations represent the majority of those involved in the discussion, for few nations even of Western Europe are comfortable with the degree to which the US seeks harmonization of communication, legal, accounting and financial systems. In addition to participating in global discussions, the EEC is developing its own, regional approach to trade in services.

One problem in decision-making is the paucity of information available about service industries; the situation is even worse for developing nations than for the developed. An increasing number of studies, largely quantitative in nature, have, however, been recently completed (for example, Daniels, 1985; Gershuny and Miles, 1983; Kaynak, 1986; Kraus, 1983; McKee, 1988). Still, not enough is known about cultural effects of service industries (Roncagliolo, 1985).

The Canadian example

The recently enacted US–Canada Free Trade Agreement offers a particularly useful example of an attempt to deal with the issue of the regulation of trade in services for several reasons: the US has made it clear it considers this agreement a model for the GATT; along with the Omnibus Trade Act of 1988 it constitutes a major revision of US trade policy; though Canada is a developed nation, cultural concerns dominated the resistance, demonstrating clearly the importance of NWIO-type issues for all nations; the opinions of a range of voices have been made available; and some of the real effects of the agreement are coming to be known as the loss of jobs and gain in cultural invasion become felt.

The issue of the trade agreement caused one of the most acrimonious elections in Canada's history in 1988. The stakes were high economically,

and a great deal had been invested in the campaign by American business interests. Three times previously such trade pacts had been rejected by Canadians (Bernier, 1988; Litvak, 1988). Those who opposed the agreement feared integration with the United States economy, which was expected to go beyond the 80 percent of Canadian exports that currently go to US markets; the linkage of computers, electrical grids and hospital organ transplant programs; and the merging of broadcast, print and other mass media audiences (Gold and Leyton-Brown, 1988; Grey, 1983). Then US Trade Ambassador Clayton Yeutter did not allay such fears when he made a comment he later tried to deny: 'The Canadians don't understand what they signed. In 20 years they will be sucked into the US economy' (quoted in Dillon, 1988: 8).

Some thought they did understand, and understood that economic integration was tied to cultural hegemony (*Transnational Data Report*, 1984; Desaulniers, 1987; Smythe, 1981). Robertson Davies (1989), the Canadian novelist who remembers being told to 'Americanize' his plots if he wanted US publication, heard in the debate a very clear statement by Canadians of the importance of non-commodity values to their cultures. David Young (1989), of Toronto's avant-garde writing and publishing community, believes the Free Trade Agreement will incrementally but fundamentally change the structure of Canadian culture over time. And Margaret Atwood (1989) ended her opinion piece in the *Toronto World & Mail* by referring to Kierkegaardian despair.

While the Free Trade Agreement specifically exempts cultural industries from its purview, as Mosco (1990) notes the very wording of the exclusion defines culture as a commodity. Further, the exemptions to the exemption leave substantial portions of the North American communications industries covered. Provisions that don't specifically deal with 'cultural industries' have an effect on those industries nonetheless, as they play such a heavy role in shaping regulatory processes and decisions, thereby playing a structural role. Finally, provisions of the Free Trade Agreement prevent either government from supporting or promoting cultural products of its own citizens or cultural groups, an area in which Canada has been extremely active since the Second World War.

Resentment of the Agreement grows as its effects are felt culturally, in jobs lost, corporate reorganizations and pressures for harmonization in other legal and regulatory affairs. There is talk of dismantling the Agreement should there be a change in Canadian government.

The example of the US–Canada Free Trade Agreement demonstrates how difficult it is even for a developed nation to find a way to accommodate the free trade thrust of the US while protecting its own cultural, social and political interests. Developing nations are much more subject to the exercise of brute force. When asked by a law student what the US response would be should developing nations refuse to go along with the effort to include trade in services under the GATT, Geza Feketekuty, then of the Office of the US Trade Representative, answered, 'We'll make them'.[4] While this is surely a facetious response, it is indicative of the attitude that has led to real US tactics in the trade arena.

Conclusions

Though little is being heard from the New World Information Order debate in some quarters, it is erupting in others. NWIO concerns about control over national information resources and the right to the value that inheres in the processing of those resources, personal and cultural privacy, access to information, sensitivity to cultural nuances in information use and intention, and the interplay between the international economic order and information flows are now the stuff of discussion within the trade arena. Both developed and developing nations are reluctant to accede to US requests that the GATT agreements, designed to regulate trade in physical goods, be extended to services.

As the NWIO debate has moved from Unesco to the GATT, however, it has evolved in response to the nuances of the new decision-making arena, distinguishable through examination of the GATT's operational definitions, modes of argument, and value hierarchies. Given history, it is not unreasonable that there are great fears of extension or multiplication of the effects of dependency should trade law come to apply to information flows. Rhetorical reliance upon 'free flow' does little to allay fears based upon historical experience, but rather provides a con-

venient hinge to flip between ideological visions having to do with libertarian notions of freedom of speech and pragmatic visions having to do with making more money by shipping more things around the world.

The operational definition of information in use in the trade arena works against NWIO-type concerns through simply denying them ontologically. Uncertainty and openness regarding modes of negotiation and the nature of regulation, however, open up a political space in which aggressive and innovative theoretical and conceptual work may have enormous structural power by shaping the way in which discussions will take place and offer new regulatory tools for use. Similarly, confusion about the locus of constitutional power and, subsequently, about dominant value hierarchies, offers a moment of opportunity to play a role by setting the terms of debate.

Since most countries, both developed and developing, are likely to choose a middle route – accommodation to the international economy to a level that is acceptable when balanced against cultural, social and political concerns – there is a need for much deeper analysis of the cultural impact of various types of information collection, processing and storage activities. The goal would be gaining sufficient knowledge to facilitate identification of a niche in the international information economy that is culturally, politically and socially compatible for every nation and culture concerned.

Last, the insistence upon sector by sector discussions within the GATT should be continued, so that books and newspapers are not treated by international law in the same way as boots and belt buckles. Convenience is not a sufficient argument for shoving everything that flows internationally under the same rug. Even the US may find it to its ultimate cultural advantage to have taken such an approach.

The results of discussions about inclusion of trade in services will have consequences not just within the trade arena but in determining the shape of the emerging international information policy regime. Thus they will have effects across the entire domain of concern to proponents of a New World Information Order. New arguments and strategies, however, must be developed to accommodate the distinct characteristics of the GATT as a decision-making arena.

Notes

1 As the line between developed and developing nations becomes what Sjostadt and Sundelius call 'diluted' (1986: 15), the GATT has come to divide countries into three categories: the Eastern trading bloc (the four 'dragonettes' of Singapore, South Korea, Hong Kong and Taiwan), developed, and developing nations. Often Brazil, India, some of the OPEC countries and/or Mexico are grouped with the Eastern trading bloc as an elite subset of developing countries called Newly Industrialized Countries (NICs).

2 To political scientists, a 'regime' is a group of operational definitions, modes of argument and value hierarchies that provide a basis for international negotiations in a policy issue area. The GATT has often been cited as an example of a successful regime. The unique characteristics of the emerging international information policy regime are explored in Braman (1990).

3 The information production chain includes the stages of information creation (via creation, generation or collection), processing (algorithmic or cognitive), storage, transportation, distribution, destruction and seeking.

4 In discussion at the University of Chicago Law Forum on Barriers to International Trade in Services, 9 February 1986.

References

Antonelli, C. (1981) *Transborder Data Flows and International Business: A Pilot Study.* Paris: OECD, Division for Science, Technology and Industry. DSTI/ICCP/81.16.

Antonelli, C. (1984) 'Multinational Firms, International Trade and International Telecommunications', *Information Economics and Policy* 1: 333–43.

Atinc, T., A. Behnain, A. Cornford, R. Glasgow, H. Skipper and A. Yusuf (1984) 'International Transactions in Services and Economic Development', *Trade and Development* 5: 141–273.

Atwood, M. (1989) 'Hard Sell, Soft Core', reprinted in *Rolling Stock* 15/16:3.

Barton, J. (1986) 'Negotiation Patterns for Liberalizing International Trade in Professional Services'. Presented to University of Chicago Law Forum, Barriers to International Trade in Services, 9 February.

Bascur, R. (1985) 'Information in the Third World: Adjusting Technologies or Strategies?', *Media, Culture and Society* 7(3): 355–68.

Bauer, R., I. Pool and L. Dexter (1963) *American Business and Public Policy: The Politics of Foreign Trade.* Chicago: Aldine.

Becker, J. (1986) 'New Information Technologies (NITs) and Transnational Culture: Is There a European Response', pp. 7–25 in G. Muskens and C. Hamelink (eds), *Global Networks and European Communities: Applied Social and Comparative Approaches.* Tilburg, FRG: Institute for Social Research at Tilburg University.

Becker, J. (1988a) 'Cultural and Media Imperialism: Two Methodological/Epistemological Problems'. Presented to International Association for Mass Communication Research, Barcelona, 24–9 July.

Becker, J. (1988b) 'Telematics and Another Foreign Development for West Germany: Applications for a New Third World–European Relationship'. Presented to International Association for Mass Communication Research, Barcelona, 24–9 July.

Bergen, T. (1987) 'Trade in Services: Toward a "Development Round" of GATT Negotiations Benefiting Both Developing and Industrialized States', *Harvard International Law Journal* 28(1): 1–30.

Bernier, J. (1988) 'A Canadian Dilemma: Free Trade with the United States', *Journal of Cultural Geography* 8(2): 135–42.

Bhagwati, J. and J. Ruggie (eds) (1984) *Power, Passions, and Purpose: Prospects for North–South Negotiations.* Cambridge: MIT Press.

Blanchard, M. (1986) *Exporting the First Amendment.* New York: Longman.

Braman, S. (1989) 'Defining Information: An Approach for Policymakers', *Telecommunications Policy* 13(3): 233–42.

Braman, S. (1990) 'The Unique Characteristics of Information Policy and their US Consequences', pp. 47–77 in V. Blake (ed.), *Information Literacies of the 21st Century.* Boston: G.K. Hall.

Bravender-Coyle, P. (1985) 'International Trade in Services and the GATT', *Australian Business Law Review* 13(4): 217–23.

Brazil (1988) *Elements for a Possible Framework.* Communication from Brazil on Trade in Services to the GATT.

Bronze, G. (1961) 'The Tariff Commission as a Regulatory Agency', *Columbia Law Review* 61: 463–89.

Bruce, R. (1983) 'A Strategic Perspective on US Telecommunications Regulation', *InterMedia* 11(4/5): 76–9.

Bruce, R. (1985) 'Definitions of Services: Line Drawing, Industry Structure and Institutional Assignments'. Second Special Session on Telecommunications Policy, OECD Committee for Information, Computer and Communications Policy.

Bruce, R., D. Cunard and M. Director (1986) *From Telecommunications to Electronic Services: A Global Spectrum of Definitions, Boundary Lines and Structures.* London: Butterworths.

Canada (1984) *Exchange of Information Pursuant to the Ministerial Decision on Services*. Submission to the GATT.

Candilis, W. (ed.) (1988) *United States Service Industries Handbook*. New York: Praeger.

Caporaso, J. (1986) *Changing International Division of Labor*. Boulder, CO: Lynne Rienner.

Carey, J. (1988) 'Taking Culture Seriously', pp. 8–18 in J. Carey (ed.), *Media, Myths, and Narratives: Television and the Press*. Beverly Hills: Sage.

Cass, R. (1987) 'The Perils of Positive Thinking: Constitutional Interpretation and Negative First Amendment Theory', *UCLA Law Review* 34(5–6): 1405–91.

Cass, R. and E. Noam (1989) 'Services Trade and Services Regulation in the United States'. Presented to Symposium on Rules for Free International Trade in Sciences, Tel-Aviv, Israel, 20–2 March.

Ciotti-Revilla, C. and R. Merritt (1982) 'Communications Research and the New World Information Order', *Journal of International Affairs* 35(2): 225–45.

Cleveland, H. (1985) *The Knowledge Executive: Leadership in an Information Society*. New York: E. P. Dutton.

Cline, W. (ed.) (1983) *Trade Policy in the 1980s*. Washington, DC: Institute for International Economics.

Cline, W., N. Kawanabe, T. Kronso and T. Williams (1978) 'Trade Negotiations and the Less Developed Countries', pp. 207–27 in *Trade Negotiations in the Tokyo Round: A Quantitative Assessment*. Washington, DC: Brookings Institution.

Cochran, T. (1960) 'Cultural Factors in Economic Growth', *Journal of Economic History* 20(4): 515–30.

Cohen, S. (1981) *The Making of United States International Economic Policy*. New York: Praeger.

Cruise O'Brien, R. (1980) 'Specialized Information and Interdependence: Problems of Concentration and Access', *Telecommunications Policy* 4(1): 42–8.

Cruise O'Brien, R. (ed.) (1983) *Information, Economics and Power: The North–South Dimension*. London: Hodder and Stoughton.

Cutajar, M. Z. (1985) *UNCTAD and the South–North Dialogue: The First Twenty Years*. Oxford: Pergamon Press.

Damon, L. (1986) 'Freedom of Information Versus National Sovereignty: The Need for a New Global Forum for the Resolution of Transborder Data Flow Problems', *Fordham International Law Journal* 10: 262–87.

Daniels, P. (1985) *Service Industries*. New York: Methuen Andover, Harts.

Davies, R. (1989) 'Signing Away Canada's Soul: Culture, Identity, and the Free Trade Agreement'. *Harper's* 278(1664): 43–7.

Desaulniers, J. (1987) 'What Does Canada Want? or L'Histoire Sans Lecon'. *Media, Culture and Society* 9(2): 149–57.

Destler, J. (1986) *American Trade Politics: System under Stress*. Washington, DC: Institute for International Economics.

Dillon, J. (1988) 'US–Canada Free Trade: Latin America is Next', *NACLA Report on the Americas* 22(4): 7–9.

Dixon, W. (1985) 'Change and Persistence in the World System: An Analysis of Global Trade Concentration, 1955–1975', *International Studies Quarterly* 29: 171–89.

Easterbrook, W. (1960) 'Problems in the Relationship of Communication and Economic History', *Journal of Economic History* 20(4): 559–65.

The Economist (1985) 'A GATT for Services' (12 Oct.): 20.

EEC (1984) *Study on International Trade in Services*. Submission to the GATT.

Eisenstadt, S. (1980) 'Comparative Analysis of State Formation in Historical Contexts', *International Social Science Journal* 32: 624–53.

Engel, C. (1989) 'Trade in Services between the European Communities and Third Countries: Its Regulation by Community Law'. Presented to Symposium on Rules for Free International Trade in Services, Tel Aviv, Israel, 20–2 March.

Evans, P. (1985) 'Transnational Linkages and the Economic Role of the State: An Analysis of Developing and Industrialized Nations in the Post-World War II Period', pp. 192–226 in P. Evans, D. Rueschmeyer and T. Skocpol (eds), *Bringing the State Back In*. Cambridge: Cambridge University Press.

Ewing, A. (1985) 'Why Freer Trade in Services is in the Interest of Developing Countries', *Journal of World Trade Law* 19: 147–69.

Federal Republic of Germany (1984) *National Study on Trade in Services*. Submission to the GATT.

Feketekuty, G. (1986) 'Trade in Professional Services – An Overview'. Presented to University of Chicago Law Forum, Barriers to International Trade in Services, 9 February.

Feketekuty, G. and J. Aronson (1984) 'Restrictions on Trade in Communication and Information Sciences', *The Information Society* 2(3/4): 217–48.

Feketekuty, G. and K. Hausar (1985) 'The Impact of Information Technology on Trade in Services', *Transnational Data Report* 8(4): 220–4.

Gasiorowski, M. (1985) 'The Structure of Third World Economic Interdependence', *International Organization* 39(2): 331–42.

GATT (1979) *Report by the Director-General of GATT. The Tokyo Round of Multilateral Trade Negotiations*. Geneva: GATT.

GATT (1986a) *General Agreement on Tariffs and Trade*. Geneva: GATT.

GATT (1986b) *Basic Instruments and Selected Documents*. Geneva: GATT, 32nd Supplement.

GATT (1986c) *International Trade 1985–86*. Geneva: GATT.

GATT (1986d) *The Texts of the Tokyo Round Agreements*. Geneva: GATT.

GATT (1987a) *Basic Instruments and Selected Documents*. Geneva: GATT.

GATT (1987b) *International Trade 1986–87*. Geneva: GATT.

GATT (1988a) *Results of Mid-Term Meeting*. MTN.TNC/11, 21 April.

GATT (1988b) *Trade Negotiations Committee Meeting at Ministerial Level*. Montreal. MTN.TNC/7 (MIN), 9 December.

Gershuny, T. and L. Miles (1983) *The New Services Economy*. London: Frances Pinter.

Gibbs, M. and M. Mashayekhi (1988) 'Services: Co-operation for Development', *Journal of World Trade Law* 22(3): 81–107.

Gold, M. and D. Leyton-Brown (eds) (1988) *Trade-offs on Free Trade: The Canada–US Free Trade Agreement*. Toronto: Carswell.

Goldhaber, M. (1983) 'Microelectronic Networks: A New Workers' Culture in Formation?', pp. 211–43 in V. Mosco and J. Wasko (eds), *Critical Communications Review*, Vol. I. Norwood, NJ: Ablex.

Goldstein, J. (1988) 'Ideas, Institutions, and American Trade Policy', *International Organization* 42(1): 179–217.

Goldthorpe, J. (1982) 'On the Service Class, Its Formation and Future', pp. 162–85 in A. Giddens and G. Mackenzie (eds), *Social Class and the Division of Labor*. Cambridge: Cambridge University Press.

Gowa, J. (1988) 'Public Goods and Political Institutions: Trade and Monetary Policy Processes in the United States', *International Organization* 42(1): 15–32.

Gray, H. (1983) 'A Negotiating Strategy for Trade in Services', *Journal of World Trade Law* 17: 377–88.

Grey, R. (1983) *Traded Computer Services: An Analysis of a Proposal for Canada/USA Agreement*. Ottawa: Grey, Clark, Shih & Associates.

Haggard, S. (1988) 'The Institutional Foundations of Hegemony: Explaining the Reciprocal Trade Agreements Act of 1934', *International Organization* 42(1): 91–119.

Hamelink, C. (1979) 'Informatics: Third World Call for New Order', *Journal of Communication* 29(3): 144–8.

Hamelink, C. (1983) *Finance and Information: A Study of Converging Interests*. Norwood, NJ: Ablex.

Hamelink, C. (1984) *Transnational Data Flows in the Information Age*. Lund, Sweden: Studentlitteratur AB.

Harter, P. and G. Eads (1985) 'Policy Instruments, Institutions, and Objectives: An Analytical Framework for Assessing "Alternatives" to Regulation', *Administrative Law Review* 37: 221–58.

Hauser, H. (ed.) (1986) *Protectionism and Structural Adjustment*. Grusch. Switzerland: Verlag Ruegger.

Hepworth, M. and K. Robins (1988) 'Whose Information Society? A View from the Periphery', *Media, Culture and Society* 10(3): 323–44.

Hills, J. (1988) 'The Domestic Dynamics of International Telecommunications Policy'. Presented to American Political Science Association, Washington, DC, September.

Hudec, R. (1975) *The GATT Legal System and World Trade Diplomacy*. New York: Praeger, especially chapter 18, 'GATT Developments, 1958–1975', pp. 195–271.

Hudec, R. (1987) *Developing Countries in the GATT Legal System*. London: Trade Policy Research Centre.

Hurwitz, L. (ed.) (1983) *The Harmonization of European Public Policy: Regional Responses to Transnational Challenges*. Westport, CT: Greenwood Press.

Hveem, H. (1987) 'Small Countries under Great Pressure: The Politics of National Vulnerability under International Restructuring', *Cooperation and Conflict* 22: 193–208.

Jackson, J. (1984) 'Perspectives on the Jurisprudence of International Trade: Costs and Benefits of Legal Procedures in the United States', *Michigan Law Review* 82: 1570–83.

Jackson, J. (1988) *International Competition in Services: A Constitutional Framework*. Washington, DC: American Enterprise Institute.

Japan (1984) *National Study on Trade in Services*. Submission to the GATT.

Kaynak, E. (ed.) (1986) *Service Industries in Developing Countries*. London: Frank Cass.

Knieps, G. and P. Spiller (1983) 'Regulating by Partial Deregulation: The Case of Telecommunications', *Administrative Law Review* 35: 391–421.

Krasner, S. (1976) 'State Power and the Structure of International Trade', *World Politics* 28: 317–47.

Kraus, I. (1983) *Services in the Domestic Economy and in World Transactions*. Cambridge, MA: National Bureau of Economic Research, Working Paper no. 124.

Krommenacker, R. (1986) 'The Impact of Information Technology on Trade Interdependence', *Journal of World Trade Law* 20: 381–400.

Labovitz, S. and J. Gibbs (1964) 'Urbanization, Technology, and the Division of Labor: Further Evidence', *The Pacific Sociological Review* 7(1): 3ff.

Lindsay, J. (1986) 'Trade Sanctions as Policy Instruments: A Reexamination', *International Studies Quarterly* 30: 153–73.

Litvak, I. (1988) 'Small Business, Competition and Freer Trade: The Canadian–US Case', *Journal of World Trade Law* 22: 33–46.

Lowenfeld, A. (1986) 'The GATT Principles and Trade in Services'. Presented at University of Chicago Legal Forum, Barriers to International Trade in Services, 9 February.

Machlup, F. and U. Mansfield (eds) (1983) *The Study of Information: Interdisciplinary Messages*. New York: John Wiley.

McKee, D. (1988) *Growth Development and the Service Economy in the Third World*. New York: Praeger.

Mexico (1988) *The Concept of Economic Development in the Uruguay Round*. Report from Mexico to the GATT.

Mosco, V. (1990) 'Toward a Transnational World Information Order: The Canada–U.S. Free Trade Agreement,' *Canadian Journal of Communication* 15(2) (Spring), pp. 46–63.

Netherlands (1984) *Exchange of Information Pursuant to the Ministerial Decision on Services*. Submission to the GATT.

Neu, W., K. Neumann and T. Schnoring (1987) 'Trade Patterns, Industry Structure and Industrial Policy in Telecommunications', *Telecommunications Policy* 11(1): 31–44.

Noam, E. (1986) 'Telecommunications Policy on Both Sides of the Atlantic: Divergence and Outlook', pp. 255–74 in M. Snow (ed.), *Marketplace for Telecommunications: Regulation and Deregulation in Industrialized Democracies*. New York: Longman.

Noyelle, T. and A. Dutka (1986) 'The Development of a World Market for Professional and Non-professional Business Services: Implications for Negotiating Trade in Services'. Presented to University of Chicago Law Forum, Barriers to International Trade in Services, 9 February.

Noyelle, T. and T. Stanback (1984) 'Technological Change and Employment: A "First Pass" at Conceptualization', working paper. New York: Columbia University, Conservation of American Resources.

Nusbaumer, J. (1987) *The Services Economy: Lever to Growth*. Boston: Kluwer Academic Publishers.

Ochel, W. and M. Wegner (1987) *Service Economies in Europe: Opportunities for Growth*. Boulder, CO: Westview Press.

Odell, J. (1985) 'The Outcomes of International Trade Conflicts: The US and South Korea, 1960–1981', *International Studies Quarterly* 29: 263–86.

O'Donnell, G. (1980) 'Comparative Historical Formations of the State Apparatus and Socio-economic Change in the Third World', *International Social Science Journal* 32: 717–29.

Patterson, E. (1986) 'Improving GATT Rules for Nonmarket Economies', *Journal of World Trade Law* 20: 185–205.

Pekelis, A. (1968) 'Legal Techniques and Political Ideologies: A Comparative Study', pp. 355–77 in B. Reinhard (ed.), *State and Society: A Reader in Comparative Political Sociology*. Boston: Little, Brown.

Perrolle, J. (1983) 'Computer Technology and Class Formation in the World System'. Presented to Conference on Communications, Mass Media and Development, Chicago.

Peters, J. (1988) 'Information: Notes Toward a Critical History', *Journal of Communication Inquiry* 12(2): 9–23.

Petersmann, E. and M. Hilf (eds) (1988) *The New GATT Round of Multilateral Trade Negotiations: Legal and Economic Problems*. Deventer, The Netherlands: Kluwer.

Petit, D. (1986) *Slow Growth and the Service Economy*. London: Frances Pinter.

Pollins, B. (1985) 'Breaking Trade Dependency: A Global Simulation of Third World Proposals for Alternative Trade Regimes', *International Studies Quarterly* 29: 287–312.

Preeg, E. (1973) *Trade and Diplomats: An Analysis of the Kennedy Round Negotiations under the General Agreements on Tariffs and Trade*. Washington, DC: Brookings Institution.

Richstad, J. and M. Anderson (eds) (1981) *Crisis in International News: Policies and Prospects*. New York: Columbia University Press.

Rivers, R., V. Slater and A. Padini (1987) 'Putting Services on the Table: The New GATT Round', *Stanford Journal of International Law* 23(1): 13–30.

Roach, C. (1987) 'The US Position on the New World Information and Communication Order', *Journal of Communication* 37(4): 36–51.

Roeder, P. (1985) 'The Ties That Bind: Aid, Trade, and Political Compliance in Soviet–Third World Relations', *International Studies Quarterly* 29: 191–216.

Roncagliolo, R. (1985) 'Information and Transnational Culture: Directions for Policy Research', *Media, Culture and Society* 7(3): 369–84.

Roth, W. (1989) 'International Free Trade in Insurance Services'. Presented to Symposium on Rules for Free International Trade in Services, Tel Aviv, Israel, 20–2 March.

Rubin, S. and M. Jones (eds) (1989) *Conflict and Resolution in US–EC Trade Relations at the Opening of the Uruguay Round*. New York: Oceana.

Ruggie, J. (1982) 'International Regimes, Transactions, and Change: Embedded Liberalism in the Postwar Economic Order', *International Organization* 36(2): 379–415.

Sauvant, K. (1985) 'The International Politics of Data Services Trade', *Transnational Data Report* 8(4): 214–16.

Sauvant, K. (1986) *Trade and Foreign Direct Investment in Data Services.* Boulder, CO: Westview Press.

Schwab, S. (1987) 'Politics, Economics and United States Trade Policy', *Stanford Journal of International Law* 23: 155–76.

Schwartz, B. (1977) 'Administrative Law: The Third Century', *Administrative Law Review* 29: 291–319.

Shaiken, H. (1986) *Work Transformed: Automation and Labor in the Computer Age.* Lexington, MA: Lexington Books, especially 'A "Technology Bill of Rights"', pp. 274–8.

Shelp, R. (1987) 'Trade in Services', *Foreign Policy* 35: 64–84.

Simon, A. and S. Waller (1986) 'A Theory of Economic Sovereignty: An Alternative to Extraterritorial Jurisdictional Disputes', *Stanford Journal of International Law* 22: 337–61.

Sjostadt, G. and B. Sundelius (eds) (1986) *Free Trade – Managed Trade Perspectives and Realistic International Trade Order.* Boulder, CO: Westview Press.

Smythe, D. (1981) *Dependency Road: Communications, Capitalism, Consciousness and Canada.* Norwood, NJ: Ablex.

Spero, J. (1981) *The Politics of International Economic Relations*, 2nd edn. New York: St Martin's Press.

Stewart, R. (1983) 'Regulation in a Liberal State: The Role of Non-Commodity Values', *The Yale Law Journal* 92: 1537–90.

Sweden (1984) *National Study on Trade in Services.* Submission to the GATT.

Transnational Data Report (1984) 'Canada Outlines Culture and Communications Future', 7(1): 14.

Trimberger, E. (1979) 'World Systems Analysis: The Problem of Unequal Development', *Theory and Society* 8: 127–37.

UN Centre on Transnational Corporations (UNCTC) (1989) *Foreign Direct Investment and Transnational Corporations in Services.* New York: UN.

UN Conference On Trade and Development (UNCTAD) (1984) *Services and the Development Process*, TD/B11008.

Unesco (1955) *Trade Barriers to Knowledge.* Paris: Unesco.

Urry, J. (1987) 'Some Social and Spatial Aspects of Services', *Environment and Planning D: Society and Space* 5: 5–26.

US (1984) *National Study on Trade in Services.* Submission to the GATT.

US (1988, May 16) *Procedures for Reading and Implementing a Multilateral Framework for Trade in Services.* Presented to Uruguay Round, GATT.

'US GATT Strategy Threatens Canada and Third World' (1986) *GATT-Fly Report* (May) 7(2): 3–4.

Walsham, G. (1979) 'Models for Telecommunications Strategy in the LDCs', *Telecommunications Policy* 3(2): 105–15.

Wuthnow, R. (1987) *Meaning and Moral Order: Explorations in Cultural Analysis.* Berkeley: University of California Press.

Yoffie, D. (1983) *Power and Protectionism: Strategies of the Newly Industrializing Countries.* New York: Columbia University Press.

Young, D. (1989) 'Cannibalizing Canada', *Rolling Stock* 15/16: 3.

Postscript: Grit in the North Atlantic Turbine: The World Trade Organization as Cultural Policy

The Uruguay Round of the General Agreements on Tariffs and Trade (GATT) – the international negotiations that concluded by establishing the World Trade Organization (WTO) in the early 1990s – was long delayed and tortured in its deliberations because of disagreements over when something was a matter of culture, and when it was not. The GATT had been established as a key part of the global economic system established after World War II to deal with trade in goods. Beginning in the 1980s, however, the United States became determined to use the Uruguay Round negotiations to extend the trading system to international information flows, or "trade in services."

The United States, as were other nations, was motivated by the need to respond to the economic implications of the fundamental social changes referred to as "informatization," the development of the information society. Many of the tools and techniques promoted by the US and, ultimately, other nation-states for this purpose provide the infrastructure and content for globalization as well, such as strengthening global organizational forms and harmonization of information and communication systems across national borders as well as across types of content. As the information economy grew, such tools and techniques have made it possible to bring within the economy types of cultural products and practices never before commodified.

The result was tensions among nation-states in the developed world as well as between the developing and developed worlds over GATT treatment of culture writ both small and large: "Small," in the sense that the US-proposed approach to trade in services included international agreements regarding specific treatment of flows of cultural goods such as television programs and films as well as cultural practices such as tourism, generating a framework within which cultural policy dealing with such goods and practices at the national level must be cast. Individual countries in both developed and developing worlds were concerned that domestic cultural industries would suffer, at the cost of local content as well as the survival of firms, professions, and industrial sectors. The question of quotas for the percentage of European television content from the US, for example, was one of the most contested over the course of the Uruguay Round negotiations. Experience with the impact of the North American Free Trade Agreement (NAFTA) on Canadian cultural industries had already made clear that such concerns were realistic.

Concerns over culture writ "large" derived from concern over the implications of the exacerbation of informatization and globalization trends that the proposed frameworks for trade would provide. Many nation-states in the developing world already experienced their relationship to the global economy as one of dependence despite the theoretical comparative advantage reliance on agriculture should have provided them within an industrialized and informatized world. Further strengthening the information economy, they feared, would only deepen the gaps between the developing and the developed.

In the end, the outcome of the Uruguay Round reflected US hegemony in a post-Cold War world. Specific rules were developed for treatment of cross-border flows of cultural goods and practices in the General Agreement on Trade in Services (GATS) and Trade Related Aspects of Intellectual Property (TRIPS) in addition to formation of the WTO to handle implementation of the GATT, GATS, and TRIPS. While each nation-state had the responsibility of crafting its own deal with the WTO in order to be accepted as a member, the degrees of freedom with which domestic policies could be drafted were severely implemented by the terms of the GATT, GATS, and TRIPS.

The WTO system reflects informatization and globalization in yet another way: While historically transfers of information, communication, and culture were perceived only when they occurred through the physical transportation of goods such as film canisters and books, today theorists and researchers also examine the flows of populations, organizational forms, and knowledge structures. In the WTO context this is acknowledged by incorporating treatment of four types of relationships within its notion of cross-border flows of services. "Cross-border supply" covers flows of services from the territory of one member into the territory of another, whether via telecommunications or physical mail. "Consumption abroad" is a type of flow that occurs when the service consumer or his or her property moves into the territory of another member state in order to obtain a service, as in tourism or ship repair. "Commercial presence" occurs when there is transportation of a service across a border via establishment of a business to deliver the service within the territory of another member state. And services also flow when individuals from one member state enter the territory of another in order to deliver a service there, what is known as the "presence of natural persons."

Half a dozen years into living with the result it has become clear that there is a third level on which these trade agreements are of interest as matters of culture, for the very notion that national governments have the right and responsibility to enter into international agreements that structure the global economy has itself come under attack. Thus today the WTO and the agreements it operationalizes are cultural policy on three levels:

- They determine the terms that govern national policy and determine the experience of cultural goods and practices; indeed, international preemption of national decision-making in these areas is explicit. This is *direct cultural policy* in its most traditional sense as decision-making elements of culture as articulated through the categories of "high" art, popular culture, and traditional cultural forms.
- They determine the rules by which the processes of informatization unfold, with all that they entail for the fundaments of cultural experience. This is *indirect cultural policy* that shapes the structures within which such elements of culture exist.
- And they constitute a culture in and of themselves that is now itself increasingly the site of conflict. This might be termed *anthropological cultural policy*, policy that promotes a particular culture as defined not in the artistic but in the anthropological sense.

In each of these areas, the tensions are still high. Restrictions on domestic support for cultural industries have led to open disputes, as in Canadian complaints over WTO constraints on its ability to tax US-based periodicals imported into Canada. Support for the commercialization of traditional music, tales, and designs (including their use in global advertising) via intellectual property rights is increasingly resented by those peoples that have spent thousands of years developing such materials and practices but are incapable of either controlling or benefiting from their use under contemporary conditions. Across the board, issues raised by treatment of specific areas covered by domestic cultural policy provide the stuff of recommendations now in place for discussion during the next round of WTO meetings: Canada would like to see the WTO decision regarding taxation of periodicals revisited, and there is a growing movement to extend the protections of TRIPS to traditional forms of knowledge and to permit intellectual property rights to be held by communities as well as by individuals.

Because of the broad way in which diverse services are defined and because each country can choose which services to include in its agreement with the WTO, the actual status of direct cultural policy provisions can only be understood through detailed analysis. "Advertising," for example, is defined as including all services used in connection with the creation, planning, placement, and distribution of advertising through any communications platform. Thus GATS provisions dealing with advertising affect not only advertising agencies and marketing experts, but also film producers, computer animators, printers, typesetters, graphic designers, website designers and programmers, carpenters, hair stylists, and so on. The content as well as the amount and placement of advertising are extremely culturally sensitive, for many countries resist the general trend towards consumption, the consumption of specific goods (such as alcohol), and/or the use of specific types of images (e.g., images of women not completely covered) in advertising. Thus of the 142 countries that had reached agreements with the WTO as of July 2001, only 51 included advertising among the services covered. In response, the US complains in its negotiating proposal for the advertising sector that reluctance to acquiesce to GATS rules regarding advertising unreasonably burdens the advertising industry, which must either spend more to craft advertisements as appropriate for diverse markets or choose not to advertise in specific restricted markets at all.

GATS rules regarding treatment of accounting, legal, and consultancy services are the most important elements of the WTO as indirect cultural policy. Each of these facilitates informatization and globalization processes. Accounting services do so in two ways. The ability of transnational accounting firms – all based in the United States – to operate globally makes it easier for them to facilitate the evolution of networked global organizational forms (increasingly oligopolistic in nature). At the same time, they provide the conceptual infrastructure for harmonization of legal systems by providing the categories through which newly-commodified forms of information, communication, and culture can be identified, quantified, tracked,

and regulated. Harmonization of legal systems is now including explicit attention to standardization of terms regarding the movement of cultural materials across borders and "transparency" regarding biases towards indigenous cultural practices as a means of attempting to ensure equal access to those "markets." In this area, developments within the WTO have effects complementary to efforts of other international organizations such as UNESCO, which is currently promoting the use of cultural policy in the service of development.

Resistance to the WTO as a culture in itself may seem trivial, for the demands of those involved in street actions such as those seen in Seattle and Genoa are rarely cast in operationalizable terms and may serve to generate more resistance than compromise. Over time, however, it has become clear that the growing numbers of individuals and groups involved in such actions is having an impact at least on public opinion. Perhaps more important, however, such activities are emblematic of the loss of belief in the political and economic principles underlying the geopolitical structures of the past several centuries. In this they demonstrate and feed the weakening of identification with the responsibilities of citizenship at the nation-state level, which in turn is one of the significant factors leading to changes in the nature of the nation-state altogether.

By the time of writing, July of 2001, efforts to launch the next round of trade talks (the Doha Round, to be held in Qatar) are already two years in, again as a result of deep tensions over cultural matters at all three levels. It is feared that should Europe and the United States not come together on even a basic agenda for the talks and countries in the developing world become convinced that it is still worth their while, the global trading system may come apart altogether. Should this occur, the systematic reduction in barriers to trade built over the last 50 years would be reversed. The results would be replacement of multilateral agreements with bilateral and regional agreements that most experts agree would best serve the strongest nations and would further decimate the ability of developing nations to effectively participate in the global economy. Innovations in the informational meta-technologies of biotechnology have even replaced the agricultural bases of many states in Africa, Asia, and Latin

America with products that can be manufactured in Europe and North America.

Sometimes the poets see it first. The late Ed Dorn, whose epic poem *Gunslinger* is arguably the most perceptive, richly nuanced, and complex analysis of the West and its interactions with capital available, provided insights into the post-World War II international trade system in *The North Atlantic Turbine*. In Dorn's vision the global trading system would exhaust all of those drawn into it in its frenzy of consumption:

> People are
> going to step *all over* property.
> They're going to put their fingers
> right through it. They are going,
> very shortly,
> to eat it *all*.
> (*The North Atlantic Turbine*, p. 20)

The engine Dorn described and that the WTO now drives is increasingly fragile. Consensus at the center is weakening. While the flag of capital accumulation still flies, it is not stable; vast fortunes come and go so quickly that they may be said to be snapping in a global trade wind. The reasons this is so have more to do with culture than with economics as narrowly defined. In an economy based on information flows this may be an example of Marshall McLuhan's prediction that, at their extreme, media effects reverse themselves. It is certainly evidence that irrespective of continued US refusal to acknowledge the cultural impact of economic, technological, and political decisions, the realm of cultural policy now encompasses them all.

Chapter 23

Crafting Culture: Selling and Contesting Authenticity in Puerto Rico's Informal Economy

Arlene Dávila

During the past decade Puerto Rico has seen what scholars have termed a "culture-oriented social movement," or the growth of a new wave of nationalism where Puerto Ricans are taking renewed pride in their culture and identity. This resurgence is often associated with the growth of grassroots cultural activities highlighting elements of Puerto Rican culture, folklore and history (Milagros González 1990; Quintero-Rivera 1991). Currently there are hundreds of such events throughout the island, organized by local groups, municipal governments and even private corporations. This growth in cultural activity, however, is also being spurred by an emergent informal economy revolving around the sale of typical food, drinks and folk arts which, though an important component feeding the growth of these events, has remained largely undocumented.[1]

The present article analyzes this culture-oriented informal economy through a discussion of the marketing of folk arts by contemporary Puerto Rican artisans. Because this sub-sector of the island's informal economy plays a key role in the local nationalist discourse, my analysis pays particular attention to how artisans' sales strategies are affected by this discourse as well as to how they simultaneously impact what is considered more or less representative of Puerto Rican culture. As such, the article explores the connections between the symbolic role that folk arts play in nationalist discourse, and their

economic importance for people's everyday subsistence.

The commodification of culture, or the rendering of culture as a thing, such as an object or a piece of folk art that has economic value that can be exchanged in the market, is a recurrent subject of contemporary analysis.[2] Studies have documented the commodification of culture for tourist consumption, where the government selects and promotes traditions for internal and external consumption, and pointed to a growing transnational network of art dealers and international markets where other people's traditions are given value, marketed and appropriated as either world music or "ethnic art" (Crain 1996; Myers and Marcus 1996; Stromberg-Pellizzi 1993). These studies remind us, as García Canclini (1993) has argued, that the "traditional" does not fade away with modernization. Instead, it is reconstituted in new forms – transformed into folk objects, nationalist or tourist symbols – and reordered around new logics of production and consumption centered on museums or the market.

Emphasis on the larger processes affecting the commodification and commerce of culture at the national or international level, however, should not distract us from the fact that these processes are also very much active at the local level where they are driven by economic need or by the same processes that render "cultural" products economically profitable. That is, it is not only nationalist elites or international dealers who manipulate or profit from culture, but increasingly also the unemployed and underemployed who turn to this sector as a viable economic choice. In fact, as research on Latin American artisans has pointed out, the marketing of crafts is evolving into an important economic resource, not only for peasant and "traditional" communities, but also, and increasingly, for urban populations and the unemployed (Nash 1993). These processes have led to a consistent increase, rather than a decline, in artisanal production alongside the processes of modernization.

Less often discussed, however, are the processes by which artisans are also involved in the commodification of their own "traditions," that is, in the transformation and appropriation of notions of traditional culture in order to join in what for many is becoming a viable and emergent economic sector. Such processes, as we shall see in the case below, are not free from contestation. Specifically, the involvement of new producers and more competitive conditions in the marketing of culture bring to the fore struggles over who can be an "authentic" producer and over what is more culturally relevant and, therefore, more profitable. Such distinctions are not elaborated solely by government representatives seeking to sanction an "authentic" folk art production, but also by artisans themselves as they in turn seek to differentiate themselves and their products in an increasingly competitive market.

What follows analyzes some of these contestations and how they impact people's ability to join in folk art sales on the island. As we will see, most of the struggles over the sale and promotion of folk arts concern the symbolic role they play within the island's nationalist discourse. Such a role both feeds a quest for authenticity and quality in its production, and compels artisans to market not only their products, but also their own authenticity in order to assert their right to participate in what will be described here as a culturally sanctioned economic field. These economic strategies, however, also have important implications for the island's nationalist discourse. For in the process of marketing themselves and their products as "culturally relevant," artisans both feed and challenge dominant discourses of cultural authenticity, sometimes incorporating dominant standards of authenticity in their own

productions and other times advancing more popular and flexible criteria for defining appropriate cultural products.

The Culture Oriented Informal Economy

The rise of the informal sector in Puerto Rico is a well known, but under-documented aspect of Puerto Rican economy. The few works that have touched on the subject have recognized its diversity, its extension to the middle classes, and its economic impact, which is estimated to be in the billions of dollars (Ortiz 1992; Pantojas 1990). Yet given the island's high rate of unemployment, which is over 20 percent, it is not too farfetched to consider the informal economy, involving any unregulated income-generating activity, an important motor of Puerto Rico's economy.[3]

In fact, whereas local scholars have been unable to define its scope, it is commonly recognized that the informal economy, along with federal welfare subsidies, is a major source sustaining what has been termed a "post-work society" (Milagros López 1994). This situation can be traced to the island's history of development strategies and economic restructuring along the lines of U.S. interests, which have consistently displaced local economic sectors and diminished the place of salaried work as a central principle in people's everyday lives.

Grassroots cultural festivals are currently an important component of the island's informal economic sector. These events are organized for a variety of purposes, such as to celebrate a regional foodstuff or to raise funds for social causes and projects, but they are always free and open to the public, providing an attractive environment for a variety of vendors. For while these events require governmental permits and pay patents for sales, their reputation as "cultural activities" renders them "safe" and shields them from the policing that characterizes public mass events on the island, such as concerts or sports events. Within these festivals, the sale of folk art is emerging as the preferred and most viable economic activity. First, unlike vendors of food, drinks and other goods attending these events, artisans constitute the symbolic base that gives any activity a "cultural" look, and they are therefore always sought after as participants. As opposed to other vendors, who may be charged thousands of dollars to sell in the most popular grassroots events, fees are waived for artisans or they are charged just a small amount, and they often even receive a small stipend or a free lunch for the duration of the event. Moreover, annual yields from the sale of folk arts in Puerto Rico are exempted from government taxes up to $6,000, a provision that gives artisans a means of disguising their financial profits if they so wish. Thus, folk art production attracts a growing informal artistic/cultural sector, which ranges from unemployed university graduates to long-term unemployed and under-employed individuals now turned into odd vendors, folk artists and performers.

In turn, the changing nature of the contemporary Puerto Rican artisan is now a recurrent subject of discussion. Artisan activists, for instance, have criticized the permanence of the government-generated romanticized notions of folk art as the "embodiment of Puerto Rican nationality," pointing instead to the major transformations undergone by folk art production (Vargas 1992; López 1993). Less discussed, however, is the fact that discussions about who is the most authentic artisan and what is the most representative folk art are being actively engaged in because of their continued importance for distinguishing who is the "rightful" Puerto Rican artisan and, thus, who can or cannot profit from the economic benefits extended to artisans. These are the issues that continue to propel many to appropriate and manipulate dominant notions that render folk arts as the embodiment of Puerto Rican culture and traditions. This criterion, in turn, benefits some but excludes others from participating in this economic sector. In order to understand these dynamics we must first analyze some of the elements that are currently employed for distinguishing authentic artisans on the island.

Arte-Sano

Local standards for defining a true Puerto Rican artisan are succinctly embodied in the pun "Arte-Sano" or "Sane Art" advanced by a radio interviewer in a program dedicated to the state folk arts in Puerto Rico that was aired live during

a Folk Arts Fair in 1993. The pun, used to introduce his "artisan" guests, summarizes the dominant coordinates around folk arts in Puerto Rico: that artisans and their creations are positive contributions to Puerto Rican culture and that folk arts are good and sane, as are, by extension, their creators.

Implied in these associations of culture and folklore is the idea that artisans are representatives of a nation's essence, a correlation that is not unique to Puerto Rico but that is a common trope of many nationalist ideologies. As Richard Handler has stated, emphasis on the "folk" is a key metaphor of Western based nationalist ideologies in which the folk is not only constructed as the essence of a nation, but also as its embodiment – as the concrete objects and elements that can "prove" the existence of a nation (Handler 1988). As such, folk art promotion became a central component of the local government's strategies for self-definition.

Thus, shortly after Puerto Rico became a Commonwealth or Free Associated State of the United States in 1952, folklore was emphasized as a key element through which to construct and disseminate an official view of the national identity. This status provided the island local autonomy for the first time since the beginning of U.S. occupation in 1898, and facilitated the establishment of cultural policies and institutions. As early as 1957 the government's primary cultural institution, the Institute of Puerto Rican Culture, sponsored the National Folk Arts Fair in Barranquitas, and since 1963 the ICP (its Spanish acronym) has hired folk arts promoters to identify appropriate representations of folk art. Most importantly, government cultural institutions, such as the Tourism Office and the Institute of Puerto Rican Culture have since helped fund and organize hundreds of folk art fairs and cultural festivals where folk arts are sold, exalted and promoted as an important expression of Puerto Rico's identity.

The role of folk art promotion, however, was not limited to the substantiation of Puerto Rico's national identity. Cultural policies and symbolic enactments of national themes are also key elements in the dissemination of dominant ideas about the content of any given national identity (Herzfeld 1997; Domínguez 1989). In Puerto Rico, these processes reproduced dominant ideas of the island's national identity revolving around a romanticized Spanish past, a traditional past, and the racial blending of Spanish, Indian and African components of society. Accordingly, the crafts selected to be promoted and identified as "representations of culture" were mostly hand-made pre-industrial products – crafts of the rural peasant, rather than the lumpen proletariat or the coastal worker – definitions directly related to Puerto Rico's peasant-based national myth that emphasizes a utopian agrarian past as the backbone of Puerto Rican nationality.

These images are still prevalent today. The government's cultural institutions still promote the image of an elderly male, rural, white peasant who inherited the craft from his immediate family and is a patriot and a true lover and defender of culture. This artisan carves "santos" (wooden images of Christian and Spanish derived iconography), does woodwork, makes hammocks associated with the indigenous tradition, or carves coconut masks, associated with the African tradition, thereby reproducing the three legacies believed to constitute Puerto Rican identity. Most importantly, the true artisan does not rely solely on his or her craft for sustenance. The economic role that crafts have historically played on the island is ignored by this conception that emphasizes only the patriotic role of folk artists as the bearers of Puerto Rican cultural traditions.

This government exaltation of the folk through cultural fairs and programs, however, soon had unexpected consequences. In particular, such stimuli simultaneously gave rise to the growth of independent grassroots artisan groups, cultural groups and folk music groups, and the marketing of anything folk as an important economic activity in its own right. This is evident in the emergence of one of the most important non-governmental folk art organizations, the "Hermandad de Artesanos," founded in 1970, which, contesting official views of artisans, began to highlight folk art's economic significance in Puerto Rican society. Founded by a group of university students, the Hermandad de Artesanos challenged the idea that the "rightful" artisan was the older master producer, highlighting instead new producers, which included university students and the unemployed. Among its goals was the promotion of new fairs as a way to increase the available markets for folk art sales and the organization of artisans as a group by uniting,

though for a brief time, all of the artisan groups of the island into a common organization. In fact, while there is no organization that presently encompasses all artisans island-wide, many artisans still popularly refer to themselves as belonging to a "gremio" or an artisanal class. These initiatives, in the 1970s, constituted some of the first challenges to the government-produced romantic view of folk art production.

The government has since recognized the growing economic role of folk arts through cultural policies and, more directly, through the creation in 1978 of the Fomento folk art office, charged with the promotion of folk art production as a sustainable economic activity. However, the symbolic role of the folk as a "representation of culture" has contributed to the maintenance of standards and regulations for defining authenticity. Thus, standards for the evaluation of artisans were institutionalized through formal evaluations during the 1970s at the same juncture when more would-be artisans began to seek participation in cultural festivities. Since then, evaluations for selecting "proper" artisans have been carried out by government cultural institutions such as the Institute of Puerto Rican Culture, the Tourism Office, and Fomento. Those selected are issued I.D. cards certifying them as artisans, a status that facilitates their participation in government-backed fairs and assures their inclusion in the official artisan registry consulted by hotels and private corporations for the organization of their own activities.[4]

The criteria upon which artisans are defined as such were explicitly listed in 1986 in Law no. 99 which stipulated, among other things, that the product "be made in Puerto Rico, that it use Puerto Rican material, and that the themes relate and reflect Puerto Rican culture, such as its history, its fauna, flora, and the symbols of the traditional life of our people." The image of the Puerto Rican artisan as an old male who loves his country and is a true master of his art continued to be reproduced in government institutions.

Yet, in sharp contrast to official views of folk artists, 52.9 percent of contemporary Puerto Rican artisans are women, most are between 31 and 40 years of age, and 56 percent live in urban areas (Vargas 1992). A study conducted by Miriam Vargas, a former director of the ICP's Popular Arts Division, referred to these artisans as "neo-artisans" because fifty-one percent were found to have been working as artisans for only the last ten years. Most of these neo-artisans learned their craft from friends, at technical schools, or even at the university. Most of them took up their craft as a means of solving unemployment problems, and most of them, irrespective of their cultural motivations for taking up the craft, increasingly respond to economic pressures. As a result, it is what sells best that guides the choice of the items they produce: souvenirs in clay and leather, decorative pots, keychains or silkscreen t-shirts. These items are decorated and therefore authenticated through decorations developing "Puerto Rican themes," such as the racial trilogy of Spanish, Indian and African elements, validating in turn the coordinates that are seen to make up the Puerto Rican national identity. These racial themes are elaborated through images of the Spanish Catholic-derived Three Kings celebration, the iconography of the indigenous Taino or through nationalist phrases and poetry.

Nevertheless, what is produced ends up challenging traditional distinctions between handicrafts, kitsch and folk arts as well as nationalist precepts about purity in folk arts as developed and maintained by government institutions. For it is jewelry and other easily manufactured goods, regarded by government agencies as handicrafts and not folk arts, that are much more common than the "traditional" folk arts (wood carving, embroidery, mask making). These require more time and training to produce and are therefore less profitable for the artisans. Moreover, the primary materials of contemporary folk arts, such as leather and clay, are mostly imported from abroad because of cheaper prices, which challenges governmental dictates that authentic crafts be made from indigenous materials. Such practices question prevalent notions of artisans as "defenders of Puerto Rican values and traditions," highlighting instead the economic needs motivating contemporary artisan production.

We Eat and Live From Culture

So far this article has established some of the coordinates by which "authentic" artisanal work is defined as well as the disjunction be-

tween such standards and the productions and motivations of present-day artisans. In the next section the focus will be on the processes by which these disjunctions are bridged and manipulated in everyday life, rendering authenticity less a matter of unattainable government-sanctioned standards, and more an issue of one's ability to present one's production as culturally relevant. As we shall see, it is through the successful manipulation of dominant ideas about folk art as a representation of culture that would-be artisans obtain government accreditation and maintain networks with those involved in the planning and organization of events. These processes, in turn, contribute to a discourse of authenticity which artisans both help to reinforce and circumvent.

For instance, in order to claim authenticity, artisans draw distinctions between culturally and economically oriented artisans, which reinforce government standards about folk arts. As Abi, a college graduate turned bead jeweler after she was unable to find a job in her field of psychology, explained: "You have to take into account that there are two types of artisans: those who do this from vocation and do it as a way of life, for money and profit. The true artisan wants to improve her art and represent our culture, not just make money." Ignoring the fact that she herself was geared to folk art because of her own inability to find employment in her field, she further noted that "folk art should not be the refuge of the unemployed."

Similar distinctions between artisans who espouse cultural motivations and those who "merely" do it as a matter of survival were advanced by artisans involved in the festival circuit who described themselves as *"luchadores"* (fighters for the nation), or *"trabajadores de la cultura"* (cultural workers) or as educators, never as just "vendors." These distinctions are also made by artisans when judging each others' attitudes toward folklore; patriotic considerations for selling folk arts are more likely to be rendered as "authentic," whereas economic motivations would disqualify commercial musicians from claiming authenticity. In this way, education and patriotism were used as synonyms of authenticity whereas selling for economic purposes was perceived as unpatriotic and illegitimate. This discourse, in turn, serves to strengthen the government-sanctioned view that folk art production should be geared to patriotic motives, furthering the goals of the policies that prioritize folklore as an intrinsic aspect of cultural identity.

While presenting themselves as "cultural" in order to assert the legitimacy on which the profitability of their work is based, it is common among contemporary artisans to define their productions as authentic and cultural according to more flexible standards. Being made by a Puerto Rican, and having Puerto Rican themes, whether peasant, Afro-Caribbean or reminiscent of Taino imagery, even when products were made with foreign materials or were mass produced, could define a product as legitimately Puerto Rican. The more flexible criteria used to define folk arts often represent an accommodation between the cultural content required of folk art, and its economic and commercial function as a means of livelihood. An informant who had been working on jewelry since she was fifteen years old and who relies on the income from her craft to supplement her part-time job stated: "My work is folklore because it is made here and by myself, a Puerto Rican. I obtained my ICP card doing something else but I continued adding beads because it is what I like and it sells much better. I am indeed a representative of Puerto Rican culture, but one who represents a contemporary aspect and a historical moment in Puerto Rican culture and history, unemployment and the socioeconomic situation."

As this young woman did, many artisans obtain their licenses by showing one "authentically made product," only to substitute them later in fairs with whatever it is they originally wanted to sell. Such is the case of Alina, another young artisan, who passed her evaluations showing leather goods inscribed with Taino iconography, and now sells fashionable leather purses which sell much better. She was well aware that the cloak of authenticity may assure participation in fairs and activities but not profitability. "Who pays me for the time and the materials?" she asked me. "Everyone wants you to do leather goods with Taino iconography because they are 'cultural' but then no one buys them. If I want to remain competitive I have to come up with something else."

In fact, while artisans are provided better sales conditions than other vendors in cultural events, they are also faced with greater pressures, as Alina soon found out when trying to live off her Taino-inspired purse bags. That is, the same processes that render them symbolically important render them a subordinate sector of Puerto Rico's informal economy, as they are faced with the pressure of "keeping truth" in their products. This pressure, in turn, limits their ability to innovate or adopt more aggressive sales strategies vis-à-vis festival vendors selling food, drinks and a variety of manufactured goods, from toys to jewelry to kitchen utensils.

This, of course, does not mean that artisans are not constantly involved in renewing their products to increase profitability. Indeed, some of their efforts in this area have led to major transformations in what is considered culturally relevant folk art in contemporary society. The changing views towards t-shirts printed with nationalist messages and patriotic slogans are a good example of these transformations. Once banned from fairs, considered a mass-produced item, they are now a must at all grassroots events, and are even being sold in the government's folk arts store in San Juan, which claims to buy only from the most noted artisans on the island. These t-shirts, in turn, are contributing to the dissemination of new aspects of Puerto Rican history and tradition. Decorated with popular slogans or images of Puerto Rico's Afro-Caribbean heritage, they are helping to enlarge the themes associated with Puerto Rican culture by celebrating salsa musicians, reggae music or beach scenes that are juxtaposed with patriotic slogans and identified as part of Puerto Rican culture.

Overall, however, contemporary developments in folk art production have not ended the need to present one's work as cultural and authentically Puerto Rican, as evidenced by the numerous practices through which people aim to circumvent government standards of authenticity. Moreover, while new means of defining authenticity are advanced through these strategies, discursive distinctions around "authenticity" remain and contribute to fostering distinctions among those who can or cannot rightfully gain a livelihood in this sector. This reproduces class and political distinctions between those who are or are not able to manipulate this discourse of authenticity because of their class and political background and educational levels. Specifically, this discourse shuns less educated vendors who may lack the ability of college educated vendors to present their products as culturally relevant.

Consider the case of Juan Sepúlveda, who found himself unemployed and engaged to be married when he was introduced to folk arts by a friend. He was aware that he needed to produce something connected to Puerto Rican culture or history if he was to be considered a proper artisan. While he claimed he did not know much about Puerto Rican history – he told me he never took a class on Puerto Rican history – he had studied agronomy at the university, a background he used to do some research on Puerto Rican autochthonous birds. He ended up crafting clay figurines after them which allowed him enough money to get married and procure subsequent invitations to other festivals. Awilda, on the other hand, who never went to school as a young woman, having spent those years working in a needlework factory, had less luck presenting herself and her products as "culturally relevant." She makes handmade clowns which she learned to do as a young woman in the needlework factory; yet, while she hand-embroiders her creations, she has had greater difficulty obtaining recognition of her clowns as representations of Puerto Rican culture. Unlike Sepúlveda, she did not research a specific topic or articulate an argument about how her dolls reflect Puerto Rican history and culture, and so had problems during the evaluation process which required her to explain her dolls' connection with the local culture. She has since been awarded her artisanal card and recognized as an official folk artist, but she still complains of being excluded from many of the most important fairs and activities which are always coordinated either by or with the assistance of the government cultural institutions.

Another form of exclusion generated by the discourse on authenticity, and perhaps the most controversial in the colonial context of contemporary society, is that taking place along partisan political lines. Puerto Rico has been debating its political future and its options of independence, U.S. statehood, or permanent commonwealth. This debate has created a highly charged and politically divided political context. Accordingly, civil jobs and patronage have historically been distributed mostly along partisan lines among the dominant parties representing U.S. statehood and commonwealth. These dynamics also affect the organization of different fairs, where invitations, prizes for production and so forth are also distributed along partisan lines, with the dominant parties (commonwealth and pro-statehood) favoring their own members whenever they are in control of the government.

Such partisan patronage in fairs, however, has most often favored pro-independence and commonwealth advocates, who have historically dominated cultural institutions. The Pro-Commonwealth Party, under whose tenure the first cultural policies were instituted in the 1950s, has since been associated and identified with the government's cultural institutions. For its part, pro-independence advocates have found in the island's cultural institutions a site for cultural resistance, in a colonial context where they were overtly and covertly persecuted. Yet, as cultural work becomes an important medium of people's livelihood, the continued association of folk art production with partisan political interests adversely affects many who are neither active in these parties, or advocate a different political ideology. Many statehood artisans, for instance, claim to receive fewer invitations to fairs than their pro-commonwealth or pro-independence counterparts despite their compliance with other criteria for assuring "authenticity" in their productions, or their economic need. A statehooder woman who beads rosaries from indigenous seeds provides a good example of how these political partisan divisions play out in the festival circuit. While she would not otherwise have problems in being credited as an authentic artisan, she claimed to be continuously rejected from some of the most important fairs because of her political views. In turn, her reaction to such a situation feeds into the existing political partisan distinctions on the island: she started to organize her own fairs, inviting her own friends, also members of her party, whom she claimed felt similarly shunned because of their political ideology.

The case above is indicative of the ongoing struggles involved in the marketing of culture, in relation to people's strategies to participate in a culturally sanctioned economic domain. Studies of the commodification of culture oftentimes reproduce distinctions between the outside marketers and local producers drawing our attention away from the local struggles involved in determining what is culturally valuable, and who and what will be included and excluded from such determinations. In part, such emphasis results from ongoing distinctions between what is "global" and "local," categories which continue to pervade contemporary analysis. Thus, studies abound about the appropriation of local traditions by nationalist elites or about their incorporation as part of an international "world of goods" (Miller 1995; Kaplan 1995; Howes 1996). As we have seen through the case at hand, however, culture is also actively sold, marketed and contested by local actors, and these processes are also characterized by struggles and contradictions. Such struggles are directly related to the island's cultural nationalist discourse, which has an impact on the processes through which folk arts can be marketed and sold. For, as highly contested and manipulated as the category of folk art may be in Puerto Rico, it continues to be enmeshed in the island's cultural nationalist discourse, which still shapes the dominant criteria for defining authenticity. As a result, whereas production has become a popular recourse for many, artisans remain constrained by the government-sanctioned discourse of authenticity: unlike other vendors, they are expected to know the "right way" to sell themselves and their products.

There is a clear need to analyze cultural revivals, such as those involving a rise in cultural activities and an interest in folk art production, in relation to wider political and economic factors. In particular, we can see in the present case how a cultural revival is also intrinsically related to the economic realities of growing unemployment and the growth of a cultural artistic sector within Puerto Rico's informal economy. Culture is also increasingly everyone's concern because more and more people eat and live from culture. Ignoring the economic dimension that folk art production plays in cultural and nationalist movements may lead us to reproduce the same romanticized view of folk art production advanced by nationalist elites, and thus feed and contribute to, rather than question, the same discourse that generates inequalities in cultural production.

Notes

1   This article is based on qualitative research on Puerto Rico's cultural politics conducted in the

summer of 1992 and in 1993–4. At that time, I visited over twenty cultural activities and folk art fairs and interviewed artisans, and organizers of cultural events along with representatives of the government cultural institutions. The fieldwork on which this article is based was supported by the Wenner-Gren Foundation for Anthropological Research, the National Science Foundation, and the City University of New York–University of Puerto Rico Academic Exchange Program.

2   The subject of commodification has been extensively researched in social science literature. For the purposes of this paper I draw on Arjun Appadurai's (1986) analysis of the processes of exchange as the key factor in commodification. Accordingly commodities are those things that are found in a "commodity phase" where "its exchangeability… for some other thing is its socially relevant feature." See also Friedman (1994).

3   I am drawing from Alejandro Portes's definition (Portes 1989), which emphasizes the unregulated component of the informal economy, focusing on any economic activity that, normally regulated, goes unregulated by institutions of society. As such, the informal economy is perceived to encompass the variety of activities people engage in as a response to unemployment and underemployment. See also Ortiz (1992).

4   For instance, one of the largest and most popular fairs, the Bacardi Folk Arts Fair, organized by the Bacardi Corporation, draws directly from the list of official artisans to assure the authenticity of the event. See Dávila (1998) for a larger discussion of this fair.

References

Appadurai, Arjun. 1986. *The Social Life of Things*. Cambridge: Cambridge University Press.

Crain, Mary. 1996. "Negotiating Identities in Quinto's Cultural Borderlands: Native Women's Performances for the Ecuadorian Tourist Market." In *Cross Cultural Consumption*. Ed. David Howes. London: Routledge.

Dávila, Arlene. 1998. *Sponsored Identities: Cultural Politics in Puerto Rico*. Philadelphia: Temple University Press.

Domínguez, Virginia. 1989. *People as Object, People as Subject*. Madison: University of Wisconsin Press.

Friedman, Jonathan. 1994. *Consumption and Identity*. Hardwood Academic Publishers.

García Canclini, Néstor. 1993. *Transforming Modernity: Popular Culture in Mexico*. Texas: University of Texas Press.

Handler, Richard. 1988. *The Politics of Culture in Quebec*. Madison: University of Wisconsin.

Herzfeld, Michael. 1997. *Cultural Intimacy, Social Poetics in the Nation State*. London: Routledge.

Howes, David. 1996. *Cross Cultural Consumption*. London: Routledge.

Kaplan, Flora. 1995. *Museums and the Making of Ourselves. The Role of Objects in National Identity*. London: Leicester University Press.

López, Ramón. 1993. "El Oficio y la Cultura, Artesanos Puertorriquenos de Hoy." *Diálogo* (December): 8–10.

Milagros González, Lydia. 1990. "Cultura y Grupos Populares en la Historia Viva de Puerto Rico Hoy," *Centro* 2 (8): 98–113.

Milagros López, Maria. 1994. "Post Work Selves and Entitlement Attitudes in Peripheral Postindustrial Puerto Rico." *Social Text* 38: 111–34.

Miller, Daniel. 1995. *Worlds Apart: Modernity through the Prism of the Local*. London: Routledge.

Myers, Fred and George Marcus. 1996. *The Traffic in Culture*. Cambridge University Press.

Nash, June. 1993. *Crafts in the World Market: The Impact of Global Exchange on Middle American Artisans*. Albany: SUNY.

Ortiz, Laura. 1992. *Al Filo de La Navaja: Los Márgenes en Puerto Rico*. Río Piedras, Puerto Rico: Centro de Investigaciones Sociales.

Pantojas, Emilio. 1990. *Development Strategies as Ideology*. Boulder, CO: Lynn Rienner Publishers.

Portes, Alejandro, Manuel Castells, and Lauren Benton. 1989. *The Informal Economy*. Baltimore: Johns Hopkins.

Puerto Rico Civil Rights Commission. 1991. "Informe sobre discrimen y persecusión por razones políticas: las prácticas gubernamentales de mantener listas, ficheros y expedientes de ciudadanos por razón de su ideología política." *Revista del Colegio de Abogados* 52 (January–March).

Quintero-Rivera, A.G. 1991. "Culture-Oriented Social Movements: Ethnicity and Symbolic Action in Latin America and the Caribbean." *Centro Bulletin* (Spring): 97–104.

Stromberg-Pellizzi, Gobi. 1993. "Coyotes and Culture Brokers: The Production and Marketing of Taxco Silverwork." In *Crafts in the World Market*. Ed. June Nash. Albany: SUNY.

Vargas, Miriam. 1992. *Artesanos y Artesanías en el Puerto Rico de Hoy*. San Juan: Centro de Estudios Avanzados.

Part IX

Urban Planning

Introduction to Part IX

Justin Lewis

It has long been fashionable to decry the more conspicuous products of urban planning, whether it's the anti-social redevelopments of the 1960s or expensive public projects like London's Millennium Dome. There is no shortage of easy targets: across the globe, urban landscapes are littered with examples of thoughtless or ill-conceived development. And, yet, regardless of foolish talk by free marketeers, there is no doubt that the growth of urban or suburban populations and the proliferation of the automobile make urban planning both difficult and necessary. Some of the most inhumane forms of urban development – notably but by no means exclusively in the developing world – are products of a lack rather than a surfeit of planning.

What constitutes "planning," however, is often demarcated along bureaucratic lines – rather than in terms of who actually makes the decisions that shape urban development. The decision of many governments to invest in and subsidize road-building rather than rapid urban transit systems has had profound implications for urban spaces, and it is often urban planners who have been asked to contain the ensuing muddle. As Kenneth Jackson points out, the growth of suburban shopping malls in the US – and the consequent decline of town and city centers – was the product of a series of government decisions (notably to favor road over rail, to keep the price of gas low, to grant certain forms of property tax relief, and the establishment of weak zoning laws) rather than a natural or inevitable form of growth. And yet these decisions were not made with the *intent* of shifting economic and cultural activity from town and city centers to suburbs and outlying strip developments. Indeed, like much government policy, they were made in *response* to certain pressures (generally pressure from business lobbies) with little serious consideration of the long-term effect on urban development. Urban planning, if it happened at all, was usually an afterthought.

A recent example of urban planning policy being made inadvertently in response to business pressure involved the failure of the US Congress to make Internet shopping subject to the same local sales taxes as brick and mortar stores. Apart from the loss of revenue for local public services, the fragility of many retailers' profit margins may make them vulnerable to even a small percentage decrease in sales. Assisted by these tax advantages, the growth of Internet retailing thus has the potential to decimate a whole tier of the less profitable retail sector (particularly smaller, locally owned businesses or shops in less affluent areas), and thereby alter the urban landscape in ways that professional planners can do little about.

Needless to say, those who are paid to plan or develop urban spaces do not have a monopoly on prescience, and the profession has a history of embracing models that have had unwelcome social and aesthetic consequences (such as the redevelopment of Boston's West End or some of the post-war British slum clearance schemes). A common feature of bad planning – if we can use such a bluntly evaluative term – is the inability to fully appreciate the popular cultural life and complex social aesthetics of urban spaces. Conversely, as Worpole and Greenhalgh (1996) point out, development that incorporates the anthropology of spatial use are more likely to be able to create diverse, dynamic and democratic environments – and it is the cultural aspects of planning and urban development that are highlighted in this section.

Thus we can differentiate between planning advocates such as Prince Charles and his concern for how buildings look (they need to look quaint) and the "new urbanism," which also draws upon pre-urban models, but does so in ways that focus on "the village" as a *cultural space* rather than an architectural style. The semiotics of public space tells us that the meaning of buildings is determined not merely by designers, artists, civil engineers or architects but by social contexts. So, for example, a public mural in an upscale urban retail setting might be used to designate the specificity of the locale amidst a swathe of clean-lined corporate emblems, while the same mural on the wall of a run-down housing estate may simply look like a cheap, messy attempt to cover up graffiti or to alleviate the drab exterior of the environment. Similarly, for a pedestrian, the roadway that takes traffic along a high street can be *experienced* in very different ways depending upon how that roadway is used (the volume of traffic, its speed, the size of the curb, the presence or absence of parked cars between curb and traffic, the number of crosswalks and so on).

How we use or experience an urban space will also depend upon how other people use it: the number of people in a given space, who they are, and how they look and behave will affect the meaning of that space. Central business districts that are bustling and dynamic in daytime can have a faintly desolate, threatening air in the evening, while the number of people on the streets of residential areas can make them seem welcoming or places to be merely hurried through. An urban center planned as a mixed-use development – one that combines business, retail, entertainment and residential use – may be less utilitarian, but its varied and fairly constant population can give it vibrancy as a public space. Residents have nearby places to eat, drink coffee, work, shop or be entertained, while their presence makes the streets busier and more secure – especially in the evening. Like all urban spaces,

mixed-use development is dependent on the presence of well-run urban transit systems or traffic control and parking facilities, and the absence of nearby shopping malls or "big box" store developments that threaten the viability of city center stores.

Crude notions of economic efficiency, whether they are put in place by planners or market forces, can, in this sense, be at odds with attempts to create livable urban space. Well-behaved "rational" consumers will shop at the Wallmart on the edge of town because it's easy to park and the prices are cheap, and in so doing appear to sanction neo-liberal policies in which such things as productivity costs and consumer sovereignty are paramount. But they may later regret the subsequent loss of a vibrant urban center, where boarded-up shop-fronts signify a spiral of downward economic decline (unable to compete, stores close, then restaurants and cafes, then theaters, and amidst the insecurity of increasingly empty streets it becomes a less desirable place to live, thereby draining the volume of disposable income). The low-wage, low-benefit jobs that Wallmart provide invariably fall short of jobs they have displaced (one of the reasons for Wallmart's efficiency, after all, is their ability to sell more with lower labor costs), while a whole range of related cultural industries are also threatened (the local paper, for example, will lose a range of local advertisers and a vital source of revenue). Some local groups, aware of these risks, have thus fought to keep Wallmart from setting up shop. Citizens' groups in Greenfield in northwestern Massachusetts, for example – a town with a fragile local economy but with a still viable mixed-use downtown – fought a long and ultimately successful battle against Wallmart. In a corporate-friendly political climate, this is no small victory: Wallmart is currently one of the forty largest economic entities on the planet. Wallmart's transnational clout means that it is well positioned to take advantage of global trade agreements, and it thereby represents a very powerful vision of the future of retailing.

Local battles against Wallmart oblige us to raise questions about the ways in which citizenry is implicated by planning and urban design. What kinds of possibilities do urban locales encourage or allow, and who is most able to benefit from these possibilities? The shift from a high street to an indoor suburban shopping mall, for example, makes certain kinds of behavior – gathering petitions or busking – less permissible, while certain forms of action (specifically, those that involve buying things) are privileged. More profoundly, feminist critiques of traditional notions of public space require us to consider the relations between domestic and outdoor space. If residential areas are removed from public spaces – parks, shopping areas and so on – people working at home (such as women with young children) are isolated by the geography of their environment and effectively excluded from that public space.

Or suppose a town that *does* successfully develop around mixed-use planning subsequently becomes seen as a more desirable place to live than surrounding towns whose centers have spilled out into strip malls? As house prices and rents go up, the shops and restaurants become more upscale, and poorer residents find themselves economically and culturally displaced. Urban planning and development is thereby implicated in class relations and taste cultures. Even if a city is designed with an egalitarian intent, the presence of attractive public spaces in the vicinity tends to inflate rents and house prices, and neighborhoods segregate in ways that make access to certain kinds of public space – whether it's a good public school or a playground – potentially restrictive. Policies like rent control and the development of affordable housing in middle-class or high-income areas are thus tools for extending or democratizing the availability of public space, as well as increasing the diversity of that space (without rent control, Manhattan loses some of its vibrancy and edge).

Questions of citizenship also abound in some of the well-known urban planning or economic development initiatives based around tourism, whether it's the accommodation of Frank Gehry's Guggenheim museum in Bilbao, Glasgow's city center refurbishment, or the expansion of tourist development in Cuba. Attracting well-heeled tourists with promises of high culture or First World comfort may, in some cases, be a way of generating local revenue, but it also runs the risk of promoting certain forms of citizenship – those who have the right tastes or enough of the right currency – and neglecting others. The challenge for tourist-based forms of economic development is to maximize economic development (to promote the development of local cultural industries, for example, so that tourists spend money on value-added local products rather than T-shirts and trinkets produced by a global sweatshop economy) while blending the aesthetics of tourist development with popular habits. Easy to say, difficult to do.

As the articles that follow demonstrate, urban development is fill of intricacies and complexities, a mish mash of thoughtful ideas, thoughtless development, good intentions, bad intentions and a host of unintended consequences (so it was, for example, that Victor Gruen, one of the designers of the prototypical US suburban shopping mall, was motivated by the desire to *limit* suburban sprawl). But all of them are concerned with urban planning as a cultural practice, and all, in their different ways, invoke democratic notions of cultural citizenship, notions very different from the corporate offerings (Citizen Disney or the Sovereign Consumer) that loom large on many urban horizons.

Reference

Ken Worpole and Liz Greenhalgh. *The Freedom of the City*. London: Demos, 1996.

Chapter 24

Re-inventing Times Square: Cultural Value and Images of "Citizen Disney"

Lynn Comella

To city planners, Disney is like a gift from heaven. No better antidote to the squalid decrepitude of Times Square could be found on earth than the company that is the very symbol of Snow White innocence and family fun. (Usborne, 1995)

This whole history of place building suggests that a cultural politics has just as frequently been at the root of the inspiration of place construction as has simple desire for profit and speculative gain. Yet the intertwining of the two is omnipresent. . . . (Harvey, 1993, p. 19)

Introduction

Part memoir, part sociological tract, Samuel Delany's *Times Square Red, Times Square Blue* (1999) pays eloquent homage to an urban landscape that is in the midst of a dramatic cultural transformation due to the twin processes of gentrification and redevelopment. With the kind of detail and "thick description" more often associated with anthropologists, Delany poignantly chronicles the people, places, social activity, and sexual culture that now face almost certain extinction as the landscape of Times Square is physically and discursively revamped (p. xi). In the two extended essays that make up the body of his book, Delany recounts and, at times, analyzes the social functions and pleasures provided by the Times Square porn theaters where his own sexual activity has thrived for nearly three decades. In doing so, he documents and brings to life a world of social-sexual activity that others – unable to see or appreciate the functions that such activity may fulfill – have simply written off as indications of urban decay and moral decline.

Delany argues that re-imagining and re-developing Times Square necessarily implies an "*a priori* major demolition, destruction, and devastation" of one of the world's most famous urban spaces. "With the rush to accommodate the new," he claims, "much that was beautiful along with much that was shoddy, much that was dilapidated with much that was pleasurable, much that was inefficient with much that was functional, is gone" (p. xviii). Whereas the physical transformation of Times Square may be more or less apparent to the naked eye – the area now boasts renovated theaters, new restaurants, and a booming tourist industry – Delany's commentary draws important attention to the cultural repercussions of urban renewal, and the complicated social processes that facilitate such a dramatic reconstruction of place. His account is significant, I think, precisely because he reminds us that people use places to organize their social worlds in a variety of ways, including sexually. Thus, economic (re)development never occurs in a cultural vacuum, but always takes place in relation – and sometimes opposition –

to the concrete realm of human experience and cultural practice.

This essay examines the ways in which notions of public culture, cultural value, and cultural enfranchisement have been simultaneously disrupted and redefined – both materially and ideologically – by a complex set of social processes commonly referred to as the Disneyfication of Times Square. I argue that the economic and cultural transformation of Times Square is the result of a state-sponsored, corporate-driven rearticulation of public culture that pivots on what David Evans describes as a "family centered moral/sexual ideology" (1993, p. 6), and on a series of cultural oppositions between family-oriented entertainment and sexual entertainment; "legitimate" versus illegitimate forms of social pleasure; and licit versus illicit forms of cultural activity.

I suggest moreover that the re-invention of Times Square is a story about a twin set of cultural policies – the public subsidy of Disney's renovation of the New Amsterdam Theater and the implementation of a city-wide zoning ordinance – that, working in tandem, cemented an economic and cultural partnership between Disney and the City of New York that has transformed the way cultural citizenship and public space are configured. In 1993 New York City planners began negotiations with Disney in the hope that the company and its wholesome, family-oriented image would become a major player in the economic revitalization of the area. Their goal was to reinvent Times Square as a vibrant entertainment showcase and corporate home for the entertainment industry, transforming it into a place that would appeal to both businesses and tourists alike. Six years later, it appears as though they have achieved their goal: Disney has renovated the historic New Amsterdam Theater, and opened both a Disney Store and the ESPN Sports Zone restaurant, all on 42nd Street; ABC's Good Morning America (a subsidiary of Disney) began broadcasting from Times Square in September, 1999; and other media giants including Reuters, Bertelsmann, Billboard Publication, Viacom's MTV, and Conde Nast, which publishes the *New Yorker*, *Vogue*, *GQ*, and *Vanity Fair*, now claim Times Square as their home. What social processes made these sweeping changes possible, and with what cultural effects?

In examining the sexual politics of Times Square's redevelopment project I use a cultural studies approach that foregrounds questions of cultural policy and the politics of urban renewal. Although the designation "cultural studies" has come to represent a "fairly dispersed array of theoretical and political positions" (Bennett, 1992, p. 23), what inevitably binds these different positions together is a shared commitment to "examining cultural practices from the point of view of their intrication with, and within, relations of power" (ibid). Because questions of power have always been central to the project of cultural studies, Bennett advocates the inclusion of policy considerations in our very definitions of and approaches to culture. Placing questions of policy at the center of our cultural analyses invariably requires us to consider the role of the state in shaping cultural practices, in turn dispelling the contemporary myth in capitalist economies of a non-interventionist state. Instead, as I argue in this essay, the state, *vis-à-vis* cultural policy, assumes an active role in producing and regulating the cultural practices and social subjectivities of its citizens, particularly in regard to sexual behavior.

Sexual Commerce and Cultural Conflict in Times Square

Times Square has served as a center for popular entertainment, sexual commerce, and tourism since the early twentieth century.[1] It is an area widely recognized not only for its more "respectable" forms of social entertainment – theaters, movie houses, arcades, and restaurants – but also for its sexual underworld and its "bawdy entertainment and erotically exciting street life" (McNamara, 1995, p. ix). Since the turn of the century, it has been a place where various forms of commercial culture and sexual entertainment have co-existed, helping to establish the area, at least in the broader cultural imagination, as an epicenter for a wide array of cultural practices. Historically, Times Square has also been one of the few areas of New York City where "social elites shared the streets and institutions of the neighborhood with more ribald elements of New York's sexual underworld" (Gilfoyle, 1996, p. 272), creating a sense of cultural democracy in an otherwise class-bound urban space.

In the essay "From Soubrette Row to Show World: The contested sexualities of Times Square, 1880–1995" (1996), Timothy Gilfoyle charts the history of sexual commerce and regulation in Times Square, demonstrating the extent to which sexual entertainment has always been part of Times Square's cultural repertoire, albeit a contested one. Gilfoyle argues that Times Square has been a site of conflict over sexual entertainment and behavior since the nineteenth century:

> For almost two hundred years, sexuality has been an integral part of New York's thriving leisure economy. From brothels, theaters, concert saloons, and dime museums in the 19th century to massage parlors, cabarets, and "call girls" in the 20th century, erotic entertainment for hire has remained an ever-present reality of New York's "underground" economy. Sex has long been treated as a commodity, bought and sold in the urban entertainment marketplace. (p. 264)

Since the early twentieth century Times Square has repeatedly been a battleground for competing forms of leisure, entertainment, and sexuality (Gilfoyle, p. 264). Indeed, various reform efforts aimed at "cleaning-up" Times Square and revamping its image are part of the area's history. According to Gilfoyle, however, more recent clean-up efforts, including the city-wide zoning ordinance that was passed in 1995, mark the most pernicious and aggressive attempts in City history to "utilize municipal or state power to restrict land and property use in regards to sexual behavior" (p. 263), a point I will return to later.[2]

As Gilfoyle's work suggests, the City's recent efforts to transform Times Square should be understood within a larger historical framework, one that demonstrates a long-standing concern over competing forms of leisure and entertainment, the regulation of sexual commerce and activity, and a crisis of representation over the "public face" of Times Square. By 1925 the theater district was firmly established in Times Square, and 42nd Street had reached the apex of its glory. The onset of the Great Depression and the era of Prohibition, however, dramatically altered the meaning (or at least the availability) of certain forms of commercial entertainment in Times Square (Newmark, 1995, p. 68). Burlesque theaters and speakeasies multiplied during this time, and, according to at least one contemporary ob-

server, "the decline of the street began." According to Newmark, the "slide continued" in the 1960s, and by the 1980s, the block of 42nd Street between 7th and 8th Avenue was considered by many to have the worst crime rate and sanitation problems of any block in New York City. Much to the dismay of City officials and many of the neighborhood's residents, the "image problem" of Times Square only worsened as the area became "a home to drug pushers and pimps and a center for child prostitutes and runaways" (ibid). Thus, not unlike other historical periods, "quality of life" concerns, particularly in regard to adult-oriented businesses and sexual entertainment, came to dominate the rhetoric of urban redevelopment.

Since the early 1980s, efforts to revive Times Square have been both economic and symbolic in nature.[3] The economic redevelopment of Times Square has ultimately depended on making the area attractive to corporations like Disney, which, in turn, has required an a priori transformation of the area's tawdry and downtrodden image. If Times Square's bold bawdiness helped make it a legend, there were many people who believed that a new found sense of respectability and propriety would make the area more appealing to more people (especially tourists) and, by extension, more profitable. Despite the fact that commercial sex has had a long and varied history in the area, representing what one current resident describes as a panoply of "inexpensive thrills," it has clearly been seen by many as an unsightly blemish, rather than a vital – or economically viable – part of the cultural landscape. Thus, as the history of Times Square suggests, the politics of economic redevelopment cannot be easily separated from a complicated politics of sexual representation and regulation.

Cultural Policy and the Disney Invasion

We're going to get rid of the filth and bring back the old values. This is the beginning of a whole new era.

Former New York Governor Mario Cuomo

When Disney formalized a deal with the City of New York in July 1995 to renovate the historic yet dilapidated New Amsterdam Theater on 42nd Street, City planners and community organizers alike declared that the "future of 42nd Street had arrived" (Pulley, 1995). For many of those who had been involved in the area's stalled plans for redevelopment, Disney's arrival "unlocked the paralysis that had afflicted efforts to rescue Times Square and its environs from the brigades of pimps, pushers, and tricksters" (Usborne, 1995). It was indeed the beginning of a new era, and Disney was paving the way. As journalist Paul Goldberger commented, "the reality is that Disney came to 42nd Street not so much because Disney was ready to become like New York as because New York was ready to become like Disney" (1996).

Disney's decision to bring its name and image to Times Square was a major departure from the carefully crafted environments that Disney was used to constructing. The company's long history of place-building is reflected in theme parks like Disneyland and Disney World, and the prefabricated community of Celebration, Florida, where even the smallest of details could be orchestrated and finessed, and where Disney's image of American wholesomeness and childlike innocence could be protected.[4] Disney was not used to blending into a pre-existing urban environment like Times Square where potentially unruly and unsavory elements might clash with the company's carefully constructed image of family-friendly order and entertainment. To maximize the business opportunities that Times Square presented, and minimize any damage to its well-polished image, Disney spent several years negotiating its terms with the City before finally agreeing to become part of a more "family-friendly" Times Square.

In the book *Variations on a Theme Park* (1992), Michael Sorkin and the collection's other authors describe the new postmodern cityscape as a *theme park*, a place where the democratic public realm is substituted for an untroubled regulated vision of pleasure that resembles the controlled environments of the theme park (p. xv). Perhaps not surprisingly, Disney actually set the standard for theme parks with the opening of Disneyland in Anaheim, California in 1955, providing a model that combined entertainment, tourism, and mass leisure. Susan Davis describes a theme park as being "commercial to its core" (1996, p. 402). "It is

the site for the carefully controlled sale of goods (souvenirs) and experiences (architecture, rides and performances), 'themed' to the corporate owner's proprietary images" (ibid). Much like the organization of shopping malls, the theme park depends on the carefully planned construction of a landscape and the orchestration of people's movements through "a cluster of commercial opportunities" (ibid.), with the ultimate goal of maximizing sales. According to Davis, not only are the meanings of the theme park centrally produced, but they are intended to be as non-conflictual as possible. Despite the appearance of a variety of cultures, histories, texts, and architectures, the message offered by a theme park is ultimately one of uniformity and homogeneity (p. 403).

Davis's work on theme parks, especially her provocative ethnography of Sea World in San Diego, California (1997), foregrounds the increasing privatization of public space in a new era of corporate penetration. For Davis, theme parks are not only a form of entertainment, but now represent an important part of an expanding global media system. Since the early 1990s, a number of large theme parks have been acquired by media conglomerates (Davis, 1996). Such acquisitions, like Time Warner's purchase of Six Flags, have created new possibilities for the cross-promotion of a variety of consumer goods. Theme parks, and now themed cities, have become another cog in the wheel of media conglomeration and corporate "synergy," where the combination of "marketing, advertising and content has become the essence of media profitability" (Davis, 1996, p. 406).

Historically then, theme parks have played an important role in the commercialization of public space. Significantly, however, as Sorkin points out in the essay, "See you in Disneyland" (1992), theme parks as a cultural form are also becoming the preferred "apparatus for keeping every urban problem out of sight" (1992, p. 230). In the case of Times Square, Disney has been positioned as a corporate knight in shining armor with the power to solve a variety of social ills associated with urban life (e.g. crime, poverty, sanitation, and public sex) by transforming the city into a homogenized and carefully policed park. Here, cultural production and cross-promotion – not to mention corporate profitability – have become intimately intertwined with the task of regulating a potentially unruly urban-based citizenry.

In his discussion of modern consumer culture and the rise of the indoor shopping mall, Kenneth Jackson reminds us that the implementation of different commercial systems and retail strategies involves policy decisions and forms of government intervention that affect the organization of our social world (1996). Jackson suggests that tax breaks, zoning, and the US government's subsidy of automobile travel as opposed to public transportation, are examples of cultural policies that helped facilitate the proliferation of suburban shopping centers to the economic and cultural detriment of urban-based central business districts. Jackson's work is instructive, particularly in regard to the Disneyfication of Times Square, because he brings questions of policy to bear on the commercial and social organization of urban space. As I have already suggested, the economic and cultural partnership between Disney and the City of New York was cemented by a twin set of cultural policies. First, Disney was provided with a generous public subsidy to assist with the renovation of the New Amsterdam Theater, which would give the company a permanent home on Broadway for its own productions. Second, and perhaps more symbolically significant, was the City's adoption of a controversial, city-wide zoning ordinance that made it illegal for adult-oriented businesses to operate within 500 feet of schools, houses of worship, residential areas, or each other. According to former New York Governor Mario Cuomo, the official policy was simple: "The policy was: get Disney's name" (quoted in Bagli and Kennedy, 1998). Working in tandem then, these two policies made Times Square more appealing to Disney, helping to facilitate a particular form of economic resurgence and the symbolic transformation of the area.

Public subsidy and tax breaks

Public funds were used to subsidize 75 percent of the estimated $34 million cost of renovating the New Amsterdam Theater. Disney agreed to contribute $8 million to the project (an amount that was less than the bonus received by Disney Chairman Michael Eisner in 1997). The City staunchly defended the deal, arguing that Disney's presence in Times Square would ultimately produce jobs and revenue in the form of taxes and tourist dollars, in addition to improving the neighborhood, and bringing other family-oriented businesses to the area.

Offering tax breaks and low-interest loans as incentives to businesses is not an unusual practice. In this case, however, Disney agreed to give the City and the State part of its gross sales from the theater, in addition to paying interest and rent, which is unusual. Disney agreed to give the City and State 2 percent a year for the first $20 million in sales and 3 percent on sales over $20 million (Finder, 1995), further solidifying the economic partnership between Disney and the City.

From the start of its negotiations with the City, however, Disney was concerned about who its new neighbors would be. "What's happening on the balance of the street is very important," said one senior vice president at Disney. "We need to have good neighbors" (quoted in Weber, 1994). Thus, before formalizing its agreement with the City, Disney required City planners to secure commitments from other companies who would also be willing to come to Times Square. Although the City successfully wooed other family-oriented businesses to the area, Disney was the only company to receive any public funds to assist with the costs of building and renovation.

Zoning

When the renovated New Amsterdam Theater was unveiled at a public ceremony in April, 1997, Disney Chairman Michael Eisner, New York City Mayor Rudolph Giuliani, and New York Governor George Pataki were all on hand to promote the "new" Times Square. Their collective presence also helped to publicly mark the growing alliance between Disney and the State. The nature of this partnership was captured when, during his closing remarks, Michael Eisner shared a story about walking along 42nd Street with the Mayor more than two years earlier. As he walked through Times Square that day, he expressed his reservations to the Mayor about bringing Disney to an area that was still dotted with porn shops, peep shows, and nude dancing. According to Eisner, the Mayor looked at him and said, "Michael, they'll be gone" (quoted in Weber, 1997).

In October, 1995, three months after Disney finalized its deal with the City to renovate the New Amsterdam Theater, New York City Council voted to adopt the controversial city-wide zoning ordinance which would regulate the location of adult-oriented businesses, effectively prohibiting their location within 500 feet of churches, schools, or residential areas. Although not specifically aimed at the adult-oriented businesses located in Times Square, the zoning ordinance made it difficult, if not impossible, for the remaining adult businesses in the area to exist alongside Disney without dramatically altering the nature of their businesses, and little effort was made by the City to downplay the fact that Disney had made the cleansing of Times Square a prerequisite for its investment in the area (see Usborne, 1995).

Prior to 1994, the Zoning Resolution of the City of New York made no distinction between commercial uses that were adult in nature and those that were not (Fahringer, 1998). As a result, adult-oriented businesses like topless bars, peep shows, video outlets, and porn theaters, were permissible in any area zoned for commercial or manufacturing use (Gilfoyle, 1996). The language of the amendment approved in October 1995, however, helped to construct and codify the distinctions between adult entertainment and other commercial uses by describing adult businesses as representing *"objectionable non-conforming uses* which are *detrimental to the character of the districts* in which [they] are located" (as quoted in Sex Panic! 1997, emphasis mine). With this in mind, the stated purpose of the zoning ordinance was to provide a mechanism that would help "guide the future use of the City's land by encouraging the development of desirable residential, commercial and manufacturing areas with appropriate groupings of compatible and related uses and thus to promote and to protect public health, safety and general welfare" (ibid). Enforced in its full capacity, the zoning ordinance would effectively eliminate an estimated 84 percent of New York's adult establishments (Fahringer, 1998), advancing Giuliani's "quality of life" campaign and, at the same time, making good on his promise to sanitize Times Square in preparation for Disney's occupation.

In February 1996, more than one hundred adult-oriented businesses initiated an action in New York State Supreme Court to have the zoning ordinance declared unconstitutional on the grounds that it violated their First Amendment rights to free speech and expression. Despite a protracted legal battle, and a series of public protests involving sex workers and peep show operators, the constitutionality of the zoning ordinance was repeatedly upheld by the Courts.[5] The zoning ordinance was put into effect in August, 1998, when the city began padlocking adult businesses that were not in compliance with the ordinance, enacting what many critics viewed as a calculated form of State sponsored censorship that had the potential to turn the "whole city into a cultural wasteland" (Mulligan, 1998). While many businesses attempted to comply with the law – which stipulated that 60 percent of all merchandise needed to be non-adult in nature – by putting bathing suits on exotic dancers and adding videos of 1970s football highlights to their stock, other businesses opted or were forced to close their doors.

Although I certainly align myself with those who oppose the zoning ordinance, it is important to recognize the limitations of opposing the ordinance solely on the basis of First Amendment rights. Framing the argument in terms of free speech versus censorship potentially risks foreclosing any discussion about the kind of role the state should play in urban planning. For example, zoning that restricts suburban development could be attacked on the same logic (that it "censors" the rights of shopping mall developers to express themselves), but the effect of this type of state intervention – to maintain the economic and cultural vitality of the city center – is quite different and part of a much more progressive politics. Significantly, the question should not be *whether* the state is involved in urban planning and redevelopment, but *how and to what end*.

In effect, New York City's zoning ordinance legitimated the state's power to eliminate commercial establishments and forms of cultural activity that were viewed as being *objectionable, non-conforming* and *detrimental* to the character of any given area. According to Gilfoyle, nowhere did the City's efforts to restrict land and property use in regard to sexual behavior take on greater symbolic meaning than Times Square, where the process of redevelopment was already well underway (1996). The zoning ordinance, therefore, in conjunction with the City's generous public subsidy of Disney, helped to rearticulate a notion of public culture that pivoted on a series of *openly acknowledged* cultural oppositions between objectionable and non-objectionable forms of cultural activity, helping to pave the way for Disney's commercial and cultural occupation of Times Square.

Cultural Value and the Reconstruction of Place

Now G-Rated, New York City's Times Square is Family-Friendly. (Ogintz, 1997)

In the essay, "From space to place and back again" (1993) David Harvey argues that the material practices and experiences involved in the construction and reconstruction of place must be "dialectically interrelated with the way places are both represented and imagined" (p. 17). Harvey discusses what he refers to as the "Lefebvrian matrix" as a way to think about place (re)construction as a complex social process. For Harvey, places are (re)constructed on three different, but interrelated levels: Places are material artifacts; they are represented in discourse; and quite significantly, they are used as representations, as "symbolic places," within the broader cultural imagination (p. 17). Harvey underscores the idea that places are constituted – and reconstituted – not only through economic forces, but, moreover, through activities of signification and representation. Our understanding of place, according to Harvey, is ultimately organized through a process of evaluation and hierarchy, and "the elaboration of some kind of mental map of the world which can be invested with all manner of personal or collective hopes and fears" (p. 22).

Harvey's work is significant, I think, not only because he provides us with a model for understanding place (re)construction as a complex set of interrelated social processes, but because he also provides us with a way to talk about the cultural transformation of Times Square in terms of a politics of representation and cultural evaluation. For if we agree with Harvey that the political-economic possibilities of place (re)construction – and indeed policy decisions – are highly influenced by the evaluative manner of

place representation, then it is important to examine how this evaluation occurs and with what effects.

Much like Harvey, Lewis also argues that addressing the question of cultural value, although difficult, is unavoidable because "our cultural values, after all, constitute the guiding principles of our cultural policy" (1990, p. 25). Although Lewis examines how systems of artistic and aesthetic value operate in regard to public funding of art, he underscores the idea that a system of cultural value is developed and maintained by the dominant power structures in society. In light of these ideas – the influence of dominant power structures on processes of cultural evaluation and policy decisions – how do we make sense of the discourse of cultural value and redevelopment advanced by Disney and the state? What implications does this value system, one steeped in what Evans refers to as a "family centered moral/sexual ideology" (1993), have for the kinds of social pleasures and forms of entertainment made available to people within the context of a public sphere increasingly dominated by, and identified with, the corporate interests of Disney?

Perhaps the best place to turn for answers to these questions are to the cultural policies themselves. For example, the public funds used to attract Disney to the area were not similarly disbursed to every business that was interested in becoming part of the new Times Square. Rather, as Mr. Cuomo stated, the policy was quite simple: The City wanted Disney, and was willing to invest a large sum of money to attract Disney – and its image – to the redevelopment project. To City planners, Disney was not just *any* entertainment company, but a widely recognized symbol of American wholesomeness, child-like innocence, and family values. Symbolically then, Disney had the kind of cultural currency that the City wanted to acquire in the hope of attracting other business, not to mention tourist dollars, to the area. From the moment it formalized its agreement with the City, Disney was positioned as a powerful agent of economic and cultural change. The company became a kind of cultural missionary, bringing its own version of family values and corporate ethos to one of the most famous red light districts in the world.

If the generous public subsidy given to Disney confirmed the symbolic significance and cultural currency associated with Disney's image, then the language of the zoning ordinance provides important clues about the cultural value (or lack thereof) assigned to adult-oriented businesses. The zoning ordinance described adult businesses *solely* in terms of their perceived negative effects. In the language of the ordinance, these businesses represented "objectionable non-conforming uses," which were seen as "detrimental to the character of the districts in which [they] are located." There was nothing in the ordinance that suggested adult businesses fulfilled any redeeming social functions whatsoever, or that they provided a livelihood to those working in the sex industry. In fact, the very language of the ordinance codified a system of cultural evaluation and hierarchy that made it extremely easy for people to pit the wholesome image of Disney against the sleazy image of Times Square's adult businesses, helping to construct two competing, and morally distinctive, images of Times Square: one before Disney and one after. What this ultimately means is that the Disneyfication of Times Square is as much about cultural politics and the assertion of family values, as it is about economic revitalization and the transformation of urban space, for the intertwining of the two, as David Harvey suggests, is omnipresent.

Sexual Citizenship versus images of "Citizen Disney"

In his discussion of the Times Square redevelopment project, Samuel Delany underscores the fact that people need *places*, including explicitly sexualized places, to congregate, meet others and, if they so choose, engage in social-sexual encounters where mutual pleasure is exchanged. For Delany, public venues for sexual activity, including bars, cruising spots, porn theaters, and peep shows, are a necessary prerequisite "for a relaxed and friendly sexual atmosphere in a democratic metropolis" (p. 127), because they ultimately fulfill needs that "most of our society does not yet know how to acknowledge" (p. 90). In pondering the impact of the Disneyfication of Times Square on his own sense of sexual enfranchisement, Delany asks "What kind of leaps am I going to have to make now between the acceptable and the unacceptable, between the legal and the illegal, to continue having a satisfactory sex life?" (p. 108).

I return to Delany's account because he consistently reminds us that Times Square is a place inhabited by *people*. Because of this, I think it is important to at least speculate about how the economic and cultural transformation of Times Square has affected those who live, work, and play within its borders, especially those like Delany who already exist at its sexual and cultural margins. How might we understand the convergence between public policy, cultural forms and practices, and citizenship rights, particularly in regard to sexual behavior? How might we frame questions of citizenship and place?

Although there is no universally-accepted definition of citizenship, recent work in the area of cultural policy has foregrounded the way "technologies of governance," which include cultural policy, produce social subjects capable of governing themselves and becoming part of an economically and socially productive citizenry (Miller, 1993, 1998; Bennett, 1995; Ouellette, 1999). Significantly, this work acknowledges that citizenship is no longer premised solely on one's connection to blood, soil or national origin, but it is something that is socially constructed. Because of this, the realm of culture, and the policies that inform some cultural forms and practices, are inevitably – and perhaps increasingly – implicated in the process of citizenship formation and regulation by helping to facilitate, strengthen, or even deny a sense of cultural representation and enfranchisement.

Like race, class, gender, and nation, sexuality also represents a sphere of social difference around which cultural forms, patterns of consumption, and citizenship rights have historically been organized. David Evans refers to this social organization as "sexual citizenship" (1993). According to Evans, sexuality is linked to the processes and power relations of modern capitalist social formations, and "mediated through the state's formal machineries and practices of citizenship" (p. 36). What is significant about Evans's model of citizenship is the articulation of sexuality and citizenship struggles to the logic of the market and the interests of the state. As I have argued throughout this essay, it is precisely this logic, and the overlapping interests between Disney and the state, that have guided the economic and cultural transformation of Times Square. In the process, two different forms of citizenship premised on distinctly different models of social pleasure, cultural values, and consumptive practices have been articulated and pitted against each other. At one end of the spectrum is a form of sexual citizenship commensurate with Delany's ideal of a sexual democracy where sexual openness and intimacy without binding obligation are part of an accessible public sphere. At the other end is an image of "Citizen Disney" predicated on a narrowly defined platform of corporatism, cross-promotion, family values, and family-oriented entertainment where shopping at the Disney store and watching the Lion King at the New Amsterdam Theater have come to define the increasingly limited forms of public culture through which people are constructed as cultural citizens and consumers. Thus, people are educated about, and encouraged to participate in, forms of social pleasure and consumptive practices premised almost entirely on the dominant family centered moral/sexual ideology constructed by Disney and the state. Meanwhile, competing forms of public culture, sexual citizenship, and urban life are effectively contained, if not entirely eliminated.

Conclusion

Feminist philosopher Iris Marion Young describes a vision of the ideal city as a place of inexhaustible difference, diversity, and an "unassimilated otherness" (1990, p. 319). For Young, the "unoppressive city" is a place where public spaces like parks, streets, and coffee houses are a fundamental and desirable part of social life, accessible and valuable to everyone. In her ideal version of city life public places provide the spaces where people congregate, meet one another, talk, appreciate and entertain each other only to "go off again as strangers" (ibid.). Young's vision of the unoppressive city resonates with Delany's notion of a democratic metropolis where people's access to public places, including sexualized places, is an integral part of social life, helping to construct and organize the world in which we live. In my own cultural imagination, cities have always represented an endless array of cultural possibilities – sexual and otherwise – that have not necessarily been available to me in other contexts. For me, part of the richness and allure of city life stems from its ability to satisfy a variety of social and cultural needs, providing a sense of

community, opportunity, freedom and, if desired, anonymity. Significantly, however, people do not typically move through the world disconnected from the people and places around them: people need access to diverse forms of public culture in order to forge meaningful social relationships and satisfy needs that otherwise might not be met.

The Disneyfication of Times Square and the trend of (re)developing the City as theme park have significant repercussions for the existence of a democratic public sphere where citizens have access to diverse forms of public culture and social entertainment. Times Square has indeed been re-invented: it has been cleaned-up, purged of almost all visible signs of public sex, and remade into a family-friendly, Disneyfied zone where tourists and their money are now, perhaps more than ever, welcome. Yet how are we to measure the cultural costs associated with the Disneyfication of Times Square in an era where the public sphere is increasingly becoming a carefully planned, regulated, and "themed" environment? The transformation of Times Square into a Disneyfied urban theme park has irrevocably altered the organization of public space by eliminating forms of public culture and commercial entertainment that stand in contradistinction to Disney's wholesome image. The idea of the city as theme park is appealing to many people precisely because it presents an economically attractive way to cleanse a "troubled urbanity of its sting, of the presence of the poor, of crime, of dirt, of work" (Sorkin, p. xv). What is lost in the process of this transformation, however, are accessible, diverse, and more democratic forms of public culture – including sexual culture – that, for many people, represent a fundamental and essential part of urban life.

Notes

1 The geographic parameters of Times Square were officially defined in 1993 as the area bounded by West 40th and West 53rd Streets, West of 6th Avenue, and including both sides of 8th Avenue (Dykstra, 1995). In addition to being a center for entertainment and tourism, Times Square is also one of the City's busiest transportation hubs, with over 200,000 people per day using the 7th Avenue station of the IRT, the 8th Avenue IND line, and the Times Square BMT line, all on 42nd Street, and

another 200,000 passing through the gates of the Port Authority Bus Terminal (McNamara, 1995). Although a more detailed history of the evolution of Times Square as a center for commercial forms of entertainment and popular culture is beyond the scope of this essay, for an interesting collection of essays see: *Inventing Times Square: Commerce and Culture at the Crossroads of the World*. Ed. William Taylor. Baltimore and London: Johns Hopkins University, 1991.

2   In the summer of 1997 a pro-sex, queer activist organization called Sex Panic! formed in New York City to counteract what many activists saw as the City's increased efforts to police various forms of public sexual culture. Sex Panic! viewed the City's adoption of the zoning ordinance as part of a larger anti-public sex backlash. For more about this see: *Policing Public Sex*. Eds. Dangerous Bedfellows. Boston: South End Press, 1996.

3   The early 1980s marked an important turning point in the history of Times Square. In 1980 the City of New York and New York State Urban Development Corporation (UDC) entered into an agreement to redevelop 42nd Street (Newmark, 1995). In 1984 the 42nd Street Development Project was created as part of the UDC, and charged with implementing the redevelopment plans. In 1988, the 42nd Street Development Project signed an agreement with a private developer, Times Square Center Associates, forging a union between the public and private sectors. In 1992 the Times Square Business Improvement District (BID), a non-profit organization that is supported by mandatory assessments on all businesses in the area, was formed. The BID has worked, at times quite aggressively, to address the "quality of life" concerns that have troubled Times Square, including, but not limited to, an assault on the adult-oriented businesses remaining in the area (Dykstra, 1995).

4   There are a number of academic studies and books relating to the cultural history and social impact of Disney. See: Henry Giroux, *The Mouse that Roared: Disney and the End of Innocence* Oxford and New York: Rowman and Littlefield Publishers, 1999; Andrew Ross, *The Celebration Chronicles: Life, Liberty and the Pursuit of Property Value in Disney's New Town*. New York: Ballantine Books, 1999; *Disney Discourses: Producing the Magic Kingdom*. Ed. Eric Snoodin. New York: Routledge, 1994.

5   Because the entertainment provided by adult-oriented businesses is, in fact, fully protected by the First Amendment, cities seeking to regulate the location of such businesses have to provide evidence demonstrating that these businesses cause some kind of social harm. Referred to as "secondary effects," the regulating locality must demonstrate an increase in crime or a decrease in property values, both of which were said to exist in the case of Times Square. Provided that the regulating locality can prove that such effects exist, they must then provide suitable sites for the relocation of these businesses. (Fahringer, 1998; Kannar, 1998).

References

Bagli, Charles and Randy Kennedy. "Disney Wished Upon Times Square and Rescued A Stalled Dream." *The New York Times*, April 5, 1998, sec. 1:1+.

Bennett, Tony. "Putting Policy into Cultural Studies." *Cultural Studies*. Eds. Lawrence Grossberg, Cary Nelson, and Paula Treichler. New York and London: Routledge, 1992: 23–37.

——. *The Birth of the Museum: History, Theory, Politics*. London and New York: Routledge, 1995.

Davis, Susan. "The theme park: global industry and cultural form." *Media, Culture, and Society* 18 (1996): 399–422.

——. *Spectacular Nature: Corporate Culture and the Sea World Experience*. Berkeley and London: University of California Press, 1997.

Delany, Samuel. *Times Square Red, Times Square Blue*. New York and London: NYU Press, 1999.

Dykstra, Gretchen. "The Times Square Business Improvement District and its role in changing the face of Times Square." *Sex, Scams and Street Life: The Sociology of New York City's Times Square*. Ed. Robert P. McNamara. Westport, CT and London: Praeger, 1995: 75–81.

Evans, David. *Sexual Citizenship: The Material Construction of Sexualities*. London and New York: Routledge, 1993.

Fahringer, Herald Price. "Zoning Out Free Expression. An Analysis of New York City's Adult Zoning Resolution." *Buffalo Law Review*, Spring, 1998.

Finder, Alan. "A Prince Charming? Disney and the City find each other." *The New York Times*, June 10, 1995, sec. 1: 21.

Gilfoyle, Timothy. "From Soubrette Row to Show World: The contested sexualities of Times Square, 1880–1995." *Policing Public Sex*. Eds. Dangerous Bedfellows. Boston: South End Press, 1996: 263–94.

Goldberger, Paul. "The New Times Square: Magic that Surprised the Magicians." *The New York Times*, October 15, 1996: C11.

Harvey, David. "From space to place and back again: Reflections on the condition of postmodernity." *Mapping the Futures: Local Cultures, Global Change*. Eds. John Bird et al. London and New York: Routledge, 1993: 3–29.

Jackson, Kenneth T. "All the World's a Mall: Reflections on the Social and Economic Consequences of the American Shopping Center." *American Historical Review*, October 1996: 1111–21.

Kannar, George. "Introduction: The First Amendment, Redeveloped." *The Buffalo Law Review*. Spring, 1998.

"Know your Enemy: New York City Zoning Law." *Sex Panic!* New York City, 1997: 34.

Lewis, Justin. *Art, Culture, Enterprise: The Politics of Art and the Cultural Industries*. London and New York: Routledge, 1990.

McNamara, Robert P. "Introduction." *Sex, Scams and Street Life: The Sociology of New York City's Times Square*. Ed. Robert P. McNamara. Westport, CT and London: Praeger, 1995: ix–xiii.

Miller, Toby. *The Well-Tempered Self: Citizenship, Culture, and the Postmodern Subject*. Baltimore and London: The Johns Hopkins University Press, 1993.

——. *Technologies of Truth: Cultural Citizenship and the Popular Media*. Minneapolis and London: University of Minnesota Press, 1998.

Mulligan, Thomas. "Cabbies, sex workers cry no fare! No fair! in New York protests: Giuliani's proposed crackdown on reckless drivers, his cleanup of Times Square prompt one-day demonstrations." *The Los Angeles Times*, May 14, 1998: A18.

Newmark, Shane. "The 42nd Street Development Project." *Sex, Scams and Street Life: The Sociology of New York City's Times Square*. Ed. Robert P. McNamara. Westport, CT and London: Praeger, 1995: 67–74.

Ogintz, Eileen. "Taking the Kids: Now G-Rated, New York City's Times Square is Family-Friendly." *The Los Angeles Times*, July 6, 1997: L2.

Ouellette, Laurie. "TV Viewing as Good Citizenship? Political Rationality, Enlightened Democracy and PBS." *Cultural Studies* (1999): 62–90.

Pulley, Brett. "Companies Reach deal for renewal in Heart of 42nd Street." *The New York Times*, July 21, 1995: A1.

——. "Disney's deal: A special report." *The New York Times*, July 29, 1995, sec. 1: 1+.

Sorkin, Michael. "See you in Disneyland." *Variations of a Theme Park: The New American City and the End of Public Space*. Ed. Michael Sorkin. New York: Hill and Wang, 1992: 205–32.

——. (ed). *Variations of a Theme Park: The New American City and the End of Public Space*. New York: Hill and Wang, 1992.

Usborne, David. "Mickey Moves in on the pimps." *The Independent* (London), August 6, 1995: B3.

Weber, Bruce. "Disney unveils restored New Amsterdam Theater." *The New York Times*, April 3, 1997: B3.

Weber, Jonathan. "Revival on Broadway; With the help of Walt Disney Company, Times Square is staging a comeback. But some fear the loss of the District's soul." *The New York Times*, June 19, 1994: D1.

Young, Iris Marion. "The ideal of community and the politics of difference." *Feminism/Postmodernism*. Ed. Linda J. Nichols. New York and London: Routledge, 1990: 300–23.

Chapter 25

All the World's a Mall: Reflections on the Social and Economic Consequences of the American Shopping Center

Kenneth T. Jackson

The Egyptians have pyramids, the Chinese have a great wall, the British have immaculate lawns, the Germans have castles, the Dutch have canals, the Italians have grand churches. And Americans have shopping centers. They are the common denominator of our national life, the best symbols of our abundance. By 1992, there were 38,966 operating shopping centers in the United States, 1,835 of them large, regional malls, and increasingly they were featuring the same products, the same stores, and the same antiseptic environment. They have been called "the perfect fusion of the profit motive and the egalitarian ideal," and one wag has remarked, only partially in jest, that either America is a shopping center or the one shopping center in existence is moving about the country at the speed of light.[1]

To be sure, the shopping center and even the shopping mall are not entirely American innovations. Merchandising outside city walls began in the Middle Ages, when traders often established markets or "fairs" beyond the gates to avoid the taxes and congestion of the urban core. For this privilege, they typically paid a fee to the lord or feudal authority who commanded the walls above the field. Similarly, enclosed shopping spaces have also existed for centuries, from the agora of ancient Greece to the Palais Royal of prerevolutionary Paris. The Jerusalem bazaar

has been providing a covered shopping experience for 2,000 years, while Istanbul's Grand Bazaar was doing the same when sultans ruled the Ottoman Empire from the nearby Topkapi Palace. In England, Chester has been famous for centuries for interconnected second-story shops, protected wonderfully from the wind and the rain, which stretch for blocks at the center of town. London's Burlington Arcade, completed in 1819, was one of the world's earliest retail shopping arcades, while the Crystal Palace Exhibition of 1851, which featured a nineteen-acre building that was entirely walled and roofed in panels of dazzling "crystal" glass, had many characteristics of the modern mall. Its designers brought the outdoors inside and made the "palace" into a giant garden, complete with an elaborate fountain and several full-grown trees. Within the mammoth structure, crowds from many nations and social classes jostled through long aisles, entertained as much by the passing parade and the spectacle as by the official displays.

The most famous pre-twentieth-century enclosed retail space is the Galleria Vittorio Emanuele II in Milan, which was built to commemorate the 1859 victory of the French and Sardinians (led by King Victor Emmanuel) over Austria at the Battle of Magenta. Located near the Duomo and opened to the public in 1867, it is really a prolongation of the public street. It houses scores of separate merchants, with a glass vault on top rather than a single, enclosed building (there are no doors). Cruciform in shape, it has a four-story interior façade that stretches 645 feet in one direction and 345 feet in the other, bordered by shops, cafés, and restaurants at the ground level and mezzanine. Despite its age, the Galleria looks and feels like a modern mall, and it remains at the center of political and commercial life in Milan.[2]

At the end of the twentieth century, the shopping mall has become a global phenomenon. Hong Kong has as many modern malls as any metropolitan region in the United States, and tourists in Kowloon might easily imagine that they are in Orlando or Spokane. In France, the Parly II Center opened outside Paris and near Versailles in 1968. It includes all-weather air-conditioning, fountains, marble floors, sculptured plaster ceilings, and scores of shops on two floors. Singapore, Taipei, Sydney, Melbourne, Hamburg, and a hundred other cities have similarly elaborate edifices; the Kaisergalerie in Berlin and GUM in Moscow are particularly notable. Even England, ever protective of its countryside, is falling victim to regional malls and the acres of parking lots that surround them. For example, seventeen miles east of central London, set among the rolling hills of Essex, is the Lakeside Centre, a 1.35 million square-foot clone of suburban America, complete with two McDonalds, a Sam Goody, and a Gap. Since the mid-1980s, a half-dozen other regional malls, as well as 250 smaller regional clusters, have gone up among the shires and sleepy hamlets of Shakespeare's scepter'd isle. By 1993, these new shopping and exurban centers were claiming more than 17 percent of the British retail market, a three-fold increase in less than fifteen years.[3]

Below-ground shopping malls have also proliferated. Since 1962, for example, Montrealers have been able to survive their harsh winters by working, shopping, and living, often for months at a time, underground – or at least inside glass and concrete. Large parts of the core city are now linked by miles of subterranean walkways, all lined with shops, restaurants, snack bars, and theaters. In posh Westmount Square, tenants in high-rise apartment buildings have only to take an elevator to find a supermarket, a bookstore, a bank, a movie theater, a bar and restaurant, or such expensive specialty shops as Givenchy and

Pierre Cardin.[4] Similarly, in Osaka, the buried-mall concept is now almost a third of a century old. There, more than a million people per day file over the lighted signs in the floor or past the giant wall maps of the connecting Umeda and Hankyu malls to buy food, clothes, toys, and even lizards and seaweed, or to pay for overseas trips. Hawkers banging tambourines urge passers-by to sample their restaurants. Even pornography shops flourish.

But, as was the case with the automobile, which also was invented in Europe, it is in the United States that the shopping center and the shopping mall have found especially fertile ground. In the North American republic, large-scale retailing, once associated almost exclusively with central business districts, began moving away from the urban cores between the world wars. Baltimore's Roland Park Shopping Center (1896) is often cited as the first of the modern genus, but Country Club Plaza in Kansas City, begun in 1923, was more influential and was the first automobile-oriented shopping center. Featuring extensive parking lots behind ornamented, Old California-style brick walls, it was the effort of a single entrepreneur, Jesse Clyde Nichols, who put together a concentration of retail stores and used leasing policy to determine the composition of stores in the concentration. By doing that, Nichols created the idea of the planned regional shopping center. At the same time, he understood, as no one had before him, that customers for the 100 shops would arrive by car. Free parking was not an afterthought; it was part of the original conception. And as Country Club Plaza expanded over the decades to encompass 978,000 square feet of retail space, the number of parking spaces multiplied as well, until by 1990 there were more than 5,000 spaces for the ubiquitous motorcar.[5]

By the mid-1930s, the concept of the planned shopping center, as a collection of businesses under one management and with convenient parking facilities, was well known and was recognized as the best method of serving the growing market of drive-in customers. But the Great Depression and World War II had a chilling effect on private construction, and as late as 1946 there were only eight shopping centers in the United States. They included Upper Darby Center in West Philadelphia (1927), Suburban Square in Ardmore, Pennsylvania (1928), Highland Park

Shopping Village outside Dallas (1931), River Oaks in Houston (1937), Hampton Village in St. Louis (1941), Colony in Toledo (1944), Shirlington in Arlington, Virginia (1944), and Belleview Square in Seattle (1946).[6]

The first major planned retail shopping center in the world went up in Raleigh, North Carolina, in 1949, the brainchild of Homer Hoyt, a well-known author and demographer best remembered for his sector model of urban growth. Another early prototype was Northgate, which opened on the outskirts of Seattle in 1950. Designed by architect John Graham, Jr., it featured a long, open-air pedestrian way lined with a number of small specialty shops and ending with a department store. The idea was that the "anchor" facility would attract people, who would then shop their way to their destination. Predictably, it went up next to a highway and provided a free 4,000-space parking lot.

The enclosed, climate-controlled indoor mall was introduced by Victor Gruen, an Austrian refugee from the Nazis, at the Southdale Shopping Center in Edina, Minnesota, a suburb of Minneapolis, in 1956. From the beginning, the 679,000 square-foot complex (later expanded to 1.35 million square feet) included two department stores, 139 shops, parking for 5,200 cars, and a two-story, sky-lit pedestrian walkway. Gruen had been inspired by Milan's Galleria and also by the markets of the Austrian and Swiss towns he had visited on bicycle as a young man. In America, ironically, he wanted to stop suburban sprawl, and he thought the shopping mall would do the trick. Because Minneapolis was so often cold, Gruen advertised that "in Southdale Center every day will be a perfect shopping day." The concept proved wildly popular, and it demonstrated that climate-controlled shopping arcades were likely to be more profitable than open-air shopping centers. Indoor malls proliferated, slowly at first but with increasing frequency, and within fifteen years anything that was not enclosed came to be considered second-rate.[7]

A few of the indoor behemoths, such as Midtown Plaza in Rochester and Chapel Square Mall in New Haven, were located downtown, but more typical were Paramus Park and Bergen Mall in New Jersey, Woodfield Mall in Schaumburg outside Chicago, King's Plaza outside Manhattan, Tyson's Corner outside Washington, and Raleigh Mall in Memphis – all of which were located on outlying highways and all of which attracted shoppers from trading areas of a hundred square miles and more. Within a mere quarter-century, they transformed the way Americans lived and worked. Indeed, reports were commonplace by the 1970s that the typical American was spending more time at the mall than at any other place other than home or work. And the shopping mall had become, along with the tract house, the freeway, and the backyard barbecue, the most distinctive product of the American postwar years.[8]

Because academic journals often publish pieces so esoteric that only a small proportion even of a specialized audience could be interested in them, the *American Historical Review* merits praise for focusing attention on the ubiquitous phenomenon of the modern shopping center. Thomas W. Hanchett's article, "U.S. Tax Policy and the Shopping-Center Boom of the 1950s and 1960s," essentially asks why and how such a profound retailing revolution could occur so quickly. By contrast, Lizabeth Cohen's "From Town Center to Shopping Center: The Reconfiguration of Community Marketplaces in Postwar America," essentially asks "so what?" Why should anyone care where I buy my socks?

Focusing on fast-growing Charlotte, North Carolina, slow-growing Cortland, New York, and declining Scranton–Wilkes Barre, Pennsylvania – all of which witnessed a transformation of shopping patterns in the quarter-century after World War II, Hanchett finds that neither rapid suburban growth nor racial strife adequately explain the shift. Instead, he points to the Internal Revenue Code, especially to a section of the 1954 law that allowed investors to depreciate real-estate investments on an accelerated basis. In practice, this meant that a particular property that was in fact performing well and even making money could be carried as a *deduction* or a *loss* on an individual's tax return. Good investments became paper losses, thus reducing tax liability and enhancing the desirability of commercial real estate as a tax shelter. Equally important, accelerated depreciation led to frequent turnovers in ownership, because as soon as one person exhausted the best tax benefits of a property, the smart thing to do was to sell it and buy another one. A new investor could utilize the favorable tax provisions all over again. The law encouraged new construction rather than maintenance or renovation because the financial advantage was in short-term depreciation. Finally, Hanchett persuasively argues that accelerated depreciation encouraged *retail* development in advance of *residential* settlement, thus reversing centuries-old patterns of human experience. In essence, the IRS created a pyramid scheme in which most of the players could not and did not lose.

Hanchett's overall point is a strong one, and he performs an important service for scholars by reminding us that government intervention, especially in the form of forgiven taxes, often shapes the world in which we live. Unfortunately, he pushes an excellent point further than the evidence will allow. For example, because tax loopholes were available to almost every income-producing structure, accelerated depreciation did not inevitably lead to investment in shopping centers. Entrepreneurs could have put their funds to dozens of alternative uses, such as drive-in theaters (the number of which instead went down in these years), or speculative office buildings (many of which went up in central cities), or livery stables (the demand for which was obviously decreasing), or hundreds of other businesses.

That investors so often channeled their interests into shopping centers and shopping malls in fact depended on other factors that Hanchett does not emphasize. First, land was often cheap on the peripheries of American cities, especially when measured against central business district (CBD) costs or comparable investment opportunities overseas. Second, American land-use controls and zoning regulations have typically been much weaker than those of other advanced nations. In Britain, for example, the government has long been determined to emphasize traditional retail patterns and to support highly compact, densely settled urban centers surrounded by mostly open green belts, where both commercial and residential development has been cautiously restricted. If, for example, a person were to purchase a farm in England and then announce an intention to develop the property as a shopping mall, local residents would think that the newcomer had lost his or her mind. They do not turn such decisions over to the investor who happens to own a parcel at any given time. It is a community decision in the full sense of the word. Similarly, Germany and France have tightened their planning regulations, never favorable to mall de-

velopment, to push developers toward town centers. Third, the United States has for generations subsidized automobile travel while asking public transit systems to operate without the substantial government handouts that are typical of Europe and Asia. Such policies clearly channel development toward the very shopping malls that offer easy and cheap access to automobiles. Fourth, shopping centers offered a range of conveniences, including light, warmth, longer hours, better security, improved store layouts, wider parking spaces, and increased self-selection, all accented by waterfalls, sculptures, fountains, landscaping, mirrors, and neon signs that downtown areas could rarely match. Accelerated depreciation helped make these innovations financially feasible, but it was only a small part of a complicated story.

Finally, Hanchett's conclusion that shopping-center development does not correlate with automobile ownership merits skepticism. It flies in the face both of conventional wisdom and of observable fact, inasmuch as an expansive parking lot not only defines the shopping center but is typically necessary to it. Perhaps the explanation for this seeming incongruity is that highways and cheap gasoline, not cars, are the crucial variables. For example, soon after a major oil crisis hit the developed world in 1973, construction starts on American shopping centers plummeted, falling 22 percent in 1974 and another 41 percent in 1975. Similarly, without the huge public expenditures on road construction that have given the United States more paved mileage per capita than any other country in the world, shopping centers would never have dominated the nation's retailing. Nor would this merchandising revolution likely have happened if the American taxpayer had not subsidized the motorist. Essentially, the federal government is the only major government in the world that fails to recapture most of the costs associated with the automobile through high taxes on gasoline. In Germany, Britain, France, Italy, and Japan, to take only the most obvious examples, the practice is to charge the consumer at the pump for the costs of the infrastructure and public health services on which the motorcar depends. Thus, in order to be convinced by Hanchett's ambitious argument, we need to know more than he has provided about highway mileage and conditions, zoning and building regulations, local shopping patterns, public transportation alternatives, and per-capita income. More systematic comparisons with Canada and Australia would be useful because their gasoline taxes are lower than Europe and Japan and higher than the United States.[9]

These comments do not mean that Hanchett's point about tax incentives is invalid, only that the decline of central business districts and the growth of regional shopping centers have continued to reshape the American landscape even as the IRS has rewritten the tax code and eliminated many earlier depreciation provisions. Indeed, more retail space has been built in the United States since 1970 than in all our national history before that time.

Lizabeth Cohen's "From Town Center to Shopping Center: The Reconfiguration of Community Marketplaces in Postwar America," is really three separate articles – the first dealing with the impact of suburban retailing on older city centers, the second with the question of free speech and the ability to hand out leaflets or otherwise protest on private property functioning as public space, and the third with the feminization of shopping. The focus is on Paramus, New Jersey, a bedroom suburb eight miles from Manhattan with no main street but with virtually every kind of store known to civilization. Along the way, Cohen disagrees with Hanchett's contention that racial discrimination had little to do with changing patterns of retailing, arguing instead that developers defined their commercial palaces in exclusionary racial and economic terms and that even the bus schedules favored white shoppers. In Paramus, it seems, both race and cars were major factors in the shopping-center revolution.

Cause and effect may never be determined, but as the malls mushroomed, older central business districts faltered. Cohen is particularly adept at tracing the changing fortunes of Paterson, a core shopping district on the traditional downtown model, as contrasted with the automobile-centered shopping centers that eventually surrounded it. In 1950, she notes, Paterson was a thriving commercial district while Paramus was, in a retail sense, only a wide place in the road. Two decades later, their positions were reversed. Paterson was losing population and sales, while Paramus was well on its way to becoming one of the most glitzy and important shopping complexes on earth. Paterson's downtown merchants and community leaders of course fought back hard,

first with Sunday blue laws, which are still on the books in Bergen County, and later with large-scale urban renewal efforts. Ultimately, nothing worked. Indeed, the failure of the Paterson CBD is instructive precisely because highly qualified planners and extensive subsidies failed to reverse the downward trend. Moreover, the success of Paramus malls was even more impressive because it took place within easy commuting distance of Manhattan, the dominant business center of the United States. It is thus easy to understand how the same phenomenon happened to smaller metropolitan areas, where the central business districts were even more easily overwhelmed by suburban competition.

These scenarios have been replayed with only slight variation across the length and breadth of the nation. Until recently, central cities were almost defined by the locally owned department stores, which dominated local life – Hudson's in Detroit, Rich's in Atlanta, Rike's in Dayton, Goldsmith's in Memphis, and Bamberger's in Newark prominent among them. All are now closed, as are dozens of other stores in similar situations. In 1993, for example, G. Fox and Company, Hartford's last downtown department store and the symbol of Connecticut's capital city, closed its flagship emporium after 145 years of service. For generations, the store had etched its own distinctive profile by its policy of free deliveries, elaborate Christmas displays, and Art Deco interior extravagance. When you thought about Hartford, you thought about G. Fox. Its empty hulk is now an eyesore.[10]

Even the Chicago Loop, the square-mile downtown business core where the rich once shopped, Frank Sinatra sang, New Year's crowds gathered, and screeching elevated trains rocked along overhead, has fallen victim to fear, changing social patterns, and the shopping-mall revolution. By the 1960s and 1970s, State Street decay was evident. Affluent shoppers soon took their business elsewhere, sometimes to the so-called Magnificent Mile just north of the Chicago River, but more often to the burgeoning suburbs on the metropolitan fringe. Downtown's formerly first-run movie palaces turned to second-run horror films and low-budget, triple X-rated features. Electronic gadget shops proliferated, as did fast-food outlets. Sears closed its famed State Street store. The last burlesque house shut down in 1977. Even sin was moving elsewhere.

Only a generation ago, Petula Clark could sing that the lights were brighter "Downtown." No longer. Yet these changes in the physical location of retail consumption are only part of the story. Equally important has been ruthless cost-cutting competition and the accompanying consumer desire, which has grown in recent decades, to choose low prices and chain stores over locally owned, independent businesses. Every city, every town, and every neighborhood in the nation has witnessed this shift from "Mom and Pop" operations to "big box" retailers.

Many contemporary observers are not unhappy with this turn of events. They regard the modern shopping mall – clean, safe, convenient, and cheerful – as superior to any downtown alternative, as in fact the re-creation of the city within a suburban setting. The mall has become the place where senior citizens walk in comfort and security, where parents lead their young to Santa Claus, where singles court, where teenagers socialize, and where everybody consumes. Indeed, a new term, "mall rats," has been coined to describe the legions of young people who spend their free time cruising indoor corridors. It is something to do when there is nothing else to do. And there is nothing else to do, according to many young people. This proliferation of uses and of customers has led to the frequent observation that regional malls are the new downtowns, the centers of informal social interaction, the successors to the traditional marketplace. Of course, this would give a new definition to the word "center," because shopping malls are often beyond town boundaries and thus outside government control or taxation. Typically, they are at the geographical centers only of parking lots.

Are shopping malls the new downtowns? Cohen rightly notes that there is something contradictory in the notion of a shopping center trying to legitimize itself as a focus of community activity even while defining that community in exclusionary socioeconomic and racial terms. An essential difference between a traditional central business district and a shopping mall is that the former is by definition open to all people at all hours. The latter is private property, owned and operated by a single corporation, and thus subject to coercive, centralized authority. The theme of their design is enclosure, protection, and control. Litter, panhandlers, vagrants, suspicious characters, protestors, and even cold winds are not toler-

ated. What happens, then, when citizens seek to exercise their constitutional right to petition the general public, to speak out about this or that outrage? A downtown street presents no constitutional problem, but urban sidewalks feature so few pedestrians that effective protest there is impossible. Shopping malls, by contrast, offer crowds but not access, because management typically prohibits activities that might be controversial or offensive. And private police forces stand ready to enforce such rules, and public-relations personnel are at the ready to justify them. Cohen focuses on this conflict between free speech and private property, concluding that, in New Jersey at least, the right to expression is guaranteed in malls. Unfortunately, New Jersey is not typical, as many state courts have thus far defended the right of mall owners to exclude political activity.[11]

Cohen's third point, the feminization of public space through the transformation of the mall culture, is compelling, albeit Gunther Barth has put this shift about a century earlier, when "the department store made the new phenomenon of a feminine public possible," and when New York's consumer palaces so catered to female customers that Manhattan's primary retail district came to be known as the "Ladies Mile." Before Alexander T. Stewart, John Wanamaker, R. H. Macy, and other early retailers adopted "departmental" organization and advertising as standard procedure, Barth alleges that women rarely ventured into commercial and business neighborhoods. Thereafter, women came literally to dominate them.[12] Cohen's contribution is to move the discussion to late twentieth-century consumption and to relate the experience and power of women to the proliferation of credit cards and of part-time employment. With imagination and insight, she demonstrates how consumer credit expanded the financial clout of married women, giving them control not only of present but of future family earnings. Part-time employment, however, was a Trojan Horse. Earlier in this century, Cohen notes, retail clerking was a respectable, middle-class occupation that paid a decent, livable wage. Shopping centers, however, experienced unusual peaks and valleys of busy and quiet periods, and they sought to use part-time female labor to cut wage costs. Unions fought desperately, and unsuccessfully, against this threat to their members' economic well-being. The bottom line is that shopping centers now rarely offer career or employment opportunities that reach a middle-class standard.

Germany provides a contrary example. There, until recently, almost all stores closed by 6:30 p.m. during the week and 2 p.m. on Saturdays. In 1966, Chancellor Helmut Kohl agreed to extend store hours until 8 p.m. during the week and 4 p.m. on Saturdays. On Sunday, everything is closed. Bakeries cannot even bake bread on Sunday. Quite simply, the German government has regulated shopping hours according to the desires of small shopkeepers and organized labor. Small stores fear that liberalized trading hours would ruin "Mom and Pop" stores and lead to American-style, big-box retailing. And organized labor believes that expanding legal shopping hours would open the door to part-time employment and thus undermine the generous benefits and income that German clerks now enjoy. Both the German and the American systems involve political choices. Thus far, Germans have chosen higher prices and higher wages; Americans have opted for cheap prices, cheap transportation, and Mammon-driven super stores.[13]

A half-century ago, almost everyone in America, whether they lived in a great metropolitan region, a medium-sized city, a small town, or a rural area, made their major consumer purchases in some sort of a centralized shopping environment. In communities of even modest pretensions, that place was at the confluence of the trolley tracks, where pedestrian traffic was the heaviest and land values the highest. Even in smaller communities, the town had a visual and clear center, if only a rural post office and a general store.

Over the past five decades, this has changed. Small towns across the nation, whether on the open plains of Nebraska or the winding rivers of West Virginia, have seen their downtown shopping districts wither and die. Old businesses and buildings are boarded up and abandoned; other structures, poorly maintained, struggle along with marginal firms as tenants. Meanwhile, several miles away, often adjacent to an interstate highway, a Wal-Mart, a K-Mart, or some other discount retailer rests in the midst of a large parking lot. Such is the physical shape of America's modern consumer culture.

There is some evidence to suggest that, in recent years, Americans have finally become bored with malls or perhaps just tired of the effort it takes to navigate them. The industry peaked in 1978, when sales per square foot of retail space averaged $197 a year. Malls have become so homogenized and predictable that they have lost much of their entertainment value. Revealingly, the number of centers under construction nationwide has been declining since 1988. Older shopping centers, in particular, have often closed or been razed. Some, like the 2.2 million square-foot Roosevelt Field complex on Long Island, with parking for 9,000 cars, have had a complete makeover in order to keep up with current trends. Smaller indoor malls, lacking the advertising budgets of larger operations, have encountered cycles of decline once associated with inner cities. The interiors of those structures have become ghost towns, with white butcher paper over the windows and specialty retail space perennially unleased. Meanwhile, new, so-called category killers like Home Depot, Price Club, Toys 'R' Us, Staples, and T. J. Maxx are taking customers from the malls. Occasionally, several category killers come together to form what is called a "power mall." It is discount with a vengeance, a place of take-no-prisoners, no-frills shopping, where the mantra is value, and where the upscale shops and elaborate fixtures of the traditional mall are dismissed as frivolous affectations of a bygone era.[14]

Nevertheless, in 1992, the largest enclosed shopping and entertainment facility in the United States opened in Bloomington, Minnesota, a suburb of Minneapolis. Known as the Mall of America, larger in square footage than Red Square, containing twice as much steel as the Eiffel Tower, and featuring 400 separate stores as well as an indoor amusement park, it is the biggest monument yet built in the United States to consumption. It takes up the equivalent of 88 football fields and features a formulaic 4.5 parking spaces for every 1,000 square feet of leasable space, which translates to 13,000 automobile spots within 300 feet of a door to the mall. The structure has already become a "destination" facility, meaning that almost 50 percent of all out-of-town visitors to the Twin Cities say that the Mall of America is their main reason for being there. Boosters like to say that it is now the third largest tourist attraction in the United States, trailing only Disney World and the country-music capital of Branson, Missouri. Meanwhile, Minneapolis and St. Paul, both perennially listed among the most "livable" American cities, lack the crowded sidewalks and colorful shopfronts that are a sign of urban health.[15]

In my view, the shopping mall and the automobile culture that makes it possible waste time, energy, and land that the United States can ill afford. Clearly, I am in the minority. The modern shopping center and shopping mall are at the core of a worldwide transformation of distribution and consumption. They represent, along with music, computers, suburbs, and skyscrapers, one of America's major contributions to twentieth-century culture and life. When historians of the twenty-first century try to sort out the nature and meaning of the retailing revolution in post-World War II America, they will have to start with the work of Thomas Hanchett and Lizabeth Cohen.

Notes

1 On the number of shopping centers, see Witold Rybezynski, "The New Downtowns," *Atlantic Monthly* 271 (May 1993): 98. See also William Severini Kowinski, *The Malling of America: An Inside Look at the Great Consumer Paradise* (New York, 1985); Howard Gillette, Jr., "The Evolution of the Planned Shopping Center in Suburb and City," *Journal of the American Planning Association* 51 (Autumn 1985): 449–60; George Sternlieb and James W. Hughes. eds., *Shopping Centers, USA* (Piscataway, N.J., 1981); William H. Whyte, *The City: Rediscovering the Center* (New York, 1988); and William Glaberson, "The Heart of the City Now Beats in the Mall," *New York Times* (March 27, 1992): A1, B4.

2 A good overview of the early development of the arcade idea is Alexander Garvin, *The American City: What Works, What Doesn't* (New York, 1996). 101–20. See also Johann Friedrich Geist, *Arcades: The History of a Building Type* (Cambridge, Mass., 1982).

3 *New York Times* (May 9, 1993): E16.

4 The Montreal complex was designed by Vincent Ponte, a native of Boston, as a way of reducing congestion on downtown streets, *New York Times*, December 17, 1976.

5 This paragraph summarizes material in Kenneth T. Jackson, *Crabgrass Frontier: The Suburbanization of the United States* (New York, 1985), 257–61. See also William S. Worley, *J. C. Nichols and the Shaping of Kansas City* (Columbia, Mo., 1990), 10–28; Rybezynski, "New Downtowns," 98–100; S. R. De Boer, *Shopping Districts* (Washington, D.C., 1937); and Yehoshua S. Cohen, *Diffusion of an Innovation in an Urban System: The Spread of*

Planned Regional Shopping Centers in the United States, 1949–1968 (Chicago, 1972).

6 John B. Rae, *The Road and the Car in American Life* (Cambridge, Mass., 1971), 230. New York City department stores began to decentralize rather early, beginning in the late 1920s, Regional Plan Association, *Suburban Branch Stores in the New York Metropolitan Region* (New York, 1951).

7 T. R. Reid, "The Magic of Malls," *Washington Post*, September 16, 1985. Late in life, after thirty years in the United States. Gruen argued that the shopping-center idea that he pioneered had been subverted and that the country was mindlessly subsidizing suburban sprawl. He retired in frustration to Vienna, Austria. Among his many writings on the subject, see especially Victor Gruen, *The Heart of Our Cities: Diagnosis and Cure* (New York, 1964).

8 William Severini Kowinski, "The Malling of America," *New Times* 10 (May 1, 1978): 31–55.

9 *Forbes*, June 1, 1976. See also "Antitrust Action in the Shopping Malls," *Business Week* (December 8, 1975): 51.

10 On the impact of malls on department stores in urban cores, see Zenia Kotval, John R. Mullin, and Edward Murray, "The Mall Comes to Town," *Economic Development* 15 (Summer 1991): 15–21. See also Kirk Johnson, "G. Fox to Close, Ending Retail Era," *New York Times*, September 12, 1992.

11 The best treatment of the phenomenon of individual rights in urban and mall type situations is Robert C. Ellickson, "Controlling Chronic Misconduct in City Spaces: Of Panhandlers, Skid Rows, and Public-Space Zoning," *Yale Law Journal* 105 (March 1996): 1165–248.

12 Gunther Barth, *City People: The Rise of Modern City Culture in Nineteenth-Century America* (New York, 1980), 181.

13 On Germany's regulated shopping hours, see "Economy Poor, Germans Yield on Store Hours," *New York Times*, June 12, 1996.

14 Dean Schwanke, *Remaking the Shopping Center* (Washington, D.C., 1994). Also see John T. McQuiston, "The Reinvention of a Shopping Mall," *New York Times*, April 23, 1993; Kirk Johnson, "Discount with a Vengeance," *New York Times*, December 7, 1993.

15 Among the dozens of newspaper and magazine articles on the Mall of America, particularly good are Neal Karlen, "The Mall That Ate Minnesota," *New York Times* (August 30, 1992): sect. V, p. 5; and Eric Hubler, "Four Million Square Feet of Mall," *New York Times* (October 25, 1992): sect. XX, p. 33.

Chapter 26

Citizenship and the Technopoles

Vincent Mosco

This chapter begins by addressing why it is important to invoke the idea of citizenship and why
it is equally important to critique it. Next, it
relates citizenship to what Manuel Castells and
Peter Hall (1994) have called the *technopoles*,
those regional concentrations of science, technology and venture capital whose icon is Silicon
Valley. I use the idea of citizenship to critique the
technopole phenomenon and conclude by considering alternative ways to think about progressive social development.

Much of what we see in the media, as well as
in academic accounts of media activity, addresses
people not as citizens but as consumers or as
members of audiences.[1] Citizenship elevates
human activity beyond the commonly accepted
view that the best way – indeed, for some, the
only way – to define human activity is by its
marketplace value, its worth as a consuming
or laboring commodity. The widely accepted
view of citizenship is that elevation has also
been accompanied by extension. Here, it is
common to invoke the work of T. H. Marshall
(1964), who charts the progress of citizenship in
modern Western society starting with the legal
sense of basic rights and protections – for
example, habeas corpus, due process, the presumption of innocence, and the right of trial by
a jury of one's peers. From here, citizenship was
extended to encompass political rights, particularly the right to vote and the right to public
assembly. Finally, social citizenship stretches
the notion to include rights to employment,
housing, health care, and other social welfare
benefits.

The media and media analysis have also invoked citizenship from time to time. The turn to
civic journalism and the movements around
community networking and public broadcasting
suggest an effort to extend media citizenship and
resist the all-consuming process of media commodification. But the very necessity to specify
journalism as *civic*, networking as *community*,
and broadcasting as *public* defines the weakness
of media citizenship. *Civic journalism* would
once have been red-penciled as a redundant expression. Now it is a hoped-for niche, however
weak, in the singularity we know as the market,
less evidence of citizenship's extension than of its
exhaustion.

These developments lead to the conclusion
that even as we welcome the insertion of citizenship into debates about communication policy,
we need to critique it. Otherwise, citizenship
dissolves into a flaccid and romantic populism
that celebrates anything outside the market as
genuinely oppositional and alternative. Witness
the communitarian movement, the not-so-Left's
version of family values, whose supporters wave
the kinship banner even as they support an end to
the very social-assistance programs necessary to
keep families together.

Discussions of citizenship today carry the
burden of Enlightenment assumptions that progress has deepened and extended citizenship to
encompass more people and more facets of
social life. Marshall's three steps in the evolution
of citizenship constitute only the most celebrated of such visions of linear progress. But
there is another view, one that I may be more

sensitive to than most because I am part of that group of people for whom citizenship was an active choice and not just a taken-for-granted birthright.

Having chosen to take Canadian citizenship and having participated actively in that never-ending Canadian pastime, the angst-ridden search for just what it means, I can appreciate that citizenship is also, if I may be excused a Foulcauldian expression, a discipline. It took about two years for me to complete the process of citizenship, and, although I have thankfully forgotten most of my march through the bureaucratic underbrush, two memories leave an aftertaste. The pamphlet whose canonical version of Canadian history and politics I was asked to study in preparation for my citizenship exam informed me that the Canadian state conferred but one citizenship benefit: the right to vote. For this I had to memorize the state's official view of history and more importantly, and this is the second image that lives on in my mind, swear allegiance to Her Majesty the Queen in a public ceremony presided over by a plum patronage-appointed citizenship judge. My active participation in this process simply drives home a more powerful version of a general lesson about contemporary citizenship. It is not only a hard-earned right fought for and won by wave after wave of working-class struggle. It is also a state-imposed discipline that controls, shapes, and confines that struggle by creating a set of rules that determine legitimate participation in national state affairs. Moreover, it is a tool of discrimination that permits the state to define who among its people can have that right. This is not to suggest that it is a natural step from *liberté*, *egalité*, and *fraternité* to the Terror. That would amount to a simplistic inversion of Marshall's vision of the progress of citizenship. Rather, citizenship is not just a pure right or an unabashed gain but a social practice defined and redefined in political struggle. This fact was not lost on the Ayatollah Khomeini, who extended full voting and civic-participation rights in Iran to anyone over the age of fifteen. What would Marshall think of this?

Moreover, it is not just a question of invoking citizenship but also a question of determining which one. For indeed, as Riesenberg tells us in his masterful work *Citizenship and the Western Tradition* (1992), the concept is ambiguous, defining civic virtue in a public arena even as it supports discrimination and exclusion: the West has experienced two different citizenships. This is where one can build a bridge to the technopole. Most of the discussion of citizenship is about what Riesenberg terms "Citizenship Two," or the rights and privileges conferred by the nation-state beginning roughly in the aftermath of the French Revolution. Discussion of this citizenship does not appear in English until about the eighteenth century, when, according to the *Oxford English Dictionary* (OED), David Hume stated that "too great disproportion among the citizens weakens any state."

But there is another citizenship, that of the city, the community, the region, or the city-state, which is canonically dated with classical Athens. The very first definition of citizen, common in English from the fourteenth century, the OED tells us, is "an inhabitant of a city or (often) of a town; esp. one possessing civic rights and privileges, a burgess or freeman of a city." It is this form of citizenship that merits reflection, but certainly not that we dust off romantic visions of a classical golden age. G. E. M. de Ste. Croix's (1981) work *The Class Struggle in the Ancient Greek World*, with its brilliant assessment of class divisions, slavery, and patriarchy, puts to rest uncritical celebrations of Athenian democracy. There are other reasons for such reflection.

Most of us would agree that in many important economic, social, and cultural arenas, nation-states around the world are in retreat, particularly with respect to those political and social rights that we have come to associate with citizenship. As a Canadian, my national government (and, by extension, the several provincial governments) are less able than they were twenty or thirty years ago to make economic policy, provide education, deliver health services, support the poor, protect our culture, or provide affordable housing. Canadians are certainly not alone in a position to conclude that the World Trade Organization and the International Monetary Fund have more to do with these matters than the government my citizenship test bought me the right to vote for. But to say that citizenship is not what it used to be is not simply to conclude that it has diminished. It has also been reshaped. Today's national citizenship is more a matter of guaranteeing other things:

protection from would-be immigrants, transmitting and adapting a global neoliberal business agenda to the particular circumstances of each nation, and, not the least, giving us national teams to root for in international competitions like the Olympic Games and the World Cup Soccer tournament.

Even if one does not fully agree with this argument, it is reasonable to conclude that we need to spend more time thinking about citizenship *across* nations, global citizenship, if only because much of our analysis begins today with global actors, primarily transnational businesses that are closely connected to regional and international associations of nation-states. Indeed, one of the few thorough reviews of the technopole phenomenon, Castells and Hall's *Technopoles of the World* (1994), admits that the primary structural revolution at work today is "the formation of a global economy, that is, the structuring of all economic processes on a planetary scale, even if national boundaries and national governments remain essential elements and key actors in the strategies played out in international competition" (p. 3). Given what we know about the formation of a global economy, it comes as no surprise to observe pleas to develop forms of global citizenship. Whether embodied in calls for global labor standards to offset sweatshops and slave labor, global environmentalism to halt emissions of greenhouse gases, or a global feminism to overcome "divide and rule" tactics that business uses to separate First World from Third World women, the many forms of global citizenship are primary grounds for resistance to the spread of commodification and the reduction of all forms of social relations to the singularity of market relations.

Technology, particularly communication and information technology, is often associated with the march of the global economy in two important ways. First, communication technology enables the expansion of practically all businesses because it expands their geographical and organizational horizons, making possible more-profitable production, distribution, and exchange relations. Second, communication technology defines an industry in its own right and, based on a variety of measures – growth rate, profitability, and stock price – it is a, if not *the*, leading sector in the global economy. It is again hardly surprising that citizenship is increasingly connected to

technology in expressions like "citizenship in the information society" and "cyber-citizenship," which make the plea for equity, access, privacy protection, and the application of other long-recognized citizenship rights to the global information economy. This line of thinking also calls for increasing use of communication technology to build the networks, however virtual, that are essential for transnational citizenship.

It is hard to quarrel with this expansion of citizenship to the global, even to the global technological arena. The times seem to demand it. Moreover, the concept itself is not new. In the West, Francis Bacon talked about it in the seventeenth century, and Thomas Paine and Oliver Goldsmith both wrote books entitled *Citizen of the World* in the eighteenth. Karl Marx's call for workers of the world to unite is another manifestation. Now, supporters maintain, technology makes it possible, indeed essential, to realize this age-old vision.

Compelling as this case may be, we would benefit from a more careful assessment of the march to globalization. It appears that no theoretical or political position is immune from the tendency to be swept away by all the end-of-geography, globalization talk (O'Brien, 1992). Marx may have started it all with his reference to capital's annihilation of space with time. Manuel Castells and Jeffrey Henderson's (1987) assessment of a world divided between placeless power and powerless places (p. 7) is another way of saying the same thing. From another perspective, James Beniger's (1986) book *The Control Revolution* is noteworthy because it offers what has to be the most extreme version of the "globalization through communication technology" theme. The computer, Beniger maintains, is the logical result of a history of organizing technologies that we have set against the second law of thermodynamics, the natural disorganizing tendency physicists call entropy, delaying, though not conquering, the inevitable heat death of us, the earth, the universe, and everything. But should we not be more careful about applying so-called laws of physics to social processes? Today, most scientists would agree with the particle physicist Lee Smolin (1997), when he concludes in *The Life of the Cosmos*, that there is no *law* of thermodynamics, just a tendency under certain closed-system conditions, and therefore no natural entropy and no inevitable heat death.

Indeed, most cosmologists see what we call the universe as a lumpy mass of energy producing galaxies embedded in a cosmic ecology of universes.

Although it is true that few social scientists have gone as far out on a limb as Beniger, we have to credit him for playing out what is implied in the many visions of geography's end, of placeless power, of friction-free capitalism, that abound in the literature. That is a primary reason that the so-called new geography is so vitally important today. Simply put, the work of people like Doreen Massey (1992) in the United Kingdom and of Saskia Sassen (1991) and Sharon Zukin (1995) in the United States remind us that capitalism, like the universe, is also lumpy, that space and place matter, as do the relationships among places, and that this conclusion has profound consequences. In the last couple of years, I have turned my attention to these lumps, these earthly versions of Smolin's energy-producing galaxies, whether defined as Massey's science parks, Sassen's global cities, Zukin's cities of the symbolic economy, or Castells' technopoles.

The technopole is a place that brings together institutions, labor, and finance that generate the basic materials of the information economy. Technopoles result from various local, national, and, in some cases, international planning activities that bring together public- and private-sector organizations to promote systematic technological innovation. The term *technopole* originated in the Japanese government's effort of the 1960s to build a science-based technopole, Tsukuba, about forty miles outside of Tokyo, and most would see Silicon Valley in California as its icon and most successful form. In their global survey, Castells and Hall (1994) refer to two dozen or so technopoles, many of which are eager to emulate the Silicon Valley model.

For the past two years, I have been taking a close look at the technopole, concentrating on a handful that, because they have recently developed, because they were overlooked, or because they did not fully qualify by the Castells and Hall criteria, are not included in their survey. I would like to turn to two of these cases now and tie my conclusions to the theme of citizenship. These are the so-called Silicon Alley district in New York City and the Multimedia Super Corridor (MSC) under construction south of Kuala Lumpur in Malaysia.

Silicon Alley is a global center for multimedia design and development, which is situated in buildings vacated by downsizing finance and investment firms (the headquarters, at 55 Broad Street, is just a block away from Wall Street). According to one report, the district anchors a new media industry that employs twenty-seven thousand in New York City and seventy-one thousand in the metropolitan area's four thousand new media firms, making it one of the largest employers of computer communication workers in North America, on a par with Silicon Valley (Coopers and Lybrand, 1996). A 1997 report by the same company concludes that New York's software, electronics, and multimedia companies have led the way, with an increase in venture capital investment of $111.3 million in 1996, more than doubling the 1995 total of $49.5 million (Coopers and Lybrand, 1996).

The growth of Silicon Alley began at a time when businesses were fleeing a city on the verge of bankruptcy with an eroding infrastructure and dwindling tax rolls (Goff, 1996). Silicon Alley is now an integral part of a revived lower Manhattan whose new, up-scale neighborhoods (Battery Park City and Tribeca) join with the artistic communities of SoHo and Greenwich Village and the Madison Avenue advertising district. These, in turn, are increasingly linked to the mass-media-rejuvenated midtown and Times Square districts, supported by major investment from the Disney Corporation and most recently by Reuters, which is building a headquarters across from a Disney theater, to produce an agglomeration of interconnected postindustrial spaces rooted in cultural production. Coopers and Lybrand's 1996 report highlights the significance of close ties among businesses in these several communities. Forty-three percent of new media companies surveyed worked principally for advertising firms, and 42 per cent for print media and entertainment firms.

The New York case invites a focus on the role of the media (especially publishing and advertising), and the arts (particularly the development of SoHo) in attracting talent to multimedia design and production, and telecommunications (for example, the regional Teleport). Additionally, there is the role of new neighborhood development (specifically Battery Park City and Tribeca) in attracting people to work and live in the city. Much is made of the role of the state and city governments in supporting the recycling (including rewiring) of vacant buildings, making it easier for multimedia start-up firms to locate in sites that meet their technical requirements. For example, the city of New York announced in 1997 that it would set aside $30 million for a Silicon Alley job-creation fund. It is also important to consider the significance of universities, particularly New York University, and networking organizations, primarily the four-thousand-member New York New Media Association, in fostering new businesses in this sector.

If New York is viewed as the information-age phoenix rising from the ashes of manufacturing decline, then Malaysia is the magic land where palm-oil plantations become Multimedia Super Corridors almost overnight. The increasingly celebrated place is a ten-by-thirty-mile tract of land south of the capital city of Kuala Lumpur. The Malaysian government proposes to spend between $8 billion and $15 billion of public and private money to turn this area of rolling countryside, rain forests, and palm-oil plantations into a postindustrial district where multinational corporations will develop and test new software and multimedia products. Much of this will be anchored in the new cities of Cyberjaya, what one pundit called "an infotech omphalos" (Greenwald, 1997, p. 98), and Putrajaya, a new cyber-ready capital (see also Rizal Rizali, 1997; Wysocki, 1997). Today, their only existing highway is a $2 billion fiber-optic network under construction. But the plan is that in these cities bureaucrats will serve the public in cyberspace, consumers will shop with smart cards, children will attend virtual schools, professors will lecture electronically at the planned Multimedia University, executives will manage through teleconferencing, and patients will be treated through telemedicine. The MSC is an effort to stem the erosion in the massive growth that Malaysia experienced based on a labor-cost advantage it enjoyed in computer and telecommunication hardware production. Having lost that advantage to other Asian nations, particularly Bangladesh, Vietnam, and China, the Malaysian government believes it can pioneer in software and product development. Malaysia proposes nothing short of making a national model out of the city-state Singapore's centrally directed, export-oriented, high-technology approach to development. Indeed, although the MSC is con-

centrated in one soon-to-be-developed region, plans exist to support the MSC with a hardware corridor in the north of Malaysia, including the island of Penang, that would attract national and foreign businesses interested in higher-end production with more-skilled labor than can be found in the lowest-wage regions of Asia (Ng, 1997, p. 23). Malaysia marks an important test of whether the once exceedingly fast-growing regions of Asia can continue to grow in the highly competitive area of software engineering and information-technology product development. It also bears close scrutiny, because Malaysia proposes to retain tight censorship, strong libel laws, and a patriarchal Islamic culture even as it welcomes foreign multinationals, inviting them to test the full range of new media products on its citizens. Recent developments in global financial and equity markets also mark this as a case to watch because massive declines in currency values, the near collapse of stock prices, and the withdrawal of foreign capital have created huge rifts between Malaysia (joined by Indonesia, Singapore, and Thailand) and First World powers that once pointed to these so-called Asian tigers as evidence for the success of traditional modernization schemes (Sanger, 1997).

The most important conclusion that I can draw from my analysis of these cases, and which by and large applies across the literature, is that there is a great deal of interest in technopoles as economic growth engines, some interest in them as new forms of cultural representation (King, 1996; Zukin 1995), and practically no interest in their political governance, that is, in addressing technopoles as sites of political power and their residents as citizens. It is not particularly surprising that the research concentrates on the technopole almost exclusively as a site for economic growth. Whether it is Silicon Valley or Silicon Alley or, for that matter, my home of Ottawa – once primarily known as the National Capital Region, now more frequently called Silicon Valley North – the technopole is researched and assessed as an engine of economic development. It is somewhat surprising that this view is shared by writers on the broadly defined Left, by people like Manuel Castells, whose book with Peter Hall provides 275 pages on the phenomenon but nothing on governance (see also Saxenian, 1994). One reason for this support may be that most technopoles confound free-market purists because they require government support and involvement in their planning and development as well as connections to local universities. Hence, the technopole naturally attracts those who would find a role for the state, for technology, for the university, and for more than a small measure of planning in the development process.

So, with the exception of the occasional critic like Bennett Harrison (1994) or Sassen (1991), the Left has proven to be as drawn to the technopole as the high-tech companies that reside there. This means that critical assessments based on a concern for governance and citizenship are muted, with the primary concern leveled, as in the work of Castells and Hall, as well as Saxenian, at the failure to deliver on economic promises, an outcome attributed to fumbling state or large corporate bureaucracies.

This is particularly unfortunate because many of the technopoles, including the New York and Malaysia cases, are not only test beds for high-tech products; they are also testing new forms of governance with significant implications for citizenship. For example, along with the creation of a new media district in New York, we find a significant transformation in governance with the formation of private-sector-run business improvement districts (BIDs) that have been put in charge of a wide range of services. They police the streets, manage the parks, haul away trash, and remove the homeless, with labor provided by private, mainly nonunion, low-wage workers. In addition, they have the authority to issue bonds (much to the consternation of city officials who fear both the competition in credit markets and the consequences of a BID default), and they pay their management well: the head of one earns more than twice the salary of the mayor. Moreover, the BID that encompasses Silicon Alley has managed to divert public and private funds to build some of the only new public spaces in New York, primarily to service upscale high-tech workers and their families. So along with high technology comes the privatization of basic services and the reorganization of urban government and civic spaces. The once public Bryant Park, adjacent to the New York Public Library and now under BID control, closes at night and contains swarms of private security guards – particularly in evidence during the many corporate-sponsored events such as fashion shows – who

prevent people with large bags, that is, the homeless, from entering the park (Birger, 1996; Breskin, 1997; Greenhouse, 1997; Zukin, 1995).

Similarly, the Malaysian government has signed agreements with several of the world's major computer and telecommunication firms under which the companies agree to set up shop in the new technopole; in return they receive a ten-year tax holiday and complete freedom to bring in their own workforce and capital and to export all products developed in the zone. They presumably would test new products in several application areas, including telemedicine, virtual schooling, and virtual government. Putrajaya is to be the new national administrative capital, operating as fully as possible in an electronic environment, including compulsory smart cards for each resident (Multimedia Development Corporation, 1997). One cannot help but conclude that this gives a whole new meaning to the responsibility of citizenship, namely, beta testing new products for transnational computer companies. Shall we call *this* virtual citizenship?

It is hard to find in the technopoles of the world any genuine source of inspiration for fresh thinking about citizenship at the local level, for ways to return to its original meaning of citizenship in the city or the community. And neither the New York nor even the Malaysian case is the most extreme. Consider Oceania (http://oceania.org). This is a planned libertarian paradise hatched by a Las Vegas entrepreneur that would be built on a concrete and steel platform eighty kilometers off the coast of Panama. The city-state, styled as a postmodern version of fifteenth-century mercantile Venice, is to serve as a "capitalist paradise" where taxation, social services, and public space would be outlawed and the number one business would be electronic financial services. Is there an alternative? The answer to this question depends on how you think about reform. On the one hand, it is tempting in the current cold climate to be modest, to weakly succumb to a kind of reform pastoralism that takes whatever we can get: a commitment to high-tech growth (whatever the consequences for governance), three hours a week of educational television (so what if stations count Jerry Springer?), or competition in telecommunications (what does it matter if most people are paying more than ever for a telephone?). On the other hand, it is just as likely that one might succumb to the opposite extreme, to a fatalistic naturalism, that removes reform from the realm of possibility.

I have been exploring the space between these views. Some of this exploration is historical: for example, there are important lessons for reinventing citizenship in the cultural industries contained in the experience of popular-front movements in the United States from the end of World War I through the 1950s. Among others, Michael Denning (1997) in his brilliant new book *The Cultural Front*, opens this period to scrutiny as no one else has. Of greater relevance to the theme of this chapter are alternatives to the technopole, regional spaces where citizenship and democracy heat up this otherwise cold climate.

One such region is Emilia-Romagna in north central Italy, which includes and extends out from the city of Bologna. In spite of its enormous economic success, which regularly places it among the fastest-growing regions of Europe, Emilia-Romagna rarely appears in any of the technopole literature, partly because high technology is not central to its development and most likely also because the region has been governed by the Communist Party of Italy, now the Democratic Party of the Left.

"The Third Italy," as it is widely known, in contrast with the heavy manufacturing region of the north and the poor, agricultural land of the south, bases its economic success on thousands of small, mainly family businesses producing customized products for the export market. In 1996, it ranked tenth among 122 regions of the European Community in per capita income and was the second-highest-income region in Italy. There are some sixty-eight thousand manufacturing firms in this region of 3.9 million, and only a handful of firms employ more than five hundred workers. Compare this with the state of New York, with 16 million people and only six thousand manufacturing firms. Moreover, the Third Italy supports a thriving cooperative sector, with sixty thousand workers in eighteen hundred so-called Red co-ops. Emilia-Romagna is particularly interesting because it emerged out of a remarkable partnership between enterprising family firms and a series of supportive regional governments of the Left.

Those who see the Third Italy as a genuine alternative to the major mainstream models of economic development build on the work of Arnaldo Bagnasco (1977), who concludes that Emilia-Romagna combines two key traits: commercial, artisanal, and financial skills based on a centuries-old set of entrepreneurial values and, equally important, strong networks of mutually supportive families. These combine to support post-Fordist production based on flexible specialization and customization for the export market. The regional governing parties of the Left have supported this development with a strong definition of cooperative citizenship: a rich social welfare system, universal trade unionism, widespread social and political networks, and regionwide agencies that pool capital for local investment, distribute business information, and coordinate global marketing efforts (Brusco and Righi, 1989; Cossentino, Pyke, and Sengenberger, 1996; Fitch, 1996; Piore and Sabel, 1984; Putnam, 1993).

Critics like Bennett Harrison (1994) and Ash Amin and Kevin Robins (1990) call our attention to the underreported influence of large national and transnational firms in the region, the brief time period that post-Fordist practices have operated, the inadequate use of new technologies, particularly communication and information technologies, that would be essential to sustain the Third Italy, and the growing reliance on immigrant labor unprotected by the "discipline" of citizenship (see also Bianchini, 1991). Nevertheless, the region invites our close scrutiny because it has, at least until recently, succeeded in weathering this cold climate and has managed to combine strong citizenship with economic success.

Communication scholars, particularly those working in the critical tradition, have tended to concentrate on the nation-state, the global structure of nation-states, and national and international businesses as their stock-in-trade units of analysis. There are important reasons for this and good reasons for continuing this pattern. Nevertheless, whatever our thoughts about technopoles and other approaches to regional development, it is time that more than a handful of communication scholars join this multidisciplinary debate on the importance of expanding to sites around the world the regional-development model pioneered in Silicon Valley. We need to enter this wider stream of thought, because it is generally barren of concern for democracy and citizenship and because of what we know about the relationship of communication, including new media, to political and economic development. Whether the rise of global cities and regional-development strategies are part of the decline of the nation-state and the return of the city-state or merely represent the latest iteration in capitalist market expansion and liberal fantasies of a beneficent capitalism, it is time that communication scholars and activists take a closer look.

Notes

I would like to thank my research assistant, Marcus Parmegianni, for his work in the completion of this chapter. I would also like to thank the Canadian Social Sciences and Humanities Research Council for a grant that assisted in the research on this chapter.

1   In fact, in a recent genealogy of the term *audience*, Lewis Kaye and I conclude that it is evidence of the immaturity of communication studies as a discipline that one of its central theoretical concepts, "the audience," has no particular warrant in disciplinary or intellectual history. The concept of the audience was hatched largely out of the marketing departments of companies with a stake in selling products through the media. Why even critics continue to use the term is an interesting question (see Mosco and Kaye, 2000).

References

Amin, A. and Robins, K. (1990). The re-emergence of regional economies? The mythical geography of flexible accumulation. *Environment and Planning B – Society and Space*, 8(1), 7–34.

Bagnasco, A. (1977). *Tre Italie: La problematica dellow sviluppo italiano*. Bologna: Il Mulino.

Beniger, J. R. (1986). *The control revolution*. Cambridge, MA: Harvard University Press.

Bianchini, F. (1991). The third Italy: Model or myth? *Ekistics*, 58, 336–46.

Birger, J. (1996, September 6). N.Y.C. is weighing ending debt power of business districts. *The Bond Buyer*, p.1.

Breskin, I. (1997, May 27). Times Square's Dykstra. *Investor's Business Daily*, p. A-1.

Brusco, S. and Righi, E. (1989). *Local government, industrial policy and social consensus: The case of Modena* (Italy). *Economy and Society*, 18(4), 405–24.

Castells, M. and Hall, P. (1994). *Technopoles of the world*. London: Routledge.

Castells, M. and Henderson, J. (1987). Techno-economic restructuring, socio-political processes and spatial transformation: A global perspective. In J. Henderson and M. Castells (Eds.), *Global restructuring and territorial development* (pp. 1–17). Beverly Hills, CA: Sage.

Coopers & Lybrand (1996, April). *The New York new media industry survey*. New York: Coopers & Lybrand.

——(1997, February). *The Coopers and Lybrand money tree*. New York: Coopers & Lybrand.

Cossentino, F., Pyke, F. and Sengenberger W. (1996). *Local and regional response to global pressure: The case of Italy and its industrial districts*. Geneva: International Institute for Labour Studies.

Denning, M. (1997). *The cultural front*. London: Verso.

De Ste. Croix, G. E. M. (1981). *The class struggle in the ancient Greek world*. London: Duckworth.

Fitch, R. (1996, May 13). In Bologna, small is beautiful: The cooperative economics of Italy's Emilia-Romagna holds a lesson for the U.S. *The Nation*, 262(19), 18.

Goff, L. (1996, April 22). Silicon Alley. *Computerworld*, 81–3.

Greenhouse, S. (1997, February 20). Unions woo business district workers. *The New York Times*, p. B4.

Greenwald, J. (1997, August). Think big. *Wired*, pp. 95–104, 145.

Harrison, B. (1994). *Lean and mean*. New York: Basic Books.

King, A. D. (Ed.). (1996). *Re-presenting the city: Ethnicity, capital, and culture in the 21st-century metropolis*. New York: New York University Press.

Marshall, T.H. (1964). *Class, citizenship, and social development: Essays*. Garden City, New York: Doubleday.

Massey, D. (1992). Politics and space/time. *New Left Review*, 196, 65–84.

Mosco, V. and Kaye, L. (2000). Questioning the concept of the audience. In I. Hagen and J. Wasko. (Eds.). *Consuming audiences*. Cresskill, N.J.: Hampton Press.

Multimedia Development Corporation Sdn Bhd. (1997). *Investing in Malaysia's multimedia supercorridor: Policies, incentives, and facilities*. Kuala Lumpur: Multimedia Development Corporation.

Ng, F. (1997, April 23). Silicon corridor set up in the north to complement MSC. *New Straits Times*, p. 23.

O'Brien, R. (1992). *Global financial integration and the end of geography.* New York: Council on Foreign Relations Press.

Piore, M. and Sabel, C. F. (1984). *The second industrial divide.* New York: Basic Books.

Putnam, R. D. (1993). *Making democracy work: Civic traditions in modern Italy.* Princeton: Princeton University Press.

Riesenberg, P. (1992). *Citizenship and the western tradition: Plato to Rousseau.* Chapel Hill: The University of North Carolina Press.

Rizal Rizali, M. (1997, April 21). Cyberjaya to pave the way for technological excellence. *New Strait Times,* p. 30.

Sanger, D. E. (1997, August 3). The overfed tiger economies. *The New York Times,* p. E3.

Sassen, S. (1991). *The global city: New York, London, Tokyo.* Princeton, N.J.: Princeton University Press.

Saxenian, A. (1994). *Regional advantage: Culture and competition in Silicon Valley and Route 128.* Cambridge, MA: Harvard University Press.

Simpson, J.A. and Weiner, E.S.C. (1989). *The Oxford English dictionary.* Oxford: Clarendon Press.

Smolin, L. (1997). *The life of the cosmos.* NY: Oxford University Press.

Wysocki, B. (1997, June 10). Malaysia is gambling on a costly plunge into a cyber future. *The Wall Street Journal,* pp. A1, A10.

Zukin, S. (1995). *The cultures of cities.* Cambridge, MA: Blackwell.

Index

Page numbers in bold type indicate a main or detailed reference.